CERTAIN DIFFICULTIES

FELT BY

ANGLICANS IN CATHOLIC TEACHING

CONSIDERED

THE WORKS OF

JOHN HENRY NEWMAN

BIRMINGHAM ORATORY

MILLENNIUM EDITION

VOLUME XVIII

SERIES EDITOR

JAMES TOLHURST DD

ASSOCIATE EDITOR

ANDREW NASH MA PhD

CERTAIN DIFFICULTIES

FELT BY ANGLICANS

IN CATHOLIC TEACHING

CONSIDERED:

In a Letter addressed to the Rev. E. B. Pusey, D.D..,
on occasion of his Eirenicon of 1864;
And in a Letter addressed to the Duke of Norfolk, on
occasion of Mr. Gladstone's Expostulation of 1874

BY

JOHN HENRY CARDINAL NEWMAN

VOL. II

With an Introduction and Notes by

JAMES TOLHURST DD

GRACEWING

Letter to Pusey first published 1866
Letter to the Duke of Norfolk first published 1875
Collected in *Difficulties felt by Anglicans
in Catholic Teaching* Vol. II, 1875; final edition 1888

Published in the Birmingham Oratory Millennium Edition
in 2023
by
Gracewing
2 Southern Avenue
Leominster
Herefordshire HR6 0QF

www.gracewing.co.uk

Typography by Andrew Nash

ISBN 978 0 85244 413 9

CONTENTS

Contents

ABBREVIATIONS

References to Newman's works are usually to the uniform edition published by Longmans, Green & Co. London.

Apo	*Apologia pro Vita Sua*
Ari	*The Arians of the Fourth Century*
Ath	*Selected Treatises of St. Athanasius,* 2 vols.
AW	*John Henry Newman Autobiographical Writings* 1956
BCP	*Book of Common Prayer*
BOA	*Birmingham Oratory Archives*
Call	*Callista: A Tale of the Third Century*
CC	*Catechism of the Catholic Church* ed. 2000.
Campaign I	*My Campaign in Ireland, Part I*
Campaign II	*My Campaign in Ireland, Part II*
CIC	*Code of Canon Law*
CS	*Catholic Sermons of Cardinal Newman* 1957

Abbreviations

DA	*Discussions and Arguments*
Dev	*An Essay on the Development of Christian Doctrine*
Diff 1 & 2	*Certain Difficulties felt by Anglicans in Catholic Teaching*
DS	*Enchiridion Symbolorum* ed. Denzinger Schönmetzer 1973.
En	*An Eirenicon In a Letter to The Author of 'The Christian Year'* by E. B. Pusey 1865
Ess 1 & 2	*Essays Critical & Historical*
GA	*An Essay in Aid of a Grammar of Assent*
HS	*Historical Sketches* 3 vols.
Idea	*The Idea of a University*
Jfc	*Lectures on the Doctrine of Justification*
LD	*The Letters and Diaries of John Henry Newman*
LG	*Loss and Gain*
Liddon	*Life of E. B Pusey DD* 4 vols. 1894
MD	*Meditations and Devotions* 1894.
Mix	*Discourses addressed to Mixed Congregations*

Abbreviations

ML	Migne *Patrologia Latina*
OS	*Sermons preached on Various Occasions*
PG	Migne *Patrologia Graeca*
PPS	*Parochial & Plain Sermons* 8 vols.
Prepos	*Lectures on the Present Position of Catholics in England*
Purcell	*Life of Cardinal Manning* 2 vols. 1895
SD	*Sermons bearing on Subjects of the Day*
SN	*Sermon Notes of John Henry Newman 1849-1878.* 1913
S 1,3,5	*John Henry Newman Sermons* 1824-1843 vols. 1, 3, 5, 1991-2012
S. Th.	*Sacrae Theologiae Summa of St. Thomas Aquinas*
TDN	*A Letter to His Grace The Duke of Norfolk*
TP	*The Theological Papers of John Henry Newman on Biblical Inspiration and on Infallibility* ed. J D. Holmes 1979
TVD	*The Vatican Decrees in Their Bearing on Civil Allegiance: An Expostulation* by W. E. Gladstone, London John Murray 1874.

Abbreviations

US	*Fifteen Sermons preached before the University of Oxford*
VM	*The Via Media* 2 vols.
VV	*Verses on Various Occasions*

A NOTE ON THE TEXT

The text used for this Gracewing volume is that of the Longmans, Green and Co. uniform edition of Newman's works. The page layout and headings are as in that edition, with the exception of the addition of the Editor's footnotes.

Newman's own footnotes are linked to his text by symbols (*, † etc), rather than numbers, and are placed below Newman's text and above the Editor's footnotes. Where a Newman footnote itself needs clarification, it has an Editor's footnote to it.

It is the practice of Newman scholars to cite his works using the uniform Longmans editions. To facilitate this in the present volume the page numbers of the Longmans edition are placed in square brackets at the appropriate places in the margins of the text. All references to the text of *Diff* 2 in the Editor's Introduction and footnotes are to these page numbers in square brackets, not to the pagination of this Gracewing volume.

The *Letter to Pusey* was first published in 1865 and the *Letter to the Duke of Norfolk* in 1874. The few editorial changes made by Newman in subsequent editions have been included as footnotes in this edition. The 'Notes' in the *Letter to Pusey* and 'Postscript' in the *Letter to the Duke of Norfolk* did not form part of their first editions. For the full printing history, see the Appendix.

DEDICATION

Most Reverend John Wilson, Archbishop of Southwark

ACKNOWLEDGEMENTS

My thanks are due to the staff of the London Library and the erudite guardians of the Lambeth Palace Library, to Dr Nicholas Richardson for his classical help and Fr. Stephen Boyle for his kind forbearance. Andrew Nash was invaluable for his comments and his editorial skill and Tom Longford as ever a faithful and understanding friend.

J.F.T.

EDITOR'S INTRODUCTION

Newman's *Letter to Pusey* and *Letter to the Duke of Norfolk* are not really letters. They are his chosen form for responding to attacks on key doctrines of the Catholic faith—about the Virgin Mary and the Papacy—made by Edward Pusey in 1865 and William Gladstone in 1872. One can see why Newman saw his responses to their attacks as naturally making up a second volume to his earlier *Difficulties of Anglicans* lectures which he had addressed in 1850 to members of the Oxford Movement who had not followed him into the Catholic Church.

I. LETTER TO PUSEY

Three old men who had "worked together vigorously in their prime", but had only corresponded since then, finally came face to face after twenty years on 12 September 1865 at John Keble's[1] rectory at Hursley, "without a common cause, or free outspoken thoughts ... now so broken up, so counter to each other. Pusey, shrinking back into a corner nursing a paunch, ponderous in his speech, full of his book, full of plans, full of meetings."[2] Keble slightly deaf, ill himself and his speech much impaired, with a sick wife upstairs in bed. They had all been Dons together at Oriel.

Edward Bouverie Pusey (1800-82) was educated at Eton and Christ Church. His father was the son of Viscount Folkestone, his mother, Lady Emily Herbert, daughter of the

---

[1] John Keble (1792-1866), Fellow at Oriel in 1811, published *The Christian Year* in 1827 and was elected professor of Poetry in 1831. He preached the Assize Sermon in 1833 and contributed Tracts 4, 13, 40, 52, 54, 57, 60, 78 and 89. Keble College was founded in 1870 in his memory.

[2] To Ambrose St. John 13 September 1865 *LD* 22 p.52 and to Mrs William Froude 16 October *LD* 22 p.76. Mrs Froude née Catherine Holdsworth (1809-78) was married to R.H. Froude's brother William in 1839. She became a Catholic in 1857.

Earl of Carnarvon. The family "was so indigenous that the place where they lived was called Pusey".[3] He became a fellow of Oriel in 1823, a year after Newman. He went to Germany to study their theology in 1826 and 1827. He married Maria Barker and became Regius Professor of Hebrew and Canon of Christchurch in 1828. Newman would pay tribute to Pusey's "vast influence, in consequence of his deep religious seriousness."[4] He would call him "A watchman on a high tower in a metropolis of religious opinion."[5] Pusey contributed Tracts 18 and 66 on 'The Benefits of the System of Fasting enjoined/prescribed[6] by the Church' and 179 pages on Tracts 67-69 on 'Scriptural Views of Holy Baptism'. Newman christened his first child who died soon after birth; his wife died in 1839 and his eldest daughter, Lucy aged 14 in 1844.

Pusey was by nature retiring and cautious, but this led to him being assailed from both sides of the theological spectrum. When he was condemned for his 1843 sermon on the Eucharist, it was "partly because of an indiscreet adoption in its literal sense of the highly figurative, mystical and incautious language of certain of the old Fathers."[7] Newman had noted this characteristic long before and wrote in the *Apologia*, "I had from the first a great difficulty in making Dr. Pusey understand such differences of opinion as existed between himself and me."[8] It was partly allied to Pusey's belief in the righteousness of his own partisan position. Newman had tasked him with it,

> What does make me anxious, is this, whenever I hear that, in spite of your evident approximation in doctrine and view of the Roman system, you are acting in hostility against it and keeping souls in a system, which you cannot bring out into

---

[3] Meriol Trevor, *Newman the Pillar of the Cloud*, London 1962 p.46.
[4] *Apo* p. 61.
[5] *Diff* 2 p.1.
[6] 'enjoined' applies to *Tr* 18, 'prescribed' to *Tr* 66. "Days of Fasting are 40 days of Lent, Ember days, Rogation days, Fridays in the Year." *BCP*
[7] Edward Hawkings (1789-1882), Fellow of Oriel 1813, Provost 1828-74 and one of the judges, in his criticism of the sermon. *Liddon* vol 2 p.317. See infra.
[8] *Apo* p. 223.

words, as I consider, or rest upon any authority besides your own.[9]

Pusey would not embrace Roman doctrine, partly because of his aristocratic background but also because he felt himself unable to accept the idea of intervention in matters of faith which were not safely identified in Scripture. He could not contemplate Newman's explanation that simultaneously maintained unity in substance but consistent evolution under the guidance of the Holy Spirit and the Magisterium of the Church. Stranded in a Tractarian past, Pusey could not or would not travel forward. Bishop Neill argued that in this way Anglo-Catholicism had been saved for the Church of England.[10]

Newman remained sympathetic but increasingly frustrated by Pusey's stance which continually produced objections to items of Catholic belief, while choosing to side-step substantial issues for fear they might undermine the unsustainability of his position. In his early days Pusey seemed close in mind and thought. Newman had said in defence of his views on baptism, "I love and revere him."[11] Pusey had returned the compliment when Newman wrote to him on the death of his wife, "I pray that God may make you what, as you say there are so few of, a 'great saint.'"[12]

In 1864 and again in 1865 Newman bought land, at the authorization of Bishop Ullathorne, for a mission at Oxford to provide for the religious need of parents who proposed to let their sons study at Protestant colleges.[13] Despite a memorandum from lay Catholics in favour, the idea was largely opposed in March 1865 by the bishops, led by Manning and supported by Ward,[14] with the backing of Propaganda. It

---

[9] To Pusey 26 February 1846 *LD* 11 p.128.
[10] Stephen Neill *Anglicanism* London 1958 p.261.
[11] Tract 82 (1837) *VM* 2 p.159.
[12] To Newman 16 July 1839 *LD* 7 p.83n. Prince Charles was present when Newman was canonized by Pope Francis 13 October 2019.
[13] To Newman 25 September 1864 *LD* 21 p.238.
[14] Richard Garnett Bellasis "told me that, from what he saw at Rome, he felt that Manning was more set against *my* going to Oxford, than merely against Catholic youths

was also opposed by Pusey, who according to Newman thought "it would cause a renew of attacks on our doctrines." Newman continued, "Yet you are doing the very thing yourself—you said that, since my day, those who agreed with you in Oxford had *ceased* to attack Rome."[15] When Pusey had published his *Eirenicon,* which would lay bare the differences, Newman took the opportunity to tell him "Now is the time if a *large and strong* body of united Anglicans could address the Council, being willing to be reconciled."[16]

Re-awakening Tract 90

Newman's conversion to Catholicism in 1845 had come as a profound shock to his two friends. Pusey's *Letter, An Eirenicon*[17] which he published in 1866 was an attempt to *harmonize* divergent opinions. He explained that he saw his book as "reviving the mode of Anglo-Catholic dialogue of Dupin and Wake."[18] Pusey dedicated his *Eirenicon* to John Keble whose Assize Sermon in 1833 was seen as the start of the Oxford Movement.

Tract 90, for Pusey was a positive theological Anglican development, and he wanted to ask Newman's permission to republish the Tract[19] and explained his reasons to Keble:

> It is chiefly a defence of ourselves against Manning, explaining our Articles in the old way, excepting against the large R.C. quasi-authoritative system, under the head of Art. 22,[20] and then speaking hopefully of ourselves, and, as we

---

going there." Journal in *AW* p.261 See also letter to W J Copeland 13 December 1864 *LD* 21 p.340 in which Newman blames Ward.

[15] To Pusey 31 October 1865 *LD* 22 p.90. Pusey persuaded Convocation to purchase the land for £9,000. *LD* 21 p.387n.

[16] To Pusey 10 July 1867 *LD* 23 p.265.

[17] Like the 2nd century *Letter to Diognetus*, it is a treatise rather than an epistle.

[18] Letter to Newman 4 September 1865 *Liddon* vol. 4 p.106 and Letter from Pusey to Keble 25 April 1865 *Liddon* vol. 4 p.106.

[19] Newman gave his permission. *Liddon* vol. 4, p.102.

[20] *Of Purgatory*: "... a fond thing vainly invented, and grounded upon no warranty of Scripture, but rather repugnant to the Word of God."

trust, our office of reuniting Christendom, following in the wake of Du Pin and Archbishop Wake.[21]

Newman thought that the movement of 1833 "was from the beginning engaged in propagating an unreality" and that the *Via Media* "scarcely had existence except on paper."[22] In contrast to Pusey he was also very blunt, saying in the 1860's, "the thought of the Thirty-Nine articles makes me shudder."[23]

Pusey existed in what Edward Short terms "alien stationariness"[24] He belonged to that fixed slice of society the landed gentry, and he had been considered acceptable for admission to the Noetic atmosphere of the Oriel Senior Common Room with Whately, Copleston, Hampden and Hawkins.[25] Pusey always felt that the Church of England was a true and lasting home for one's faith[26] and was faithful to "the only principles by which the Church of Christ is really defensible as an institution among men."[27] He wrote in 1844 "I sign the Articles as I ever have since I have known what Catholic Antiquity is (to which our Church guides us) ..."[28] The title of Pusey's *Letter* also reveals *his* mind, *"The Church of England, a portion of Christ's One Holy Catholic, and a Means of Restoring Visible Unity."* Pusey argued his position:

---

[21] Bishop William Wake (1657-1737), Archbishop of Canterbury 1716, author of *Principles of the Christian Religion* 1700. In 1718 he discussed reunion between the Church of England and the French Church with Louis Ellies Dupin (1657-1719), author of *Nouvelle Bibliothèque des auteurs écclesiastiques* (which was put on the index by Innocent XI in 1685). Wake said, "We are not in most things so far removed from one another that we may not be mutually reconciled". See also *Liddon* vol 4 p.108 and *En* pp.213, 217.

[22] *Diff* 1, p.48, *VM* I p.xxiv

[23] Newman writing in the *Globe* newspaper 28 June 1862 *LD* 20 p.214. His harsh tone is explained by the continuing newspaper reports that he was about to return to the Church of England.

[24] Edward Short *Newman and his Contemporaries* New York 2001 p.128.

[25] Richard Whately (1787-1863), Fellow of Oriel 1811-21, became Archbishop of Dublin in 1831. Edward Copleston (1776-1849), Provost of Oriel 1814-28, became Bishop of Llandaff in 1827 and Archbishop of Dublin in 1831. Renn Dickson Hampden (1793-1868), elected Fellow in 1814 and Professor of Divinity in 1836, became Bishop of Hereford in 1847. Edward Hawkins, see supra.

[26] The title on the cover of his *Eirenicon* was *The Truth and Office of the English Church*.

[27] *Liddon* vol 1 p.269.

[28] To the Editor of *The English Churchman* December 17 1844 *LD* 10 p.464.

The saying that "the Church of England *is* in God's hands, the great bulwark against infidelity in this land," relates plainly only to a present fact. It does not aver, that the Church of England is the best possible bulwark; but only, as a matter of fact that it *is* at this moment in God's Providence a real and chief bulwark against it."[29]

Newman, on the other hand, maintained that he had been misquoted and that,

The National Church has hitherto been a *serviceable breakwater* against doctrinal errors, more fundamental than its own.[30]

He does not use the word *bulwark* because, he explains, "A bulwark is an integral part of the thing it defends,[31] whereas the word 'breakwater' implies such a protection of the Catholic truth as is, in its nature, accidental and *de facto* and again, such a protection as does not utterly exclude error, but detracts from its value and face. *Serviceable* also implies something external to the thing served."[32] Newman admired his friends, but he did not 'stand still' like Pusey.

Three Eirenicons

In his quest for a formula which would facilitate Christian unity, Pusey undertook not one *Eirenicon,* but *three.* After the Letter to Keble which was *Eirenicon I* in 1865,[33] he wrote *First Letter to the Very Revd. J H Newman DD*[34] (*Eirenicon Part II*) in Lent 1869. It was subtitled *In Explanation chiefly in regard to the Reverential Love due to the Ever-Blessed Theotokos, and the Doctrine of her Immaculate Conception.* Both *Eirenicons*

---

[29] *En* p.8. Manning maintained that the Church of England was "the cause and spring of the existence of that unbelief ... and this by detaching the truths which it has received from the divine voice of the Church." *En* p.14.

[30] "A breakwater against the deluge" *Apo* p.244. See also Note E *Apo* p.342.

[31] Therefore "The Mother of God has ever been the bulwark of our Lord's divinity" 'Maternity of Mary' Sermon 14 October 1849 *Sermon Notes of John Henry Cardinal Newman 1849-1878* Millennium Edition ed. James Tolhurst Leominster 2000 p.22.

[32] *Diff* 2 p.11.

[33] It sold 3,000 copies by March. *Liddon* vol 4 p.126.

[34] John Keble died 29th March 1866. Pusey died 16th September 1882.

dealt with the possibility of a decree on the infallibility of the Pope, which "if passed, would be one more difficulty in the way of the reunion of Christendom, one more ground of severance between the Roman and the Greek Church; an insoluble difference between the modern Roman and the ancient Church."[35] To this was added the obstacle of the Catholic exaltation of the Virgin Mary. Newman commented, "Dr Pusey has now finally given up any prospect of ever being in communion with Rome. To me this is a great pain."[36] In Part III Pusey expanded the argument in his first *Eirenicon, A Second Letter to The Very Revd. J.H. Newman DD*, subtitled '*Is Healthful Reunion Impossible*' which he finished in November 1869 and intended to be 'a real Eirenicon.'[37] He changed the wording in subsequent editions to *Healthful Reunion, as conceived possible before the Vatican Council*. Pusey had thoroughly researched the subject in depth as a learned Professor from an Anglican perspective but had not fully taken into consideration that "Newman, like Manning and other Roman Catholic writers, regards Pusey's ideas as impracticable."[38]

His *Eirenicon* I, which he was 'full of' at Hursley, although addressed to Keble was aimed at Manning[39] in response to his pamphlet in 1864 *The Workings of the Holy Spirit in the Church of England*.[40] In it, Manning was brutally frank: "If the Catholic faith be the perfect revelation of Christianity, the Anglican Reformation is a cloud of heresies; if the Catholic Church be the organ of the Holy Ghost, the Anglican Church is not only no part of the Church, but no Church of divine

---

[35] *En* p.121.
[36] To an anonymous correspondent 31 August 1870 *LD* 32 p.311. At the same time Newman was certain that "the Holy See will never admit Anglican Orders, on the ground of its having sanctioned conditional baptism in England—for if Baptism is given conditionally, so certainly must Orders, to those who are to continue the Ministerial Office." To James Hope Scott 26 November 1865 *LD* 22 p.113.
[37] *Liddon* vol. 4 p.183.
[38] Wilfrid Ward *The Life of John Henry Cardinal Newman* vol 2 p.109.
[39] Henry Edward Manning (1808-92). Fellow of Merton 1832, Archdeacon of Chichester 1841, received into the Church 1851, Archbishop of Westminster 1865.
[40] "It is chiefly a defence of ourselves against Manning, explaining our Articles in the old way." Pusey to J. Keble 25 April 1865 *Liddon* vol 4 p.105.

foundation. It is a human institution sustained as it was founded by a human authority, without priesthood, without sacraments, without absolution without the real presence of Jesus upon its altars."[41] He did not recognize the grace of the Church of England as such because "grace works not *by* it, nor *through* it, but *in* it and among those who, without faults of their own, are detained by it, from the true Church of their baptism." He added—just to make matters clear—the grace "was granted not to detain them in the Church of England but to call them out of it."[42] Pusey could hardly fail to respond to that attack on his cherished beliefs. In response, he assembled what he considered a multi-pronged approach concentrating on the nature and exercise of the power of the papacy, "The chief controversy I hold to be about the sovereignty of the Pope."[43]

But, as with Gladstone in his later *Expostulation*, the occasion which prompted it was also the *action* of that papal sovereignty, proclaiming infallibility. For Pusey it was the Bull *Ineffabilis Deus* which defined the Immaculate Conception of the Blessed Virgin Mary on December 8th 1854. Pius IX had declared that Mary "was from the first moment of her conception, by the singular grace and privilege of almighty God and in view of the merits of Christ Jesus the Saviour of the human race, preserved immune from all stain of original sin."[44] Pusey greeted the announcement "in silent sorrow."[45] He considered that the teaching was a "pious opinion,"[46] even part of Catholic devotion, but maintained that its basis was disputed by many; and its being made a dogma was an example of unwarranted power. He made clear to Newman,

> I merely meant to put out what are our difficulties. I did not, as a mere presbyter, wish to put down formally what I thought should be the formula of union, nor had I any idea of wishing to interfere with others devotions.

---

[41] *Workings* p.42.
[42] Ibid pp.18, 20.
[43] *En* p.63
[44] *DS* 2803.
[45] *En* p.123.
[46] November 2, 1865 *Liddon* vol 4 p.122.

and in a postscript not in Liddon:

> I thought my line much the same as yours when answering me. I wanted that a quasi-authoritative system should be declared not to be authoritative [not de fide] and that, if we were united, we should not be obliged to receive, what I have put down. I wanted to work for an union, minus certain things, but then I wanted it authoritatively explained that those things are not 'de fide.' I fear that I have made a confused mess of this explanation, repeating the same things.[47]

Newman as an Anglican had been careful not to go beyond the words of Scripture with regard to the dignity of Mary.[48] He told his congregation, "Let us not suppose that she is different from ourselves in any other way than that she is better."[49] But largely under the influence of Richard Hurrell Froude,[50] who "fixed deep in me the idea of devotion to the Blessed Virgin,"[51] he began to appreciate her exalted role and would venture to preach in 1832, "Who can estimate the holiness and perfection of her, who was chosen to be the Mother of Christ? If to him that hath, more is given, and holiness and Divine favour go together (and this we are expressly told), what must have been the transcendent purity of her, whom the Creator Spirit condescended to overshadow with His miraculous presence?"[52] Then as he wrote his *Essay on the Development of Doctrine* he saw the place of Mary in the teaching of the Fathers as the first among created beings and the new Eve.[53] By this time it seems

---

[47] *Liddon* vol 4 p.121-2 and *LD* 22 p.93.
[48] Article 22 says that "the Romish doctrine concerning ... the invocation of Saints is a fond thing vainly invented."
[49] Sermon No 137 19 February 1826 *S* 5 p.391.
[50] Richard Hurrell Froude (1803-36) was the brother of James Anthony Froude and became a fellow of Oriel in 1826. He journeyed to the Mediterranean with Newman in 1832-3; he was responsible for Tracts 9 and 59. His posthumously published *Remains* (1838, 1839) revealed his asceticism and deep spirituality.
[51] *Apo* p.25.
[52] 'The Annunciation' 25 March 1832 *PPS* 2 pp.131-2.
[53] "The parallel between 'the Mother of all living' and the Mother of the Redeemer may be gathered from a comparison of the first chapters of Scripture with the last." *Dev* pp.415-16.

that he privately believed in the Immaculate Conception.[54] Eight years later as a Catholic while preaching that the Immaculate Conception had been a point of controversy, he added, "Do I think any holy person in any age has ever really denied it; if they seemed to do so, it was something else they oppose …. Though the Church has never proposed it as a point of faith, it is not difficult to conceive it should be one, and there has been a growing wish that the Church could find that it was part of the original dogma … for if no venial sin, *must* there not be Immaculate Conception."[55] Edward Caswell[56] who joined the Oratory in 1849 wrote in his hymn "How could one so highly favoured share the guilt of Adam's crime?"[57]

Pusey's reservations

Pusey focused on the definition, seeing it as an obstacle to achieving Christian unity as he saw it. He argued that it was one of a myriad of pious opinions and popular beliefs in the minds of many Englishmen that could be imposed by papal authority (especially if any were proclaimed to be infallible) upon anyone who would wish to be received into the Catholic Church. He considered the Church of England at the sixteenth century "to have been purified of such devotional and erroneous excesses."[58] He wanted more clarification about what could and what could not be defined and wrote to Newman explaining his concern:

> What I wanted, I thought I had explained at the beginning of p.100-1, that that should be declared to be alone *de fide* which the Council of Trent had laid down on the subject of Invocation, I mean that if the explanation of Milner, which I quoted in p.100, were laid down authoritatively, so that all

---

[54] Lutgart Govaert *Kardinal Newmans Mariologie und sein persönlicher Werdegang.* Salzburg pp. 48, 58-9.

[55] December 8, 1853. *Sermon Notes of John Henry Cardinal Newman 1849-1878,* ed. James Tolhurst, Leominster 2000 p.106.

[56] Edward Caswall (1814-78). Hymn-writer, received into the Church in 1847 and joined the Oratory on the death of his wife; author of 'See amid the winter's snow'.

[57] 'Holy Light on Earth's Horizon' in *Lyra Catholica,* 1849.

[58] Philip Boyce *The Virgin Mary in the Life and Writings of John Henry Newman,* Leominster 2001 p.40.

besides should be left as pious opinion, an immense step would be gained.... I thought that none of the system of the B.V. had been *de fide* and this is what I wished to be said by your authorities indirectly... I wanted that a quasi-authoritative system should be declared not to be authoritative [not de fide] and that, if we were united, we should not be obliged to receive, what I have put down. I wanted to work for an union, minus certain things, but then I wanted it authoritatively explained that those things are not 'de fide.'[59]

When Bishop Dupanloup[60] asked him about Pusey's theology, Newman replied in Latin saying that this was a new proposition since Pusey had previously repudiated the Canons of the Council of Trent[61] and there still remained serious obstacles on the road to unity.[62] Newman mused ironically, "Union *is possible* as soon as Italy and England, having the same faith and the same centre of unity, are allowed to hold severally their own theological opinions."[63]

For Pusey the Immaculate Conception was 'a perplexity'. He accepted the theological fact that our Lord was born of a Virgin Mother and was St Mary, the Virgin. But this excluded at that time devotion to her in any Roman sense, such as statues, candles and prayers such as the rosary.[64] Pusey himself was somewhat of a perplexity: he had fostered the practice of private confession in the Church of England, been suspended from preaching for two years for declaring his belief in the Real Presence[65] and was involved in establishing the first Anglican

---

[59] To Newman 2 November 1865. *Liddon* vol 4 pp 122-3; and for the postscript *LD* 22 p.93n.

[60] Bishop Dupanloup. Félix Antoine Philibert Dupanloup (1802-78) was Superior of the Seminary at St-Nicholas-du-Chardonnet (1837-45). He reconciled Talleyrand on his death bed and became Bishop of Orléans in 1849.

[61] "At the beginning of the Tracts for the Times the Council of Trent was considered to be the act of apostasy." Newman to Miss M. R. Giberne 29 January 1866 *LD* 22 p.143. See *Tr*. 15 'On the Apostolical Succession in the English Church' (1833) p.10.

[62] To Bishop Felix Dupanloup 25 January 1866 *LD* 22 pp.138-9.

[63] *Diff* 2 p.[116].

[64] "The Homilies illustrate what it is, which our Articles condemn, viz., Invocations, which seem to interfere with the all-sufficiency of the Intercession of our Divine Redeemer, or any act of devotion which is 'proper unto God.'" *En* p.108.

[65] In his sermon on 14 May 1843 'The Holy Eucharist, a Comfort to the Penitent' which "implied rather than stated even the doctrine of the Real Objective Presence" for which

sisterhood.[66] He could not understand that there was always going to be a reluctance on the part of officialdom to accept practices that were seen as expressions of Roman Catholic belief however they were interpreted and justified.[67] That painful conclusion had been forced on Newman by the very publication of Tract 90. With his failure to accept the profound differences between Anglican and Roman Catholic beliefs, it is not surprising that Pusey could ask how a 'pious opinion' (the Immaculate Conception) could be *imposed* on people's faith.[68] Newman answered, "So far from being a tyrannical infliction on the Catholic world, it was received everywhere on its promulgation with the greatest enthusiasm."[69] Admittedly Pusey was goaded by the triumphalist outpourings of Ward, Manning and Mgr. Capel[70] as he made plain to Newman:

> I have had to deprecate the Ultramontanism, which in the *Dublin Review,* goes beyond Bellarmine as to the infallibility of the Pope and the large development of the Blessed Virgin."[71]

In *Eirenicon* I his treatment of devotion to the Blessed Virgin occupies a quarter of the text, the larger part being devoted to "a vindication of the claims of the English Church to be a portion of the Catholic Church in doctrine and Sacraments."[72]

---

he was suspended from preaching for two years, as this teaching was "in discordance with the Formularies of our Church." *Liddon* vol. 2 pp.306, 308, 328-9. According to him the Real Presence lies not in the *oblata* [the offerings] but in the communion. Note 2 in *VM* 2 p.352.

[66] The Sisterhood of the Holy Cross (1845-1956) at 17 Park Village, Camden, in 1845. *Liddon* vol 3 pp.14-17, 21-5, 31, 191.

[67] Edward King (1829-1910), Bishop of Lincoln, was prosecuted in 1888 by the Church Association for mixing water with wine in the chalice and having lighted candles. The judgement by Archbishop Benson in 1890 supported the bishop but said that if the chalice was mixed, it should be done before the service.

[68] *En* p.127.

[69] *Apo* p.255. It was in consequence of the unanimous petition presented from all parts of the Church to the Holy See. See Pusey's letter on p.xvi.

[70] Thomas John Capel (1836-1911) was a chaplain to Lord Bute and was made a papal chamberlain by Pius IX. He became the Rector of Manning's University College in Kensington in 1878 but was asked to resign in 1879. He eventually settled in California.

[71] To Newman 4 September 1865 *Liddon* 4 p.106.

[72] *Liddon* vol. 4 p.107.

When he came to write *Eirenicon* II in 1869 he devoted the whole text to consider Mary as Theotokos,[73] using patristic and scriptural arguments "because", as he wrote to Newman,

> I thought that your people had not the case fully before them, and that those who prepared for the decision were one-sided. The grave question now seems to me the tradition.[74]

The 'cultus' of St. Mary

Pusey assembled evidence to show how there was exaggeration 'to the point of error' in the Roman attitude to Mary. His position was the same as Bishop Pearson's:

> Far be it from any Christian to derogate from that special privilege granted her, which is incommunicable to any other. We cannot bear too reverend a regard unto the *Mother of Our Lord,* so long as we give her not that worship which is due unto the Lord Himself.[75]

In traditional Anglicanism there exists that distinction between the doctrinal fact of Mary's eminence and the concept that she might have a very powerful role of her own. Pusey provided evidence in Roman Catholic writings "in no figurative or general way"[76] that she is "not only the middle point of mankind, but the centre of the whole universe,"[77] "Co-Redemptress" and "placed by God between Christ and the Church."[78] She is addressed by Catholics as "Authoress and Cause of everlasting joy" is also "a Priestess, and He is our High Priest"[79] and "Complement of the Trinity."[80] "As Jesus

---

[73] *Eirenicon* II pp. xiv-526 pp. In *Eirenicon* I pp.127-89, 329-34 and 351-409 concern the Blessed Virgin.

[74] To Newman 10 June 1869. *Liddon* vol. 4 p.164.

[75] John Pearson (1612-86), Lady Margaret Professor of Divinity and Bishop of Chester. *An Exposition of the Creed.* Oxford 1864 p.321.

[76] *En* p.165.

[77] *En* p.166. Ferdinand Chirinos de Salazar (1575-1626), Jesuit author of *A Defence on behalf of the Immaculate Conception of the Blessed Virgin* (1618).

[78] *En.* p.151. The Archbishop of Syracuse.

[79] *En* p.63. Oswald *Dogmatische Mariologie* (Paderborn 1850) p.174. See supra.

[80] *En* p.167. Archbishop of Trani.

sits at the Right Hand of God, so she is at His Right Hand."[81] "What I say absolutely of Jesus Christ, I say relatively of our Blessed Lady."[82] "As baptised, we are souls born of God *and* Mary."[83] He devotes some space to the teaching that "The Blood of the Lord and the lac of the Blessed Virgin, as also her soul, are present in the Eucharist."[84] Mary "in her office of Advocate, is named 'Omnipotency kneeling,' or 'interceding Omnipotency'";[85] her intercession is held to be "co-extensive with His, 'who ever liveth to make intercession for us,' our Divine Lord, and to be the access to his intercession."[86] "No creature obtained any grace from God, save according to the dispensation of His holy mother."[87] She has a "consanguity with Christ, as God."[88] In fact "'douleia' melts very much into the 'latreia' or the worship due to God."[89] "Jesus is altogether in Mary and Mary is altogether in Jesus, so that to pray to Mary is to pray to Jesus in her."[90] "No one would impute to the Marian writers that they mean that she is *Dea*, although, notoriously, some of them have called her so. But they speak of what comes to the same, of her 'delegated omnipotency.'"[91] He concludes, "It is difficult to see how direct heresy should not be suggested by sentences such as these".[92]

Most would argue that this appeared to contradict Scripture and at the same time threatened deep Anglican sensitivities, although Pusey admitted "that the devotion of the people to the Blessed Virgin outruns the judgment of the priests," while at

---

[81] *En* p.163. Oswald Dogmatische *Mariologie* p.174.

[82] *En* p.165. St Louis-Marie Grignion de Montfort (1673-1716) founder of the Company of Mary 1712 and author of *True Devotion to the Blessed Virgin* (English translation 1843); pp.49-50. Newman refers to him as de Montfort.

[83] *En* p.164. De Montfort ibid pp.74, 126. The emphasis is Pusey's.

[84] *En* p.169 Oswald *Dogmatische Mariologi,* pp.174-86.

[85] *En* p.182. Oswald Ibid p.216.

[86] *En* p.101 Alphonsus Liguori, *Glories of Mary* v.1. St Alphonsus Liguori (1696-1787), founder of the Redemptorists and author of *Glories of Mary* 1850.

[87] *En* p.108. Bernadine of Siena Sermon 61 Tr. i. Art. 8. St Bernadino of Siena (1380-1444), Franciscan theologian and famous preacher.

[88] Cajetan 1469-1534. 2-2 q.103 a 4 ad 2.

[89] *En* p.184. *Dulia* is the honour given to angels and saints and the special veneration paid to Mary as Mother of God.

[90] *En* p.184.De Montfort *True Devotion to the Blessed Virgin* p.171.

[91] *En* p.182. *Dea*: Goddess.

[92] *En* p.183.

the same time adding that "the Pope favours with his authority such popular devotions." There is in his arguments a mish-mash between what is acceptable in devotion and what is an exaggeration. Pusey also confuses the idea of Mary's intercession and that of her invocation, quoting a theologian (Suarez) in support of intercession and a devotional author (St. Bernadine) for the power of her invocation.[93] When he deals with Mary as "The Complement of the Trinity", he adds that this was founded originally on a strange mistake in the understanding of the term by an unknown author. But he adds that it is still said to be "one which she has merited, and was attributed to the celebrated Hesychius of Jerusalem,[94] who explained it to mean that she added the last complement to the Holy Trinity. Moreover, through the Incarnation of our Lord in her, the Virgin Mother of God filled up the capacity which the Trinity had, of a natural paternity and a natural filiation, and a bond of both in time."[95] But then Pusey has to admit that Salazar,[96] whom he has previously quoted, rejected the expression.

Pusey failed to allow that the devotion to Mary 'co-present' *in* the Eucharist was forbidden at the highest level,[97] not only by Benedict XIV but also by Gregory XVI.[98] He later admitted that Pius IX "had forbidden some new and extravagant titles which had been given to the Blessed Virgin."[99] This was at a

---

[93] *En* p.102. "I will never say, even though St Bernadine said it, that no one is saved who is not devout to her." Newman to Keble 8 October 1865 *LD* 22 p.68. See also Newman to Pusey 31 October 1875 *LD* 22 p.90.

[94] Biblical exegete according to St. Jerome (342-420), secretary to Pope Damasus, who settled in Bethlehem in 386 and translated most of the Bible into Latin.

[95] *En* p.167.

[96] Salazar. See supra p.98.

[97] B. C. Butler, *The Church and Infallibility* London 1954, comments "Like many non-Catholics, while denying the doctrinal basis of papal authority, he complains that this authority is so often inert in face of what he believes to be scandalous" p.76. Basil Christopher Butler (1902-86), after academic prowess in Cambridge, was received into the Church in 1928 and became a monk, later abbot of Downside, Abbot President in Vatican II and in 1966 auxiliary bishop of Westminster.

[98] *Diff* 2 pp.165-70 *A Scandalous Tenet concerning the Blessed Virgin*. See also Letter to Pusey 31 October 1865 *LD* 22 p.89. A prayer to 'Our Lady of the Blessed Sacrament' asks her to "awaken in all believers a lively devotion toward the Most Holy Eucharist." Pius X Audience 9 December 1906.

[99] *VM* I p.xlviii (1877).

time when there would in fact be increasing criticism in the *Home and Foreign Review*[100] that Rome was interfering *too much* in local matters. Pusey was willing to amass a list of 'Marian devotions' because he saw them as obstacles to reunion, because they went against the firm teaching of the Articles, "For Holy Scripture doth set out unto us that only the Name of Jesus Christ, whereby men must be saved."[101] However he was prepared to admit such devotions in the interests of Christian Unity, "provided *he* is not obliged to use the Italian devotions to our Lady, he will let what he calls popular devotions take their course in Italy etc."[102] To an Established Church dignitary like Pusey, any derogation from the Mediatorship of the Son of God was seen as a betrayal of Scripture and "an intolerable offence of having added to the faith".[103] Newman had already dealt with this in his *Essay on the Development of Christian Doctrine*:

> When Roman Catholics are accused of substituting another Gospel for the primitive Creed, they answer that they hold, and can show that they hold, the doctrines of the Incarnation and Atonement, as firmly as any Protestant can state them. To this it is replied that they do certainly profess them, but that they obscure and virtually annul them by their additions; the *cultus* of St. Mary and the Saints is no development of the truth, but a corruption and a religious mischief to those doctrines of which it is the corruption, because it draws away the mind and heart from Christ. But they answer that, so far from this, it

---

[100] *Home and Foreign Review*. Sir John Emerich Edward Dalberg, eighth baronet (1834-1902), succeeded Newman as editor of the *Rambler* in 1859 and converted it into the *Home and Foreign Review* in 1862. He opposed the *Syllabus* and strongly resisted a definition of infallibility. He was appointed Regius Professor of Modern History at Cambridge in 1895.

[101] Article 18.

[102] Newman mentions this to Miss M R Giberne 29 January 1866 *LD* 22 p.102. Maria Rosina Giberne (1802-85) met Newman in 1827 and was received into the Church in 1845, taking Newman as her director. She collected witnesses for the Achilli trial and became a Visitation nun at Autun in 1856 as Sister Maria Pia. He intended to visit her after receiving the Cardinalate in Rome but was too sick. She continued to correspond with Newman throughout her life.

[103] See *Apo* p.107.

subserves, illustrates, protects the doctrine of our Lord's loving kindness and mediation.[104]

He told Coleridge that Pusey's mind-set was different from that of Keble, whom he envisaged "like the dew from the fountain."[105]

Keble had from his youth a great drawing to Catholicism, and that Pusey had never had.[106]

Keble's *The Christian Year* had included a poem on the Annunciation which resonated with Roman Catholic spirituality:

Ave Maria ! Mother blest,
To whom caressing and caressed,
Clings the Eternal Child …
Ave Maria, thou whose name
All by adoring love may claim."

But Roman Catholicism possessed a foreign 'aura' particularly in Oxford Common Rooms which regarded it "as a form of national treachery".[107] Podsnap in *Our Mutual Friend* (which had just been published) considered it 'Not English'. Newman would patiently explain this to Fr. Gallwey who was thinking of starting a new Catholic periodical,

I think that Protestants are accustomed to look upon Catholics, as an un-English body, who take no interest in national questions, nay, are unable to do so, and useless or hostile to the public, and the mere instruments of a foreign power.[108]

---

[104] *Dev* p.202. Newman notes July 10 1866 "As to the Cultus, to me it is no increase in devotion, but in sentimentality." *TP* p.144.
[105] To Henry James Coleridge 20 April 1866 *LD* 22 p.218. Coleridge (1822-93) was a Fellow at Oriel in 1845 and became a Jesuit in 1856 and editor of the *Month* 1865-81.
[106] To Henry James Coleridge 3 April 1866 *LD* 22 p. 202.
[107] Richard J Evans *The Pursuit of Power* New York 2016 p.456.
[108] To Peter Gallwey SJ 26 February 1865 *LD* 31 p.80* Peter Gallwey (1820-1906). an Irishman from Killarney, became a Jesuit in 1852. He was based at Farm Street in London from 1857 and Provincial 1873-6.

Newman's critique

Newman was reluctant to criticize Pusey, but having read the book, he considered he had a 'call' to reply.[109] When he came to analyse Pusey's evidence he found his approach uneven. He noticed that he had Suarez quoting Eadmer,[110] when in fact it was Irenaeus,[111] and he had mixed authentic Church documents with a host of quotations often out of context. Newman also observed that there was an occasional bias in his interpretation. He told Lady Fullerton that Pusey's *doctrinal* notes in his volumes in the Oxford Library of the Fathers on Cyprian's *Epistles* and Tertullian's *Apology* were 'grossly unfair'.[112] Newman wrote to Allies rather brutally,

> As to Pusey, it is harsh to call any mistakes of his, untruthfulness. I think they arise from the same slovenly habit which some people would recognize in his dress, his beard, etc. He never answers letters, I believe, which do not lie in the line of the direct *work* which he has on hand. And so, in composing a book, he takes uncommon pains about some points, as in his analysis of the Episcopal Replies in re Immaculate Conception; but he will combine this with extreme carelessness in respect to other statements. Then, from that radical peculiarity of mind which interferes with his being a Catholic, he goes by books, not by persons. Thus he is tempted to trust to what he gathers himself from the text of the Bull *Ineffabilis*,[113] more than to the testimony of its meaning borne by a score of Bishops... Then again (speaking antecedently, for it is 20 years since I actually knew him) surely a habit of carelessness in stating and ruling points must be generated from the fact of his position, as being testis, judex et magister to so many people.[114]

---

[109] *Diff* 2 p.[20].

[110] Eadmer or Edmer (1064-1124) A monk and member of Anselm's household, he was a historian who wrote his life and a treatise on the doctrine of the Immaculate Conception. He was elected Bishop of St Andrews in 1120 but never consecrated.

[111] To Pusey 10 November 1865 *LD* 22 pp.100-1.

[112] To Lady Fullerton 1 January 1853 *LD* 15 p.236.

[113] Bull defining the dogma of the Immaculate Conception in 1854 *DS* 2803.

[114] To T. W. Allies 19 February 1866 *LD* 22 p.158. *Testis, judex et magister*: witness, judge and teacher. Thomas William Allies (1813-1903) was Chaplain to Bishop Blomfield. He became a Catholic in 1850 and was Professor of Church History at the Catholic University in Dublin in 1855.

Newman made the point that he did not question Pusey's devotion, but went to the heart of the argument: "You really do love and venerate her, though you do not evidence it in your book. I am glad then in this place to insist on a fact which will lead those among us who know you not, to love you from their love of her, in spite of what you refuse to give her."[115] But Newman measured his approach to the subject with what we would nowadays term 'ecumenical sensitivity.' He told Fr Coleridge, "I do not call exposing a man's mistakes 'speaking against him.'"[116]

Newman informed his friend that the Letter was "calculated to wound those who love you well, but love truth more."[117] He also called it "rhetorical and unfair."[118] In a letter he wrote to Pusey about his response, he said that his aim was "If not to hinder, for that is not in my power, but to balance and neutralize other things which may be written against it.... I am taking the greatest possible pains not to say a word which I should be sorry for afterwards."[119] He still wanted Pusey to understand,

> Your frequent references in your volume to what I have lately or formerly written, are caused by your strong desire to be still one with me as far as you can, and by that true affection, which takes pleasure in dwelling on such sayings of mine as you can still accept with the full approbation of your judgment.[120]

He insisted that his main aim was a desire to correct what he saw as a one-sided view:

> You must not be made anxious that I am going to publish a Letter on your Irenicon. I wish to accept it as such and shall write in that spirit. And I write, if not to hinder, for that is not in my power, but to balance and neutralize other things which

---

[115] *Diff* 2 p.[90].
[116] To H. J. Coleridge 24 October 1866 *LD* 22 p.307. Ambrose St John maintained Newman in Ireland "was too mild to be effective." Meriol Trevor *Light in Winter* London 1962 p.63.
[117] *Diff* 2 p.[6].
[118] To T. W. Allies 11 October 1865 *LD* 22 p.72.
[119] To Pusey 8 December 1865 *LD* 22 p.119.
[120] *Diff* 2 p.[9].

may be written upon it. If I shall say anything which is in the way of remonstrance, it will be, because, unless I were perfectly honest, I should not only do no good, but carry no one with me—but I am taking the greatest possible pains not to say a word which I should be sorry for afterwards.[121]

Newman conceded that Ward's approach to Catholic practice—in the *Dublin Review*—was too confrontational: "I do so dislike Ward's way of going on that I cannot get myself to read the *Dublin*."[122] He also remarked that, "It is more difficult at once to praise Mary, and to dispraise her imprudent votaries."[123] At the same time he told Pusey that Mary was not "of a different nature from that of her parents, and from that of fallen Adam, that she incurred his debt, as we do; but that, for the sake of Him who was to redeem her and us upon the Cross, to her the debt was remitted by anticipation."[124] He made the point that a gift had been given to Adam also, before Mary and she was as fully endowed with grace as Eve."[125]

As far as Mary's relationship to us is concerned, she "is only our mother by divine appointment, given us from the Cross; her presence is above, not on earth; her office is eternal not within us. Her name is not heard in the administration of the Sacraments. Her work is not one of ministration towards us; her power is indirect."[126] He had already pointed out in the *Apologia,* "The Catholic Church allows no image of any sort, material or immaterial, no dogmatic symbol, no sacrament, no Saint, not even the Blessed Virgin herself, to come between the soul and its Creator. It is face to face, 'solus cum solo', in all matters between man and God. He alone creates; He alone has redeemed."[127] He reiterates, "It is her prayers that avail, and her

---

[121] To Pusey December 8, 1865 *LD* 22 p.119.

[122] To Pusey September 5 1865 *LD* 22 p.44.

[123] To Mary Imelda Poole (1815-1873): Maria Spencer Ruscombe Poole, Sister Imelda, a Dominican sister at St Catherine's Convent at Clifton 2 April 1866 *LD* 22 p.200.

[124] *Diff* 2 p.[48]. "... by a special privilege of God." Council of Trent Session 6 Canon 23 *DS* 1574.

[125] *Diff* 2 p.[45].

[126] *Diff* 2 p.[84].

[127] *Apo* p.195. "Conscience is the most secret core and sanctuary of man, where he finds himself alone with God." Vatican II, *Gaudium et Spes* n.16.

prayers are effectual by the *fiat* of Him who is our all in all…
She and we are both saved by the grace of Christ… On Him we
solely depend."[128]

> Most assuredly, without any derogation from the honour of our
> Lord, is Mary His Mother called the Star of the Sea, and the
> more so because even on her head she wears a crown of twelve
> stars. Jesus is the Light of the world, illuminating every man
> who cometh into it, opening our eyes with the gift of faith,
> making souls luminous by His Almighty grace; and Mary is
> the star, shining with the light of Jesus.[129]

Her place at the birth of the Church is clearly indicated by St.
Luke when we are told that in waiting for the coming of the
Holy Spirit at Pentecost, all the apostles were at prayer together
with 'Mary the Mother of Jesus' (Acts 1:14).[130] Newman
introduces the parable of Dives and Lazarus, "It is usual to pass
over this striking passage with the remark that it is a Jewish
mode of speech; whereas, Jewish belief or not it is recognized
and sanctioned by our Lord himself. What do Catholics teach
about the blessed Virgin more wonderful than this? If
Abraham, not yet ascended on high, had charge of Lazarus
what offence is it to affirm the like of her, who was not merely
as Abraham 'the friend' but the very 'Mother of God'"[131] When
Pusey talks of Mary as Co-Redemptress, the term can be
understood as a fulfilment of Mary's unique share, united with
the redemptive suffering and death of her Son: "in bearing him
corporally, she became spiritually the Mother of all the
members of Christ".[132] Vatican II makes clear that Mary
"totally consecrated herself as handmaid of the Lord to the
person and the work of her Son, serving the mystery of

---

[128] *Diff* 2 pp.[84, 49, 99].

[129] 'Ave Maris Stella' *MD* pp.361-2.

[130] Bishop Moriarty of Kerry wrote that having read Newman's *Letter*, "Nothing better,
safer or sounder was, as far as my knowledge goes ever written by theologian on the
cultus Deiparae." 19 March 1866 *LD* 22 p.187n. David Moriarty (1814-77) became
President of All Hallows Drumcondra in 1847, Coadjutor, then Bishop of Kerry from
1854. He was an inopportunist at Vatican I.

[131] *Diff* 2 p.[72]. See Luke 15:11-32.

[132] Augustine *De Sancta Virginitate* n.6 ML 40.402. See Benedict XV's comment in
footnote to p.[79].

redemption *in subservience to him and together with him* by the grace of Almighty God."[133] Newman tactfully omitted to mention the place that Marian piety played in the life of pre-Reformation England with its important shrine of Our Lady of Walsingham, and the fact that the country was known throughout Europe since the eleventh century as the *Dowry of Mary*.

Newman made the objection that Pusey should call his Letter an *Eirenicon*—as an attempt at peace and harmony. He mentioned to Keble,

> If Pusey is writing to hinder his own people from joining us, well and good, he has a right to write as he has done—but how can he fancy that to exaggerate, instead of smoothing contrarieties, is the way to make us listen to him?[134]

Pusey however claimed that his own reply was "no declamation: it is simply historical."[135] So Newman asks what is Pusey's basic premise?

> An Irenicon smooths difficulties; I am sure people will think that you increase them. And forgive me if I do not recollect what you have exactly said, but I do not think you have said definitely *what you* ask as a condition of union,[136] in respect to the cultus of the Blessed Virgin. This would be something *practical*. Do you wish us to deny her Intercession? or her Invocation? or the *forms* of devotion? or what? Had this been clearly done, people would have thought you practical—but forgive me if I say that your pages read like a declamation.[137]

Newman added, "But we at least have not professed to be composing an Irenicon, when we were treating you as foes.[138]

---

[133] *Lumen Gentium* n.56.
[134] To Keble 8 October 1866 *LD* p.67.
[135] To Newman 4 September 1865 *Liddon* vol. 4 p.106.
[136] See supra pp. xxii.
[137] To Pusey 32 October 1865 *LD* 22 p.90.
[138] Newman had previously written more generously to Pusey, "I wish to accept it [your Irenicon] as such, and I shall write in that spirit. And I write, if not to hinder, for that was not in my power, but to balance and neutralize other things which may be written upon it." 8 December 1865. Pusey replied, "I am safe in your hands." *LD* 22 p.119n.

There was one of old time who wreathed his sword in myrtle; excuse me—you discharge your olive branch as if from a catapult."[139] He was going to quote to Pusey "If anyone ask for a fish, will he give him a stone ?"[140] But Keble begged him not to use the quote because it would hurt Pusey too much."[141] But he felt bound to say,

> It is true, that your book disappointed me. It does seem to me that 'Eirenicon' is a misnomer; and that it is calculated to make most Catholics very angry. And that because they will consider it rhetorical and unfair.[142]

Faith and devotion

Newman never disparaged devotion because, as he explained pithily to Lord Blachford, "The Catholic Church is at once, first a devotion, secondly a philosophy, thirdly a polity."[143] Newman had always taught that, "Prayer, praise, thanksgiving, contemplation, are the peculiar privilege and duty of the Christian."[144] But he always bore in mind St Paul's words to Timothy, "Hold fast the form of sound words."[145] He chose to explain his thoughts in greater detail to Mrs Froude:

> There is a marked contrast in Catholicity between the views presented to us by doctrine and devotion respectively. Doctrines never change, devotions vary with each individual. Catholics allow each other accordingly the greatest licence,

---

[139] *Diff* 2 p.[7]. "Wreathed in myrtle my sword I conceal." The Ode to Aristogeiton and Harmodius was translated by Edgar Allan Poe in 1827.

[140] Matt 7: 9, 10. Newman combines the verses.

[141] To Henry James Coleridge 24 November 1865 *LD* 22 p.110. A 'harsh' article on the Eirenicon was published in The *Month* in December, 'Dr Pusey as a Controversialist'.

[142] To Pusey 31 October 1865 *LD* 22 p.89.

[143] To Fredrick Rogers, Lord Blachford 3 June 1874 *LD* 27 p.70. Frederic Rogers (1811-89) Fellow of Oriel 1833. Lawyer, Secretary of State for the Colonies 1860-71. He became Baron Blachford in 1871.

[144] 'Moral Effect of Communion with God' *PPS* 4 p.227 10 December 1837.

[145] 2 Tim 1:13. See Sermons 124 and 125, 31 January and 7 February 1830 *S* 1 pp.60, 70.

and are if I may so speak, utter *liberals*,[146] as regard devotions, whereas they are sensitive about doctrine. That Mary is the Mother of God is a point of faith—that Mary is to be honoured and exalted in this or that way is a point of devotion... I really do think then, no objection can be made to 'We praise thee O Mary—etc' except that is it 'very bad taste.' And if this is all, let us recollect that, using our own judgment, we should call the Orientalisms of Scripture 'very bad taste.' Every nation and age has its own taste—and though there are invariable principles, we must allow a great latitude for such accidents.[147]

He had already explained in 1850 "the dogmatic truth of the prerogatives of the Blessed Virgin may be said to have grown upon the consciousness of the faithful."[148]

Newman outlined how he proposed to broach the subject in the proposed *Letter*: "The doctrine of Catholics about the Blessed Virgin is plain and simple; there are no varieties of opinion... All I had to animadvert on was a certain extravagance of devotion in details ..."[149] "Newman did not consider Faber "representative of English Catholic devotion"[150] especially in his edition of Grignion de Montfort,[151] where Faber translates him speaking against those "who did not believe that the Holy Trinity has made the Blessed Virgin the dispensatrix of all which They possess and will to bestow upon man"[152] Newman also said that he did not accept or follow Alphonsus Liguori's views about Mary even if he recognized his system of theology[153] but would not "dispute the right of

---

[146] Newman is making the point that Catholics remain absolutely free to choose their own devotions, in spite of various revelations and religious orders promoting their preferences; the *Raccolta* offered a wide range.

[147] To Mrs William Froude 2 January 1855 *LD* 16 p.341.

[148] *Diff* 1 p.395.

[149] February 26, 1866. *TP* p.111.

[150] *Diff* 2 p.[99].

[151] See *Diff* 2 pp.[98-9]. De Montfort see supra. Fr. Faber translated his *Devotion to the Blessed Virgin* (1866). Frederick William Faber (1814-63), Fellow of University College 1837, Rector of Elton 1842, received into the Church 1843, Head of the London Oratory 1849.

[152] *En* p.258.

[153] To Pusey 10 November 1865 *LD* 22 p.100. Dr Russell had sent Newman a volume of Liguori's sermons in October 1842 and explained what was doctrinally accurate and what was over exuberant. *LD* 9 pp.154-5. See *Apo* pp.194-5. Alphonsus Liguori (1696-

whoso will to use devotions to the Blessed Virgin which seem to me unnatural and forced."[154] But he made the proviso, "while they keep clear of offending in their devotional impulses, any doctrine of the Church."[155] This harks back to what Newman said when he talked in 1835 about the danger of "detaching yourself from the Church's discipline."[156] He frankly admitted that some devotions to the Blessed Virgin did not go down well in England, "English taste is severe, and Englishmen will consider such devotions to be in very bad taste."[157] Pusey had quoted Liguori that "From Mary we have received Jesus Christ, through Whose merits we receive all graces."[158] It is a valid point, but such has been the development of doctrine that Mary's closeness to her Son has given her a powerful role which allows people to approach her as a supreme advocate, while not using the term, as "a sacrament of mercy".[159] Similarly Newman stressed a truly theological devotion to the Mother of God in any series of devotions: "This being the faith of the Fathers, we need not wonder that it should in no long time be translated into devotion."[160] Keble put it to Pusey that Newman "was conceding your ground for hoping that something might be one day said or done to moderate the excessive worship of [the Blessed Virgin]".[161] Newman had reminded his audience at his 1850 Lenten Lectures in London of the 'strange mysteries' of popular Catholicism such as,

> Some appearance of our Lady (the like of which has really seen before and since) but on no authority except popular report,

---

1787); his *Glories of Mary* was published in 1850. He is famous for his *Theologia Moralis* (2 vols. 1753, 1755). See infra.

[154] To Pusey 5 September 1865 *LD* 22 p.44.

[155] To Keble 9 October 1865 *LD* 22 p.69.

[156] 'Religious Worship a Remedy for Excitement' *PPS* 3 p.342.

[157] To R. B. Forsaith 12 December 1876 *LD* 28 p.145. Robert E. Forsaith was a Congregationalist minister at Hertford. See also letter to J. D.Sandford 22 May 1876 *LD* 28 p.359.

[158] *En* p.102.

[159] *En* p.107.

[160] *Diff* 2 p.[65].

[161] Keble to Pusey 8 November 1865 *Liddon* vol. 4 p.124. See infra on *Lumen Gentium* in Vatican II.

and in no shape but that which popular caprice has given it.[162]

There is no doubt that Catholics regard pre-eminent sanctity in the Blessed Virgin Mary as co-natural because she is the Mother of God. Newman regarded the Incarnation as "the central aspect of Christianity."[163] In two memorable phrases he says "... that Man is God and God is man; that in Mary they meet.... The Creator and the creature met together and became one in her womb."[164] He addresses a congregation, "In Jesus Christ is the fulness of the Godhead with all its infinite sanctity. In Mary is reflected the sanctity of Jesus... Her very image is as a book in which we may read at a glance the mystery of the Incarnation and the mercy of the Redemption."[165]

Newman emphasizes that both in the Fathers and in Catholic devotion, Mary is seen not as a mere physical instrument in the Incarnation but an "intelligent, responsible cause" and "had a real meritorious co-operation" by her faith and constant loving acceptance of her role.[166] Mary freely admits, being 'full of grace' because "The almighty has done great things for me."[167] Mary in her humanity is chosen out of all creation to bring the Saviour into the world but "He who charges us with making Mary a divinity is thereby denying the divinity of Christ."[168] Newman told Lady Chatterton,[169]

In speaking of her, we are honouring him; as he likes to be petitioned by his chosen ones, so does he especially love the petitions which she offers him; and in asking her to intercede

---

[162] *Diff* 1 p.287.

[163] *Dev* p.36.

[164] *Diff* 2 pp.[87, 104]. John Paul II summarizes Newman's words as "Mother of her Creator" *In God's Hands* p.231.

[165] A Short Service for Rosary Sunday *MD* p.357.

[166] *Diff* 2 pp.[35, 36, 41, 43]. John Moress had to abjure his opinion that the Virgin Mary was nothing "but *a sakk* (sack)." St Nicholas Church Rochester Register, fol. 41v 17 May 1505.

[167] Luke 1:28, 49.

[168] *Diff* 2 p.[85].

[169] Lady Henrietta Georgina Maria Lascelles Chatterton (1806-76) married William Abraham Chatterton, who died in 1855 and then married Edward Dering. Both were received into the Church in 1865.

for us, we are pleasing both her and him.[170]

He pointed out that "those nations and countries have lost their faith in the divinity of Christ, who have given up devotion to His Mother, and that those on the other hand, who had been foremost in her honour, have retained their orthodoxy."[171] Newman had stressed in his 1859 article, "I have always fancied that, when Catholics were accused of hyperbolical language towards the Blessed Virgin, it was replied that devotion was not the measure of doctrine."[172] This was against the background of the great heresies (Gnosticism, Arianism, Nestorianism). It also explains the ebb and flow of devotion, with one practice falling out of favour while another finds acceptance: "We cannot indeed, be devout without faith but we may believe without feeling devotion. Of this phenomenon every one has experience both in himself and in others."[173]

He had put it to Pusey in 1845, "Multitudes of people flocked to the Holy Robe of Trèves just now — and cures were wrought — Faith might thus be rewarded, even though the Robe was not a genuine relic."[174] In a new preface to *Via Media* in 1877 Newman later says, "While the Catholic Church is ever most precise in her enunciation of doctrine, and allows no liberty of dissent from her decisions, (for on such objective matters she speaks with the authority of infallibility), her tone is different, in the sanction she gives to devotions, as they are of a subjective and personal nature. Here she neither prescribes measure, nor forbids choice, nor, except so far as they imply doctrine, is she infallible in her adoption or use of them." [175] Any authentic devotion struggles to express some deep truth of

---

[170] To Lady Chatterton 29 March 1866 *LD* 22 p.194.

[171] *Diff* 2 p.[92].

[172] 'On Consulting the Faithful in Matters of Doctrine' ed. Colson. London 1961. p.60.

[173] *Diff* 2 p.[26].

[174] To Pusey 14 March 1845 *LD* 10 p.593. Newman is talking of the Seamless Robe or Tunic of Trèves/Trier. Over half a million pilgrims came between 18 August and 6 October 1844. In 1996 it drew a million. The robe was thought to have been woven by the Blessed Virgin and discovered by St Helena in the Holy Land in 327 or 328.

[175] *VM* 1 p.lxxv (1877).

faith which is illustrated by Bernadette Soubirous[176] who, when shown the statue erected in the Grotto of Lourdes remarked that it was very fine, but "It was not her"; sculpture could not express the full reality of what she had seen.

Devotions have changed and developed with the times. "In the course of years, some of them spring up, others decline and die."[177] Newman notes, "A large liberty is accorded to private judgment and inclination as regards matters of devotion."[178] Catholics hardly say any longer the chaplet of the Holy Spirit or the Seven Days Devotion of St. Bonaventure,[179] and the rosary and the Stations of the Cross have both had additions. People did, however, honour the Immaculate Conception and the Assumption before they became dogmas and the Crowning of Mary as Queen of Heaven, long before it was made a feast in 1954.[180] Episcopal or papal authority have always been ready to step in to ensure that no devotion contradicts dogma.[181]

Ian Ker draws attention to Pusey's emphasis in his *Letter* on a certain kind of extreme 'devotionalism' among Roman Catholics.[182] Newman gradually comes round to this part of the argument. He begs to point out that "Faith and devotion are as distinct in fact, as they are in idea. We cannot, indeed be devout without faith, but we may believe without feeling devotion."[183] This was perfectly expressed in his *Dream of Gerontius*.[184] Manning had questioned Newman's attitude to devotion:

---

[176] St Bernadette Soubirous (1844-79). The Virgin Mary appeared to her at Lourdes in 1858. She became a nun at Nevers in 1866.

[177] *Diff* 2 p.[29].

[178] *Diff* 2 p.[28].

[179] The Chaplet of the Holy Spirit. Apostolic Brief 24 March 1902. Seven Days Devotion, A Prayer to the Immaculate Mother of God. Apostolic Brief December 9, 1856, from the *Raccolta*.

[180] "It is a simple fact to say that Catholics have not come to believe it (the Immaculate Conception) because it is defined, but that it was defined because they believed it." *Apo* p.255 and St. Amadeus (1110-39) Bishop of Lausanne in his Homily 7 on Our Lady as Queen.

[181] See reference to Peter Canisius pp.[108, 153ff], and Gregory XVI p.[107].

[182] *John Henry Newman* Oxford (2nd ed.) 2009 p.580.

[183] *Diff* 2 p.[26].

[184] It was published in the *Month* in May 1865. It includes the hymn *Praise to the Holiest. VV* pp.327-8.

I see much danger of an English Catholicism, of which Newman is the highest type. It is the old Anglican, patristic, literary, Oxford tone transplanted into the Church. It takes the line of deprecating exaggerations, foreign devotions, Ultramontanism, anti-national sympathies. In one word, it is worldly Catholicism and it will have the worldly on its side, and will deceive many.[185]

But Newman did not see his idea of Catholicism connected with any brand of Anglicanism, arguing, "From my point of view, I cannot conceive…the Establishment running into Catholicism, more than I can conceive the Thames running into the Wash."[186] Catholic devotion also possessed its own particular character and had an organic growth, as he told Charlotte Wood,[187]

The definition of the Immaculate Conception was not the work of a Council—and was the consequence of the spontaneous growth of belief through centuries in the Church.[188]

He had enlarged on the point to Alleyne in a long letter in answer to his questions about the Immaculate Conception,

The *devotion* to her has gradually and slowly extended through the Church; the *doctrine* about her being always the same from the first. But the *gradual* growth of the devotion was a cause why that doctrine, in spite of its having been from the first should have been but slowly recognized, slowly defined.[189]

---

[185] Manning to Mgr. Talbot 25 February 1866 *Purcell* vol. 2 p.323. George Talbot (1816-86), Fifth son of third Baron Talbot of Malahide, was received into the Church in 1842 and ordained in 1846. A priest at St. George's Southwark, he was appointed a Canon of St Peter's and Papal Chamberlain in 1849.

[186] To Ambrose Phillipps de Lisle 3 March 1866 *LD* 22 p.172.

[187] See supra.

[188] To Charlotte Wood 14 April 1870 *LD* 25 p.100. Charlotte Wood (1789-1873), the widow of William Wood, Canon on Canterbury. When she was about to become a Catholic in 1845, Archbishop Howley sent his Domestic chaplain, a Tractarian, Benjamin Harrison to try to dissuade her. She and her daughter were received. Her son Granville a naval captain was also received in 1849 and became a Jesuit. She lived in the Isle of Wight and was a frequent correspondent.

[189] To Arthur Osborne Alleyne, Rector of St Edmund's Exeter, (a living in his own gift). 15 June 1860 *LD* 19 p.364.

Newman is also clear about Mary's status, "She is not the rival but the minister to her Son."[190] Vatican II would later be explicit: "This very special devotion, as it has always existed in the Church, for all its uniqueness, differs essentially from the adoration, which is given to the incarnate Word and equally to the Father and the Holy Spirit, and greatly fosters this adoration."[191] But devotion grows not in a vacuum but with the rhythm of a faithful people: "to be *devout* is to be devoted."[192] In Newman's novel *Loss and Gain*, Mr. Vincent had voiced the typical Anglican criticism of Italian Catholicism:

> Such heaps of beggars in the streets of Rome or Naples; so much squalidness and misery; no cleanliness; an utter want of comfort; and such superstition; and such an absence of all true and evangelical seriousness. They push and fight while Mass is going on; they jabber their prayers at railroad speed; they worship the Virgin as a goddess; and they see miracles at the corner of every street. Their images are awful and their ignorance prodigious.[193]

Newman admitted that there was some substance in Pusey's pained comments, saying "I like some of those you quote as little as you do"[194] but felt the need to make the comparison between Keble's approach and Pusey's,

> The first duty of charity is to try and enter into the mind and feelings of others. This is what I love so much in you ... but I must desiderate it in this new book of Pusey's—and I deplore the absence of it there.[195]

A people's religion

Pusey expected to discover a staid decorum and instead he was confronted with vulgarity: 'the carnal tastes of the

---

[190] *Diff* 2 p.[93]. Since patristic times the Saturday memorial to Our Lady has commemorated Mary's faith during the time her Son was in the tomb on Holy Saturday.

[191] *Lumen Gentium* n.66.

[192] *MD* p.72.

[193] *LG* p.176.

[194] *Diff* 2 p.[103].

[195] To Keble 8 October 1865 *LD* 22 p.69.

multitude.'[196] Newman talked of "spectacles of idleness, slovenliness, want of spirit, disorder, dirt and dishonesty,"[197] even the breath of superstition—which Pusey found distasteful and therefore an obstacle to Christian reunion. Yet, as Newman had earlier observed,

> Not the highest in rank, not the meanest, not the most refined, not the rudest is beyond the influence of the Church; she includes specimens of every class among her children. She is the solace of the forlorn, the chastener of the prosperous, and the guide of the wayward. She keeps a mother's eye for the innocent, bears with a heavy hand upon the wanton, and has a voice of majesty for the proud. She opens the mind of the ignorant and she prostrates the intellect of even the most gifted.[198]

And now he pointed out that,

> Religion acts on the affections; who is to hinder these, when once roused, from gathering in their strength and running wild … the religion of the multitude is ever vulgar and abnormal; it ever will be tinctured with fanaticism and superstition, while men are what they are. A people's religion is ever a corrupt religion.[199]

There was that strange contradiction about Catholicism, as Newman had put it to his congregation in Birmingham,

> So much good and so much evil—so much evil which revolts him, so much good which amazes and troubles him.[200]

There was "the soul of the single wild bandit of Calabria", "the whining beggar of Palermo", "a poor Neapolitan crone who chatters to her crucifix", and "the troubadour offered tapers and paid for Masses, for his success in some lawless attachment;" all weighed in the balance against the wonders of railway

---

[196] *VM* 1 p.xxx.
[197] *Diff* 1 p.230.
[198] *Mix* 'The Catholic Missioner' (May 1849) p.253.
[199] *Diff* 2 pp.[79, 81].
[200] 'Christ upon the Waters' *OS* (1850) p.150.

travel![201] Newman asked ironically whether "the standard of civil prosperity and political aggrandizement is the truest test of grace and the largest measure of salvation?"[202]

Such popular devotion would appear either a profound mystery or a scandal to respectable Anglicans. Yet Newman distinguishes, "There is a healthy devotion and there is an artificial ...".[203] "True devotion consists neither in vain and passing feelings but arises out of a true faith."[204] St. Teresa of Avila exclaims, "From foolish devotions may God deliver us!"[205] The reason for such apparent contrasts of good and evil was inherent in Christianity itself: "It is eminently an objective religion. For the most part it tells us of persons and facts in simple words, and leaves that announcement to produce its effect on such hearts as are prepared to receive it."[206] Lady Chatterton[207] two years before she became a Catholic had written to Newman about "the tawdry and doll-like figures of the Blessed Virgin in Belgium's churches," and he replied,

> If a divine system, when committed to men, becomes at once mixed up with human weakness and *corruption* (as the parables and other portions of the New Testament seem to predict of the gospel dispensation,) it is not wonderful that defects, which are *short* of sin yet repulsive to the beholder, much of extravagance, of fanaticism, or ignorance, and of bad taste, also should be grafted upon or infused into it. Christianity was intended for whole populations; now a popular religion is necessarily deformed by the errors and bad taste of the multitude. As the religion of barbarous times will ever be fierce and superstitious, as the religion of the schools will ever tend to be subtle land pedantic, so the religion of a nation will ever partake of the peculiar faults of the national character. The most sublime truths take a vulgar shape and bear a forbidding aspect, when reflected back by the masses of

---

[201] *Diff* 1 pp.240, 280.
[202] *Diff* 1 p.260.
[203] *Diff* 2 p.[100].
[204] 'The Cult of the Blessed Virgin in the Church' *Lumen Gentium* n.67.
[205] *Life* ch.13.
[206] *Diff* 2 p.[86].
[207] See supra.

human society—nay, often cannot be made intelligible to them, or at least cannot be made to reach them, till thrown into words or actions which are offensive to educated minds. The Church cannot countenance any such misstatement of the truth, much less any degradation or depravation of it—yet, when it has actually taken place she may find it quite impossible to root out the tares without rooting out the wheat with them—and is obliged to let them grow together till the harvest.[208] At least, she is obliged to be patient, and waits her time—hoping that an evil will at length die of itself—or again that some favourable opportunity may occur, when she may be able to do what she has no means of doing at present.[209]

He later reminded her, "Abraham doubtless found his life in Canaan not so pleasant to him, as his native Mesopotamia. We ever much sacrifice something, to gain great blessings. If the Catholic Church is from God, to belong to her is a make-up for many losses."[210]

What Newman objected to in Pusey's *Letter* was his failure to *appreciate* the Catholic attitude, including "his one-sided view of our teaching about Mary."[211] At least he would attempt to discriminate what is its substance from its accidents.[212] But they had long been talking at cross-purposes. Pusey for instance was disturbed that "devotions to the Blessed Virgin have been and are assigned as penance in the Roman Church," and went on to say, "consequently as a condition of forgiveness of sin."[213] He failed to understand the nature of 'satisfaction/penance' which should in some measure reflect the sin 'in accordance with the quality and number of sins confessed'.[214] A prayer to Our Lady or any other religious prayer or act is that means of showing sorrow, and in no way involves the Blessed Virgin in the actual forgiveness of sin in the sacrament. Newman remarked to Coleridge, "If there is one

---

[208] Matt 13: 29-30.
[209] To Lady Chatterton 16 June 1863 *LD* 20 pp.470-1.
[210] Ibid 29 March 1866 *LD* 22 p.194.
[211] *Diff* 2 p.[7].
[212] See *Diff* 2 p.[19].
[213] *En* p.111.
[214] *CIC* 981.

thing more than another to shock and alienate those whom we wish to convert, it is to ridicule their objects of worship. It is wounding them in their most sacred part."[215] When he came to discuss the Catholic outlook, he was blunt:

> Ordinary human weakness are coupled with the intense absolute faith which Catholics have and Protestants have not.[216]

There is in Catholicism that strange light of faith which tends to explain the 'contrarities'. He pointed out that it is normal for Catholics "to begin the day with Our Lord and then go on to His Mother,"[217] referring to daily Mass and then Marian devotions, and reminded Pusey of the Eucharistic presence of Jesus in every tabernacle alongside the statue to Mary. He had earlier explained to a correspondent,

> The devotion of the Blessed Sacrament, our Lord Himself Present and Unseen, has acted as a sufficient balance to keep the whole system of doctrine and worship in aequilibrio.[218]

He told a London chemist whose 'great difficulty was 'Mariolatry' in the Church',

> Before a person is a judge, whether our devotions to the Blessed Virgin and the Saints are idolatrous or not, he must place himself in the position towards them in which, as a matter of faith, we hold ourselves to be. We believe in a family of God, of which the Saints are the heavenly messengers and we the earthly—yet one family embracing earth and heaven. We believe we have access to the heavenly members, and are at liberty to converse with them—and that we can ask them for benefits and they can gain them for us... Our language towards Our Lady and the Saints is not so much above that which is

[215] To Henry James Coleridge 24 October 1866 *LD* 22 p.306

[216] To Emily Bowles 15 October, 1874 *LD* 27 p.139

[217] *Diff* 2 p.[95]. The various altars and statues would contrast with the one altar or table in Protestant Churches.

[218] To Daniel Radford 15 October 1862 *LD* 20 p.307. Radford, a partner in a Stockbrokers in Liverpool, was a High Church Anglican.

used towards great personages on earth, as immortal blessedness if above temporal power.[219]

Newman did not share the views of devotees of Italianate Marian devotions.[220] He says in the *Apologia,*

> Such devotional manifestations in honour of our Lady had been my great *crux* as regards Catholicism; I say frankly, I do not fully enter into them now; I trust I do not love her the less, because I cannot enter into them. They may be fully explained and defended; but sentiment and taste do not run with logic: they are suitable for Italy, but they are not suitable for England.[221]

He told Hope-Scott that his initial project "will be the most inoffensive way of alluding to Faber and Ward, if I can write without hurting Pusey."[222] In a letter to Newman, Pusey had said,

> I have had to deprecate the Ultramontanes, which in the *Dublin Review* goes beyond Bellarmine as to the Infallibility of the Pope and the large development of the system as to the Blessed Virgin.[223]

"I had established a moderate view…"

In favour of true devotion, Newman preferred "to represent what is a nobler and more elevated side of the system to which he has attached himself."[224] Newman notes in his *Theological Papers* "In my first pamphlet I had established a moderate view about the Blessed Virgin as against other extreme writers."[225] This was on a par with his attitude to liturgy generally. Lisle Phillips was informed in 1848,

---

[219] To Edward Bedoe 2 October 1865, *LD* 22 p. 64-5. He was a London chemist who had read the *Apologia* and had become interested in Catholicism. He was received into the Church in 1866.

[220] Newman refers to "Italian compositions" p.[22].

[221] *Apo* p.195.

[222] To James Hope-Scott 26 November 1865, *LD* 22 p.112.

[223] Pusey to Newman 4 September 1865, *LD* 22 p.44n.

[224] Dean Church *Occasional Papers* vol 1 p.415.

[225] *TP* iam cit, 26 February 1866 p.111.

> [As an Anglican] I never committed myself to the Rubric movement, nor allowed of innovations, though for the better, in St. Mary's—much less gave in to such extravagances as they at present practice at Margaret Street Chapel.[226]

Newman was not alone with his concerns. Dr. John Milner, one of the Vicars Apostolic, had been more forthright:

> Cursed be every goddess-worshipper, that believes the Blessed Virgin Mary to be any more than a creature; that worships her, or puts his trust in her more than in God; that believes her above her Son, or that she can in anything command his Amen.[227]

Bishop Brown of Newport wrote saying that Newman's "reasoning was irresistible, and I am specially gratified by your rejection of the ill-advised terms whereby some writers have sought to exalt our Blessed Lady."[228] Dr. Russell, Professor of Church History at Maynooth, on reading Pusey's *Letter* wrote to Newman,

> Frankly I *am* both startled and pained by the expressions and views to which you refer [Pusey's quotations from Salazar, de Montford, Oswald etc.]. My instincts and sympathies are all against such views... I own I cannot accept *a share in the Redemption...*[229]

Dr Griffiths also strongly objected "to certain foreign 'Saints'

---

[226] To Ambrose Lisle Phillips 15 June, 1848 *LD* 12 p.222. The Tractarian Frederick Oakley (1802-80) was in charge of the Margaret St Chapel 1839-45 when he converted to Catholicism. The Church was built on the site 1850-9 by William Butterfield with the support of the Ecclesiological Society in Gothic revival mode.

[227] *End of Religious Controversy* Letter 33 p.174. John Milner (1752-1826) was appointed Vicar Apostolic of the Midland District in 1803 and published his *End of Religious Controversy* in 1818.

[228] To Newman 21 February 1866 *LD* 22 p.163n.

[229] Charles William Russell (1812-80) was made Professor in 1845 and became President in 1857. In 1841 Newman had written to him about "the extreme honours paid to St. Mary and other saints." He replied to Newman on 6 December 1865, *LD* 22 p.117n.

Lives' and devotional works, as being unsuitable to England"[230] and specifically warned Newman against books of devotion of the Italian school.[231]

Newman told Pusey,

I prefer English habits of belief to foreign from the same causes and by the same right which justified foreigners in preferring their own. In following those of my people, I show less singularity, and created less disturbance than if I made a flourish with what is novel and exotic.[232]

He had earlier explained to Miss Holmes that

The great benefit I feel in Roman books of devotion is their great and business-like practicalness, if I may so speak. They do for one what one wants, as being the writings of persons who *knew* the wants of people.[233] As to the weakness of the writers (intellectually) I do not think that what you allude to proves it. The truth is R Cs cannot write English. Our literature is essentially Protestant—All our great writers are such—all the strength, richness, and elegance of the language is devoted to the maintenance of Protestantism. R Cs are driven to foreign writers—they write their own language in consequence, like foreigners.[234]

He also privately noted that he could deal with a certain extravagance of devotion in detail, "by throwing this off as being foreign."[235] An example of this would be Louis Grignion de Montfort's encouragement of 'l'esclavage de Marie,' which

---

[230] See *Diff* p.[21]. Dr Thomas Griffiths (1791-1847) was Vicar Apostolic of the London District from 1836-47. "A very amiable taking person—not at all what I expected. Our talk was almost general—but satisfactory." Newman to Ambrose St. John 20 November 1845 *LD* 11 p.37.

[231] *Diff* 2 p.[21].

[232] Ibid. pp.20-21. Newman is referring to Faber's *Lives of the Saints*. See *Ker* pp.582-3.

[233] Newman gives a list of spiritual reading in *Dev* pp.432-6.

[234] To Mary Holmes 8 March 1843 *LD* 9 p.273. Mary Holmes was a governess and friend of Thackeray and Trollope. She met Newman in 1842 and was received into the Church in 1844.

[235] *TP* p.111.

tended to grate on English ears.[236] But he also told a congregation in 1848,

> If you cannot enter into the warmth of foreign books of devotion, it is a deficiency in you. To use strong words will not mend the matter; it is a fault within which can only gradually be overcome, but it is a deficiency, for this reason if for no other. Depend upon it, the way to enter into the sufferings of the Son is to enter into the sufferings of the mother. Place yourselves at the foot of the Cross, see Mary standing there, looking up and pierced with the sword. Imagine her feelings, make them your own. Let her be your great pattern.[237]

Wilfrid Ward remarks that Newman's "personal taste in devotion was always far more in sympathy with the continental forms than was that of the old Catholics (i.e. those who had remained faithful from the time of the Reformation). The Birmingham Oratory adopted Roman rather than Gothic vestments."[238] Newman was not overly demonstrative and shrank from some expressions of devotion while accepting an element of *schmaltz*, along with most Victorians.[239] He would strongly endorse Catholic spiritual authors[240] and would express "the greatest affection for Fr Faber's hymn *Eternal Years*, "and ... when I came to die, I should like to have it sung

---

[236] See *Diff* 2 p.[98]. "I choose you this day for my Mother and Queen. I deliver and consecrate myself to you as your slave, my body and soul." *Devotion to the Blessed Virgin* Supplement. Act of Consecration. See supra.

[237] *Our Lady in the Gospel* 26 March 1848 *CS* p.103.

[238] Wilfrid Ward *Life of John Henry Cardinal Newman* vol 1 London 1921 p.204 n2.

[239] See his *The Pilgrim Queen* which he wrote in 1850:

> "Here I sit desolate."
> sweetly said she,
> "Though I'm a queen,
> and my name is Marie;
> Robbers have rifled
> my garden and store,
> Foes they have stolen
> my heir from my bower..." *VV* pp.281-3.

[240] Newman had recommended 'R.C. books of devotion' such as Thomas à Kempis and Lorenzo Scupoli to Mary Holmes (see supra) in 1843 adding, 'if you leave out the Invocations.' *LD* 9 pp.274-5.

to me."[241] But he would add—just to confuse things—that he did not dispute "the right of who so will, to use devotions to the Blessed Virgin which seem to me unnatural and forced."[242] Affection can always be combined with reverence. Evelyn Waugh describes one aspect of the English Catholic attitude is to be 'at ease with the Awesome.'[243] Newman had to remind Faber that in hagiography, as in devotion there was the English perspective to be considered and that his own type of Italianate devotion should not lead him to condemn the habits of English Catholics as Protestant:[244]

> The lives of foreign saints, however edifying in their respective countries, are unsuited to England and unacceptable [offensive] to Protestants.[245]

Did Newman completely change his mind after 1845? Did he still remain attached to his loving friends with their kind and affectionate hearts[246] as not to depict Mary in a way that would cast scorn on any of their devotion? There would seem to be an undercurrent in much of his writings, including his *Letter,* which expressed his abiding sympathy for those he had left behind in 1845. Pusey would have been consoled to read the balanced words of Vatican II which "earnestly exhorts theologians and preachers of the word of God carefully to avoid all false exaggeration and equally a too narrow mentality in considering the special dignity of the Mother of God."[247]

---

[241] When he was very ill in 1889, it was sung for him accompanied by a harmonium and a violincello. Edward Bellasis *Coram Cardinali* Longmans 1917 pp.47-8.

[242] To Pusey 5 September 1865 *LD* 33 p.44.

[243] *Sword of Honour* London 2011 p.33.

[244] Meriol Trevor *The Pillar and the Cloud* London 1962 p.443.

[245] To Faber 30 October 1848 *LD* 12 p.316.

[246] 'The Parting of Friends' *SD* p.409.

[247] 'The Cult of the Blessed Virgin in the Church' *Lumen Gentium* n.67. The *Eirenicon* was put on the Index of Prohibited Books "in company with two heretical or unbelieving works," which" pained Pusey a good deal, and he has almost resolved to give up eirenicizing". Newman to Miss M. R. Giberne 30 December 1866 *LD* 22 p.334.

Newman on Catholic devotion

Jan Walgrave maintains that when it came to Mariology, Newman "took great pains to distinguish ... between the data of faith and the manifestations of piety."[248] Newman told William Walker, "I hoped to undeceive Anglicans on the subject of Our Lady."[249] He had always insisted "the doctrine about the Blessed Virgin is plain and simple; there are no varieties of opinion."[250] But devotion ought to go hand-in-hand with doctrine and not try to outstep it. There was always a possibility that popular devotion could threaten orthodoxy.

But when people now began to complain that Newman was somehow against Marian devotion, Bishop Ullathorne sprang to his defence.[251] He remonstrated in a long letter to the *Tablet* "... about the ungrateful attitude towards a man who wrote a masterly exposition of the subject most difficult for a Protestant to comprehend, and which has made that subject classical in the English tongue. The apprehension that Dr Newman is encouraging a dry and formal devotion towards the Blessed Virgin and the saints needs to be removed". Newman, he states, "took the name of Mary in Confirmation"[252] and "dedicated the Birmingham Oratory to the Immaculate Conception."[253] In Ireland he placed the University under the patronage of Maria Sedes Sapientiae.[254] The Birmingham Oratory was also the first in the country to introduce a cycle of Marian devotions.[255] Newman was quite candid:

---

[248] J. H. Walgrave *Newman the Theologian* London 1950 p.59.

[249] To William Walker 17 February 1866 *LD* 22 p.156. William Walker (1820-93) Rector of St Peter's Lancaster and Provost of the Liverpool Chapter.

[250] *TP* p.111.

[251] Newman had given him some of the details in a postscript to a letter of 1 April 1866 *LD* 22 p.199. Ullathorne's letter to *The Tablet* 4 April 1866 is an appendix in *LD* 22 pp.341-4.

[252] When he wrote to Pius IX asking for the papal blessing on the English foundation of the Oratory at Alcester Street in Birmingham, he signed his letter Giovanni M [Maria] Newman. 20 June 1847 *LD* 12 p.87.

[253] In 1851, three years before the proclamation of the dogma.

[254] *Mary, Seat of Wisdom*. One of the invocations in the *Litany of Loreto*.

[255] See Newman's letter to *The Tablet* 4 April 1866 *LD* 22 pp. 341-2. See the pages of Meditations for the Month of May *MD* pp. 3-113, *MD* 13-68.

I have ever been under her [Mary's] shadow, if I may say it. My College was St. Mary's, and my Church; and when I went to Littlemore, there, by my own previous disposition our Blessed Lady was waiting for me.[256] Nor did she do nothing for me in that low habitation, of which I always think with pleasure.[257]

It is interesting to note that in Newman's *A Short Road to Perfection* which he wrote in 1856, he makes the point that one should not gabble the words or allow them to become a sort of sacred mantra, but recite them in a reflective way or, in other words, "say the Rosary well."[258] He would also speak lyrically in his sermon in Oscott, in 1852, known as 'The Second Spring':

Arise Mary, and go forth in thy strength into that North country, which once was thy own, and take possession of a land which knows thee not. Arise, Mother of God, and with thy thrilling voice, speak to those who labour with child, and are in pain, till the babe of grace leaps within them! Shine on us, dear Lady. With thy bright countenance, O harbinger of peace, till our year is one perpetual May. From thy sweet eyes, from thy pure smile, from thy majestic brow, let ten thousand influences rain down, not to confound, or over-whelm, but to persuade, to win over thine enemies. O Mary, my hope, O Mother undefiled, fulfil to us the promise of this Spring.[259]

Pusey maintained that Catholics in their devotion distorted the reverence due to Christ. But Newman argued "As a body was prepared for Him, so was the place of that body prepared

---

[256] Littlemore Church was dedicated to St. Mary and St. Nicholas in September 1836.
[257] To Henry Wilberforce 12 January 1848 *LD* 12 pp153-4. Henry William Wilberforce (1807-73) was the youngest son of the philanthropist. He became Newman's pupil at Oriel in 1826 and later was presented to the living of East Farleigh at the wish of Prince Albert, which he resigned in 1850 when he, his wife and children were received into the Church. He was secretary of the Catholic Defence Association in Dublin and owner and editor of the *Weekly Register*. Newman preached at his funeral.
[258] *MD* p.383. See "Those who, at their prayers, think neither of God nor of what they say, do not pray well; but they offend God, if their distractions are willful." *Catechism of Catholic Doctrine* n.143.
[259] 13 July 1852 *OS* p.177.

also."[260] He added, "He is a God made low, she is a woman made high."[261] There is a revered place for Mary, because God had so honoured her and filled her with his grace. As Newman preached to his congregation in Birmingham in 1848,

> Every Church which is dedicated to her, every altar which is raised under her invocation, every image which represent her, every litany in her praise every Hail Mary for her continual memory does but remind us that there was One who though He was blessed from all eternity yet for the sake of sinners, 'did not shrink from the Virgin's womb.'[262]

As an Anglican, he had always had that firm regard for the dignity of Mary which enabled him to accept the veneration that Catholics gave:

> What must have been her gifts who was chosen to be the only earthly relative of the Son of God?[263]

> The power of the Mother and of the Son is all one. She being by her omnipotent Son made herself omnipotent [quoting Bossuet].[264]

He also emphasized that the Blessed Virgin is "*All*-Powerful, because she has, more than anyone else, more than all Angels and Saints, this great, prevailing gift of prayer. No one has access to the Almighty as His Mother has; none has merit such as hers. Her Son will deny her nothing that she asks; and herein lies her power."[265] He insisted on this to Pusey, reminding him that Mary is the Mother of God and "her office above is one of perpetual intercession for the faithful militant,"[266] a special presence in the Mystery of the Church.

---

[260] *CS* p.96 (1848). St Athanasius of Alexandria said, "Who is your equal in greatness, O dwelling place of God the Word?" *Homily of the Papyrus of Turin* ed. T. Lefort in *Le Muséon* 1958 p.216.

[261] *Diff* 2 p.[93].

[262] Discourse 17 'The Glories of Mary for the sake of her Son' *Mix* pp.348-9.

[263] *PPS* 2 'The Reverence due to the Virgin Mary' (March 25, 1832) p.132.

[264] Tract 71 (1836) *VM* 2 p.122.

[265] *MD* pp.103-104 'On the Assumption'.

[266] *Diff* 2 pp.[73, 84].

When it came to the question of considering Mary's sinlessness, from conception to the grave, Newman insisted that Mary always remained God's humble servant.[267] In Catholic devotion, together with the concept of Mary's sinlessness, developed the notion of her own sufferings which resonated with one's own personal distress. It can be argued that that the Church could not have defined the Immaculate Conception earlier than the nineteenth century because only by then had the theology and the spiritual insight on the part of the *sensus fidelium* come to that point.[268] Pusey concentrated on the need for Mary to be subject to the law of sin and not discern any difference between the Roman and Anglican doctrine of Original Sin. So he could dispute Newman's view that Catholics thought it as something negative and Anglicans as something positive.[269] Newman replied that Original Sin was not a radical change of nature but "the *deprivation* of that supernatural grace which Adam and Eve had on their first formation."[270] He explained to Pusey, "It was the *consequence* of deprivation. My words are 'deprivation and its consequences.'[271] A nature is a very different state which has never had grace, and which has forfeited it, as a dethroned and beggared prince is worse off than one who never was rich or great."[272] "Eve was created without sin like Mary"[273] but Mary is not specially created but born 'of Adam's race' into our sinful world yet preserved from sin. Newman insisted to a solicitor friend of Manning's that Mary was always 'in debt' to God for her immaculate state:

> What I have said in my letter was but a matter of fact, viz. that the Decree of 1854 did not deny that our Lady was under the debitum [debt]—that no Catholic was called to deny it—that I

---

[267] Luke 1:48.
[268] See B. C. Butler op. cit. supra pp.67-8.
[269] *Diff* 2 p.[48].
[270] Ibid. Council of Trent Session 6 *DS* 1551.
[271] *DS* 1553.
[272] To Pusey 12 February 1865 *LD* 22 p.152.
[273] *Diff* 2 p.[48].

did not deny it—that Suarez, the greatest theological authority of these latter times, affirmed it.[274]

If Eve had this supernatural inward gift given her from the first moment of her personal existence, is it possible to deny that Mary had this gift from the very first moment of her personal existence?"[275]

In considering Pusey's catalogue of Roman Catholic extravagances, Newman was at pains to point out that he had been very selective in his patristic sources. In contrast, Newman's selection of texts is chosen to represent the opinion of the universal Church taken from Fathers in Africa, Rome and Asia Minor. He also included (in his *Note 4*) Eastern liturgical sequences, because "before they were confessed by the church or even taught by the theologians they had already been believed and celebrated by the liturgy and devotion of the people,"[276] bearing in mind that Pusey was held in great renown in the Greek Church.[277] He pointed out that "the Eastern Churches … go further than we do… What have the Latins done so bold, as the substitution of the name of Mary for the name of Jesus at the end of the collects and petitions in the Breviary, nay, in the Ritual and Liturgy… To make a rule of substituting Mary with all Saints for Jesus in the public service, has more 'Mariolatry' in it, than to alter the Te Deum to her honour in private devotion."[278] He also reminded Pusey of their mutual acquaintance William Palmer, who was the author of Tract 15,[279] and told Hope-Scott,

---

[274] To M. J Rhodes 25 April 1866 *LD* 22 p.225. Matthew John Rhodes (1817-91) was admitted to the Inner Temple in 1837. He was received into the Church by Manning in 1852 and was the author of *The Visible Unity of the Catholic Church* London 1870. See *Diff* 2 p.[48]. Francisco de Suarez (1548-1617), Jesuit Professor and theologian, known as Doctor Eximius, in his *De Mysteriis Vitae Christi d* 3 (1592).

[275] *Diff* 2 p.46. This has been further emphasized among Catholics by the devotion to the Immaculate Heart of Mary since the apparitions at Fatima in 1917.

[276] Jaroslav Pelikan *The Christian Tradition* vol 2 Chicago 1977 p.141.

[277] *Diff* 2 p.[2].

[278] *Diff* 2 pp.[90-1]. "The Fathers of the eastern tradition call the Mother of God 'The All-Holy' *Panagia.*" *CC* 493

[279] 'On the Apostolic Succession in the English Church' (December 1833). William Palmer (1811-79), Fellow of Magdalen and also author of *Dissertations on Subjects relating to the Orthodox or Eastern-Catholic Communion* (1853), became a Catholic

He [Pusey] must not suppose that I mean to be lax ... so I go into the Patristic view of the B.V.M and ask him whether it is not a high one—and then expostulate with him, for making so much of what is but a slight addition to what the Fathers teach.[280]

Pusey and Newman on Scripture and Tradition

Newman had answered the problem, brought up by Pusey, about 'contradictory' views of famous theologians on the subject.[281] He had already explained in his *Apologia* the scruples of St Bernard[282] and the argument of St Thomas Aquinas being opposed to the Immaculate Conception from different doctrinal perspectives.[283] He mentioned in this respect, "Had they lived into this [day], would have rejoiced to accept it for its own sake."[284]

Pusey in his Tracts 67-69 on Baptism made use of the Fathers, but concentrated on Anglican authorities to support his argument. He adopts the same procedure in his *Eirenicon*, emphasizing doubts expressed by bishops and theologians alongside Patristic evidence. Newman was familiar with the attitude because when he had been asked to contribute to a 'History of the Councils' he was told "to give us a work on the Articles."[285] On rejecting the final work, he was told by the editors that "Mr. Newman's notions about tradition appears directly adverse to that which Protestant writers of our own church have contended".[286] It was much the same attitude

---

in 1855. Newman edited and published his *Notes of a Visit to the Russian Church* in 1882.

[280] To James Hope-Scott 26 November 1865 *LD* 22 p.113. Pusey selects texts which support his argument and ignores the overall witness.

[281] *En* pp.176-8.

[282] St Bernard applied the text "In iniquities was I conceived" (Ps 51:5) to everyone except Jesus but included Mary. *Letter* 174. *ML* 182, 333.

[283] St Thomas says in *S.T.* 3 a. 27 a. 2 "It is only a rational soul that is susceptible of guilt. The foetus that is conceived before the infusion of the soul is not subject to guilt ... the sanctification of the Blessed Virgin took place after her animation."

[284] *Apo* p.255.

[285] H. J. Rose to Newman 69 March 1831 *LD* 2 p.321.

[286] From W.R. Lyall to H. J. Rose 19 October 1843 *LD* 2 p.105. The resulting work was *The Arians of the Fourth Century* (1833).

towards Tradition, which would be reflected by Pusey in his *Letter*.

Newman first produced an argument from Scripture using texts from St John. The marriage feast of Cana points to Mary's intercessory role and Revelation Chapter 12 "would not have spoken of the Church under this particular image, *unless* there had existed a blessed Virgin Mary, who was exalted on high."[287] When he came to consider the "goodly fellowship of the Fathers"[288] he asked, "What dignity can be too great to attribute to her who is as closely bound up, as intimately one, with the Eternal Word, as Mother of God?"

> I hold, as you know, a process of development in Apostolic truth as time goes on, such development does not supersede the Fathers, but explains and completes them. And, in particular, as regards our teaching concerning the Blessed Virgin.[289]

He put it to Lady Chatterton,[290] "The earliest Fathers, St Justin, St. Irenaeus etc. contrast her with Eve, while they contrast our Lord with Adam."[291] He reminded Pusey, "The *primâ facie* view of her person and office, the broad outline laid down of her, the aspect under which she comes to us, in the writings of the Fathers. She is the Second Eve."[292]

He brought in the witness of the East (especially in his 'Postscript'), knowing how much Pusey valued their importance. He made his methodology plain to Robert Wilberforce in a 'Memorandum on the Immaculate Conception':

---

[287] *Diff* 2 pp.[57-61, 72-3].

[288] Tract 82 reprinted in *VM* 2 p.164.

[289] *Diff* 2 p.[24].

[290] See supra.

[291] To Lady Chatterton 2 October 1865 *LD* 22 p.66. Newman cites representatives of the second century and from the fourth and fifth centuries, making the point with Jerome that they speak for the whole world, p.42. "Many of the Fathers of early times declare in their preaching that 'the knot of Eve's disobedience was untied by Mary's obedience.'" *Lumen Gentium* n. 56.

[292] *Diff* 2 p.[31].

Now I wish it observed *why* I adduce the Fathers and Scripture. Not to *prove* the doctrine, but to rid it of any such monstrous improbability as would make a person *scruple* to accept it *when* the Church declares it. A Protestant is apt to say: 'Oh, I really never, never can accept such a doctrine from the hands of the Church, and I had a thousand thousand times rather determine that the Church spoke falsely, than that so terrible a doctrine was true.'[293]

He takes up Pusey's point about the Fathers' occasional inconsistencies, and says that they were concentrating on defeating heresy and their teaching "commends itself as the one true interpretation, from its appositeness,—because no other view of doctrine, which can be ascribed to the inspired writers, so happily solves the obscurities and seeming inconsistencies of their teaching."[294] The theological argument from Tradition demands a *general accord* among Fathers which allows for the odd divergence.

Pusey conceded that Newman had made a good case when he provided more patristic quotations in *Enchiridion II* but gave prominence to the contrary opinion of Cardinal de Turrecremata on the Immaculate Conception.[295] His argument (which sweeps aside Newman's abundant patristic evidence), was that Pius IX's Bull *Ineffabilis* "appears to assert only one side of the doctrine. If it means more than what it asserts, it will have to be in acknowledged contradiction to the whole teaching of the universal Church in all ages, with the exception of the Roman Catholic Church at that moment."[296] Newman pointed out to Pusey that,

---

[293] *MD* p.124. Robert Isaac Wilberforce (1802-57) became a Catholic in 1854.
[294] *Diff* 2 p.[57].
[295] Juan de Torquemada OP (1388-1463). Papal theologian at the Council of Basle in 1433. His treatise, *De Veritate Conceptionis Beatae Virginis*, which rejected the doctrine, was published in 1547. Pusey quotes him in *En* p.334. Newman would later point out to Pusey that "your quotation from Cardinal Turrecremata is not to be found in him." 7 October 1866 *LD* 22 p.297. Pusey would bring out his own edition of Turrecremata's work in 1869. *Liddon* vol. 4 pp.181-2.
[296] *Liddon* vol. 4 p.163.

It has always been trusted that the received belief of the faithful and the obligations of piety would cover a larger circuit of doctrinal matters that was formally claimed, and secure a more generous faith than was imperative on the conscience. Hence there has never been a wish on the part of the Church to cut clean between doctrine revealed and doctrine not revealed; first indeed because she actually *cannot* do so at any given moment, but is illuminated from time to time as to what was revealed in the beginning on this or that portion of the whole mass of teaching which is now received; but secondly, because for that very reason she would be misrepresenting the real character of the dispensation, as God has given it.[297]

There was in Pusey's whole position a reluctance to give Mary undue affection. He could not understand the 'human' place which went with her theological position that she had in the Catholic church. Newman pointed out to him, "I have not found any one (I think) who has not been repelled by what has been thought your hostile tone."[298] It was "rhetorical and unfair".[299] He also complained, "Have you even hinted that our love for her is anything ese than an abuse? Have you thrown her one kind word yourself all through your book?"[300] Pusey failed to understand that Catholics instinctively felt that Mary was close to them, being able to feel the full extent of human weakness, precisely *because* she had not known sin,[301] whereas Pusey could not think along those lines. Newman added something which would also question the foundation of Pusey's deepest hopes for Christian unity: "They have not done you justice here; because in truth, the honour of our Lady is dearer to them [Roman Catholics] than the conversion of England."[302]

---

[297] To Pusey 22 March 1867 *LD* 23 p.99.
[298] To Pusey July 4 1869 *LD* 24 p.284.
[299] To Keble 8 October 1865 *LD* 22 p.67.
[300] *Diff* 2 p.[116].
[301] "Not having known sin, she is able to have compassion on every kind of weakness. She understands sinful man and loves him with a Mother's love." John Paul II *Veritatis Splendor* (1993) n.120.
[302] Ibid.

Original projects

Newman decided that he would cut short his original project. When asked about a second pamphlet, he told W. G. Ward "I should be obliged to have a few sentences to the effect that the Pope's infallibility was not a point of faith—that would be all."[303] But then in March he said it would be "about the Pope's infallibility in *some* means, and about the subject matter of the Church's infallibility."[304] He decided in the end to limit himself to Pusey's objections to Marian devotion, because he had been ill and was exhausted;[305] and as an additional justification, "it would not come into the right number of pages."[306] He referred to the matter in his Journal:

> I laid down two subjects for discussion—the prerogatives of our Lady, and their abuse—and those of the Holy See and their abuse. I wished to consider each subject argumentatively, and to ascertain the intellectual view to be taken of each. The former took up so any pages, and the latter subject was so large and intricate that I published on the subject of the Bl. Virgin, leaving the subject of the Holy See for a separate pamphlet. When I did so, some anonymous Catholic wrote in a Protestant paper that I was forbidden, or certainly should be forbidden at Rome, did I attempt to write upon my second subject.[307]

He noted at the time, "I have not enough to say, nor would it be *tanti*, [too little] to write simply against *him* [Pusey] unless I did something to establish a moderate view about the Pope and the church, as against Ward, as in my first Pamphlet I had established a moderate view about the Blessed Virgin as

---

[303] To W. G. Ward 18 February 1866 *LD* 22 p.157.

[304] To Canon Walker 12 March 1866 *LD* 22 p.178.

[305] To David Moriaty Bishop of Kerry. "I found myself so fatigued when I came to the end of it" 23 March 1866 *LD* 22 p.187.

[306] To Mrs. F. R. Ward 17 December 1865 *LD* 22 p.122. Mrs. Francis Ward (1817-89) became a Catholic with her husband and brother, the Vicar of St. Saviour's, Leeds, in 1857.

[307] *Journal* 29 January 1868 *AW* p.265. George Williams, a High Churchman and Fellow of King's College Cambridge so wrote to the *Guardian* 21 March 1866. Newman had to contradict it in a letter to the Editor 23 March 1866 *LD* 22 p.186.

against other extreme writers."[308] He also did not want to get involved in Archbishop Manning's ecclesiological views, which had prompted Pusey in the first place. Newman could argue that the subject of the Papacy was covered by Fr. Ignatius Ryder's work 'in answer to Mr. Ward', which was published two years later.[309]

Meriol Trevor remarks that there was another reason. He had to put it aside "in the face of the violent opposition in the Catholic press."[310] She is referring to the Rome correspondent of the *Tablet*, E. R. Martin, who attacked Newman for taking Mary's prerogative to pieces, "not reverently, not lovingly, not devotionally, but coldly, dogmatically and drily."[311] But Wilfrid Ward said Fr. Neville told him "that, when writing the letter to Pusey, Newman decided after much thought and prayer that it was not wise to deal at that moment with so delicate and burning a topic as the papal claims."[312] Newman told Fr William Walker, that "there was far more difference among Catholics on questions connected with the Church than on those arising out of our doctrine about the Blessed Virgin."[313]

Newman argued that Catholic Marian belief, far from being an exaggeration, reinforced devotion to her Son. He wrote to Emily Bowles,

> What I have done, I have tried to do well—but a reader will say "*This* is all! *I* have no difficulties about the Blessed Virgin.

---

[308] 26 February 1866 *TP* p.111. He intended that the second letter would be "about the Pope's infallibility in *some* measure, and about the subject matter of the Church's infallibility." To Canon Walker 12 March 1866 *LD* 22 p.176.

[309] Henry Ignatius Dudley Ryder (1837-1907) *Idealism in Theology, A Review of Dr. Ward's Scheme of Dogmatic Authority* London 1867. He was the eldest son of George Ryder who joined the Birmingham Oratory in 1856 taking the name of Ignatius. He was Superior 1890-1907. See *Diff* 2 p.[17]n and Newman's letter to W. G. Ward 30 April 1867 *LD* 23 p.197.

[310] Meriol Trevor *Prophets and Guardians* London 1969 p.112.

[311] *Tablet* 10 March 1866. Edwin Roper Martin had recently become a Catholic and was studying privately for the priesthood while acting as Rome correspondent. He also attacked Newman about his plan for an Oratory in Oxford. He was ordained for the Shrewsbury diocese in 1869 and died in 1877. See *LD* 22 p.178n.

[312] Wilfrid Ward vol. 2 p.107.

[313] To William Walker 28 February 1866 *LD* 22 p.168 William Walker (1820-93). Professor at Ushaw College 1835-1845, Rector of St. Peter's Lancaster 1869-93 and Provost of the Liverpool Chapter.

Pusey only goes off on the old story, which I heard about years ago.[314]

Newman told W. G. Ward that.

As to writing a volume on the Pope's infallibility, it never so much as entered my thoughts. I am a controversalist, not a theologian. And I should have nothing to say about it. I have ever thought it likely to be true, never thought it certain.[315]

Newman noticed that Pusey in *Eirenicon III,* pursuing his search for Christian Reunion, returned to the subject of "idolatry in the *cultus of the Blessed Virgin*" but went on to express his objections at "interference with Christian liberty from an arbitrary, boundless authority of the Pope or some interference with the due authority of a Christian sovereign in matters temporal."[316] Newman came to feel that there were parallels between those who exaggerated Marian devotion and the exuberance of Ultramontanes in their attitude to the exercise of papal power. He would combine both *Letters* in 1876, feeling he could promote the authentically moderate Catholic viewpoint, while at the same time answering both Pusey and Gladstone's objections, adding five appendices (*Notes*) to his original *Letter.*

II. A LETTER ADDRESSED TO THE DUKE OF NORFOLK

Unlike the *Letter to Pusey* which was written to him, the *Letter to the Duke of Norfolk* was really addressed to William Gladstone. Newman wanted to respond to a political diatribe directed at Catholic teaching in a calm and reasonable manner; pointing out how his information was at fault, while treating it as an explanation to one of his former students who had the

---

[314] To Emily Bowles 18 January 1866 *LD* 22 p.129.
[315] To W. G. Ward 18 February 1866 *LD* 22 p.157
[316] *Eirenicon* III pp 39, 40.

hereditary position of Earl Marshall of England[317] and was "the special representative and the fitting example of a laity as zealous for the Catholic religion as it is patriotic."[318]

William Gladstone never really understood the essence of Roman Catholicism. He thought that it might evolve in the fulness of time into a variant of Anglicanism, despite having a problem with certain aspects of Church teaching and its exercise of papal authority. But while expressing his distaste of the decree of infallibility he wanted at the same time to direct his remarks to moderate Catholics "to help them to do their duty" as he put it to his fellow member of the Cabinet, the Earl of Granville.[319] He was hoping to provoke a response and called his pamphlet *A Political Expostulation*, which was published, hardly by accident on Guy Fawkes day.[320] He argued, with no sense of sophistry that in it that he would "eschew not only religious bigotry but likewise religious controversy"[321] and "that his part was not that of a theological partisan but simply of a good citizen."[322]

Newman, having initially told W. G. Ward, "As to writing a volume on the Pope's infallibility, it never so much entered into my thoughts,"[323] was finally urged to reply by several of

---

[317] Henry Fitzalan-Howard (1847-1917). He succeeded his father as 15th Duke in 1860 and went to the Oratory School, 1861-4. He volunteered for the Boer War at the age of 52, and as a personal friend he played a role in securing Newman's Cardinalate in 1879. He was sent by Queen Victoria as her personal representative to the Vatican in 1887.

[318] *Diff* 2 p.[175].

[319] *Political Correspondence of Mr. Gladstone and Lord Granville 1868-1876*. Agatha Ramm ed. Oxford 1952 vol 2, p.458. The 2nd Earl of Granville (1815-91) was colonial secretary in 1868 and foreign secretary 1870-4. Newman writing to Lord Blachford on 2 October 1874 said "He [Gladstone] will do us a service, if he gives us an opportunity of speaking." *LD* 27 pp.122-3.

[320] *The Vatican Decrees in Their Bearing on Civil Allegiance. A Political Expostulation*, published by John Murray 5 November 1874. Gladstone sold nearly 150,000 copies of his pamphlet by the end of December and had received £2,000, the modern equivalent of nearly £200,000. The *Guardian* commented on 2 December, "This is unquestionably the greatest success ever achieved by a political pamphlet." *LD* 32 p.346 n.3.

[321] He renounces this in *TVD* p.14 but returns to questions of divinity on p.15. See *Diff* 2 p.[309].

[322] *TVD* pp.9, 57.

[323] To W. G. Ward 18 February 1866 *LD* 22 p.154. William George Ward (1812-82). Fellow of Balliol until deprived of it for writing *The Ideal of the Christian Church* in

his friends including Bishop Brown of Newport, and Dr. Russell.[324] He had thought of Monsell[325] as a possible respondent but asked him, "Would it not affect you in some ways which I do not know and you only *do* ? How would it affect your political position in Ireland to quarrel with Dr Cullen and his Bishops?"[326] He told Ambrose Philipps later that he felt he had to tackle it himself, "as a matter of duty."[327] He had then been "hard at it for five or six hours a day for five or six weeks and had produced nothing."[328] On December 6th he said Mass 'for my attempt', began again and completed it in four weeks: "Life seemed to come into me all of a sudden, and from that day I wrote straight off without stopping".[329] Published on 14 January, the day that Gladstone resigned as Leader of the Liberal Party, it ran to 150 closely-printed pages. It was like the experience he had with the *Apologia* all over again, yet he was now seventy-four and it would turn out to be

---

1844. He was received into the Church with his wife in 1845, taught philosophy and theology at St. Edmund's Ware and was editor of *Dublin Review* 1863-78.

[324] Bishop Ullathorne, in support of Newman, told Cardinal Franchi in 1875 that the *Letter* was in response to the requests of several prominent Catholics. Appendix 1 *LD* 27 p.404. William Bernard Ullathorne (1806-89). As a Benedictine monk he volunteered as Vicar General for Australia in 1832. Returning to England, he became Vicar Apostolic for the Western District in 1846 and Bishop of Birmingham in 1850. Bishop Thomas Joseph Brown (1798-1880) was Prior of Downside and in 1850 Bishop of Newport. He delated Newman's *Rambler* article to Rome but later wanted him to be his peritus at the Council. Charles William Russell (1812-80) was Professor of Church History at Maynooth and President in 1857.

[325] William Monsell (1812-94). He was at Oriel in 1831 and was MP for Limerick 1847-74; he was received into the Church in 1850. He had various posts in Liberal governments and was created Lord Emly in 1874.

[326] To William Monsell 12 January 1865 *LD* 21 p.385. Dr Paul Cullen (1803-78) became bishop of Armagh in 1849 and was translated to Dublin in 1852; he was trying to negotiate with the government the status of the Catholic University of Ireland. Monsell on his side was being kept in touch by Sir George Grey who had been Colonial Secretary and Home Secretary.

[327] To Ambrose Phillips de Lisle 29 November 1875 *LD* 32 p.363. William Neville noted that the writing began in earnest on St. Clement's day (24 November), to whom Newman "had a great devotion." (*BOA*) Ambrose Lisle March Philipps (1809-78) was received into the Church in 1824 and co-founded AUPC in 1838 with Frederick Lee. See supra.

[328] To William Monsell, Lord Emly 23 November 1874 *LD* 27 p.159.

[329] To R. W. Church 18 January 1875 *LD* 27 p.194. Richard William Church (1815-90). Fellow of Oriel in 1838-52 when he became Rector of Whately. He became Dean of St. Paul's in 1871 and wrote a history of the Oxford Movement which was published posthumously.

his last complete book. Although it was aimed at Gladstone, he followed convention and addressed the *Letter* not to the politician but to the first peer of the realm, the young Duke of Norfolk[330] who was "the special representative and the fitting sample of a laity as zealous for the Catholic religion as it is patriotic."[331] The *Letter* was published on 14 January 1875. By 10th August Newman had received £500, the modern equivalent of nearly £50,000, from his publisher B. M. Pickering who wrote, "Seldom a day goes by but I sell a copy."[332]

Newman later combined both Pusey's and Gladstone's *Letters* in volume 2 of *Certain Difficulties felt by Anglicans in Catholic Teaching Considered*.[333] He felt that both letters in their way argued the need to defend Catholic doctrine and differentiate traditional teaching from extremist views. Gladstone had himself linked the two subjects when he wrote, "The growth of what is often termed among Protestants, 'Mariolatry'"[334] and a belief in Papal Infallibility, "that was notoriously advancing but it seems not fast enough to satisfy the dominant party."[335]

W. E. Gladstone

Gladstone was first introduced to Newman by Frederic Rogers[336] in 1831, when Newman, who had been Rogers' tutor had begun work on *Arians* and was Vicar of St. Mary's. Gladstone was interested in things spiritual and admitted at the time, "his mental life was concentrated in the Church."[337] He was also friends with contemporaries Hope Scott[338] at Christ

---

[330] See supra p.lxiv.

[331] *Diff* 2 p.[175].

[332] *LD* 27 p.340 n.4.

[333] See Appendix on Printing History. *Diff* 2 was published by B M Pickering in 1876.

[334] *TVD* p.14.

[335] *TVD* p.xxvi.

[336] Gladstone noted in his diary for 20 August "… had tea with Rogers at Iffley to meet Newman as he kindly asked me." *The Gladstone Diaries* I 1825-1832 ed. M. R. D. Foot, Oxford 1968.

[337] *The Prime Minister's Papers W E. Gladstone* eds. J Brooke and M. Sorenson (1971-81) 4 vols vol 1 p.145.

[338] James Robert Hope-Scott (1812-73) See supra.

Church and Henry Manning at Balliol.[339] Newman was his senior by eight years, but Gladstone attended his Sermons and read the Tracts. They met up from time to time,[340] until he took a First in *Literae Humaniores* [Greats], and politics began to claim him. Yet he would at the same time, in a somewhat cryptic phrase, "honestly aim at enabling the Church to develop her own intrinsic means."[341]

William Ewert Gladstone was born in Liverpool in 1809, but with Scottish ancestry. His grandfather had come from Biggar and the family name was Gledstanes. William Ewert was his father's business partner in the corn and tobacco markets and was largely responsible for the Liverpool Corn Exchange. By 1820 he was worth more than a third of a million pounds, a generous proportion coming from his investments in plantations in Demerara; and this enabled him to live in some splendour in Seaforth House in Crosby. In 1829 John Gladstone bought an estate at Fasque in Kincardineshire where the family would move in 1833. By this time, Gladstone had resolved his religious turmoil and decided (with his father's prompting) on a political career. Edward Short has drawn attention to an unresolved tension that would always be present in his life, "Gladstone longed to be free of what he considered to be the slavery of politics so he could devote himself to God."[342] He was a good slave nevertheless, allowing himself to be returned—thanks to the influence of the Duke of Newcastle—as a young member of Parliament for Newark in January 1830, but mentioning on the hustings a defence of the established Church of Ireland. There was that underlying religious emphasis, which he mentioned when he wrote to Manning,

---

[339] Henry Edward Manning See supra.
[340] See Diary *LD* 4 pp.98, 191n; *LD* 5 p.13.
[341] *The Gladstone Diaries 1825-1896* eds. M. R. D Foot and H. C. G. Matthew 14 vols 1968-94. 27 March 1842.
[342] Edward Short *Newman and his Contemporaries.* New York 2011 p.242.

Politics would become an utter blank to me, were I to make the discovery that we were mistaken in maintaining their association with religion.[343]

Gladstone always retained certain reservations about Newman. He told Lord Acton after Newman's death, "I was not a friend of his but only an acquaintance treated with extraordinary kindness."[344] He identified more with Manning and in 1838, after his wife had died, holidayed with him in Rome. Newman on his part saw fine qualities in him and remarked to Hurrell Froude in 1834, "Gladstone is very promising, good and staunch fellow we know he is."[345] In December 1834 the promising fellow would be offered by Robert Peel the post of under-secretary in the Colonial Office, and his London address was L2, The Albany, Piccadilly. Although he had abandoned the idea of the Anglican ministry, he still saw his career in a religious context: "Restrict the sphere of politics to earth, and it becomes a secondary science."[346] He went to church every day, concerned himself with religious fraternities and joined a lay brotherhood founded by Thomas Dyke Acland[347] which was involved in works of mercy and charity. He served on projects to revitalize Anglicanism, of which in September 1840 he had "ten plans in view". His interests would always remain church politics and "the moral efficacy of religion."[348]

As he climbed the political ladder, he became Colonial Secretary in 1845, MP for Oxford in 1847, leader of the Liberal Party in 1867 and Prime Minister four times. Early on, Gladstone began to note the emerging conflict between the Government and the Church and felt the need to bridge the gap. His first contribution in 1838 was *The State in Relations with the Church*. In it he outlined a plan by which the English State

---

[343] 5 April 1835 *The Gladstone Papers* British Library.

[344] John Morley *Life of W. E. Gladstone* London 1903 vol. 3 pp.421-2.

[345] To R. H. F. Froude 14 June 1834 *LD* 4 p.277. Hurrell Froude see supra.

[346] Comment made in 1832. Perry Butler, *Gladstone, Church, State and Tractarianism, 1809-1859* London.1982 p.42.

[347] Thomas Dyke Acland (1808-98). Fellow of All Souls 1831-7 and MP for West Somerset 1837-47; a friend of Newman as an undergraduate and later a Tractarian.

[348] Edward Short iam cit. p.221.

should be obliged by its Christian conscience to enter into a renewed and improved joint partnership with the Anglican Church.[349] The *Times* commented,

> He has done little else than disturb questions which, under the present temper and settled arrangements of society no discreet Christian or constitutionalist should have ventured to revive much less in the spirit of slavish mysticism with which his work is unhappily imbue. If this gentleman's views of the Church of England, as a tame dilution of Romanism, could be supposed to obtain extensive credit she may henceforth write *Ichabod*[350] on all her gates, for assuredly her doom were sealed.[351]

Gladstone would always have a somewhat broader vision which would include "a new reconciliation of Christianity and mankind."[352] He never quite saw how the partnership would work, yet he had a sense of vocation and unashamedly declared in 1868, "The Almighty seems to sustain me for some purpose of His own, deeply unworthy as I know myself to be."[353]

Gladstone and Newman

Newman appreciated Gladstone's perspective, although he could see problems ahead, "When the Isis flows back and St Mary's spire turns into a railroad train, he will begin to waver and repent of his book. I believe he is a sure man, as far as he commits himself."[354] Gladstone was in no way put off by his critics and issued its companion volume, *Church Principles Considered in their Results*, in 1840. Newman, willing to see the good in people, observed to Rogers that "Gladstone's book is not open to the objection I feared; it is doctrinaire and (I think) somewhat self-confident, but it will do good." But then he added, interestingly, "Somehow there is great earnestness,

---

[349] Richard Shannon, *Gladstone, God and Politics* p.21.

[350] "The glory has departed", literally "Where is the glory?" 1 Sam 4:21.

[351] *The Times* 21 January 1839 p.4.

[352] To Newman 18 February 1866 *LD* 22 p.162.

[353] Richard J Evans iam cit. p.573.

[354] To Miss M. R. Giberne 11 July 1839 *LD* 7 p.103. Miss Giberne see supra.

but a want of amiableness in him."[355] Nevertheless he regretted that Gladstone was "the leader of a mixed multitude, who profess a Babel of religions or none at all."[356] Some would describe Gladstone as "tall, fanatical and verbose."[357] Queen Victoria herself told her daughter that Mr. Gladstone "was so wonderfully unsympathetic"[358] but on other occasions "a half-mad firebrand."[359] John Brown, Queen Victoria's man servant, maintained that he was a secret papist.[360] In fact Gladstone's whole attitude combined elements of Pietism with political economy. He confessed to Manning:

> Everything, of course, but conscience should be surrendered for the sake of peace. On the other hand, I am afraid our people generally are not impressed yet with the *duty* of seeking unity, nor do they comprehend that genuine elasticity in the principles of Catholic Communion which permits, and what alone safely permits, a large toleration in matters not of faith…
> I have, as I have ventured to tell you, my own private apprehensions of Oxford opinions, particularly as regards the doctrine of justification. I believe it might be a blessing to our theology, if the word would be forgotten altogether, for I do not know what idea it conveys to any mind that is not carried by one of the two terms pardon and sanctification. I cannot tell in Newman's book [*Jfc*] what the thing really is for which he is arguing: I dread beyond measure, I confess to you, the doctrine of human *desert,* come it in what form it may, and a sermon in his fifth volume [*PPS* 5, 12] staggers me exceedingly.[361] I dread the working out of, not his notions, for I do not understand them, but his propositions—the time when

---

[355] To Rogers 26 December 1840 *LD* 7 p.470.

[356] To F. G. Lee 5 April 1872 *LD* 26 p.55. Frederick George Lee (1832-1902). The Vicar of All Saints' Lambeth, one of the founders of the Association for the Propagation of the Unity of Christendom (A.P.U.C.) in 1857. He became a Catholic in 1901.

[357] A. N. Wilson *Victoria, A Life*. London 2014 p.307.

[358] R. Fulford ed. *Darling Child: Private Correspondence of Queen Victoria and the German Crown Princess,* 1871-78 London 1976 p.29.

[359] Paula Bartley *Queen Victoria* London 2016 p.231.

[360] According to Baron Arthur Ponsonby, Queen Victoria's Private Secretary. Edward Short op. cit. p.232.

[361] 'The New Works of the Gospel'. In it Newman said, "Let us aim at doing nothing in a dead way; let us beware of dead works, dead forms, dead professions. Let us pray to be filled with the spirit of love," p.177.

they shall have become popular, practical, familiar among us… My crude idea of justifying faith is naked perception of the Redeemer.[362]

He conceded however, having read Newman's "noble volume of sermons, "… I think it would be the basis of a high and permanent reputation."[363] At the same time Gladstone praised Manning's *The Unity of the Church* (the volume was dedicated to Gladstone), saying,

I wish for the interest of truth that this had been more sedulously enforced upon public attention by the Oxford writers in the Tracts and other publications with which they have been connected.[364]

Gladstone and Catholicism

Gladstone's grand ideas suffered a jolt when his sister Helen indicated in 1842 that she wanted to become a Roman Catholic. He noted in his diary that if it was in his power, he "would drag a woman by the hair, to save her from drowning.[365] He later told Robert Wilberforce[366] (who was not at that time a Catholic), "In quitting the Church of England you inflict on it the worst injury it can receive." When Newman took the step he described it as "The greatest crisis, and the sharpest that the Church has known since the Reformation."[367] He would later reflect, "His [Newman's] secession from the Church of England has never yet been estimated among us at anything like the full amount of its calamitous importance.… much greater than the partial secession of John Wesley."[368] Gladstone's contribution to the debate was in the form of an Essay, *Catholic development in the Church of England or Catholicism and Protestantism in the*

---

[362] To Henry Manning 22 April 1841 *LD* 8 p.179n.
[363] *Diary* 24 July 1842 *LD* 9 p.47n.
[364] To Henry Manning 30 June 1842, *Purcell* vol 1 p.271. Manning commented that "it was the best apology I could make for the Anglican Church—and the last."
[365] Diary 29 May 1842 *LD* 9 p.24n.
[366] *LD* 9 p.205n. Robert Isaac Wilberforce (1802-57). See supra.
[367] To Henry Manning 24 October 1843 *The Gladstone Papers* British Library 44274, 177. Manning dedicated his *The Unity of the Church* to his friend Gladstone.
[368] *Vaticanism: An Answer to Replies and Reproofs*. London 1875. pp.10-11.

Church of England.[369] Newman expressed his appreciation of the author:

> I never would presume to criticize any act of yours except in the abstract. I have too heartfelt a respect for qualities which it would be a disrespect to mention more particularly, to make the person who owns them a subject of remark or complaint.[370]

He told Bowden that Gladstone was

> Very kind, but like a statesman he takes a mere practical view of the matter, and gives no solution of the difficulties which cause our present distress. When persons have got it into their head that a union with Rome is *necessary* for their being Catholics, it is in vain to tell them, that they have no chance of making the *English Nation* submit itself to Rome. They have no *plans,* but view the matter as a personal one.[371]

When Newman retired finally to Littlemore, Gladstone noted in his diary that he "saw Newman and conv. [convent] on the road." But according to Newman, he did call,[372] and he also noted in his diary that he came with a party that afternoon to Evensong.[373] Gladstone could not bring himself to admit it.

Newman's secession was followed by the double blow of the 'going' of Manning and Hope[374] in 1851, as a result of the Gorham judgement,[375] which at the same time showed up the one-sidedness of the partnership between Church and State. More 'blows' would follow. Gladstone's Anglicanism did not

---

[369] *Foreign and Colonial Review* October 1843.

[370] To Gladstone 22 January 1845 *LD* 10 p.503

[371] To J. W Bowden (1799-1844) 31 October 1843 *LD* 9 p.594. Newman's friend when he was at Trinity. He was a Tractarian and wrote Tracts 5, 29, 30 and 56.

[372] Diary 17 April 1843 *LD* 9 p.308n.

[373] Diary Tuesday 18 April 1843 *LD* 9 p.310.

[374] James Robert Hope Scott. See supra.

[375] Revd. Charles Gorham's doubts about baptismal regeneration in 1847 caused bishop Phillpotts of Exeter not to institute him to a living (Phillpotts was the model for Trollope's Archdeacon Grantley). On appeal, the Judicial Committee of the Privy Council overturned the bishop's decision.

seem troubled either by the Jerusalem bishopric affair[376] or the Gorham judgement; but he was disturbed by the emergence of English Catholicism, which added point to Newman's observation that "Protestantism is, or it has been for centuries, the religion of England"[377] The year before there had been the proclamation of a Roman Catholic hierarchy in the exuberant tones of Wiseman's first pastoral letter, 'Out of the Flaminian Gate' proclaiming, "Catholic England has been restored to its orbit in the ecclesiastical firmament from which its light had long vanished." Such *Romanitá* came as an insult to Gladstone's idea of the identification of Englishness and Anglicanism and was seen generally by the country as 'Papal Aggression.'[378] He talked in his *Expostulation* of being susceptible to the "aggressive activity and imagined growth of the Roman Church, as well as the efforts of some Anglican clergy to romanise the Church and the people of England."[379]

A Question of Loyalty

An appeal to nationalism has always been a winning formula in England, especially when allied to a jealous regard for private judgement and a rejection of any foreign interference: "Meetings are held, denunciations lauded, calumnies spread abroad."[380] In former times it ineluctably led to cries of anti-Popery: The English were willing to believe the malign inventions of Titus Oates and to condemn Archbishop Oliver Plunkett, the Primate of Ireland, to a cruel death at Tyburn in 1681. At the trial the judge berated him for his religion,

> Ten times worse than all the heathenish superstitions; the most dishonourable and derogatory to God and his glory of all religions or pretended religions whatsoever, for it undertakes

---

[376] In 1841 an Anglican bishopric for Jerusalem was established, to be nominated by England and Prussia alternately. The scheme collapsed in 1886, and Jerusalem came under Anglican jurisdiction and an Archbishopric in 1957.
[377] *Diff* 1 p.20.
[378] The name given by the British press to the action of Pius IX restoring the Catholic hierarchy in 1850 and its reference to the Church of England as 'the Anglican Schism'.
[379] *TVD* pp.5, 6.
[380] *Diff* 1 p.viii.

to dispense with God's laws and to pardon the breach of them.[381]

This national sentiment was responsible for the emergence of the *Little Englander* movement which began with Manchester industrialists in 1859 and was taken up by Gladstone and the Liberal party. Wesley in his day had referred to Quakerism, Fanaticism and Popery in the same breath,[382] and Charles Dickens knew the Gordon Riots of 1780 as a backdrop for *Barnaby Rudge* (published in 1841) would guarantee success.

Newman himself would be the victim in the Achilli affair,[383] but the actual presence in the country of a Cardinal at the head of a hierarchy in 1850 managed to produce an outburst of jingoism,[384] seeing Catholics as 'Johnny Foreigners' and disloyal. Gladstone at the time remarked, "Has not a foreign power a hold on their consciences?" Years later he described his friend Dr. Manning not as Archbishop of Westminster but as 'Head of the Papal Church in England'[385] and said,

The name of Popery, which was formerly imposed *ad invidiam* [an argument that appeals to popular hatred] by heated antagonists, and justly resented by Roman Catholics, appears now to be perhaps the only name which describes, at once with point and accuracy, the religion promulgated from the Vatican in 1870.[386]

---

[381] Tomàs ò Fiaich and Desmond Forristal *Oliver Plunket. His Life and Letters* Huntington Ind. 1975 p.239. See also Jane Lane *Titus Oates* London 1949 pp.260, 364. Titus Oates (1649-1705). His plot lasted from 1678-81.

[382] *Works* III p.152.

[383] Dr. Giovanni Giacinto Achilli (1803-60). The former Dominican priest was brought to England by the Evangelical Alliance in 1850. See the excellent treatment of anti-Catholicism in Andrew Nash's Introduction to *Prepos* Newman Millennium Edition Vol. I. Leominster 2000 pp.xvi-xxi, 427-8.

[384] Jingoism. A contemporary expression at the time of the Russo-Turkish War of 1877-8 made popular by G. W. Hunt's song: 'We don't want to fight, but by jingo if we do, We've got the ships, we've got the men, and got the money too.' The magazine *Punch* in November 1850 portrayed the Pope as 'The Guy Fawkes of 1850' distributing mitres, (labelled Clapham, Pimlico, Margate, Mile-End and Westminster) instead of gunpowder, 'preparing to blow up all England'.

[385] *Diff* 2 p.[190]. *TVD* p.52.

[386] *Vaticanism* p.92. See supra.

The English Protestant Association declared, "To design the advancement of Popery is to design the ruin of the State."[387] Lord John Russell, the Whig Prime Minister wrote to the *Times,*

> I feel persuaded that we are strong enough to repel any outward attacks. The liberty of Protestantism has been enjoyed to long in England to allow any successful attempt to impose a foreign yoke upon our minds and consciences. No foreign prince or potentate will be at liberty to foster his fetters upon a nation that has so long and so nobly vindicated its right to freedom of opinion, civil, political and religious.[388]

Two decades later when Gladstone's Irish University Bill was defeated in February 1873, he saw 'the hand of Rome' in it'[389] and offered the first of his resignations. There remained an underlying spirit of anti-Catholicism which was expressed by the Ecclesiastical Titles Bill: the prohibition of tolling a bell in Catholic Churches and the banning of religious habits in the street.[390] Pius IX's secular policy was seen "as especially distasteful to Englishmen."[391] The *Times* at the time gave a hint that "since there was need of a cry, perhaps a party might be formed on the basis of the 'No Popery.'"[392]

When the Vatican Council declared the infallibility of the Pope, it brought the whole question of allegiance to the fore. Newman made a point of denying that the question of

---

[387] Bishop Sherlock's appeal in 1779. See Antonia Fraser, *The King and the Catholics.* London 2018 p.8. See *Diff* 2 p.[241].

[388] To Edward Maltby, Bishop of Durham 4 November 1850. Lord John Russell (1792-1878) was the uncle of Odo Russel (1829-84), the unofficial envoy to the Holy See 1858-60. He became Lord Ampthill.

[389] The Irish bishops had previously rejected the establishment of the Queens Colleges. See Newman's *My Campaign in Ireland Part I* pp.223-6. Gladstone said in *Vaticanism*, "No pledge from Catholics was of any value to which Rome was not a party." *Diff* 2 p.[351].

[390] Newman had a bag of flour poured over him in Birmingham when he wore his habit. Ronald Chapman *Father Faber* London 1961 p.221. The Redemptorists at Clapham nevertheless went ahead with their belfry in 1851. See note infra *Diff* 2 p.[270].

[391] To The Birmingham Annual Catholic Reunion 27 January 1880. *Addresses to Cardinal Newman with his replies*, ed. William Neville. London 1905 p.242.

[392] To Lord Emly 4 November 1874 *LD* 27 p.148.

infallibility was one of civil allegiance[393] or that the Pope was "a trespasser on ground which belonged to civil authority."[394] Gladstone's case was that the Irish bishops would not compromise their allegiance to the Crown and so had denied in the past that Infallibility was an article of faith. It was true that Dr. Doyle, the Bishop of Kildare and Leighlin, had appeared before parliamentary committees and had said to Lord Liverpool in 1826, "My Lord, what have we do to do with Popes?"[395] But Newman questioned the importance of Dr. Doyle and asked Lord Emly, whether the British Government had applied direct to Rome or to any authorized representative?[396] When Emly replied that there had never been any such application, Newman was satisfied that it remained an Irish Catholic issue and the bishops were acting in the national interest.[397] Gladstone, however, implied that if there was any doubt about the Bishops' allegiance in the 1820's, then Catholic Emancipation in 1829 would not have gone forward with *his* backing, and it showed that Catholics were always indebted first to Rome and then to their own government. But Newman pointed out that years earlier Archbishop Troy of Dublin said that "the Pope, when teaching the universal Church as their supreme visible head and pastor, as successor of St Peter, and heir to the promises of special assistance made to him by Jesus Christ, is infallible... but it is not an article of faith."[398] Newman was obviously not completely satisfied with how he had put this because he added a further clarification in his 'Postscript':

---

[393] *Diff* 2 p.[351].

[394] *TVD* p.12.

[395] *TVD* pp.29-30. James Warren Doyle (1786-1834). He had been a soldier and interpreter in the British Army in the Peninsular War and became an Augustinian friar. He was appointed Bishop in 1819 and gave evidence to Parliamentary committees in 1824 and 1826. He was a supporter of Daniel O'Connell 'The Liberator.' Robert Jenkinson, 2nd Earl of Liverpool was Prime Minister 1812-27.

[396] To Lord Emly 24 November 1874 *LD* 27 pp.159-60. Newman used the term 'headquarters'. See *Diff* 2 pp.[350-6].

[397] *Diff* 2 p.[188]. Letter to Lord Emly 6 and 31 December 1874 *LD* 27 pp.165, 180n; and see 'The Controversy between Newman and Gladstone over the Question of Civil Allegiance' *Dublin Review* 217 (October 1945) p.174.

[398] Pastoral 1793. *Diff* 2 p.[188]. John Troy (1786-1823) was Archbishop of Dublin 1786-1823.

The North of Catholic Christendom took a different view of Papal infallibility from the South....The Gallican party, towards which England and Ireland inclined, thought the other simply extravagant; but with the Ultramontanes stood Rome itself. Ministers do not commonly believe all the representations of deputations who come to them with the advocacy of particular measures, though those deputations may be perfectly sincere in what they aver. The Catholics of England and Ireland in 1826 were almost as one man in thinking lightly of the question.[399]

Newman reminded Gladstone that "he did not give absolute obedience either to the Pope or the Queen",[400] although he thought it necessary to state, "I recognize my loyalty to the constitution, the laws and the government of England"[401] and my allegiance to Queen Victoria.[402] He considered that no Catholics would commit themselves "to any step of a treasonable nature,"[403] and saw "no inconsistency in my being at once a good Catholic and a good Englishman."[404] But *The Times* still thundered at the time,

The loyalty of our civil allegiance is, not in spite of the teaching of the Catholic Church, but because if it.... A simple devotion to the commands of the HOLY FATHER, in temporal and ecclesiastical matters, is the one great command of the modern Catholic law, and this, as experience has shown, does not include a good many ordinary matters, which all

---

[399] *Diff* 2 p.[353].

[400] *Diff* 2 pp.[233, 240, 243].

[401] *Diff* 2 p.[177]. Manning made the same point, without mentioning Newman's *Letter*: "The Vatican Council has not touched our Civil allegiance at all; that the laws which govern our Civil allegiance are as old as the revelation of Christianity, the Divine constitution of the Church and the immutable duties of natural morality.... We were bound by all these obligations before the Vatican Council existed." *The Vatican Decrees in their Bearing on Civil Allegiance* London 1875. *Purcell* vol 2 p.480.

[402] *Diff* 2 p.[194].

[403] *Diff* 2 p.[238].

[404] *Diff* 2 p.[177]. James Bryce (1838-1922). An Ulsterman, a barrister, and an MP. Appointed Regius Professor of Civil Law at Oxford in 1870. He entered Gladstone's Cabinet in 1892, became Chief Secretary for Ireland, Ambassador to Washington and a Viscount in 1914. He called on Newman on 28 February 1875 and wrote about it afterwards, "He was not a priest in his manner—still an Englishman more than a R. Catholic." 8 March 1875 *LD* 27 p.238n.

human societies have agreed to consider as of quite primary importance.

and a few days, later commenting on the stance of President Ulysses Grant,[405]

> The coming struggle will be, as the President predicts, between the free thought and activity of Republican America and the league between superstition and ambition, which the policy of Rome has forged.... As through a chink, we see the burning lava and the implacable wrath of Rome.[406]

For Gladstone there was a conflict between the infallibility of God in heaven and the exercise by any human being of "such universal dominion which was obsolete and beyond revival."[407] This responded to that traditional English opposition to foreign tyranny. Henry VIII in 1532 invoking his interpretation of praemunire,[408] had told a Commons delegation,

> We believe that the clergy of our realm were wholly our subjects but we have now seen clearly that they are only half subjects of ours, that is, that they are really not subjects at all, for all clergy swear an oath to the Pope that totally contradicts the one they give to us, so that they appear to be more his subjects than ours.[409]

This would later give rise to the 'Bloody Question':

> If an army promising to restore the Catholic faith invaded England, whom would you support? The Pope or the Queen?[410]

---

[405] Ulysses Simpson Grant (1822-85). In 1864 he was offered supreme command of the Federal Army, was elected 18th President in 1868 and re-elected in 1872.

[406] *The Times* 7 November 1874; 2 October, 5 October, 19 October.

[407] *DVD* p.26.

[408] *Praemunire*: appealing to a foreign jurisdiction on a matter that is subject to a royal court.

[409] The Speaker and twelve representatives on 11 May 1832. Edward Hall *Chronicle: The Union of the Two Noble and Illustre Families of Lancastre and Yorke* (1548) ed. C. Whibley London 1904.vol 2 p.210.

[410] Either deny your faith or be guilty of treason. It was attributed to William Cecil, Lord Burleigh, Queen Elizabeth's Secretary of State. See John Bellamy *The Tudor Law of Treason* London 1979 p.108.

Gladstone reminded his readers, "The Rome of the Middle Ages claimed universal monarchy"[411] and maintained, "Individual servitude, however abject, will not satisfy the party now dominant in the Latin Church, the State must also be a slave."[412] For Gladstone there was what Professor Matthew calls "a sense of organic nationality."[413] Newman, however, made the point that we accept the authority of the Law of the land: "The thraldom and irksomeness is nothing compared with the great blessings which the Constitution and Legislature secure to us;" and in the case of the medical man who "exercises a 'supreme direction' over those who put themselves under him, do not therefore say, even of him, that he interferes with our daily conduct, and that we are his slaves."[414]

Gladstone referred to the Papacy as "an Asian monarchy: nothing but one giddy height of despotism and one dead level of religious subservience."[415] Newman retorted that "since 1874 he [Gladstone] had attacked wantonly the Holy Roman Church and the Holy See, in the person of Pius IX,[416] which he had described as "the present perilous Pontificate."[417] At the time Gladstone was thinking of his projected journey in September 1874 to meet up again with Dr. Döllinger,[418] who had been excommunicated by the Archbishop of Munich in 1871 for his opposition to the Vatican decree. Gladstone found Döllinger's position as a theologian, "both sympathetic and sustaining."[419] His views were further influenced by his friend

---

[411] *TVD* p.11. Gregory VII maintained "Only the Pope's feet are to be kissed by all princes."

[412] *TVD* p.40. He would withdraw this in *Vaticanism* p.14. See *Diff* 2 p.[349].

[413] H.C.G. Matthew 'Gladstone and the Question of the East' in Derek Butler *Studies in Church History* Oxford 1978 vol 1 p.44.

[414] *Diff* 2 pp.[228, 231-2].

[415] See Philip Magnus *Gladstone, a Biography* 1958 p.236.

[416] To R. Bosworth Smith 22 December 1885 *LD* 31 p.104. Bosworth Smith (1839-1908). Fellow of Trinity 1863, appointed classics master at Harrow where he spent 30 years. He defended the Church of England against what he saw as Gladstone's attempts at disestablishment but was a liberal churchman himself.

[417] *TVD* p.14.

[418] Dr Johan Joseph Ignaz Döllinger (1799-1890), Professor of Church history at Munich 1826-1873. He had translated Newman's *Prepos* in 1853. Gladstone had last met him in 1845. When they resumed contact in 1871 they were unfortunate to encounter the Archbishop by accident on a walk.

[419] Roy Jenkins *Gladstone* Macmillan London 1985 p.385.

and cabinet colleague the Marquis of Ripon becoming a Catholic,[420] one of those convert aristocrats that he would refer to caustically as "a severance of a certain number of Lords of the soil from those who till it."[421] He inserted an attachment to his article in the *Contemporary Review* after meeting Döllinger[422] which argued that ritualistic practices by some clergymen did not imply a romanization of the Church of England. In his *Expostulation* he mentioned that this had not happened "since the bloody days of Mary"[423] and repeated his expressions of outrage at the Vatican Decrees:

> A 'convert' now joining the Papal Church, not only gives up certain rights and duties of freedom, but surrenders them by a conscious and deliberate act... No one can become her convert without renouncing all moral and mental freedom, and placing his civil loyalty at the mercy of another... It has been possible in the seventeenth or eighteenth centuries, it would still have impossible in the nineteenth; when Rome has substituted for the proud boast of *semper eadem*[424] a policy of violence and change of faith; when she has refurbished and paraded anew every rusty tool she was fondly thought to have misused; when no one can become her convert without renouncing all moral and mental freedom, and placing his civil loyalty and duty at the mercy of another... For the natures and claims of the Papal power, it was not possible for the consistent Roman Catholic to pay the Crown of this country an entire allegiance... a Catholic first and an Englishman afterwards.[425]

The *Times* went further and said on the day after Ripon was received into the Church, that his action betrayed "An irreparable weakness of character. To become a Roman

---

[420] George Frederick Samuel Robinson (1827-1909) inherited the title of Marquis of Ripon 1859 and became a Catholic in 1874. Together with the Duke of Norfolk he approached Manning to ask Leo XIII to make Newman a Cardinal in 1878. Ripon was appointed Viceroy of India in 1880.

[421] *TVD* p.62. Newman wrote about such comments, "May they who have spoken or written harshly of recent converts to the Catholic Church, receive at the Great Day more lenient measure than they have in this case given!" *Ess* 2 p.427.

[422] 'Ritualism and Ritual' October 1874.

[423] *TVD* p.6.

[424] *Semper eadem*: 'always the same'.

[425] *TVD* pp.24, 25, 26, 61.

Catholic and remain a thorough Englishman are—it cannot be disguised—almost incompatible conditions... A statesman who becomes a convert forfeits at once the confidence of the English people.[426]

However, Newman made careful distinctions between demands of the civil authority and those of the Pope, arguing that there was no conflict unless the edges were blurred, or the temporal powers of the Papacy were extravagantly exalted, as they were by the Ultramontanes.

The lesson of history

Newman could sympathize with Gladstone over the 'loss' of his friends since the 1840's. He had admired his intellectual grasp—Gladstone usually managed to read a book a day. But he could not agree that the recent acts of the papacy represented "a violent breach with history"[427] and put the matter quite bluntly:

> Does any Anglican Bishop for the last three hundred years recall to our minds the image of St. Basil?... Can we dress up any civil functionary in the vestments of divine authority?[428]

Newman had grasped the importance of an infallible authority in the 1840's. He had written to Henry Wilberforce in 1849:

> There is a great virtue in a Pope—it is something to fall back on. It is a present avenger of the champions of truth. St Athanasius found it so in his day—and lesser and little men have found it ever since. There was I in the English Church with nothing to support me—no basis. 'I said. I can do any thing if I have some authority—give me liturgy, or articles, or Bishop, or Caroline Divine, or Canons—but all is against me—but *here* laity may be secularized, and Churchmen timid, but *there* is the *infallible,* keensighted, un-wearied, undaunted tribunal in the background, undaunted amid all worldly

---

[426] 8 September 1874

[427] *TVD* p.xxv.

[428] *Diff* 2 pp.[207, 226]. "Basil, who issued from the solitudes of Pontus to rule like a king, and minister like the lowest in the kingdom." *HS* 2 p.29.

troubles and reverses, to inspire a salutary awe into the shufflers and to animate Xt's little ones.[429]

He expanded this in his *Essay on Development of Doctrine*:

> To suppose that the doctrine of a permanent authority in matters of faith interferes with our free will and responsibility is, as before, to forget that there were infallible teachers in the first age and heretic and schismatics in the ages subsequent. There may have been a supreme authority from first to last, and a moral judgement from first to last.[430]

Clearly, although Gladstone had read his 1845 version of the *Essay*, he continued to see a contradiction imbedded in the teaching of the Roman Church and saw "a system of development, through which somebody's private opinion of to-day may become matter of faith for all the to-morrows of the future."[431] Gladstone argued, "There was an unmeasured power of the theory of development, ever ready to open, adopt and shape doctrine according to the times"... as against "the unbroken and absolute identity of belief from the days of our Saviour until now."[432] Rome has made "a great change and irreversible".[433] Newman remained frustrated that Gladstone did not fully understand what he had said in his *Essay* about "the legitimate growth and complement, that is, the natural and necessary development of the doctrine of the early Church"[434] and had made clear in 1851: "The Church of God cannot change; what she was that she is."[435] He reminds Gladstone,

> Such change as has taken place (which I should prefer to call doctrinal development), is in itself a positive argument in

---

[429] See supra.

[430] *Dev* (1845 ed.) pp.121, 124. See also *Ari* p.285.

[431] Newman said in his 'Postscript' that Gladstone "should give some proof of this." *Diff* 2 p.378.

[432] *TVD* p.13.

[433] *Diff* 2 p.[341].

[434] *Dev* p.169.

[435] *Prepos* p.399.

favour of the Church's identity from first to last; for a growth in its creed is a law of its life.[436]

Behind Gladstone's arguments lurked the fundamental difference for Anglicans: "They do not believe that Christ set up a visible society, or rather kingdom for the propagation and maintenance of His religion, for a necessary home and a refuge for His people, but we do."[437] Newman added that early Christians were, from the State's point of view, 'the enemies of the human race.'[438] He also gently reminded one who was a leading politician with liberal sympathies of "that tradition of Apostolical independence and freedom of speech which in the eyes of men is her great offence now."[439] It all but resembled Gladstone's "free-spoken dauntless Church of old."[440] Newman quoted a German historian, familiar to him, in his support:

> The rise of Christianity involved the liberation of religion from all political elements... In this separation of the Church from the State consists, perhaps, the greatest, the most pervading and influential peculiarity of all Christian times.[441]

In his *Essay on the Development of Christian Doctrine* he had developed the point: "Christianity, though represented in prophecy as a kingdom, came into the world as an idea rather than an institution, and has had to wrap itself in clothing and fit itself with armour of its own providing... As creation argues continual governance, so are Apostles harbinger of Popes."[442] At the end of three hundred years the position of Rome was unchallenged: "The Pope is the heir of the Ecumenical Hierarchy of the fourth century.... No one else claims or

---

[436] *Diff* 2 p.[356].
[437] *Diff* 2 p.[207].
[438] See *Diff* 2 p.196. 'hostes humani generis." Tacitus *Annals* 15, 44. See *Dev* p.230.
[439] Ibid p.197.
[440] *TVD* p.198.
[441] Leopold von Ranke *Die römischen Päpste, ihre Kirche und ihre Staat* 3 vols 1834-1836. See *Diff* 2 p.[204].
[442] *Dev* pp.116, 124. The apostles were collectively infallible to bear witness to Christ whereas over and above them, Peter and his successors were personally and absolutely infallible. See Gasser's *Relatio* of July 11, 1870 n.6.

exercises its rights or its duties."[443] Newman provided the historical evidence of the plenitude of power accorded to the one who occupied the throne of St. Peter not only from the acts of Constantine but also from the reaction of Napoleon when he was excommunicated by Pius VII in 1807. The evidence of history argued in favour of the "Church's definitive recognition of the doctrine thus gradually manifested in her."[444] This process had resulted in the eventual declaration of the dogma of the Immaculate Conception as "step by step was taken *towards* it."[445]

Ultramontanist extremists[446]

Gladstone had described Manning and his ilk as 'Vaticanists'[447] Newman agreed with Gladstone that the Ultramontanes are "now the sole legitimate party of the Latin Church"[448] and painfully admitted that they were guilty of "chronic extravagances."[449] He told Dr. Russell "I had spoken of them as extravagant and tyrannous, and as having set the house on fire."[450] But on his side he made it a point to mention for the sake of those who questioned his Catholic credentials, that with the Pope "are found the claims, the prerogatives, and duties which we identify with the kingdom set up by Christ."[451]

Alongside the standpoint of the Catholic Church, Newman made the case that there was no condemnation of those outside because "it was possible to belong to the soul of the Church

---

[443] *Diff* 2 pp.[207-11].

[444] *Diff* 2 p.[310].

[445] See *Diff* 2 p.[314] and letter to Reginald Buckler OP 15 April 1870 *LD* 27 p.100.

[446] Ultramontanists. 'Beyond the mountains', i.e. the Alps; therefore in favour of the centralizing power of Rome and the Curia as opposed to local bishops. Technically they should be called neo-Ultramontanes, since Ultramontanism can be traced back to St. Robert Bellarmine in 1586. See B. C. Butler *The Church and Infallibility* London 1954 p.90.

[447] To Charles Russell 6 February 1875 *LD* 27 p.215. Newman dedicated *LG* to Russell and was a regular correspondent.

[448] *TVD* p.50

[449] *Diff* 2 p.[177]. Pusey said, "They seem to be drifting off further from the principles of the early undivided Church." *En* p.287.

[450] To Charles Russell 6 February 1875 *LD* 27 p.215.

[451] *Diff* 2 p.[208].

without belonging to the body."[452] Along with the demands of extremists there was the added concern which he confessed to Robert Whitty in Rome: "It would seem as if a grave dogmatic question was being treated merely as a move in ecclesiastical politics."[453] Newman, writing to Bishop Ullathorne in a confidential letter (which later became public) referred to Ultramontanes as "an aggressive insolent faction" who made "the heart of the just mourn, whom the Lord hath not made sorrowful."[454] Their position has elsewhere been described as "a kind of theological puritanism, narrow and exclusive."[455] Ultramontanism would lead to a desperate insularity, as he pointed out to Emily Bowles,

> We are sinking into a sort of Novatianism, the heresy which the early Popes so strenuously resisted. Instead of aiming at being a world-wide power, we are shrinking into ourselves, narrowing the lines of communion, trembling at freedom of thought and using the language of dismay and despair at the prospect before us, instead of, with the high spirit of the warrior, going out conquering and to conquer.[456]

Newman mentioned a further effect: "They are creating much uneasy feeling among lay converts, and unsettling their minds, they are hindering the chances of such as Pusey joining the Church."[457] He included W. G. Ward as editor of the *Dublin Review* under that heading and told Pusey, "I do so dislike

---

[452] Ibid pp.[244, 335].

[453] To Robert Whitty 12 February 1870 *LD* 25 p.95. Robert Whitty (1817-75). Ordained by Bishop Griffiths in 1840, he corresponded with Newman in 1843 and tried his vocation in the Oratory. Wiseman made him Vicar General in 1850 and Provost. He became a Jesuit in 1857 and was English Provincial and later Assistant to the General in Rome.

[454] To Ullathorne 28 January 1870 *LD* 25 p.19. Ullathorne admitted that he had shown the confidential letter to Bishop Errington and Bishop Clifford and blamed the latter. (Champ p.373). Extracts were published in the *Standard* 14 March 1870. It proved providential because although it reflected Newman's views, he could not be accused of publishing them. "I said nothing to imply that on reflection I agreed to every proposition which I set down on my *prima facie* view of the matter." *Diff* 2 p.[371].

[455] Meriol Trevor *Newman Light in Winter* London 1962 p.410.

[456] To Emily Bowles 11 November 1866 *LD* 22 p.314. Emily Bowles (1818-1903) became a Catholic in Rome in 1843. Author of religious books and a regular correspondent.

[457] To Miss M R Giberne 20 August 1868 *LD* 24 p.128.

Ward's way of going on."[458] He objected to the particular slant which Ward gave as editor:

> The Pope, in virtue of his ecclesiastical office has the power of deposing any sovereign, whose government he may consider injurious to the spiritual welfare of that country ... [and the Temporal Power] is the very bulwark and citadel of Catholic order, liberty and progress.[459]

Newman in response was blunt, telling him, "You are making a Church within a Church, as the Novatians of old did.[460]

Ward had quoted Cardinal Patrizi: "The faithful, who show themselves such in word and act, recognize in the voice of the Church's visible head *the very word of God*."[461] Ignatius Ryder maintained that Ward was "not so much a theologian as a *theo-politician*."[462] Ward was supported by Herbert Vaughan[463] as editor of *The Tablet*. The Ultramontane lobby was supported by the contributions of Louis Veuillot[464] who became editor of *L'Univers* and in Rome by Mgr. George Talbot[465] and *La Civiltà Cattolica,* edited by the Jesuits. It tended to make the Pope, according to Fr. Dessain, "an oracle independent of the Church"[466]—and not surprisingly fueled Gladstone's resentment.

---

[458] To Pusey 5 September 1866 *LD* 22 p.44. "W G Ward writes to Dr Ivers that what they have to oppose in England, as their great mischief, is Fr. Newman." To Ambrose St John 3 May 1867 *LD* 23 p.202.

[459] *Dublin Review* (October 1874) p.298.

[460] To W. G. Ward 9 May 1867 *LD* 23 p.217. The Novatians were rigorist third century schismatics who opposed the papal policy of leniency to those who had lapsed, and permanently excluded them from the Church as convicted of grave sin. See Gibbon *Decline and Fall* 2, 21 and *Diff* p.[203]n.

[461] *Dublin Review* April 1865 p.449. Cardinal Patrizzi (1798-1876) was Dean of the College of Cardinals. The italics are in the original.

[462] In his *Idealism in Theology*, quoted in Meriol Trevor *Newman Light in Winter* p.450.

[463] Herbert Vaughan (1832-1903). Ordained priest in 1854 and was Vice-President of St. Edmund's College Ware and editor and owner of the *Tablet* 1868. He became bishop of Salford in 1872 and worked closely with Manning, whom he succeeded as Archbishop in 1892.

[464] Louis Veuillot (1813-83). He was editor of *L'Univers* 1843-83 and strongly supported the temporal power of the Pope and papal infallibility.

[465] Mgr. George Talbot. See supra. Newman told Pusey in 1868 that "Talbot has done a great deal of harm." 24th May 1868 *LD* 24 p.79.

[466] C. S. Dessain *Newman's Spiritual Themes.* Dublin 1977 p.28.

Newman himself talks of people "having papal claims as if in defiance flourished in their faces."[467] He thought that there were some who wanted definitions "to become as plentiful as blackberries."[468] At the same he told Maskell, "I have full confidence that such extravagance as marks some Pastorals is but for the moment—things will in time gradually settle down and find their level... The Council cannot force things—the voice of the Schola Theologorum of the whole Church diffusive, will in time make itself heard... but what we have wanted, ever since Cardinal Wiseman drifted from his first policy, and took up an ultra line, has been some periodical organ of moderate views, yet unassailable in point of theology."[469] This was made worse both by the then current state of theological research—tending towards a sterile scholasticism—which revolutionary turmoil had exacerbated by closing down seminaries and expelling religious orders. He discussed the whole question with Lord Blachford:

I think, when you were here last, I said to you our great want just now was theological schools, which the great French Revolution has destroyed. This has been the occasion of our late and present troubles. Where would Ward have been, if there had been theological schools in England? Again, the Archbishop is not a theologian, and so theology has gone out of fashion. This is the only reason which made me regret not going to Oxford—and why Ward did all he could at Rome, and successfully, to hinder me going. I don't profess to be a theologian, but at all events I should have been able to show a side of Catholic religion more theological more exact than his. Where there is such a lack of theological science, I must not take it for granted as yet that I am out of the wood, for I may still receive some cuff from the political Ultra-Devotional party—but I don't think it can be very bad. This I may say for my comfort—the only great, now going is the Jesuit School,

---

[467] *Diff* 2 p.[177].
[468] To Lady Chatterton 6 August 1870 *LD* 25 p.174.
[469] To William Maskell 12 February 1871 *LD* 25 p.284. William Maskell (1814-90). A student at University College in 1832, he was a Tractarian and interested in liturgy. He was examining chaplain to Bishop Phillpotts of Exeter. He was received into the Church in 1850 and was an inopportunist at the time of the Council. When widowed he lived in Cornwall.

and they have always been for me—not always agreeing with me (about that I know nothing) tho', *often* agreeing, but always taking my part and backing me up.[470]

It all contributed to the Ultramontane reaction which he described to John Wallis:

a reign of terror has begun, a reign of denunciation, secret tribunals and moral assassination… It is not at all easy to break that formidable conspiracy, which is in action against the theological liberty of Catholics.[471]

Gladstone saw in the recent history and the dogma itself a blatant exercise of Roman domination. He maintained, "My charges are against what the Germans[472] call Vaticanismus. Then against its authors and promoters whom I cannot affect to treat as innocent… I have made no charge against the Roman Catholics of England."[473] Presumably Catholics were allowed to obey their Church but not the Person who lived in the Vatican.

Newman himself was under no illusions about 'Roman malaria'[474] and even that "the annals of the Church are stained with human sin and error."[475] He candidly admitted, "There are certain acts of Popes in which no one would like to have part,"[476] but added "I am far from saying that Popes are never

---

[470] To Lord Blachford 5 February 1875 *LD* 27 p.212. This was especially true of Frs. Giovanni Perrone, Henry Coleridge, Peter Gallwey and James Jones.

[471] To John Wallis 23 April 1867 *LD* 23 p.187. John Wallis (1821-88). A barrister, he was editor of the *Tablet* 1856-68 when it was bought and edited by Herbert Vaughan. He was Consul in Port Said and Judge of the International Court at Cairo 1882-88.

[472] Gladstone is referring to Dr Döllinger, Professor Reusch of Bonn and other supporters.

[473] To Newman 17 January 1875 *LD* 27 p.194. He would call his subsequent volume *Vaticanism; An Answer to Replies and Reproofs* London 1875.

[474] "Now the Rock of St. Peter on its summit enjoys a pure and serene atmosphere, but there is a great deal of Roman *malaria* at its foot." *Diff* 2 p.[297]. See editorial footnote.

[475] *Diff* 2 p.[309].

[476] See *Diff* 2 p.[187]. "Such acts as the conduct of Paul III or Pius IV towards England; nor again to the conduct of Vigilius, Honorius, John XXII etc." *TP* p.135. Newman might have liked to add Stephen VI, John XII, Clement VI, Alexander VI, and Sergius II, not to mention those like Paul III who had lived unholy lives before becoming admirable popes.

in the wrong[477] and are nevertheless to be resisted; or that excommunications always avail"[478] He made the same point to his nephew J R Mozley: "Certainly I would maintain firmly, with most writers on the Evidences,[479] that, as the Church has a dark side, so (as you do not seem to admit) it has a light side also, and that its good has been more potent and permanent and evidently intrinsic to it than its evil."[480] He had earlier told Lady Chatterton,

> I do not believe there ever was a time when the gravest scandals did not exist in the Church, and act as impediments to its mission. Those scandals have been the occasion of momentous secessions and schisms... It is also a fact, that, in spite of them still, the Church has ever got on and made way, to the surprise of the world.[481]

Newman would like Gladstone to accept the principle that,

> The greater part of the Church has long thought that the Pope has the power which he and the bishops of the majority have declared *is* his; and that, if the Church is the work and ordinance of God, we must have a little faith in Him, and be assured that he will provide that there is no abuse of the Pope's power.[482]

The underlying difficulty was that neither Gladstone nor Pusey could grasp the essence of the Catholic 'soul'. Newman remarked, "I wish Protestants would throw themselves into our

---

[477] When he wrote the Third Preface to *Via Media* in 1877, he added a 'Note 2' in which Cardinal Aeneas Piccolomini after he became Pius II admitted he had previously held conciliarist views, saying, "We are human, and have erred as humans do." *VM* I, pp.187.

[478] *Diff* 2 p.[216-17]. Such comments did not go down well in the Curia.

[479] The most famous was William Paley (1743-1805) who wrote *View of the Evidences of Christianity* in 1794. See *Diff* 1 p.3.

[480] To J. R. Mozley 1 April 1874 *LD* 27 p.262. John Rickards Mozley (1840-1931) was the second son of Newman's sister Jemima. A fellow of King's College, Cambridge, he became Professor of Pure Mathematics at Owens College Manchester 1865-85.

[481] To Lady Chatterton 10 June 1863 *LD* 20 p.465.

[482] To W.J. Daunt 7 August 1870 *LD* 25 p.175. William Joseph O'Neill Daunt (1807-94). Born in Tullamore, he became a Catholic in 1827. MP for Mallow, a Nationalist in favour of a repeal of the Union with England Bill of 1800. Secretary to Daniel O'Connell and author of a novel *The Wife Hunter* 1839.

minds upon this point."[483] It would seem that they both found it hard to accept the full impact of the Incarnation: God becoming Flesh which is "a meeting with the living Truth and the living Love,"[484] and that truth expressed most fully in the witness of the successor of St Peter in essential matters of faith and morals.

Although Gladstone did not waiver in his meticulous religious allegiance he combined this with his politically liberal position and this would find expression in his "opposing all coercive powers, great or small—Empires, Papacies, Parliaments, Sultans, Colonial Offices, Trade Unions—which do not rest their authority on consent, habitual or expressed."[485] In this bombastic vein he happily rejoiced that "the fangs of the medieval Popedom had been drawn and its claws torn away."[486] It was still of recent memory that Pius IX had been ruler of the papal states with all the trappings of government as well as being spiritual head of the Catholic Church.

'Temporal Sovereign in his own home…'

Gladstone was particularly annoyed at the Ultramontane stance taken by Manning and his confreres with regard to papal sovereignty. A contemporary catechism had asked, "Does the Holy Law of God permit rebellion against the legitimate temporal sovereign? No, never, because the temporal power comes from God."[487] Manning's own position was clear. He explained his views in a series of lectures 'On the Temporal Sovereignty of the Popes', 'The Last Glories of the Holy See greater than the first' and 'The Present Crisis of the Holy See

---

[483] *Diff* 2 p.[207].

[484] Karol Wojtyla *Sign of Contradiction* London 1979 p.4.

[485] George Malcolm Young 'Mr Gladstone' in *Today and Yesterday.* London 1948 pp.34-5.

[486] *TVD* p. 26.

[487] The counter-revolutionary catechism of Monaldo Leopardi, *Catechismo cattòlico sulle Rivoluzioni* 1832. Gregory XVI, confronted in 1831 by a popular uprising demanding greater democracy in the Papal States, had called on the help of Austrian troops (who rapidly crushed it), and he turned to them again later when disorder recurred. Pius IX was restored to Rome in 1850 and then defended by French troops. See infra Newman's disapproval of papal recourse to arms.

tested by Prophecy',[488] as well as in a sermon on 'Rome, the Capital of Christendom.'[489] He vigorously maintained that the Pope had 'both spiritual and temporal sovereignty.'[490] In another book he committed himself to the statement that the temporal power of the pope would in due course be defined as an article of faith and that the temporal power was necessary for the liberty of the Church and the spiritual independence of the papacy.[491] Gladstone was familiar with the position of papal power, having translated a four volume Italian work.[492] He quoted Manning arguing that the destruction of Temporal Power would result in the laws of nations falling into ruins.[493] Manning branded the invaders of Rome as 'public malefactors.'[494] He followed this with his *Caesarism and Ultramontanism* in 1874 (and sent a copy to Gladstone). This supported Pusey's description, "The civil princedom of the Apostolic See."[495] Newman told Lord Blachford that Manning's extremism was Gladstone's excuse for writing as he did.[496] He further vented his frustration to an Anglican Canon,

> In the first definition there are many open questions; and partizans of the Pope as if to compensate for his temporal loss, wish to close them in favour of the extremist sense of them.[497]

Fr. Gallwey the influential Jesuit preacher[498] had thoroughly endorsed these sentiments in a pamphlet, with gusto:

---

[488] Manning translated his lectures into Italian and sent them to Rome in 1860. They were censured and threatened with the Index. After some amendments these were considered acceptable. *Purcell* vol. 2 p.152-3

[489] *Purcell* vol 2 p.461.

[490] *The Present Crisis of the Holy See* London 1861 p.74.

[491] *Purcell* vol 2 pp 152-3, 161. In a volume entitled *The Temporal Power of the Vicar of Jesus Christ* (1861).

[492] Luigi Carlo Farini, *The Roman State: from 1815-1850* Trs. Gladstone 4 vols, London 1851-54.

[493] *TVD* p.52.

[494] *Tablet* 8 October 1870.

[495] *En* p. 301.

[496] To Lord Blachford 2 October 1874 *LD* 27 p.122.

[497] To Robert Charles Jenkins (1815-90) Rector of Lyminge and Honorary Canon of Canterbury 25 February 1875 *LD* 27 p.234.

[498] See supra.

Even if the exaggerated foreboding should have its fulfilment, so that the time should come when we might expect some new definition every morning, yet so long as the watchful providence of God is pledged not to suffer any false oracle to emanate from the Apostolic See, such daily pronouncements, so far from being an evil, would be like the daily provision of manna.[499]

Ward who had published *De Infallibilitatis Extensione*[500] Herbert Vaughan[501] saw the Pope as supreme head on earth of the perfect society and the Definition as 'the increased executive force' needed in the Church. Newman later wrote to Mrs. William Froude:

I am told some wicked men, not content with their hitherto cruel conduct are trying to bring in this doctrine of inherent infallibility of which there is not a hint in the definition. perhaps they would like to go on to call him a Vice-God, as some one actually did, or sole God to us.[502]

Giovanni Maria Mastai-Ferretti had been fifty-four when he succeeded Gregory XVI in 1846 and took the title of Pius IX (Pio Nono). The Pope would reign until 1878, even now the longest pontificate in the history of the Church. Gladstone saw him as a despot, Ward, as a triumphant monarch. For Newman, there were tender thoughts. He would recall in his sermon preached at a time when a day of prayer for Pius IX was enjoined by the hierarchy, that he was the Pope who, as one of his first acts, "was to call me to Rome; then, when I got there, he bade me send for my friends to be with me, and he formed us into an Oratory."[503] He also painted the larger picture: "He has brought us together, has given us Bishops and created out

---

[499] 'St Joseph and the Vatican Council' 1870 *LD* 25 p.174n. It was suggested that Ward would welcome such with his morning *Times*. Wilfrid Ward *The Life of John Henry Cardinal Newman* London 1921 vol 2 p.213.

[500] *De infallibilitatis extensione theses quasdam et quaestiones theologorum judicio* Certain theses and questions concerning the extension of infallibility subject to the judgement of theologians. London 1869.

[501] See supra.

[502] To Mrs William Froude, 8 August 1870, *LD* 25, p.176. See supra.

[503] 'The Pope and the Revolution' *OS* p.290.

of us a body politic, which (please God), as time goes on, will play an important part in Christendom."[504] He added with absolute sincerity, "Great equally are the claims on us of his personal character and of his many virtues. He is one whom to see is to love."[505] Newman could in that sense say *he* was an Ultramontanist.[506]

Newman was not alone as an admirer who appreciated his efforts for the Church. However, he was not blind to Pius's attachment to Ultramontanism and that there were occasions when he did not know all the facts.[507] He also considered in his Memorandum of 1870 on the Catholic University, that he was not well served by his advisors.

> I had been accustomed to believe that, over and above that attribute of infallibility which attached to the doctrinal decisions of the Holy See, a gift of sagacity had in every age characterized its occupants, so that we might be sure, as experience taught us, without its being a dogma of faith that what the Pope determined was the very measure, or the very policy expedient for the Church at the time when it was determined... I am obliged to say that a sentiment which history has impressed upon me, and impresses me still, has been considerably weakened as far as the present Pope is concerned by the experience of the result of the policy which his chosen Counsellors have led him to pursue. I cannot help thinking in particular, that, if he known more or the state of things in Ireland he would not have taken up the quarrel about the higher education which his predecessor left him... I was a poor innocent as regards the actual state of things in Ireland when I went there and did not dare to think about it, for I relied on the word of the Pope, but from the event I am led to think it not rash to say that I knew as much about Ireland as he did.[508]

---

[504] Ibid p.289.

[505] *OS* p.290

[506] *Diff* 2 p.[208].

[507] To Lady Simeon, 18 November 1870, *LD* 25, p.231."He has no one to contradict him, does not know fact, and does cruel things without meaning it!" Louisa Edith Simeon (1843-95) was the daughter of Sir John Simeon. She consulted Newman over her religious difficulties. She married the son of F.R. Ward in 1872.

[508] 'Memorandum on my Connection with the Catholic University', *AW* p.320. See Paul Shrimpton's Introduction in *Campaign I*, Newman Millennium Edition Vol. XVI Gracewing 2021, and *Campaign II*, Millennium Edition Vol. XVII Gracewing 2022.

He adds in the *Letter*:

> orders which issue from him [the Pope] for the observance of
> particular countries, or political or religious classes, have no
> claim to be utterances of his infallibility. If he enjoins upon the
> hierarchy of Ireland to withstand mixed education, this is no
> exercise of infallibility…. I say this the more freely because
> Urban VIII when urged to excommunicate the Kings of France
> and Sweden said, "Wisdom does not teach us to imitate Pius
> V or Clement VII, but Paul V, who, in the beginning, being
> many times urged by the Spaniards to excommunicate James,
> King of England, never would consent to it.[509]

In the first two years of his pontificate Pius IX had granted
a constitution to the papal states and a general amnesty to
political prisoners. He had also showed himself open to the idea
of Italian unity. In 1848 revolutions broke out across Europe in
Paris, Vienna, Berlin and also in Rome. Count Pellegrino Rossi
was appointed Prime Minister in September but was
assassinated three months later for opposing a union with
Savoy. Pius fled Rome in disguise and took refuge in Gaeta,
under the protection of the Prince of Naples. Among Catholics
there was great sympathy and growing popularity, thanks,
according to Wilfrid Ward, to the series of tableaux brought
before the public in the newspapers of his reception of visitors
in the Vatican after his return.[510] Faber preached sermons in
1860 and 1861 on Pius IX as 'Christ suffering in the world'.
Newman took an unapologetic view of the papacy and the
impact it should have on the Church,

> In his administration of Christ's kingdom, in his religious acts,
> we must never oppose his will, or dispute his word, or criticize
> his policy, or shrink from his side. There are kings of the earth
> who have despotic authority, which their subjects obey indeed
> but disown in their hearts; but we must never murmur at that
> absolute rule which the Sovereign Pontiff has over us, because

---

[509] *Diff* 2 pp.[332, 217n].
[510] To the Birmingham Annual Catholic Reunion 27 January 1880. *Addresses to Cardinal Newman and his Replies* ed. William Neville London 1905 p.52.

it is given to him by Christ, and in obeying him, we are obeying his Lord. We must never suffer ourselves to doubt, that, in his government of the Church, he is guided by an intelligence more than human. His yoke is the yoke of Christ; and to his *Lord* he must render account, not to us. Even in secular matters it is ever safe to be on his side, dangerous to be on the side of his enemies.[511]

Newman did not have any real problem about the Pope's Temporal Power.[512] He urged people "to pray for Rome as the seat, not only of his spiritual government, but of his temporal … and that he may continue King of Rome"[513] but at the same time hedged his bets. "He is right in [maintaining] defending his temporal right to territory, and that it is the Providential way for his safeguarding his independence (nay, as a point of doctrine that he is a sovereign *in se* independently of all terrritory, and has the right of being no one's subject). While I have never been anxious about his losing his temporal power [his temporals], being sure that, if Providence dispensed with one way, He would find another."[514] Later he told Miss Munro that he did not think the papacy would lose temporal power, "No one but the reds wish him to lose it—no one but extreme ultramontanes think he can lose no part of it."[515] On his accession Pius IX was ruler of the Papal States. But then there followed the defeat of papal forces by the Piedmontese at Castelfidardo and Ancona[516] and the annexation of Romagna and the Marches, which left only Rome and the Patrimony of St Peter—and that had to be defended by Napoleon III's army. Newman felt the situation was repugnant, as he told Charlotte Wood,[517]

---

[511] 'The Pope and the Revolution' *OS* p.286. Newman said this did not imply inherent papal inspiration.

[512] Unlike Gladstone who called it, "That foul blot on the face of creation".

[513] *OS* p.108.

[514] Introductory Notes [IV] 1866 *TP* p.107.

[515] To Miss Munro 8 October 1866 *LD* 22 p.297. Miss Munro was known to Pusey, became a Catholic in 1845 and thought of becoming a nun. She took Newman as her director and died c. 1913.

[516] 18th and 30th September 1860. Newman called the invading army 'sacrilegious robbers' *OS* p.307.

[517] See supra.

I cannot think it right that the Holy Father should be protected against his own people by foreign bayonets. It is a great scandal. Any thing is better than that. When he is persecuted, he is in his proper place—not when he persecutes.[518]

Newman concluded that full spiritual and temporal power did not go easily together. But he noted in 1866 that "Pius IX laid down a doctrine about the necessity of the temporal power for the spiritual, and it was taken for a practical instruction."[519] He told William Monsell, "Is it possible in the disposition of Providence that the same man should be both infallible in spirituals and absolute in temporals?"[520] Newman concluded, as the clouds gathered in 1870, that something must give:

Whatever to the good of evil of the Temporal Power it certainly seems now sure to go—and gradually, not at once, a new system must supersede the old; and one better suitable to modern times.[521]

Pius IX surrendered to the Italian army under General Cordona on 20 September 1870. Newman did not mince his words about papal policy when he subsequently wrote to Canon Walker,

Don't you think, if it is pious to criticize, that the Pope, to be consistent with his antecedents, ought to have left Rome, when the Italians came? The dignified course is to say to his people 'It is your look out—I don't want to force myself on you. I am not your tyrant or conqueror, but your Father'. And it *is* the fault of his people that the Italians came in. Do you mean to tell me, that, if they had stood out and rallied around him against the battalions of Victor Emmanuel, every man in England would not have taken part with the weaker, and applauded him and them? I think he is in a false position,

---

[518] To Charlotte Wood 20 October 1870 *LD* 25 p.217.
[519] 12 December 1866 *TP* p.144.
[520] To William Monsell 12 December 1866 *LD* 25 p.245
[521] To John Pym Pym Yeatman (1830-1910) 26 September 1870 *LD* 25 p.213. He became a Catholic in 1866 after reading *Letter to Pusey* and was a lawyer interested in genealogy. He had nine children, one of whom became an Ursuline nun.

remaining in Rome. Of course he might 20 years ago have made terms—but he took the 'Non Possumus'[522] line. That line, I think required him to shake the dust of his sandals, and to have left Rome. Now people pity him, or condemn him—and he has to bear numberless less insults.[523]

Newman took a pragmatical approach that weighed up the cost of temporal power and the advantages which would accrue if the Pope made a courageous decision to lay it aside. The new Italian legislature had recognized Pius as a head of state, provided diplomatic immunity for foreign members of the curia and assigned a generous annual income but the settlement was rejected.[524] It was destined to leave the Pope as 'a prisoner of the Vatican' for the next fifty years. Newman remarked that the loss of temporal power "may effectually prevent a tyrannous use of his spiritual power."[525] Prophetically he thought that it "may be (if it is ratified by time) the first step towards an emancipation parallel though unlike, to that which Hildebrand effected."[526] Newman also told Bishop Moriarty at the time that there was bound to be a trade-off involving papal infallibility: "The Papacy cannot mount to the summit in things ecclesiastical, without a secular downfall."[527]

However, Veuillot in *L'Univers* maintained the authority and omnipotence of the Pope as the source of all authority, spiritual and temporal:[528] 'Rex est imperator in regno suo,' (the King is the emperor in his own realm),[529] effectively harking

---

[522] Non Possumus: We cannot (take any other decision).

[523] To Canon Walker 28 December 1871 *LD* 25 pp.454-5. John Walker (1800-73) Parish priest of Scarborough 1835-73 and a Canon of Beverley diocese in 1851. A regular correspondent.

[524] Richard J Evans *The Pursuit of Power* iam cit. p.463.

[525] To Mrs William Froude 2 January 1871 *LD* 25 p.262.

[526] To William Maskell 12 February 1871 *LD* 25 p.282.

[527] To Bishop Moriarty 2 March 1871 *LD* 25 p.297. Bishop David Moriarty See supra.

[528] The papal tiara with its three crowns, symbolized that the Pope is 'Father of princes and kings, Ruler of the world and Vicar of our Saviour Jesus Christ'- words said by the cardinal deacon at the ceremony. Pope John Paul reinterpreted this as indicating the three-fold mission of Christ as Priest, Prophet and King in which the whole People of God share. (*Inaugural Homily* 16 October 1978).

[529] *Decretal* of Innocent III 1202. Leo XIII in his Instruction to Cardinal Rampolla said on 15 June 1883 before sending him as nuncio to Spain, "The freedom of the Popes has been the temporal sovereign power, and when these means were lacking the

back to an older tradition. The *Dublin Review* had quoted Cardinal Patrizzi, "It is necessary for enabling the Pope freely to govern the Church without subjection to an earthly ruler.[530] The same message was conveyed by the *Syllabus* which condemned the Error: "The abolition of the temporal power of which the Apostolic See is possessed would contribute in the greatest degree to the liberty and prosperity of the Church."[531]

Manning said much the same thing, "The temporal power was necessary to the liberty of the Church and the spiritual independence of the Papacy." He argued that without the temporal power "the laws of nations would at once fall into ruin."[532] Later, in a Note on the Roman Question to Disraeli's Cabinet, he wrote: "The Holy Father is bound by an oath never to cede Rome and the States of the Church."[533]

Newman explained *his* position in a long letter to Lord Emly:

There is no addition whatever in it [the Vatican decree] to the Pope's power. Not a word is said in it about practical obedience to the command of a Pope. The duty remains what it was in the time of Bellarmine.[534] It remains what it was in Elizabeth's reign, when her Catholic subjects with great zeal took part in the defence of the country against an Armada[535] blessed by the Pope...[536] Supposing the Prince of Wales became a Catholic,[537] and the Pope bade Catholic members of

---

Pontiffs were always either persecuted or imprisoned or exiled, or certainly in a condition of dependence."

[530] *Dublin Review* April 1865 p.449. Quoted by Pusey *En* p.304. See supra.

[531] § 76. *DS* 2976.

[532] *The Temporal Power of the Vicar of Jesus Christ* 1861; *Three Lectures on the Temporal Sovereignty of the Popes* 1860 pp 58-9. See also Leo XIII 15 June 1887 where he sees the temporal power 'as the only means provided by Providence."

[533] 'Memorandum of 1875 at the request of Sir John Pope Hennessy.' *Purcell* 1 Vol. 2 p.523.

[534] St. Robert Bellarmine (1542-1621), Jesuit Cardinal, outlined the power of the Pope in 'De Romano Pontifice' in his *Disputationes de Controversiis Christianae Fidei adversus hujus temporis Haereticos* 3 vols. 1586-93. The same point was made by Manning: "The loyalty of our civil allegiance is, not in spite of the teaching of the Catholic Church, but because of it." *Times* 7 November 1874.

[535] Such dutiful action was praised by Gladstone *TVD* p.25.

[536] See supra under Sixtus V.

[537] George IV when Prince of Wales was married to Mrs. Maria Fitzherbert (1756-1837), a Roman Catholic widow, in 1785 in a secret ceremony in London by one of

Parliament to accept him as their king, in spite of their oath[538] to the contrary, it would be their duty, while the nation enforced the oath, and they were in the House, to refuse that allegiance was demanded of them... In two respects then I consider G[ladstone] to be wrong —1, in supposing that the particular precepts or commands of the Pope to be infallible, whereas only general propositions on religion and morals are such, not propositions on matters of expedience, but about things intrinsically good or evil, right or wrong, and therefore few and rare and at best only indirectly bearing on the conduct of individuals... Lastly, if it be said that, putting aside formal commands, it is impossible a Catholic should not be influenced in his political acts by the Pope's wishes, or by what he knows will be for the advantage of the Catholic religion. I answer, This is no *new* difficulty and it is on the change of a Catholic's duties since the Council on which G. relies and insists. 2, it applies to all class interests—eg. Anglican members of Parliament support the Church of England, dissenters oppose it—men sent in by the Railway interest or the publican interest[539] support those interests respectively.[540]

In his sermon on the papacy he said that God maintains the Church by various means (including what Newman called the 'Papal monarchy').[541] A gathering of bishops in Rome in December 1867 made the important point in a declaration that temporal authority was "in praesenti rerum humanorum statu."[542] Newman would write in 1882 expressing sympathy for the loss of Pius IX's territory, but he added, "I will not allow that the Temporal Power is the only way in which the spiritual power can be preserved.... Further, I have no reason to suppose

---

his royal chaplains, which contravened the Royal Marriage Act of 1772 and required consent of the sovereign. He subsequently married Caroline of Brunswick in 1795.

[538] "That the sacrifice of the Mass and the invocation of the Blessed Virgin Mary and other saints, as now practised in the Church of Rome, are impious and idolatrous." Gladstone told Newman there was no oath, it was simply a matter of statute law. 15 January 1875 *LD* 27 pp.192-3.

[539] Brewers, distillers and the many private railway limited liability companies had members of their board in parliament. See Newman's comments on railways to J. R. Mozley infra n. p.217.

[540] To Lord Emly 9 October 1874 *LD* 27 pp.133-4.

[541] 'The Pope and the Revolution' *OS* p.296.

[542] "In the *present state* of human affairs." The bishops were there for the canonization of the Japanese martyrs on 9 December 1867. See *LD* 22 p.305.

that our present Holy Father Leo XIII, differs from such a statement." In that he would be mistaken.[543]

Robert Bellarmine, who was quoted frequently in Vatican I, was well aware that according to *Unam Sanctam*[544] the Pope was said to possess two swords, symbolizing his universal temporal and spiritual authority or 'plenitudo potestatis' (the fulness of power), when theologians argued that for the maintenance of unity the most suitable form of government was a monarchy.[545] But he interpreted this in the light of the teaching of St. Thomas Aquinas who said that although the Pope possessed the pinnacle of both powers, this did not include *direct* temporal jurisdiction outside the Papal States.[546] He argued that in spiritual matters the Pope was to be obeyed, but the civil authority could justly claim power in civil matters.[547] Jean Gossselin, a French Sulpician Father, writing in 1839 insisted that papal power was not a divine prerogative resting on doctrinal grounds but was based on historical constitutional law. It was ultimately founded on historical events.[548] Newman adds, "The exercise of this right is limited to the ages of faith... and the Pope is not infallible in the exercise of this right."[549]

Canon lawyers also maintained that the Church's authority was spiritual and not temporal.[550] Bishop Joseph Fessler, the General Secretary to the Vatican Council, wrote, "The

---

[543] *Memorandum* 22 May 1882 *LD* 30 p.90. However, Leo XIII said in 1885, "All ought to hold that it was not without a singular disposition of God's providence, that this power of the Church was provided with a civil sovereignty as the surest safeguard of her independence". Encyclical *Immortale Dei* n.12.

[544] Boniface VIII's Bull 18 November 1302 on the position of the Pope as Head of the Church. St. Roberto Francesco Romolo Bellarmino (1542-1621). Jesuit Professor and Controversialist made Cardinal.in 1598.

[545] Avery Dulles *The Catholicity of the Church* Oxford 1987 p.135. Boniface VIII retorted to King Albert I's envoys, seeking his election as Holy Roman Emperor, "I am the King of the Romans. I am an Emperor." *Monumenta Germaniae Historica. SS* vol 12 p.58.

[546] *Commentarius in Epistolas omnes Pauli* cap.13.

[547] *De Summo Pontifice* lib. 5 cap.5.

[548] *The Power of the Pope during the Middle Ages; or an Historical Inquiry into the Origin of the Temporal Power of the Holy See, and the Constitutional Laws of the Middle Ages relating to the Deposition of Sovereigns.* London 1853.

[549] *Diff* 2 pp.[221-2].

[550] See *Diff* 2 pp.[291-2].

definition at the end of the Bull *Unam Sanctam* only asserted the Catholic doctrine of the spiritual primacy of the Pope."[551] Gregory XVI himself had argued that the power of the Pope to depose rulers, as claimed by Gregory VII,[552] had to be considered in its historical context and not as a theological precedent, and in any case it was not linked to infallibility. In a *Memorandum* for a letter to Pusey in 1865, Newman had written, "It may be in the Providence of God, that, if the H[oly] S[ee] lost the temporal power, it should gain the definition of infallibility."[553]

Newman did not conceal his concerns about the timeliness of any dogma given the prevailing atmosphere.[554] But there was a further point (which he had made earlier) that complicated the issue for him: "Since the infallibility of the Church has not been defined, it must be defined, if any thing on the subject is defined, before we come to define the infallibility of the Pope."[555] But he was quite definite about the *extent* of papal jurisdiction, and painted it in graphic terms to leave Pusey in no doubt,

> As a matter of principle, the Pope must have universal jurisdiction; and then comes the question to what extent? Now the Church is a Church Militant, and, as the commander of the army is despotic, so must the visible head of the Church be; and therefore in its idea the Pope's jurisdiction can hardly be limited.[556]

---

[551] Joseph Fessler Bishop of Sankt Pölten *Die wahre und die falshe Unfehlbarkeit der Päpste*. Vienna 1871. English translation by Ambrose St John, *The True and False Infallibility of the Popes*, London 1875; pp. 6-9 *LD* 27 p.173n.

[552] Hildebrand. St. Gregory VII Pope, (1073-85) issued his *Dictatus papae* in 1075 on the powers of the Pope. See H. E. J Cowdrey *The Register of Pope Gregory VII 1073-1085*.Oxford 2002, 2, 55a.

[553] *TP* p.103.

[554] He pointed to the defection of Dr. Döllinger and the Falk laws and Kulturcampf in Germany in a letter to Miss Rowe 16 July 1873 *LD* 26 p.367. In later editions, he changed '*opportuneness* of its definition' to 'the fact of its definition' See infra p.[193]n.

[555] *TP* July 10, 1866 p.143. *Lumen Gentium* n.25 "gives concrete effect to the infallibility *of the Church* itself." Karl Rahner in *Commentary on the Documents of Vatican II* ed. Vol 1. Ed. Herbert Vorgrimler New York 1969 p. 212.

[556] To Pusey 23 March 1867 *LD* 23 p.106

Newman was clear that papal infallibility was a necessary part of Catholic faith but he was precise about the extent of that authority and had written in 1863 to a clergyman with leanings towards Rome,

> To submit to the Church means this, first that you will receive as *de fide* whatever she pronounces *de fide*; that you will submit to the decisions of the Schola Theologorum, when unanimous in matters of faith and morals, as being so sure that it is forbidden to contradict them—that you obey the commands of the Church in act and deed, though as a matter of policy, prudence etc., you may think other commands may be better. You are not called on to believe *de fide* any thing but what has been promulgated as such—you are not called on to exercise an internal belief of any doctrine which Sacred Congregations, Local Synods, or particular Bishops or the Pope as a private Doctor, may enunciate. You are not called upon even to believe or act against the moral law at the command of any superior. You are not bound to put yourself under the direction of any Priest, except as a matter of counsel.[557]

Newman had explained in 1846 how the 'subjective word' becomes objective in the Church by showing that when controversy grows serious "appeal is made to Peter, asking him to pronounce on the case and a Council is assembled. Then the matter is disposed of peacefully. Opinions are advanced and questions raised from all sides. Different views of the Council fathers are elucidated. Dogmas of faith already accepted are examined straightforwardly and at length. These become the seeds from which an apostolic definition grows that deals with the matter in hand. Newman had described himself as a Developmentist[558] and said that finally, under God's direction

---

[557] To Rev W. R. Brownlow 25 October 1863 *LD* 20 p.545. William Robert Brownlow (1830-1901). Student of Trinity College Cambridge. He became curate at Moor Lane London in 1863 and was received that November by Newman. He joined the Plymouth diocese and was Vicar General and later bishop of Clifton in 1894.

[558] To Francis Richard Wegg-Prosser 20 February 1852 *LD* 15 p.39. Francis Richard Wegg-Prosser (1824-1911), Rector of Nuneham Courtenay and Prebendary of Durham. MP for Herefordshire 1847-52, when he was received into the Church by Bishop Grant. He financed the Church and monastery at Belmont.

at his silent bidding after a hard birth a new dogma comes into being."[559] But there needed to be a full discussion:

> Turn to the first Council, in Acts xv, and there you find that before the settlement there was 'magna conquisitio'.[560]

This would involve a clear statement about the ambit and limitations of supreme papal authority:

> Any how the doctrine of Papal Infallibility must be fenced round and limited by *conditions*. The gift must be defined, and the circumstances of its exercise."[561]

The Syllabus *and* Quanta Cura

Newman was slightly ambiguous in his general attitude towards those officials of the Curia surrounding the Pope (whom Gladstone termed "the Myrmidons of the Apostolic Chamber");[562] some, he appreciated for their service to the Church; others he blamed for the advice they gave to the Pope. He had mentioned, in his 'Memorandum' of 1870-3, their influence with Pius IX in his dealings with Ireland.[563] But from his many political friends he knew the contribution made by the British civil service, and that even without a temporal kingdom there was still "the rule of Pope and Curia."[564] Ullathorne would also not be browbeaten when instructed by the Curia on 5 February 1875 to ask Newman to retract his comments about the papacy. Cardinal Franchi, Prefect of Propaganda complained in a confidential note that "Newman had markedly expressed views about the Pope and the Acts of the Council which have caused harm to the minds of the

---

[559] 'On the Subjective Word of God in the Catholic Church' Newman's Thesis 3. Giovanni Perrone SJ to whom Newman submitted the paper would comment "I should not be so bold as to say that". James Gaffney *Roman Catholic Writings on Doctrinal Development by John Henry Newman.* Kansas 1997 p.21.

[560] To Reginald Buckler 15 April 1870 *LD* 25 pp.100-1. Acts 15:7 "when there had been much disputing".

[561] To Peter Le Page Renouf 21 June 1868 *LD* 24 p.92.

[562] *TVD* p.65.

[563] 'Memorandum about my Connection with the Catholic University' *AW* p.320.

[564] *VM* I p.xl.

faithful."[565] The Bishop—having experienced a similar request concerning the Oxford mission—when he was asked to approach Newman 'blande suaviterque',[566] replied in Latin pointing out that "shameful acts and the errors of history affirmed, rather than undermined doctrine"[567] and if anything was required, Newman should be written to "directly and openly". Cardinal Cullen then intervened with a Lenten Pastoral in which he said "The grounds on which this statesman founded his expostulation have been admirably answered by the venerable Dr. Newman."[568] It was decisive. Ullathorne heard nothing more and chose to ignore his instructions.[569]

Ward continued to argue his case:

> A very large number of bishops, from the Cardinal Vicar of Rome downwards, have officially and most emphatically pronounced it infallible; and moreover—the former being a manifest and overt fact—no one bishop has so much as publicly hinted any different view. The Cardinal Vicar of Rome declared it was to be received 'as the very word of God' Ergo & etc. You reply that I do not myself *maintain* it should be so received. But I do. If God has conferred on Pius IX the gift of infallibility, then we are bound to accept all his infallible utterances, 'as the very Word of God', who guarantees them from error.[570]

This would have confirmed Gladstone's worst nightmares. Newman told a correspondent quite the opposite:

---

[565] *LD* 27 p.401. Propaganda objected to eleven points where Newman referred among other things to the Pope being 'heir by default', Popes being called 'ambitious', 'those who gave themselves up to luxury' as well as Newman's contention that 'Popes are never in the wrong and are never to be resisted.' and 'ceasing to be Pope by reason of heresy.' *Diff* 2 pp.[206, 212, 254, 216, 377]. See Appendix 1 *LD* 27 pp. 408-9. Franchi called such remarks "troppo irreverente" and even "ereticale". Cardinal Alessandro Franchi (1819-78) became a Cardinal in 1873, Prefect of Propaganda in 1875 and Secretary of State under Leo XIII.

[566] *blande suaviterque*: soothingly and sweetly. *LD* 21 p.331 n.2.

[567] Appendix 1 *LD* 27 p.406.

[568] *LD* 27 p.xvi.

[569] C. S. Dessain *John Henry Newman* Oxford 1980 p.146. See also Appendix 1 *LD* 27 pp.410-11.

[570] 'A Brief Summary' *Dublin Review* 11 July-October 1868 appendix to July issue p.17.

As to the syllabus, I think it will not be passed by the Council—but really if you ask me there is little in it which when I was young, the Tory party did not hold and which I did not hold myself.[571]

Newman considered that the *Syllabus* had no special sanction except as bearing the authority of Cardinal Antonelli,[572] the Secretary of State, who had sent it to the bishops with a copy of *Quanta Cura*[573] "with the mere coincidence of time, and as a fact, each condemnation having only the weight which it had in the original papal document."[574] The Syllabus itself was not signed by the Pope and therefore not an official act... The Pope was not teaching dogmatically and infallibly".[575] It had to be taken "with obedience" but "obedience is concerning with doing, but faith with affirming. Now when we are told to avoid certain propositions, we are told primarily and directly not to do something; whereas, in order to affirm we must have positive statements put before us."[576]

Newman told Oxenham "It would be most rash in me to pronounce that, looking back in the year 2000 at the recent Syllabus or errors condemned in 1864, an impartial posterity will not pronounce it to be a wise, bold, and necessary manifesto. And this seems to be clear, that it condemns little which would not have been condemned by all Anglican High Church men thirty years ago."[577] But in essence they were

---

[571] To Lady Henrietta Georgina Marcia Lascelles Chatterton (1806-76). Newman would add, "All this was called Toryism, and men gloried in the name; now it is called Popery and reviled." *Diff* 2 p.[263].

[572] Cardinal Antonelli. Giacomo Antonelli (1806-78) was Pius IX's Secretary of State 1848-76.

[573] Encyclical 8 December 1864 which instructed the bishops to tell their charges "to abstain from evil pastorage which Jesus Christ does not till" and "kingdoms rest upon the foundation of the Catholic faith." *DS* 2890-6.

[574] To Pusey 17 November 1865 *LD* 22 p.104.

[575] *Diff* 2 pp.[278, 375]. Robert Whitty told Newman that "The Syllabus was prepared and published without asking the advice of a single Father of the Society upon it." 23 February 1870 *LD* 25 p.92n.

[576] *Diff* 2 p.[366].

[577] To Henry Nutcombe Oxenham 25 January 1865 *LD* 21 p.392. Henry Oxenham (1829-88) was a Tractarian and one of the founders of the A.P.U.C. In 1857 he was received into the Church by Manning. In 1858 he had welcomed Pusey's *Eirenicon*;

'*abstract propositions*'[578] and did not involve infallibility:

> If a Bishop asked the Pope 'Is this the meaning of your holiness's "Pastor Aeternus,"' and he answered in conversation before witnesses, or in other informal way, 'Yes it is' or 'no it isn't', the interpretation, so announced by him, would not be de fide. Or again if the Pope said to a deputation in his answer to them 'I hope you uphold the Syllabus, which I assure you is de fide' that would not make it de fide.[579]

This did not mean that he opposed the stand taken against rationalism and indifferentism, (both were included by Gladstone in the category of 'modern thought,') which Rome had repudiated.[580] Newman pointed out that Gladstone jumped to the conclusion that the Pope condemns something he does not condemn "which is neither just nor logical."[581] The condemnation of 'absolute liberty of conscience' or licence was only a repetition of the words used by Gregory XVI in *Singulari Nos*.[582] Newman reminded Gladstone (who hadn't taken the point) that even the libertarian John Stuart Mill could not admit of a freedom to harm others.[583] As far as the Syllabus went,

> There is not a word in it of the Pope's own writing; there is nothing in it at all, but the Erroneous Propositions themselves... It has no mark or seal put upon it which gives it a direct relation to the Pope ... it is nothing more than a digest of certain Errors made by an anonymous writer ... the Syllabus then has no dogmatic force.[584]

---

he helped Gladstone in his pamphlet *Vaticanism,* tried his vocation in the Oratory and was a master at the Oratory School.

[578] To Ambrose St John 8 January 1865 *LD* 21 p.378.

[579] To William Maskell 12 February 1876 *LD* 28 p.25.

[580] *TVD* p.12. "The faith in Christ is detrimental to human reason; and divine revelation not only is of no use but is even harmful to man's perfection." *Syllabus of Errors* n. 4. *DS* 2906.

[581] *Diff* 2 p.[275].

[582] Encyclical *Singulari Nos* (1834) n.29.

[583] See *Diff* 2 pp.[274-5, 363].

[584] *Diff* 2 pp.[277, 281]. Newman notes that the Pope could have given it his infallible sanction but did not do so.

He added later, in light vein, "The propositions may be as false as heathenism, but they have this redeeming virtue, that the Pope denounces them."[585]

The authority of conscience

When Gladstone implied that such an authoritative intervention by the Pope amounted to "the moral murder of stifling conscience and conviction",[586] Newman highlighted the power of conscience, before toasting the Pope.[587] He had initially pondered "our divinely-enlightened sense of duty and our right feeling implicitly; and though (alas!) we continually transgressed, and thereby impaired this inward guide, at least we did not question its authority no longer recognized as an independent arbiter of action."[588] "Conscience implies a relation between the soul and a something exterior, and that, moreover, superior to itself; a relation to an excellence which it does not possess, and to a tribunal over which it has no power."[589] As St. Pope John Paul II was later to put it, "It is by listening to the voice of God in the depth of our hearts and abiding by his commandments that we reach the liberty for which we yearn."[590] Newman had explained his point in 1856 that Conscience is

> A certain commanding dictate not a mere sentiment not a mere opinion or impression, or view of things, but a law, an authoritative voice, bidding him do certain things and avoid others... This is conscience; and, from the nature of the case, its very existence carries on our minds to a Being exterior to ourselves; for elsewhere when did it come? and to a Being superior to ourselves; else when its strange peremptoriness?[591]

---

[585] *Diff* 2 p.[367].
[586] *TVD* p.21.
[587] See p.261.
[588] *PPS* I p.312.
[589] *US* 'The Influence of Natural and Revealed Religion Respectively' (18 April 1830), p.18.
[590] *Address* at Denver 14 April 1993.
[591] 'Dispositions for Faith' *OS* pp.64-5.

Somehow to confuse this with 'liberty of conscience' is to blur the whole issue, because liberty is frequently expressed in opposition to right mindedness; we can always make our conscience the servant of our wishes. There are always those "who follow the dictates of their own hard hearts."[592] Newman argues if we take this to an extreme we would not allow the police to visit a notorious place like Hollywell Street, of which Gladstone in his regular nocturnal social work would be familiar.[593] It was an agreed maxim that "the supremacy of conscience is the essence of natural religion; the supremacy of Apostle, or Pope, or Church, or Bishop."[594] He now argues, "Conscience has rights because it has duties; but in this age, with a large portion of the public, it is the very right and freedom of conscience to dispense with conscience, to ignore a Lawgiver and Judge, to be independent of unseen obligation."[595] He asks a rhetorical question, "The State ought to have a conscience, but what if it happened to have half-a-dozen, or a score, or a hundred, in religious maters, each different from each other?"[596]

There is no argument about conscience's preeminent authority, because the Pope is himself subject to conscience as the supreme law, for conscience is "the aboriginal Vicar of Christ."[597] It is "that Divine Authority, on which in truth the Church herself is built."[598] Newman adds, to forestall objections, "No Pope ever will be able, as the objection supposes, to create a false conscience for his own ends." [599] In his letter to the *Times* concerning an article on the St Bartholomew's day massacre and the involvement of Gregory XIII, Newman pointed out "No Pope has any power over those eternal moral principles which God has implanted on our hearts and consciences. If any Pope has, with his eyes open, approved

---

[592] Jer 13:10.
[593] See *Diff* 2 p.[364]. Hollywell Street, now demolished to make way for the Aldwich in 1901, had a very shady reputation.
[594] *Dev* (1ˢᵗ edition 1845) p.124.
[595] *Diff* 2 p.[250].
[596] Ibid p.[267].
[597] Ibid p.[248].
[598] Ibid p.[252].
[599] Ibid p.[258].

of treachery or cruelty, let those defend that Pope who can."[600]
He went so far as to say that it was "a suicidal act to speak
against conscience."[601] Thomas More said the same at his trial:
"Every true and good subject is more bound to have respect to
his said conscience and to his soul than to any other thing in all
the world besides."[602] Newman pointed out,

> It praises, it blames, it promises, it threatens, it implies a future,
> and it witnesses to the unseen. It is more than a man's own
> soul.[603]

It is quite another matter when the individual chooses to pit
his own conscience against the teaching authority of the
Church,[604] because one is not in the same position or possessing
the same authority as the successor of Peter and the other
apostles. Newman had much earlier made the point about faith:
"They substitute for it something or other, a feeling, notion,
sentiment, conviction, or act of reason, which they may hang
over, and doat[605] upon. They rather aim at experiences (as they
are called) within them, than at Him that is without them."[606]

The definition of infallibility

The actual circumstances of the vote did pose the question of
whether the authority of the Council as represented by the

---

[600] To the Editor of *The Times* 9 September 1872 *LD* 26 pp.163-4. Newman and John
William Bowden (1798-1844), who was a Tractarian and author of the *Life and
Pontificate of Gregory VII*, had jointly composed *St Bartholomew's Eve, A Tale of the
Sixteenth Century in Two Cantos* (Oxford 1821 but published anonymously, *LD* 1 p.61)
as a lament for the murder of the Huguenots on 24 August 1572. Newman noted "This
design so pleasing to the court of Rome" p.45. Historians acknowledge that the causes
were political, and Gregory XIII who became Pope in May 1572 played no part in the
event. Nevertheless, when he received the news he celebrated with a solemn *Te Deum*
in thanksgiving and had a commemorative medal struck. *Diff* 2 p.[257].
[601] Ibid p.[252].
[602] Nicholas Harpsfield, *Life and Death of Sir Thomas More*. EETS ed. E.V. Hitchcock
Oxford 1932 p.56.
[603] 'Dispositions for Faith' *OS* p.64.
[604] "What happens when there is a conflict between the Pope's utterances and one's
individual conscience?" John Cornwell *Newman's Unquiet Grave* London 2010
pp.199.
[605] *doat*: an uncommon variant of dote.
[606] *Jfc* p.336.

whole college of bishops remained valid when a large number dissented or abstained. At the time of the draft Constitution on 13 July 1870, of the 601 bishops present, 451 voted *placet*, 62 *iuxta modum* and 88 *non placet*.[607] At the time of the final vote on 18 July (the day before the outbreak of the Franco-Prussian war) only 435 bishops were present, and all but two voted *placet*.[608] Newman initially pondered on all those who had left before the final vote,[609] because he wanted to be sure that this fulfilled the conditions of being a truly oecumenical council with decisions decided in full session i.e. 'conciliariter.'[610] He pointed out to Bishop Ullathorne that a moral unanimity was indispensable.[611] There was the situation at Ephesus in 431 where there was a minority which disagreed and who eventually put forward its views in the *Latrocinium* or Robber Council in 449. But Leo's famous Tome[612] "had the effect of turning a great mass of Bishops right round, as if he were infallible" in the Council of Chalcedon in 451.[613] Newman explained to Ambrose Phillips when the definition was announced,

> The *primâ facie* argument is in favour of its having that authority [of an Ecumenical Council]. The Council was legitimately called; it was more largely attended than any Council before it; and innumerable prayers from the whole of Christendom have preceded it and attended it and merited a happy issue of its proceedings. Were it not then for certain circumstances, under which the Council made the definition, I should receive that definition at once. Even as it is, if I were

---

[607] *placet*: equivalent to agree (it pleases); *placet iuxta modum*: agree with reservations; *non placet*: disagree.

[608] Of the English bishops, Clifford and Errington voted *non placet* and Bishop Ullathorne *iuxta modum*. Bishop Edward Fitzgerald of Little Rock Arkansas also voted *non placet* but when the dogma was proclaimed, said "Holy Father, I now believe."

[609] Of the English bishops, these included Turner, Brown, Roskill and Amherst, Grant having died suddenly in Rome. Andrew Beck and Bernard Griffin eds. *The English Catholics* London 1950 p.205.

[610] *Diff* 2 p.[305].

[611] To Bishop Ullathorne 6 June 1870 *LD* 25 p.138.

[612] *Letter 28 to Patriarch Flavian* 13th June 449. *DS* 290-5.

[613] *Diff* 2 pp.[305-7, 372-5]. Letter to Isy Froude 24 April 1875 *LD* 27 p.287. Eliza Margaret (Isy) was the eldest daughter of William Froude. She became a Catholic in 1859 and married Baron Anatole von Hugel, (brother of Friedrich) in 1880.

called upon to profess it, I should be unable, considering it came from the Holy Father and the competent local authorities, at once to refuse to do so. On the other hand it cannot be denied that there are reasons for a Catholic, till better informed, to suspend his judgment on its validity... Again, if the Council continues to sit, if the dissentient Bishops more or less take part in it, and concur in its acts; if there is a new Pope, and he continues the policy of the present, and if the Council terminates without any reversal or modification of the definition, or any effective movement against it on the part of the dissentients, then again there will be good reason for saying that the want of moral unanimity has not been made out.[614]

He had considered the impact of a minority dissent when writing to Frederick Rymer at the time:

Supposing that protest came to nothing, supposing the subscribers did not act as a body, and did not carry it out in their own diocese then I should think that the definition was valid.[615]

It was a case of applying the principle of 'securus iudicat orbis terrarum'; as he said to Pusey, "Universal reception is a more striking test than antiquity because it can be more easily ascertained."[616] He had already accepted Fr. Perrone's argument, "The strength of the 'sensus commnis fidelium' can make up (e.g.) for the silence of the Fathers... Although at various times infallibility is not strictly *in* that consensus, but rather the consensus is an indicium or instrumentum to us of the judgement of that Church which *is* infallible."[617]

Newman was quite clear that infallibility was part of the deposit of faith, but this did not amount to an admission that it was linked to any act of the Pope's supreme authority.

---

[614] To Ambrose Phillipps de Lisle 24 July 1870 *LD* 25 pp.164-5.

[615] To Fredrick Rymer 15 August 1870 *LD* 27 p.186. Frederick Rymer was the President of St. Edmund's College Ware 1861-8. He was removed from his post because he was an inopportunist in 1870.

[616] To Pusey 4 July 1869 *LD* 24 p.283. *Securus iudicat orbis terrarium*: 'The judgement of the whole Church has no chance of being wrong.'

[617] 'On Consulting the Faithful in Matters of Doctrine' pp.66-7. See James Tolhurst *The Church ... a Communion* Leominster 1988 pp.140-1.

> The Pope is infallible in actu, not in—in his particular pronouncements ex Cathedra, not in his state of illumination as an Apostle might be, which would be inspiration. I am told some wicked men, not content with their hitherto cruel conduct are trying to bring in this doctrine of inherent infallibility, of which there is not a hint in the definition.[618]

Newman did not need to mention Manning, who issued a two hundred page pastoral in October in which he said that dogmatic facts, papal censures, the canonization of saints and the approbation of religious orders were subject to papal infallibility.[619] Both he and Ward tended to regard infallibility as a personal attribute of the Pope for use in the furtherance of his office. Ward was adamant, "In a figurative sense Pius IX may be said never to have ceased from one continuous *ex cathedra* pronouncement."[620] Such a position justified Gladstone's worst fears and he maintained that papal power was "without any practical limit or reserve" and that "the reach of infallibility is as wide as it may prompt the Pope to make it."[621] As Newman later said in his 1878 third preface to *Via Media* II, "It is so ordered on high that in our day holy church should present just that aspect to my countrymen which is most consonant with their ingrained prejudice against her, most unpromising for their conversion."[622]

He had consistently maintained that there were limits to papal supreme authority: "Infallibility cannot act outside of a definite circle of thought and it must in all its decisions or *definitions,* as they are called, profess to be keeping within it. The great truths of the moral law of natural religion, and of Apostolic faith, are both its boundary and its foundation... And

---

[618] To Mrs. William Froude 8 August 1870 *LD* 25 p.178.
[619] See Robert Gray *Cardinal Manning, a Biography.* London 1985 p.235. Newman noted in 1866 "Yes—de fide—Tanner, Valentia a Castro. Those who do not say that it is de fide say that it is *certain.* Suarez, Vasquez etc. Lambertini *leaves it doubtful* till the Pope decides... The Pope infallible, not in the canonization but in the commending cults etc, i.e. in the act, not in the doctrine. Amort vol. 1 p.333. *TP* XVIII iii p.128.
[620] *Essays on the Church's Doctrinal Authority* London 1880 p.510.
[621] *TVD* pp.32 49.
[622] *VM* 1 p.xxxviii.

it must ever profess to be guided by Scripture and tradition."[623] He wrote to Mansell, "I could not have publicly given my assent of the definition without also saying that I thought there was a great deal much to be regretted in the way of passing it.[624] He pointed out that "there never was a time when her Bishops, and notably the Bishop of Rome, were slow to give their testimony in behalf of the moral and revealed law and to suffer for their obedience to it." [625]

The Council had been prorogued until November 11; it had not closed.[626] This could be said to have left things open, as he mentioned to Pusey,

> As to the Council, I don't consider the question of infallibility quite settled—that is, it is just possible, before the Council closes, there might be some modification, especially if there is a new Pope.[627]

He later wrote,

> I think it is not usual, to promulgate a dogma till the end of the Council, as far as I know—and next, this has been carried out under such very special circumstances. I look for the Council to *right itself* in some way before it ends. It looks like a house divided against itself, which is a great scandal.[628]

When it became obvious that the prorogation of the Council was brought to an end by the Pope formally suspending the proceedings on October 20, the status of the definition had to be examined on its merits.[629] Newman had already considered the possibility when he wrote to Ambrose Phillips,

---

[623] *Apo* p.253.
[624] To William Monsell 20 January 1872 *LD* 26 p.21.
[625] *Diff* 2 p.[197].
[626] General Congregations, comprising 120 bishops, continued into September.
[627] To Pusey 28 August 1870 *LD* 25 p.1897. Pius IX was seventy-eight and had been seriously ill.
[628] To Mrs. William Froude 8 August 1870 *LD* 25 p.176.
[629] Vatican I was only formerly closed by John XXIII in 1960, announcing the calling of Vatican II.

And further, if the definition is eventually received by the whole body of the faithful, as valid or as the expression of a truth, then too it will claim our assent by the force of the great dictum, 'Securus judicat orbis terrarum.' This indeed is the broad principle by which all acts of the rulers of the Church are ratified... Nor, in saying this, do I forget that the definition if valid has been passed under the Presence and Aid of the Holy Ghost; for thought the supernatural promise guarantees its truth, it does not therefore guarantee the Christian prudence, the spirit and temper of its promulgators.[630]

The crux of the argument

Newman had gone over the facts in 1866, noting "It may be said that the Pope seems to appeal to himself and the See of Peter—but that is because by *divine right* he governs—because he has the strong presage that he will not be wrong *because he has consulted* the Bishops beforehand and perhaps altered or modified his prospective act at their suggestion, and because he *has to appeal to himself* in a way, viz in General Council."[631] He told Frederick Rymer, "I consider the self-assertion, the *ipse dixit* of the Popes for 1800 years a great and imposing argument for the validity of their claims."[632] He now told Ambrose St John much the same thing: that the definition could stand *on the authority of the Pope himself,* as being "a thousand bishops in himself at once."[633] He says bluntly in the *Postscript* "the Pope, if the Bishops in the Council, few or many, held back, might define a doctrine without them. A council of Bishops of the world is only one of the various modes in which he exercises his infallibility. The seat of infallibility is in him, and they [the bishops] are adjuncts"[634] He put it to Ambrose St John,

I have ever, since a Catholic held the Pope's Infallibility as a matter of opinion, at least I see nothing in the definition which

---

[630] To Ambrose Phillipps de Lisle 24 July 1870 *LD* 25 pp.165-6.
[631] 25 February 1866 *TP* p.110. Pius IX issued *Ubi Primum* in 1849; see note p.[188].
[632] To Frederick Rymer 15 August 1870 *LD* 25 p.186.
[633] *Diff* 2 p.[212].
[634] *Diff* 2 p.[371].

necessarily contradicts Scripture, Tradition or History. *I* can obey without *inconvenience*; and the Doctor Ecclesiae [Pius IX], whether exceeding his authority or not, bids me obey. Therefore I have an obligation of accepting the definition as a dogma. In this case I do not receive it on the word of the Council, but on the Pope's self-assertion. And I confess, as I said to you the other day, the fact that all along for so many centuries, the head of the Church and the teacher of the faithful and the Vicar of Christ has been allowed by God to assert virtually his infallibility, is a great argument in favour of the validity of his claim.[635]

Although Gladstone saw Pio Nono as the supreme enemy in all this (and the Pope would return the compliment by describing him as 'a viper'[636]), it was by no means clear that, as Pope, he drove the debate on Infallibility. The subject was not mentioned in the preparatory *Schemata* for the Council.[637] When Joseph de Maistre, with his exalted view of monarchy, advocated in 1819 the infallible sovereignty of the Papacy, Rome did not show any enthusiasm,[638] a fact that Pusey in his *Eirenicon* failed to mention. Newman noted that the question of infallibility was not raised at the beginning of the beginning of the Council.[639] He told Monsell, "There is no talk of bringing forward the infallibility, except at *last*—" which was in fact what happened.[640] Unlike the dogmatic declaration on the Immaculate Conception, Pius did *not* consult the Bishops on the likelihood of a declaration on infallibility before the Council. On 9 May 1870 the Commission *de fide* produced two documents: a Constitution on the Pope and a Report summarizing the suggestions made by several bishops *and* the objections raised against the doctrine of infallibility. The

---

[635] To Ambrose St. John 27 July 1870 *LD* 25 p.168.

[636] Reported in the *Western Times* 12 November 1874.

[637] *Diff* 2 p.[376].

[638] Comte Joseph Marie de Maistre (1753-1821). Philosopher and diplomat, in his *Le Pape* 1819 and *de l'Église gallicane* 1821. See note *Diff* 2 p.[10]. *En* pp.260-1.

[639] *Diff* 2 p.[376].

[640] To William Monsell 9 December 1869 *LD* 24 p.386. There was a preliminary discussion on 30 December but no formal schema.

moving spirit was the threat of Pistoia[641] rearing its head again. As expressed by Bossuet it states "That only to be *de fide*, which is *received* and sanctioned *by the whole Church*."[642] Dr. Döllinger was moving at that time towards the idea of a national Catholic Church in Germany, free of State control, which chimed in with Gladstone's own ideas.[643] He was not ready to accept a *definition* of infallibility but claimed that his views accorded with *moderate* Ultramontanism. He acknowledged:

> his (the Pope's) right to (be) *consultor* to *convoke* the episcopal body, by the possibility in which he is of acting always in concert with it, possessed in virtue of the Divine order the assured means to *give* infallibility to his dogmatic judgements … [but] apart from the episcopal body, the Pontiff is not infallible.[644]

Newman did not side with those who favoured the Gallican[645] argument introduced by Cardinal Filippo Guidi,[646] who wanted to see incorporated in any decree: "The Pope is assisted by the counsel of the bishops, manifesting the tradition of the Churches."[647] Newman regarded such manoeuvres as "the Anglican theory made real. It would be an ecclesiastical communism."[648] He told Maskell that the Pope "can decide a

---

[641] The Synod of Pistoia in 1786 adopted the Four Gallican Articles of 1682. Pius VI condemned the propositions in *Auctorem Fidei* in 1794 *DS* 2600-2700.

[642] Quoted by Pusey in *En* p.37.

[643] *Gladstone Diaries* 22 November 1850. Newman told Alfred Plumer, "Döllinger is not an Anglican getting nearer to the truth but a Catholic receding from it." 6 October 1874 *LD* 27 p.129.

[644] Quoted in Manning *Petri Privilegium: Three Pastoral Letters to the Clergy of the Diocese.*vol 2 London 1871 pp.139-40.

[645] Gallican argument. See p.[189]n. "The Gallican party, towards which England and Ireland inclined," p.353.

[646] Cardinal Guidi. Filippo Maria Guidi (1815-79). A Dominican, he was Professor of Theology in Vienna 1857-63 and was created Cardinal in 1863. He was a Presiding Officer of the Council.

[647] Bishop Gasser in his *relatio* made the point, "Who will decide what number is sufficient? Who will make a choice, since in this respect the bishops are completely equal among themselves?" July 11 1870 n.40.

[648] See p.[211]. The Paris commune of 1871 was still in people's minds. R. E. Brown has said, "If the papacy one day faces a situation wherein Protestants are open to the bishop of Rome as a spokesman for a united Church, how could such a concept of

point infallibly which never came before any council."[649] Neither was he a supporter of those who took up the case of Popes Liberius and Honorius, which Le Page Renouf[650] and Döllinger espoused.[651] He told Willis Nevins, "The question is whether you can properly say that Honorius, in countenancing the Monophysite doctrine, spoke ex cathedrâ."[652]

In an earlier book Newman had written, "Pope Liberius might sign a Eusebian formula at Sirmium[653], and the mass of Bishops at Ariminum[654] or elsewhere, and yet they might, in spite of this error, be infallible in their *ex cathedrâ* decisions."[655] Before the Council he had explained to Mrs Helbert, "Dogmatic epistles to the Eastern Patriarchs will not be *enough* to be an ex cathedrâ act. See how tightly the *cases* of an ex cathedrâ decision will be restricted."[656] He wrote again in 1870 to Frederick Rymer,

> Now *my own* lines of thought run thus. (1) As things stand, I have not information, I have not grounds sufficient for

jurisdiction be adapted to meet their needs?" *Crisis Facing the Church* London 1975 p.78. Christopher Dawson called it 'ecclesiastical constitutionalism' in *Medieval Christianity* London 1935 p.23.

[649] To William Maskell 15 February 1876 *LD* 32 p.367.

[650] Le Page Renouf. See pp.315, 374n. Renouf Peter le Page Renouf (1822-97). He was received into the Church in 1842, became Professor of Ancient History in Dublin in 1854 and wrote a pamphlet *The Condemnation of Pope Honorius* in 1868 which was put on the Index. Pusey had also brought up the case of Honorius and Liberius *En* pp.35, 124. *The Condemnation of Pope Honorius* was put on the index.

[651] Ignaz von Döllinger's 'Letters of Quirinus'. Newman thought Döllinger had been badly treated but that his position was wrong. He returned to the question of Liberius when he revised *Ari* in 1876 pp.464-5.

[652] To J. H. Willis Nevins 16 June 1872 *LD* 26 p.117. Willis Nevins was a clerk in the Equity and Law Life Assurance Society. He became a Catholic in 1868 but left the Church over infallibility and became an Anglican curate at Southsea. He returned to the Church in 1873.

[653] The Council of Sirmium in 357 asserted the subordination of the Son to the Father and forbade the term 'substance'. See *Ari* pp.311-14. The Eusebian formula, named after Eusebius Bishop of Caesarea (260-340), admitted of an orthodox interpretation but also of an heretical. *Ath* 2 pp.282ff.

[654] The Synod of Ariminum (Rimini) in 359 endorsed an Arian Creed. See *Ari* pp.448-9.

[655] *Ari* p.464.

[656] To Mrs. Helbert 28 September 1869 *LD* 24 p.339. Magdalene Helbert, married with four children, corresponded with Newman in 1869 but was only received into the Church before her death in 1874. See note p.[187].

accepting the definition. The protest of 80 bishops on the day of voting is a bar. (2) but, *supposing* that protest came to nothing, supposing its subscribers did not act in a body, and did not carry it out in their own dioceses, then I should think that the definition was valid...(3) BUT again, even though the bar remains, and though there is not the clear and undeniable 'judicium orbis terrarum'[657] still for myself (and here perhaps you will not follow me) I consider the self-assertion, the ipse dixit of the Popes for 1800 years a great and imposing argument for the validity of their claims... I should consider the fact of the Pope being able by his power of jurisdiction practically to enforce his claim of infallibility was practically an intimation that that claim was well founded, and I should receive the dogma as a dogma.[658]

It was a matter which he had considered in the July 1859 *Rambler* article:

In the preparation of a dogmatic definition, the faithful are consulted. Doubtless their advice, their opinion, their judgment on the question of definition is not asked; but the matter of fact, viz. their belief, *is* sought for, as a testimony to that apostolical tradition, on which alone any doctrine whatsoever can be defined...the *sense of the faithful is not left out of the question* by the Holy See among the preliminary acts of defining a doctrine.[659]

The words used in the final decree were, as Newman envisaged, both moderate and at the same time, limiting. But he also said puzzlingly that the terms were both "vague and comprehensive."[660] An annotation to the first draft of the formula stated, "The Supreme Pontiff does not perform his duty as teacher without interaction and union with the Church." Whereas Gladstone saw the Pope in absolute terms as a monarch, Newman saw him even supernaturally as "Lord of a vast empire."[661] There is an inexact parallel for his rule in the

---

[657] A judgement of the universal Church.

[658] To Frederick Rymer 15 August 1870 *LD* 25 p.186.

[659] 'On Consulting the Faithful in Matters of Doctrine,' pp. 54-6.

[660] To Ambrose Phillipps de Lisle 24 July 1870 *LD* 25 p.164. *Diff* 2 p.[301].

[661] *Diff* 2 p.[223].

British Constitution where Henry de Bracton says "The King is under God and the law" [662] The Pope has always been similarly constrained not only by Scripture and Tradition—in other words, "without revelation it cannot be brought into exercise."[663] He told Lady Simeon,

> If you look into history, you find Popes continually completing the acts of their predecessors, and councils too—sometimes only half the truth is brought out at one time—I doubt not a coming Pope, or a coming Council, will so explain and guard what has been now passed by [the] late Council as to clear up all that troubles us now ... other definitions are necessary, and were intended, and will be added, if we are patient to reduce this dogma to its proper proportions and place it in the Catholic system. This is just what took place in the history of the 5th century, as regards the doctrine of the Incarnation.[664]

Gladstone was fixated on what he saw as a supreme dictat coming out of the blue. Newman understood his attitude and that there was some basis in his (unfounded) fears. But he considered that Gladstone overrated the Pope's powers in political and social matters.[665] As far as the spiritual power of the Pope there was no argument: "As what is expressively called Popery, it exalts the will and pleasure of the existing Church above all authority whether of Scripture or Antiquity, interpreting the one and disposing of the other by its absolute and arbitrary decree."[666] In this vein he replied to Canon Jenkins,

> The decrees on the Popes have a side on which all Catholics are agreed, but there is a side on which they admit of a variety of interpretations—just as the Council of Nicæa settled once for all the question of Our Lord's divinity, leaving open the

---

[662] Henry de Bracton Judge in the King's central court and writer on law (d. 1268) in his *Treatise on the Laws and Customs of England* (1250-56).

[663] *TP* (1866) p.107.

[664] To Lady Simeon 26 April and 15 October 1871 *LD* 25 pp.322, 415. Newman said to William Monsell "Will not the next century demand Popes who are not Italian?" 12 January 1865 *LD* 21 p.386.

[665] To Gladstone 23 December 1881 *LD* 30 p.37.

[666] *VM* 1 p.xliv.

question how that divinity stood in relation to 'The Word was made flesh' and now in the first definition there are many open questions; and partizans of the Pope, as if to compensate for his temporal losses, wish to close them in favour of the extremist sense of them. At the same time, when it is asked what has actually been passed at the Vatican Council, I do not think it is more than I have stated in my Pamphlet [*A Letter to the Duke of Norfolk*].[667]

Certain clear limits ...

Newman had reflected on this matter in 1864 in the *Apologia*:

Infallibililty cannot act outside of a definite circle of thought, and it must in all its decisions, or *definitions,* as they are called, profess to be keeping within it. The great truths of the moral law or natural religion, and of Apostolical faith, are both its boundary and its foundation. It must not go beyond them, and it must ever appeal to them.[668]

In 1871 there was an exchange of letters between William Maskell the liturgist and Archbishop Manning over the definition. Manning put his answer in the form of a syllogism:

The infallibility of the Church is of faith. The *extension* of that infallibility is not yet defined, and is therefore matter of theology. The same is true of the Head of the Church. His infallibility is of faith. The *extension* of his infallibility is matter of theology.[669]

When Maskell passed on the correspondence, Newman replied,

He [Manning] and his are looking out for a definition *extending* the province of infallibility of the Church, over politics, science, etc., etc. Not a word will be said about the *Pope's* infallibility—for (since he has the *same* infallibility as

---

[667] To Canon Jenkins 25 February 1875 *LD* 27 pp.234-5. Robert Charles Jenkins (1815-96). Educated at Trinity College, Cambridge. He was Rector of Lyminge and honorary Canon of Canterbury in 1869.
[668] *Apo* p.253.
[669] Manning to William Maskell 19/20 October 1871 *LD* 25 p.420 n.2.

the Church's) *his* infallibility will be extended indirectly, when such a decree is passed about the *Church. Whether* it *will* be ever, depends on the will of God.[670]

Gladstone, however, made the point about 'morals', saying that "three-fourths of life are thus handed over."[671] Newman sought to counter this, giving a Canon Lawyer's response:

It may be added that the field of morals contains so little that is unknown and unexplored, in contrast with revelation and doctrinal fact which form the domain of faith, that is difficult to say what portions of moral teaching in the course of 1800 years actually have proceeded from the Pope, or from the Church, or where to look for such. Nearly all that either oracle has done in this respect, has been to condemn such propositions as in a moral point of view are false, or dangerous or rash.[672]

Newman left aside the question of how far authority could extend in general but noted that ultimately moral law was "that primary revelation to us from God".[673] He had already said in the *Apologia*, "Infallibility cannot act outside of a definite circle of thought, and it must in all its decisions, or *definitions,* as they are called profess to be keeping within it. The great truths of the moral law or natural religion, and of Apostolic faith, are both its boundary and its foundation. It must not go beyond them, and it must ever appeal to them."[674] In a later reply to Bishop Clifford Newman wrote,

It is a further question of course whether the Vatican Council has *defined* the Pope's infallibility in praeceptis morum,[675] and

---

[670] To William Maskell 22 October 1871 *LD* 25 p.420.

[671] *TVD* pp.32, 49.

[672] *Diff* 2 p.[332]. "'Offensive to pious ears', 'scandalous'—these too are declarations of matters of fact". 'The Censures' *TP* p.135.

[673] *Diff* 2 p.[331].

[674] *Apo* p.253. More recently it has been stated that "infallibility … extends to all the elements of doctrine, including moral doctrine, without which the saving truths of the faith cannot be preserved, expounded or observed." *CC* n.2051.

[675] *praeceptis morum*: in moral matters.

I am very glad you have started it. Certainly the infallibility is made in the *Pastor Aeternus* to attach to 'doctrina' only.[676]

He does not here seem to have noticed that the definition *did* refer to "doctrine concerning faith and morals."[677] But he also made the point "The Pope, who comes of Revelation, has no jurisdiction over Nature, *i.e.* The natural law."[678] Some have taken this to imply that in his exercise of infallibility the Pope is severely restricted to doctrine,[679] but Newman was thinking more in terms of "the fact that things happen according to fixed circumstances, and not without them, and at random: that is, that they happen in an order,"[680] which makes it impossible for the Pope to violate such a law.[681] He maintained as a private opinion in his *Postscript* that "a heretical Pope, *ipso facto,* ceases to be Pope by reason of his heresy."[682] This would apply to his doctrinal pronouncements.

Newman added that the Pope is not infallible either in his administration or in his public policy,[683] but he was quite definite about the broad extent of papal authority: "As to this particular doctrine (Papal Infallibility), I am not at all sure it will increase the Pope's power—it may restrict it. Hitherto he has done what he would, because its limits were not defined— now he must act by rule."[684] Newman was quite definite that the Pope could not issue injunctions ordering lotteries in parishes, advocating vegetarianism or instructing priests to argue in favour of teetotalism[685]—the latter was a particular concern of Manning. Such things were matters for debate but were not within the remit of infallibility in the Catholic Church.

---

[676] To Bishop Clifford 5 February 1875 *LD* 27 p.214
[677] *DS* 3074.
[678] *Diff* 2 p.[254].
[679] Francis A Sullivan *Magisterium* London 1983 p.138. Hans Küng *Infallible?* London 1971 p.33ff.
[680] *GA* pp.68-9.
[681] *Diff* 2 p.[358].
[682] *Diff* 2 p.[359].
[683] *Diff* 2 pp.[240-1].
[684] To Anna Whitty 9 September 1870 *LD* 25 p.204. Mrs Michael James Anna Neill Whitty wife of the journalist who founded the *Liverpool Daily Post* in 1855. A convert, she died in 1873.
[685] *Diff* 2 p.[260] and *Idea* pp.221-2, 472.

Newman adds an extract from the Swiss Bishops which received the Pope's approbation,

> It in no way depends upon the caprice of the Pope, or upon his good pleasure, to make such and such a doctrine, the object of a a dogmatic definition. He is tied up and limited to the divine revelation, and to the truths which that revelation contains. He is tied up and limited by the Creeds, already in existence, and by the preceding definitions of the Church. He is tied up and limited by the divine law, and by the constitutions of the Church. Lastly, he is tied up and limited by that doctrine, divinely revealed.[686]

It could not be argued that the condemnation of Galileo's opinions in 1633 was in any way an infallible decision, not only because it was a decision of a Roman Congregation but also because it did not define doctrine.[687] Newman points out to a correspondent "Infallibility is not a *habit,* or a state of mind— but, as the decree says, that infallibility which the Church has."[688] He enlarges on this, in an important letter in July 1870 to Isy Froude:

> ... the *infallibility* of the Church (or of the Pope) is, as far as I know, a novel phrase. The infallibility of the Church has never been defined as a dogma (except indirectly in the late Vatican Council). The form which the doctrine took was to say that the point in dispute, when once decided, was 'irreformable', it was settled once for all—it was part of the Catholic faith— Therefore attention was centred in the *thing* not in the person... 'If the *Schola* Theologorum, decides the meaning of a Pope or a Council's words, the Schola is infallible, not *they* or *he*'. ... Some power then is needed to determine the general sense of authoritative words—to determine their direction drift, limits, and comprehension, to hinder gross perversions. This power is virtually the *passive infallibility* of the whole

---

[686] *Diff* 2 p.[339].

[687] See *Diff* 2 pp.[257, 326].

[688] To Anon 17 September 1872 *LD* 26 p.171, possibly Richard Frederick Littledale, an Anglo Catholic controversialist. See *Diff* 2 p.[321]. "The supreme degree of participation in the authority of Christ is ensured by the charism of infallibility." *CC* n. 2035.

body of the Catholic people.[689] The active infallibility lies in the Pope and the Bishops—the passive the 'universitas' of the faithful. Hence the maxim 'Securus judicat orbis terrarum.' The body of the faithful can never misunderstand what the Church determines by the gift of its active infallibility.[690]

He further explains the rather untidy process that is involved when Councils meet, in order to subdue the fears of Mrs Wilson:

There has ever been a great deal of disturbance after any new definition of faith. If there was none at Trent, it must be recollected it went on for 20 years, and good part of the trouble went before it, and the rest during it. The *Reformation* created the trouble—in our case, alas, an unscrupulous Church faction has created the trouble. We were going on quite well when they meddled. However, God overrules all things. If the whole Church accepts the late definition, then it will stand on its proper ground, universal acceptance (according to St Augustine's maxim, 'Securus judicat orbis terrarum—' 'The judgment of the whole Church has no chance of being wrong') At present it is a great shame to hurry people on.[691]

Gladstone does not seem to have endeavoured to "enter into scientific distinctions and traditionary rules of interpretation",[692] and this prevented him from fully understanding and interpreting the theology behind the actual words of the decree: "The Roman Pontiff, when he speaks *ex cathedrâ,* that is when, as supreme pastor and teacher of all Christians, he defines with his supreme apostolic authority a doctrine concerning faith or morals to be hold by the universal Church, through the divine assistance promised to him in St. Peter, is possessed of *that infallibility with which the divine*

---

[689] Newman had republished his essay 'On Consulting the Faithful in Matters of Doctrine' in *Ari* third edition as an appendix pp.445-68.

[690] To Isy Froude 28 July 1875 *LD* 27 pp.337-8.

[691] To Mrs Margaret Wilson 24 October 1871 *LD* 25 pp.219-20. She had complained that she had been received into the Church precipitately and was troubled about infallibility. See *Diff* 2 pp.[303, 372] on acceptance of the definition and understanding of 'ratified'.

[692] *Diff* 2 p.[177].

Redeemer willed his Church to be endowed in defining doctrine concerning faith and morals: and therefore such definitions of the Roman Pontiff are irreformable of themselves and not from the consent of the Church."[693] He further showed his lack of comprehension by pronouncing, "There is no established or accepted definition of the phrase *ex cathedrâ*, and he [the Pope] has no power to obtain and no guide to direct him in his choice among some twelve theories on the subject."[694] Newman said that the words of the definition *were* quite clear about the conditions for an infallible statement. The scope of *ex cathedra*, short of being formally defined as dogma, would be a teaching by the Pope on matters of faith or morals "in the name and with the authority of the Apostles" formally intended "with the purpose of binding every member of the church to accept and believe his decision."[695] This means that "The Roman Pontiff, head of the college of bishops, enjoys this infallibility in virtue of his office when, as supreme pastor and teacher of all the faithful—who confirms his brethren in the faith—he proclaims in an absolute decision a doctrine pertaining to faith or morals."[696] John Paul II made such a pronouncement on the reservation of priestly ordination to men alone.[697]

Newman, makes the distinction that although the Apostles *were* inspired, the Pope is *not* inspired, although he is *assisted*.[698] He describes this as "an external guardianship, keeping them off from error (as a man's good angel) … saving

---

[693] *DS* 3074.

[694] *TVD* p. xlvi.

[695] *Diff* 2 p.[325].

[696] *Lumen Gentium* n.25.

[697] "A matter which pertains to the Church's divine constitution itself, and in virtue of my ministry of confirming the brethren I declare that the Church has no authority whatsoever to confer priestly ordination on women and that this judgment is to be definitively held by all the Church's faithful," *Ordinatio Sacerdotalis* 22 May 1994 n.4. *CIC* 1024. This was further confirmed by Pope Francis in his Apostolic Exhortation *Querida Amazonia* (2002) n.102.

[698] Newman notes "a divine *assistentia*, not in any sense an inspiration" July 10 1866 *TP* p.143. "Never have Catholics taught that the gift of infallibility is given by God to the Church after the manner of inspiration" Perrone *Praeelectiones Theologicae* vol 2 p.253. See infra pp.[328, 338, 377]. Benedict XVI told an audience in Aosto in July 2005, "The Pope is not an oracle."

them, as far as their ultimate decisions are concerned, from the effects of their inherent infirmities."[699] In another letter he says, the Pope "has no inherent gift of divine knowledge but when he speaks ex Cathedrâ he may say little or much, but he is simply protected from saying what is untrue."[700] He also added, "Infallibility is not impeccability".[701]

Newman had previously outlined the alternative theological positions 'if the Pope and Bishops differ':

> Infallibility lies with the Bishops by themselves [or] Infallibility lies in the Pope by himself. In the Council of the Vatican, the last answer has been made de fide.[702]

He explained the historical exercise of papal authority to Isy Froude,

> Now the Pope ever acted in company *with* the Church, sometimes before the hierarchy, sometimes after, sometimes simultaneously with, the hierarchy. He always showed, as the *voice* of the Church. The Vatican Council has decided that he is not only the instrumental head or organ of the Church, not only has a power of veto, not only is a co-operating agent in *de fide* decisions, but that in him lies the root of the matter, that his decision viewed separate even from the Bishops, is gospel... I might have taken a higher ground, for long before the Vatican Council, though not perhaps in the time of Honorious, Popes have realized to themselves their own infallibility, and from the first, as we see in the history of St. Victor, St Stephen, St Dionysius in the Ante-nicene times –

---

[699] *Diff* 2 p.[328].

[700] To Mrs. Froude 5 March 1871 *LD* 25 p.299. See supra about his comment in his *Memorandum* on the Catholic University about Pius IX's grasp of Irish affairs.

[701] To The Editor of *The Times* 9 September 1872 *LD* 26 p.164.

[702] To Thomas Edwards 13 April 1875 *LD* 27 pp. 277-8. Frederick Thomas Edwards, author of *An Appeal to High Churchmen* (1867) was received into the Church the same year by Newman. He became a priest in Plymouth diocese in 1876 and died in 1917. The *Nota Praevia* appended to *Lumen Gentium* states "The Pope, as supreme pastor of the Church, may exercise his power at any time, as he sees fit, by reason of his office." n.4.

they have acted as if their Word was *law,* without making nice distinctions.[703]

The Pope, a brother among his bishops

Despite the exclamations of 'Viva il Papa Infallibile!' when the dogma was announced, Pius IX hastened to tell the assembled bishops,

> This supreme authority of the Roman Pontiff does not oppress but helps, does not destroy but builds up, confirms in dignity, unites in charity, and strengthens and protects the rights of his Brethren the Bishops.[704]

The final text states, "This power of theirs is asserted, supported and defended by the supreme and universal pastor."[705] Vatican II echoed this when it declared,

> Just as, in accordance with the Lord's decree St Peter and the rest of the apostles constitute a unique apostolic college, so in like fashion the Roman Pontiff, Peter's successor, and the bishops, the successors of the apostles are related with and united to one another.[706]

So Pius neatly answered Gallican arguments and satisfied Bishop Ullathorne. Newman had made the point, "What a Bishop is to his Church—such [is] the Pope to all Bishops and the whole Church. A Bishop of Bishops."[707] It can be seen that the authority of the individual bishop is inextricably interwoven with, and depends upon the supreme authority of the Pope; as is made clear in the apostolic letter from the Pope

---

[703] To Isy Froude 28 July 1875 *LD* 27 pp.336-7.338. See *Ess* 2 p.101. Newman preached on 15 April 1850, "The Christian people cannot be wrong. Vox populi etc." *SN* p.77. See also "The whole body of the faithful who have an anointing that comes from the holy one cannot err in matters of belief." *Lumen Gentium* n.12.

[704] Cuthbert Butler *The Vatican Council 1869-1870* ed. B. C. Butler. London 1967 p.414.

[705] *DS* 3061.

[706] *Lumen Gentium* n.22.

[707] *TP* 25 February 1866 p.110. In a collective declaration the German hierarchy stated in 1875 "It is in virtue of the same divine institution upon which the papacy rests that the episcopate also exists." *DS* 3115.

or *Mandate,* appointing him to the diocese read at the beginning and in the promise made during the ordination ceremony "to render obedience faithfully to the successor of the blessed Apostle Peter".[708] Newman added in a new preface to *Via Media,*

> I will but say in passing, that I must not in this argument be supposed to forget that the Pope, as the Vicar of Christ, inherits these offices and acts for the Church in them. This is another matter; I am speaking here of the Body of Christ, and the Sovereign Pontiff would not be the visible head of that Body, did he not first belong to it. He is not himself the Body of Christ, but the chief part of the Body.[709]

Bishop Ullathorne put it in his Advent Pastoral Letter before the Council opened,

> It is for the bishops, then, in Council to bear witness, to deliberate, and to deliver their judgements by their votes on the matter in hand; and it is for the Pope to confirm or withhold consent from their decision. The Church does not consist of body alone, or of head alone, but of head and body moving in joint action;[710] but the head is the crowning authority, alike in the Church's capacity of teacher, of lawgiver, and of ruler.[711]

Bishop Brown in his 1870 Pastoral said,

> Popes were only to define after inquiring as to what was held throughout the Church, and then in their capacity of supreme Pontiff as part of the Deposit entrusted to the apostles and their

---

[708] In earlier times English bishops bound themselves "to be faithful and obedient to the Holy Roman Church and to further and defend the authority and privileges of the Holy See."

[709] *VM* 1 p.xl.

[710] Ullathorne would seem to be making use of Newman's "*pastorum* ac fidelium *conspiratio ... which is not in the pastors alone*" in his 'On Consulting the Faithful in Matters of Doctrine,' pp.72, 103. Newman wrote to Robert Whitty, "The Church moves as a whole, it is not a mere philosophy, it is a communion." 12 April 1870 *LD* 25 p.93. See James Tolhurst *The Church ... A Communion* Leominster 1988 pp.138-43.

[711] Cuthbert Butler *Life and Times of Bishop Ullathorne 1806-1889* London 1926 vol. 2 p.49.

successors in the ministry and for the guidance of the Universal Church.[712]

Such a measured approach, which eschewed support for any Gallicanist sympathies, brought even those who doubted the opportuneness of the dogma eventually into acceptance. Despite their difference of opinion, there was no animosity and when Gladstone called on Newman in 1888 and was unable to meet him owing to his illness, Newman wrote in his own hand,

> It is a great kindness and compliment your asking to see me. I have known and admired you so long. But I can't write nor talk nor walk and hope you will take my blessing which I give from my heart.[713]

But in emphasizing the apostolic role of bishops the decree also provided a further understanding of the nature and exercise of the papacy. Vatican II reminds us that the Bishops "gather together the universal Church, which the Lord *founded upon the apostles* and *built upon blessed Peter their leader*, the chief corner-stone being Christ Jesus himself."[714]

In the years since Newman wrote, there still remains an underlying issue both for Gladstone and for Pusey. It was put succinctly by Bishop Butler when he asked, "Whether visible unity is only a goal to be aimed at, or whether it is a divinely guaranteed endowment?"[715] Newman leaves us in no doubt,

> We must either give up the belief in the Church as a divine institution altogether, or we must recognize it at this day in that communion of which the Pope is the head. With him alone and round about him are found the claims, the prerogatives, and duties which we identify with the kingdom set up by Christ. We must take things as they are; to believe in a Church, is to

---

[712] See *LD* 25 p.220n.

[713] To Gladstone 6 November 1888 *LD* 31 p.266. Gladstone wrote from Edgbaston, where he was staying, "In case he should be altogether able, and also kindly disposed, to see me. I should hold myself in readiness at any time tomorrow, or in the forenoon of Thursday, to wait upon him."

[714] *Lumen Gentium* n.19.

[715] B. C. Butler *The Church and Unity* London 1979 p.226.

believe in the Pope. And thus this belief in the Pope and his attributes, which seems so monstruous to Protestants, is bound up with our being Catholics at all; as our Catholicism is bound up with our Christianity. There is nothing then of wanton opposition to the powers that be, no dinning of novelties in their startled ears in what is often unjustly called Ultramontane doctrine; there is no pernicious servility to the Pope in our admission of his pretensions. I say, we cannot help ourselves— Parliament may deal as harshly with us as it will; we should not believe in the Church at all, unless we believe in its visible head."[716]

James Tolhurst

---

[716] *Diff* 2 p.[208].

A LETTER ADDRESSED TO THE REV. E. B. PUSEY, D.D.,

ON THE OCCASION OF HIS EIRENICON

A LETTER,[1]

&c.

NO one who desires the union of Christendom after its many and long-standing divisions, can have any other feeling than joy, my dear Pusey, at finding from your recent Volume,[2] that you see your way to make definite proposals to us for effecting that great object, and are able to lay down the basis and conditions on which you could co-operate in advancing it. It is not necessary that we should concur in the details of your scheme, or in the principles which it involves, in order to welcome the important fact, that, with your personal knowledge of the Anglican body, and your experience of its composition and tendencies, you consider the time to be come when you and your friends may, without imprudence, turn your minds to the contemplation of such an enterprise. Even were you an individual member

---

[1] Newman prefaced his text with a quotation from the Gelasian Sacramentary (for the 4th Sunday of Advent) "Veni. Domine, et noli tardare, relaxa facinora plebis tuae; et revoca dispersos in terram tuam": "Come, Lord and do not delay, remit the misdeeds of your people and call back to your land those who have been scattered."

[2] *The Church of England A Portion of Christ's One Holy Catholic Church, and a Means of Restoring Visible Unity. An Eirenicon., in a Letter to The Author of 'The Christian* Year' (1865). John Keble (1792-1866) published *The Christian Year* in 1827.

3

of that Church, a watchman upon a high tower[3] in a metropolis of religious opinion, we should naturally listen with interest to what you had to report of the state of the sky and the progress of the night, what stars were mounting up or what clouds gathering,[4]—what were the prospects of the three great parties which Anglicanism contains within it[5], and what was just now the action upon them respectively of the politics and science of the time. You do not go into these matters; but the step you have taken is evidently the measure and the issue of the view which you have formed of them all.

[2]

However, you are not a mere individual; from early youth you have devoted yourself to the Established Church, and, after between forty and fifty years of unremitting labour in its service, your roots and your branches stretch out through every portion of its large territory. You, more than any one else alive, have been the present and untiring agent by whom a great work has been effected in it; and, far more than is usual, you have received in your lifetime, as well as merited, the confidence of your brethren. You cannot speak merely for yourself; your antecedents, your existing influence, are a pledge to us, that what you may determine will be the determination of a multitude. Numbers, too, for whom you cannot properly be said to speak, will be moved by your authority or your arguments; and, numbers, again, who are of a school more recent than your own, and who are only not your followers because they have outstripped you in their free speeches and demonstrative acts in our behalf, will, for the occasion,

---

[3] Walter Scott in *Marmion* speaks of William Pitt as "A watchman on the lonely tower."

[4] Luke 12:54.

[5] The High Church, the Broad Church and the Low Church or Evangelical.

accept you as their spokesman.[6] There is no one anywhere,—among ourselves, in your own body, or, I suppose, in the Greek Church,—who can affect so large a circle of men, so virtuous, so able, so learned, so zealous, as [3] come, more or less, under your influence; and I cannot pay them a greater compliment than to tell them they ought all to be Catholics, nor do them a more affectionate service than to pray that they may one day become such. Nor can I address myself to an act more pleasing, as I trust, to the Divine Lord of the Church, or more loyal and dutiful to His Vicar on earth, than to attempt, however feebly, to promote so great a consummation.

I know the joy it would give those conscientious men, of whom I am speaking, to be one with ourselves. I know how their hearts spring up with a spontaneous transport at the very thought of union; and what yearning is theirs after that great privilege, which they have not, communion with the see of Peter, and its present, past, and future. I conjecture it by what I used to feel myself, while yet in the Anglican Church. I recollect well what an outcast I seemed to myself, when I took down from the shelves of my library the volumes of St. Athanasius[7] or St. Basil,[8] and set myself to study them; and how, on the contrary, when at length I was brought into Catholic communion,[9] I kissed them with delight, with a feeling that in them I had more than all that I

---

[6] "Dr Pusey was a person who commanded the utmost interest and reverence; he was more in communication with the great world outside than Oxford people generally, and lived much in retirement from Oxford society; but to all interested in the movement he was its representative and highest author." R. W Church *The Oxford Movement 1839-1843* London 1891 p.160.

[7] St. Athanasius (c. 296-373). He succeeded Bishop Alexander as Patriarch of Alexandria in 328. He defended faith in the Incarnation against Arianism and suffered exile for it.

[8] St Basil the Great (c. 330-79). He lived as a hermit 358-64 when he was persuaded to become Bishop of Caesarea. He is responsible for the Eastern Church's monastic rule.

[9] 1st ed, "Catholicism".

had lost; and, as though I were directly addressing the glorious saints, who bequeathed them to the Church, how I said to the inanimate pages, "You are now mine, and I am now yours, beyond any mistake."[10] Such, I conceive, would be the joy of the persons I speak of, if they could wake up one morning, and find themselves rightfully possessed of Catholic traditions and hopes, without violence to their own [4] sense of duty; and, certainly, I am the last man to say that such violence is in any case lawful, that the claims of conscience are not paramount, or that any one may overleap what he deliberately holds to be God's command, in order to make his path easier for him or his heart lighter.

I am the last man to quarrel with them for this jealous deference to the voice of their conscience, whatever be the judgment that others may form of them[11] in consequence, for this reason, because their present circumstances[12] have once, as you know, been my own. You recollect well what hard things were said against us twenty-five years ago, which we knew in our hearts we did not deserve. Accordingly, I am now in the position of the fugitive Queen in the well-known passage; who, "non ignara mali"[13] herself, had learned to sympathize with those who were the inheritors of her past wanderings. There were Priests, good men, whose zeal outstripped their knowledge, and who in consequence spoke confidently, when it would have been wiser in them to have suspended their adverse judgment of

---

[10] "The writings of the Fathers, so far from prejudicing at least one man against the modern Catholic Church, have been simply and solely the one intellectual cause of his having renounced the religion in which he was born and submitted himself to her." *Diff* 1 p.367.

[11] 1st ed. "the voice of our conscience ... may form of us"

[12] 1st ed. "because their case, as it as present stands, has ..."

[13] Virgil *Aeneid* Book 1, l.630, "non ignara mali miseris succurrere disco". Trojan fugitives including Aeneas seek refuge which Queen Dido grants. The Carthagian Queen Dido says, "I know nothing so fine, so full of meaning, so touching, so true as these words." *Aeneid* Book 1 l.330.

those whom, in no long time, they had to welcome as brethren in communion. We at that time were in worse plight than your friends are now, for our opponents put their very hardest thoughts of us into print. One of them wrote thus in a Letter addressed to one of the Catholic Bishops:—

"That this Oxford crisis is a real progress to Catholicism, I have all along considered a perfect delusion ... I look upon Mr. Newman, Dr. Pusey, and their associates, as wily and crafty, though unskilful guides ... The embrace of Mr. Newman is the kiss that would betray us ... But,—what is [5] the most striking feature in the rancorous malignity of these men,—their calumnies are often lavished upon us, when we should be led to think that the subject-matter of their treatises closed every avenue against their vituperation. The three last volumes [of the Tracts] have opened my eyes to the craftiness and the cunning, as well as the malice, of the members of the Oxford Convention ... If the Puseyites are to be the new Apostles of Great Britain, my hopes for my country are lowering and gloomy ... I would never have consented to enter the lists against this strange confraternity ... if I did not feel that my own Prelate was opposed to the guile and treachery of these men ... I impeach Dr. Pusey and his friends of a deadly hatred of our religion ... What, my lord, would the Holy See think of the works of these Puseyites? ..."[14]

Another priest, himself a convert, wrote:—

"As we approach towards Catholicity, our love and respect increases, and our violence dies away; but the bulk of these men become more rabid as they become like Rome,—a plain proof of their designs ... I do not believe

---

[14] *Are the Puseyites Sincere? A Letter Most Respectfully Addressed to a Right Reverend Catholic Lord Bishop on the Oxford Movement by Rev. Joseph Rathbone.* London 1841, pp.4, 6, 12, 13, 15-16, 21, 29. Fr. Joseph Rathbone (1807-42) became Parish Priest of St Thomas', Cowes (1830-42).

that they are any nearer the portals of the Catholic Church than the most prejudiced Methodist and Evangelical preacher ... Such, Rev. Sir, is an outline of my views on the Oxford movement."[15]

I do not say that such a view of us was unnatural; and, for myself, I readily confess, that I had at one time used about the Church such language, that I had no claim on Catholics for any mercy. But, after all, and in fact, they [6] were wrong in their anticipations,—nor did their brother Catholics[16] agree with them at the time. Especially Dr. Wiseman (Co-adjutor[17] Bishop as he was then) took a larger and more generous view of us,[18] nor did the Holy See interfere against us,[19] though the writer of one of these passages invoked its judgment. The event showed that the more cautious line of conduct was the more prudent; and one of the Bishops, who had taken part against us, with a supererogation of charity, sent me on his deathbed an expression of his sorrow for having in past years mistrusted me. A faulty conscience, faithfully obeyed, through God's mercy, had in the long-run brought me right.

Fully, then, do I recognize the rights of conscience in this matter. I find no fault with your stating, as clearly and completely as you can, the difficulties which stand in the way of your joining us. I cannot wonder that you begin with stipulating conditions of union, though I do not concur in them myself and think that in the event you yourself would be content to let them drop. Such representations as yours

---

[15] Revd. James Austin Mason (1785-1844), formerly a Methodist minister, later Parish Priest of Stourbridge. His comments occur on p.19 of Rathbone's tract.

[16] 1st edition: "... brethren"

[17] 1st edition: "Coadjutor" is omitted.

[18] Dr Wiseman, Bishop of Melipotamus, was co-adjutor to Bishop Baines. He had written *A Letter on Catholic Unity, addressed to the Right Honourable, the Earl of Shrewsbury* in 1841 which he sent to Newman *LD* 8 pp.282-5. John Talbot (1791-1852) succeeded to the title in 1827 as 16th Earl.

[19] 1st ed. omits "... against us".

are necessary to open the subject in debate; they ascertain how the land lies, and serve to clear the ground. Thus I begin:—but after allowing as much as this, I am obliged in honesty to add what I fear, my dear Pusey, will pain you. Yet I am confident, my very dear friend, that at least you will not be angry with me if I say, what I must say if I say anything at all, viz., that there is much, both in the matter and in the manner of your Volume, calculated to wound those who love you well, but love truth more. So it is; with the best motives and kindest intentions,—"Cædimur, et   [7] totidem plagis consumimus hostem."[20] We give you a sharp cut, and you return it. You complain of our being "dry, hard and unsympathizing;" and we answer that you are unfair and irritating. But we at least have not professed to be composing an Irenicon, when we were treating you as foes. There was one of old time who wreathed his sword in myrtle;[21] excuse me—you discharge your olive-branch as if from a catapult.

Do not think I am not serious; if I spoke as seriously as I feel, I should seem to speak harshly. Who will venture to assert, that the hundred pages which you have devoted to the subject of the Blessed Virgin give other than a one-sided view of our teaching about her, little suited to win us? This may be a salutary castigation of us, if any of us have fairly provoked it; but it is not making the best of matters; it is not smoothing the way for an understanding or a compromise. Your representation of what we hold,[22] leads a writer in the most moderate and liberal Anglican newspaper of the day,

---

[20] Horace *Ars Poetica*: "Like Samnite gladiators in slow conflict at early candle-light, we receive blows, and wear out our antagonist enemies by as many in return." Horace *Epistles* Book II, 2, 2, 97.
[21] From *Song of Harmodius* by Callistratus (4th century BC Athenian general and orator).
[22] "Your representation of what we hold ..." omitted in 1st ed.

the *Guardian*,[23] to turn away from us, shocked and dismayed. "It is language," says your reviewer, "which, after having often heard it, we still can only hear with horror. We had rather not quote any of it, or of the comments upon it." What could an Exeter Hall[24] orator, what could a Scotch commentator on the Apocalypse, do more for his own side of the controversy in the picture he drew of us? You may be sure that charges which create horror on one side, will be repelled by indignation on the other; and these are not the most favourable dispositions of mind for a peace conference. I had been accustomed to

[8] Suppose,[25] that you, who in times past were ever less declamatory in controversy than myself, now that years had gone on, and circumstances changed, had come to look on our old warfare against Rome as cruel and inexpedient. Indeed, I know that it was a chief objection urged only last year against the scheme then in agitation of introducing the Oratory into Oxford,[26] that such an undertaking on my part would be a signal for the rekindling of that fierce style of polemics which is now long out of date. I had fancied you shared in that opinion; but now, as if to show how imperative you deem the renewal of that old violence, you actually bring to life one of my own strong sayings in 1841, which had long been in the grave, that "the Roman Church

---

[23] A weekly newspaper founded by R. W. Church, Frederick Rogers and others in 1846 to express Tractarian views.

[24] Exeter Hall, dating from 1830, a building in the Strand often used by Evangelicals for their meetings.

[25] 1st ed "to think"

[26] In August 1864 Newman was offered a five-acre plot in Oxford. He thought it could be a future Oratory, but he was not allowed to go ahead because it was felt this might encourage Catholics to attend Oxford. See *LD* 21 pp.165ff. The scheme failed, with Newman saying that it looked as if Manning and Ward were "co-operating to fulfil Pusey's wish of keeping me out of Oxford." *LD* 21 p.340. In 1864 edition "… which at that time was in prospect."

comes as near to idolatry as can be supposed in a Church,[27] of which it is said, 'The idols He shall utterly abolish.'"[28]——P. 111.[29]

---

[27] "If the note of schism on the one hand lies against England, an antagonist disgrace lies upon Rome, the Note of idolatry." 'Private Judgement' in *British Critic* (July 1841) *Ess* 2 p.367.

[28] Is 2:18.

[29] Pusey refers to Newman's comment that "Romanists are almost unchurched by their superstitions" in 'Private Judgement' *Ess* 2 pp.369-70.

§ 2.—*Remarks on various statements introduced into the Eirenicon.*[1]

I KNOW, indeed, and feel deeply, that your frequent references, in your Volume, to what I have lately or formerly written, are caused by your strong desire to be still one with me as far as you can, and by that true affection, which takes pleasure in dwelling on such sayings of mine as you can still accept with the full approbation of your judgment. I trust I am not ungrateful or irresponsive to you in this respect; but other considerations have an imperative claim to be taken into account. Pleasant as it is to agree with you, I am bound to explain myself in cases in which I have changed my mind, or have given a wrong impression of my meaning, or have been wrongly reported; and, while I trust that I have higher than mere personal motives for addressing you in print, yet it will serve to introduce my main subject, and give me an opportunity for remarks which bear upon it indirectly, if I dwell for a page or two on such matters contained in your Volume as concern myself.

1.[2] The mistake which I have principally in view is the belief which is widely spread, that I have publicly spoken of the Anglican Church as "the great *bulwark* against infidelity in this land." In a pamphlet of yours a year old, you spoke of "a very earnest body of Roman Catholics," who "rejoice in all the workings of God the Holy Ghost in the Church of England (whatever they think of her), and are saddened by what weakens her who is, in God's hands, the great *bulwark*

---

[1] Subheading not in the 1st edition.
[2] Numbering not in the 1st edition.

against infidelity in this land."[3] The concluding words you were thought to quote from my *Apologia.* In consequence, Dr. Manning, now our Archbishop,[4] replied to you, asserting, as you say, "the contradictory of that statement." In that counter-assertion, he was at the time generally considered (rightly or wrongly as it may be),[5] though writing to you, to be really glancing at my *Apologia,* and correcting it, without introducing my name, where he thought it needed correction.[6] Further, in the Volume, which you have now published, you recur to the phrase; and you speak of its author in term which, did I not know your partial kindness for me, would hinder me from identifying him with myself. You say, "The saying was not mine, but that of one of the deepest thinkers and observers in the Roman Communion." P.7. A friend has suggested to me that you mean De Maistre;[7] and, from an anonymous letter which I have receive from Dublin, I find it is certain that the very words in question were once used by Archbishop Murray;[8] however, you speak of the author of them as if now alive. At length, a reviewer of your Volume in the "Weekly Register,"[9] distinctly attributes them to me by name, and gives me the first opportunity I have had of disowning them; and this I now do. What, at some time or

---

[3] *En* p.7. Newman would "recognize in the Anglican Church, a time-honoured institution of noble historical memories, a monument of ancient wisdom, a momentous arm of political strength." *Apo* pp.340.

[4] Henry Edward Manning (1808-92), Fellow of Merton. He married Caroline Sargent in 1833 and became Rector of Lavington and Archdeacon of Chichester in 1841. He became a Catholic in 1851, succeeded Nicholas Wiseman as Archbishop in 1865 and was made a Cardinal in 1875.

[5] Mgr George Talbot (1816-86), a Canon of St. Peter's, regarded such remarks about Manning as "Most uncatholic and unchristian." *Purcell* vol 2 p.322.

[6] "where he thought it needed correction" was not in the 1st ed.

[7] Joseph de Maistre (1753-1821). Proponent of Ultramontane views, author of *Le Pape* (1819).

[8] Daniel Murray (1768-1852). He became Archbishop in 1823, having been coadjutor since 1809. He met Pusey during his visit to Dublin in 1841.

[9] *The Weekly Register was* amalgamated with *The Catholic Standard* in 1853. Henry William Wilberforce (1807-73), a pupil of Newman at Oriel who became a Catholic in 1850, was the owner and editor 1854-63.

[11] other, I may have said in conversation or in private letter, of course I cannot tell; but I have never, I am sure, used the word "*bulwark*" of the Anglican Church deliberately, or speaking of it in its religious aspect, nor, as I think, at all.*[10] What I said in my *Apologia* was this: that that Church was "a serviceable *breakwater* against errors more fundamental than its own."[11] A bulwark is an integral part of the thing it defends; whereas the word[12] "breakwater" implies such a protection of the Catholic truth, as is, in its nature, accidental an *de facto*, - and again, such a protection as does not utterly exclude error, but detracts from its volume and force. "Serviceable,"[13] too, implies a something external to the thing served. Again, in saying that the Anglican Church is a defence against "errors more fundamental than its own" I imply that it has errors, and those fundamental.

2. There is another passage of your book, at p. 337, which it may be right to observe upon. You have made a collection of passages from the Fathers, as witnesses in behalf of your doctrine that the whole Christian faith is contained in Scripture, as if, in your sense of the words, Catholics contradicted you here. And you refer to my Notes on St. Athanasius[14] as contributing passages to your list; but, after all, neither do you, nor do I in my Notes, affirm any doctrine which Rome denies. Those Notes also make frequent

---

* In the former of these volumes, p.1, speaking of 'Institutions' (i.e. 'the Church and Universities of the nation'), I call them 'the only *political* bulwarks' remaining of the 'dogmatic principle'.

---

[10] "...or speaking of it in its religious aspect, nor, as I think at all" is not in the 1st edition.

[11] *Apo* p.298.

[12] 1st ed. inserts "serviceable".

[13] *Apo* p.342. He adds, "How long this will last in the years now before us, it is impossible to say, for the Nation drags down its Church to its own level."

[14] *Select Treatises of St. Athanasius, archbishop of Alexandria in controversy with the Arians, translated with notes and appendices.* Oxford 1842.

reference to a traditional teaching, [15] which (be the faith ever so certainly contained in Scripture), still is necessary as a Regula Fidei,[16] for showing us that it is contained there; vid. pp. 283, 341;† and this tradition, I know, you uphold as fully as I do in the Notes in question. In consequence, you allow that there is a two-fold rule, Scripture and Tradition; and this is all that Catholics say. How, then, do Anglicans differ from Rome here? I believe the difference is merely one of words; and I shall be doing, so far, the work of an Irenicon,[17] if I make clear what this verbal difference is. Catholics and Anglicans (I do not say Protestants), attach different meanings to the word "proof," in the controversy as to whether the whole faith is, or is not, contained in Scripture. We mean that not every article of faith is so contained there, that it may thence be logically proved, *independently* of the teaching and authority of the Tradition; but Anglicans mean that every article of faith is so contained there, that it may thence be proved, *provided* there be added the illustrations and compensations supplied by the Tradition. And it is in this latter sense that the Fathers also speak in the passages which you quote from them. I am sure at least that St. Athanasius frequently adduces passages in proof of points in controversy, which no one would see to be proofs, unless Apostolical Tradition were taken into account, first as suggesting, then as authoritatively ruling their meaning. Thus *you* do not say,[18] that the whole revelation is in Scripture in

[12]

† Oxford Edition.

---

[15] "It has always been taught in the Church, that the tradition of the first centuries was to be kept to, as well for discipline as for doctrine" (Fleury *En* p.238). "Take thou and hold that faith only as a learner and in profession, which is by the Church delivered to thee, and is established from all Scripture." St Cyril of Jerusalem" (*En* p.341).
[16] Rule of faith.
[17] Alternative spelling - one who attempts to harmonize opposing views.
[18] 1st ed. "Thus you do not deny ..."

such sense that pure unaided logic can draw it from the sacred text; nor do *we* say, that it is not in Scripture, in an improper sense,[19] in the sense that the *Tradition* of the Church is able to recognize and determine it there. You do not profess to dispense with Tradition; nor do we forbid the idea of [13] probable, secondary, symbolical, connotative, senses of Scripture, over and above those which properly belong to the wording and context. I hope you will agree with me in this.

3. Nor is it only in isolated passages that you give me a place in your Volume. A considerable portion of it is written with a reference to two publications of mine, one of which you name and defend, the other you implicitly protest against; Tract 90, and the Essay on Doctrinal Development. As to Tract 90, you have from the first, as all the world knows, boldly stood up for it, in spite of the obloquy which it brought upon you, and have done me a great service.[20] You are now republishing it with my cordial concurrence;[21] but I take this opportunity of noticing, lest there should be any mistake on the part of the public, that you do so with a different object from that which I had when I wrote it. Its original purpose was simply that of justifying myself and others in subscribing to the Thirty-nine Articles, while professing many tenets which had popularly been considered distinctive of the Roman faith. I considered that my interpretation of the Articles, as I gave it in that Tract, would stand, provided the parties imposing them allowed it; otherwise, I thought it could not stand; and, when in the event

---

[19] 1st ed. "... This you do not deny, that the whole is not in Scripture in such a sense that pure unaided logic can draw it from the sacred text ..."

[20] See Pusey's *The Articles Treated on in Tract 90 Reconsidered And Their Interpretation Vindicated in a Letter to the Rev. R. W. Jelf* Oxford Parker 1841 "in which he identifies himself unreservedly with Newman and his work". *Liddon* 2 p.213.

[21] *Tract 90. On Certain Passages in the 39 Articles ... with a historical preface by the Rev. E. B. Pusey* Oxford 1865. See Newman's letter to Henry James Coleridge, in which he points to certain changes Pusey made to the original Tract 20 October 1865 *LD* 22 pp.78-9.

the Bishops and public opinion did not allow it, I gave up my Living, as having no right to retain it. My feeling about the interpretation is expressed in a passage in "Loss and Gain," which runs thus:—

"'Is it,' asked Reding, 'a received view?' 'No view is received,' said the other; 'the Articles themselves are received, but there is no authoritative interpretation of them at all.' 'Well,' said Reding, 'is it a tolerated view?' 'It certainly has been strongly opposed,' answered Bateman; 'but it has never been condemned.' 'That is no answer,' said Charles. 'Does any one Bishop hold it? Did any one Bishop ever hold it? Has it ever been formally admitted as tenable by any one Bishop? Is it a view got up to meet existing difficulties, or has it an historical existence?' Bateman could give only one answer to these questions, as they were successively put to him. 'I thought so,' said Charles; 'the view is specious certainly. I don't see why it might not have answered, had it been tolerably sanctioned; but you have no sanction to show me. As it stands, it is a mere theory struck out by individuals. Our Church *might* have adopted this mode of interpreting the Articles; but, from what you tell me, it certainly has not done so.'"—Ch. 15.[22]

[14]

However, the Tract did not carry its object and conditions on its face, and necessarily lay open to interpretations very far from the true one. Dr. Wiseman (as he then was),[23] in particular, with the keen apprehension which was his characteristic, at once saw in it a basis of accommodation between Anglicanism and Rome.[24] He suggested broadly that the decrees of the Council of Trent should be made the rule of interpretation for the Thirty-nine Articles, a proceeding, of

---

[22] *LG* pp.134-5.
[23] Nicholas Wiseman (1802-65), Coadjutor to Bishop Walsh in the Midland District and President of Oscott College.
[24] *Letter on Catholic Unity addressed to the Right Honourable, the Earl of Shrewsbury* 1841 See *LD* 8 pp.282n. See p.[6].

which Sancta Clara,[25] I think, had set the example; and as you have observed, published a letter to Lord Shrewsbury on the subject, of which the following are extracts:—

[15] "We Catholics must necessarily deplore [England's] separation as a deep moral evil,—as a state of schism, of which nothing can justify the continuance. Many members of the Anglican Church view it in the same light as to the first point—its sad evil, though they excuse their individual position in it as an unavoidable misfortune. ... We may depend upon a willing, an able, and most zealous co-operation with any effort which we may take, towards bringing her into her rightful position, into Catholic unity with the Holy See and the Churches of its obedience,—in other words, with the Church Catholic. Is this a visionary idea? Is it merely the expression of a strong desire? I know that many will so judge it; and, perhaps, were I to consult my own quiet, I would not venture to express it. But I will, in simplicity of heart, cling to hopefulness, cheered, as I feel it, by so many promising appearances ...

"A natural question here presents itself;—what facilities appear in the present state of things for bringing about so happy a consummation, as the reunion of England to the Catholic Church, beyond what have before existed, and particularly under Archbishops Laud or Wake.[26] It strikes me, many. First, &c. ... A still more promising circumstance I think your Lordship will with me consider the *plan* which the eventful Tract No. 90 has pursued, and in which Mr. Ward,[27]

---

[25] Franciscus a Sancta Clara (1598-1680), an alias of Christopher Davenport who became a Franciscan theologian and was chaplain to Henrietta Maria. He wrote *Letter on Catholic Unity* to the Earl of Shrewsbury.

[26] William Laud (1573-1645) became Archbishop of Canterbury in 1633. He maintained in his debate in 1622 with 'Fisher the Jesuit' that the Church of England and the Roman Church were part of the same Church Catholic. Wake, see Editor's Introduction, p.xvi.

[27] William George Ward (1812-62) A Fellow of Balliol and Tractarian, author of *The Ideal of a Christian Church* (1844) and deprived of his degrees for heresy in 1845. He became a Roman Catholic the same year.

Mr. Oakeley,[28] and even Dr. Pusey have agreed. I allude to the method of *bringing their doctrines into accordance with ours by explanation*. A foreign priest has pointed out to us a valuable document for our consideration,—'Bossuet's[29] Reply to the Pope,'—when consulted on the best method of reconciling the followers of the Augsburg Confession with the Holy See. The learned Bishop observes, that Providence had allowed so much Catholic truth to be preserved in that Confession, that full advantage should be taken of the circumstance; that no retractations should be demanded, but an explanation of the Confession in accordance with Catholic doctrines. Now, for such a method as this, the way is in part prepared by the demonstration that such interpretation may be given of the most difficult Articles, as will strip them of all contradiction to the decrees of the Tridentine Synod. The same method may be pursued on other points; and much pain may thus be spared to individuals, and much difficulty to the Church."—Pp. 11, 35, 38. [16]

This use of my Tract, so different from my own, but sanctioned by the great name of our Cardinal, you are now reviving; and I gather from your doing so, that your Bishops and the opinion of the public are likely now, or in prospect, to admit what twenty-five years ago they refused. On this point, much as it rejoices me to know your anticipation, of course I cannot have an opinion.

4. So much for Tract 90. On the other hand, as to my hypothesis of Doctrinal Development, I am sorry to find you do not look upon it with friendly eyes; though how, without its aid, you can maintain the doctrines of the Holy Trinity and

---

[28] Frederick Oakeley (1802-80), Rector of Margaret Chapel 1839-45 when he was received into the Roman Catholic Church. He became a Canon of Westminster diocese.

[29] Jacques Bénigne Bossuet (1627-1704), Bishop of Meaux (1681), declared that the Church of Rome was ready to make concessions on matters of discipline but not on Articles of Faith relating to the unity of the Catholic Church in communion with the Roman Pontiff as defined by Trent. He corresponded with Leibnitz (1683-1700) on the best means of achieving Christian reunion.

Incarnation, and others which you hold, I cannot understand. You consider my principle may be the means, in time to come, of introducing into our Creed, as portions of the necessary Catholic faith, the Infallibility of the Pope, and various opinions, pious or profane, as it may be, about our [17] Blessed Lady. I hope to remove your anxiety as to the character of these consequences, before I bring my observations to an end;* at present I notice it as my apology for interfering in a controversy which at first sight is no business of mine.

5. I have another reason for writing; and that is, unless it is rude in me to say so, because you seem to think writing does not become me, as being a convert. I do not like silently to acquiesce in such a judgment. You say at p. 98:—

"Nothing can be more unpractical than for an individual to throw himself into the Roman Church, because he could accept the *letter* of the Council of Trent. Those who were born Roman Catholics, have a liberty, which, in the nature of things, a person could not have, who left another system, to embrace that of Rome. I cannot imagine how any faith could stand the shock of leaving one system, criticizing *it*, and cast himself into another system, criticizing *it*. For myself, I have always felt that had (which God of His mercy avert hereafter also) the English Church, by accepting heresy, driven me out of it, I could have gone in no other way than that of closing my eyes, and accepting whatever was put before me. But a liberty which individuals could not use, and explanations, which so long as they remain individual, must be unauthoritative, might be formally made by the Church of Rome to the Church of England as the basis of reunion."

[18]   And again, p. 210:—

---

* Father Ryder of the Oratory removed the necessity of my fulfilling this intention as far as Infallibility is concerned, by his able pamphlets in answer to Mr. Ward.

"It seems to me to be a psychological impossibility for one who has already exchanged one system for another to make those distinctions. One who, by his own act, places himself under authority, cannot make conditions about his submission. But definite explanations of our Articles have, before now, been at least tentatively offered to us on the Roman and Greek side, as sufficient to restore communion; and the Roman explanations too were, in most cases, mere supplements to our Articles, on points upon which our Church had not spoken."

Now passages such as these seem almost a challenge to me to speak; and to keep silence would be to assent to the justice of them. At the cost, then, of speaking about myself, of which I feel there has been too much of late, I observe upon them as follows:—Of course, as you say, a convert comes to learn, and not to pick and choose. He comes in simplicity and confidence, and it does not occur to him to weigh and measure every proceeding, every practice which he meets with among those whom he has joined. He comes to Catholicism as to a living system, with a living teaching, and not to a mere collection of decrees and canons, which by themselves are of course but the framework, not the body and substance of the Church. And this is a truth which concerns, which binds, those also who never knew any other religion, not only the convert. By the Catholic system, I mean that rule of life, and those practices of devotion, for which we shall look in vain in the Creed of Pope Pius.[30] The convert comes, not only to believe the Church, but also to trust and obey her priests, and to conform himself in charity to her people. It would never do for him to resolve that he never would say a Hail Mary, never avail himself of an indulgence,[31] never kiss [19]

---

[30] Creed of Pope Pius. Issued by Pius IV in 1564, summarizing the teaching of the Council of Trent and condemning Protestant errors. *DS* 1862ff.

[31] The remission by the Church of the temporal punishment due to forgiven sins which the individual pledges to undertake by performing certain prayers or actions.

a crucifix, never accept the Lent dispensations,[32] never mention a venial sin[33] in confession. All this would not only be unreal, but would be dangerous, too, as arguing a wrong state of mind, which could not look to receive the divine blessing. Moreover, he comes to the ceremonial, and the moral theology, and the ecclesiastical regulations, which he finds on the spot where his lot is cast. And again, as regards matters of politics, of education, of general expedience, of taste, he does not criticize or controvert. And thus surrendering himself to the influences of his new religion, and not risking the loss of revealed truth altogether by attempting by a private rule to discriminate every moment its substance from its accidents, he is gradually so indoctrinated in Catholicism, as at length to have a right to speak as well as to hear. Also in course of time a new generation rises round him; and there is no reason why he should not know as much, and decide questions with as true an instinct, as those who perhaps number fewer years of life than he numbers Easter communions.[34] He has mastered the fact and the nature of the differences of theologian from theologian, school from school, nation from nation, era from era. He knows that there is much of what may be called fashion in opinions and practices, according to the circumstances of time and place, according to current politics, the character of the Pope of the day, or the chief Prelates of a particular country;—and that fashions change. His experience tells him, that sometimes what is denounced in one place as a great offence, or preached up as a first principle, has in another nation been immemorially regarded in just a contrary sense, or has made no sensation at all, one way or the other, when brought before public opinion; and that loud talkers are apt to carry all before

[20]

---

[32] Regarding days of fasting and abstinence and restrictions on the solemnization of marriage during the Lenten season.

[33] Venial sin does not deprive the sinner of sanctifying grace.

[34] The Fourth Commandment of the Roman Catholic Church is "to receive the Blessed Sacrament at least once a year, and that at Easter or thereabouts."

them in the Church, as elsewhere, while quiet and conscientious persons commonly have to give way. He perceives that, in matters which happen to be in debate, ecclesiastical authority watches the state of opinion and the direction and course of controversy, and decides accordingly; so that in certain cases to keep back his own judgment on a point, is to be disloyal to his superiors.

So far generally; now in particular as to myself. After twenty years of Catholic life, I feel no delicacy in giving my opinion on any point when there is a call for me,—and the only reason why I have not done so sooner or more often than I have, is that there has been no call. I have now reluctantly come to the conclusion that your Volume *is* a call. Certainly, in many instances in which theologian differs from theologian and country from country, I have a definite judgment of my own; I can say so without offence to any one, for the very reason that from the nature of the case it is impossible to agree with all of them. I prefer English habits of belief and devotion to foreign, from the same causes, and by the same right, which justifies foreigners in preferring their own. In following those of my people, I show less singularity, and create less disturbance than if I made a [21] flourish with what is novel and exotic. And in this line of conduct I am but availing myself of the teaching which I fell in with on becoming a Catholic; and it is a pleasure to me to think that what I hold now, and would transmit after me if I could, is only what I received then. The utmost delicacy was observed on all hands in giving me advice: only one warning remains on my mind, and it came from Dr. Griffiths,[35] the late Vicar-Apostolic of the London district. He warned me against books of devotion of the Italian school, which were just at that time coming into England; and when I asked him

---

[35] Dr. Thomas Griffiths (1791-1847) was President of St Edmund's College 1818-33 and then became co-adjutor to Bishop Bramston, Vicar-Apostolic of the London District, whom he succeeded in 1840.

what books he recommended as safe guides, he bade me get the works of Bishop Hay.[36] By this I did not understand that he was jealous of all Italian books, or made himself responsible for all that Dr. Hay happens to have said; but I took him to caution me against a character and tone of religion, excellent in its place, not suited for England.

When I went to Rome, though it may seem strange to you to say it, even there I learned nothing inconsistent with this judgment. Local influences do not form the atmosphere of its institutions and colleges, which are Catholic in teaching as well as in name. I recollect one saying among others of my Confessor, a Jesuit Father, one of the holiest, most prudent men I ever knew. He said that we could not love the Blessed Virgin too much, if we loved our Lord a great deal more. When I returned to England, the first expression of theological opinion which came in my way, was *apropos* of the series of translated Saints' Lives which the late Dr. Faber originated.[37] That expression proceeded from a wise prelate, who was properly anxious as to the line which might be taken by the Oxford converts,[38] then for the first time coming into work. According as I recollect his opinion, he was apprehensive of the effect of Italian compositions, as unsuited to this country, and suggested that the Lives should be original works, drawn up by ourselves and our friends from Italian sources. If at that time I was betrayed into any acts which were of a more extreme character than I should approve now, the responsibility of course is my own; but the impulse came, not from old Catholics or superiors, but from

[22]

---

[36] George Hay (1729-1811), Vicar Apostolic of the Lowland District in 1778. He was the author of T*he Scripture Doctrine of Miracles Displayed* (1775) and *The Sincere Christian instructed in the Law of Christ* (1783). An edition of his works in five volumes was published in 1871.

[37] The series of *Lives of the Saints* which began in 1844 was at first edited by Newman but was discontinued by him after two numbers (*Apo* pp.211-13.). Fr. Frederick William Faber (1814-63) became the Provost of the London Oratory in 1848.

[38] See reference to Dr. Griffiths supra.

men whom I loved and trusted, who were younger than myself. But to whatever extent I might be carried away, and I cannot recollect any tangible instances, my mind in no long time fell back to what seems to me a safer and more practical course.

Though I am a convert, then, I think I have a right to speak out; and that the more because other converts have spoken for a long time, while I have not spoken; and with still more reason may I speak without offence in the case of your present criticisms of us, considering that, in the charges you bring, the only two English writers you quote in evidence, are both of them converts, younger in age than myself. I put aside the Archbishop of course, because of his office. These two authors are worthy of all consideration, at once from their character and from their ability. In their respective lines they are perhaps without equals at this particular time; and they deserve the influence they possess. One is still in the vigour of his powers; the other has departed amid the tears of hundreds.[39] It is pleasant to praise them for their real excellences; but why do you rest on them as authorities? You say of the one that he was "a popular writer;" but is there not sufficient reason for this in the fact of his remarkable gifts, of his poetical fancy, his engaging frankness, his playful wit, his affectionateness, his sensitive piety, without supposing that the wide diffusion of his works is caused by a general sympathy with his particular sentiments about the Blessed Virgin? And as to our other friend, do not his energy, acuteness, and theological reading, displayed on the vantage ground of the historic "Dublin Review,"[40] fully account for the sensation he has produced, without supposing that any great number of our body go his lengths in their view of the Pope's infallibility? Our silence as regards their writings is

[23]

---

[39] Fr. Faber had died in 1863.
[40] The *Dublin Review* first appeared in 1836. W.*G.* Ward (qv supra) was the editor 1863-78.

very intelligible: it is not agreeable to protest, in the sight of the world, against the writings of men in our own Communion whom we love and respect. But the plain fact is this,—they came to the Church, and have thereby saved their souls; but they are in no sense spokesmen for English Catholics, and they must not stand in the place of those who have a real title to such an office. The chief authors of the passing generation, some of them still alive, others gone to their reward, are Cardinal Wiseman,[41] Dr. Ullathorne,[42] Dr. Lingard,[43] Mr. Tierney,[44] Dr. Oliver,[45] Dr. Rock,[46] Dr. Waterworth,[47] Dr. Husenbeth,[48] and Mr. Flanagan;[49] which of these ecclesiastics has said anything extreme about the prerogatives of the Blessed Virgin or the infallibility of the Pope?

[24] I cannot, then, without remonstrance, allow you to identify the doctrine of our Oxford friends in question, on the two subjects I have mentioned, with the present spirit or the prospective creed of Catholics; or to assume, as you do, that, because they are thorough-going and relentless in their statements, therefore they are the harbingers of a new age, when to show a deference to Antiquity will be thought little

---

[41] Nicholas Wiseman (1802-65). See supra.

[42] William Bernard Ullathorne (1806-89), a descendant of Thomas More, became a monk of Downside in 1824 and Bishop of Birmingham in 1850.

[43] John Lingard (1771-1851), priest and historian, published his *History of England* in 8 volumes (1830).

[44] Mark Aloysius Tierney (1795-1862), Canon Penitentiary of Southwark diocese in 1852; historian and antiquarian who crossed swords with Wiseman and Lingard.

[45] George Oliver (1781-1861), Provost of the Plymouth chapter and ecclesiastical historian.

[46] Daniel Rock (1799-1871), medieval historian who had been chaplain at Alton Towers before moving to Buckland.

[47] William Waterworth (1811-82), Jesuit priest in charge of the Church in Worcester from 1854.

[48] Frederick Charles Husenbeth (1796-1872), antiquary who was chaplain to Lord Stafford at Cossey and a Catholic controversialist.

[49] John Stanislas Flanagan (1821-1905) joined the Oratory in 1848 but returned to Ireland and became parish priest of Adare. Newman corresponded with him on theological matters.

else than a mistake. For myself, hopeless as you consider it, I am not ashamed still to take my stand upon the Fathers, and do not mean to budge. The history of their times is not yet an old almanac to me. Of course I maintain the value and authority of the "Schola,"[50] as one of the *loci theologici*;[51] nevertheless[52] I sympathize with Petavius[53] in preferring to the "contentious and subtle theology" of the middle age, that "more elegant and fruitful teaching which is moulded after the image of erudite Antiquity." The Fathers made me a Catholic, and I am not going to kick down the ladder by which I ascended into the Church. It is a ladder quite as serviceable for that purpose now, as it was twenty years ago. Though I hold, as you know, a process of development in Apostolic truth as time goes on, such development does not supersede the Fathers, but explains and completes them. And, in particular, as regards our teaching concerning the Blessed Virgin, with the Fathers I am content;—and to the subject of that teaching I mean to address myself at once. I do so, because you say, as I myself have said in former years, that "That vast system as to the Blessed Virgin ... to all of us has been the special *crux* of the Roman system."—P. 101. Here, let me say, as on other points, the Fathers are enough for me. [25] I do not wish to say more than they suggest to me, and will not say less. You, I know, will profess the same; and thus we can join issue on a clear and broad principle, and may hope to come to some intelligible result. We are to have a Treatise on the subject of our Lady soon from the pen of the Most Reverend Prelate;[54] but that cannot interfere with such a mere

---

[50] The decisions of theologians throughout the world. See letter to James Fitzjames Stephen 7 September 1866 *LD* 22 p.284.

[51] The sources of theological knowledge: Magisterium, Scripture, Tradition, the Fathers of the Church, the theologians and the liturgy.

[52] 1st ed. has "Still I sympathize with …"

[53] Dionysius Petavius/Denis Pétau (1583-1652), Jesuit Professor of Dogmatic Theology in Paris (1621), who accepted the idea of doctrinal development.

[54] *The Anglican Theory of Union, as maintained in the 'Appeal to Rome' and Dr Pusey's 'Eirenicon'. A second letter to the clergy of Birmingham* 1865.

argument from the Fathers as that to which I shall confine myself here. Nor indeed, as regards that argument itself, do I profess to be offering you any new matter, any facts which have not been used by others,—by great divines, as Petavius,—by living writers, nay, by myself on other occasions.[55] I write afresh nevertheless, and that for three reasons; first, because I wish to contribute to the accurate statement and the full exposition of the argument in question; next, because I may gain a more patient hearing than has sometimes been granted to better men than myself; lastly, because there just now seems a call on me, under my circumstances, to avow plainly what I do and what I do not hold about the Blessed Virgin, that others may know, did they come to stand where I stand, what they would, and what they would not, be bound to hold concerning her.

---

[55] See *PPS* 2. 12; *Sermon* 291 *S3* pp.116-21; *US* pp. 312-13; *Ath* 2 pp.210-15; *Dev* pp.143-4; *SD* pp. 32-7; *CS* pp.92-104; *VV* pp.279-86; *MD* pp.10-129. "Our whole line … has been a sort of domestic one - easy, familiar and not rigid – with a special devotion to St Mary." Letter to J. D. Dalgairns 31 December 1846 *LD* 11 pp.304-5. John Dobrée Dalgairns (1818-76) was received into the Church by Fr Dominic Barberi in 1845 and joined Newman in Rome in 1847. He succeeded Faber as Provost of the London Oratory.

§ 3.—*The Belief of Catholics concerning the Blessed Virgin, as distinct from their Devotion to her.*[1]

I begin by making a distinction which will go far to remove good part of the difficulty of my undertaking, as it presents itself to ordinary inquirers,—the distinction between faith and devotion. I fully grant that *devotion* towards the blessed Virgin has increased among Catholics with the progress of centuries; I do not allow that the *doctrine* concerning her has undergone a growth, for I believe that it has been in substance one and the same from the beginning.

By "faith" I mean the Creed and assent to the Creed; by "devotion" I mean such religious honours as belong to the objects of our faith, and the payment of those honours. Faith and devotion are as distinct in fact, as they are in idea. We cannot, indeed, be devout without faith, but we may believe without feeling devotion. Of this phenomenon every one has experience both in himself and in others; and we bear witness to it as often as we speak of realizing a truth or not realizing it. It may be illustrated, with more or less exactness, by matters which come before us in the world. For instance, a great author, or public man, may be acknowledged as such for a course of years; yet there may be an increase, an ebb and flow, and a fashion, in his popularity. And if he takes a [27] lasting place in the minds of his countrymen, he may gradually grow into it, or suddenly be raised to it. The idea of Shakespeare as a great poet, has existed from a very early date in public opinion; and there were at least individuals then who understood him as well, and honoured him as much,

---

[1] 1st ed. has heading "The Blessed Virgin the Second Eve."

as the English people can honour him now; yet, I think, there is a national devotion to him in this day such as never has been before. This has happened, because, as education spreads in the country, there are more men able to enter into his poetical genius, and, among these, more capacity again for deeply and critically understanding him; and yet, from the first, he has exerted a great insensible influence over the nation, as is seen in the circumstance that his phrases and sentences, more than can be numbered, have become almost proverbs among us. And so again in philosophy, and in the arts and sciences, great truths and principles have sometimes been known and acknowledged for a course of years; but, whether from feebleness of intellectual power in the recipients, or external circumstances of an accidental kind, they have not been turned to account. Thus the Chinese are said to have known of the properties of the magnet from time immemorial, and to have used it for land expeditions, yet not on the sea. Again, the ancients knew of the principle that water finds its own level, but seem to have made little application of their knowledge. And Aristotle was familiar with the principle of induction; yet it was left for Bacon[2] to develope[3] it into an experimental philosophy. Illustrations such as these, though not altogether apposite, serve to convey that distinction between faith and devotion on which I am

[28] insisting. It is like the distinction between objective and subjective truth. The sun in the spring-time will have to shine many days before he is able to melt the frost, open the soil, and bring out the leaves; yet he shines out from the first notwithstanding, though he makes his power felt but gradually. It is one and the same sun, though his influence day by day becomes greater; and so in the Catholic Church it is the one Virgin Mother, one and the same from first to last,

---

[2] Francis Bacon (1561-1626), was made Lord Chancellor in 1618 and is the author of *Novum Organum* (1620) where he provides a list of instances which point toward the theory.

[3] *develope*: alternative spelling

and Catholics may have ever acknowledged her; and yet, in spite of that acknowledgment, their devotion to her may be scanty in one time and place, and overflowing in another.

This distinction is forcibly brought home to a convert, as a peculiarity of the Catholic religion, on his first introduction to its worship. The faith is everywhere one and the same, but a large liberty is accorded to private judgment and inclination as regards matters of devotion. Any large church, with its collections and groups of people, will illustrate this. The fabric itself is dedicated to Almighty God, and that, under the invocation of the Blessed Virgin, or some particular Saint; or again, of some mystery belonging to the Divine Name or the Incarnation, or of some mystery associated with the Blessed Virgin. Perhaps there are seven altars or more in it, and these again have their several Saints. Then there is the Feast proper to this or that day; and during the celebration of Mass, of all the worshippers who crowd around the Priest, each has his own particular devotions, with which he follows the rite.[4] No one interferes with his neighbour; agreeing, as it were, to differ, they pursue independently a common end, and by paths, distinct but converging, present themselves before God. Then there are confraternities attached to the church,— of the Sacred Heart, or of the Precious Blood; associations of prayer for a good death,[5] or for the repose of departed souls, or for the conversion of the heathen; devotions connected with the brown, blue, or red scapular;[6] not to speak of the great ordinary Ritual observed through the four seasons, or of the constant Presence of the Blessed Sacrament, or of its ever-recurring rite of Benediction, and its extraordinary forty

[29]

---

[4] Newman describes the liturgy before the Vatican II renewal.

[5] The Archconfraternity of the Bona Mors was founded in 1648 to honour the Passion of Jesus Christ and the Sorrows of the Blessed Virgin so as to obtain the grace of a happy death.

[6] The Scapular is a piece of cloth joined across the shoulders, the brown for Our Lady of Mount Carmel, the blue for the Immaculate Conception and the red for the Passion, worn as an act of devotion.

hours' Exposition.[7] Or, again, look through such manuals of prayers as the *Raccolta*,[8] and you at once will see both the number and the variety of devotions, which are open to individual Catholics to choose from, according to their religious taste and prospect of personal edification.

Now these diversified modes of honouring God did not come to us in a day, or only from the Apostles; they are the accumulations of centuries; and, as in the course of years some of them spring up, so others decline and die. Some are local, in memory of some particular Saint, who happens to be the Evangelist, or Patron, or pride of the nation, or who lies[9] entombed in the church or in the city where it is found;[10] and these devotions, necessarily, cannot have an earlier date than the Saint's day of death or interment there. The first of these sacred observances, long before such national memories, were the devotions paid to the Apostles, then those which were paid to the Martyrs; yet there were Saints nearer to our Lord than either Martyrs or Apostles; but, as if these sacred persons were immersed and lost in the effulgence of His glory, and because they did not manifest themselves, when in the body,[11] in external works separate from Him, it happened that for a long while they were less dwelt upon.[12] However, in process of time, the Apostles, and then the Martyrs, exerted less influence than before over the popular mind, and the local Saints, new creations of God's power, took their place, or again, the Saints of some religious order here or

[30]

---

[7] The Forty Hours (Quarant' Ore), exposition of the Blessed Sacrament in honour of the time spent by Our Lord in the tomb, was introduced in the sixteenth century and approved by Pius IV in 1560.

[8] *Raccolta di orazioni e pie opera*. A Collection of Prayers and Good Works. The Manual containing indulgenced prayers and devotions issued periodically by the Sacred Apostolic Penitentiary of the Vatican was translated into English by Fr. Ambrose St. John.in 1857.

[9] 1st ed has "is entombed ..."

[10] 1st ed has "where it stands ..."

[11] 1st ed. ed omits "when in the body"

[12] 1st ed. has "... less dwelt upon"

there established. Then, as comparatively quiet times succeeded, the religious meditations of holy men and their secret intercourse with heaven gradually exerted an influence out of doors, and permeated the Christian populace, by the instrumentality of preaching and by the ceremonial of the Church. Hence at length those luminous stars rose in the ecclesiastical heavens, which were of more august dignity than any which had preceded them, and were late in rising, for the very reason that they were so specially glorious. Those names, I say, which at first sight might have been expected to enter soon into the devotions of the faithful, with better reason might have been looked for at a later date, and actually were late in their coming. St. Joseph furnishes the most striking instance of this remark; here is the clearest of instances of the distinction between doctrine and devotion. Who, from his prerogatives and the testimony on which they come to us, had a greater claim to receive an early recognition among the faithful than he? A Saint of Scripture, the foster-father of our Lord, he was an object of the universal and absolute faith of the Christian world from the first, yet the devotion to him is comparatively of late date.[13] When once it began, men seemed surprised that it had not been thought of before; and now, they hold him next to the Blessed Virgin in their religious affection and veneration. [31]

As regards the Blessed Virgin then, I shall postpone the question of devotion for a while, and inquire first into the doctrine of the undivided Church[14] (to use your controversial phrase), on the subject of her prerogatives.

---

[13] The cult began in the East with the account of his happy death in the *History of Joseph the Carpenter* (5th-6th century). His feast was celebrated in Winchester and Ely before 1100 but more widely spread by St Teresa of Avila and St. Ignatius in the sixteenth century. In 1870 Pius IX declared him a Patron of the Universal Church.

[14] "Unknown in face, in place separate, different in language, opposed alas! In some things to one another, still before the throne of God they are One Holy Catholic Apostolic Church." *En* p.57.

1.[15]

What is the great rudimental teaching of Antiquity from
its earliest date concerning her? By "rudimental teaching," I
mean the *primâ facie* view of her person and office, the broad
outline laid down of her, the aspect under which she comes
to us, in the writings of the Fathers. She is the Second Eve.[*16]
Now let us consider what this implies. Eve had a definite,
essential position in the First Covenant. The fate of the
human race lay with Adam; he it was who represented us. It
was in Adam that we fell; though Eve had fallen, still, if
Adam had stood, we should not have lost those supernatural
privileges which were bestowed upon him as our first father.
Yet though Eve was not the head of the race, still, even as
regards the race, she had a place of her own; for Adam, to
whom was divinely committed the naming of all things,
named her "the Mother of all the living,"[17] a name surely
expressive, not of a fact only, but of a dignity; but further, as
she thus had her own general relation to the human race, so
[32] again had she her own special place, as regards its trial and
its fall in Adam. In those primeval events, Eve had an integral
share. "The woman, being seduced, was in the
transgression."[18] She listened to the Evil Angel; she offered
the fruit to her husband, and he ate of it. She co-operated, not
as an irresponsible instrument, but intimately and personally
in the sin: she brought it about. As the history stands, she was

[*] Vide Essay on Development of Doctrine, 1845, p.384, &c.

[15] Not in 1st ed.

[16] "Our received doctrine is, after St. Justin and St. Irenaeus, as we interpret them,
that as Eve had a secondary part in the fall so had blessed Mary in the redemption."
To Keble 8 October 1865 *LD* 22 p.68.

[17] Gen 3:20. Newman further explains, "The comparison between Eve and Mary is
in all the Fathers 'mystical throughout', not literal. Our Lord is Adam – and Mary
is Eve. Unless there is a likeness, there would be no mystical relation." To R. C.
Jenkins, 26 February 1866 *LD* 22 p.164.

[18] 1 Tim 2:14.

34

a *sine-qua-non*,[19] a positive, active, cause of it. And she had her share in its punishment; in the sentence pronounced on her, she was recognized as a real agent in the temptation and its issue, and she suffered accordingly. In that awful transaction there were three parties concerned,—the serpent, the woman, and the man; and at the time of their sentence, an event was announced for a distant future, in which the three same parties were to meet again, the serpent, the woman, and the man; but it was to be a second Adam and a second Eve, and the new Eve was to be the mother of the new Adam. "I will put enmity between thee and the woman, and between thy seed and her seed."[20] The Seed of the woman is the Word Incarnate, and the Woman, whose seed or son He is, is His mother Mary. This interpretation, and the parallelism it involves, seem to me undeniable; but at all events (and this is my point) the parallelism is the doctrine of the Fathers, from the earliest times; and, this being established, we are able, by the position and office of Eve in our fall, to determine the position and office of Mary in our restoration.

I shall adduce passages from their writings,[21] noting their respective countries and dates; and the dates shall extend from their births or conversions to their deaths, since what [33] they propound is at once the doctrine which they had received from the generation before them, and the doctrine which was accepted and recognized as true by the generation to whom they transmitted it.

---

[19] an indispensable part.
[20] Gen. 3:15.
[21] Newman admitted he quoted extensively from *Dev* pp.143-8 in his letter to Archbishop Manning 9 February 1866 *LD* 22 p.149.

First, then, St. Justin Martyr[22] (A.D. 120-165), St. Irenæus[23] (120-200), and Tertullian[24] (160-240). Of these Tertullian represents Africa and Rome; St. Justin represents Palestine; and St. Irenæus Asia Minor and Gaul;—or rather he represents St. John the Evangelist, for he had been taught by the Martyr St. Polycarp,[25] who was the intimate associate of St. John, as also of other Apostles.

    1.   St. Justin:*—

"We know that He, before all creatures, proceeded from the Father by His power and will, ... and by means of the Virgin became man, that by what way the disobedience arising from the serpent had its beginning, by that way also it might have an undoing. For Eve, being a Virgin and undefiled, conceiving the word that was from the serpent, brought forth disobedience and death; but the Virgin Mary, taking faith and joy, when the Angel told her the good tidings, that the Spirit of the Lord should come upon her and the power of the Highest overshadow her, and therefore the Holy One that was born of her was Son of God, answered, 'Be it to me according to thy word.'"—*Tryph.*[26] 100.

[34]   2. Tertullian:—

"God recovered His image and likeness, which the devil had seized, by a rival operation. For into Eve, as yet a virgin, had crept the word which was the framer of death. Equally into a virgin was to be introduced the Word of God which

---

*I have attempted to translate literally without caring to write English. The original passages are in Note I. infra.

---

[22] St. Justin became a Christian in 130 and opened a school in Rome. He was an apologist for the faith and was beheaded in 165. See 'Note I' p.119.

[23] St. Irenaeus was a native of Smyrna where he knew Polycarp, but after studying in Rome he became bishop of Lyons in 178. He was an opponent of Gnosticism and author of *Adversus Hæreses - Against all the Heresies.*

[24] Quintus Septimus Florens Tertullian was brought up in Carthage and became a Christian c.193 but left the Church in 203 to join the Montanists.

[25] St. Polycarp (c.69-c.155), Bishop of Smyrna and disciple of John the Apostle.

[26] *Dialogue with Trypho the Jew* (c.150) 12, 17. *ML* 2, 827-8.

was the builder-up of life; that, what by that sex had gone into perdition by the same sex might be brought back to salvation. Eve had believed the serpent; Mary believed Gabriel; the fault which the one committed by believing, the other by believing has blotted out."—*De Carn. Christ.* 17.[27]

3. St. Irenæus:—

"With a fitness, Mary the Virgin is found obedient, saying, 'Behold Thy handmaid, O Lord; be it to me according to Thy word.' But Eve was disobedient; for she obeyed not, while she was yet a virgin. As she, having indeed Adam for a husband, but as yet being a virgin ... becoming disobedient, became the cause of death both to herself and to the whole human race, so also Mary, having the predestined man, and being yet a Virgin, being obedient, became both to herself and to the whole human race the cause of salvation ... And on account of this the Lord said, that the first should be last and the last first. And the Prophet signifies the same, saying, 'Instead of fathers you have children.' For, whereas the Lord, when born, was the first-begotten of the dead, and received into His bosom the primitive fathers, He regenerated them into the life of God, He Himself becoming the beginning of the living, since Adam became the beginning of the dying. Therefore also Luke, commencing the line of generations from the Lord, referred it back to Adam, signifying that He [35] regenerated the old fathers, not they Him, into the Gospel of life. And so the knot of Eve's disobedience received its unloosing through the obedience of Mary; for what Eve, a virgin, bound by incredulity, that Mary, a virgin, unloosed by faith."—*Adv. Hær.* iii. 22, 34.[28]

And again,—

"As Eve by the speech of an Angel was seduced, so as to flee God, transgressing His word, so also Mary received the good tidings by means of the Angel's speech, so as to bear

---

[27] *Treatise on the Flesh of Christ* (c. 208-12) *ML* 2, 782.
[28] *Adversus Haereses* (c.180/199) *PG* 7, 959-60.

God within her, being obedient to His word. And, though the one had disobeyed God, yet the other was drawn to obey God; that of the virgin Eve the Virgin Mary might become the advocate. And, as by a virgin the human race had been bound to death, by a virgin it is saved,* the balance being preserved, a virgin's disobedience by a Virgin's obedience."—*Ibid.* v. 19.[29]

Now, what is especially noticeable in these three writers, is, that they do not speak of the Blessed Virgin merely as the physical instrument of our Lord's taking flesh, but as an intelligent, responsible cause of it; her faith and obedience being accessories to the Incarnation, and gaining it as her reward. As Eve failed in these virtues, and thereby brought on the fall of the race in Adam, so Mary by means of the same [36] had a part in its restoration. You surely imply, pp. 151-156,[30] that the Blessed Virgin was only a physical instrument of our redemption; "what has been said of her by the Fathers as the chosen *vessel* of the Incarnation, was applied *personally* to her," (that is, by Catholics,) p. 151, and again "the Fathers speak of the Blessed Virgin as the *instrument* of our salvation, *in that* she gave birth to the Redeemer," pp. 155, 156; whereas St. Augustine, in well-known passages, speaks of her as more exalted by her sanctity than by her relationship to our Lord.† However, not to go beyond the doctrine of the Three Fathers, they unanimously declare that she was *not* a mere instrument in the Incarnation, such as David, or Judah,

---

* Salvatur; some MSS. read Solvatur, "[that] it might be loosed;" and so Augustine contr. Jul. i. n. 5. This variety of reading does not affect the general sense of the passage. Moreover, the word "salvation" occurs in the former of these two passages.[31]

† Opp. t. 3, p. 2. col. 369, t. 6, col. 342.[32]

---

[29] *PG* 7. 1175.
[30] 1st ed: erroneously "pp. 255-6."
[31] This did not appear in the first edition.
[32] *Sermo* 318.1 *ML* 38. 1440.

may be considered; they declare she co-operated in our salvation not merely by the descent of the Holy Ghost upon her body, but by specific holy acts, the effect of the Holy Ghost within her soul; that, as Eve forfeited privileges by sin, so Mary earned privileges by the fruits of grace; that, as Eve was disobedient and unbelieving, so Mary was obedient and believing;[33] that, as Eve was a cause of ruin to all, Mary was a cause of salvation to all;[34] that as Eve made room for Adam's fall, so Mary made room for our Lord's reparation of it; and thus, whereas the free gift was not as the offence, but much greater, it follows that, as Eve co-operated in effecting a great evil, Mary co-operated in effecting a much greater good.[35]

And, besides the run of the argument, which reminds the reader of St. Paul's antithetical sentences in tracing the analogy between Adam's work and our Lord's work,[36] it is well to observe the particular words under which the Blessed Virgin's office is described. Tertullian says that Mary "blotted out" Eve's fault, and "brought back the female sex," or "the human race, to salvation;"[37] and St. Irenæus says that "by obedience she was the cause or occasion" (whatever was the original Greek word) "of salvation to herself and the whole human race;"[38] that by her the human race is saved; that by her Eve's complication is disentangled; and that she is Eve's Advocate, or friend in need. It is supposed by critics, Protestant as well as Catholic, that the Greek word for

[37]

---

[33] Justin says, "The Virgin Mary conceived with faith and joy" *Dialogue with Trypho* 100. *PG* 6 710.

[34] Compare Newman's words in his 'Memorandum on the Immaculate Conception', "Mary *undoes* what Eve has done; mankind is *saved through* a virgin." *MD* p.122.

[35] Newman would add, "As regards the Blessed Virgin, it was God's will that she should undertake willingly and with full understanding to be the Mother of our Lord, and not to be a mere passive instrument whose maternity would have no merit and no reward" *MD* p.37.

[36] "As in Adam all die, so also in Christ shall all be made alive." 1 Cor. 15:22.

[37] *De carne Christi* 17.4 *ML* 2. 809.

[38] *Adversus Hæreses* 5, 19. *PG* 7, 960.

Advocate in the original was Paraclete;[39] it should be borne in mind, then, when we are accused of giving our Lady the titles and offices of her Son, that St. Irenæus bestows on her the special Name and Office proper to the Holy Ghost.

So much as to the nature of this triple testimony; now as to the worth of it. For a moment put aside St. Irenæus, and put together St. Justin in the East with Tertullian in the West. I think I may assume that the doctrine of these two Fathers about the Blessed Virgin, was the received doctrine of their own respective times and places; for writers after all are but witnesses of facts and beliefs, and as such they are treated by all parties in controversial discussion. Moreover, the coincidence of doctrine which they exhibit, and again, the antithetical completeness of it, show that they themselves did not originate it. The next question is, Who did? for from one definite organ or source, place or person, it must have come. Then we must inquire, what length of time would it take for [38] such a doctrine to have extended, and to be received, in the second century over so wide an area; that is, to be received before the year 200 in Palestine, Africa, and Rome. Can we refer the common source of these local traditions to a date much later than that of the Apostles, since St. John died within twenty years of St. Justin's conversion and sixty of Tertullian's birth?[40] Make what allowance you will for whatever possible exceptions can be taken to this representation; and then, after doing so, add to the concordant testimony of these two Fathers the evidence of St. Irenæus, which is so close upon that of the School of St. John himself in Asia Minor. "A three-fold cord," as the wise man says, "is not quickly broken."[41] Only suppose there were so early and

---

[39] *Ibid* 5.19 *PG* 7. 1175. Newman pointed out that this meant "Intercessor, Helper, Advocate or Paraclete" in a letter to Keble 8 October 1865 *LD* 22 p.68. Newman says Mary "is nothing more than an advocate, and not a source of mercy." p.101.

[40] 1st ed. "...St John dying within thirty or forty years of St. Justin's conversion and Tertullian's birth."

[41] Eccl 4:12.

so broad a testimony, to the effect that our Lord was a mere man, the son of Joseph; should we be able to insist upon the faith of the Holy Trinity as necessary to salvation? Or supposing three such witnesses could be brought to the fact that a consistory of elders governed the local churches, or that each local congregation was an independent Church, or that the Christian community was without priests, could Anglicans maintain their doctrine that the rule of Episcopal succession is necessary to constitute a Church? And then recollect that the Anglican Church especially appeals to the ante-Nicene centuries, and taunts us with having superseded their testimony.

Having then adduced these Three Fathers of the second century, I have at least got so far as this: viz., that no one, who acknowledges the force of early testimony in determining Christian truth, can wonder, no one can [39] complain, can object, that we Catholics should hold a very high doctrine concerning the Blessed Virgin, unless indeed stronger statements can be brought for a contrary conception of her, either of as early, or at least of a later date. But, as far as I know, no statements can be brought from the ante-Nicene literature, to invalidate the testimony of the Three Fathers concerning her; and little can be brought against it from the fourth century, while in that fourth century the current of testimony in her behalf is as strong as in the second; and, as to the fifth, it is far stronger than in any former time, both in its fulness and its authority. That such is the concordant verdict of "the undivided Church"[42] will to some extent be seen as I proceed.

4. St. Cyril of Jerusalem (315-386)[43] speaks for Palestine:—

---

[42] "That such is the concordant verdict of 'the undivided Church'" does not appear in the 1st ed.

[43] St. Cyril (c.315-86) became Bishop of Jerusalem c.349. He delivered his 24 *Catecheses* c.350.

"Since through Eve, a Virgin, came death, it behoved, that through a Virgin, or rather from a Virgin, should life appear; that, as the Serpent had deceived the one, so to the other Gabriel might bring good things."—*Cat*. xii. 15.[44]

5. St. Ephrem Syrus[45] (he died 378) is a witness for the Syrians proper and the neighbouring Orientals, in contrast to the Græco-Syrians. A native of Nisibis on the farther side of the Euphrates, he knew no language but Syriac

"Through Eve, the beautiful and desirable glory of men was extinguished; but it has revived through Mary."—*Opp. Syr*. ii. p. 318.[46]

Again:—

[40] "In the beginning, by the sin of our first parents, death passed upon all men; today, through Mary we are translated from death unto life. In the beginning, the serpent filled the ears of Eve, and the poison spread thence over the whole body; today, Mary from her ears received the champion of eternal happiness: what, therefore, was an instrument of death, was an instrument of life also."—iii. p. 607.[47]

I have already referred to St. Paul's contrast between Adam and our Lord in his Epistle to the Romans, as also in his first Epistle to the Corinthians.[48] Some writers venture to say that there is no doctrinal truth, but a mere rhetorical display, in those passages. It is quite as easy to say so, as to attempt so to dispose of this received comparison, in the writings of the Fathers, between Eve and Mary.

---

[44] *Catechetical Lecture* 12 *PG* 33.741.

[45] St. Ephrem Syrus (c.306-73). Ordained deacon, he lived in Edessa (now Urfa in Southern Turkey) where he wrote exegetical and dogmatic works mostly in verse and was renowned for his great devotion to the Mother of God.

[46] *Opera omnia in sex tomos distributa ad MSS, Codices Vaticanos aliosque castigata, etc: nunc primum sub auspicies S.P. Clementis Pontificis Max e Bibl. Vaticana proderint* ed. J. S. Assemani (Romae 1732-43.) Completed by Overbeck (Oxford 1865). vol. 2 p.318. Cf. "You have conquered the death of Eve in the daughter of Eve" *Hymns on Virginity* 34, 2.

[47] Ibid vol 3 p.607.

[48] Rom 5:14; 1 Cor 15:45.

6. St. Epiphanius (320-400)[49] speaks for Egypt, Palestine, and Cyprus:—

"She it is, who is signified by Eve, enigmatically receiving the appellation of the Mother of the living ... It was a wonder, that after the transgression she had this great epithet. And, according to what is material, from that Eve all the race of men on earth is generated. But thus in truth from Mary the Life itself was born in the world, that Mary might bear living things, and become the Mother of living things. Therefore, enigmatically, Mary is called the Mother of living things ... Also, there is another thing to consider as to these women, and wonderful,—as to Eve and Mary. Eve became a cause of death to man ... and Mary a cause of life; ... that life might be instead of death, life excluding death which came from the woman, viz., He who through the woman has become our life."—*Hær*. 78. 18.[50]   [41]

7. By the time of St. Jerome[51] (331-420), the contrast between Eve and Mary had almost passed into a proverb. He says (*Ep.* xxii. 21, *ad Eustoch.*),[52] "Death by Eve, life by Mary." Nor let it be supposed that he, any more than the preceding Fathers, considered the Blessed Virgin a mere physical instrument of giving birth to our Lord, who is the Life. So far from it, in the Epistle from which I have quoted, he is only adding another virtue to that crown which gained for Mary her divine Maternity. They have spoken of faith, joy, and obedience; St. Jerome adds, what they had only suggested, virginity. After the manner of the Fathers in his own day, he is setting forth the Blessed Mary to the high-born Roman Lady, whom he is addressing, as the model of the

---

[49] St. Epiphanius, (c.315-403). Born in Palestine, he was elected Bishop of Salamis and Metropolitan of Cyprus in 367. His *Panarion* is also known as *Refutation of all Heresies.*

[50] *Panarion* 78.18 *PG* 42. 728-30. Newman quotes this in *Dev* p.146.

[51] St. Jerome. Eusebius Hieronymus (c.342-420) was ordained by Paulinus in Antioch and after many journeys settled in Bethlehem in 386 where he translated the Bible into Latin (The Vulgate).

[52] *Ep. ad Eustochium* (c.383-4). 22, 21. *ML* 22, 407-8.

virginal life; and his argument in its behalf is, that it is higher than the marriage-state, not in itself, viewed in any mere natural respect, but as being the free act of self-consecration to God, and from the personal religious purpose which it involves.

"Higher wage," he says, "is due to that which is not a compulsion, but an offering; for, were virginity commanded, marriage would seem to be put out of the question; and it would be most cruel to force men against nature, and to extort from them an angel's life."—20.

I do not know whose testimony is more important than St. Jerome's, the friend of Pope Damasus[53] at Rome, the pupil of St. Gregory Nazianzen at Constantinople,[54] and of Didymus in Alexandria,[55] a native of Dalmatia, yet an inhabitant, at different times of his life, of Gaul, Syria, and Palestine.

[42]

8. St. Jerome speaks for the whole world, except Africa; and for Africa in the fourth century, if we must limit so world-wide an authority to place, witnesses St. Augustine (354-430). He repeats the words as if a proverb, "By a woman death, by a woman life" (*Opp. t.* v. *Serm.* 232),[56] elsewhere he enlarges on the idea conveyed in it. In one place he quotes St. Irenæus's words, as cited above (*adv. Julian* i. n. 5.).[57] In another he speaks as follows:—

"It is a great sacrament that, whereas through woman death became our portion, so life was born to us by woman; that, in the case of both sexes, male and female, the baffled devil should be tormented, when on the overthrow of both sexes he was rejoicing; whose punishment had been small, if

---

[53] St. Damasus, Spanish Pope (366-84) who succeeded Liberius. Jerome was his secretary.

[54] St Gregory Nazianzen (329-89) studied in Athens and eventually became Bishop of Constantinople in 381 but resigned the see that year. *Ep 101 MG* 37. 177-80.

[55] Didymus the Blind (c.318-98) headed the catechetical school in Alexandria and taught Gregory Nazianzen, in his *De Trinitate* 1, 31 *MG* 39.422.

[56] Sermon 232.2 *ML* 38. 1108.

[57] *Adversus Julian* ('the Apostate') 1.2.5 *PL* 44.644. Julian (331-63) became Emperor in 361. He promoted paganism as a rival to Christianity.

44

both sexes had been liberated in us, without our being liberated through both."—*Opp. t.* vi. *De Agon. Christ.* c. 24.[58]

9. St. Peter Chrysologus (400-450),[59] Bishop of Ravenna, and one of the chief authorities in the 4th General Council:—

"Blessed art thou among women; for among women, on whose womb Eve, who was cursed, brought punishment, Mary, being blest, rejoices, is honoured, and is looked up to. And woman now is truly made through grace the Mother of the living, who had been by nature the mother of the dying ... Heaven feels awe of God, Angels tremble at Him, the creature sustains Him not, nature sufficeth not; and yet one maiden so takes, receives, entertains Him, as a guest within her breast, that, for the very hire of her home, and as the price [43] of her womb, she asks, she obtains peace for the earth, glory for the heavens, salvation for the lost, life for the dead, a heavenly parentage for the earthly, the union of God Himself with human flesh."—*Serm.* 140.[60]

It is difficult to express more explicitly, though in oratorical language, that the Blessed Virgin had a real meritorious co-operation, a share which had a "hire" and a "price," in the reversal of the fall.

10. St. Fulgentius,[61] Bishop of Ruspe in Africa (468-533). The Homily which contains the following passage, is placed by Ceillier[62] (t. xvi. p. 127), among his genuine works:—

"In the wife of the first man, the wickedness of the devil depraved her seduced mind; in the mother of the Second Man, the grace of God preserved both her mind inviolate and her flesh. On her mind it conferred the most firm faith; from her flesh it took away lust altogether. Since then man was in

---

[58] *De agonia Christi* c.24 *ML* 40. 303.
[59] St Peter Chrysologus (c.400-50), Bishop of Ravenna, named *golden-worded* to distinguish him from golden-mouthed St John Chrysostom.
[60] *PL* 52. 576-7.
[61] He became Bishop of Ruspe in 502 or 507 but was banished to Sardinia soon after, being finally allowed back in 523.
[62] Remi Ceillier (1688-1763), ecclesiastical historian who wrote *Histoire générale des auteurs sacrés et ecclésiastiques* in 23 volumes.

a miserable way condemned for sin, therefore without sin was in a marvellous way born the God-man."—*Serm.* 2, p. 124. *De Dupl. Nativ.*[63]

Accordingly, in the Sermon which follows (if it is his), he continues thus, illustrating her office of universal Mother, as ascribed to her by St. Epiphanius:—

"Come ye virgins to a Virgin, come ye who conceive to her who conceived, ye who bear to one who bore, mothers to a mother, ye that suckle to one who suckled, young girls to the young girl. It is for this reason that the Virgin Mary has taken on her in our Lord Jesus Christ all these divisions of [44] nature, that to all women who have recourse to her, she may be a succour, and so restore the whole race of women who come to her, being the new Eve, by keeping virginity, as the new Adam the Lord Jesus Christ, recovers the whole race of men."[64]

Such is the rudimental view, as I have called it, which the Fathers have given us of Mary, as the Second Eve, the Mother of the living: I have cited ten authors. I could cite more, were it necessary: except the two last, they write gravely and without any rhetoric. I allow that the two last write in a different style, since the extracts I have made are from their sermons; but I do not see that the colouring conceals the outline. And after all, men use oratory on great subjects, not on small;—nor would they, and other Fathers whom I might quote, have lavished their high language upon the Blessed Virgin, such as they gave to no one else, unless they knew well that no one else had such claims, as she had, on their love and veneration.[65]

And now, I proceed to dwell for a while upon two inferences, which it is obvious to draw from the rudimental

---

[63] His sermon on 'The Two-Fold Nativity of Christ' *ML* 65. 728.
[64] Sermon 36 *ML* 65. 899-900.
[65] 1st ed title heading "Her Immaculate Conception".

doctrine itself; the first relates to the sanctity of the Blessed Virgin, the second to her dignity.

1. Her sanctity. She holds, as the Fathers teach us, that office in our restoration which Eve held in our fall:—now, in the first place, what were Eve's endowments to enable her to enter upon her trial? She could not have stood against the wiles of the devil, though she was innocent and sinless, without the grant of a large grace. And this she had;—a heavenly gift, which was over and above and additional to that nature of hers, which she received from Adam, a gift which had been given to Adam also before her, at the very time (as it is commonly held) of his original formation.[66] This is Anglican doctrine, as well as Catholic; it is the doctrine of Bishop Bull.[67] He has written a dissertation on the point. He speaks of the doctrine which "many of the Schoolmen affirm, that Adam was created in grace, that is, received a principle of grace and divine life from his very creation, or in the moment of the infusion of his soul; of which," he says, "for my own part I have little doubt." Again, he says, "It is abundantly manifest from the many testimonies alleged, that the ancient doctors of the Church did, with a general consent, acknowledge, that our first parents in the state of integrity, had in them something more than nature, that is, were endowed with the divine principle of the Spirit, in order to a supernatural felicity."

[45]

Now, taking this for granted, because I know that you and those who agree with you maintain it as well as we do, I ask you, have you any intention to deny that Mary was as fully endowed as Eve? is it any violent inference, that she, who was to co-operate in the redemption of the world, at least was not less endowed with power from on high, than she who,

---

[66] 1st ed has "original creation"

[67] George Bull (1634-1710) became Bishop of St. David's in 1705. He was the author of *The State of Man before the Fall*, "Adam was *creatus in gratia...*" Discourse 5. *Works of George Bull* Edited by Edward Burton. Oxford. 1846 Vol 2 p.91. See Newman's reference in *Dev* pp.135-8 and *Diff* 1 pp.2, 139.

given as a help-mate to her husband, did in the event but cooperate with him for its ruin? If Eve was raised above human nature by that indwelling moral gift which we call grace, is it rash to say that Mary had even a greater grace?[68] And this consideration gives significance to the Angel's salutation of her as "full of grace,"—an interpretation of the [46] original word which is undoubtedly the right one, as soon as we resist the common Protestant assumption that grace is a mere external approbation or acceptance, answering to the word "favour,"[69] whereas it is, as the Fathers teach, a real inward condition or superadded quality of soul. And if Eve had this supernatural inward gift given her from the first moment of her personal existence, is it possible to deny that Mary too had this gift from the very first moment of her personal existence? I do not know how to resist this inference:—well, this is simply and literally the doctrine of the Immaculate Conception. I say the doctrine of the Immaculate Conception is in its substance this, and nothing more or less than this (putting aside the question of degrees of grace); and it really does seem to me bound up in the doctrine of the Fathers, that Mary is the second Eve.

It is indeed to me a most strange phenomenon that so many learned and devout men stumble at this doctrine; and I can only account for it by supposing that in matter of fact they do not know what we mean by the Immaculate Conception;[70] and your Volume (may I say it?) bears out my suspicion. It is a great consolation to have reason for thinking so,—reason for believing that in some sort the persons in question are in the position of those great Saints in former

---

[68] 1st ed. "...had an even greater grace"

[69] κεχαριτωμένη from χαριζ (grace or favour) in Luke 1:28. Augustine talks of the excess of grace with which Mary was endowed in order to bear Him who had no sin, *Of Nature and Grace* see infra.

[70] The dogma (1854) states "that the most Blessed Virgin Mary in the first instant of her conception, by a unique grace and privilege of the omnipotent God and in consideration of the merits of Jesus Christ the Saviour of the human race, was preserved from all stain of original sin." *DS* 2803.

times, who are said to have hesitated about the doctrine, when they would not have hesitated at all, if the word "Conception" had been clearly explained in that sense in which now it is universally received. I do not see how any one who holds with Bull the Catholic doctrine of the supernatural endowments of our first parents, has fair reason for doubting our doctrine about the Blessed Virgin. It has no reference [47] whatever to her parents, but simply to her own person; it does but affirm that, together with the nature which she inherited from her parents, that is, her own nature, she had a superadded fulness of grace, and that from the first moment of her existence.[71] Suppose Eve had stood the trial, and not lost her first grace; and suppose she had eventually had children, those children from the first moment of their existence would, through divine bounty, have received the same privilege that she had ever had; that is, as she was taken from Adam's side, in a garment, so to say, of grace, so they in turn would have received what may be called an immaculate conception. They would have then been conceived in grace, as in fact they are conceived in sin. What is there difficult in this doctrine? What is there unnatural? Mary may be called, as it were, a daughter of Eve unfallen. You believe with us that St. John Baptist had grace given to him three months before his birth,[72] at the time that the Blessed Virgin visited his mother.[73] He accordingly was *not* immaculately conceived, because he was alive before grace came to him; but our Lady's case only differs from his in this respect, that to her the grace of God came, not three months

---

[71] "By virtue of the richness of the grace of the beloved Son, by reason of the redemptive merits of Him who willed to become her Son, Mary was preserved from the inheritance of sin" St. John Paul II Encyclical *Redemptoris Mater* (1987) n.10.

[72] Compare Newman's words in his 'Memorandum on the Immaculate Conception': "Does he not believe that St. John the Baptist had the grace of God – *i.e.* was regenerated, even before his birth?" *MD* p.116.

[73] "Behold, when the voice of your greeting came to my ears, the babe in my womb leaped for joy" Luke 1:44.

merely before her birth, but from the first moment of her being, as it had been given to Eve.

But it may be said, How does this enable us to say that she was conceived without *original sin*? If Anglicans knew what we mean by original sin, they would not ask the question. Our doctrine of original sin is not the same as the Protestant doctrine. "Original sin," with us, cannot be called sin, in the mere ordinary sense of the word "sin;"[74] it is a term denoting Adam's sin as transferred to us, or the state to which Adam's sin reduces his children;[75] but by Protestants it seems to be understood as sin, in much the same sense as actual sin. We, with the Fathers, think of it as something negative, Protestants as something positive. Protestants hold that it is a disease, a radical change of nature, an active poison internally corrupting the soul, infecting its primary elements, and disorganizing it;[76] and they fancy that we ascribe a different nature from ours to the Blessed Virgin, different from that of her parents, and from that of fallen Adam.[77] We hold nothing of the kind; we consider that in Adam she died, as others; that she was included, together with the whole race, in Adam's sentence; that she incurred his debt, as we do; but that, for the sake of Him who was to redeem her and us upon the Cross, to her the debt was remitted by anticipation,[78] on

[48]

---

[74] "Original sin is contracted without consent whereas actual sin is committed with consent." Innocent III, Letter to Humbert Archbishop of Arles 1201 *Maiores Ecclesiae Causas*, *DS* 780

[75] In the first edition Newman wrote, "it denotes the *imputation* of Adam's sin, or the state to which Adam's sin reduces his children" See *LD* 22 p.154n.

[76] 1st ed: "Protestants hold that it is [a disease, a change of nature, a poison internally corrupting the soul and propagated from father to son [after the manner of a bad constitution]. … We hold nothing of the kind." See *LD* 22 p.154n

[77] See Note II, 'Suarez on the Immaculate Conception' pp.[125-7]. This Note did not appear in the 1st ed. Francisco de Suarez (1548-1617), a Jesuit, lectured on Thomist theology at the Roman College and was then appointed by Philip II to the University of Coimbra in 1597. He differed from St Thomas in his theory of knowledge by which God foresees man's free acts by 'scientia media'. He was named Doctor Eximius by Pope Paul V.

[78] "We say that she, of all mere children of Adam, is in the truest sense the fruit and purchase of His Passion." 'Memorandum' *MD* p.117.

her the sentence was not carried out, except indeed as regards her natural death, for she died when her time came, as others.*
All this we teach, but we deny that she had original sin; for by original sin we mean, as I have already said, something negative, viz., this only, the *deprivation* of that supernatural unmerited grace which Adam and Eve had on their first formation,—deprivation and the consequences of deprivation. Mary could not merit, any more than they, the restoration of that grace; but it was restored to her by God's free bounty, from the very first moment of her existence, and thereby, in fact, she never came under the original curse, which consisted in the loss of it. And she had this special privilege, in order to fit her to become the Mother of her and our Redeemer, to fit her mentally, spiritually for it; so that, by the aid of the first grace, she might so grow in grace, that, when the Angel came and her Lord was at hand, she might be "full of grace," prepared as far as a creature could be prepared, to receive Him into her bosom. [49]

I have drawn the doctrine of the Immaculate Conception, as an immediate inference, from the primitive doctrine that Mary is the second Eve. The argument seems to me conclusive: and, if it has not been universally taken as such, this has come to pass, because there has not been a clear understanding among Catholics, what exactly was meant by the "Immaculate Conception." To many it seemed to imply that the Blessed Virgin did not die in Adam, that she did not come under the penalty of the fall, that she was not redeemed, that she was conceived in some way inconsistent with the verse in the *Miserere* Psalm.[79] If controversy had in earlier days so cleared the subject as to make it plain to all, that the doctrine meant nothing else than that in fact in her case the

* Vid. Note II. Infra.

---

[79] "O see in guilt I was born, a sinner was I conceived" Ps 51/50:7.

general sentence on mankind was not carried out, and that, by means of the indwelling in her of divine grace from the first moment of her being (and this is all the decree of 1854[80] has declared), I cannot believe that the doctrine would have ever been opposed; for an instinctive sentiment has led [50] Christians jealously to put the Blessed Mary aside when sin comes into discussion. This is expressed in the well-known words of St. Augustine, All have sinned "except the Holy Virgin Mary, concerning whom, for the honour of the Lord, I wish no question to be raised at all, when we are treating of sins" (*de Nat. et Grat.* 42[81]); words which, whatever was St. Augustine's actual occasion of using them (to which you refer, p. 176), certainly, in the spirit which they breathe, are well adapted to convey the notion, that, though her parents had no privilege beyond other parents, she had not personally any part in sin whatever. It is true that several great Fathers of the fourth century do imply or assert that on one or two occasions she did sin venially or showed infirmity.[82] This is the only real objection which I know of; and as I do not wish to pass it over lightly, I propose to consider it at the end of this Letter.[*]

2. Now, secondly, her dignity.[83] Here let us suppose that our first parents had overcome in their trial; and had gained for their descendants for ever the full possession, as if by right, of the privileges which were promised to their obedience,—grace here and glory hereafter. Is it possible that

[*] Vid.[See] Note III. infra.[84]

---

[80] Bull *Ineffabilis Deus*, *DS* 2800.
[81] *De natura et gratia* (415) 36, 42. *ML* 44, 267. Pusey had said, "S. Augustine does not even rule that she never sinned actually, by any sin of infirmity; he marks it to be uncertain, by the contrast which he draws with our Lord." *En* p.176.
[82] See Note III pp.[128-52].
[83] In 1st ed. "her greatness". Title heading "Her Exaltation in Scripture".
[84] p.128.

those descendants, pious and happy from age to age in their temporal homes, would have forgotten their benefactors? Would they not have followed them in thought into the heavens, and gratefully commemorated them on earth? The history of the temptation, the craft of the serpent, their steadfastness in obedience,—the loyal vigilance, the [51] sensitive purity of Eve,—the great issue, salvation wrought out for all generations,—would have been never from their minds, ever welcome to their ears. This would have taken place from the necessity of our nature. Every nation has its mythical hymns and epics about its first fathers and its heroes. The great deeds of Charlemagne, Alfred, Coeur de Lion, Louis the ninth, Wallace, Joan of Arc,[85] do not die; and though their persons are gone from us, we make much of their names. Milton's Adam, after his fall, understands the force of this law and shrinks from the prospect of its operation.

> "Who of all ages to succeed, but, feeling
> The evil on him brought by me, will curse
> My head? Ill fare our ancestor impure,
> For this we may thank Adam."[86]

If this anticipation of the first man has not been fulfilled in the event, it is owing to the exigencies of our penal life, our state of perpetual change, and the ignorance and un-belief incurred by the fall; also because, fallen as we are, still from the hopefulness of our nature, we feel more pride in our national great men, than dejection at our national

---

[85] Charlemagne or Charles I (742-814), emperor in 771. Alfred the Great (849-99) became king of Wessex in 871. Richard I, *Coeur-de-Lion* (1157-99) became king in 1189 and led his army in the Third Crusade. St. Louis IX (1214-70) became king in 1225   and went on the First Crusade in 1248. He was canonized in 1297. Sir William Wallace (1272-1305), Scottish patriot. He became Guardian of Scotland, having defeated the English in 1297, but was declared an outlaw and finally executed. Joan of Arc (1413-31), France's second patron, rode to battle at the siege of Orléans. She was canonized in 1920.
[86] *Paradise Lost* Book 10.

misfortunes. Much more then in the great kingdom and people of God;—the Saints are ever in our sight, and not as mere ineffectual ghosts or dim memories, but as if present bodily in their past selves. It is said of them, "Their works do follow them;"[87] what they were here, such are they in heaven and in the Church. As we call them by their earthly names, so we contemplate them in their earthly characters and histories. Their acts, callings, and relations below, are types [52] and anticipations of their present mission above. Even in the case of our Lord Himself, whose native home is the eternal heavens, it is said of Him in His state of glory, that He is "a Priest for ever;"[88] and when He comes again, He will be recognized by those who pierced Him,[89] as being the very same that He was on earth. The only question is, whether the Blessed Virgin had a part, a real part, in the economy of grace, whether, when she was on earth, she secured by her deeds any claim on our memories; for, if she did, it is impossible we should put her away from us, merely because she is gone hence, and should not look at her still according to the measure of her earthly history, with gratitude and expectation. If, as St. Irenæus says, she acted the part of an Advocate,[90] a friend in need, even in her mortal life, if as St. Jerome and St. Ambrose say, she was on earth the great pattern of Virgins, if she had a meritorious share in bringing about our redemption, if her maternity was gained by her faith and obedience, if her Divine Son was subject to her, and if she stood by the Cross with a mother's heart and drank in to the full those sufferings which it was her portion to gaze upon, it is impossible that we should not associate these characteristics of her life on earth with her present state of

---

[87] Rev 14: 13.

[88] Heb. 5:6. "Thou art a priest for ever, after the order of Melchizedek."

[89] Rev 1:7; John 19:37.

[90] See supra Irenaeus' reference to Mary as Paraclete.

blessedness; and this surely she anticipated, when she said in her hymn that all "generations should call her blessed."[91]

I am aware that, in thus speaking, I am following a line of thought which is rather a meditation than an argument in controversy, and I shall not carry it further; but still, before turning to other topics, it is to the point to inquire, whether the popular astonishment, excited by our belief in the blessed [53] Virgin's present dignity, does not arise from the circumstance that the bulk of men, engaged in matters of this world, have never calmly considered her historical position in the gospels, so as rightly to realize (if I may use the word a second time) what that position imports. I do not claim for the generality of Catholics any greater powers of reflection upon the objects of their faith, than Protestants commonly have; but, putting the run of Catholics aside, there is a sufficient number of religious men among us who, instead of expending their devotional energies (as so many serious Protestants do) on abstract doctrines, such as justification by faith only,[92] or the sufficiency of Holy Scripture,[93] employ themselves in the contemplation of Scripture facts, and bring out before their minds in a tangible form the doctrines involved in them, and give such a substance and colour to the sacred history, as to influence their brethren; and their brethren, though superficial themselves, are drawn by their Catholic instinct to accept conclusions which they could not indeed themselves have elicited, but which, when elicited, they feel to be true. However, it would be out of place to pursue this course of reasoning here; and instead of doing so, I shall take what perhaps you may think a very bold step,—I shall find the doctrine of our Lady's present exaltation in Scripture.

---

[91] Luke 1:48.
[92] Article 11 *BCP*.
[93] Article 6 *BCP*.

I mean to find it in the vision of the Woman and Child in the twelfth chapter of the Apocalypse:[*]—now here two objections will be made to me at once; first that such an interpretation is but poorly supported by the Fathers, and secondly that in ascribing such a picture of the Madonna (as it may be called) to the Apostolic age, I am committing an anachronism.

[54]

As to the former of these objections, I answer as follows:—Christians have never gone to Scripture for proof of their doctrines, till there was actual need, from the pressure of controversy;—if in those times the Blessed Virgin's dignity was unchallenged on all hands, as a matter of doctrine, Scripture, as far as its argumentative matter was concerned, was likely to remain a sealed book to them. Thus, to take an instance in point; the Catholic party in the Anglican Church (say, the Nonjurors),[94] unable by their theory of religion simply to take their stand on Tradition, and distressed for proof of their doctrines, had their eyes sharpened to scrutinize and to understand in many places the letter of Holy Scripture, which to others brought no instruction. And the peculiarity of their interpretations is this,—that these have in themselves great logical cogency, yet are but faintly supported by patristical commentators. Such is the use of the word $\pi o\iota\epsilon\tilde{\iota}v$ or *facere* in our Lord's institution of the Holy Eucharist, which, by a reference to the Old Testament, is found to be a word of sacrifice. Such again

---

[*] Vid. Essay on Doctr. Development, p. 384, and Bishop Ullathorne's work on the Immaculate Conception, p. 77.[95]

---

[94] Those members of the Church of England who refused to take oaths accepting William and Mary as sovereigns because they had already sworn allegiance to James II.

[95] Ullathorne published *The Immaculate Conception: An Exposition* in 1855, which "described the definition of the dogma as a triumph for episcopal authority and popular devotion". Judith Champ *William Bernard Ullathorne A Different Kind of Monk*, Leominster 2006 p.224.

is λειτουργούντων in the passage in the Acts "As they *ministered* to the Lord and fasted,"[96] which again is a sacerdotal term. And such the passage in Rom. xv. 16, in which several terms are used which have an allusion to the sacrificial Eucharistic rite.[97] Such too is St. Paul's repeated message to the *household* of Onesiphorus,[98] with no mention of Onesiphorus himself, but in one place with the addition of a prayer that "he might find mercy of the Lord"[99] in the day of judgment, which, taking into account its wording and the known usage of the first centuries, we can hardly deny is a prayer for his soul. Other texts there are, which ought to find a place in ancient controversies, and the omission of which by the Fathers affords matter for more surprise; those for instance, which, according to Middleton's rule,[100] are real proofs of our Lord's divinity, and yet are passed over by Catholic disputants; for these bear upon a then existing controversy of the first moment, and of the most urgent exigency.

[55]

As to the second objection which I have supposed, so far from allowing it, I consider that it is built upon a mere imaginary fact, and that the truth of the matter lies in the very contrary direction. The Virgin and Child is *not* a mere modern idea; on the contrary, it is represented again and again, as every visitor to Rome is aware, in the paintings of the Catacombs. Mary is there drawn with the Divine Infant in her lap, she with hands extended in prayer, He with His hand in the attitude of blessing. No representation can more forcibly convey the doctrine of the high dignity of the Mother, and, I will add, of her influence with her Son. Why

---

[96] Acts 13:2.
[97] "a minister…in the priestly service [ἱερουργοντα] of the gospel"
[98] Letter to Philemon 10.
[99] 2 Tim 1:18-19.
[100] Thomas Fanshawe Middleton (1769-1822), first (Anglican) Bishop of Calcutta and author of *The Doctrine of the Greek Article applied to the Criticism and Illustration of the New Testament* (1808).

should the memory of His time of subjection be so dear to Christians, and so carefully preserved? The only question to be determined, is the precise date of these remarkable monuments of the first age of Christianity. That they belong to the centuries of what Anglicans call the "undivided Church"[101] is certain; but lately investigations have been pursued, which place some of them at an earlier date than any one anticipated as possible. I am not in a position to quote largely from the works of the Cavaliere de Rossi,[102] who has thrown so much light upon the subject; but I have his "Imagini Scelte," published in 1863, and they are sufficient for my purpose. In this work he has given us from the Catacombs various representations of the Virgin and Child; the latest of these belong to the early part of the fourth century, but the earliest he believes to be referable to the very age of the Apostles.[103] He comes to this conclusion from the style and the skill of its composition, and from the history, locality, and existing inscriptions of the subterranean in which it is found. However he does not go so far as to insist upon so early a date; yet the utmost concession he makes is to refer the painting to the era of the first Antonines,[104] that is, to a date within half a century of the death of St. John. I consider then, that, as you would use in controversy with Protestants, and fairly, the traditional doctrine of the Church in early times, as an explanation of a particular passage of Scripture, or at least as a suggestion, or as a defence, of the

[56]

---

[101] "All the true churches in the world, which are all but one whole Church united in Christ their Head" William Sherlock *A Vindication of the Doctrine of the Trinity* p.35(1690). See *En* pp.10, 287.

[102] Giovanni Battista de Rossi (1822-94) with Giuseppe Marchi SJ became famous for excavating and describing the catacombs. Rossi's *Immàgine Scelte della Beata Virgine tratte dalle Catacombe Romane/Selected Images of the Blessed Virgin from the Roman Catacombs* (1863) was one of his many publications.

[103] Scholars date the portrait of the Madonna and child with the prophet Balaam in the catacomb of Priscilla as early as the second century. Herbert A. Musurillo, ed., *The Fathers of the Primitive Church* New York 1966 p.112.

[104] Antonius Pius, Emperor (138-61).

sense which you may wish to put upon it, quite apart from the question whether your interpretation itself is directly traditional, so it is lawful for me, though I have not the positive words of the Fathers on my side, to shelter my own interpretation of the Apostle's vision in the Apocalypse[105] under the fact of the extant pictures of Mother and Child in the Roman Catacombs. Again, there is another principle of Scripture interpretation which we should hold as well as you, viz., when we speak of a doctrine being contained in Scripture, we do not necessarily mean that it is contained there in direct categorical terms, but that there is no satisfactory way of accounting for the language and expressions of the sacred writers, concerning the subject-matter in question, except to suppose that they held concerning it the opinion which we hold,—that they would not have spoken as they have spoken, *unless* they held it. For myself I have ever felt the truth of this principle, as regards the Scripture proof of the Holy Trinity; I should not have found out that doctrine in the sacred text without previous traditional teaching; but, when once it is suggested from without, it commends itself as the one true interpretation, from its appositeness,—because no other view of doctrine, which can be ascribed to the inspired writers, so happily solves the obscurities and seeming inconsistencies of their teaching. And now to apply what I have been saying to the passage in the Apocalypse. [57]

If there is an Apostle on whom, *à priori*, our eyes would be fixed, as likely to teach us about the Blessed Virgin, it is St. John, to whom she was committed by our Lord on the Cross;[106]—with whom, as tradition goes, she lived at Ephesus till she was taken away. This anticipation is confirmed *à posteriori*; for, as I have said above, one of the earliest and fullest of our informants concerning her dignity, as being the

---

[105] Rev 12.
[106] John 19:26.

second Eve, is Irenæus, who came to Lyons from Asia Minor, and had been taught by the immediate disciples of St. John. The Apostle's vision is as follows:—

[58]

"A great sign appeared in heaven: A woman clothed with the Sun, and the Moon under her feet; and on her head a crown of twelve stars. And being with child, she cried travailing in birth, and was in pain to be delivered. And there was seen another sign in heaven; and behold a great red dragon ... And the dragon stood before the woman who was ready to be delivered, that, when she should be delivered, he might devour her son. And she brought forth a man child, who was to rule all nations with an iron rod; and her son was taken up to God and to His throne. And the woman fled into the wilderness."[107] Now I do not deny of course, that under the image of the Woman, the Church is signified; but what I would maintain is this, that the Holy Apostle would not have spoken of the Church under this particular image, *unless* there had existed a blessed Virgin Mary, who was exalted on high, and the object of veneration to all the faithful.[108]

No one doubts that the "man-child" spoken of is an allusion to our Lord: why then is not "the Woman" an allusion to His Mother? This surely is the obvious sense of the words; of course they have a further sense also, which is the scope of the image; doubtless the Child represents the children of the Church, and doubtless the Woman represents the Church; this, I grant, is the real or direct sense, but what is the sense of the symbol under which that real sense is conveyed? *who* are the Woman and the Child? I answer, they are not personifications but Persons. This is true of the Child, therefore it is true of the Woman.

But again: not only Mother and Child, but a serpent is introduced into the vision. Such a meeting of man, woman, and serpent has not been found in Scripture, since the

---

[107] Rev 12:1-6.
[108] See Newman's treatment on the *Office of the Blessed Virgin* in *Dev* pp.415-16.

60

beginning of Scripture, and now it is found in its end. [59]
Moreover, in the passage in the Apocalypse,[109] as if to supply,
before Scripture came to an end, what was wanting in its
beginning, we are told, and for the first time, that the serpent
in Paradise was the evil spirit. If the dragon of St. John is the
same as the serpent of Moses,[110] and the man-child is "the
seed of the woman," why is not the woman herself she,
whose seed the man-child is? And, if the first woman is not
an allegory, why is the second? if the first woman is Eve, why
is not the second Mary?

But this is not all. The image of the woman, according to
general Scripture usage, is too bold and prominent for a mere
personification. Scripture is not fond of allegories. We have
indeed frequent figures there, as when the sacred writers
speak of the arm or sword of the Lord;[111] and so too when
they speak of Jerusalem or Samaria in the feminine; or of the
Church as a bride or as a vine; but they are not much given
to dressing up abstract ideas or generalizations in personal
attributes. This is the classical rather than the Scriptural style.
Xenophon places Hercules between Virtue and Vice,
represented as women;[112] Æschylus introduces into his drama
Force and Violence;[113] Virgil gives personality to public
rumour or Fame,[114] and Plautus to Poverty.[115] So on
monuments done in the classical style, we see virtues, vices,
rivers, renown, death, and the like, turned into human figures
of men and women. Certainly I do not deny there are some
instances of this method in Scripture, but I say that such
poetical compositions are strikingly unlike its usual method.
Thus, we at once feel the difference from Scripture, when we

---

[109] Rev 12.
[110] Num 21:8.
[111] Pss 89:13; 7:12.
[112] Xenophon's *Memorabilia 10* ch. 2.1 21-30.
[113] In *Prometheus Bound*.
[114] In the *Aeneid* 4 1-299.
[115] Titus Maccius Plautus in his *Aulularia*.

[60] betake ourselves to the Pastor of Hermas,[116] and find the Church a woman; to St. Methodius, and find Virtue a woman;[117] and to St. Gregory's poem,[118] and find Virginity again a woman. Scripture deals with types rather than personifications. Israel stands for the chosen people, David for Christ, Jerusalem for heaven. Consider the remarkable representations, dramatic I may call them, in Jeremiah, Ezechiel, and Hosea: predictions, threatenings, and promises, are acted out by those Prophets. Ezechiel is commanded to shave his head, and to divide and scatter his hair;[119] and Ahias tears his garment, and gives ten out of twelve parts of it to Jeroboam.[120] So too the structure of the imagery in the Apocalypse is not a mere allegorical creation, but is founded on the Jewish ritual. In like manner our Lord's bodily cures are visible types of the power of His grace upon the soul; and His prophecy of the last day is conveyed under that of the fall of Jerusalem. Even His parables are not simply ideal, but relations of occurrences, which did or might take place, under which was conveyed a spiritual meaning. The description of Wisdom in the Proverbs[121] and other sacred books, has brought out the instinct of commentators in this respect. They felt that Wisdom could not be a mere personification, and they determined that it was our Lord: and the later-written of these books, by their own more definite language, warranted that interpretation. Then, when it was found that the Arians used it in derogation of our Lord's divinity, still, unable to tolerate the notion of a mere allegory, commentators applied the description to the Blessed Virgin. Coming back then to [61] the Apocalyptic vision, I ask, If the Woman ought to be some

---

[116] *Vision* 2.4.1. *PG* 2.897.

[117] *Symposium.* Hymn 16.

[118] Gregory of Nazianzen's *Poemata Arcana, PG* 38.91.

[119] Ezek 5:1.

[120] Ahias/Ahijah I Kings 1:30.

[121] "Wisdom has built her house, she has set up her seven columns... She calls from the heights out over the city." Wis 8:1,3.

real person, who can it be whom the Apostle saw, and intends, and delineates, but that same Great Mother to whom the chapters in the Proverbs are accommodated? And let it be observed, moreover, that in this passage, from the allusion made in it to the history of the fall, Mary may be said still to be represented under the character of the Second Eve. I make a farther remark: it is sometimes asked, Why do not the sacred writers mention our Lady's greatness? I answer, she was, or may have been alive, when the Apostles and Evangelists wrote;—there was just one book of Scripture certainly written after her death, and that book does (so to say) canonize and crown her.[122]

But if all this be so, if it is really the Blessed Virgin whom Scripture represents as clothed with the sun, crowned with the stars of heaven, and with the moon as her footstool, what height of glory may we not attribute to her? and what are we to say of those who, through ignorance, run counter to the voice of Scripture, to the testimony of the Fathers, to the traditions of East and West, and speak and act contemptuously towards her whom her Lord delighteth to honour?

2.[123]

Now I have said all I mean to say on what I have called the rudimental teaching of Antiquity about the Blessed Virgin; but after all I have not insisted on the highest view of her prerogatives, which the Fathers have taught us. You, my dear Friend, who know so well the ancient controversies and Councils, may have been surprised why I should not have yet [62] spoken of her as the Theotocos;[124]—but I wished to show on

---

[122] Rev 12:1. 1st ed. does not have "and crown".

[123] 1st ed. title heading "The Blessed Virgin The Theotocos".

[124] Newman later comments, "Christians were accustomed from the first to call the Blessed Virgin 'Mother of God' because they saw that it was impossible to deny her

how broad a basis her dignity rests, independent of that wonderful title; and again I have been loth to enlarge upon the force of a word, which is rather matter for devotional thought than for polemical dispute. However, I might as well not write to you at all, as altogether be silent upon it.

It is then an integral portion of the Faith fixed by Ecumenical Council, a portion of it which you hold us well as I, that the Blessed Virgin is Theotocos, Deipara,[125] or Mother of God; and this word, when thus used, carries with it no admixture of rhetoric, no taint of extravagant affection,—it has nothing else but a well-weighed, grave, dogmatic sense, which corresponds and is adequate to its sound. It intends to express that God is her Son, as truly as any one of us is the son of his own mother. If this be so, what can be said of any creature whatever, which may not be said of her? what can be said too much, so that it does not compromise the attributes of the Creator? He indeed might have created a being more perfect, more admirable, than she is; He might have endued that being, so created, with a richer grant of grace, of power, of blessedness: but in one respect she surpasses all even possible creations, viz., that she is Mother of her Creator. It is this awful title, which both illustrates and connects together the two prerogatives of Mary, on which I have been lately enlarging, her sanctity and her greatness. It is the issue of her sanctity; it is the origin[126]

[63] of her greatness. What dignity can be too great to attribute to her who is as closely bound up, as intimately one, with the Eternal Word, as a mother is with a son? What outfit of sanctity, what fulness and redundance[127] of grace, what exuberance of merits must have been hers, when once we admit the supposition, which the Fathers justify, that her

---

that title without denying St John's words, 'the Word' (that is God the Son) was made flesh.'" *MD* p.56.

[125] God-bearer.

[126] 1st ed has "*source* of her greatness."

[127] redundance: outpouring, overflowing

Maker really did regard those merits, and take them into account, when He condescended "not to abhor the Virgin's womb"?[128] Is it surprising then that on the one hand she should be immaculate in her Conception? or on the other that she should be honoured with an Assumption, and exalted as a queen with a crown of twelve stars, with the rulers of day and night to do her service? Men sometimes wonder that we call her Mother of life, of mercy, of salvation; what are all these titles compared to that one name, Mother of God?

I shall say no more about this title here. It is scarcely possible to write of it without diverging into a style of composition unsuited to a Letter; so I will but refer to the history and to instances of its use.

The title of *Theotocos** as ascribed to the Blessed Mary, begins with ecclesiastical writers of a date hardly later than that at which we read of her as the second Eve. It first occurs in the works of Origen[129] (185-254); but he, witnessing for Egypt and Palestine, witnesses also that it was in use before his time; for, as Socrates informs us, he "interpreted how it was to be used, and discussed the question at length" (*Hist.* vii. 32) Within two centuries of his time (431), in the General Council held against Nestorius,[130] it was made part of the [64] formal dogmatic teaching of the Church. At that time, Theodoret, who from his party connexions might have been supposed disinclined to its solemn recognition, owned that

---

* Vid. Oxford Translation of St. Athanasius, pp. 420, 440, 447; and Essay of Doct. Development, pp. 407-409.[131]

---

[128] From the *Te Deum*, a Latin hymn of praise to the Father and the Son used in the Catholic Office of Readings on Sundays and feast days and prescribed for daily use in Matins in the *BCP*. Author unknown, though formerly attributed to St. Ambrose.
[129] Origen (c.185-254). Head of the Catechetical School in Alexandria but transferred to Caesarea in 231 and was imprisoned in 250. He is famous for his biblical commentaries.
[130] The Council of Ephesus. *DS* 252-263.
[131] *Select Treatise of St. Athanasius in controversy with the Arians* was Newman's translation 2nd edition 1881. This note is not in the 1864 edition.

"the ancient and more than ancient heralds of the orthodox faith taught the use of the term according to the Apostolic tradition."[132] At the same date John of Antioch,[133] the temporary protector of Nestorius, whose heresy lay in the rejection of the term, said, "This title no ecclesiastical teacher has put aside. Those who have used it are many and eminent; and those who have not used it, have not attacked those who did." Alexander[134] again, one of the fiercest partisans of Nestorius, witnesses to the use of the word, though he considers it dangerous; "That in festive solemnities," he says, "or in preaching or teaching, *theotocos* should be unguardedly said by the orthodox without explanation is no blame, because such statements were not dogmatic, nor said with evil meaning."[135] If we look for those Fathers, in the interval between Origen and the Council, to whom Alexander refers as using the term, we find among them no less names than Archelaus of Mesopotamia,[136] Eusebius of Palestine,[137] Alexander of Egypt,[138] in the third century; in the fourth, Athanasius,[139] who uses it many times with emphasis, Cyril

---

[132] Theodoret of Cyrrhus (c. 393-c. 466) stated this in 436 in his *Haereses* 4.12. See *HS* 2 p.360.

[133] John of Antioch (d. 441), bishop who supported Nestorius in his conflict with Cyril of Alexandria. Socrates *Ecclesiastical History* Book 7 c.34.

[134] Alexander bishop of Hierapolis (fl. 431), 'holy and beloved of his people' but stubborn at Ephesus. "He fully allows the ancient reception of the word though only into popular use, from which came what he considers the doctrinal corruption" (*Ath* 2 p. 211). Eventually banished by the Emperor to the mines of Pharmuthin in Egypt, where he died.

[135] Alexander, in his *Proverbs of the Council* Felix in Artur Haase, 'Die Koptischen Quellen zum Konzil von Nicaea, Kap. 34-5, *Studien zur Geschichte und Kultur des Altertums* 10 (1929) pp.50ff.

[136] Archelaus, Bishop of Carrhae (fl. 278), disputed with Manichean heretics.

[137] Eusebius, Bishop of Caesarea (c. 260-340), termed "the Father of Church history".

[138] Alexander, Patriarch of Alexandria (d. 328). He excommunicated Arius in 321.

[139] Athanasius, Bishop of Alexandria (c. 296-373). He succeeded Alexander and was the great opponent of Arianism, *De virginitate* 3. *PG* 28. 256.

of Palestine,[140] Gregory Nyssen[141] and Gregory Nazianzen of Cappadocia,[142] Antiochus of Syria,[143] and Ammonius of Thrace:[144]—not to refer to the Emperor Julian,[145] who, having no local or ecclesiastical domicile, is a witness for the whole of Christendom. Another and earlier Emperor, Constantine,[146] in his speech before the assembled Bishops at [65] Nicæa, uses the still more explicit title of "the Virgin Mother of God;"[147] which is also used by Ambrose of Milan,[148] and by Vincent[149] and Cassian[150] in the south of France, and then by St. Leo.[151]

[152]So much for the term; it would be tedious to produce the passages of authors who, using or not using the term, convey the idea. "Our God was carried in the womb of Mary," says Ignatius, who was martyred A.D. 106.[153] "The Word of God,"

---

[140] Cyril of Jerusalem author of the 24 *Catecheses.* See supra.

[141] Gregory of Nyssa (c. 330-95), brother of St. Basil and author of *Oratio catechetica,* Letter 3. *PG* 46. 1024A.

[142] Gregory of Nazianzus (329-89), Bishop of Constantinople during the Council of Constantinople in 381. *Ep.* 101, *PG* 37.177-80.

[143] Antiochus of Syria, Bishop of Ptolemais in Phoenicia at the time of John Chrysostom. See Socrates *Ecclesiastical History* Book 6 ch. 11.

[144] Ammonius Saccas (c. 175-243) studied in the Catechetical School of Alexandria and influenced Origen. See Eusebius *Ecclesiastical History* Book 6 ch. 19.

[145] Emperor Julian, qu. Cyril of Alexandria *Contra Julianum* ,8. *PG* 76.901.

[146] Constantine., sole emperor 324-37. He presided at the Council of Nicaea in 325.

[147] Constantine's *Oration* is found in Ambrose *De Virg.* 2.7.

[148] Ambrose (c. 339-97), Bishop of Milan 384, author of *De institutione virginis et sanctae Mariae virginitate perpetua ad Eusebium liber unus* (391). 2.2.7 *ML* 16.209.

[149] Vincent (d. before 450), monk of Lérins and author of the *Vincentian Canon*: 'what everywhere, what always, what by everyone must be believed.'

[150] John Cassian, (c. 360-435), Abbot of Marseilles, author of monastic rules and of *De incarnatione Christi adversus Nestorium*: "You deny that God was born of the Virgin, and that Mary, the Mother of Our Lord Jesus Christ may be called *Theotokos,* meaning the mother of God", Book 2 ch 2., ed. Bertram, Gracewing 2018 p.12.

[151] St Leo (d. 461), Pope 440-61. His *Tome* was accepted as normative at the Council of Chalcedon in 451. John Pearson (1613-86), Bishop of Chester, says the phrase 'Mater Dei' originated with St. Leo in his *Exposition of the Creed* (quoted in *Ath* 2 p. 212). *Letter to Flavian* 28,2. *ML* 54. 759.

[152] In the 1st ed. there is a heading here, "Zeal of the Fathers for the Blessed Virgin".

[153] *Letter to the Ephesians* 7.2 *PG* 5. 649; 18.2. *PG* 5.660.

says Hippolytus,[154] "was carried in that Virgin frame." "The Maker of all," says Amphilochius,[155] "is born of a Virgin." "She did compass without circumscribing the Sun of justice,—the Everlasting is born," says Chrysostom.[156] "God dwelt in the womb," says Proclus.[157] "When thou hearest that God speaks from the bush," asks Theodotus,[158] "in the bush seest thou not the Virgin?" Cassian says, "Mary bore her Author."[159] "The One God only-begotten," says Hilary,[160] "is introduced into the womb of a Virgin." "The Everlasting," says Ambrose, "came into the Virgin."[161] "The closed gate," says Jerome, "by which alone the Lord God of Israel enters, is the Virgin Mary."[162] "That man from heaven," says Capriolus,[163] "is God conceived in the womb." "He is made in thee," says St. Augustine, "who made thee."[164]

This being the faith of the Fathers about the Blessed Virgin, we need not wonder that it should in no long time be

[154] Hippolytus (c. 170-236), church writer and historian, author of *Contra haeresim Noetii* 17 *PG* 10. 826-7.
[155] Amphilochius (c. 340-95), Bishop of Iconium from 373 *On Christmas* 4 *PG* 39, 40.
[156] John Chrysostom (c. 347-407), Patriarch of Constantinople 398 but frequently banished; author of *The Proof that Christ was God* (381). In his *Second Christmas Homily* he says, "The virgin gave birth and I believe that God begot him out of time." *PG* 58. 387.
[157] Proclus (d. 446/447), Bishop of Constantinople in 434, in *Prayers in Praise of the Blessed Virgin Mary PG* 65 715-22. He preached on the *Theotokos* in 428 in the presence of Nestorius.
[158] Theodotus (d. c. 445), Bishop of Ancyra and opponent of Nestorius (whom he had at first supported) at the Council of Ephesus in 431. *Homily 4 on the Holy Mother of God, PG* 77, 1394. Theodoret of Cyrrhus (qv) uses the same symbolism in his *Eranistes* Dialogue 1.
[159] John Cassian (qv supr.) *Contra haeresim Noetii* Book 4 ch. 2, "She procreated her own creator, she was the mother of her own Father." Bertram iam cit supra p.49.
[160] Hilary (c.315-67), Bishop of Poitiers. He wrote his *On the Trinity* against the Arians.2. 24-25. *PL* 10.66.
[161] Ambrose (qv supr.) *De Fide ad Gratianum* 5. 54. *PL* 16. 687.
[162] St. Jerome (qv supr.) *Dialogus adversis Pelagianos* 2.4 *PL* 23. 563.
[163] Capreolus (d. c. 437), Bishop of Carthage in c.430, prevented from attending the Council of Ephesus by the Vandals who had invaded the province, wrote a letter in support of doctrine, and against Nestorius, "Let them tell us how is that Man from heaven, if He be not God conceived in the womb?" *PL* 53.843.
[164] Augustine (354-430), Bishop of Hippo Regius in 395. *Homily* 186, 1 *ML* 38. 999.

transmuted into devotion. No wonder if their language should become unmeasured, when so great a term as "Mother of God" had been formally set down as the safe limit of it. No [66] wonder if it should be stronger and stronger as time went on, since only in a long period could the fulness of its import be exhausted. And in matter of fact, and as might be anticipated, (with the few exceptions which I have noted above, and which I am to treat of below), the current of thought in those early ages did uniformly tend to make much of the Blessed Virgin and to increase her honours, not to circumscribe them. Little jealousy was shown of her in those times; but, when any such niggardness of affection occurred, then one Father or other fell upon the offender, with zeal, not to say with fierceness. Thus St. Jerome inveighs against Helvidius;[165] thus St. Epiphanius denounces Apollinaris,[166] St. Cyril Nestorius,[167] and St. Ambrose Bonosus;[168] on the other hand, each successive insult offered to her by individual adversaries did but bring out more fully the intimate sacred affection with which Christendom regarded her. "She was alone, and wrought the world's salvation and conceived the redemption of all," says Ambrose;[*][169] "she had so great grace, as not only to preserve virginity herself, but to confer it on

---

[*] Essay on Doctr. Dev. *ubi supra.*[170]

---

[165] *Adversus Helvidium: de virginitate perpetua Mariae virginis* (381) *ML* 23 183-206. Helvidius was a 4th century theologian who said that the brethren of the Lord were the natural sons of Joseph and Mary.

[166] Epiphanius (qv supr.) (c. 315-403), Bishop of Salamis who attacked Apollinarius' teaching on the humanity of Christ. *Adversus Haereses* 78.18 *PG* 42 728.

[167] Cyril (d. 444), Patriarch of Alexandria, defended the title of *Theotokos* applied to the Virgin Mary against Nestorius who became Patriarch of Constantinople in 428 but was deposed in 431. *Against those not wishing to admit the Virgin to be Mother of God* n. 4 *PG* 76. 260.

[168] Bonosus (d. c. 400), Bishop Sardico in Illyria. In a *Letter on the Case of Bonosus* which was probably written by Pope Siricius (according to Tillemont), Bonosus is said to deny the perpetual virginity of Mary. His teaching was condemned at the Council of Capua in 391.

[169] *Letter* 49, 2 *PL* 16.1154.

[170] This note does not appear in the 1866 first edition.

those whom she visited."[171] "She is the rod out of the stem of Jesse,"[172] says St. Jerome, "and the Eastern gate through which the High Priest alone goes in and out, which still is ever shut."[173] "She is the wise woman," says Nilus, who "hath clad believers, from the fleece of the Lamb born of her, with the clothing of incorruption, and delivered them from their spiritual nakedness."[174] "She is the mother of life, of beauty, of majesty, the morning star," according to Antiochus.[175] "The mystical new heavens," "the heavens carrying the Divinity," "the fruitful vine," "by whom we are translated from death unto life," according to St. Ephrem[176]. "The manna, which is delicate, bright, sweet, and virgin, which, as though coming from heaven, has poured down on all the people of the Churches a food pleasanter than honey," according to St. Maximus.[177]

[67]

Basil of Seleucia[178] says, that "she shines out above all the martyrs as the sun above the stars, and that she mediates between God and men." "Run through all creation in your

---

[171] "This woman is the model of virginity. For such was Mary, that the life of this one woman may be an example for all." *De virginibus* 2,15. *PL* 12.222 See *Dev* p.146.

[172] *Dev* p.146.

[173] *Ep. 22, 19 ad Eustochium* in which he uses the analogy of Is 11:1 and *Commentary on the Gospel of Luke*, *PL* 25. 430.

[174] Nilus (d. 436), a disciple of John Chrysostom and founder of a monastery near Ancyra in *Letter 270*, *PG* 79. 181.

[175] Newman quotes from St. Cyril of Alexandria's *De Recta Fide ad Reginas*, "Antiochus speaks of Him as Saviour 'with whom yesterday in an immaculate bearing Mary travailed, the Mother of life, of beauty, of majesty, the Morning Star, &c.'" *Ath. 2* p.213.

[176] *Sermon on Our Lord* 4,1. Newman is using Gerhard Vessius, *Sancti Ephraemi Opera Omnia*, 3 vols, Rome 1589.

[177] Maximus 'the Confessor' (c. 580-66), Secretary to the Emperor and later Abbot of Chrysopolis and theologian, stressed the crucial place in history of the Incarnate Word. See *Dev* p.146.

[178] Basil of Seleucia (d. c. 458), Archbishop of Seleucia in Isauria. He supported Chalcedon and attended the Synod of Constantinople which condemned Dioscurus of Alexandria for his Eutychian views. His *Homily 42 On the Annunciation of the Most Holy Mother of God, MG* 85, 449C-452A, is thought to be by Procus. In place of Basil of Seleucia 1st ed. has "Proclus calls her 'the unsullied shell which contains the pearl of price', 'the Church's diadem, the expression of orthodoxy'".

thought," says Proclus, "and see if there be one equal or superior to the Holy Virgin, Mother of God."[179] "Hail, Mother, clad in light, of the light which sets not," says Theodotus, or some one else at Ephesus;[180] "hail, all undefiled mother of holiness; hail, most pellucid fountain of the life-giving stream." And St. Cyril too at Ephesus, "Hail, Mary, Mother of God, majestic common-treasure of the whole world, the lamp unquenchable, the crown of virginity, the sceptre of orthodoxy, the indissoluble temple, the dwelling of the Illimitable, Mother and Virgin, through whom He in the holy gospels is called blessed who cometh in the name of the Lord, ... through whom the Holy Trinity is sanctified, ... through whom Angels and Archangels rejoice, devils are put to flight, ... and the fallen creature is received up into the heavens, &c., &c."* Such is but a portion of the panegyrical language which St. Cyril used in the third Ecumenical Council.[181]

3.[182]   [68]

I must not close my review of the Catholic doctrine concerning the Blessed Virgin,[183] without directly speaking of her intercessory power, though I have incidentally made mention of it already. It is the immediate result of two truths, neither of which you dispute;—first, that "it is good and

* Opp. t. 6, p. 355.[184]

---

[179] Proclus of Constantinople qv supr. *Homily* 5, 2. *PG* 65. 717.
[180] Newman mentions his intervention at Ephesus, quoting Philippe Labbe (1607-67) *Sacrosancta Concilia ad Regiam Editionem exacta* (1671-73) p.1529, in *Dev* p.147.
[181] The Council of Ephesus (431).
[182] 1st ed. has the title heading "Her Intercessory Power".
[183] Newman revisits many of these references in his *Select Treatises of S. Athanasius in Controversy with the Arians* pp.440ff. and in *Annotations on Theological Subjects. Ath* 2 pp.204-15.
[184] *Homily 4 preached against Nestorius. PG* 77, 992.

useful," as the Council of Trent says, "suppliantly to invoke the Saints and to have recourse to their prayers;"[185] and secondly, that the Blessed Mary is singularly dear to her Son and singularly exalted in sanctity and glory. However, at the risk of becoming didactic, I will state somewhat more fully the grounds on which it rests.

To a candid pagan it must have been one of the most remarkable points of Christianity, on its first appearance, that the observance of prayer formed so vital a part of its organization; and that, though its members were scattered all over the world, and its rulers and subjects had so little opportunity of correlative action, yet they, one and all, found the solace of a spiritual intercourse and a real bond of union, in the practice of mutual intercession. Prayer indeed is the very essence of all religion; but in the heathen religions it was either public or personal; it was a state ordinance, or a selfish expedient for the attainment of certain tangible, temporal goods. Very different from this was its exercise among Christians, who were thereby knit together in one body, different, as they were, in races, ranks, and habits, distant from each other in country, and helpless amid hostile [69] populations. Yet it proved sufficient for its purpose. Christians could not correspond; they could not combine; but they could pray one for another. Even their public prayers partook of this character of intercession; for to pray for the welfare of the whole Church was in fact a prayer for all the classes of men and all the individuals of which it was composed. It was in prayer that the Church was founded. For ten days all the Apostles "persevered with one mind in prayer and supplication, with the women, and Mary the Mother of Jesus, and with his brethren."[186] Then again at Pentecost "they were all with one mind in one place; and the converts then

---

[185] Session 25 3-5 December 1563 *On Invocation, Veneration and Relics of the Saints and on Sacred Images. DS* 1821.
[186] Acts 1:14.

made are said to have "persevered in prayer."[187] And when, after a while, St. Peter was seized and put in prison with a view to his being put to death, "prayer was made without ceasing" by the Church of God for him; and, when the Angel released him, he took refuge in a house "where many were gathered together in prayer."[188]

We are so accustomed to these passages as hardly to be able to do justice to their singular significance; and they are followed up by various passages of the Apostolic Epistles. St. Paul enjoins his brethren to "pray with all prayer and supplication at all times in the Spirit, with all instance and supplication for all saints," to "pray in every place," "to make supplication, prayers, intercessions, giving of thanks, for all men." And in his own person he "ceases not to give thanks for them, commemorating them in his prayers," and "always in all his prayers making supplication for them all with joy."[189]

Now, was this spiritual bond to cease with life? or had [70] Christians similar duties to their brethren departed? From the witness of the early ages of the Church, it appears that they had; and you, and those who agree with you, would be the last to deny that they were then in the practice of praying, as for the living, so for those also who had passed into the intermediate state[190] between earth and heaven. Did the sacred communion extend further still, on to the inhabitants of heaven itself? Here too you agree with us, for you have adopted in your Volume the words of the Council of Trent which I have quoted above. But now we are brought to a higher order of thought.[191]

---

[187] Acts 2:1, 14.

[188] Acts 12:5, 12.

[189] Eph 6:18; 1 Tim 2:1; Eph 1:16; Phil 1:4.

[190] *intermediate state*: purgatory. Newman wrote Tract 79 on Purgatory in 1836 and also in §6 in Tract 90. See *Tracts for the Times* ed. Tolhurst, Leominster 2013 pp.263-332, 405-30.

[191] "The Council of Trent requires only that '*due* honour and veneration should be paid them". *En* pp.99-100.

It would be preposterous to pray for those who are already in glory; but at least they can pray for us, and we can ask their prayers, and in the Apocalypse at least Angels are introduced both sending us their blessing and offering up our prayers before the Divine Presence. We read there of an angel who "came and stood before the altar, having a golden censer;" and "there was given to him much incense, that he should offer of the prayers of all saints upon the golden altar which is before the Throne of God."[192] On this occasion, surely the Angel performed the part of a great Intercessor or Mediator above for the children of the Church Militant below. Again, in the beginning of the same book, the sacred writer goes so far as to speak of "grace and peace" coming to us, not only from the Almighty, "but from the seven Spirits that are before His throne,"[193] thus associating the Eternal with the ministers of His mercies; and this carries us on to the remarkable passage of St. Justin, one of the earliest Fathers, who, in his Apology, says, "To Him (God), and His Son who came from Him and taught us these things, and the host of the other good Angels who follow and resemble Him, and the Prophetic Spirit, we pay veneration and homage."[194] Further, in the Epistle to the Hebrews, St. Paul introduces, not only Angels, but "the spirits of the just" into the sacred communion: "Ye have come to Mount Zion, to the heavenly Jerusalem, to myriads of angels, to God the Judge of all, to the spirits of the just made perfect, and to Jesus the Mediator of the New Testament."[195] What can be meant by having "come to the spirits of the just," unless in some way or other, they do us good, whether by blessing or by aiding us? that is, in a word, to speak correctly, by praying for us, for it is surely by prayer that the creature above is able to bless and aid the creature below.

[71]

---

[192] Rev 8:3, 4.
[193] Rev 1:4.
[194] *Apologia* 1, 6. *PG* 6, 336.
[195] Heb. 12:22-4.

Intercession thus being a first principle of the Church's life, next it is certain again, that the vital force of that intercession, as an availing power, is, (according to the will of God), sanctity. This seems to be suggested by a passage of St. Paul, in which the Supreme Intercessor is said to be "the Spirit:"—"the Spirit Himself maketh intercession for us; He maketh intercession for the saints according to God."[196] And, indeed, the truth thus implied, is expressly brought out for us in other parts of Scripture, in the form both of doctrine and of example. The words of the man born blind speak the common-sense of nature:—"if any man be a worshipper of God, him He heareth."[197] And Apostles confirm them:—"the prayer of a just man availeth much,"[198] and "whatever we ask, we receive, because we keep his commandments."[199] Then, [72] as for examples, we read of the Almighty's revealing to Abraham and Moses beforehand, His purposes of wrath, in order that they by their intercessions might avert its execution.[200] To the friends of Job it was said, "My servant Job shall pray for you; his face I will accept."[201] Elias by his prayer shut and opened the heavens.[202] Elsewhere we read of "Jeremias, Moses, and Samuel;"[203] and of "Noe, Daniel, and Job,"[204] as being great mediators between God and His people. One instance is given us, which testifies the continuance of this high office beyond this life. Lazarus, in the parable, is seen in Abraham's bosom.[205] It is usual to pass over this striking passage with the remark that it is a Jewish

---

[196] Rom 8:2.
[197] John 9:31.
[198] Jas 5:16.
[199] 1 John 3:22.
[200] Gen 18:17ff. Ex 32:7ff.
[201] Job 42:8.
[202] 1 Kings 17:1.
[203] Jer 15:1.
[204] Ezek 14:14.
[205] Luke 16:24. "Father Abraham, have mercy on me, and send Lazarus to dip the end of his finger in water and cool my tongue, for I am in anguish in this flame."

mode of speech; whereas, Jewish belief or not, it is recognized and sanctioned by our Lord Himself. What do Catholics teach about the Blessed Virgin more wonderful than this? If Abraham, not yet ascended on high, had charge of Lazarus,[206] what offence is it to affirm the like of her, who was not merely as Abraham, "the friend,"[207] but was the very "Mother of God"?

It may be added, that, though, if sanctity was wanting, it availed nothing for influence with our Lord, to be one of His company, still, as the Gospel shows, He on various occasions actually did allow those who were near Him, to be the channels of introducing supplicants to Him or of gaining miracles from Him, as in the instance of the miracle of the loaves; and if on one occasion, He seems to repel His Mother, when she told Him that wine was wanting for the guests at the marriage feast, it is obvious to remark on it, that, by saying that she was then separated from Him ("What have I to do with thee?") *because* His hour was not yet come,[208] He implied, that when that hour was come, such separation would be at an end. Moreover, in fact He did at her intercession work the miracle to which her words pointed.[209]

[73]

I consider it impossible then, for those who believe the Church to be one vast body in heaven and on earth, in which every holy creature of God has his place, and of which prayer is the life, when once they recognize the sanctity and dignity of the Blessed Virgin, not to perceive immediately, that her office above is one of perpetual intercession for the faithful militant, and that our very relation to her must be that of clients to a patron, and that, in the eternal enmity which exists between the woman and the serpent, while the serpent's strength lies in being the Tempter, the weapon of the Second Eve and Mother of God is prayer.

---

[206] In the parable, Luke 16:23.
[207] 2 Chron 20:7.
[208] John 2:4.
[209] 1st ed. adds "… which she desired."

As then these ideas of her sanctity and dignity gradually penetrated the mind of Christendom, so did that of her intercessory power follow close upon them and with them. From the earliest times that mediation is symbolized in those representations of her with up-lifted hands, which, whether in plaster or in glass, are still extant in Rome,—that Church, as St. Irenæus says, with which "every Church, that is, the faithful from every side, must agree, because of its more powerful principality;"[210] "into which," as Tertullian adds, "the Apostles poured out, together with their blood, their whole doctrine."[211] As far indeed as existing documents are concerned, I know of no instance to my purpose earlier than A.D. 234, but it is a very remarkable one; and, though it has been often quoted in the controversy, an argument is not weaker for frequent use. [74]

St. Gregory Nyssen,[212]* then, a native of Cappadocia in the fourth century, relates that his namesake, Bishop of Neo-Cæsarea in Pontus, surnamed Thaumaturgus,[213] in the century preceding, shortly before he was called to the priesthood, received in a vision a Creed, which is still extant, from the Blessed Mary at the hands of St. John. The account runs thus:—He was deeply pondering theological doctrine, which the heretics of the day depraved. "In such thoughts," says his namesake of Nyssa, "he was passing the night, when one appeared, as if in human form, aged in appearance, saintly in the fashion of his garments, and very venerable both in grace of countenance and general mien. Amazed at the sight, he started from his bed, and asked who it was, and why he came;

* Vid. *Dev.*, p.386.

---

[210] *Adversus Haereses* 3.3.2. *PG* 7, 848.

[211] *De praesciptione haereticorum* 36, 1. *ML* 2, 49.

[212] Gregory of Nyssa (c. 330-95), Bishop of Nyssa in 371 and in 380 Bishop of Sebaste, younger brother of St. Basil (qv supr). He is famous for his catechetical homilies and his exegetical works.

[213] Gregory Thaumaturgus/Wonderworker (c. 213-70), Bishop of Neocaesarea, received a vision of the Blessed Virgin Mary according to Gregory of Nyssa.

but, on the other calming the perturbation of his mind with his gentle voice, and saying he had appeared to him by divine command on account of his doubts, in order that the truth of the orthodox faith might be revealed to him, he took courage at the word, and regarded him with a mixture of joy and fright. Then, on his stretching his hand straight forward and pointing with his fingers at something on one side, he followed with his eyes the extended hand, and saw another appearance opposite to the former, in shape of a woman, but more than human ... When his eyes could not bear the apparition, he heard them conversing together on the subject [75] of his doubts; and thereby not only gained a true knowledge of the faith, but learned their names, as they addressed each other by their respective appellations. And thus he is said to have heard the person in woman's shape bid 'John the Evangelist' disclose to the young man the mystery of godliness; and he answered that he was ready to comply in this matter with the wish of 'the Mother of the Lord,' and enunciated a formulary, well-turned and complete, and so vanished. He, on the other hand, immediately committed to writing that divine teaching of his mystagogue, and henceforth preached in the Church according to that form, and bequeathed to posterity, as an inheritance, that heavenly teaching, by means of which his people are instructed down to this day, being preserved from all heretical evil." He proceeds to rehearse the Creed thus given, "There is One God, Father of a Living Word," &c. Bull, after quoting it in his work on the Nicene Faith,[214] alludes to this history of its origin, and adds, "No one should think it incredible that such a providence should befall a man whose whole life was conspicuous for revelations and miracles, as all ecclesiastical writers who have mentioned him (and who has not?) witness with one voice."

---

[214] George Bull (1634-1710) Bishop of St David's who was a High Churchman and wrote *Defensio Fidei Nicaenae* in1685 and *Judicium Ecclesiae Catholiae* in 1694.

Here our Lady is represented as rescuing a holy soul from intellectual error. This leads me to a further reflection. You seem, in one place of your Volume, to object to the Antiphon, in which it is said of her, "All heresies thou hast destroyed alone."[215] Surely the truth of it is verified in this age, as in former times, and especially by the doctrine concerning her, on which I have been dwelling. She is the great exemplar of   [76] prayer in a generation, which emphatically denies the power of prayer *in toto*, which determines that fatal laws govern the universe, that there cannot be any direct communication between earth and heaven, that God cannot visit His own earth, and that man cannot influence His providence.

---

[215] Antiphon used in pre-Vatican II Office of Feasts of the Blessed Virgin Mary, Matins. 3rd Nocturn Antiphon 7. Pusey quotes this in *En* p.124.

§ 4.—*Belief of Catholics concerning the Blessed Virgin, as coloured by their Devotion to her.*[1]

I CANNOT help hoping that your own reading of the Fathers will on the whole bear me out in the above account of their teaching concerning the Blessed Virgin. Anglicans seem to me simply to overlook the strength of the argument adducible from the works of those ancient doctors in our favour; and they open the attack upon our mediæval and modern writers, careless of leaving a host of primitive opponents in their rear. I do not include you among such Anglicans, as you know what the Fathers assert; but, if so, have you not, my dear Friend, been unjust to yourself in your recent Volume, and made far too much of the differences which exist between Anglicans and us on this particular point? It is the office of an Irenicon to smoothe difficulties; I shall be pleased if I succeed in removing some of yours. Let the public judge between us here. Had you happened in your Volume to introduce your notice of our teaching about the Blessed Virgin, with a notice of the teaching of the Fathers concerning her, which you follow, ordinary men would have considered that there was not much to choose between you and us. Though you appealed ever so much, in your defence, to the authority of the "undivided Church,"[2] they would have

[78] said that you, who had such high notions of the Blessed Mary, were one of the last men who had a right to accuse us of quasi-idolatry. When they found you with the Fathers

---

[1] 1st ed. has the title heading "True and False Devotion".

[2] "It is matter of faith that the whole Church shall never be led into any formal acceptance of error by virtue of our Lord's promise; and on this ground the Church of England receives the Six Councils." *En* p.93. See also p.31.

calling her Mother of God, Second Eve, and Mother of all Living, the Mother of Life, the Morning Star, the Mystical New Heaven, the Sceptre of Orthodoxy, the All-undefiled Mother of Holiness, and the like, they would have deemed it a poor compensation for such language, that you protested against her being called a Co-redemptress[3] or a Priestess. And, if they were violent Protestants, they would not have read you with the relish and gratitude with which, as it is, they have perhaps accepted your testimony against us. Not that they would have been altogether fair in their view of you;—on the contrary I think there is a real difference between what you protest against, and what with the Fathers you hold; but unread men of the world form a broad practical judgment of the things which come before them, and they would have felt in this case that they had the same right to be shocked at you, as you have to be shocked at us;—and further, which is the point to which I am coming, they would have said, that, granting some of our modern writers go beyond the Fathers in this matter, still the line cannot be logically drawn between the teaching of the Fathers concerning the Blessed Virgin and our own. This view of the matter seems to me true and important; I do not think the line *can* be satisfactorily drawn, and to this point I shall now direct my attention.

It is impossible, I say, in a doctrine like this, to draw the line cleanly between truth and error, right and wrong. This is ever the case in concrete matters, which have life. Life in this world is motion, and involves a continual process of change. Living things grow into their perfection, into their decline, [79]

---

[3] "Some of us, who do not read Marian books, have heard now for the first time, that she was ever our 'Co-Redemptress.'" *En* p.151. Benedict XV said, "Insofar as it was in her power to satisfy the justice of God, it can rightly be said that she redeemed mankind together with Christ." Apostolic Letter *Inter Sodalicia* 22 March 1918 *AAS* 10 (1919) p.182.

into their death.[4] No rule of art will suffice to stop the operation of this natural law, whether in the material world or in the human mind. We can indeed encounter disorders, when they occur, by external antagonism and remedies; but we cannot eradicate the process itself, out of which they arise. Life has the same right to decay, as it has to wax strong. This is specially the case with great ideas. You may stifle them; or you may refuse them elbow-room; or again, you may torment them with your continual meddling; or you may let them have free course and range, and be content, instead of anticipating their excesses, to expose and restrain those excesses after they have occurred. But you have only this alternative; and for myself, I prefer much wherever it is possible, to be first generous and then just; to grant full liberty of thought, and to call it to account when abused.

If what I have been saying be true of energetic ideas generally, much more is it the case in matters of religion. Religion acts on the affections; who is to hinder these, when once roused, from gathering in their strength and running wild? They are not gifted with any connatural principle within them, which renders them self-governing, and self-adjusting. They hurry right on to their object, and often in their case it is, the more haste, the worse speed. Their object [80] engrosses them, and they see nothing else. And of all passions love is the most unmanageable; nay more, I would not give much for that love which is never extravagant, which always observes the proprieties, and can move about in perfect good taste, under all emergencies. What mother, what husband or wife, what youth or maiden in love, but says a thousand foolish things, in the way of endearment, which the speaker would be sorry for strangers to hear; yet they are not on that account unwelcome to the parties to whom they are

---

[4] Newman had written in *Dev*, "It is the rule of creation, or rather of the phenomena which it presents, that life passes on to its termination by a gradual, imperceptible course of change" p.199.

addressed. Sometimes by bad luck they are written down, sometimes they get into the newspapers; and what might be even graceful, when it was fresh from the heart, and interpreted by the voice and the countenance, presents but a melancholy exhibition when served up cold for the public eye. So it is with devotional feelings. Burning thoughts and words are as open to criticism as they are beyond it. What is abstractedly extravagant, may in particular persons be becoming and beautiful, and only fall under blame when it is found in others who imitate them. When it is formalized into meditations or exercises, it is as repulsive as love-letters in a police report. Moreover, even holy minds readily adopt and become familiar with language which they would never have originated themselves, when it proceeds from a writer who has the same objects of devotion as they have; and, if they find a stranger ridicule or reprobate supplication or praise which has come to them so recommended, they feel it as keenly as if a direct insult were offered to those to whom that homage is addressed. In the next place, what has power to stir [81] holy and refined souls is potent also with the multitude; and the religion of the multitude is ever vulgar and abnormal; it ever will be tinctured with fanaticism and superstition, while men are what they are. A people's religion is ever a corrupt religion, in spite of the provisions of Holy Church.[5] If she is to be Catholic, you must admit within her net fish of every kind, guests good and bad, vessels of gold, vessels of earth.[6] You may beat religion out of men, if you will, and then their excesses will take a different direction; but if you make use of religion to improve them, they will make use of religion to

---

[5] Newman had preached in 1832, "They who are not superstitious without the Gospel, will not be religious with it: and I would that even in us, who have the Gospel, there were more of superstition than there is; for much it is to be feared that our security about ourselves arises from defect in self-knowledge rather than in fullness of faith, and that we appropriate to ourselves promises which we cannot read." *US* p.118.

[6] Matt 13:47; 2 Tim 2:20.

corrupt it. And then you will have effected that compromise of which our countrymen report so unfavourably from abroad:—a high grand faith and worship which compels their admiration, and puerile absurdities among the people which excite their contempt.

Nor is it any safeguard against these excesses in a religious system, that the religion is based upon reason, and develops into a theology. Theology both uses logic and baffles it; and thus logic acts both for the protection and for the perversion of religion. Theology is occupied with supernatural matters, and is ever running into mysteries, which reason can neither explain nor adjust. Its lines of thought come to an abrupt termination, and to pursue them or to complete them is to plunge down the abyss. But logic blunders on, forcing its way, as it can, through thick darkness and ethereal mediums. The Arians went ahead with logic for their directing principle,[7] and so lost the truth; on the other [82] hand, St. Augustine[8] intimates that, if we attempt to find and tie together the ends of lines which run into infinity we shall only succeed in contradicting ourselves, when, in his Treatise on the Holy Trinity,[9] he is unable to find the logical reason for not speaking of three Gods as well as of One, and of one Person in the Godhead as well as of Three.[10] I do not mean to say that logic cannot be used to set right its own error, or that in the hands of an able disputant it may not trim the balance of truth.[11] This was done at the Councils of Antioch and Nicæa, on occasion of the heresies of Paulus and Arius.[12] But

---

[7] "The Arian school has already been attributed to Antioch as its birth-place and its character determined to be what we may call Aristotelico-Judaic." *Ari* p.109.

[8] His five books on the Trinity date from 399-419.

[9] *De Trinitate libri quindecim.*

[10] *On the Trinity* I 4,7 *ML* 42. 824.

[11] 1st ed. has "in the hands of and able disputant...the balance of truth may not be lessened."

[12] Paul of Samosata (3rd century) became Bishop of Antioch in 260 and was condemned at the Synod of Antioch and deposed form his see in 268. Arius (c.250-

84

such a process is circuitous and elaborate; and is conducted by means of minute subtleties which will give it the appearance of a game of skill in matters too grave and practical to deserve a mere scholastic treatment. Accordingly St. Augustine, in the Treatise above mentioned, does no more than simply lay it down that the statements in question are heretical, that is to say there are three Gods is Tritheism, and to say there is but one Person, Sabellianism.[13] That is, good sense and a large view of truth are the correctives of his logic. And thus we have arrived at the final resolution of the whole matter, for good sense and a large view of truth are rare gifts; whereas all men are bound to be devout, and most men busy themselves in arguments and inferences.[14]

Now let me apply what I have been saying to the teaching of the Church on the subject of the Blessed Virgin. I have to recur to a subject of so sacred a nature, that, writing as I am for publication, I need the apology of my purpose for venturing to pursue it. I say then, when once we have mastered the idea, that Mary bore, suckled, and handled the [83] Eternal in the form of a child, what limit is conceivable to the rush and flood of thoughts which such a doctrine involves? What awe and surprise must attend upon the knowledge, that a creature has been brought so close to the Divine Essence? It was the creation of a new idea and of a new sympathy, of a new faith and worship, when the holy Apostles announced that God had become incarnate; then a supreme love and devotion to Him became possible, which seemed hopeless before that revelation. This was the first consequence of their preaching. But, besides this, a second range of thoughts was

---

336) was a priest in Alexandria and through the instrumentality of Athanasius was condemned by the Council of Nicaea.

[13] "The Sabellians agreed with the Arians, as far as words went, in considering the Logos as a creative attribute, but some of them held that the Logos actually took flesh, escaped the mystery of God subsisting in Two Persons only by falling into the heterodox notion that his nature was compounded of substance and attribute." *Ath* 2 pp.255-6.

[14] 1st ed. has "… where most men think they can argue and conclude."

opened on mankind, unknown before, and unlike any other, as soon as it was understood that that Incarnate God had a mother. The second idea is perfectly distinct from the former, and does not interfere with it. He is God made low, she is a woman made high. I scarcely like to use a familiar illustration on the subject of the Blessed Virgin's dignity among created beings, but it will serve to explain what I mean, when I ask you to consider the difference of feeling, with which we read the respective histories of Maria Theresa and the Maid of Orleans;[15] or with which the middle and lower classes of a nation regard a first minister of the day who has come of an aristocratic house, and one who has risen from the ranks. May God's mercy keep me from the shadow of a thought, dimming the purity or blunting the keenness of that love of Him, which is our sole happiness and our sole salvation! But surely when He became man, He brought home to us His [84] incommunicable attributes with a distinctiveness, which precludes the possibility of our lowering Him merely by our exalting a creature. He alone has an entrance into our soul, reads our secret thoughts, speaks to our heart, applies to us spiritual pardon and strength. On Him we solely depend. He alone is our inward life; He not only regenerates us, but (to use the words appropriated[16] to a higher mystery) *semper gignit*;[17] He is ever renewing our new birth and our heavenly sonship. In this sense He may be called, as in nature, so in grace, our real Father. Mary is only our mother by divine appointment[18], given us from the Cross;[19] her presence is above, not on earth; her office is external, not within us. Her name is not heard in the administration of the Sacraments.

---

[15] Maria Theresa (1717-80) ruler of the Holy Roman Empire and daughter of Charles VI. The Maid of Orléans was Joan of Arc (1412-31), the shepherdess and daughter of a peasant who helped in the relief of Orléans during the Hundred Years' War.

[16] 1st ed. has "alluded to"

[17] 'continually brings to birth'. Augustine uses the expression in reference to the process of the Son from the Father. *De Trinitate* 2. 5 n7.

[18] 1st ed. has "only our adopted mother".

[19] "Woman, behold your mother... [son] behold your mother." John 19: 26-7.

Her work is not one of ministration towards us; her power is indirect. It is her prayers that avail, and her prayers are effectual by the *fiat* of Him who is our all in all. Nor need she hear us by any innate power, or any personal gift; but by His manifestation to her of the prayers which we make to her. When Moses was on the Mount, the Almighty told him of the idolatry of his people at the foot of it,[20] in order that he might intercede for them; and thus it is the Divine Presence which is the intermediating Power by which we reach her and she reaches us.

Woe is me, if even by a breath I sully these ineffable truths! but still, without prejudice to them, there is, I say, another range of thought quite distinct from them, incommensurate with them, of which the Blessed Virgin is the centre. If we placed our Lord in that centre, we should [85] only be dragging Him from His throne, and making Him an Arian kind of a God;[21] that is, no God at all. He who charges us with making Mary a divinity, is thereby denying the divinity of Jesus. Such a man does not know what divinity is. Our Lord cannot pray for us, as a creature prays, as Mary prays; He cannot inspire those feelings which a creature inspires. To her belongs, as being a creature, a natural claim on our sympathy and familiarity, in that she is nothing else than our fellow. She is our pride,—in the poet's words, "Our tainted nature's solitary boast".[22] We look to her without any fear, any remorse, any consciousness that she is able to read us, judge us, punish us. Our heart yearns towards that pure Virgin, that gentle Mother, and our congratulations follow her, as she rises from Nazareth and Ephesus, through the choirs of angels, to her throne on high, so weak, yet so strong; so delicate, yet so glorious; so modest and yet so mighty. She has sketched for us her own portrait in the Magnificat. "He

---

[20] Ex 32:7ff.

[21] One who is less than God although reflecting his likeness was the teaching of Arius. See above.

[22] Wordsworth *The Virgin* in Part II of his *Ecclesiastical Sonnets* 1822.

hath regarded the low estate of His hand-maid; for, behold, from henceforth all generations shall call me blessed. He hath put down the mighty from their seat; and hath exalted the humble. He hath filled the hungry with good things, and the rich he hath sent empty away."[23] I recollect the strange emotion which took by surprise men and women, young and old, when, at the Coronation of our present Queen, they gazed on the figure of one so like a child, so small, so tender, so shrinking,[24] who had been exalted to so great an inheritance and so vast a rule, who was such a contrast in her own person to the solemn pageant which centred in her. Could it be otherwise with the spectators, if they had human affection? And did not the All-wise know the human heart when He took to Himself a Mother? did He not anticipate our emotion at the sight of such an exaltation in one so simple and so lowly? If He had not meant her to exert that wonderful influence in His Church, which she has in the event exerted, I will use a bold word, He it is who has perverted us. If she is not to attract our homage, why did He make her solitary in her greatness amid His vast creation? If it be idolatry in us to let our affections respond to our faith, He would not have made her what she is, or He would not have told us that He had so made her; but, far from this, He has sent His Prophet to announce to us, "A Virgin shall conceive and bear a Son, and they shall call His name Emmanuel,"[25] and we have the same warrant for hailing her as God's Mother, as we have for adoring Him as God.

Christianity is eminently an objective religion. For the most part it tells us of persons and facts in simple words, and leaves that announcement to produce its effect on such hearts as are prepared to receive it. This at least is its general

[86]

---

[23] Luke 1:48, 52-3.
[24] Victoria was 18 in 1837 and only five feet tall.
[25] Matt 1:23 (quoting Is 7:14.)

character; and Butler recognizes it as such in his Analogy[26], when speaking of the Second and Third Persons of the Holy Trinity:— "The internal worship," he says, "to the Son and Holy Ghost is no farther matter of pure revealed command than as the relations they stand in to us are matters of pure revelation; for the relations being known, the obligations to such internal worship are *obligations of reason arising out of those relations themselves*."* It is in this way that the revealed doctrine of the Incarnation exerted a stronger and a broader influence on Christians, as they more and more apprehended and mastered its meaning and its bearings. It is contained in the brief and simple declaration of St. John, "The Word was made flesh;"[27] but it required century after century to spread it out in its fulness, and to imprint it energetically on the worship and practice of the Catholic people as well as on their faith. Athanasius[28] was the first and the great teacher of it. He collected together the inspired notices scattered through David, Isaias, St. Paul, and St. John, and he engraved indelibly upon the imaginations of the faithful, as had never been before, that man is God, and God is man, that in Mary they meet, and that in this sense Mary is the centre of all things. He added nothing to what was known before, nothing to the popular and zealous faith that her Son was God; he has left behind him in his works no such definite passages about her as those of St. Irenæus[29] or St. Epiphanius;[30] but he

[87]

* Vid. Essay on Doctr. Dev., p. 50.

---

[26] Joseph Butler (1692-1752) became Bishop of Durham in 1750. He was the author of *The Analogy of Religion Natural and Revealed to the Constitution and the Course of Nature* (1736) pp. 143-4.

[27] John 1:14.

[28] Athanasius, see supra. "The Word begottten of the Father from on high, inexpressibly, inexplicably, incomprehensibly and eternally, is He that is born in time here below, of the Virgin Mary, the Mother of God." *De incarnatione Dei Verbi et contra Arianos.* 8 *PG* 26, 996.

[29] St. Irenaeus, see supra.

[30] St. Epiphanius, see supra.

brought the circumstances of the Incarnation home to men's minds, by the multiform evolutions of his analysis, and thereby secured it to us for ever from perversion. Still, however, there was much to be done; we have no proof that [88] Athanasius[31] himself had any special devotion to the Blessed Virgin; but he laid the foundations on which that devotion was to rest, and thus noiselessly and without strife, as the first Temple was built in the Holy City, she grew up into her inheritance, and was "established in Sion and her power was in Jerusalem."[32]

---

[31] St. Athanasius, see supra.
[32] Sir 24:15.

§ 5.—*Anglican Misconceptions and Catholic Excesses in Devotion to the Blessed Virgin*[1]

SUCH was the origin of that august *cultus* which has been paid to the Blessed Mary for so many centuries in the East and in the West. That in times and places it has fallen into abuse, that it has even become a superstition, I do not care to deny; for, as I have said above, the same process which brings to maturity carries on to decay, and things that do not admit of abuse have very little life in them.[2] This of course does not excuse such excesses, or justify us in making light of them, when they occur. I have no intention of doing so as regards the particular instances which you bring against us, though but a few words will suffice for what I need say about them:—before doing so, however, I am obliged to make three or four introductory remarks in explanation.[3]

1. I have almost anticipated my first remark already. It is this: that the height of our offending in our devotion to the Blessed Virgin would not look so great in your Volume as it does, had you not deliberately placed yourself on lower ground than your own feelings towards her would have spontaneously prompted you to take. I have no doubt you had some good reason for adopting this course, but I do not know [90] it; what I do know is, that, for the Fathers' sake who so exalt her, you really do love and venerate her, though you do not

---

[1] 1st ed. has title heading "Explanations".

[2] Newman uses similar words in *Dev*: "Such are the superstitions which pervade a population, like some ingrained dye or inveterate odour, and which at length come to an end, because nothing lasts for ever but which run no course and have no history; such was the established paganism of classical times" p.205.

[3] 1st ed. omits "in explanation".

evidence it in your book. I am glad then in this place to insist on a fact which will lead those among us, who know you not, to love you from their love of her, in spite of what you refuse to give her; and lead Anglicans, on the other hand, who do know you, to think better of us, who refuse her nothing, when they reflect that, if you come short of us, you do not actually go against us in your devotion to her.

2. As you revere the Fathers, so you revere the Greek Church; and here again we have a witness on our behalf, of which you must be aware as fully as we are, and of which you must really mean to give us the benefit. In proportion as the Greek ritual is known to the religious public, that knowledge will take off the edge of the surprise of Anglicans at the sight of our devotions to our Lady. It must weigh with them, when they discover that we can enlist on our side in this controversy those "seventy millions" (I think they do so consider them) of Orientals, who are separated from our communion. Is it not a very pregnant fact, that the Eastern Churches, so independent of us, so long separated from the West, so jealous for Antiquity, should even surpass us in their exaltation of the Blessed Virgin? That they go further than we do is sometimes denied, on the ground that the Western devotion towards her is brought out into system, and the Eastern is not; yet this only means really, that the Latins have more mental activity, more strength of intellect, less of [91] routine, less of mechanical worship among them, than the Greeks. We are able, better than they, to give an account of what we do; and we seem to be more extreme, merely because we are more definite.[4] But, after all, what have the Latins done so bold, as that substitution of the name of Mary for the Name of Jesus at the end of the collects and petitions in the Breviary, nay, in the Ritual and Liturgy? Not merely in local or popular, and in semi-authorized devotions, which are the kind of sources that supply you with your matter of

---

[4] See Note IV pp.153-64. Omitted in 1st ed.

accusation against us, but in the formal prayers of the Greek Eucharistic Service, petitions are offered, not in "the name of Jesus Christ," but in that "of the Theotocos."[5] Such a phenomenon, in such a quarter, I think ought to make Anglicans merciful towards those writers among ourselves, who have been excessive in singing the praises of the Deipara. To make a rule of substituting Mary with all Saints for Jesus in the public service, has more "Mariolatry" in it, than to alter the Te Deum to her honour in private devotion.[*]

3. And thus I am brought to a third remark, supplemental to your accusation of us. Two large views, as I have said above, are opened upon our devotional thoughts in Christianity; the one centering in the Son of Mary, the other in the Mother of Jesus. Neither need obscure the other; and in the Catholic Church, as a matter of fact, neither does. I wish you had either frankly allowed this in your Volume, or proved the contrary. I wish, when you report that "a certain proportion" of Catholics, "it has been ascertained by those [92] who have inquired, do," in their devotions, "stop short in her," p. 107,[6] that you had added your belief, that the case was far otherwise with the great bulk of Catholics. Might I not have expected such an avowal?[7] May I not, without sensitiveness, be somewhat pained at the omission? From mere Protestants, indeed, I expect nothing better. They content themselves with saying that our devotions to our Lady *must necessarily* throw our Lord into the shade; and thereby they relieve themselves of a great deal of trouble.

* Vid. Note IV. infra.

---

[5] The *Penitential Troparia* in Evening Prayer ends "Open unto us the door of your loving kindness, O blessed Mother of God; in that we set our hope on thee, we may not go astray; but through thee, may we be delivered from all adversities. For thou art the salvation of all Christian people." *Manual of Eastern Prayers* SPCK 10th ed. London 1983 p.13.

[6] Pusey prefaces this by saying that in India Roman Catholic Churches are called "Mary-Churches" and some Catholics "confine their prayers to the Blessed Virgin.".

[7] 1st ed. omits "such an avowal".

Then they catch at any stray fact which countenances or seems to countenance their prejudice. Now I say plainly, I never will defend or screen any one from your just rebuke, who, through false devotion to Mary, forgets Jesus. But I should like the fact to be proved first; I cannot hastily admit it. There is this broad fact the other way;—that, if we look through Europe, we shall find, on the whole, that just those nations and countries have lost their faith in the divinity of Christ, who have given up devotion to His Mother, and that those on the other hand, who had been foremost in her honour, have retained their orthodoxy. Contrast, for instance, the Calvinists with the Greeks, or France with the North of Germany, or the Protestant and Catholic communions in Ireland. As to England, it is scarcely doubtful what would be the state of its Established Church, if the Liturgy and Articles were not an integral part of its Establishment; and, when men bring so grave a charge against us, as is implied in your [93] Volume, they cannot be surprised if we in turn say hard things of Anglicanism.* In the Catholic Church Mary has shown herself, not the rival, but the minister of her Son; she has protected Him, as in His infancy, so in the whole history of the Religion. There is then a plain historical truth in Dr.

---

* I have spoken more on this subject in my Essay on Development, p. 488, "Nor does it avail to object, that, in this contrast of devotional exercises, the human is sure to supplant the Divine, from the infirmity of our nature; for, I repeat, the question is one of fact, whether it has done so. And next, it must be asked, *whether the character of Protestant devotion towards our Lord, has been that of worship at all*; and not rather such as we pay to an excellent human being ... Carnal minds will ever create a carnal worship for themselves; and to forbid them the service of the saints, will have no tendency to teach them the worship of God. Moreover, ... great and constant as is the devotion which the Catholic pays to St. Mary, it has a special province, and *has far more connexion with the public services and the festive aspect of Christianity*, and with certain extraordinary offices which she holds, *than with what is strictly personal and primary* in religion." Our late Cardinal, on my reception, singled out to me this last sentence, for the expression of his especial approbation.

94

Faber's words, which you quote to condemn, "Jesus is obscured, because Mary is kept in the background."[8]

This truth, exemplified in history, might also be abundantly illustrated, did my space admit, from the lives and writings of holy men in modern times. Two of them, St. Alfonso Liguori[9] and the Blessed Paul of the Cross, for all their notorious devotion to the Mother, have shown their supreme love of her Divine Son, in the names which they have given to their respective Congregations, viz. that "of the Redeemer," and that "of the Cross and Passion."[10] However, I will do no more than refer to an apposite passage in the Italian translation of the work of a French Jesuit, Fr. Nepveu, "Christian Thoughts for every Day in the Year," which was [94] recommended to the friend who went with me to Rome,[11] by the same Jesuit Father there,[12] with whom, as I have already said, I stood myself in such intimate relations; I believe it is a fair specimen of the teaching of our spiritual books.

"The love of Jesus Christ is the most sure pledge of our future happiness, and the most infallible token of our predestination. Mercy towards the poor, devotion to the Holy Virgin, are very sensible tokens of predestination; nevertheless they are not absolutely infallible; but one cannot have a sincere and constant love of Jesus Christ, without being predestinated ... The destroying angel, which bereaved

---

[8] *En* p.118.

[9] St Alphonsus Liguori (1696-1787), a Neapolitan, became a lawyer aged seventeen but joined the Oratory and was ordained in 1726. He founded the Congregation of the Most Holy Redeemer or Redemptorists in 1732, described as 'the Salvation Army of the Church'. Famous as a moral theologian, he published his *Theologia Moralis* in 1748. He is also the author of *The Glories of Mary* (1750). Newman would "hold by his numerous spiritual books but I do not accept and follow views which he expresses about the Blessed Virgin." To Pusey 10 November 1865 *LD* 22 p.100.

[10] St Paul of the Cross (1694-1775) was the founder of the Order of the Cross and Passion or Passionists, canonized in 1867. Blessed Dominic Barberi (1792-1849) who received Newman into the Catholic Church in 1845 was a Passionist.

[11] François Nepveu SJ (1639-1708), *Thoughts or Christian Reflections for every day of the Year* (1702).

[12] Giacomo Mazio SJ (1800-51). See C. Michael Shea *Newman's Early Roman Catholic Legacy 1845-1854* Oxford University Press 2017 pp.136ff.

the houses of the Egyptians of their first-born, had respect to all the houses which were marked with the blood of the Lamb."[13]

And it is also exemplified, as I verily believe, not only in formal and distinctive Confessions, not only in books intended for the educated class, but also in the personal religion of the Catholic populations. When strangers are so unfavourably impressed with us, because they see Images of our Lady in our churches, and crowds flocking about her, they forget that there is a Presence within the sacred walls, infinitely more awful, which claims and obtains from us a worship transcendently different from any devotion we pay to her. That devotion to her might indeed tend to idolatry, if it were encouraged in Protestant churches, where there is nothing higher than it to attract the worshipper: but all the images that a Catholic church ever contained, all the Crucifixes at its Altars brought together, do not so affect its [95] frequenters, as the lamp which betokens the presence or absence there of the Blessed Sacrament.[14] Is not this so certain, so notorious, that on some occasions it has been even brought as a charge against us, that we are irreverent in church,[15] when what seemed to the objector to be irreverence was but the necessary change of feeling, which came over those who were in it, on their knowing that their Lord was no longer there, but away?[16]

The Mass again conveys to us the same lesson of the sovereignty of the Incarnate Son; it is a return to Calvary, and Mary is scarcely named in it.[17] Hostile visitors enter our churches on Sunday at midday, the time of the Anglican

---

[13] Ex 12:13.

[14] "A special lamp which indicates and honours the presence of Christ is to shine continually before a tabernacle in which the Most Holy Eucharist is reserved." *CCC* 940.

[15] See the picture painted by Newman in *Diff* 1 pp. 284-7 and *LG* p.176.

[16] 1st ed. "their Lord was away."

[17] At the time Newman was writing the name of Mary occurred as an Offertory Prayer and in the *Communicantes* during the Canon.

Service. They are surprised to see the High Mass perhaps poorly attended, and a body of worshippers leaving the music and the mixed multitude who may be lazily fulfilling their obligation, for the silent or the informal devotions which are offered at an Image of the blessed Virgin. They may be tempted, with one of your informants, to call such a temple, not a "Jesus church," but a "Mary church". But, if they understood our ways, they would know that we begin the day with our Lord and then go on to His Mother. It is early in the morning that religious persons go to Mass and Communion. The High Mass, on the other hand, is the festive celebration of the day, not the special devotional service; nor is there any reason why those who have been at low Mass already, should not at that hour proceed to ask the intercession of the Blessed Virgin for themselves and all that is dear to them.

Communion, again, which is given in the morning,[18] is a solemn unequivocal act of faith in the Incarnate God, if any can be such; and the most gracious of admonitions, did we need one, of His sovereign and sole right to possess us. I knew a lady, who on her deathbed was visited by an excellent Protestant friend. The latter, with great tenderness for her soul's welfare, asked her whether her prayers to the Blessed Virgin did not, at that awful hour, lead to forgetfulness of her Saviour. "Forget Him?" she replied with surprise, "Why, He was just now here." She had been receiving Him in communion. When then, my dear Pusey, you read anything extravagant in praise of our Lady, is it not charitable to ask, even while you condemn it in itself, did the author write nothing else? Had he written on the Blessed Sacrament? had he given up "all for Jesus?"[19] I recollect some lines, the happiest, I think, which that author wrote, which bring out strikingly the reciprocity, which I am dwelling on, of the respective devotions to Mother and Son:—

[96]

---

[18] At that time there was a required fast from midnight.

[19] *All for Jesus* by Fr. Faber was published in 1853.

"But scornful men have coldly said
    Thy love was leading me from God;
And yet in this I did but tread
    The very path my Saviour trod.

"They know but little of thy worth
    Who speak these heartless words to me;
For what did Jesus love on earth
    One half so tenderly as thee?

"Get me the grace to love thee more;
    Jesus will give, if thou wilt plead;
And, Mother, when life's cares are o'er,
    Oh, I shall love thee then indeed.

"Jesus, when His three hours were run,
    bequeath'd thee from the Cross to me;
And oh! how can I love thy Son,
    Sweet Mother, if I love not thee."[20]

[97]   4. Thus we are brought from the consideration of the sentiments themselves, of which you complain, to the persons who wrote, and the places where they wrote them. I wish you had been led, in this part of your work, to that sort of careful labour which you have employed in so masterly a way in your investigation of the circumstances of the definition of the Immaculate Conception.[21] In the latter case you have catalogued the bishops who wrote to the Holy See, and analyzed their answers. Had you in like manner discriminated and located the Marian writers as you call them, and observed the times, places, and circumstances of their works, I think, they would not, when brought together, have had their present startling effect on the reader. As it is, they inflict a vague alarm upon the mind, as when one hears

---

[20] *Mother of Mercy, Day by Day* was Fr. Faber's Hymn for Good Friday.
[21] *En* pp.119-53, 351-409.

a noise, and does not know whence it comes and what it means. Some of your authors, I know are Saints; all, I suppose, are spiritual writers and holy men; but the majority are of no great celebrity, even if they have any kind of weight. Suarez[22] has no business among them at all, for, when he says that no one is saved without the Blessed Virgin, he is speaking not of devotion to her, but of her intercession. The greatest name is St. Alfonso Liguori; but it never surprises me to read anything extraordinary in the devotions of a saint. Such men are on a level very different from our own, and we cannot understand them. I hold this to be an important canon in the Lives of the Saints, according to the words of the Apostle, "The spiritual man judges all things, and he himself is judged of no one."[23] But we may refrain from judging, without proceeding to imitate. I hope it is not disrespectful to so great a servant of God to say, that I never have read his Glories of Mary;[24] but here I am speaking generally of all Saints, whether I know them or not;—and I say that they are beyond us, and that we must use them as patterns, not as copies. As to his practical directions, St. Alfonso wrote them for Neapolitans, whom he knew, and we do not know. Other writers whom you quote, as De Salazar,[25] are too ruthlessly logical to be safe or pleasant guides in the delicate matters of devotion. As to De Montford[26] and Oswald,[27] I never even

[98]

---

[22] See supra.

[23] 1 Cor 2:15.

[24] See St. Alphonsus Liguori supra.

[25] De Salazar. Ferdiando Chirinos de Salazar (1575-1646), Jesuit theologian, author of A *Defence on behalf of the Immaculate Conception of the Blessed Virgin* (1618) in which he says, "She acted as mediatrix with the Mediator... The salvation of the world was granted by the Eternal Father, not only to Christ, but also to the Virgin." Ch. 19, nn.3-7.

[26] Louis Grignion de Montfort (1673-1716), priest and founder of the Company of Mary and author of *True Devotion to the Blessed Virgin* (1712) translated into English by Fr. Faber in 1863 (his preface is quoted in *Eirenicon* p.118). Newman writes to Pusey that Faber's translation "is *very* incorrect. He did it when he was too near death to be able to be accurate." 25 September 1866, *LD* 22 p.294.

[27] Oswald Johann Heinrich Sigismund Oswald.(1817-1903) See supr. He argues in his *Dogmatische Mariologie* (Paderborn 1850) that Mary is a priestess, "Ascending

met with their names, till I saw them in your book; the bulk of our laity, not to say of our clergy, perhaps know them little better than I do. Nor did I know till I learnt it from your Volume, that there were two Bernardines. St. Bernardine of Sienna,[28] I knew of course, and knew too that he had a burning love for our Lord. But about the other, "Bernardine de Bustis,"[29] I was quite at fault. I find from the Protestant Cave,[30] that he, as well as his namesake, made himself also conspicuous for his zeal for the Holy Name, which is much to the point here. "With such devotion was he carried away," says Cave, "for the bare Name of Jesus, (which, by a new device of Bernardine of Sienna, had lately begun to receive divine honours,) that he was urgent with Innocent VIII[31] to assign it a day and rite in the Calendar."

One thing, however, is clear about all these writers; that not one of them is an Englishman. I have gone through your book, and do not find one English name among the various [99] authors to whom you refer, except of course the name of the author whose lines I have been quoting, and who, great as are his merits, cannot, for the reasons I have given in the opening of my Letter* be considered a representative of English Catholic devotion. Whatever these writers may have said or not said, whatever they may have said harshly, and whatever

---

* Supra p. 22.

the ladder to heaven leads first to the Mother; from the Mother to the Son, from the Son to the Mother. We might, indeed, passing over the lowest Court, turn direct to the Son; but we can also spring over the middle step and go direct to the Godhead." p.58

[28] St Bernardino of Sienna (1380-1444), Vicar General of the Observant Franciscans in 1437. He had a great devotion to the Holy Name of Jesus in his preaching and of the *written* name of Jesus in the form of the monogram HIS. He was also a promoter of Mary as the Mediatrix of graces merited by her son.

[29] Bernardine de Bustis or Busti (1450-1513), Milanese Catholic theologian and Mariologist. He is the author of *Corona della Vergine Maria*. See *Miscellanea bibiliographica in memoria di Don Tommaso Accurti R*ome 1947 pp.103-24.

[30] William Cave (1637-1713), ecclesiastical historian and patristic scholar.

[31] Innocent VIII was Pope 1484-92. The feast was put in the Church's calendar in 1721 and is now celebrated on January 3rd.

capable of fair explanation, still they are foreigners; we are not answerable for their particular devotions; and as to themselves, I am glad to be able to quote the beautiful words which you use about them in your letter to the *Weekly Register* of November 25th last. "I do not presume," you say, "to prescribe to Italians or Spaniards, what they shall hold, or how they shall express their pious opinions; and least of all did I think of imputing to any of the writers whom I quoted that they took from our Lord any of the love which they gave to His Mother." In these last words too you have supplied one of the omissions in your Volume which I noticed above.[32]

5. Now then we come to England itself, which after all, in the matter of devotion, alone concerns you and me; for though doctrine is one and the same everywhere, devotions, as I have already said, are matters of the particular time and the particular country. I suppose we owe it to the national good sense, that English Catholics have been protected from the extravagances which are elsewhere to be found. And we owe it also to the wisdom and moderation of the Holy See, which, in giving us the pattern for our devotion, as well as the rule of our faith, has never indulged in those curiosities [100] of thought which are both so attractive to undisciplined imaginations and so dangerous to grovelling hearts. In the case of our own common people I think such a forced style of devotion would be simply unintelligible; as to the educated, I doubt whether it can have more than an occasional or temporary influence. If the Catholic faith spreads in England, these peculiarities will not spread with it. There is a healthy devotion to the Blessed Mary, and there is an artificial; it is possible to love her as a Mother, to honour her as a Virgin, to seek her as a Patron, and to exalt her as a

---

[32] See Letter from Pusey to Newman 9th December 1865 *Liddon* vol 4 p.131.

Queen, without any injury to solid piety and Christian good sense:—I cannot help calling this the English style. I wonder whether you find anything to displease you in the Garden of the Soul, the Key of Heaven, the Vade Mecum, the Golden Manual, or the Crown of Jesus.[33] These are the books to which Anglicans ought to appeal, who would be fair to us in this matter. I do not observe anything in them which goes beyond the teaching of the Fathers, except so far as devotion goes beyond doctrine.

There is one collection of Devotions besides, of the highest authority, which has been introduced from abroad of late years. It consists of prayers of very various kinds which have been indulgenced by the Popes; and it commonly goes by the name of the *Raccolta*.[34] As that word suggests, the language of many of the prayers is Italian, while others are in Latin. This circumstance is unfavourable to a translation, which, however skilful, must ever savour of the words and idioms of the original; but, passing over this necessary disadvantage, I consider there is hardly a clause in the goodsized volume in question which even the sensitiveness of English Catholicism would wish changed. Its anxious observance of doctrinal exactness is almost a fault. It seems afraid of using the words "give me," "make me," in its addresses to the Blessed Virgin, which are as natural to adopt in speaking to her, as in addressing a parent or friend. Surely we do not disparage Divine Providence when we say that we are indebted to our parents for our life, or when we ask their blessing; we do not show any atheistical leaning, because we say that a man's recovery must be left to nature, or that nature supplies brute animals with instincts. In like manner it seems to me a simple purism, to insist upon minute accuracy of

[101]

---

[33] *The Garden of the Soul* by Richard Challoner qv supr. (1740). *The Key of Heaven* by John Milner, qv supr. (1752). *The Catholic's Vade Mecum* (1851) by Anon. *The Golden Manual* by Anon (1850). *The Crown of Jesus* by Anon (1862). See *Dev* p.503 where Newman refers to Catholic devotional books.
[34] qv supra.

expression in devotional and popular writings.[35] However, the *Raccolta*, as coming from responsible authority, for the most part observes it. It commonly uses the phrases "gain for us by thy prayers," "obtain for us," "pray to Jesus for me," "speak for me, Mary," "carry thou our prayers," "ask for us grace;" "intercede for the people of God," and the like, marking thereby with great emphasis that she is nothing more than an Advocate, and not a source of mercy. Nor do I recollect in this book more than one or two ideas to which you would be likely to raise an objection. The strongest of these is found in the Novena[36] before her Nativity, in which, *apropos* of her Birth, we pray that she "would come down again, and be reborn spiritually in our souls;"—but it will occur to you that St. Paul speaks of his wish to impart to his converts, "not only the gospel, but his own soul;"[37] and writing to the Corinthians, he says he has "begotten them by the gospel,"[38] and to Philemon, that he had "begotten Onesimus, in his bonds;"[39] whereas St. James, with greater accuracy of expression, says "of His own will hath God begotten us with the word of truth."[40] Again, we find the petitioner saying to the Blessed Mary, "In thee I place all my hope;" but this is explained by another passage, "Thou art my best hope after Jesus." Again, we read elsewhere, "I would I had a greater love for thee, since to love thee is a great mark of predestination;" but the prayer goes on, "Thy Son deserves of us an immeasurable love; pray that I may have this grace, a great love for Jesus," and further on, "I covet no good of the earth, but to love my God alone."

[102]

---

[35] "The Catholic Church ... allows no liberty of dissent from her decisions... her tone is different in the sanction she gives to devotions, as they are of a subjective and personal nature." *VM* I p.lxxv.

[36] A nine day series of prayers, suggested by the nine months from the Incarnation to the birth of Jesus.

[37] 1 Thess 2:8.

[38] 1 Cor 4:15.

[39] Philem 10.

[40] Jas 1:18.

Then again, as to the lessons which our Catholics receive, whether by catechising or instruction, you would find nothing in our received manuals to which you would not assent, I am quite sure. Again, as to preaching, a standard book was drawn up three centuries ago, to supply matter for the purpose to the parochial clergy. You incidentally mention, p. 153, that the comment of Cornelius à Lapide[41] on Scripture is "a repertorium[42] for sermons;" but I never heard of this work being so used, nor indeed can it, because of its size. The work provided for the purpose by the Church is the "Catechism of the Council of Trent,"[43] and nothing extreme about our Blessed Lady is propounded there. On the whole I am sanguine that you will come to the conclusion, that [103] Anglicans may safely trust themselves to us English Catholics, as regards any devotions to the Blessed Virgin which might be required of them over and above the rule of the Council of Trent.

6. And, now at length coming to the statements, not English, but foreign, which offend you in works written in her honour, I will allow that I like some of those which you quote as little as you do. I will frankly say that, when I read them in your volume, they affected me with grief and almost anger; for they seemed to me to ascribe to the Blessed Virgin a power of "searching the reins and hearts,"[44] which is the attribute of God alone; and I said to myself, how can we any longer prove our Lord's divinity from Scripture, if those cardinal passages which invest Him with divine prerogatives, after all invest Him with nothing beyond what His Mother shares with Him? And how, again, is there anything of incommunicable greatness in His death and passion, if He

---

[41] Cornelius a Lapide (1567-1637). Cornelis Cornelissen van den Steen, Flemish Jesuit, Professor of exegesis in Rome and author of biblical commentaries.
[42] catalogue or inventory
[43] *Catechism of the Council of Trent* or *Roman Catechism* issued in 1556. Part I Ch. 4 Question 9; Part 4 Ch. 6 Question 8.
[44] "For the righteous God trieth the hearts and reins." Ps 7:9.

who was alone in the garden, alone upon the cross, alone in the resurrection, after all is not alone, but shared His solitary work with His Blessed Mother,—with her to whom, when He entered on His ministry, He said for our instruction, not as grudging her her proper glory, "Woman, what have I to do with thee?"[45] And then again, if I hate those perverse sayings so much, how much more must she, in proportion to her love of Him? and how do we show our love for her, by wounding her in the very apple of her eye? This I felt and feel; but then on the other hand I have to observe that these strange words after all are but few in number, out of the many passages you cite; that most of them exemplify what I said above about the difficulty of determining the exact point where truth passes into error, and that they are allowable in one sense or connection, though false in another. Thus to say that prayer (and the Blessed Virgin's prayer) is omnipotent, is a harsh expression in every-day prose; but, if it is explained to mean that there is nothing which prayer may not obtain from God, it is nothing else than the very promise made us in Scripture.[46] Again, to say that Mary is the centre of all being, sounds inflated and profane; yet after all it is only one way, and a natural way, of saying that the Creator and the creature met together, and became one in her womb; and as such, I have used the expression above. Again, it is at first sight a paradox to say that "Jesus is obscured, because Mary is kept in the background;"[47] yet there is a sense, as I have shown above, in which it is a simple truth.

[104]

And so again certain statements may be true, under circumstances and in a particular time and place, which are abstractedly false; and hence it may be very unfair in a controversialist to interpret by an English or a modern rule, whatever may have been asserted by a foreign or medieval

---

[45] John 2:4.

[46] "Ask and it will be given you... For everyone who asks receives." Matt 7:7.8.

[47] *En* p.118 iam cit. supra.

author. To say, for instance, dogmatically, that no one can be saved without personal devotion to the Blessed Virgin, would be an untenable proposition; yet it might be true of this man or that, or of this or that country at this or that date; and, if that very statement has ever been made by any writer of consideration (and this has to be ascertained), then perhaps it was made precisely under these exceptional circumstances. [105] If an Italian preacher made it, I should feel no disposition to doubt him, at least if he spoke of Italian youths and Italian maidens.

Next I think you have not always made your quotations with that consideration and kindness which is your rule. At p. 106, you say, "It is commonly said that, if any Roman Catholic acknowledges that 'it is good and useful to pray to the saints,' he is not bound himself to do so. Were the above teaching true, it would be cruelty to say so; because, according to it, he would be forfeiting what is morally necessary to his salvation." But now, as to the fact, by whom is it said that to pray to our Lady and the Saints is necessary to salvation? The proposition of St. Alfonso is, that "God gives no grace except through Mary;" that is through her intercession. But intercession is one thing, devotion is another. And Suarez[48] says, "It is the universal sentiment that the intercession of Mary is not only useful, but also in a certain manner necessary;" but still it is the question of her intercession, not of our invocation of her, not of devotion to her. If it were so, no Protestant could be saved; if it were so, there would be grave reasons for doubting of the salvation of St. Chrysostom or St. Athanasius, or of the primitive Martyrs; nay, I should like to know whether St. Augustine, in all his voluminous writings, invokes her once. Our Lord died for those heathens who did not know Him; and His Mother intercedes for those Christians who do not know her; and she [106] intercedes according to His will, and, when He wills to save

---

[48] See supra.

a particular soul, she at once prays for it. I say, He wills indeed according to her prayer, but then she prays according to His will. Though then it is natural and prudent for those to have recourse to her, who from the Church's teaching know her power, yet it cannot be said that devotion to her is a *sine-quâ-non* of salvation. Some indeed of the authors, whom you quote, go farther; they do speak of devotion; but even then, they do not enunciate the general proposition which I have been disallowing. For instance, they say, "It is morally impossible for those to be saved who *neglect* the devotion to the Blessed Virgin;" but a simple omission is one thing, and neglect another. "It is impossible for any to be saved who *turns away* from her," yes; but to "turn away" is to offer some positive disrespect or insult towards her, and that with sufficient knowledge; and I certainly think it would be a very grave act, if in a Catholic country (and of such the writers were speaking, for they knew of no other), with Ave-Marias sounding in the air, and images of the Madonna in every street and road, a Catholic broke off or gave up a practice that was universal, and in which he was brought up, and deliberately put her name out of his thoughts.

7. Though, then, common sense may determine for us, that the line of prudence and propriety has been certainly passed in the instance of certain statements about the Blessed Virgin, it is often not easy to convict them of definite error logically; and in such cases authority, if it attempt to act, would be in the position which so often happens in our courts of law, when the commission of an offence is morally certain, but the government prosecutor cannot find legal evidence sufficient to insure conviction. I am not denying the right of [107] sacred Congregations, at their will, to act peremptorily, and without assigning reasons for the judgment they pass upon writers; but, when they have found it inexpedient to take this severe course, perhaps it may happen from the circumstances of the case, that there is no other that they can take, even if

they would. It is wiser then for the most part to leave these excesses to the gradual operation of public opinion, that is, to the opinion of educated and sober Catholics; and this seems to me the healthiest way of putting them down. Yet in matter of fact I believe the Holy See has interfered from time to time, when devotion seemed running into superstition; and not so long ago. I recollect hearing in Gregory the XVI.'s[49] time, of books about the Blessed Virgin, which had been suppressed by authority; and in particular of a pictorial[50] representation of the Immaculate Conception which he had forbidden; and of measures taken against the shocking notion that the Blessed Mary is present in the Holy Eucharist, in the sense in which our Lord is present; but I have no means of verifying the information I then received.*

Nor have I time, any more than you have had, to ascertain how far great theologians have made protests against those various extravagances of which you so rightly complain. Passages, however, from three well-known Jesuit Fathers have opportunely come in my way, and in one of them is introduced in confirmation, the name of the great Gerson[51]. They are Canisius,[52] Petavius,[53] and Raynaudus;[54] and as they speak very appositely, and you do not seem to know them, I will here make some extracts from them:—

[108]

* Vid. Note V. infr.[55]

---

[49] Gregory XVI Bartolomeo Alberto Cappellari, Camaldolese monk, Pope 1831-46.

[50] 1st ed. omits "pictorial"

[51] Jean le Charlier de Gerson (1363-1429), Chancellor of Notre Dame 1395

[52] St. Peter Canisius (1521-97), Jesuit theologian who participated in the Council of Trent and was the author of a number of catechisms.

[53] Denis Petau. (1583-1652), Professor of Dogmatic Theology in Paris in 1621 and author of *De Theologicis Dogmatibus* (1644ff)

[54] Théophile Raynaud (1583-1663), Jesuit theologian. His works were published in 19 volumes; volume 8 is *Marialia.*

[55] This note does not appear in the 1866 edition. Newman writes to Pusey 25 September 1866, "The last number of the Roman *Analecta* ... is to disown extreme sayings about the Blessed Virgin." *LD* 22 p.294.

(1.) Canisius:—

"We confess that in the *cultus* of Mary it has been, and is possible for corruptions to creep in; and we have a more than ordinary desire that the Pastors of the Church should be carefully vigilant here, and give no place to Satan, whose characteristic office it has ever been, while men sleep, to sow the cockle amid the Lord's wheat[56] ... For this purpose it is his wont gladly to avail himself of the aid of heretics, fanatics, and false Catholics, as may be seen in the instance of this *Marianus cultus.*[57] This *cultus*, heretics, suborned by Satan, attack with hostility ... Thus too, certain mad heads are so demented by Satan, as to embrace superstitions and idolatries instead of the true *cultus*, and neglect altogether the true measures whether in respect to God or to Mary. Such indeed were the Collyridians[58] of old ... Such that German herdsman a hundred years ago, who gave out publicly that he was a new prophet, and had had a vision of the Deipara, and told the people in her name to pay no more tributes and taxes to princes[59] ... Moreover, how many Catholics does one see who, by great and shocking negligence, have neither care nor regard for her *cultus*; but, given to profane and secular objects, scarce once a year raise their earthly minds to sing her praises or to venerate her."—*De Mariâ Deiparâ*, p. 518.

(2.) Father Petau[60] says, when discussing the teaching of the Fathers about the Blessed Virgin (*de Incarn.* xiv. 8):—

"I will venture to give this advice to all who would be [109] devout and panegyrical towards the Holy Virgin, viz., not to exceed in their piety and devotion to her, but to be content with true and solid praises, and to cast aside what is otherwise. This kind of idolatry, lurking, as St. Augustine

---

[56] Matt 13:25
[57] Marian veneration.
[58] 4th century Thracian heretical sect who worshipped Mary by offering up cakes (κολλυρίς). See St. Epiphanius *Against the Heresies* 3.2.
[59] Only one of many apparitions which fail to be approved by Church authorities.
[60] See supra.

says, nay implanted in human hearts, is greatly abhorrent from Theology, that is, from the gravity of heavenly wisdom, which never thinks or asserts anything, but what is measured by certain and accurate rules. What that rule should be, and what caution is to be used in our present subject, I will not determine of myself; but according to the mind of a most weighty and most learned theologian, John Gerson,[61] who in one of his Epistles proposes certain canons, which he calls truths, by means of which are to be measured the assertions of theologians concerning the Incarnation ... By these truly golden precepts Gerson brings within bounds the immoderate licence of praising the Blessed Virgin, and restrains it within the measure of sober and healthy piety. And from these it is evident that that sort of reasoning is frivolous and nugatory, in which so many indulge, in order to assign any sort of grace they please, however unusual, to the Blessed Virgin. For they argue thus; 'Whatever the Son of God could bestow for the glory of His Mother, that it became Him in fact to furnish;' or again, 'Whatever honours or ornaments He has poured out on other saints, those altogether hath He heaped upon His Mother;' whence they draw their chain of reasoning to their desired conclusion; a mode of argumentation which Gerson treats with contempt as captious and sophistical."

[110] He adds, what of course we all should say, that, in thus speaking, he has no intention to curtail the liberty of pious persons in such meditations and conjectures, on the mysteries of faith, sacred histories, and the Scripture text, as are of the nature of comments, supplements, and the like.

(3.) Raynaud[62] is an author, full of devotion, if any one is so, to the Blessed Virgin; yet in the work which he has composed in her honour (*Diptycha Mariana*), he says more than I can quote here, to the same purpose as Petau. I abridge some portions of his text:—

---

[61] See supra p.107.
[62] See supra p.108.

"Let this be taken for granted, that no praises of ours can come up to the praises due to the Virgin Mother. But we must not make up for our inability to reach her true praise, by a supply of lying embellishment and false honours. For there are some whose affection for religious objects is so imprudent and lawless, that they transgress the due limits even towards the saints. This Origen[63] has excellently observed upon in the case of the Baptist, for very many, instead of observing the measure of charity, considered whether he might not be the Christ," p. 9. ... "St. Anselm,[64] the first, or one of the first champions of the public celebration of the Blessed Virgin's Immaculate Conception, says, *de Excell. Virg.*, that the Church considers it indecent, that anything that admits of doubt should be said in her praise, when the things which are certainly true of her supply such large materials for laudation. It is right so to interpret St. Epiphanius also, when he says that human tongues should not pronounce anything lightly of the Deipara; and who is more justly to be charged with speaking lightly of the most Holy [111] Mother of God, than he, who, as if what is certain and evident did not suffice for her full investiture, is wiser than the aged, and obtrudes on us the toadstools of his own mind, and devotions unheard of by those Holy Fathers who loved her best? Plainly, as St. Anselm says, that she is the Mother of God, this by itself exceeds every elevation which can be named or imagined, short of God. About so sublime a majesty we should not speak hastily from prurience of wit, or flimsy pretext of promoting piety; but with great maturity of thought; and whenever the maxims of the Church and the oracles of faith do not suffice, then not without the suffrages of the Doctors ... Those who are subject to this prurience of innovation, do not perceive how broad is the difference

---

[63] See supra.
[64] St Anselm (c.1033-1109), Archbishop of Canterbury 1093, succeeding Lanfranc. His most famous work is *Cur Deus Homo* (1098), but he also preached *Homily* 7 on Mary and wrote *The Excellences of Mary*.

between subjects of human science, and heavenly things. All novelty concerning the objects of our faith is to be put far away; except so far as by diligent investigation of God's Word, written and unwritten, and a well-founded inference from what is thence to be elicited, something is brought to light which though already indeed there, has not hitherto been recognized. The innovations which we condemn are those which rest neither on the written nor unwritten Word, nor on conclusions from it, nor on the judgment of ancient sages, nor sufficient basis of reason, but on the sole colour and pretext of doing more honour to the Deipara," p. 10.

In another portion of the same work, he speaks in particular of one of those imaginations to which you especially refer, and for which, without strict necessity (as it seems to me) you allege the authority of à Lapide.[65]

[112]   "Nor is that honour of the Deipara to be offered, viz. that the elements of the body of Christ, which the Blessed Virgin supplied to it, remain perpetually unaltered in Christ, and thereby are found also in the Eucharist ... This solicitude for the Virgin's glory must, I consider, be discarded; since, if rightly considered, it involves an injury towards Christ, and such honour the Virgin loveth not. And first, dismissing philosophical bagatelles about the animation of blood, milk, &c., who can endure the proposition that a good portion of the substance of Christ in the Eucharist should be worshipped with a *cultus* less than *latria*? viz. by the inferior *cultus* of *hyperdulia*?[66] The preferable class of theologians contend that not even the humanity of Christ, is to be materially abstracted from the Word of God, and worshipped by itself; how then shall we introduce a *cultus* of the Deipara in Christ, which is inferior to the *cultus* proper to Him? How is this other than a casting down of the substance of Christ from His

---

[65] See supra.

[66] *Hyperdulia* is the special veneration (*cultus*) paid to Mary. "This very special devotion differs essentially from the adoration which is given to ... God." *CCC* 971; *dulia* is the veneration paid to saints; *latria* is the worship paid to God.

Royal Throne, and a degradation of it to some inferior sitting place? It is nothing to the purpose to refer to such Fathers, as say that the flesh of Christ is the flesh of Mary, for they speak of its origin. What will hinder, if this doctrine be admitted, our also admitting that there is something in Christ which is detestable? for, as the first elements of a body which were communicated by the Virgin to Christ, have (as these authors say) remained perpetually in Christ, so the same *materia*, at least in part, which belonged originally to the ancestors of Christ, came down to the Virgin from her father, unchanged, and taken from her grandfather, and so on. And thus, since it [113] is not unlikely that some of these ancestors were reprobate, there would now be something actually in Christ, which had belonged to a reprobate, and worthy of detestation."—p. 237.

8. After such explanation, and with such authorities, to clear my path, I put away from me, as you would wish, without any hesitation, as matters in which my heart and reason have no part, (when taken in their literal and absolute sense, as any Protestant would naturally take them, and as the writers doubtless did not use them), such sentences, and phrases, as these:—that the mercy of Mary is infinite; that God has resigned into her hands His omnipotence; that it is safer to seek her than to seek her Son; that the Blessed Virgin is superior to God;[67] that our Lord is subject to her command; that His present disposition towards sinners, as well as His Father's, is to reject them, while the Blessed Mary takes His place as an Advocate with Father and Son; that the Saints are more ready to intercede with Jesus than Jesus with the Father; that Mary is the only refuge of those with whom God is angry; that Mary alone can obtain a Protestant's conversion; that it would have sufficed for the salvation of men if our Lord had died, not in order to obey His Father, but to defer to the decree of His Mother; that she rivals our Lord in being

---

[67] "Some one said now that we ought not to pray to God at all, but only to the Blessed Virgin." To Mrs. William Froude 8 August 1870 *LD* 25 p.176.

God's daughter, not by adoption, but by a kind of nature; that Christ fulfilled the office of Saviour by imitating her virtues; that, as the Incarnate God bore the image of His Father, so [114] He bore the image of His Mother; that redemption derived from Christ indeed its sufficiency, but from Mary its beauty and loveliness; that, as we are clothed with the merits of Christ, so we are clothed with the merits of Mary; that, as He is Priest, in a like sense is she Priestess; that His Body and Blood in the Eucharist are truly hers and appertain to her; that as He is present and received therein, so is she present and received therein; that Priests are ministers as of Christ, so of Mary; that elect souls are born of God and Mary; that the Holy Ghost brings into fruitfulness His action by her, producing in her and by her Jesus Christ in His members; that the kingdom of God in our souls, as our Lord speaks, is really the kingdom of Mary in the soul; that she and the Holy Ghost produce in the soul extraordinary things; and that when the Holy Ghost finds Mary in a soul He flies there.

Sentiments such as these I freely surrender to your animadversion;[68] I never knew of them till I read your book, nor, as I think, do the vast majority of English Catholics know them. They seem to me like a bad dream. I could not have conceived them to be said. I know not to what authority to go for them, to Scripture, or to the Fathers, or to the decrees of Councils, or to the consent of schools, or to the tradition of the faithful, or to the Holy See, or to Reason. They defy all the *loci theologici*.[69] There is nothing of them in the Missal, in the Roman Catechism, in the Roman *Raccolta*, in the

---

[68] 1st ed omits "I freely surrender to your animadversion".
[69] *loci theologici*: see supra.

Imitation of Christ, in Gother,[70] Challoner,[71] Milner[72] or Wiseman,[73] as far as I am aware. They do but scare and confuse me. I should not be holier, more spiritual, more sure of perseverance, if I twisted my moral being into the reception of them; I should but be guilty of fulsome frigid flattery towards the most upright and noble of God's creatures, if I professed them,—and of stupid flattery too; for it would be like the compliment of painting up a young and beautiful princess with the brow of a Plato and the muscle of an Achilles. And I should expect her to tell one of her people in waiting to turn me off her service without warning. Whether thus to feel be the *scandalum parvulorum* in my case, or the *scandalum Pharisæorum*,[74] I leave others to decide; but I will say plainly that I had rather believe (which is impossible) that there is no God at all, than that Mary is greater than God. I will have nothing to do with statements, which can only be explained, by being explained away. I do not, however, speak of these statements, as they are found in their authors, for I know nothing of the originals, and cannot believe that they have meant what you say; but I take them as they lie in your pages. Were any of them the sayings of Saints in ecstasy, I should know they had a good meaning; still I should not repeat them myself; but I am looking at them, not as spoken by the tongues of Angels, but according to that literal sense which they bear in the mouths of English men and English women. And, as spoken by man to man, in

[115]

---

[70] John Gother (d.1704), a Presbyterian who converted to Catholicism, wrote in defence of his faith and became chaplain at Warkworth Castle where he taught Challoner.

[71] Richard Challoner (1691-1781) became Vicar Apostolic of the London district in 1758. He was responsible for a revised version of the Douay-Rheims Bible and for compiling *The Garden of the Soul.*

[72] John Milner (1752-1826), Vicar Apostolic of the Midland district in 1803, was a forthright defender of Catholicism and author of *The End of Religious Controversy* (1818).

[73] See supra.

[74] 'the scandal of the little ones' (see Matt 18:6) or 'the scandal of the Pharisees' (see Matt 15:12).

England, in the nineteenth century, I consider them calculated to prejudice inquirers, to frighten the unlearned, to unsettle consciences, to provoke blasphemy, and to work the loss of souls.

[116] 9. And now, after having said so much as this, bear with me, my dear Friend, if I end with an expostulation. Have you not been touching us on a very tender point in a very rude way? is it not the effect of what you have said to expose her to scorn and obloquy, who is dearer to us than any other creature? Have you even hinted that our love for her is anything else than an abuse? Have you thrown her one kind word yourself all through your book? I trust so, but I have not lighted upon one. And yet I know you love her well. Can you wonder, then,—can I complain much, much as I grieve,— that men should utterly misconceive of you, and are blind to the fact that you have put the whole argument between you and us on a new footing; and that, whereas it was said twenty-five years ago in the British Critic,[75] "Till Rome ceases to be what practically she is, union is *impossible* between her and England," you declare on the contrary, "Union *is possible*, as soon as Italy and England, having the same faith and the same centre of unity, are allowed to hold severally their own theological opinions"? They have not done you justice here; because in truth, the honour of our Lady is dearer to them than the conversion of England.

Take a parallel case, and consider how you would decide it yourself. Supposing an opponent of a doctrine for which you so earnestly contend, the eternity of punishment, instead of meeting you with direct arguments against it, heaped together a number of extravagant descriptions of the place, mode, and circumstances of its infliction, quoted Tertullian as a witness for the primitive Fathers, and the Covenanters

---

[75] 'Catholicity of the Anglican Church' in *The British Critic,* January 1840, republished in *Ess* 2 p.72. *The British Critic* was a theological quarterly magazine founded by Hugh James Rose in 1827. Newman was editor 1838-41.

and Ranters[76] for these last centuries; brought passages from the Inferno of Dante, and from the Sermons of Wesley and Whitfield;[77] nay, supposing he confined himself to the chapter on the subject in the work, which has the sanction of Jeremy Taylor,[78] on "The State of Man," or to his Sermon on "The Foolish Exchange,"[79] or to particular passages in Leighton,[80] South,[81] Beveridge,[82] and Barrow,[83] would you think this a fair and becoming method of reasoning? and if he avowed that he should ever consider the Anglican Church committed to all these accessories of the doctrine, till its authorities formally denounced Beveridge, and Whitfield, and a hundred others, would you think this an equitable determination, or the procedure of a theologian?

[84]So far concerning the Blessed Virgin; the chief but not the only subject of your volume. And now, when I could wish

[117]

---

[76] Presbyterians who covenanted in the 16th and 17th centuries to uphold their faith. *Ranters* were a group of religious libertarians who flourished after the death of Charles I and were falsely identified with Quakers. They believed in spiritual liberty and denied the authority of Scripture, the Creeds and authority in general. See Nigel Smith, *Spiritual Liberty and Sexual Freedom in the English Revolution* London 2014.

[77] John Wesley (1703-91), founder of Methodism and itinerant preacher. George Whitefield (1714-70) was a Methodist evangelist with Calvinist leanings. See the 1845 edition of *An Essay on the Development of Christian Doctrine* edited by James Tolhurst Leominster 2018 pp.535-8.

[78] Jeremy Taylor (1613-67) had been a chaplain in the Royalist army and imprisoned. He was appointed Bishop of Down and Connor in 1660. He was a renowned preacher.

[79] Sermon 17 'What is a man profited, if shall gain the whole world, and lose his own soul?' Matt 16:26.

[80] Robert Leighton (1611-84), Archbishop of Glasgow in 1670 who hoped to reconcile Presbyterians and Episcopalians but without success.

[81] Robert South (1634-1716) became Canon of Christ Church in 1670 and published his *Sermons Preached on Several Occasions* in 1679.

[82] William Beveridge (1637-1708), author of an *Exposition of the Thirty-Nine Articles*; he became Bishop of St. Asaph in 1704.

[83] Isaac Barrow (1630-77), Classical scholar, mathematician, author of *Treatise on the Pope's Supremacy* (1680).

[84] In 1st ed. there is a heading here "CONCLUSION".

to proceed,[*] she seems to stop all controversy, for the Feast of her Immaculate Conception is upon us;[85] and close upon its Octave, which is kept with special solemnities in the Churches of this town, come the great Antiphons,[86] the heralds of Christmas. That joyful season, joyful for all of us, while it centres in Him who then came on earth, also brings before us in peculiar prominence that Virgin Mother, who bore and nursed Him. Here she is not in the background, as at Easter-tide, but she brings Him to us in her arms. Two great Festivals, dedicated to her honour, tomorrow's and the [118] Purification,[87] mark out and keep the ground, and, like the towers of David, open the way to and fro, for the high holiday season of the Prince of Peace. And all along it her image is upon it, such as we see it in the typical representation of the Catacombs. May the sacred influences of this tide bring us all together in unity! May it destroy all bitterness on your side and ours! May it quench all jealous, sour, proud, fierce antagonism on our side; and dissipate all captious, carping, fastidious refinements of reasoning on yours! May that bright and gentle Lady, the Blessed Virgin Mary, overcome you with her sweetness, and revenge herself on her foes by interceding effectually for their conversion!

I am,

Yours, most affectionately,

JOHN H. NEWMAN.

THE ORATORY, BIRMINGHAM,
  Dec. 7, 1865.[88]

---

[*] The sequel to this letter never was written. Vid. supra., note p.17.[89]

---

[85] Newman finished his text on December 7th (the eve of the feast day)

[86] Known as the *O Antiphons*, at Vespers 17th–24th December.

[87] February 2nd.

[88] 1st ed: "In fest. S. Ambrosii 1865." (The feast of St. Ambrose on 7th December is also the eve of the Immaculate Conception.)

[89] This note did not appear in the 1st edition.

NOTES

NOTE I. PAGE 33.

TESTIMONIES OF THE FATHERS TO THE DOCTRINE THAT MARY IS THE SECOND EVE

ST. JUSTIN:—*Ψἱὸν Θεοῦ γεγραμμένον αὐτον ἐν τοῖζ ἀπομνηονεύασι τῶν ἀποστολων αὐτοῦ ἔχουτεζ, καὶ υἱον αὐτον λέγοντεζ, νενοήκμεν, καὶ πρὸ πάντων ποιημάτων ἀπὸ τοῦ πατρὸς δυνάμει αὐτοῦ καὶ βουλῇ προελθόντα .... καὶ διπάντων τῆς παρθένου ἄνθρωπος [ον] γεγονέναι, ἵνα καὶ δι' ἧς ὁδοῦ ἡ ἀπὸ τοῦ ὄφεως παρακοὴ τὴν ἀρχὴν ἔλαβε, καὶ δια ταύτηζ τῆς ὁδοῦ καὶ κατάλυσιν λάβῃ· παρθένοζ γαρ οὖσα Εὔα καὶ ἄφθοποζ τὸν λόγον τὸν ἀπὸ τοῦ ὄφεωζ συλλαβοῦσα, παρακοὴν καὶ θάνατον ἔτεκε· πίστιν δὲ καὶ χαρὰν λαβοῦσα Μαρία ἡ παρθένος, εὐαγγελιζομένου αὐτῇ Γαβριὴλ ἀγγέλου, ὅτι Πνεῦμα Κυρίου ἐπ' αὐτὴν ἐπελεύσεται, &c....ἀπεκρίνατο, Γένοιτό μοι κατὰ τὸ ῥῆμά σου. — Tryph. 100.*[1]

---

[1] "Since it is written of Him in the Memoirs of the Apostles that He is the Son of God, and since we call Him Son, we have understood that before all creatures He proceeded from the Father by His will and power – for in the words of the Prophets He is addressed in one way or another as Wisdom and Day and East and Sword and Stone and Rod and Jacob and Israel – and that He became Man by the Virgin so that the course which was taken by disobedience in the beginning through the agency of the serpent, might be also the very course by which it would be put down. For Eve, a virgin and undefiled, conceived the word of the serpent, and bore disobedience and death. But the Virgin Mary received faith and joy when the angel Gabriel announced to her the glad tidings that the Spirit of the Lord

2. Tertullian:—"Ne mihi vacet incursus nominis Adæ, unde Christus Adam ab Apostolo dictus est, si terreni non fuit census homo ejus? Sed et hic ratio defendit, quod Deus imaginem et similitudinem suam a diabolo captam æmula operatione recuperavit. In virginem enim adhuc Evam irrepserat verbum ædificatorium mortis. In virginem æque introducendum erat Dei verbum extructorium vitæ; ut quod per ejusmodi sexum abierat in perditionem, per eundem sexum redigeretur in salutem. Crediderat Eva serpenti; credidit Maria Gabrieli; quod illa credendo deliquit, hæc credendo delevit."—*De Carn. Chr.* 17.[2]

[120]

3. St. Irenæus:—"Consequenter autem et Maria virgo obediens invenitur, dicens, Ecce ancilla tua, Domine, fiat mihi secundum verbum tuum. Eva vero inobediens: non obedivit enim, adhuc quum esset virgo. Quemadmodum illa, virum quidem habens Adam, virgo tamen adhuc existens (erant enim utrique nudi in Paradiso, et non confundebantur, quoniam, paullo ante facti, non intellectum habebant filiorum generationis; oportebat enim illos primo adolescere, dehinc sic multiplicari), inobediens facta, et sibi et universo generi humano causa facta est mortis: sic et Maria, habens prædestinatum virum, et tamen virgo, obediens, et sibi et universo generi humano causa facta est salutis. Et propter hoc Lex eam, quæ desponsata erat viro, licet virgo sit adhuc, uxorem ejus, qui desponsaverat, vocat;

---

would come upon her and the power of the Most High would overshadow her for which reason the Holy One being born of her is the Son of God. And she replied, 'Be it done unto me according to thy word.'" *Dialogus cum Tryphone* 100 *PG* 6. 709.

[2] "Indeed I am permitted to consider the name of Adam, which the Apostle relates to Christ (I Cor. 15:47), if the first man was not considered from the earth? But, and here reason supports it, that God recovered by skillful deception his image and likeness from the Devil. As yet, Eve, as a virgin, had grasped the death-dealing word. Equally, as a virgin God would introduce the life-giving word; so that in the same way sex would be the cause of perdition and in the same way sex would bring about salvation. Eve believed in the serpent; Mary believed in Gabriel; what one lost by believing, one succeeded in wiping out, by believing." *De carne Christi* 17.5 *ML* 2 .828.

eam quæ est à Maria in Evam recirculationem significans: quia non aliter quod colligatum est solveretur, nisi ipsæ compagines alligationis reflectantur retrorsus; ut primæ conjunctiones solvantur per secundas, secundæ rursus liberent primas. Et evenit primam quidem compaginem à secundâ colligatione solvere, secundam vero colligationem primæ solutionis habere locum. Et propter hoc Dominus dicebat, primos quidem novissimos futuros, et novissimos primos. Et propheta autem hoc idem significat, dicens, 'Pro patribus nati sunt tibi filii.' 'Primogenitus' enim 'mortuorum' natus Dominus et in sinum suum recipiens pristinos patres, regeneravit eos in vitam Dei, ipse initium viventium factus, quoniam Adam initium morientium factus est. Propter hoc et Lucas initium generationis a Domino inchoans, in Adam retulit, significans, quoniam non illi hunc, sed hic illos in Evangelium vitæ regeneravit. Sic autem et Evæ inobedientiæ nodus solutionem accepit per obedientiam Mariæ. Quod enim alligavit virgo Eva per incredulitatem, hoc virgo Maria solvit per fidem."—*S. Iren. contr. Hær.* iii. 22.[3]

[121]

---

[3] "Consequently, then, Mary the Virgin is found to be obedient, saying: 'Behold, O Lord, your handmaid; be it done to me according to your word.' Eve, however, was disobedient; and when yet a virgin, she did not obey. Just as she having Adam for a husband and still a virgin, (for in Paradise they were both naked but were not ashamed; for, having been created only a short time, they had no understanding of the procreation of children and it was necessary that they first come to maturity before beginning to multiply), but having become disobedient, was made the cause of death for herself and for the whole human race. And on account of this the Law by which a virgin is pledged to a man so as to be called his wife which we see signified in the unwinding of the parallel of Mary and Eve. What was joined, is released; the first joining freed by the second. It happened that the first was freed by the second but the second takes the place of the first. And on account of this the Lord said, 'The first will be last and the last first' (Matt 19:30). And the prophet said the same 'For to fathers will be born sons' (Ps. 44:17). The Lord is the first-born from the dead and in his bosom received the fathers of old, bringing them rebirth by the life of God. He who was the beginning of life as Adam was the beginning of death. On account of this Luke traces the ancestry of the Lord from Adam, signifying that from him comes the Gospel of life. Thus the knot of Eve's disobedience was undone by the obedience of Mary. What the virgin

"Quemadmodum enim illa per Angeli sermonem seducta est, ut effugeret Deum, prævaricata verbum ejus; ita et hæc per Angelicum sermonem evangelizata est, ut portaret Deum, obediens ejus verbo. Et si ea inobedierat Deo; sed hæc suasa est obedire Deo, uti Virginis Evæ Virgo Maria fieret advocata. Et quemadmodum adstrictum est morti genus humanum per Virginem, salvatur [solvatur] per Virginem, æqua lance disposita, virginalis inobedientia, per virginalem obedientiam."—*Ibid.* v. 19.[4]

4. St. Cyril:—Διὰ παρθένου τῆς Εὔας ἦλθεν ὁ Θάνατος, ἔδει διὰ παρθένου, μᾶλλον δὲ ἐκ παρθένου, φανῆναι τὴν ζωήν· ἵνα ὥσπερ ἐκείνην ὄφις ἠπάτησεν, οὕτω καὶ ταύτην Γαβριὴλ εὐαγγελίσηται. — *Cat.* xxi.1.[5]

5. St. Ephrem.:—"Per Evam nempe decora et amabilis hominis gloria extincta est, quæ tamen rursus per Mariam refloruit"—*Opp. Syr.* ii. p. 318.[6]

"Initio protoparentum delicto in omnes homines mors pertransiit; hodie vero per Mariam translati sumus de morte ad vitam. Initio serpens, Evæ auribus occupatis, inde virus in totum corpus dilatavit; hodie Maria ex auribus perpetuæ felicitatis assertorem excepit. Quod ergo mortis fuit, simul et vitæ extitit instrumentum"—iii. p. 607.[7]

[122]

Eve tied by disbelief the virgin Mary undid by faith." Irenaeus *Adversus Haereses* 3. 22. *PG* 959-60.

[4] "Eve was seduced by the word of the [fallen] angel and transgressed God's word, so that she fled from him. In the same way, [Mary] was evangelized by the word of an angel and obeyed God's word, so that she carried him. And while the former was seduced into disobeying God, the later was persuaded to obey God, so that the Virgin Mary became the advocate of the Virgin Eve. And just as the human race was tied to death because of a virgin, so it was set free from death by a Virgin, since the disobedience of one virgin was counterbalanced by a Virgin's obedience" Ibid v. 19. *PG* 7. 1175-6.

[5] *PG* 33.741. See p.[39].

[6] "Through Eve, the beautiful and desirable glory of men was extinguished; but it has revived through Mary." *Opera Omnia in six tomos distributa* 2 p.318, ed. Assemani and Mobarek Rome 3 vols. 1732-46.

[7] "In the beginning, by the sin of our first parents, death passed upon all men; today, through Mary we are translated from death to life. In the beginning, the serpent filled the ears of Eve, and the poison spread over the whole body; today,

Note I

6. ST. EPIPHANIUS:—*Αὐτὴ ἐστὶν ἡ παρὰ μὲν τῇ Εὔᾳ σημαινομένη δι' αἰνίγματος λαμβοῦσα το καλεῖσθαι μήτηρ ζώντων.... καὶ ἦν θαῦμα ὅτι μετὰ τὴν παράβασιν ταύτην τὴν μεγάλην ἔσχεν ἐπωνυμίαν. καὶ κατὰ μὲν τὸ αἰσητὸν, ἀπ' ἐκείνης τῆς Εὔας πᾶσα τῶν ἀνθρώπων ἡ γέννησις ἐπὶ γῆς γεγέννηται· ὧδε δὲ ἀληθῶς ἀπὸ Μαρίας αὐτὴ ἡ ζωὴ τῷ κόσμῳ γεγέννηται· ἵνα ζῶντα γεννήσῃ, καὶ γέννηται ἡ Μαρία μήτηρ ζώντων· δι' αἰνίγματος οὖν ἡ Μαρία μήτηρ ζώντων κέκληται ... ἀλλὰ καὶ ἕτερον περὶ τούτων διανοεῖσθαί ἐστι θαυμαστὸν, περὶ δὲ τῆς Εὔας καὶ τῆς Μαρίας· ἡ μὲν γὰρ Εὔα πρόφασις γεγέννηται θανάτου τοῖς ἀνθρώποις· ... ἡ δὲ Μαρία πρόφασις ζωῆς ... ἵνα ζωὴ ἀντὶ θανάτου γέννηται, ἐκκλείσασα τὸν θάνατον τὸν ἐκ γυναικὸς, πάλιν ὁ διά γυναικὸς ἡμῖν ζωὴ γεγεννημένος.* —*Hær.* 78. 18.[8]

7. St. Jerome:—"Postquam vero Virgo concepit in utero, et peperit nobis puerum ... soluta maledictio est. Mors per Evam, vita per Mariam."—*Ep.* 22. *ad Eustochium,* 21.[9]

8. St. Augustine:—"Huc accedit magnum sacramentum, ut, quoniam per feminam nobis mors acciderat, vita nobis per feminam nasceretur: ut de utrâque naturâ, id est, femininâ et masculinâ, victus diabolus cruciaretur, quoniam de ambarum subversione lætabatur, cui parum fuerat ad pœnam si ambæ naturæ in nobis liberarentur, nisi etiam perambas liberaremur".—*De Agone Christ.*c. 24.[10]

9. St. Peter Chrysologus:—"Benedicta tu in mulieribus. Quia in quibus Eva maledicta puniebat viscera; tunc in illis

---

Mary from her ears received the champion of eternal happiness; what therefore, was an instrument of death, was an instrument of life also." Ibid 3 p.607.

[8] See pp.[40-1]. *Adversus Haereses* 78. 18 *PG* 42. 728-9.

[9] "After the Virgin conceived and brought forth a son ... the curse is ended. Death through Eve, life through Mary." *Ep. 22 ad Eustochium* 21 (385). *ML* 22.407-8. See p.[41].

[10] "This is a great sacrament, that whereas death came through a woman, life was born for us through a woman; so by both natures, feminine and masculine, the conquered devil would be punished and by the overcoming of both there should be joy. For both were destined for punishment until both were freed. *De agone christiano* c. 24. *ML* 40.302. See p.[42].

[123]   gaudet, honoratur, suspicitur Maria benedicta. Et facta est vera nunc mater viventium per gratiam quæ mater extitit morientium per naturam ... Quantus sit Deus satis ignorat ille, qui hujus Virginis mentem non stupet, animum non miratur: pavet cœlum, tremunt Angeli, creatura non sustinet, natura non sufficit, et una puella sic Deum in sui pectoris capit, recipit, oblectat hospitio, ut pacem terris, cœlis gloriam, salutem perditis, vitam mortuis, terrenis cum cœlestibus parentelam, ipsius Dei cum carne commercium, pro ipsa domus exigat pensione, pro ipsius uteri mercede conquirat, et impleat illud Prophetæ: Ecce hæreditas Domini, filii merces fructus ventris. Sed jam se concludat sermo ut de partur Virginis, donante Deo, et indulgente tempore, gratius proloquamur."—*Serm.* 140.[11]

    10. St. Fulgentius:—"In primi hominis conjuge, nequitia diaboli seductam depravavit mentem: in secundi autem hominis matre, gratia Dei et mentem integram servavit, et carnem: menti contulit firmissimam fidem, carni abstulit omnino libidinem. Quoniam igitur miserabiliter pro peccato damnatus est homo, ideo sine peccato mirabiliter natus est Deus homo."—*Serm.* ii.[12]

---

[11] "Blessed are you among women. As the womb of women was punished by wretched Eve, so they may rejoice in Mary's blessedness. Truly now she is Mother of the living by that grace by which she extinguished what was the curse of death. How can God not be sufficiently aware that the mind is not amazed at the Virgin, the soul does not wonder: the heavens quake and the angels tremble, creatures cannot imagine, it is beyond nature that a girl could take and receive God in her womb, give him welcome, so bring peace to the earth, glory to heaven, salvation to the lost, life to the dead, joining heaven to earth, connecting God with human flesh, for her home, payment is demanded, for her womb a reward must be collected so that the prophecy might be fulfilled: Behold the inheritance of the Lord the reward of the son, the fruit of the womb.[Ps. 126/127:3] But already the sermon is ended but on the part of the Virgin, God giving and time allowing, we could go on longer." Sermo 2. *ML* 52. 576. See pp.[42-3].

[12] "In the first man, the mind of his wife was perverted and seduced by the wickedness of the devil: in the second man, his mother, with a mind and body preserved by the grace of God: with strength of faith and no wantonness of flesh. Whereas man was miserably condemned for his sin, the God-man is wonderfully born without sin." *Sermo* 2.6 *De Dupl. Nativitate* Sermo 2, 6. *ML* 65.728

Note I

"Venite, virgines, ad virginem; venite, concipientes, ad concipientem; venite, parturientes, ad parturientem; venite, matres, ad matrem; venite, lactantes, ad lactantem; venite, juvenculæ, ad juvenculam. Ideo omnes istos cursus naturæ virgo Maria in Domino nostro Jesu Christo suscepit, ut omnibus ad se confugientibus fœminis subveniret, et sic restauraret omne genus fœminarum ad se advenientium nova Eva servando virginitatem, sicut omne genus virorum Adam novus recuperat dominus Jesus Christus."—*Ibid.* iii.[13]

I have omitted, among the instances of the comparison [124] of Eve with Mary, the passage at the end of the Epistle to Diognetus, a testimony which would be most important from the great antiquity of that work, from the religious beauty of its composition, and the stress laid upon it by Protestants. But I cannot construe it satisfactorily as it stands in the received text. Should not the semicolon be placed after *φθείρεται*, not, as in the editions, after *πιστευεναι*? thus:—*ὡν ὄφιζ οὐκ ἅπτεται οὐδε πλανη συγχωριζεται, οὐδε Εὑα φθειρεται αλλα παρθενος πιστευεται, και σωτηριον δεικνυται, k.t.l.*[14]

---

[13] "Come virgins to the Virgin; come pregnant to her who was pregnant; come you who are about to give birth to her who gave birth; come mothers to the Mother; come you who gave your milk to her who gave hers; come young women to the young Woman. Therefore the Virgin Mary naturally underwent all these things in the life of our Lord Jesus Christ so that she could come to the support of all women and so restore the feminine race, serving their virginity as the new Eve, just as the new Adam, our Lord Jesus Christ restored a new humanity to men." *Ibid* Sermo 36. *PL* 65.728. See pp.[43-4].

[14] "Blessings which no serpent can touch, no deceit defile by its contact. Then Eve is not seduced; on the contrary a virgin can be trusted." *Ancient Christian Writers* 6, Westminster Md 1948 p.147. *PG* 2. 1189. This whole paragraph only appeared in the third edition. In its place Newman had written in the 1st ed. "I should add that the sixth Oratio of St Proclus quoted in a later page, is suspected by Tillemont not to be his. It is, however, the work of some writer within the period of what Anglicans consider to be 'the Undivided Church." Louis Sébastien Le Nain Tillemont (1637-98), French Church historian who published *Mémoires pour server à l'histoire ecclésiastique des six premiers siècles* (1693-1712).

NOTE II. PAGE 48.

SUAREZ ON THE IMMACULATE CONCEPTION

ABRIDGED from Suarez. Opp. t. 17, p. 7—Ed. Venet. 1746:—[1]

"1. Statuendum est B. Virginem fuisse a Christo redemptam, quia Christus fuit universalis redemptor totius generis humani, et pro omnibus hominibus mortuus est."[2]— p. 15.

"2. Præterea constat indiguisse Virginem redemptione, quia nimirum descendebat ex Adamo per seminalem generationem."[3]—p. 7.

"3. Tanquam certum statuendum est, B. Virginem procreatam esse ex viri et fœminæ commixtione carnali, ad modum aliorum hominum. Habetur certâ traditione et communi consensu totius Ecclesiæ."—p. 7.[4]

"4. Absolute et simpliciter fatendum B. Virginem in Adam peccasse."[5]—p. 16.

---

[1] Francisco de Suarez's *Opera Omnia* were published in 23 volumes in Venice (1740-51).

[2] "It must be a matter of faith that the B. Virgin was redeemed by Christ, because Christ was the absolute redeemer of the whole human race, and died for all men."

[3] "In addition, the redemption of the Virgin is demanded because she surely came by normal human generation from Adam."

[4] "It must also be a matter of faith that the B. Virgin was conceived by the human intercourse between a man and a woman. This is the established tradition and common acceptance of the whole Church."

[5] "It is fully and completely established that the B. Virgin sinned in Adam."

"5. B. Virgo peccavit in Adamo, ex quo tanquam ex radice infecta per seminalem rationem est orta; hæc est tota ratio contrahendi originale peccatum, quod est ex vi conceptionis, nisi gratia Dei præveniat."[6]—p. 16.

"6. Certum est B. Virginem fuisse mortuam saltem in Adamo. Sicut in Christo vitam habuit, ita et in Adam fuit mortua. Alias B. Virgo non contraxisset mortem aliasve corporis pœnalitates ex Adamo; consequens [autem] est omnino falsum. Habuit B. Virgo meritum mortis saltem in Adamo. Illa vere habuit mortem carnis ex peccato Adami contractam."[7]—p. 16.

[126]

"7. B. Virgo, ex vi suæ conceptionis fuit obnoxia originali peccato, seu debitum habuit contrahendi illud, nisi divinâ gratiâ fuisset impeditum."[8]—p. 16.

"8. Si B. Virgo non fuisset (ut ita dicam) vendita in Adamo, et de se servituti peccati obnoxia, non fuisset vere redempta."[9]—p. 16.

"9. Dicendum est, potuisse B. Virginem præservari ab originali peccato, et in primo suæ conceptionis instanti sanctificari."[10]—p. 17.

"10. Potuit B. Virgo ex vi suæ originis esse obnoxia culpæ, et ideo indigere redemptione, et nihilominus in eodem

---

[6] "The B. Virgin sinned in Adam - arising from the fact that she is the seed of an infected rootstock; the whole reason for contracting original sin is by way of conception, unless the grace of God should prevent it."

[7] "It is certain that the B. Virgin suffers death through Adam. As she had life in Adam, so she had death; that she did not contact death and other corporal defects from Adam is completely false. The B. Virgin at least was destined to die, and her death was contracted by the sin of Adam."

[8] "The B. Virgin by means of her own conception was subject to original sin, or in other words paid the debt to nature for it, unless prevented by divine grace."

[9] "If the B. Virgin was not (as is said) 'sold' into death by Adam and was subject to the slavery of sin she would not have been truly redeemed."

[10] "It is maintained that the B. Virgin could be preserved from original sin, and be sanctified from the first moment of her conception."

momento, in quo erat obnoxia, præveniri, ne illam contraheret."[11]—p. 14.

"11. Dicendum B. Virginem in ipso primo instanti conceptionis suæ fuisse sanctificatam, et ab originali peccato præservatam."[12]—p. 19.

"12. Carnem Virginis fuisse carnem peccati … verum est, non quia illa caro aliquando fuit subdita peccato aut informata anima carente gratia, sed quia fuit mortalis et passibilis ex debito peccati, cui de se erat obnoxia, si per Christi gratiam non fuisset præservata."[13]—p. 22.

"13. Quod B. Virgo de se fuerit obnoxia peccato, (si illud revera nunquam habuit) non derogat perfectæ ejus sanctitati et puritati."[14]—pp. 16, 17.

[127] Cornelius à Lapide, Comment. in Ep. ad Rom. v. 12, says:—

"The Blessed Virgin sinned in Adam, and incurred this necessity of contracting original sin; but original sin itself she did not contract in herself in fact, nor had it; for she was anticipated by the grace of God, which excluded all sin from her, in the first moment of her conception."

In 2 Ep. ad Corinth. v. 15:—

"All died, namely, in Adam, for in him all contracted the necessity of sin and death, even the Deipara; so that both herself and man altogether needed Christ as a Redeemer and His death. Therefore the Blessed Virgin sinned and died in Adam, but in her own person she contracted not sin and the

---

[11] "The B. Virgin, because of her human origin was subject to the guilt of sin and therefore in need of redemption, and at the same time, as far as the guilt was concerned, she could have been prevented from contracting it."

[12] "It is maintained that the B. Virgin from the first moment of her conception was sanctified and preserved from original sin."

[13] "The flesh of the Virgin was sinful flesh…The truth is that not because that flesh was ever subject to sin and informed by a soul lacking grace, but because she was mortal and subject to the debt of sin to which she was exposed, unless preserved by the grace of Christ."

[14] "The fact that the B. Virgin was subject to sin (even given that she never had any) in no way affected her perfect holiness and purity."

death of the soul, for she was anticipated by God and God's grace."

If any one wishes to see our doctrine drawn out in a Treatise of the present day, he should have recourse to Dr. Ullathorne's Exposition of the Immaculate Conception, a work full of instruction and of the first authority.

NOTE III. PAGE 50.

THE ANOMALOUS STATEMENTS OF ST. BASIL, ST. CHRYSOSTOM, AND ST. CYRIL ABOUT THE BLESSED VIRGIN

I HAVE admitted that several great Fathers of the Church of the fourth and fifth centuries speak of the Blessed Virgin in terms which we never should think of using now, and which at first sight are inconsistent with the belief and sentiment concerning her, which I have ascribed to their times. These Fathers are St. Basil,[1] St. Chrysostom[2], and St. Cyril of Alexandria;[3] and the occasion of their speaking is furnished by certain passages of Scripture on which they are commenting. It may in consequence be asked of me, why I do not take these three, instead of St. Justin, St. Irenæus, and Tertullian, as my authoritative basis for determining the doctrine of the primitive times concerning the Blessed Mary: why, instead of making St. Irenæus, &c., the rule, and St. Basil, &c., the exception, I do not make the earlier Fathers the exception, and the latter the rule. Since I do not, it may be urged against me that I am but making a case for my own opinion, and playing the part of an advocate.

Now I do not see that it would be illogical or nugatory, though I did nothing more than make a case; indeed I have worded myself in my Letter as if I wished to do little more. For so much as this would surely be to the purpose, considering that the majority of Anglicans have a supreme

---

[1] See supra.
[2] See supra.
[3] St Cyril of Alexandria (d. 444), Patriarch in 412, opposed Nestorius and was primarily responsible for his condemnation at Ephesus in 431.

confidence that no case whatever can be made in behalf of our doctrine concerning the Blessed Virgin from the ancient Fathers. I should have gained a real point if I did anything to destroy this imagination; but I intend to attempt something more than this. I shall attempt to invalidate the only grounds on which any teaching contrary to the Catholic can be founded on Antiquity.

1.

First, I set down the passages which create the difficulty, as they are found in the great work of Petavius,[4] a theologian too candid and fearless to put out of sight or explain away adverse facts, from fear of scandal, or from the expedience of controversy.

1. St. Basil then writes thus, in his 260th Epistle, addressed to Optimus:[5]—

"[Symeon] uses the word 'sword,'[6] meaning the word which is tentative and critical of the thoughts, and reaches unto the separation of soul and spirit, of the joints and marrow. Since then every soul, at the time of the Passion, was subjected in a way to some unsettlement (*διακρίσει*), according to the Lord's word, who said, 'All ye shall be scandalized in Me,'[7] Symeon prophesies even of Mary herself, that, standing by the Cross, and seeing what was doing, and hearing the words, after the testimony of Gabriel, after the secret knowledge of the divine conception, after the great manifestation of miracles, Thou wilt experience, he says, a certain tossing (*σάλος*) of thy soul. For it beseemed [130] the Lord to taste death for every one, and to become a propitiation of the world, in order to justify all in His blood. And thee thyself who hast been taught from above the things concerning the Lord, some unsettlement (*διάκρισις*) will

---

[4] See supra.
[5] To Optimus, Bishop of Antioch in Pisidia (377) *PG* 32.965.
[6] Luke 2:35.
[7] Matt 26:31.

reach. This is the sword; 'that out of many hearts thoughts may be revealed.' He obscurely signifies, that, after the scandalizing which took place upon the Cross of Christ, both to the disciples and to Mary herself, some quick healing should follow upon it from the Lord, confirming their heart unto faith in Him."

2. St. Chrysostom, in Matth. Hom. iv.:—

"'Wherefore,' a man may say, 'did not the Angel do in the case of the Virgin [what he did to Joseph?'" viz., appear to her after, not before, the Incarnation], "'why did he not bring her the good tidings after her conception?' lest she should be in great disturbance and trouble. For the probability was, that, had she not known the clear fact, she would have resolved something strange (ἄτοπον) about herself, and had recourse to rope or sword, not bearing the disgrace. For the Virgin was admirable, and Luke shows her virtue when he says that, when she heard the salutation, she did not at once become extravagant, nor appropriated the words, but was troubled, searching what was the nature of the salutation. One then of so refined a mind (διηκριβωμένη) would be made beside herself with despondency, considering the disgrace, and not expecting, whatever she may say, to persuade any one who hears her, that adultery had not been the fact. Lest then these things should occur, the Angel came before the conception; for it beseemed that that womb should be without disorder, which the Creator of all entered, and that that soul should be rid of all perturbation, which was counted worthy to become the minister of such mysteries."[8]

[131]

In Matth. Hom. xliv.[9] (vid. also in Joann. Hom. xxi.):—

"Today we learn something else even further, viz., that not even to bear Christ in the womb, and to have that wonderful childbirth, has any gain without virtue. And this is especially true from this passage, 'As He was yet speaking to

---

[8] *PG* 57.45.
[9] *PG* 57.465.

the multitude, behold His Mother and His brethren stood without, seeking to speak to Him,' &c.[10] This He said, not as ashamed of His Mother, nor as denying her who bore Him; for, had He been ashamed, He had not passed through that womb; but as showing that there was no profit to her thence, unless she did all that was necessary. For what she attempted, came of overmuch love of honour; for she wished to show to the people that she had power and authority over her Son, in nothing ever as yet having given herself airs (φανταζομένη) about Him. Therefore she came thus unseasonably. Observe then her and their rashness (ἀπόνοιαν) ... Had He wished to deny His Mother, then He would have denied, when the Jews taunted Him with her. But no: He shows such care of her as to commit her as a legacy on the Cross itself to the disciple whom He loved best of all,[11] and to take anxious oversight of her. But does He not do the same now, by caring for her and His brethren? ... And consider, not only the words which convey the considerate rebuke, but also ... who He is who utters it ... and what He aims at in uttering it; not, that is, as [132] wishing to cast her into perplexity, but to release her from a most tyrannical affection, and to bring her gradually to the fitting thought concerning Him, and to persuade her that He is not only her Son, but also her Master."

3. St. Cyril, in Joann. lib. xii. 1064:—

"How shall we explain this passage? He introduces both His Mother and the other women with her standing at the Cross, and, as is plain, weeping. For somehow the race of women is ever fond of tears; and especially given to laments, when it has rich occasions for weeping. How then did they persuade the blessed Evangelist to be so minute in his account, as to make mention of this abidance of the women? For it was his purpose to teach even this, viz., that probably even the Mother of the Lord herself was scandalized at the

---

[10] Matt. 12:47.
[11] John 19:27.

unexpected Passion, and that the death upon the Cross, being so very bitter, was near unsettling her from her fitting mind; and in addition to this, the mockeries of the Jews, and the soldiers too, perhaps, who were sitting near the Cross and making a jest of Him who was hanging on it, and daring, in the sight of His very mother, the division of His garments.[12] Doubt not that she admitted (εἰσεδέξατο) some such thoughts as these:—I bore Him who is laughed at on the wood; but, in saying He was the true son of the Omnipotent God, perhaps somehow He was mistaken. He said He was the Life, how then has He been crucified? how has He been strangled by the cords of His murderers? how prevailed He not over the plot of His persecutors? why descends He not from the Cross, though He bade Lazarus to return to life, and amazed all Judæa with His miracles?[13] And it is very natural that the woman in her (τὸ γύναιον), not knowing the mystery, should slide into some such trains of thought. For we must conclude, if we judge well, that the gravity of the circumstances was enough to overturn even a self-possessed mind; it is no wonder then if a woman (τὸ γύναιον) slipped into this reasoning. For if Peter himself, the chosen one of the holy disciples, once was scandalized ... so as to cry out hastily, Be it far from Thee, Lord ... what paradox is it, if the soft mind of womankind was carried off to weak ideas? And this we say, not idly conjecturing, as it may strike one, but entertaining the suspicion from what is written concerning the Mother of the Lord. For we remember that Simeon the Just, when he received the Lord as a little child into his arms, ... said to her, 'A sword shall go through thine own soul, that out of many hearts thoughts may be revealed.' By sword he meant the sharp excess of suffering cutting down a woman's mind into extravagant thoughts. For temptations test the

[133]

---

[12] Matt 27:35.
[13] John 11:45.

hearts of those who suffer them, and make bare the thoughts which are in them."

Now what do these three Fathers say in these passages?

1. St. Basil imputes to the Blessed Virgin, not only doubt, but the sin of doubt. On the other hand, 1. he imputes it only on one occasion; 2. he does not consider it to be a grave sin; 3. he implies that, in point of spiritual perfection, she is above the Apostles.

2. St. Chrysostom, in his first passage, does not impute sin [134] to her at all. He says God so disposed things for her as to shield her from the chance of sinning; that she was too admirable to be allowed to be betrayed by her best and purest feelings into sin. All that is implied repugnant to a Catholic's reverence for her, is, that her woman's nature, viewed in itself and apart from the watchful providence of God's grace over her, would not have had strength to resist a hypothetical temptation,—a position which a Catholic will not care to affirm or deny, though he will feel great displeasure at having to discuss it at all. This, moreover, at least is distinctly brought out in the passage, viz., that in St. Chrysostom's mind, our Lady was not a mere physical instrument of the Incarnation, but that her soul, as well as her body, "ministered to the mystery," and needed to be duly prepared for it.

As to his second most extraordinary passage, I should not be candid, unless I simply admitted that it is as much at variance with what we hold, as it is solitary and singular in the writings of Antiquity. The saint distinctly and (*pace illius*[14]) needlessly, imputes to the Blessed Virgin, on the occasion in question, the sin or infirmity of vainglory. He has a parallel passage in commenting on the miracle at the marriage-feast. All that can be said to alleviate the startling character of these passages is, that it does not appear that St.

[14] with all due respects to him

Chrysostom would account such vainglory in a woman as any great failing.

3. Lastly, as to St. Cyril, I do not see that he declares that Mary actually doubted at the Crucifixion, but that, considering she was a woman, it is likely she was tempted to doubt, and nearly doubted. Moreover, St. Cyril does not seem to consider such doubt, had it occurred, as any great sin.

Thus on the whole, all three Fathers, St. Basil and St. Cyril explicitly, and St. Chrysostom by implication, consider that on occasions she was, or might be, exposed to violent temptation to doubt; but two Fathers consider that she actually did sin, though she sinned lightly;—the sin being doubt, and on one occasion, according to St. Basil; and on two occasions, the sin being vainglory, according to St. Chrysostom.

However, the strong language of these Fathers is not directed against our Lady's person, so much as against her nature. They seem to have participated with Ambrose, Jerome, and other Fathers, in that low estimation of woman's nature which was general in their times. In the broad imperial world, the conception entertained of womankind was not high; it seemed only to perpetuate the poetical tradition of the "Varium et mutabile semper."[15] Little was then known of that true nobility, which is exemplified in the females of the Gothic and German races, and in those of the old Jewish stock, Miriam, Deborah, Judith, and Susanna,[16] the forerunners of Mary. When then St. Chrysostom imputes vainglory to her, he is not imputing to her anything worse than an infirmity, the infirmity of a nature, inferior to man's, and intrinsically feeble; as though the Almighty could have created a more excellent being than Mary, but could not have made a greater woman. Accordingly Chrysostom does not say that she sinned. He does not deny that she had all the

[135]

---

[15] Virgil *Aeneid* 4.569 "unstable and forever changing" (referring to Dido).
[16] Ex 15:20; Judg 4:4; Judith; Dan 13.

perfections which woman could have; but he seems to have [136]
thought the capabilities of her nature were bounded, so that
the utmost grace bestowed upon it could not raise it above
that standard of perfection in which its elements resulted, and
that to attempt more, would have been to injure, not to benefit
it. Of course I am not stating this as brought out in any part
of his writings, but it seems to me to be the real sentiment of
many of the ancients.

I will add that such a belief on the part of these Fathers,
that the Blessed Virgin had committed a sin or a weakness,
was not in itself inconsistent with the exercise of love and
devotion to her (though I am not pretending that there is proof
of any such exercise on their part in fact); and for this simple
reason, that if sinlessness were a condition of inspiring
devotion, we should not feel devotion to any but our Lady,
not to St. Joseph, or to the Apostles, or to our Patron saints.

Such then is the teaching of these three Fathers; now how
far is it in antagonism to ours? On the one hand, we will not
allow that our Blessed Lady ever sinned; we cannot bear the
notion, entering, as we do, into the full spirit of St.
Augustine's words, "Concerning the Holy Virgin Mary, I
wish no question to be raised at all, when we are treating of
sins."[17] On the other hand, we admit, rather we maintain, that,
except for the grace of God, she might have sinned; and that
she may have been exposed to temptation in the sense in
which our Lord was exposed to it, though as His Divine
Nature made it impossible for Him to yield to it, so His grace
preserved her under its assaults also. While then we do not
hold that St. Simeon prophesied of temptation, when he said [137]
a sword would pierce her, still, if any one likes to say he did,
we do not consider him heretical, provided he does not
impute to her any sinful or inordinate emotion as the
consequence to it. In this way St. Cyril may be let off

---

[17] *De natura et gratia* (415), *ML* 44.267.

altogether; and we have only to treat of the *paradoxa* or *anomala*[18] of those great Saints, St. Basil and St. Chrysostom. I proceed to their controversial value.

2.

I mean, that having determined what the Three Fathers say, and how far they are at issue with what Catholics hold now, I now come to the main question, viz., What is the authoritative force in controversy of what they thus say in opposition to Catholic teaching? I think I shall be able to show that it has no controversial force at all.

1. I begin by observing, that the main force of passages which can be brought from any Father or Fathers in controversy, lies in the fact that such passages represent the judgment or sentiment of their own respective countries; and again, I say that the force of that local judgment or sentiment lies in its being the existing expression of an Apostolical tradition. I am far, of course, from denying the claim of the teaching of a Father on our deference, arising out of his personal position and character; or the claims of the mere sentiments of a Christian population on our careful attention, as a fact carrying with it, under circumstances, especial weight; but, in a question of doctrine, we must have recourse to the great source of doctrine, Apostolical Tradition, and a Father must represent his own people, and that people must be the witnesses of an uninterrupted Tradition from the Apostles, if anything decisive is to come of any theological statement which is found in his writings; and if, in a particular case, there is no reason to suppose that he does echo the popular voice, or that that popular voice is transmitted from Apostolic times,—or (to take another channel of Tradition) unless the Father in question receives and reports his doctrine from the Bishops and Priests who instructed him on the very

[138]

---

[18] self-contradictory statements and irregularities.

understanding and profession that it is Apostolical,—then, though it was not one Father but ten who said a thing, it would weigh nothing against the assertion of only one Father to the contrary, provided it was clear that that one Father witnessed to an Apostolical Tradition. Now I do not say that I can decide the question by this issue with all the exactness which is conceivable, but still this is the issue by which it must be tried, and the issue by which I shall be enabled, as I think, to come to a satisfactory conclusion upon it.

2. Such, I say, being the issue, viz., that a doctrine reported by the Fathers, in order to have dogmatic force, must be a Tradition in its *source* or *form*, next, what is a Tradition, considered in its *matter*? It is a belief, which, be it *affirmative* or *negative*, is *positive*.[19] The mere absence of a tradition in a country, is not a tradition the other way. If, for instance, there was no tradition in Syria and Asia Minor that the phrase "consubstantial with the Father,"[20] came from the Apostles, that would not be a tradition that it did not come from the Apostles; though of course it would be necessary for those who said that it did, to account for the ignorance of those countries as to the real fact.   [139]

3. The proposition "Christ is God," serves as an example of what I mean by an affirmative tradition; and "no one born of woman is born in God's favour," is an example of a negative tradition. I observe then, in the third place, that a tradition does not carry its own full explanation with it; it does but land (so to say) a proposition at the feet of the Apostles, and its interpretation has still to be determined,— as the Apostles' words in Scripture, however much theirs, need an interpretation. Thus I may accept the above negative Tradition, that "no one woman-born is born in God's favour,"

---

[19] Newman would argue, "The two main sources of Revelation are Scripture and Tradition; that these constitute one Rule of Faith, and that, sometimes as a composite rule, sometimes as a double and co-ordinate, sometimes as an alternative under the *magisterium*, of course, of the Church." *Ath* 2 p.312.
[20] Creed of Chalcedon (451) *DS* 300.

yet question its strict universality, as a point of criticism, saying that a general proposition admits of exceptions, that our Lord was born of woman, yet was the sinless and acceptable priest and sacrifice for all men. So again the Arians allowed that "Christ was God," but they disputed about the meaning of the word "God."

4. Further, there are *explicit* traditions and *implicit*. By an explicit tradition I mean a doctrine which is conveyed in the letter of the proposition which has been handed down; and by implicit, one which lies in the force and virtue, not in the letter of the proposition. Thus it might be an Apostolical tradition that our Lord was the very Son of God, of one nature with the Father, and in all things equal to Him; and again a tradition that there was but one God: these would be explicit, but in them would necessarily be conveyed, moreover, the implicit tradition, that the Father and the Son were [140] numerically one. Implicit traditions are positive traditions, as being strictly conveyed in positive.

5. Lastly, there are at least two ways of determining an Apostolical tradition:—(l.) When credible witnesses declare that it *is* Apostolical; as when three hundred Fathers at Nicæa stopped their ears at Arius's blasphemies:[21] (2.) When, in various places, independent witnesses enunciate one and the same doctrine, as St. Irenæus, St. Cyprian, and Eusebius assert, that the Apostles founded a Church, Catholic and One.

3.

Now to apply these principles to the particular case on account of which I have laid them down.

---

[21] See *Select Treatises of S. Athanasius in Controversy with the Arians* p.3n, Library of the Fathers, Oxford 1877.

1. That "Mary is the new Eve,"[22] is a proposition answering to the *idea* of a Tradition. I am not prepared to say that it can be shown to have the first of the above two tests of its Apostolicity, viz. that the writers who record it, profess to have received it from the Apostles; but I conceive it has the second test, viz. that the writers are independent witnesses, as I have shown at length in the course of my Letter.

It is an explicit tradition; and by the force of it follow two others, which are implicit:—first (considering the condition of Eve in paradise), that Mary had no part in sin, and indefinitely large merits), that she has been exalted to glory proportionate to that grace.

This is what I have to observe on the argument in behalf of the Blessed Virgin. St. Justin, St. Irenæus, Tertullian, are witnesses of an Apostolical tradition, because in three [141] distinct parts of the world they enunciate one and the same definite doctrine. And it is remarkable that they witness just for those three seats of Catholic teaching, where the truth in this matter was likely to be especially lodged. St. Justin speaks for Jerusalem, the see of St. James; St. Irenæus for Ephesus, the dwelling-place, the place of burial, of St. John; and Tertullian, who made a long residence at Rome, for the city of St. Peter and St. Paul.

2. Now,[23] what can be produced on the other side, parallel to an argument like this? A tradition in its matter is a positive statement of belief; in its form it is a statement which comes from the Apostles: (1.) now, first in point of matter, what definite statement of belief at all, is witnessed to by St. Basil, St. Chrysostom, and St. Cyril? I cannot find any. They do but interpret certain passages in the Gospels to our Lady's disadvantage; is an interpretation a distinct statement of belief? but even if it was, there is no joint interpretation in

---

[22] See Newman's comment "As to the primitive notion about our Blessed Lady, really, the frequent contrast of Mary with Eve seems very strong indeed..." *Memorandum for R. I. Wilberforce, MD* p.116ff. Also see Note I supra.

[23] 1st ed.: "Now let us inquire what can be produced..."

this case; they do not all three interpret one and the same passage. Nor do they agree together in their interpretation of those passages, which either one or other of them interprets so harshly; for, while St. Chrysostom holds that our Lord spoke in correction of His Mother at the wedding feast, St. Cyril on the contrary says that He wrought a miracle which He was Himself unwilling to work, in order to show "reverence to His Mother," and that she "having great authority for the working of the miracle, got the victory, persuading the Lord, as being her Son, as was fitting." But, taking the statements which are in her disparagement as we find them, can we generalize them into one proposition? Shall we make it such as this, viz. "The Blessed Virgin during her earthly life committed actual sin"? If we mean by this, that there was a positive recognition of such a proposition in the country of St. Basil or St. Chrysostom, this surely is not to be gathered merely from their separate and independent comments on passages of Scripture. All that can be gathered thence legitimately is, that, had there been a positive belief in her sinlessness in those countries, the Fathers in question would not have spoken of her in the terms which they have used; in other words, that there was no belief in her sinlessness then and there; but the absence of a belief is not a belief to the contrary, it is not that positive statement, which, as I have said, is required for the matter of a tradition.

(2.) Nor do the passages which I have quoted from these Fathers, supply us with any tradition, viewed in its form, that is, as a statement which has come down from the Apostles. I have suggested two tests of such a statement:—one, when the writers who make it so declare that it was from the Apostles; and the other when, being independent of one another, they bear witness to one and the same positive statement of doctrine. Neither test is fulfilled in this case. The three Fathers of the 4th and 5th centuries are but commenting on Scripture; and comments, though carrying with them of course, and betokening, the tone of thought of the place and time to which they belong, are, *primâ facie*, of a private and personal character. If they are more than this, the *onus probandi*[24] lies with those who so maintain. Exegetical theology is one department of divine science, and dogmatic is another. On the other hand, the three Fathers of the 2nd century are all writing on dogmatic subjects, when they compare Mary to Eve.

[143]

4.

Now to take the Three later Fathers, viewed as organs of tradition, one by one :—

1. As to St. Cyril, as I have said, he does not, strictly speaking, say more than that our Lady was grievously tempted. This does not imply sin, for our Lord was "tempted in all things like as we are, yet without sin."[25] Moreover, it is this St. Cyril who spoke at Ephesus of the Blessed Virgin in terms of such high panegyric, as to make it more consistent in him to suppose that she was sinless, than that she was not.

2. St. Basil derives his notion from Origen, that the Blessed Virgin at the time of the Passion admitted a doubt about our Lord's mission, and Origen, so far from professing to rest it on Tradition, draws it as a theological conclusion from a received doctrine. Origen's characteristic fault was to prefer scientific reasonings to authority; and he exemplifies it in the case before us. In the middle age, the great obstacle to the reception of the doctrine of the Blessed Mary's immaculate conception, was the notion that, unless she had been in some sense a sinner, she could not have been redeemed. By an argument parallel to this, Origen argues, that since she was one of the redeemed, she must at one time or another have committed an actual sin. He says: "Are we to

---

[24] the burden of proof
[25] Heb 4:15.

[144] think, that the Apostles were scandalized, and not the Lord's Mother? If she suffered not scandal at our Lord's passion, then Jesus died not for her sins. If all have sinned and need the glory of God, being justified by His grace, and redeemed, certainly Mary at that time was scandalized." This is precisely the argument of Basil, as contained in the passage given above; his statement then the Blessed Virgin's wavering in faith, instead of professing to be the tradition of a doctrine, carries with it an avowal of its being none at all.

However, I am not unwilling to grant that, whereas Scripture tells us that all were scandalized at our Lord's passion, there was some sort of traditional interpretation of Simeon's words, to the effect that she was in some sense included in that trial. How near the Apostolic era the tradition existed, cannot be determined; but such a belief need not include the idea of sin in the Blessed Virgin, but only the presence of temptation and darkness of spirit. This tradition, whatever its authority, would be easily perverted, so as actually to impute sin to her, by such reasonings as that of Origen. Origen himself, in the course of the passage to which I have referred, speaks of "the sword" of Simeon, and is the first to do so. St. Cyril, who, though an Alexandrian as well as Origen, represents a very different school of theology, has, as we have seen, the same interpretation for the piercing sword. It is also found in a Homily attributed to St. Amphilochius;[26] and in that sixth Oration of Proclus,[27] which, according to Tillemont[28] and Ceillier[29], is not to be considered genuine. It is also found in a work incorrectly attributed to St. Augustine.

[145] 3. St. Chrysostom is, *par excellence*, the Commentator of the Church. As Commentator and Preacher, he, of all the Fathers, carries about him the most intense personality. In

[26] See supra.
[27] See supra p.[67].
[28] See supra Note 1 p.[124].
[29] See supra p.[43].

this lies his very charm, peculiar to himself. He is ever overflowing with thought, and he pours it forth with a natural engaging frankness, and an unwearied freshness and vigour. If he really was in the practice of deeply studying and carefully criticizing what he delivered in public, he had in perfection the rare art of concealing his art. He ever speaks from himself, not of course without being impregnated with the fulness of a Catholic training, but, still, not speaking by rule, but as if, "trusting the lore of his own loyal heart." On the other hand, if it is not a paradox to say it, no one carries with him so little of the science, precision, consistency, gravity of a Doctor of the Church,[30] as he who is one of the greatest. The difficulties are well known which he has occasioned to school theologians: his *obiter dicta* about our Lady are among them.

On the whole then I conclude that these three Fathers supply no evidence that, in what they say about her having failed in faith or humility on certain occasions mentioned in Scripture, they are reporting the enunciations of Apostolical Tradition.

5.

Moreover, such difficulties as the above are not uncommon in the writings of the Fathers. I will mention several:—

1. St. Gregory Nyssen is a great dogmatic divine; he too, like St. Basil, is of the school of Origen; and, in several passages of his works, he, like Origen, declares or suggests [146] that future punishment will not be eternal. Those Anglicans who consider St. Chrysostom's passages in his Commentary on the Gospels to be a real argument against the Catholic belief of the Blessed Virgin's sinlessness, should explain why they do not feel St. Gregory Nyssen's teaching in his

---

[30] A title given in the Catholic Church to theologians who are distinguished for orthodoxy, personal sanctity, learning and commendation by the Church.

Catechetical Discourse, an argument against their own belief in the eternity of punishment.

2. Again, Anglicans[31] believe in the proper Divinity of our Lord, in spite of Bull's saying of the Ante-Nicene Fathers, "Nearly all the ancient Catholics, who preceded Arius, have the appearance of being ignorant of the invisible and incomprehensible (*immensam*) nature of the Son of God;"[32] an article of faith expressly contained in the Athanasian Creed, and enforced by its anathema.

3. The Divinity of the Holy Ghost is an integral part of the fundamental doctrine of Christianity; yet St. Basil, in the fourth century, apprehending the storm of controversy which its assertion would raise, refrained from asserting it on an occasion when the Arians were on watch as to what he would say. And, on his keeping silence, St. Athanasius took his part. Such inconsistencies take place continually, and no Catholic doctrine but suffers from them at times, until what has been preserved by Tradition is formally pronounced to be Apostolical by definition of the Church.

6.

Before concluding, I shall briefly take notice of two questions which may be asked me.

[147]

1. How are we to account for the absence, at Antioch or Cæsarea, of a tradition of our Lady's sinlessness? I answer that it was obliterated or confused for the time by the Arian troubles in the countries in which those Sees are situated.[33]

It is not surely wonderful, if, in Syria and Asia Minor, the seat in the fourth century of Arianism and Semi-Arianism, the prerogatives of the Mother were obscured together with the essential glory of the Son, or if they who denied the

---

[31] 1st edition: 'they'
[32] See supra p.[75].
[33] 1st ed: 'are included'

tradition of His divinity, forgot the tradition of her sinlessness. Christians in those countries and times, however religious themselves, however orthodox their teachers, were necessarily under peculiar disadvantages.

Now let it be observed that Basil grew up in the very midst of Semi-Arianism, and had direct relations with that portion of its professors who had been reconciled to the Church and accepted the Homoüsion.[34] It is not wonderful then, if he had no firm habitual hold upon a doctrine which (though Apostolical) in his day was as yet so much in the background all over Christendom, as our Lady's sinlessness.

As to Chrysostom, not only was he in close relations with the once Semi-Arian Cathedra of Antioch,[35] to the disowning of the rival succession there, recognized by Rome and Alexandria, but, as his writings otherwise show, he came under the teaching of the celebrated Antiochene School, celebrated, that is, at once for its method of Scripture criticism, and (orthodox as it was itself) for the successive outbreaks of heresy among its members. These outbreaks began in Paul of Samosata,[36] were continued in the Semi-Arian pupils of Lucian,[37] and ended in Nestorius. The famous Theodore,[38] and Diodorus, of the same school, who, though not heretics themselves, have a bad name in the Church, were, Diodorus[39] the master, and Theodore the fellow-pupil, of St. Chrysostom. (Vid. *Essay on Doctr. Devel.* chap. v. § 2.) Here then is a natural explanation, why St. Chrysostom, even more than St. Basil, might be wanting, great doctor as he was, in a clear perception of the place of the Blessed Virgin in the Evangelical Dispensation.

[148]

---

[34] The Father and the Son are '*of the same substance*'.

[35] The Semi-Arians supported the formula *Homoioüsion*: '*of similar substance*'.

[36] Paul of Samosata (3rd century), Bishop of Antioch in 260 but deposed in 268.

[37] Lucian of Antioch (d. 312), Presbyter of Antioch, Arian theologian.

[38] Theodore of Mopsuestia (c.350-428) entered the school of Diodorus in Antioch with John Chrysostom and became bishop of Mopsuestia in 392.

[39] Diodore (d. c.390) became bishop of Tarsus in 378 and was a native of Antioch.

2. How are we to account for the passages in the Gospels which are the occasion of the three Fathers' remarks to her disparagement? I answer, they were intended to discriminate between our Lord's work who is our Teacher and Redeemer, and the ministrative office of His Mother.

As to the words of Simeon, indeed, as interpreted by St. Basil and St. Cyril, there is nothing in the sacred text which obliges us to consider the "sword" to mean doubt rather than anguish; but Matth. xii. 46-50, with its parallels Mark iii. 31-35, and Luke viii. 19-21: and with Luke xi. 27, 28, and John ii. 4, requires some explanation.

I observe then, that, when our Lord commenced His ministry, and during it, as one of His chief self-sacrifices, He separated Himself from all ties of earth, in order to fulfil the typical idea of a teacher and priest; and to give an example to His priests after Him; and especially to manifest by this action the cardinal truth, as expressed by the Prophet, "I am the Lord, and there is no Saviour besides Me."[40] As to His Priests, they, after Him, were to be of the order of that Melchizedech, who was "without father and without mother;"[41] for "no man, being a soldier to God, entangleth himself with secular business:"[42] and "no man putting his hand to the plough, and looking back, is fit for the kingdom of God."[43] Again, as to the Levites, who were His types in the Old Law, there was that honourable history of their zeal for God, when they even slew their own brethren and companions who had committed idolatry; "who said to his father and to his mother, I do not know you, and to his brethren, I know you not, and their own children they have not known."[44] To this His separation even from His Mother He refers by anticipation at twelve years old in His words,

[149]

---

[40] Is 43:11.
[41] Heb 7:3.
[42] 2 Tim 2:4.
[43] Luke 9:62.
[44] Deut 33:9.

"How is it that you sought Me? Did you not know that I must be about My Father's business?"[45]

The separation from her, with whom He had lived thirty years and more, was not to last beyond the time of His ministry. She seems to have been surprised when she first heard of it, for St. Luke says, on occasion of His staying in the Temple, "they understood not the word that He spoke to them." Nay, she seems hardly to have understood it at the marriage-feast; but He, in dwelling on it more distinctly then, implied also that it was not to last long. He said, "Woman, what have I to do with thee? My hour is not yet come,"[46]— that is, the hour of His triumph, when His Mother was to take her predestined place in His kingdom. In saying the hour was not yet come, He implied that the hour would come, when He would have to "do with her," and she might ask and obtain from Him miracles. Accordingly, St. Augustine thinks that that hour had come, when He said upon the Cross, [150] "*Consummatum est,*"[47] and, after this ceremonial estrangement of years, He recognized His Mother and committed her to the beloved disciple. Thus, by marking out the beginning and the end of the period of exception, during which she could not exert her influence upon Him, He signifies more clearly by the contrast, that her presence with Him, and Her power, was to be the rule of His kingdom. In a higher sense than He spoke to the Apostles, He seems to address her in the words, "Because I have spoken these things, sorrow hath filled your heart. But I will see you again, and your heart shall rejoice, and your joy no man shall take from you."[48] (*Vid. Sermon* iii. *in Sermons on Subjects of the*

---

[45] Luke 2:49.
[46] John 2:4.
[47] "It is accomplished" John 19:30.
[48] John 1:22.

Day.[49] Also the comment of St. Irenæus, &c., upon John ii. 4, in my note on Athanas. Orat. iii. 41.)[50]

Also, I might have added the passage in Tertullian, Carn. Christ. § 7, as illustrating, by its contrast with § 17 (quoted above, p. 34), the distinction between doctrinal tradition and personal opinion, if it were clear to me that he included the Blessed Virgin in the unbelief which he imputes to our Lord's brethren; on the contrary, he expressly separates her off from them. The passage runs thus on the text, "Who is My Mother? and who are My Brethren?"[51]

"The Lord's brothers had not believed in Him, as is contained in the Gospel published before Marcion.[52] His Mother, equally, *is not described* (non demonstratur) *as having adhered to Him*, whereas other Marthas and Maries are frequent in intercourse with him. In this place at length their (eorum) incredulity is evident; while He was teaching the way of life, was preaching the kingdom of God, was working for the cure of ailments and diseases, though strangers were riveted to Him, these, so much the nearest to Him (tam proximi), were away. At length they come upon Him, and stand without, nor enter, not reckoning forsooth on what was going on within."[53]

Additional Note, Ed. 5.—It may be added to the above, that Fr. Hippolyto Maracci,[54] in his "Vindicati Chrysostomica," arguing in behalf of St. Chrysostom's belief

[151]

---

[49] 1st ed: "And as at his first feast, he had seemed to turn from his Mother's prayer, while he granted it, because of the time, so to his apostles he foretold, at his second feast, what the power of their prayers should be hereafter, by way of cheering them on his departure." 'Our Lord's Last Supper and his First.' The rest was omitted.

[50] *Select Treatises of St. Athanasius in controversy with the Arians*, Library of the Fathers, Oxford 1877, p.458.

[51] Matt 12:48.

[52] Marcion (d. c.160). Wealthy shipowner who rejected the Old Testament and was excommunicated in 144.

[53] These two paragraphs appear in the third edition.

[54] Ippolito Maracci (1604-75), Vicar General of the Clerks Regular of the Mother of God and author of many Mariological titles.

in the Blessed Virgin's Immaculate Conception, maintains that a real belief in that doctrine is compatible with an admission that she was not free from venial sin, granting for argument's sake that St. Chrysostom held the latter doctrine. If this be so, it follows that we cannot at once conclude that either he or the other two Fathers deny the doctrine of the Immaculate Conception, because here and there in their writings they impute to the Blessed Virgin infirmities or faults. He writes as follows:—

"Demus, quod dandum non est, scilicet Chrysostomum tribuisse Deiparæ Virgini peccatum actuale veniale, nunquid ex hoc potest solidè inferri ipsum eidem tribuisse etiam peccatum originale? Minimè quidem. Non enim apparet necessaria connexio inter carentiam peccati venialis et carentiam originalis, ita ut ex unâ possit inferri alia. Potuit Chrysostomus liberare B. Virginem à peccato originali, licet non liberaverit à veniali. Peccatum veniale, juxta doctrinam Angelici Doctoris, non causat maculam in animâ, nec spiritualem pulchritudinem in eâ demolitur, stareque potest cum elogiis 'immaculatæ,' 'incontaminatæ,' 'impollutæ,' &c. Cæterùm peccatum originale, cùm penitus omnem gratiæ ornatum explodat, cum decore immaculatæ, incontaminatæ, impollutæ &c., minimè potest consistere. Chrysostomus arbitratus est, minùs indecorum fuisse Christo nasci ex matre, quæ levi veniali maculâ afficeretur, quam quæ originali ignominiâ dehonestaretur. Præservare Virginem a peccato originali majus privilegium et excellentius beneficium est ex parte Dei, quàm eam non permittere maculâ veniali aliquantulum opacari. Stante enim præservatione à peccato originali, nec anima Dei inimicitiam bushcontrahit, nec diaboli mancipium evadit, nec denique redditur inepta ad recipienda plura auxilia gratiæ annexa, quibus plura peccata venialia declinare posset. Ex aliâ parte, peccatum veniale ex se his bonis recipiendis obicem non adeo ponit, nec animæ [152] pulchritudini, nec amicitiæ, nec charitati machinatur exilium."[55]

---

[55] "Let us give what should not be given, namely that Chrysostom might have attributed actual venial sin to the Virgin Mother of God, it can in no way be solidly inferred that he also attributed original sin? Certainly not. For there does not appear to be a necessary connection between the absence of venial sin and that of original sin, so that from one you can infer the other. Chrysostom could have freed the Blessed Virgin from original sin and not freed her from venial sin. Venial sin, according to the teaching of the Angelic Doctor [Thomas Aquinas] does not leave a stain on the soul nor is the beauty of holiness destroyed in her, so she can be praised as immaculate, untarnished, unpolluted etc. Besides, someone adorned with every grace, immaculate, untarnished, unpolluted could not be envisaged because original sin would be driven out. Chrysostom argued that it would be less fitting for Christ to be born of a mother lightly affected by venial sin than to dishonour her by the ignominy of original sin. Preserving the Virgin from original sin is, from the part of God the far greater privilege and reward, than not allowing her the slightest shade of any stain of venial sin. The preservation from original sin means that the soul is not alienated from God, escapes the Devil's clutches, and is open to receive the many graces which would not be possible with venial sin. In addition venial sin of itself does not place any barrier to the good things received nor brings about any exclusion either to beauty of soul, or of friendship or charity." [Added to the 5th edition]

NOTE IV. PAGE 91.

ON THE TEACHING OF THE GREEK CHURCH ABOUT THE BLESSED VIRGIN

CANISIUS,[1] in his work *de Mariâ Deiparâ Virgine*,[2] p. 514, while engaged in showing the carefulness with which the Church distinguishes the worship of God from the *cultus* of the Blessed Virgin, observes, "Lest the Church should depart from *Latria* (i.e. the worship of God) she has instituted the public supplications in the Liturgy in perpetuity in such wise as to address them directly to God the Father, and not to the Saints, according to that common form of praying, 'Almighty, everlasting God,' &c.; and the said prayers which they also call 'Collects,' she generally ends in this way, 'through Jesus Christ, Thy Son, our Lord.'" He says more to the same purpose; but the two points here laid down are sufficient; viz. that as to the Latin Missal, Ritual, and Breviary,[3] (1.) Saints are not directly addressed in these authoritative books: and (2.) in them prayers end with the name of Jesus. An apposite illustration of both of these, that is, in what is omitted and what is introduced, is supplied by the concluding prayer of the Offertory in the Latin Mass. If in any case the name of "our Lady and all Saints" might at the end of a prayer be substituted for our Lord's name, it would be when the object addressed is, not God the Father, [154]

---

[1] See supra.

[2] *De Beata Maria Virgine incomparabili* Ingolstadt 1577.

[3] The Breviary is the Office or Liturgy of the Hours used by clergy and religious.

but the Son, or the Holy Trinity; but let us observe how the prayer in question runs:—

"Suscipe, Sancta Trinitas"—"Receive, *O Holy Trinity*, this oblation which we make to Thee, in memory of the Passion, Resurrection, and Ascension of our Lord Jesus Christ, and *in honour of* the Blessed Mary, Ever-Virgin, of Blessed John Baptist, and of the Holy Apostles Peter and Paul, and of these and all Saints, that it may avail for their honour and our salvation, and that they may vouchsafe to intercede for us in heaven, whose memory we celebrate on earth, *Through the same Christ our Lord.* Amen."[4]

When in occasional Collects the intercession of the Blessed Mary is introduced, it does not supersede mention of our Lord as the Intercessor. Thus in the Post-Communion on the Feast of the Circumcision,[5]—

"May this Communion, O Lord, purify us from guilt; and at the intercession of the Blessed Virgin Mary, Mother of God, make us partakers of the heavenly remedy, through the same our Lord Jesus Christ. Amen."

In like manner, when the Son is addressed, and the intercession of Mary and the Saints is supplicated, His atoning passion is introduced at the close, as on the Feast of the Seven Dolours:[6]—

"God, at whose passion, according to the prophecy of Simeon, the most sweet soul of the glorious Virgin-Mother Mary was pierced through with the sword of sorrow, mercifully grant, that we, who reverently commemorate her [155] piercing and passion, may, by the intercession of the glorious merits and prayers of the Saints who faithfully stood by the Cross, *obtain the happy fruit of Thy Passion*, who livest and reignest, &c."

---

[4] Since the reform of Vatican II this prayer is no longer part of the Offertory.

[5] Feast kept on January 1, "when eight days were accomplished" Luke 2:21.

[6] Friday in Passion week, included in the Roman calendar in 1727 by Benedict XIII but now replaced by the feast of Our Lady of Sorrows on September 15th.

Note IV

"We offer to Thee, Lord Jesus Christ, our prayers and sacrifices, humbly supplicating, that we, who renew in our prayers the piercing of the most sweet soul of Thy Blessed Mother Mary, by the manifold compassionate intervention of both her and her holy companions under the Cross, *by the merits of Thy death*, may merit a place with the Blessed, who livest, &c."

Now let us observe how far less observant of dogmatic exactness, how free and fearless in its exaltation of the Blessed Virgin, is the formal Greek devotion:—

1. "We have risen from sleep, and we fall down before Thee, O good God; and we sing to Thee the Angelic Hymn, O powerful God. Holy, holy, holy art Thou, God; have mercy on us through the Theotocos.

"Thou hast raised me from my bed and slumber, O God. Lighten my mind, and open my heart and lips, to sing of Thee, Holy Trinity. Holy, holy, holy art Thou, God; have mercy on us through the Theotocos.

"Soon will come the Judge, and the deeds of all will be laid bare ... Holy, holy, holy art Thou, God; have mercy on us through the Theotocos."—*Horologium*,[7] p. 2, *Venet.* 1836: vide also, pp. 34, 48, 52. Also *Eucholog.*[8] *Venet.* p. 358.

2. "O God, who lookest on the earth, and makest it tremble, deliver us from the fearful threatenings of earthquake, Christ our God; and send down on us Thy rich mercies, and save us, at the intercessions (πρεσβείαις) of the Theotocos."—*Ibid.* p. 224. Vid. also *Pentecostar.*[9] p. 14. [156]

3. "O Holy God, ... visit us in Thy goodness, pardon us every sin, sanctify our souls, and grant us to serve Thee in holiness all the days of our life, at the intercessions

---

[7] The liturgical book giving the parts of the Office throughout the year.

[8] The book giving the essential texts and rubrics for the liturgy.

[9] The book used for prayers and lections between Easter and the Sunday after Pentecost.

(πρεσβείαις) of the Holy Theotocos and all the Saints, &c."—
Euchologium, p. 64. *Venet*. 1832.

4. "Again, and still again, let us beseech the Lord in peace.
Help, save, pity, preserve us, O God [through] her, the all-
holy, Immaculate, most Blessed, and glorious (διαφύλαξον
ἡμᾶς ὁ Θεὸς τῆς παναγίας), &c."—*Euchologium*, p. 92.
Venet. 1832. Vid. also *Pentecostar*, p. 232; and *passim*.

5. "Lord, Almighty Sovereign, ... restore and raise from
her bed this Thy servant, &c. ... at the intercession
(πρεσβείαις) of the all-undefiled Theotocos and all the
Saints."—*Ibid*. p. 142.

6. "Have mercy and pardon, (for Thou alone hast power
to remit sins and iniquities,) at the intercession of Thy all-
holy Mother and all the Saints."—*Ibid*. p. 150.

7. "O Lord God Almighty, ... bless and hallow Thy place
... at the intercession (πρεσβείαις) of our glorious Lady,
Mary, Mother of God and Ever-Virgin."—*Eucholog*. p. 389.

Is the Blessed Virgin ever called "our Lady," as here, in
the Latin Prayers? whereas it is a frequent title of her in the
Greek.

8. "Save me, my God, from all injury and harm, Thou who
art glorified in Three Persons ... and guard Thy flock at the
intercessions (ἐντεύξεσιν) of the Theotocos."—
Pentecostarium, p. 50. *Venet*. 1820. Vid. also Goar,[10]
Eucholog. p. 30.

9. "In the porch of Solomon there lay a multitude of sick[11]
... Lord, send to us Thy great mercies at the intercession
(πρεσβείαις) of the Theotocos."—*Pentecostar*. p. 84. Vid.
also Goar, *Eucholog*. pp. 488, 543.

10. "O great God, the Highest, who alone hast immortality
... prosper our prayer as the incense before Thee ... that we
may remember even in the night Thy holy Name, ... and rise

[157]

---

[10] Jacques Goar (1601-54), French Dominican liturgiologist who published his
Rituale Graecorum in 1647.
[11] Acts 5:12.

anew in gladness of soul ... bringing our prayers and supplications to Thy loving kindness in behalf of our own sins and of all Thy people, whom visit in mercy at the intercessions (πρεσβείαις) of the Holy Theotocos."—*Ibid*. p. 232. Vid. *Horolog*. p. 192. *Venet*. 1836.

11. Between the Trisagion[12] and Epistle in Mass. "O Holy God, who dwellest in the holy place, whom with the voice of their Trisagion the Seraphim do praise, &c. ... sanctify our souls and bodies, and grant us to serve Thee in holiness all the days of our life, at the intercession (πρεσβείαις) of the Holy Theotocos and all the Saints."—*Eucholog*. p. 64. *Venet*. 1832.

12. In the early part of Mass. "Lift up the horn of Christians, and send down on us Thy rich mercies, by the power of the precious and life-giving Cross, by the grace of Thy light-bringing, third-day resurrection from the dead, at the intercession (πρεσβείαις) of our All-holy Blessed Lady, Mother of God and Ever-Virgin, and all Thy Saints."— Assemani, *Codex Liturg*. t. v. p. 71. *Rite of St. James*.

13. At the Offertory at Mass. "In honour and memory of [158] our singularly blessed and glorious Queen, Mary Theotocos and Ever-Virgin; at whose intercession, O Lord, receive, O Lord, this sacrifice unto Thy altar which is beyond the heavens."—Goar, *Euchol*. p. 58. *Rite of St. Chrysostom*.

14. In the Commemoration at Mass. "*Cantors*. Hail, Mary, full of grace, &c. &c. ... for thou hast borne the Saviour of our souls. *Priest*. [Remember, Lord] especially the most Holy Immaculate, &c. ... Mary. *Cantors*. It is meet truly to bless (μακαρίζειν) thee, the Theotocos ... more honourable than the Cherubim, &c. ... thee we magnify, who art truly the Theotocos. O Full of Grace, in thee the whole creation rejoices, the congregation of Angels, and the race of men, O

---

[12] "Holy God, Holy and mighty, Holy and immortal, have mercy on us." Chanted before the Lections.

sanctified shrine, and spiritual Paradise, boast of virgins,"
&c.—Assemani,[13] t. v. p. 44. *Jerusalem Rite.*

15. In the Commemoration at Mass. "*Priest.* Especially
and first of all, we make mention of the Holy, glorious, and
Ever-Virgin Mary, &c. *Deacon.* Remember her, Lord God,
and at her holy and pure prayers be propitious, have mercy
upon us, and favourably hear us. *Priest.* Mother of our Lord
Jesus Christ, pray for me to thy Son Only-begotten, who
came of thee, that, having remitted my sins and debts, He
may accept from my humble and sinful hands this sacrifice,
which is offered by my vileness on this altar, through thy
intercession, Mother most holy."—*Ibid.* p. 186. *Syrian Rite.*

16. Apparently, after the Consecration. "*The Priest
incenses thrice before the Image (or Picture, imagine) of the
Virgin and says*: Rejoice, Mary, beautiful dove,[14] who hast
borne for us God, the Word; thee we salute with the Angel
Gabriel, saying, Hail, full of grace, the Lord is with thee,
Hail, Virgin, true Queen; hail, glory of our race, thou hast
borne Emmanuel. We ask, remember us, O faithful advocate,
in the sight of our Lord Jesus Christ, that He put away from
us our sins."—*Ibid.* t. vii., *pars 2da. in fin.* p. 20. *Alexandrian
Rite.*

[159]

17. At the Communion in Mass. "Forgive, our God, remit,
pardon me my trespasses as many as I have committed,
whether in knowledge or in ignorance, whether in word or in
deed. All these things pardon me, as Thou art good and kind
to men, at the intercession (πρεσβείαις) of Thy all-undefiled
and Ever-Virgin Mother. Preserve me uncondemned, that I
may receive Thy precious and undefiled Body, for the
healing of my body and soul."—Goar, *Euchologium*, p. 66.

---

[13] The family name of Stephen Evodius (1707-82). He edited *Bibliothecae
Medicineae-Laurentianae et Palatinae Codicum MSS Orientalium Catalogus* in
1742. Like his relatives he was a Maronite Orientalist; he worked in the Vatican
library.

[14] Song 4:1; 5:2.

18. After Communion at Mass. "O Lord, be merciful to us, bless us, let Thy countenance be seen upon us, and pity us, Lord, save Thy people, bless Thine heritage, &c., ... through the prayers and addresses (orationes) which the Lady of us all, Mother of God, the divine (diva) and Holy Mary, and the four bright holy ones, Michael," &c., &c.— Renaudot,[15] *Liturg. Orient.* t. i. p. 29. *Coptic Rite of St. Basil.* Vid. also *ibid.* pp. 29, 37, 89, 515, *of St. Basil, Coptic*; *of St. Gregory, Coptic*; *of Alexandria, Greek*; *and of Ethiopia.*

19. After Communion at Mass. "We have consummated this holy service (λειτουργίαν), as we have been ordered, O Lord ... we, sinners, and Thine unworthy servants, who have been made worthy to serve at Thy holy altar, in offering to Thee the bloodless sacrifice, the immaculate Body, and the precious Blood of the Great God, our Saviour Jesus Christ, to Thy glory, the unoriginate Father, and to the glory of Him, Thy only-begotten Son, and of the Holy Ghost, good, life-giving, and consubstantial with Thee. We ask a place on Thy right hand in Thy fearful and just day through the intercession (διά τῶν πρεσβειῶν) and prayers of our most glorious Lady, Mary, Mother of God, and Ever-Virgin, and of all saints."— Assemani, *Cod. Liturg.* t. vii. p. 85. *Rite of Alexandria.* [160]

20. After Communion at Mass. "We thank Thee, Lord, Lover of men, Benefactor of our souls, that also on this day Thou hast vouchsafed us Thy heavenly and immortal mysteries. Direct our way aright, confirm us all in Thy fear, &c, ... at the prayers and supplications of the glorious Theotocos and Ever-Virgin Mary, and of all Thy saints."— *Eucholog.* p. 86. *Venet.* 1832.

21. Concluding words of Mass. "Blessed is He who has given us His holy Body and precious Blood. We have received grace and found life, by virtue of the Cross of Jesus

---

[15] Eusèbe Renaudot (1646-1720), a member of the Académie Française in 1689, was a historian and Orientalist. His *Liturgiarum Orientalium Collectio* was published in 1713.

Christ. To Thee, O Lord, we give thanks, &c. Praise to Mary, who is the glory of us all, who has brought forth for us the Eucharist."—Renaudot, *Liturg. Orient.* t. i. p. 522. *Rite of Ethiopia.*

I will add some of the instances, which have caught my eye in these ecclesiastical books, of expressions used of the Blessed Virgin, which, among Latins, though occurring in some Antiphons, belong more to the popular than to the formal and appointed devotions paid to her.

22. "Thee we have as a tower and harbour, and an [161] acceptable ambassadress (πρέσβιν) to the God whom thou didst bear, Mother of God who hadst no spouse, the salvation of believers."—*Pentecostar.* p. 209. *Venet.* 1820.

23. "O Virgin alone holy and undefiled, who hast miraculously (ἀσπόρως) conceived God, intercede (πρεσβεύε) for the salvation of the soul of thy servant."—*Eucholog.* p. 439. *Venet.* 1832.

24. "Show forth thy speedy protection and aid and mercy on thy servant, and still the waves, thou pure one, of vain thoughts, and raise up my fallen soul, O Mother of God. For I know, O Virgin, I know that thou hast power for whatever thou willest."—*Ibid.* p. 679.

25. "Joachim and Anna[16] were set free from the reproach of childlessness, and Adam and Eve from the corruption of death, O undefiled, in thy holy birth. And thy people keeps festival upon it, being ransomed from the guilt of their offences in crying to thee. The barren bears the Theotocos, and the nurse of Life."—*Horolog.* p. 198. *Venet.* 1836.

26. "Let us now run earnestly to the Theotocos, sinners as we are, and low, and let us fall in repentance, crying from the depths of our souls, Lady, aid us, taking compassion on us. Make haste, we perish under the multitude of our offences. Turn us not, thy servants, empty away; for we have thee as

---

[16] Joachim and Anna were first mentioned in the 2nd century *Protoevangelium of St. James* as the parents of the Blessed Virgin Mary.

our only hope."—*Ibid.* p. 470. Vid. "My whole hope I repose in thee."—*Triodion,*[17] p. 94. *Venet.* 1820.

27. "We have gained thee for a wall of relief, and the all-perfect salvation of souls, and a relief (πλατυσμὸν) in afflictions, and in thy light we ever rejoice; O Queen, even now through suffering and danger preserve us."—*Ibid.* p. 474. [162]

28. "By thy mediation, Virgin, I am saved."—*Triod.* p. 6. *Venet.* 1820.

29. "The relief of the afflicted, the release of the sick, O Virgin Theotocos, save this city and people; the peace of those who are oppressed by war, the calm of the tempest-tost, the sole protection of the faithful."—Goar,[18] *Eucholog.* p. 478.

30. All through the Office Books are found a great number of Collects and Prayers to the Blessed Virgin, called Theotocia,[19] whereas in the Latin Offices addresses to her scarcely get beyond the Antiphons. There are above 100 of them in the Euchology, above 170 in the Pentecostarium, close upon 350 in the Triodion. These, according to Renaudot, are sometimes collected together into separate volumes. (*Liturg. Orient.* t. ii. p. 98.)

31. At p. 424 of the *Horologium* there is a collection of 100 invocations in her honour, arranged for the year.

32. At page 271 of the *Euchologium*, is a form of prayer to her "in the confession of a sinner," consisting of thirty-six collects, concluding with a Gospel, supplication, &c. If there were any doubt of the difference which the Greeks make between her and the Saints, one of these would be evidence of it. "*Take with you* (παράλαβε) the multitude of Archangels and of the heavenly hosts, and the Forerunner, &c., ... and

---

[17] The book containing variable parts of the liturgy between the 4th Sunday before Lent until the Saturday before Easter. The canons usually contain three odes instead of nine.

[18] See supra.

[19] Stanzas in hymns addressed to the Blessed Virgin.

make intercession (*πρεσβειαν*), Holy one, in my behalf with God," p. 275. *Vid.* also *ibid.* p. 390, &c.

[163] 33. There is another form of prayer to her at p. 640, of forty-three collects or verses, "in expectation of war," arranged to form an Iambic acrostic, "O undefiled, be the ally of my household." Among other phrases we read here, "Thou art the head commander (*ὁ ἀρχιστράτηγος*) of Christians; ... "They in their chariots and horses, we, thy people, in thy name;" "with thy spiritual hand cast down the enemies of thy people;" "Thy power runs with thy will (*σύνδρομον ἔχεις*)," &c. "Deliver not thine heritage, O holy one, into the hands of the heathen, lest they shall say, Where is the Mother of God in whom they trusted?" "Hear from thy holy Temple, thy servants, O pure one, and pour out God's wrath upon the Gentiles that have not faithfully called upon thy glorious name."

34. It is remarkable, that, not only the Jacobites,[20] but even the Nestorians[21] agree with the Orthodox in the unlimited honours they pay to the Blessed Virgin. "No one," says Renaudot, "has accused the Orientals of deficiency in the legitimate honours, which are the right of the Deipara; but many have charged them with having sometimes been extravagant in that devotion, and running into superstition, which accusation is not without foundation."—t. i. p. 257.

Another remark of his is in point here. The extracts above made are in great measure from Greek service-books of the day; but even those which are not such are evidence, according to their date and place, of opinions and practices, then and there existing. "Their weight does not depend on the

---

[20] Monophysites who denied the two natures in Christ and were followers of Jacob Baradeus (c.500-78) who became Bishop of Edessa in 542. They became the national Church of Syria

[21] Followers of Nestorius (d. c.451) who studied under Theodore of Mopsuestia (qv) and became Bishop of Constantinople. Nestorius denied that Christ was one Person, God and man. His teaching was condemned by Pope Celestine in 430, and he was banished in 436.

authority of the writers, but on the use of the Churches. Those prayers had their authors, who indeed were not known; but, [164] when once it was clear that they had been used in Mass, who their authors were ceased to be a question."—t. i. p. 173. The existing manuscripts can hardly be supposed to be mere compositions, but are records of rites.

I say then, first:—That usage, which, after a split has taken place in a religious communion, is found to obtain equally in each of its separated parts, may fairly be said to have existed before the split occurred. The concurrence of Orthodox, Nestorian, and Jacobite in the honours they pay to the Blessed Virgin, is an evidence that those honours were in the irsubstance[22] paid to her in their "Undivided Church."

Next:—Passages such as the above, taken from the formal ritual of the Greeks, are more compromising to those who propose entering into communion with them, than such parallel statements as occur in unauthoritative devotions of the Latins.

---

[22] essential quality

NOTE V. PAGE 107.

ON A SCANDALOUS TENET CONCERNING THE BLESSED VIRGIN

I FIND the following very apposite passage at note t, p. 390, of vol. i. of Mr. Morris's "Jesus the Son of Mary,"[1] a work full of learning, which unhappily I forgot to consult, till my Letter was finished and in type.

"An error of this sort [that our Lady is in the Holy Eucharist] was held by some persons, and is condemned in the following language by Benedict XIV. [i.e. by Cardinal Lambertini],[2] as has been pointed out to me by my old and valued friend, Father Faber:[3] 'This doctrine was held to be erroneous, dangerous, and scandalous, and the *cultus* was reprobated, which in consequence of it they asserted was to be paid to the most Blessed Virgin in the Sacrament of the Altar.'

"Lambertini de Canonizatione Sanctorum, lib. iv. p. 2, c. 31, n. 32.

"De cultu erga Deiparam in Sacramento Altaris.[4]

---

[1] John Brande Morris, *Jesus the Son of Mary or the Doctrine of the Church Upon the Incarnaion of God the Son* (1851). He had become a Catholic in 1846.

[2] Prospero Lorenzo Lambertini had been Promoter of the Faith (in charge of canonizations) and was Pope from 1740-to 1758. Newman also refers to "new and extravagant titles" given to the Blessed Virgin which had been condemned by Pius IX *VM* 1 p.xlviii.

[3] See supra p.[22].

[4] On the worship of the Mother of God in the Sacrament of the Altar. "Not many years ago there was a book produced on the worship directed toward the Mother of God in the Sacrament of the Altar, by the author Fr. Zepherin de Someire, a

Franciscan Recollect, in which it was asserted that Mary was present in some way in the Sacrament of the Altar, in other words, her flesh enlivened by her holy soul and the blood contained in her veins and the milk from her full breasts. In addition we have not only the blood of the Mother of God, in so far as the flesh and bones of Christ are changed, but also some of the blood in its original form; not only her true flesh but some of her members because the blood and the milk which formed and nourished the body of Christ were furnished by each and every member of the Blessed Virgin.

Also Cristóbal de Vega in a substantial book entitled *Theologia Mariana* edited in Lyon in 1653 covered virtually the same subject: but Théophile Raynaud in his *Marian Diptych* t. 7 p. 65 rejects what has been argued and asserts that it is heresy according to Guy the Carmelite in his *Summa* on his Tract on the Heresies of the Greeks. 13, where he says, "The thirteenth error of the Greeks is that they say, what remains of the consecrated Bread are remains of the body of the Blessed Virgin. This error is full of lies and stupidity. For the body of Christ remains in its totality under each part of the consecrated host. Therefore each part however divided and separated is truly the body of Christ. It is moreover heretical and stupid to say that the body of Christ is the body of his Virgin mother, as heretical to say that Christ is the Blessed Virgin: because distinct men have distinct bodies and so much honour is due to the body of a virgin as is due to the body of Christ, for which reason the honour of *latria* is due to the divine Person of Christ not to the body of the Virgin. Therefore to say that the remains of the consecrated hosts are remains of the body of he Blessed Virgin is manifest heresy."

In addition, the foremost of theologians, St. Thomas in his III Pars Q. 31 a. 5 teaches firstly that the body of Christ was 'conceived of the most chaste and pure blood of the Blessed Virgin, specifically brought into this world with the capacity to make it suitable for the purpose of conception'. Since the conception of Christ was entirely of the natural order: the most pure blood as suitable matter for the working of the Holy Spirit in the womb of the Blessed Virgin and the forming of the infant. Secondly, the body of Christ could not have been formed by any other substance than the flesh and bones of the Blessed Virgin since they are integral parts of her body: therefore you cannot take them away without corruption and diminution. When we say that Christ took flesh from the Blessed Virgin, it must be understood and explained not that the material of the body was actual flesh but blood with the potential of becoming flesh. Thirdly, how could one take away some part from the body of Adam without causing a diminution, since Adam is in a certain way the progenitor of humanity, he ought to have extra personal parts of his body which could be taken away to form Eve without harming his bodily integrity: which would not have been possible in the case of the Blessed Virgin, who as a unique individual had a most perfect human body, with a most suitable material structure to form the body of Christ from the feminine aspect, and as relates to giving birth. From this it follows that you cannot take anything from the substance of her body without harming the integrity of the Blessed Virgin.

Therefore since this teaching, allied expressly to the principles of faith rejects the assertions in the said book of Fr. Zepherin and his teaching as erroneous, dangerous and scandalous, it also rejects his assertion of worship of the Blessed Virgin in the Sacrament of the altar. The formula which says the Flesh of Mary is the Flesh of Christ is not accepted by a considerable number of the Fathers. The flesh of Mary is

"Non multis abhinc annis prodiit Liber de cultu erga Deiparam in Sacramento altaris, auctore Patre Zephyrino de Someire Recollecto Sancti Francisci,[5] in quo asserebatur, in Sacramento altaris aliquam illius partem adesse, eandem videlicet carnem, quam olim ejus sanctissima anima [166] vivificavit, eumdemque illum sanguinem, qui in ejus venis continebatur, et ipsum lac, quo ejus ubera plena erant. Addebatur, nos habere in Sacramento non tantum sanguinem Deiparæ, quatenus in carnem et ossa Christi mutatus est, sed etiam partem sanguinis in propria specie; neque solum veram carnem ipsius, sed etiam aliquid singulorum membrorum, quia sanguis, et lac, ex quibus formatum et nutritum fuit corpus Christi, missa fuerunt ab omnibus et singulis membris Beatissimæ Virginis.

---

given to us to eat for our salvation should be understood not in the sense that in Christ there is something which is of Mary but Christ was conceived of the Virgin Mary: she giving him body and form, and therefore he is her son. So, because the flesh of Christ was from David as it is said expressly in Romans "descended from David according to the flesh" [Rom 1:3] David is likened to Christ, as Augustine says in his *Ennarationes* on Psalm 144 "Praise of David should be understood as praise of Christ." And further, "Because from David according to the flesh, so it is with Christ. And we see the same use in the solemn words of Scripture, speaking of parents when the flesh of one calls to the other, as with Laban when Jacob in Gen 29 says, "Os meum es, et caro mea" ["You are my bone and my flesh" Gen 29:14] and Judah, speaking of his brother Joseph, says in Gen 27 "Frater enim, et caro nostra est" ["For he is our brother and of our own flesh." Gen 37:27] and Lev. 18 says, "Soror patris tui caro est patris tui, et soror matris tuae caro est matris tuae" ["because she is the flesh of thy father ... of thy father's sister; because she is the flesh of thy father" Lev 18:12-13]. From which it can be inferred that in Jacob there was some actual part of the body of Laban, and in Joseph some part of Judah: in the son some part of the father. Therefore it can only be allowed that in the Sacrament there is the flesh of Christ taken from Mary, or as St. Ambrose says in the canon *Omnia de Consecratione distincta 2* in these words, "This my flesh is life for the world and what is wonderful to say, it is not plainly any other than was born of Mary, suffered on the cross and rose from the tomb; this is say it is the same flesh." And speaking elsewhere of the body of Christ, "Clearly this is the very same body taken from the Virgin which suffered and was buried." [Pusey treats of this, mentioning Cornelius a Lapide, Salazar and Faber's *The Precious Blood, En* pp.169-72.]

[5] Zepherin de Semeire *La devotion à la mère de Dieu dans le très Saint Sacrement de l'autel, fondé sur les unions, qui sont entre son fils et elle en ce divin mystère* . His book was put on the index 30 September, 1698.

Note V

Etiam Christophorus de Vega[6] in volumine satis amplo, quod inscribitur "Theologia Mariana," Lugduni edito ann. 1653, fusius ea omnia prosecutus est: sed Theophilus Raynaudus in suis Diptychis Marianis, t. 7, p. 65, ea reprobat, asseritque hæresim sapere juxta Guidonem Carmelitam in Summa de hæresibus tract. de hæresi Græcorum, c. 13, cujus arenim, quod reliquiæ Panis consecrati sunt reliquiæ corporis Beatæ Virginis. Hic error stultitiæ et amentiæ plenus est. Nam corpus Christi sub qualibet parte hostiæ consecratæ integrum manet. Itaque quælibet pars, a tota consecrata hostia divisa et separata, est verum corpus Christi. Hæreticum autem est et fatuum dicere, quod corpus Christi sit corpus Virginis matris suæ, sicut hæreticum esset dicere, quod Christus esset Beata Virgo: quia distinctorum hominum distincta sunt corpora, nec tantus honor debetur corpori virginis, quantus debetur corpori Christi, cui ratione Divini Suppositi debetur honor latriæ, non corpori Virginis. Igitur dicere, reliquias hostiæ consecratæ esse reliquias corporis Beatæ Virginis est hæreticum manifesto."

Porro Theologorum Princeps B. Thomas, 3 part. quæst. 31, art. 5, docet primo, Christi corpus conceptum fuisse ex Beatæ Virginis castissimis et purissimis sanguinibus non quibuscunque, sed "perductis ad quamdam ampliorem digestionem per virtutem generativam ipsius, ut essent materia apta ad conceptum," cum Christi conceptio fuerit secundum conditionem naturæ; materiamque aptam, sive purissimum sanguinem in conceptione Christi sola Spiritus Sancti operatione in utero Virginis adunatum, et in prolem formatum fuisse; ita ut vere dicatur corpus Christi ex purissimis et castissimis sanguinibus Beatæ Virginis fuisse formatum. Docet secundo, non potuisse corpus Christi formari de aliqua substantia, videlicet de carne et ossibus Beatissimæ Virginis, cum sint partes integrantes corpus ipsius: ideoque subtrahi non potuissent sine corruptione, et [167]

---

[6] Cristóbal de Vega (1595-1672), Spanish Jesuit author of *Theologia Mariana*.

ejus diminutione: illud vero, quod aliquando dicitur, Christum de Beata Virgine carnem sumpsisse, intelligendum esse et explicandum, non quod materia corporis ejus fuerit actu caro, sed sanguis qui est potentia caro. Docet demum tertio, quomodo subtrahi potuerit ex corpore Adam aliqua ejus pars absque ipsius diminutione, cum Adam institutus ut principium quoddam humanæ naturæ, aliquid habuerit ultra partes sui corporis personales, quod ab eo subtractum est pro formanda Heva, salva ipsius integritate in ratione perfecti corporis humani: quæ locum habere non potuerunt in Beatissima Virgine, quæ uti singulare individuum habuit perfectissimum corpus humanum, et aptissimam materiam ad Christi corpus formandum, quantum est ex parte feminæ, et [168] ad ejus naturalem generationem. Ex quo fit, ut non potuerit, salva integritate Beatæ Virginis, aliquid subtrahi, quod dici posset de substantia corporis ipsius.

Itaque, cum per hanc doctrinam, Fidei principiis conjunctissimam, directe et expressis verbis improbata remanserint asserta in citato libro Patris Zephyrini, ejus doctrina habita est tanquam "erronea, periculosa, et scandalosa," reprobatusque fuit cultus, quem ex ea præstandum Beatissimæ Virgini in Sacramento altaris asserebat. Loquendi autem formulæ a nonnullis Patribus adhibitæ, Care Mariæ est caro Christi etc. Nobis carnem Mariæ manducandum ad salutem dedit, ita explicandæ sunt, non ut dicamus, in Christo aliquid esse, quod sit Mariæ; sed Christum conceptum esse ex Maria Virgine, materiam ipsa ministrante in similitudinem naturæ et speciei, et ideo filium ejus esse. Sic, quia caro Christi fuit sumpta de David, ut expresse dicitur ad Romanos 1: "Qui factus est ex semine David secundum carnem," David dicitur Christus, ut notat S. Augustinus enarrat, in Psalm. 144, num. 2: "Intelligitur laus ipsi David, laus ipsi Christo." Christus autem secundum carnem David, quia Filius David." Et infra: "Quia itaque ex ipso Christus secundum carnem, ideo David." Est item solemnis Scripturæ usus, loquendo de parentibus, ut caro unius vocitetur caro alterius. Sic Laban, Gen. 29, dixit Jacob: "Os meum es, et caro mea;" et Judas, loquendo de fratre suo Joseph, Gen. 27, ait: "Frater enim, et caro nostra est;" et Lev. 18 legitur: "Soror patris tui caro est patris tui, et soror matris tuæ caro est matris tuæ;" abaque eo quod hinc inferri possit, ut in Jacob fuerit aliqua actualis pars corporis Laban, aut in [169] Joseph pars Judæ, aut in filio pars aliqua patris. Igitur id solum affirmare licet, in Sacramento esse carnem Christi assumptam ex Maria, ut ait Sanctus Ambrosius relatus in canone Omnia, de Consecrat. distinct. 2 his verbis: "Hæc caro mea est pro mundi vita, et, ut mirabilius loquar, non alia plane quam quæ nata est de Maria, et passa in cruce, et resurrexit de sepulcro; hæc, inquam, ipsa est." Et infra loquens de corpore Christi: "Illud vere, illud sane, quod sumptum est de Virgine, quod passum est, et sepultum."[7]

So much for Fr. de Someire's wild notion. As to Oswald,[8] his work is on the Index.[9] Vide page 5 of "Appendix Librorum Prohibitorum a die 6 Septembris, 1852, ad mensem Junium, 1858."[10]

Additional Note, Ed. 5.—As another and recent instance of the jealousy with which the Holy See preserves the bounds, within which both tradition and theology confine the *cultus* of the Blessed Virgin, I refer to a Decree of Inquisition of February 28, 1875, addressed to the Bishop of Presmilia,

---

[7] In the 1st ed. the Note ends here. The paragraphs which follow only appeared in the second edition.

[8] Johann Heinrich Oswald. See supra.

[9] The Index of Prohibited Books was compiled by the Congregation of the Index as a result of a resolution of the Council of Trent in 1571. It was supressed in 1917 and its duties transferred to the Congregation for the Doctrine of the Faith. The Index was abandoned in 1966 and the rules for the censorship of books radically revised.

[10] Newman mentions instances of books about the Blessed Virgin which Pope Gregory XVI had censured about Our Lady's presence in the Eucharist in a letter to Pusey 31 October 1865 *LD* 22 p.89.

in which the title of "*Queen* of the Heart of Jesus," as well as a certain novelty in the representation of Madonna and Child, as in use in a certain Sodality,[11] are condemned, on the ground that they may be understood in a sense inconsistent with the true faith. It will be found in the "Irish Ecclesiastical Record" for April, 1875.

The Bishop had forbidden the above innovations, and the Sacred Congregation, "to which the examination of the matter was committed by the Holy Father," says to the Bishop, it cannot but "acknowledge and praise your Excellency's zeal and care in defending the purity of the faith, especially in these days, when it seems not to be held in much account by men, who, whatever their piety, are led by a sovereign love of novelty to neglect the danger, incurred in consequence by the simple among the faithful, of deviating from the right sense of piety and devotion by means of strange and foreign doctrines.

"To obviate this danger," the letter proceeds to say, the Sacred Congregation has at other times (*altre volte*) interposed, "to warn and reprehend" those who, by such language about the Blessed Virgin, "have not sufficiently conformed to the right Catholic sense," but "ascribe power to her, as issuing from her divine maternity, beyond its due limits; as if this new title had brought her an accession of greatness and glory hitherto unknown, and, in the notion of her sublime dignity hitherto held by the Church according to the doctrine of the Holy Fathers, there were something still wanting, not considering that, although she has the greatest influence (*possa moltissimo*) with her Son, still it cannot be piously affirmed that she exercises command over Him (*eserciti impero*)."

[170]

---

[11] A religious confraternity, from the Latin *sodalitas*: fellowship. The Jesuit Sodality of the Blessed Virgin was founded by Jean Leunis SJ in Rome in 1563 for the students of the Roman College. See *CIC* Canon 298.

Note V

Further, in order apparently to mark the ministrative office of the Blessed Virgin, and her dependence as a creature on her Son, "it has been ruled by the Sovereign Pontiff, that the images or pictures to be consecrated to the *cultus* in question, must represent the Virgin as carrying the infant Jesus, not placed before her knees, but in her arms."[12]

---

[12] See supra p.[55].

A LETTER ADDRESSED TO

HIS GRACE THE DUKE OF NORFOLK

ON OCCASION OF

MR. GLADSTONE'S RECENT EXPOSTULATION

TO HIS GRACE THE DUKE OF NORFOLK[1]

HEREDITARY EARL MARSHAL OF ENGLAND, ETC., ETC.

MY DEAR DUKE OF NORFOLK,

WHEN I yielded to the earnest wish which you, together with many others, urged upon me, that I should reply to Mr. Gladstone's recent expostulation,[2] a friend suggested that I ought to ask your Grace's permission to address my remarks to you. Not that for a moment he or I thought of implicating you, in any sense or measure, in a responsibility which is solely and entirely my own; but on a very serious occasion, when such heavy charges had been made against the Catholics of England by so powerful and so earnest an adversary, it seemed my duty, in meeting his challenge, to gain the support, if I could, of a name, which is the special representative and the fitting sample of a laity, as zealous for the Catholic Religion as it is patriotic.

---

[1] 1875 ed.: This was subtitled 'on occasion of Mr. Gladstone's recent expostulation.' The text used here is the 1888 Longmans edition.

[2] *The Vatican Decrees In Their Bearing On Civil Allegiance, A Political Expostulation.* November 1874 Murray London 72pp.

[176]   You consented with something of the reluctance[3] which I had felt myself when called upon to write; for it was hard to be summoned at any age, early or late, from a peaceful course of life and the duties of one's station, to a scene of war. Still, you consented; and for myself, it is the compensation for a very unpleasant task, that I, who belong to a generation that is fast flitting away, am thus enabled, in what is likely to be my last publication,[4] to associate myself with one, on many accounts so dear to me,—so full of young promise—whose career is before him.

I deeply grieve that Mr. Gladstone has felt it his duty to speak with such extraordinary severity of our Religion and of ourselves. I consider he has committed himself to a representation of ecclesiastical documents which will not hold, and to a view of our position in the country which we have neither deserved nor can be patient under. None but the *Schola Theologorum*[5] is competent to determine the force of Papal and Synodal utterances, and the exact interpretation of them is a work of time. But so much may be safely said of the decrees which have lately been promulgated, and of the faithful who have received them, that Mr. Gladstone's account, both of them and of us, is neither trustworthy nor charitable.

Yet not a little may be said in explanation of a step, which so many of his admirers and well-wishers deplore. I own to a deep feeling, that Catholics may in good measure thank themselves, and no one else, for having alienated from them so religious a mind. There are those among us, as it must be confessed, who for years past have conducted themselves as if no responsibility attached to wild words and overbearing

---

[3] "My feeling was one of shyness at the idea of your letter coming out addressed to one so unimportant an individual as myself." 17 December 1874 *LD* 27 p. 177n.

[4] He would in fact publish *VM* 1 with a ninety-four page preface in 1877 and the completely recast *Dev* in 1878.

[5] The various theological schools, i.e. Thomism, Suarezianism etc.

deeds; who have stated truths in the most paradoxical form,[6] [177]
and stretched principles till they were close upon snapping;
and who at length, having done their best to set the house on
fire, leave to others the task of putting out the flame. The
English people are sufficiently sensitive of the claims of the
Pope, without having them, as if in defiance, flourished in
their faces. Those claims most certainly I am not going to
deny; I have never denied them. I have no intention, now that
I have to write upon them, to conceal any part of them. And
I uphold them as heartily as I recognise my duty of loyalty to
the constitution, the laws and the government of England. I
see no inconsistency in my being at once a good Catholic and
a good Englishman.[7] Yet it is one thing to be able to satisfy
myself as to my consistency, quite another to satisfy others;
and, undisturbed as I am in my own conscience, I have great
difficulties in the task before me. I have one difficulty to
overcome in the present excitement of the public mind
against our Religion, caused partly by the chronic
extravagances of knots of Catholics here and there, partly by
the vehement rhetoric which is the occasion and subject of
this Letter.[8] A worse difficulty lies in getting people, as they
are commonly found, to put off the modes of speech and
language which are usual with them, and to enter into
scientific distinctions and traditionary rules of interpretation,
which as being new to them, appear evasive and unnatural.
And a third difficulty, as I may call it, is this—that in so very
wide a subject, opening as great a variety of questions, and
of opinions upon them, while it will be simply necessary to
take the objections made against us and our faith, one by one, [178]
readers may think me trifling with their patience, because

---

[6] Newman is referring to those who hold Ultramontane extravagant views.
[7] Gladstone said, "Too commonly the spirit of the neophyte is expressed in the
words, which have become notorious: 'A Catholic first, an Englishman afterwards'"
p.23.
[8] 1874 ed.: "… of my writing to you."

they do not find those points first dealt with, on which they lay most stress themselves.

But I have said enough by way of preface; and without more delay turn to Mr. Gladstone's pamphlet.

§ 1. *Introductory Remarks.*

THE main question which Mr. Gladstone has started I consider to be this:—Can Catholics be trustworthy subjects of the State? has not a foreign Power a hold over their consciences such, that it may at any time be used to the serious perplexity and injury of the civil government under which they live?[1] Not that Mr. Gladstone confines himself to these questions, for he goes out of his way, I am sorry to say, to taunt us with our loss of mental and moral freedom, a vituperation which is not necessary for his purpose at all. He informs us too that we have "repudiated ancient history," and are rejecting modern "thought," and that our Church has been "refurbishing her rusty tools," and has been lately aggravating, and is likely still more to aggravate, our state of bondage. I think it unworthy of Mr. Gladstone's high character thus to have inveighed against us; what intellectual manliness is left to us according to him? yet his circle of acquaintance is too wide, and his knowledge of his countrymen on the other hand too accurate, for him not to know that he is bringing a great amount of odium and bad feeling upon excellent men,

---

[1] "...the people of this country who fully believe in their loyalty, are entitled on purely civil grounds to expect from them some declaration or manifestation of opinion in reply to that ecclesiastical party in their Church who have laid down in their name, principles adverse to the purity and integrity of civil allegiance." *TVD* p.4.

[180] whose only offence is their religion. The more intense is the prejudice with which we are regarded by whole classes of men, the less is there of generosity in his pouring upon us superfluous reproaches. The graver the charge which is the direct occasion of his writing against us, the more careful should he be not to prejudice judge and jury to our disadvantage. No rhetoric is needed in England against an unfortunate Catholic at any time; but so little is Mr. Gladstone conscious of his treatment of us, that in one place of his Pamphlet, strange as it may seem, he makes it his boast that he has been careful to "do nothing towards importing passion into what is matter of pure argument," pp. 15, 16. I venture to think he will one day be sorry for what he has said.

However, we must take things as we find them; and what I propose to do is this—to put aside, unless it comes directly in my way, his accusation against us of repudiating ancient history, rejecting modern thought, and renouncing our mental freedom, and to confine myself for the most part to what he principally insists upon, that Catholics, if they act consistently with their principles, cannot be loyal subjects;—I shall not, however, omit notice of his attack upon our moral uprightness.[2]

The occasion and the grounds of Mr. Gladstone's impeachment of us, if I understand him, are as follows:—He was alarmed, as a statesman, ten years ago by the Pope's Encyclical of December 8, and by the Syllabus of Erroneous Propositions[3] which, by the Pope's authority, accompanied its transmission to the

---

[2] See Postscript p.[349-50].
[3] *Quanta cura* and *Syllabus Pii IX seu Collectio Errorum*, 8 December 1864.

bishops.[4] Then came the Definitions of the Vatican
Council in 1870, upon the universal jurisdiction and
doctrinal infallibility of the Pope. And lastly, as the
event which turned alarm into indignation, and into the
duty of public remonstrance, "the Roman Catholic
Prelacy of Ireland thought fit to procure the rejection of
the Irish University Bill of February, 1873,[5] by the direct
influence which they exercised over a certain number of
Irish Members of Parliament," &c. p. 60. This step on
the part of the bishops showed, if I understand him, the
new and mischievous force which had been acquired at
Rome by the late acts there, or at least left him at liberty,
by causing his loss of power,[6] to denounce it. "From that
time forward the situation was changed," and an
opening was made for a "broad political discussion" on
the subject of the Catholic religion and its professors,
and "a debt to the country had to be disposed of." That
debt, if I am right, will be paid, if he can ascertain, on
behalf of the country, that there is nothing in the
Catholic Religion to hinder its professors from being as
loyal as other subjects of the State, and that the See of
Rome cannot interfere with their civil duties so as to
give the civil power trouble or alarm.[7] The main ground
on which he relies for the necessity of some such inquiry
is, first, the text of the authoritative documents of 1864

---

[4] See p.[283].

[5] Trinity College was to be separated from the University of Dublin, which was to become an examining body to which Magee in Ulster, St Patrick's Maynooth and a College in Dublin would be affiliated with financial support from the State. The Irish Bishops condemned the Bill 28 February 1873. It was defeated by 284 to 287 votes. on March 10. Gladstone resigned on March 13.

[6] By the Law of Guarantees (13 May 1871) the Pope was deprived of temporal sovereignty.

[7] Newman makes clear that the Pope cannot override civil responsibilities, thus undermining Gladstone's argument.

and 1870; next, and still more, the *animus* which they breathe, and the sustained aggressive spirit which they disclose; and thirdly, the daring deed of aggression in 1873, when the Pope, acting (as it is alleged) upon the Irish Members of Parliament, succeeded in ousting from their seats a ministry who, besides past benefits, were at [182] that very time doing for Irish Catholics, and therefore ousted for doing, a special service.

Now, it would be preposterous and officious in me to put myself forward as champion for the Venerable Prelacy of Ireland, or to take upon myself the part of advocate and representative of the Holy See. "Non tali auxilio;"[8] in neither character could I come forward without great presumption; not the least for this reason, because I cannot know the exact points which are really the *gist* of the affront, which Mr. Gladstone conceives he has sustained, whether from the one quarter or from the other; yet in a question so nearly interesting myself as that February bill, which he brought into the House, in great sincerity and kindness, for the benefit of the Catholic University in Ireland, I may be allowed to say thus much—that I, who now have no official relation to the Irish Bishops,[9] and am not in any sense in the counsels of Rome, felt at once, when I first saw the outline of that bill, the greatest astonishment on reading one of its provisions, and a dread which painfully affected me, lest Mr. Gladstone perhaps was acting on an understanding with the Catholic Prelacy. I did not see how in honour they could accept it. It was possible, did

---

[8] The full quotation is 'Non tali auxilio, nec defensoribis istis tempus eget': 'The times require other aid and other defenders than those you bring.' Virgil *Aeneid* l. 520.

[9] Newman had been Rector of the Catholic University of Ireland 1854-8.

182

the question come over again, to decide in favour of the Queen's Colleges,[10] and to leave the project of a Catholic University alone. The Holy See might so have decided in 1847.[11] But at or about that date, three rescripts had come from Rome in favour of a distinctively Catholic Institution; a National Council had decided in its favour; large offers of the Government had been rejected; great commotions had been caused in the political world; munificent contributions had been made;—all on the sole principle [183] that Catholic teaching was to be upheld in the country inviolate. If, then, for the sake of a money grant,[12] or other secular advantage, this ground of principle was deserted, and Catholic youths after all were allowed to attend the lectures of men of no religion, or of the Protestant, the contest of thirty years would have been stultified, and the Pope and the Bishops would seem to have been playing a game, while putting forward the plea of conscience and religious duty. I hoped that the clause in the Bill, which gave me such uneasiness, could have been omitted from it;[13] but, anyhow, it was an extreme relief to me when the papers announced that the Bishops had expressed their formal dissatisfaction with it.

---

[10] The 1873 Bill proposed that the Queen's Colleges in Belfast Galway and Cork be attached to the Queen's University of Ireland in Dublin.

[11] The idea was first proposed to the Congregation of Propaganda at the Vatican in 1847.

[12] There had been a previous grant in 1844 to the seminary in Maynooth which Gladstone had first opposed but then supported.

[13] "The teaching of religion would be separated from secular education.... In the Catholic institutions certain areas of secular teaching would be under strict reservation and certain 'controversial' areas would not be examinable." Richard Shannon *Gladstone, God and Politics*, Continuum 2008 p.250.

They determined to decline a gift laden with such a condition, and who can blame them for so doing? who can be surprised that they should now do what they did in 1847?[14] what new move in politics was it, if they so determined? what was there in it of a factious character? Is the Catholic Irish interest the only one which is not to be represented in the House of Commons? Why is not that interest as much a matter of right as any other? I fear to expose my own ignorance of Parliamentary rules and proceedings, but I had supposed that the railway interest, and what is called the publican interest,[15] were very powerful there: in Scotland, too, I believe, a government has a formidable party to deal with; and, to revert to Ireland, there are the Home-rulers,[16] who have objects in view quite distinct from, or contrary to, those of the Catholic hierarchy. As to the Pope, looking at the surface of things, there is nothing to suggest that he [184] interfered, there was no necessity of interference, on so plain a point; and, when an act can be sufficiently accounted for without introducing an hypothetical cause, it is bad logic to introduce it. Speaking according to my lights, I altogether disbelieve the interposition of Rome in the matter. In the proceedings which they adopted, the Bishops were only using civil rights, common to all, which others also used and in their own way. Why might it not be their duty to promote the

---

[14] Gladstone had proposed to the Irish of a national system of education which would give the Church a larger say in higher education but appeared to encroach on the right of Catholics to their own education system as was the case in 1868. See infra.
[15] The brewers of Allsop, Bass and Guinness were all ennobled, named by the press 'The Brewerage'.
[16] The Irish Home Rule movement began in 1871. It was led by John Redmond, Charles Stewart Parnell and Isaac Butt but was associated with the Liberal Party and Gladstone, who would introduce two Bills in 1886 and 1893.

interests of their religion by means of their political opportunities? Is there no Exeter Hall[17] interest? I thought it was a received theory of our Reformed Constitution that Members of Parliament were representatives, and in some sort delegates of their constituents, and that the strength of each interest was shown, and the course of the nation determined, by the divisions in the House of Commons. I recollect the *Times* intimating its regret, after one general election, that there was no English Catholic in the new House, on the ground that every class and party should be represented there.[18] Surely the Catholic religion has not a small party in Ireland;[19] why then should it not have a corresponding number of exponents and defenders at Westminster? So clear does this seem to me, that I think there must be some defect in my knowledge of facts to explain Mr. Gladstone's surprise and displeasure at the conduct of the Irish Prelacy in 1873; yet I suspect none; and, if there be none, then his unreasonableness in this instance of Ireland makes it not unlikely that he is unreasonable also in his judgment of the Encyclical, Syllabus, and Vatican Decrees.

However, the Bishops, I believe, not only opposed [185] Mr. Gladstone's bill, but, instead of it, they asked for some money grant towards the expenses of their University.[20] If so, their obvious argument was this— that Catholics formed the great majority of the

---

[17] A building in The Strand erected in 1830 used especially for Evangelical (and 'No Popery') meetings.
[18] The Catholic Relief Act of April 1829 finally allowed Catholics to become MPs.
[19] "A country ... the wonder by reason of its knowledge, sacred and profane, and the asylum of religion, literature and science." *Idea* p. 15.
[20] The Earl of Mayo, Chief Secretary for Ireland, had previously offered an endowment to the Catholic University of Ireland in 1868.

population of Ireland, and it was not fair that the Protestant minority should have all that was bestowed in endowment or otherwise upon education. To this the reply, I suppose, would be, that it was not Protestantism, but liberal education that had the money, and that, if the Bishops chose to give up their own principles and act as Liberals, they might have the benefit of it too.[21] I am not concerned here with these arguments, but I wish to notice the position which the Bishops would occupy in urging such a request:—I must not say that they were Irishmen first and Catholics afterwards, but I do say that in such a demand they spoke not simply as Catholic Bishops, but as the Bishops of a Catholic nation. They did not speak else in the world. It is their comfort, their joy, their treasure, their boast, their compensation for a hundred worldly disadvantages; but who can deny that in politics their conduct at times—nay, more than at times—has had a flavour rather of their nation than of their Church? Only in the last general election this was said, when they were so earnest for Home Rule. Why, then, must Mr. Gladstone come down upon the Catholic Religion, because the Irish love dearly the Green Island, and its interests? Ireland is not the only country in which politics, or patriotism, or party, has been so closely associated with religion in the nation or a class, that it is difficult to say which of the various motive principles was uppermost. "The Puritan," says Macaulay, "prostrated himself in the dust before his Maker, but he

[186]

---

[21] In 1852 Newman wrote, "Ecclesiastical authority ... has interposed in favour of a pure University system for Catholic youth, forbidding compromise or accommodation of any kind." *Idea* p.10.

set his foot on the neck of his king:"[22] I am not accusing such a man of hypocrisy on account of this; having great wrongs, as he considered, both in religious and temporal matters, and the authors of these distinct wrongs being the same persons, he did not nicely discriminate between the acts which he did as a patriot and the acts which he did as a Puritan. And so as regards Irishmen, they do not, cannot, distinguish between their love of Ireland and their love of religion; their patriotism is religious, and their religion is strongly tinctured with patriotism; and it is hard to recognize the abstract and Ideal Ultramontane, pure and simple, in the concrete exhibition of him in flesh and blood as found in the polling-booth or in his chapel. I do not see how the Pope can be made answerable for him in any of his political acts during the last fifty years.

This leads me to a subject, of which Mr. Gladstone makes a good deal in his pamphlet. I will say of a great [187] man, whom he quotes, and for whose memory I have a great respect, I mean Bishop Doyle,[23] that there was just a little tinge of patriotism in the way in which, on one occasion, he speaks of the Pope. I dare say any of us would have done the same, in the heat of a great struggle for national liberty, for he said nothing but what was true and honest; I only mean that the energetic language which he used was not exactly such as would have suited the atmosphere of Rome. He says to Lord

---

[22] Thomas Babington Macaulay, from his 'Essay on Milton' which appeared in 1825 in *The Edinburgh Review* but subsequently was published (1898), p.53.

[23] James Warren Doyle (1786-1834). He became Bishop of Kildare and Leighlin in 1819 and was the author of *A Vindication of the Religious and Civil Liberties of the Irish Catholics* (1824). He gave evidence to parliamentary committees in 1830 on the current state of Ireland.

Liverpool,[24] "We are taunted with the proceedings of Popes. What, my Lord, have we Catholics to do with the proceedings of Popes, or why should we be made accountable for them?" p. 27. Now, with some proceedings of Popes, we Catholics have very much to do indeed; but, if the context of his words is consulted, I make no doubt it would be found that he was referring to certain proceedings of certain Popes, when he said that Catholics had no part of their responsibility. Assuredly there are certain acts of Popes in which no one would like to have part.[25] Then, again, his words require some pious interpretation when he says that "the allegiance due to the king and the allegiance due to the Pope, are as distinct and as divided in their nature as any two things can possibly be," p. 30. Yes, in their nature, in the abstract, but not in the particular case; for a heathen State might bid me throw incense upon the altar of Jupiter,[26] and the Pope would bid me not to do so. I venture to make the same remark on the Address of the Irish Bishops to their clergy and laity in 1826,[27] quoted at p. 31, and on the Declaration of the Vicars Apostolic in England,[28] *ibid*.

[188]   But I must not be supposed for an instant to mean, in what I have said, that the venerable men, to whom I have

---

[24] *An Essay on the Catholic Claims addressed to the Right Hon the Earl of Liverpool* Dublin 1826 (the Earl was Prime Minister 1812-27).

[25] Newman wrote to Mrs Helbert, "As to the scandalous lives of some Popes, to which you refer we not only allow but glory in, as showing the Divine Care of the Church, that, even in the case of those very men, the See of Peter spoke truth, not falsehood." 10 September 1869 *LD* 24 p.328. See also pp.[216, 254].

[26] i.e. compromise one's principles. To cast a few grains on Jupiter's altar was a sign of loyalty to the Emperor.

[27] See *Quarterly Review* Vol 133 (1840) p.90.

[28] The Declaration on "The Misrepresentation of the Catholic Religion", January 1829.

188

referred, were aware of any ambiguity either in such statements as the above, or in others which were denials of the Pope's infallibility. Indeed, one of them at an earlier date, 1793, Dr. Troy,[29] Archbishop of Dublin, had introduced into one of his Pastorals the subject which Mr. Gladstone considers they so summarily disposed of. The Archbishop says, "Many Catholics contend that the Pope, when teaching the universal Church, as their supreme visible head and pastor, as successor to St. Peter, and heir to the promises of special assistance made to him by Jesus Christ, is infallible; and that his decrees and decisions in that capacity are to be respected as rules of faith, when they are dogmatical or confined to doctrinal points of faith and morals. Others deny this, and require the expressed or tacit acquiescence of the Church, assembled or dispersed, to stamp infallibility on his dogmatical decrees. Until the Church shall decide upon this question of the Schools,[30] either opinion may be adopted by individual Catholics, without any breach of Catholic communion or peace. The Catholics of Ireland have lately declared, that it is not an article of the Catholic faith; nor are they thereby required to believe or profess that the Pope is infallible, without adopting or abjuring either of the recited opinions which are open to discussion, while the Church continues silent about them." The Archbishop thus addressed his flock, at the time when he was informing them that the Pope had altered the oath which was taken by the Catholic Bishops.[31]

---

[29] John Thomas Troy (1739-1823) was Archbishop of Dublin 1787-1823. See p.[190].

[30] See supra.

[31] The oath of allegiance was part of the Catholic Relief Act of 1793.

[189]   As to the language of the Bishops in 1826, we must recollect that at that time the clergy, both of Ireland and England, were educated in Gallican[32] opinions. They took those opinions for granted, and they thought, if they went so far as to ask themselves the question, that the definition of Papal Infallibility was simply impossible. Even among those at the Vatican Council, who themselves personally believed in it, I believe there were Bishops who, until the actual definition had been passed, thought that such a definition could not be made. Perhaps they would argue that, though the historical evidence was sufficient for their own personal conviction, it was not sufficiently clear of difficulties to be made the ground of a Catholic dogma.[33] Much more would this be the feeling of the Bishops in 1826. "How," they would ask, "can it ever come to pass that a majority of our order should find it their duty to relinquish their prime prerogative, and to make the Church take the shape of a pure monarchy?" They would think its definition as much out of the question, as the prospect that, in twenty-five years after their time, there would be a hierarchy of thirteen Bishops in England, with a cardinal for Archbishop.[34]

But, all this while, such modes of thinking were foreign altogether to the minds of the *entourage* of the

---

[32] The first of the Four Gallican Articles drawn up by Bishop J. B. Bossuet in the Paris Assembly of 1682 declared that the Pope had no dominion over temporal matters. The second maintained the authority of General Councils over the Pope. The third insisted on the inalienable rights of the Gallican Church and the fourth said that the judgement of the Pope was not irreformable.

[33] 1875 ed.: "...to make it safe to impose it on Catholics as a dogma"

[34] The Catholic hierarchy was established on 29 September 1850 by the Bull *Universalis Ecclesiae* Cardinal Wiseman was appointed Archbishop of Westminster.

Holy See. Mr. Gladstone himself says, and the Duke of Wellington[35] and Sir Robert Peel[36] must have known it as well as he, "The Popes have kept up, with comparatively little intermission, for well-nigh a thousand years, their claim to dogmatic infallibility," p. 28. Then, if the Pope's claim to infallibility was so patent a fact, could they ever suppose that he could be [190] brought to admit that it was hopeless to turn that claim into a dogma? In truth, Wellington and Peel[37] were very little interested in that question; as was said in a Petition or Declaration,[38] signed among others by Dr. Troy, it was "immaterial in a political light;" but, even if they thought it material, or if there were other questions they wanted to ask, why go to Bishop Doyle? If they wanted to obtain some real information about the probabilities of the future, why did they not go to headquarters? Why did they potter about the halls of Universities in this matter of Papal exorbitances, or rely upon the pamphlets or examinations of Bishops whom they never asked for their credentials? Why not go at once to Rome?

The reason is plain: it was a most notable instance, with a grave consequence, of what is a fixed tradition with us the English people, and a great embarrassment to every administration in its dealings with Catholics. I recollect, years ago, Dr. Griffiths,[39] Vicar Apostolic of

---

[35] Arthur Wellesley (1769-1852), created Duke of Wellington in 1814, became Prime Minister in 1828 and carried through Catholic Emancipation in 1829.

[36] Robert Peel (1788-1850), Home Secretary under Wellington, became Prime Minister 1834-9;1841-5.

[37] 1874 ed.: "…these ministers"

[38] In 1791. See Marianne Elliott 'The Origins and Transformation of Early Irish Republicanism' *International Review of Social History* 23 (1978) pp.405-28.

[39] Thomas Griffiths (1791-1847) became Vicar Apostolic of the London District in 1836. See supra p.[21].

the London District, giving me an account of an interview he had with the late Lord Derby,[40] then I suppose Colonial Secretary. I understood him to say that Lord Derby was in perplexity at the time, on some West India matter,[41] in which Catholics were concerned, because he could not find their responsible representative. He wanted Dr. Griffiths to undertake the office, and expressed something of disappointment when the Bishop felt obliged to decline it. A chronic malady has from time to time its paroxysms, and the history on which I am now engaged is a serious instance of it. I think it is impossible that the British government could have entered into formal negotiations with the Pope, without its transpiring in the course of them, and its becoming perfectly clear, that Rome could never be a party to such a pledge as England wanted, and that no pledge from Catholics was of any value to which Rome was not a party.[42]

[191]

But no; they persisted in an enterprise which was hopeless in its first principle, for they thought to break the indissoluble tie which bound together the head and the members,—and doubtless Rome felt the insult, though she might think it prudent not to notice it. France was not the keystone of the ecumenical power, though her Church was so great and so famous; nor could the hierarchy of Ireland, in spite of its fidelity to the Catholic faith, give any pledge of the future to the

---

[40] Edward George Geoffrey Stanley, Lord Derby (1799-1869), was Colonial Secretary under Peel in 1841, Foreign Secretary under Disraeli and later Prime Minister in 1842, 1858 and 1866.

[41] A Bill was introduced for the freeing of slaves 14 May 1833 when he was Chief Secretary of State for Ireland. There was a wish to consult the Catholic viewpoint.

[42] See Postscript pp.[350-6].

statesmen who required one; there was but one See, whose word was worth anything in the matter, "that church" (to use the language of the earliest of our Doctors) "to which the faithful all round about are bound to have recourse."[43] Yet for three hundred years it has been the official rule with England to ignore the existence of the Pope, and to deal with Catholics in England, not as his children, but as sectaries of the Roman Catholic persuasion. Napoleon said to his envoy,[44] "Treat with the Pope as if he was master of 100,000 men."[45] So clearly did he, from mere worldly sagacity, comprehend the Pope's place in the then state of European affairs, as to say that, "if the Pope had not existed, it would have been well to have created him for that occasion, as the Roman consuls created a dictator in difficult circumstances." (Alison's *Hist*. ch. 35.[46]) But [192] we, in the instance of the greatest, the oldest power in Europe, a church whose grandeur in past history demanded, one would think, some reverence in our treatment of her, the mother of English Christianity, who, whether her subsequent conduct had always been motherly or not, had been a true friend to us in the beginning of our history; her we have not only renounced, but, to use a familiar word, we have absolutely cut. Time has gone on and we have no relentings; today, as little as yesterday, do we

---

[43] "To this Church, every Church, that is, the faithful from every side must resort." Irenaeus of Lyons *Adversus Haereses* 3.3.2 *PG* 7.848.

[44] Cardinal Joseph Fesch, his uncle, was appointed by Napoleon in 1803. See p.[361].

[45] *The Times* quoted, "Traiter toujours le Pape comme s'il avait une armée de *300,000 hommes* derrière lui." 19 October 1875 p.5.

[46] Sir Archibald Alison (1792-1867) published a ten volume *History of Europe* (1833-43).

193

understand that pride was not made for man, nor the cuddling of resentments for a great people. I am entering into no theological question: I am speaking all along of mere decent secular intercourse between England and Rome. A hundred grievances would have been set right on their first uprising, had there been a frank diplomatic understanding between two great powers; but, on the contrary, even within the last few weeks, the present Ministry has destroyed any hope of a better state of things by withdrawing from the Vatican the makeshift channel of intercourse which had of late years been permitted there.[47]

The world of politics has its laws; and such abnormal courses as England has pursued have their *Nemesis.* An event has taken place which, alas, already makes itself felt in issues, unfortunate for English Catholics certainly, but also, as I think for our country. A great Council has been called; and as England has for so long a time ignored Rome, Rome, I suppose, it must be said, has in turn ignored England. I do not mean of set purpose ignored, but as the natural consequence of our [193] act. Bishops brought from the corners of the earth, in 1870, what could they know of English blue book[48] and Parliamentary debates in the years 1826 and 1829? It was an extraordinary gathering, and its possibility, its purpose, and its issue, were alike marvellous, as depending on a coincidence of strange conditions,

---

[47] Disraeli's Conservative government, unlike Gladstone's, was not interested in continuing the semi-official diplomatic arrangement and recalled Henry Clark Jervoise in 1874. They argued that it made no economic sense to continue dealing with a non-existent state since the Pope was no longer a sovereign. Diplomatic relations were not restored until 1914 with the appointment of Sir Henry Howard.
[48] An almanac of economic statistics, originally bound in blue.

which, as might be said beforehand, never could take place. Such was the long reign of the Pope, in itself a marvel, as being the sole exception to a recognized ecclesiastical tradition.[49] Only a Pontiff so unfortunate, so revered, so largely loved, so popular even with Protestants, with such a prestige of long sovereignty, with such claims on the Bishops around him, both of age and of paternal gracious acts, only such a man could have harmonized and guided to the conclusion which he pointed out, an assembly so variously composed. And, considering the state of theological opinion seventy years before, not less marvellous was the concurrence of all but a few out of so many hundred Bishops in the theological judgement, so long desired at Rome; the protest made by some eighty or ninety, at the termination of the Council, against the proceedings of the vast majority lying, not against the truth of the doctrine then defined, but against the fact of its definition.[50] Nor less to be noted is the neglect of the Catholic powers to send representatives to the Council, who might have laid before the Fathers its political bearings. For myself, I did not call it inopportune,[51] for times and seasons are known to God alone, and persecution may be as opportune, though not so pleasant as peace; nor in accepting as a dogma what I had ever

---

[49] Pius IX had already reigned for 29 years, passing what was traditionally seen as St Peter's 25 years.

[50] The 1875 ed.: "… but against its opportuneness."

[51] Newman, writing five years after the definition and regarding his correspondence as private, fully accepted the definition and considered it opportune; but in those still contentious times he did not wish to undermine people's faith or give ammunition to enemies. He chose not to disclose that he had had his own serious misgivings about its timeliness and its possible impact (see the Editor's Introduction).

[194]   held as a truth, could I be doing violence to any theological view or conclusion of my own; nor has the acceptance of it any logical or practical effect whatever, as I consider, in weakening my allegiance to Queen Victoria; but there are few Catholics, I think, who will not deeply regret, though no one be in fault, that the English and Irish Prelacies of 1826 did not foresee the possibility of the Synodal determinations of 1870, nor can we wonder that Statesmen should feel themselves aggrieved, that stipulations, which they considered necessary for Catholic emancipation, should have been, as they may think, rudely cast to the winds.

And now I must pass from the mere accidents of the controversy to its essential points, and I cannot treat them to the satisfaction of Mr. Gladstone, unless I go back a great way, and be allowed to speak of the ancient Catholic Church.

§ 2. *The Ancient Church*

WHEN Mr. Gladstone accuses us of "repudiating ancient history," he means the ancient history of the Church; also, I understand him to be viewing that history under a particular aspect. There are many aspects in which Christianity presents itself to us; for instance, the aspect of social usefulness, or of devotion or again of theology; but, though he in one place glances at the last of these aspects, his own view of it is its relation towards the civil power. He writes "as one of the world at large;" as a "layman who has spent most and the best years of his life in the observation and practice of politics"[1] (p. 7); and, as a statesmen, he naturally looks at the Church on its political side. Accordingly, in his title-page, in which he professes to be expostulating with us for accepting the Vatican Decrees, he does so, not for any reason whatever, but because of their incompatibility with our civil allegiance. This is the key-note of his impeachment of us. As a public man, he has only to do with the public action and effect of our Religion, its aspect upon national affairs, on our civil duties, on our foreign interests; and he tells us that our Religion has a bearing and behaviour towards the State utterly unlike that of [196] ancient Christianity, so unlike that we may be even said to repudiate what Christianity was in its first centuries,

---

[1] He added "… not aggressive but defensive".

so unlike to what it was then, that we have actually forfeited the proud boast of being "Ever one and the same;"[2] unlike, I say, in this, that our action is so antagonistic to the State's action, and our claims so menacing to civil peace and prosperity.

Indeed! then I suppose[3] that St. Ignatius of Antioch,[4] and St. Polycarp of Smyrna,[5] and St. Cyprian of Carthage,[6] and St. Laurence of Rome,[7] that St. Alexander[8] and St. Paul of Constantinople,[9] that St. Ambrose of Milan,[10] that Popes Leo,[11] John,[12] Sylverian,[13] Gregory,[14] and Martin,[15] all members of the "undivided Church," cared supremely and laboured successfully, to cultivate peaceful relations with the government of Rome. They had no doctrines and precepts, no rules of

---

[2] "Rome has substituted for the proud boast of *semper eadem* a policy of violence and change of faith; when she has reburnished and paraded anew every rusty tool she was fondly thought to have disused." (*TVD* p.12) 'Semper eadem' ('always the same') was the motto of Elizabeth I.

[3] 1875 ed.: "I suppose that Our Lord and his Apostles, St Ignatius …"

[4] St. Ignatius of Antioch (d. c. 108), martyred in Rome.

[5] St Polycarp (c. 69-155), bishop and martyr.

[6] St Cyprian (d. 258), Bishop of Carthage, martyr; author of *On the Unity of the Catholic Church PL* 4.498.

[7] St Laurence of Rome (d. 258), martyr, one of the seven deacons under Pope Sixtus II.

[8] St. Alexander, Bishop of Alexandria (d. 328), opponent of Arianism; attended Nicaea (Eusebius *Ecclesiastical History* IV, 1).

[9] St. Paul of Constantinople (d. c.352), bishop, opponent of Arianism who appealed to Pope Julius I.

[10] St Ambrose of Milan (c 339-397), in his commentary on Luke 1.4. *PL* 5.1633; St Leo (d. 461) *Sermo 3 PL* 54.145; resisted the Emperor Valentinian II and Empress Justina who supported Arianism.

[11] Pope St Leo the Great (c. 400-61); persuaded Attila the Hun not to invade Italy.

[12] Pope St John I, (d. 526); died following imprisonment by King Theodoric, ruler of Italy.

[13] Pope St Sylverius, (d. 537) was deposed by the general Belisarius and starved to death on the island of Palmarola.

[14] Pope St. Gregory the Great (540-604) greatly strengthened papal supremacy (See p.[214]).

[15] Pope St. Martin I (649-655) "won praise for this See" according to Pius VII in Encyclical *Diu Satis* (1800). See Newman 'Papal Primacy' *Dev* pp.148-65.

life, no isolation and aggressiveness, which caused them to be considered, in spite of themselves, the enemies of the human race![16] May I not, without disrespect, submit to Mr. Gladstone that this is very paradoxical? Surely it is our fidelity to the history of our forefathers, and not its repudiation, which Mr. Gladstone dislikes in us.[17] When, indeed, was it in ancient times that the State did not show jealousy of the Church? Was it when Decius and Dioclesian slaughtered their thousands who had abjured the religion of old Rome?[18] or, was it when Athanasius was banished to Treves?[19] or when Basil, on the Imperial Prefect's crying out, "Never before did any man make so free with me," answered, "Perhaps you never before fell in with a Bishop"?[20] or when Chrysostom was sent off to Cucusus, to be worried to death by an Empress?[21] Go through the long annals of Church History, century after century, and say, was there ever a time when her Bishops, and notably the Bishop of Rome, were slow to give their testimony in behalf of the moral and revealed law and to suffer for their obedience to it? ever a time when they forgot that they had a message to deliver to the world,—not the task merely of administering spiritual consolation, or of making the sick-bed easy, or of training up good

[197]

---

[16] "humani generis hostes" Tacitus. *Annals* 15,44. See *Dev* p.230.

[17] See Postscript p.[196-205].

[18] Caius Messius Quintus Decius Emperor 249-51. Valerius Diocletianus Emperor from 284-305. See Edward Gibbon *Decline and Fall of the Roman Empire* chs. 10 and 13.

[19] Athanasius was exiled to Trier by Constantine in 335.

[20] The Prefect of the East, Modestus, threatened Basil with exile, torture and death. Socrates *Ecclesiastical History* 4, 26.

[21] John Chrysostom (347-407), Archbishop of Constantinople, was exiled to Cucusus in Armenia and then ordered further away. He died on the journey. *HS* 2 pp. 240, 291.

members of society, or of "serving tables"[22] (though all this was included in their range of duty),—but specially and directly, a definite message to high and low, from the world's Maker, whether men would hear or whether they would forbear? The history surely of the Church in all past times, ancient as well as medieval, is the very embodiment of that tradition of Apostolical independence and freedom of speech which in the eyes of man is her great offence now.

Nay, that independence, I may say, is even one of her Notes or credentials; for where shall we find it except in the Catholic Church? "I spoke of Thy testimonies," says the Psalmist, "even before kings, and I was not ashamed."[23] This verse, I think Dr Arnold[24] used to say, rose up in judgment against the Anglican Church,[25] in spite of its real excellences. As to the Oriental Churches, every one knows in what bondage they lie, whether they are under the rule of the Czar or of the Sultan. Such is the actual fact that, whereas it is the very mission of Christianity to bear witness to the Creed and Ten [198] Commandments in a world which is averse to them, Rome is now the one faithful representative, and thereby is heir and successor, of that free-spoken dauntless

[22] Acts 6:2.

[23] Ps 119[118]: 46.

[24] Dr. Thomas Arnold (1795-1842), Fellow of Oriel 1815-1819 and Headmaster of Rugby School. Chevalier Christian Karl Josias Baron von Bunsen said that no one had spoken "so extensively against the assumptions of the clergy church." *Church of the Future* p.221.

[25] Dean Church said of Dr. Arnold that "Church organization was, according to circumstances, partly inevitable or expedient, partly mischievous but in no case of divine authority." *The Oxford Movement 1833-1845* London 1891 p.6. Arnold's pamphlet, 'The Principles of Church Reform' (1833) proposed that all sects should be united by Act of Parliament with the Church of England.

Church of old, whose political and social traditions Mr. Gladstone says the said Rome has repudiated.

I have one thing more to say on the subject of the "semper eadem." In truth, this fidelity to the ancient Christian system, seen in modern Rome, was the luminous fact which more than any other turned men's minds at Oxford forty years ago to look towards her with reverence, interest, and love. It affected individual minds variously of course; some it even brought on eventually to conversion, others it only restrained from active opposition to her claims; but none of us could read the Fathers, and determine to be their disciples, without feeling that Rome, like a faithful steward, had kept in fulness and in vigour what our own communion had let drop. The Tracts for the Times[26] were founded on a deadly antagonism to what in these last centuries has been called Erastianism[27] or Cæsarism. Their writers considered the Church to be a divine creation, "not of men, neither by man, but by Jesus Christ,"[28] the Ark of Salvation, the Oracle of Truth, the Bride of Christ, with a message to all men everywhere, and a claim on their love and obedience; and, in relation to the civil power, the object of that promise of the Jewish prophets, "Behold, I will lift up My Hand to the Gentiles, and will set up My standard to the peoples: kings and their queens shall how down to thee with their face toward the earth, and they shall lick up the dust of thy feet."[29]

---

[26] By various authors, including Newman, between 1833 and 1841.

[27] The theory of state control of the Church-from Swiss theologian Thomas Erastus (1524-1583). Newman maintained to Ambrose Phillips de Lisle about the Church of England that "I say, all parties [Anglo-Catholic, Evangelical and Liberal] ever have been Erastian." 1 March 1866 *LD* 22 p. 171.

[28] Gal 1:1.

[29] Is 49:23

[199] No Ultramontane (so called) could go beyond those writers in the account which they gave of her from the Prophets, and that high notion is recorded beyond mistake in a thousand passages of their writings.

There is a fine passage of Mr. Keble's in the *British Critic*, in animadversion upon a contemporary reviewer. Mr. Hurrell Froude,[30] speaking of the Church of England, had said that "she was 'united' to the State as Israel to Egypt." This shocked the reviewer in question, who exclaimed in consequence, "The Church is *not* united to the State as Israel to Egypt; it is united as a believing *wife* to a *husband* who threatened to apostatize; and, as a Christian wife so placed would act ... clinging to the connexion ... so the Church must struggle even now, and save, not herself, but the State, from the crime of a *divorce*." On this Mr. Keble says, "We had thought that the Spouse of the Church was a very different Person from any or all States, and her relation to the State through Him *very unlike that of hers, whose duties are summed up in 'love, service, cherishing, and obedience.'*[31] And since the one is exclusively of this world, the other essentially of the eternal world, *such an Alliance* as the above sentence describes, would have seemed to us, *not only fatal but monstrous!*"* And he quotes the lines,—

* Review of Gladstone's "The State in its Relations with the Church", October, 1839.[32]

---

[30] Richard Hurrell Froude (1803-36), Fellow of Oriel 1826, was from the beginning closely associated with Newman and Keble and author of Tracts 59 and 63. He went with his family and Newman to Southern Europe in 1832-33. The quotation is in Froude's *Remains* I p. 302.

[31] Words used in the solemnization of matrimony.

[32] In 'Oxford Theology' in *Quarterly Review* 63-64 (1839) p.311.

"Mortua quinetiam jungebat corpora vivis,
  Componens manibusque manus, atque oribus ora:
  Tormenti genus!"[33]

It was this same conviction that the Church had rights which the State could not touch, and was prone to ignore, and which in consequence were the occasion of great troubles between the two, that led Mr. Froude at the beginning of the movement to translate the letters of St. Thomas Becket,[34] and Mr. Bowden to write the Life of Hildebrand.[35] As to myself, I will but refer, as to one out of many passages with the same drift, in the books and tracts which I published at that time, to my Whit-Monday and Whit-Tuesday Sermons.[36]

[200]

I believe a large number of members of the Church of England at this time are faithful to the doctrine which was proclaimed within its pale in 1833,[37] and following years; the main difference between them and Catholics being, not as to the existence of certain high prerogatives and spiritual powers in the Christian Church, but that the powers which we give to the Holy See, they lodge in her Bishops and Priests, whether as a body or individually. Of course, this is a very important difference, but it does not interfere with my argument here. It does seem to me preposterous to charge the

---

[33] "He even bound the bodies of the dead to the living, joining together hands to hand and face to face, a horrid kind of torture" Virgin *Aeneid* Book 4 l. 485. Cicero ascribed this kind of torture to 'Tuscans in general'.

[34] See *British Magazine 2* (September 1832) and *Remains of the Late Reverend Richard. Hurrell. Froude* eds. Newman and Keble 1838-1839 Part 2 v. 2.

[35] *The Life and Pontificate of Gregory VII.* London 1840.

[36] 'Wisdom as Contrasted with Faith and with Bigotry' Whit-Tuesday 1 June 1841 *US* 14 pp. 278-311; 'Connection between Personal and Private Improvement' June 4, 1843 *SD* 19 pp. 126-36.

[37] Keble's *Assize Sermon* 14 July 1833, the beginning of the Oxford Movement.

Catholic Church of today with repudiating ancient history by certain political acts of hers, and thereby losing her identity, when it was her very likeness in political action to the Church of the first centuries, that has in our time attracted even to her communion, and at least to her teaching, not a few educated men, who made those first centuries their special model.

[201]

But I have more to say on this subject, perhaps too much, when I go on, as I now do, to contemplate the Christian Church, when persecution was exchanged for establishment, and her enemies became her children. As she resisted and defied her persecutors, so she ruled her convert people.[38] And surely this was but natural, and will startle those only to whom the subject is new. If the Church is independent of the State, so far as she is a messenger from God, therefore, should the State, with its high officials and its subject masses, come into her communion, it is plain that they must at once change hostility into submission.[200] There was no middle term; either they must deny her claim to divinity or humble themselves before it,—that is, as far as the domain of religion extends, and that domain is a wide one. They could not place God and man on one level. We see this principle carried out among ourselves in all sects every day, though with greater or less exactness of application, according to the supernatural power which they ascribe to their ministers or clergy. It is a sentiment of nature, which anticipates the inspired command,

---

[38] "Time after time they resisted the authority of the magistrate... The justification of such disobedience lies simply in the necessity of obeying the higher authority of some divine law." *Dev* p. 235.

"Obey them that have the rule over you, and submit yourselves, for they watch for your souls."[39]

As regards the Roman Emperors, immediately on their becoming Christians, their exaltation of the hierarchy was in proportion to its abject condition in the heathen period. Grateful converts felt that they could not do too much in its honour and service. Emperors bowed the head before the Bishops, kissed their hands and asked their blessing. When Constantine entered into the presence of the assembled Prelates at Nicæa, his eyes fell, the colour mounted up into his cheek, and his mien was that of a suppliant; he would not sit, till the Bishops bade him, and he kissed the wounds of the Confessors.[40] [202] Thus he set the example for the successors of his power, nor did the Bishops decline such honours. Royal ladies[41] served them at table; victorious generals[42] did penance for sin and asked forgiveness. When they quarrelled with them, and would banish them, their hand trembled when they came to sign the order,[43] and after various attempts they gave up their purpose. Soldiers raised to sovereignty asked their recognition and were refused it. Cities under imperial displeasure sought their intervention, and the master of thirty legions found himself powerless to withstand the feeble voice of some aged travel-stained stranger.

---

[39] Heb 13:17.
[40] Eusebius, *Life of Constantine.* St. Paphnutius (d. 360) who had been tortured in 303 under Emperor Maximinus had his eyes kissed by Emperor Constantine.
[41] 1875 ed.: "Emperor's wives served them."
[42] 1875 ed.: "…when they did wrong they did penance"
[43] 1875 ed.: "… sign the order and refused to do its office, and after various attempts…"

Laws were passed in favour of the Church; Bishops could only be judged by Bishops,[44] and the causes of their clergy were withdrawn from the secular courts. Their sentence was final, as if it were the Emperor's own, and the governors of provinces were bound to put it in execution. Litigants everywhere were allowed the liberty of referring their causes to the tribunal of the Bishops, who, besides, became arbitrators on a large scale in private quarrels; and the public, even heathens, wished it so. St. Ambrose was sometimes so taken up with business of this sort, that he had time for nothing else. St. Austin[45] and Theodoret[46] both complain of the weight of such secular engagements, as were forced upon them by the importunity of the people. Nor was this all; the Emperors showed their belief in the divinity of the Church and of its creed by acts of what we should now call persecution. Jews were forbidden to proselytize a Christian;[47] Christians were forbidden to become pagans; pagan rights were abolished, the books of heretics and infidels were burned wholesale; their chapels were razed to the ground, and even their private meetings were made illegal.

[203]

These characteristics of the convert Empire were the immediate, some of them the logical, consequences of its new faith. Had not the Emperors honoured Christianity in its ministers and in its precepts, they would not properly have deserved the name of converts.

---

[44] Council of Sardica (343).

[45] St. Augustine: "I was weighed down with the encumbrance of this world" *Confessions* 8.12.

[46] Theodoret (c. 393-466) Bishop of Cyrrhus. "He was both a Bishop and a monk … What time had he over for duties not eremitical, nor pastoral?" *HS* 2 p. 327.

[47] Arcadius (394-408) re-enacted Constantius' decrees. The 3rd and 4th Council of Orleans (538. 548) issued prohibitions against proselytism.

Nor was it unreasonable in litigants voluntarily to frequent the episcopal tribunals, if they got justice done to them there better than in the civil courts. As to the prohibition of heretical meetings, I cannot get myself quite to believe that Pagans, Marcionites,[48] and Manichees[49] had much tenderness of conscience in their religious profession, or were wounded seriously by the Imperial rescripts to their disadvantage. Many of these sects were of a most immoral character, whether in doctrine or practice; others were forms of witchcraft; often they were little better than paganism. The Novatians[50] certainly stand on higher ground; but on the whole, it would be most unjust to class such wild, impure, inhuman rites with even the most extravagant and grotesque of American sectaries now.[51] They could entertain no bitter feeling that injustice was done them in their repression. They did not make free thought or private judgment their watch-words. The populations of the Empire did not rise in revolt when its religion was changed. There were two broad conditions which accompanied the grant of all this ecclesiastical power and privilege, and made the exercise of it possible; first, that the people consented to it, secondly, that the law of the Empire enacted and enforced it. Thus high and low   [204]

---

[48] Followers of Marcion who was excommunicated in 144 for rejecting the Old Testament and insisting that St Paul alone understood the Gospel of Love.

[49] Followers of Manes (c.216-276) who believed in a Gnostic conflict of light overcoming darkness, with 'Elect' and 'Hearers' in their hierarchy.

[50] Followers of Novatian, a Roman presbyter who was put to death under Valerian in 257-258. They were doctrinally orthodox but rigorist. See *Dev* p. 251.

[51] Newman would have had in mind the American sects he had mentioned in 'The Anglo-American Church', *Ess* I, pp.325-27, which included the Seed and Snake Baptists who taught that Eve had mated with the Serpent to produce Cain whose descendants were all damned; and the followers of Ann Lee who practised shaking dancing as evidence of sin leaving their bodies and believed that she was the woman described in Revelation ch.12.

opened the door to it. The Church of course would say that such prerogatives were justly hers, as being at least congruous grants made to her, on the part of the State, in return for the benefits which she bestowed upon it. It was her right to demand them, and the State's duty to concede them. This seems to have been the basis of the new state of society. And in fact these prerogatives were in force and in exercise all through those troublous centuries which followed the break-up of the Imperial sway: and, though the handling of them at length fell into the hands of one see exclusively (on which I shall remark presently), the see of Peter, yet the substance and character of these prerogatives, and the Church's claim to possess them, remained untouched. The change in the internal allocation of power did not affect the existence and the use of the power itself.

Ranke,[52] speaking of this development of ecclesiastical supremacy upon the conversion of the Empire, remarks as follows:—

"It appears to me that this was the result of an internal necessity. The rise of Christianity involved the liberation of religion from all political elements. From this followed the growth of a distinct ecclesiastical class with a peculiar constitution. In this separation of the Church from the State consists, perhaps the greatest, the most pervading and influential peculiarity of all Christian times. The spiritual and secular powers may come into near contact, may even stand in the closest community; but they can be thoroughly incorporated

---

[52] Leopold von Ranke (1795-1886), German historian and professor of history in Berlin from 1825-1886. His history of the Popes, *Die römischen Päpste, ihre Kirche und ihr Staat* (3 vols. 1834-1836) was remarkably free from polemics and based on meticulous research.

only at rare conjunctures and for a short period. Their [205] mutual relations, their positions with regard to each other, form, from this time forward, one of the most important considerations in all history."—*The Popes*, vol. i. p. 10, *transl.*

§ 3. *The Papal Church.*

NOW we come to the distinctive doctrine of the Catholic Religion, the doctrine which separates us from all other denominations of Christians however near they may approach to us in other respects, the claims of the see of Rome, which have given occasion to Mr. Gladstone's Pamphlet and to the remarks which I am now making upon it. Of those rights, prerogatives, privileges, and duties, which I have been surveying in the ancient Church, the Pope is historically the heir. I shall dwell now upon this point, as far as it is to my purpose to do so, not treating it theologically (else I must define and prove from Scripture and the Fathers the "Primatus jure divino Romani Pontificis,"[1] which of course I firmly hold), but historically,* because Mr. Gladstone appeals to history. Instead of treating it theologically I wish to look with (as it were) secular, or even non-Catholic eyes at the powers claimed during the last thousand years by the Pope—that is, only as they lie in the nature of the case, and on the surface of the facts which come before us in history.

1. I say the Pope is the heir[2] of the Ecumenical Hierarchy

---

* History never serves as the measure of dogmatic truth in its fulness. *Vide infra.* § 8.[3]

---

[1] 'The Primacy of the Roman Pontiff by divine law.'
[2] 1875 ed.: "… the Pope is historically the heir"
[3] This footnote was not in the 1875 edition.

of the fourth century,[4] as being, what I may call, heir by default. No one else claims or exercises its rights or its duties. Is it possible to consider the Patriarch of Moscow or of Constantinople, heir to the historical pretensions of St. Ambrose or St. Martin? Does any Anglican Bishop for the last 300 years recall to our minds the image of St. Basil?[5] Well, then, has all that ecclesiastical power, which makes such a show in the Christian Empire, simply vanished, or, if not, where is it to be found? I wish Protestants would throw themselves into our minds upon this point;[6] I am not holding an argument with them; I am only wishing them to understand where we stand and how we look at things. There is this great difference of belief between us and them: they do not believe that Christ set up a visible society, or rather kingdom, for the propagation and maintenance of His religion, for a necessary home and a refuge for His people; but we do.[7] We know the kingdom is still on earth: where is it? If all that can be found of it is what can be discerned at Constantinople or Canterbury, I say, it has disappeared; and either there was a radical corruption of Christianity from the first, or Christianity came to an end, in proportion as the type of the Nicene Church faded out of the world: for all that we know of Christianity, in ancient history, as a concrete fact, is the Church of Athanasius[8] and his fellow Bishops: it is nothing else historically but that bundle of phenomena, that combination of claims, prerogatives, and corresponding acts,

---

[4] "Its bishops were not mere local officers, but possessed a quasi-ecumenical power, extending wherever a Christian was to be found... Such was the admirable unity of the Church Catholic in those days, and the blessed harmony and consent of her bishops among one another." *Dev* p. 266.

[5] St. Basil (c.330-79) became bishop of Caesarea in 370. He is called 'The Great' for his holiness and his influence on Eastern monasticism. He built a new town called Basilead, complete with hospital and a soup kitchen for the poor.

[6] Newman had made the same point to Pusey in his attitude to Catholic devotion to the Blessed Virgin p.[116].

[7] "She is the Church of all lands and of all times." 'Christ upon the Waters' (1850) *OS* p. 145.

[8] See supra.

[208] some of which I have recounted above. There is no help for it then; we cannot take as much as we please, and no more, of an institution which has a monadic existence.[9] We must either give up the belief in the Church as a divine institution altogether, or we must recognize it at this day in that communion of which the Pope is the head. With him alone and round about him are found the claims, the prerogatives, and duties which we identify with the kingdom set up by Christ. We must take things as they are; to believe in a Church, is to believe in the Pope. And thus this belief in the Pope and his attributes, which seems so monstrous to Protestants, is bound up with our being Catholics at all; as our Catholicism is bound up with our Christianity. There is nothing then of wanton opposition to the powers that be, no dinning of novelties in their startled ears in what is often unjustly called Ultramontane doctrine; there is no pernicious servility to the Pope in our admission of his pretensions. I say, we cannot help ourselves—Parliament may deal as harshly with us as it will; we should not believe in the Church at all, unless we believe in its visible head.

So it is; the course of ages has fulfilled the prophecy and promise, "Thou art Peter, and upon this rock I will build My Church; and whatsoever thou shalt bind on earth, shall be bound in heaven, and whatsoever thou shalt loose on earth shall be loosed in heaven."[10] That which in substance was possessed by the Nicene Hierarchy,[11] that the Pope claims now. I do not wish to put difficulties in my way: but I cannot conceal or smooth over what I believe to be a simple truth, though the avowal of it will be very unwelcome to

[209] Protestants, and, as I fear, to some Catholics. However, I do not call upon another to believe all that I believe on the subject myself. I declare it, as my own judgment, that the

---

[9] of a fundamental singular entity.
[10] Matt 16:18, 19.
[11] i.e. at the time of the First Council of Nicaea (325).

prerogatives, such as, and in the way in which, I have described them in substance, which the Church had under the Roman Power, those she claims now, and never, never will relinquish; claims them, not as having received them from a dead Empire, but partly by the direct endowment of her Divine Master, and partly as being a legitimate outcome of that endowment; claims them, but not except from Catholic populations, not as if accounting the more sublime of them to be of every-day use, but holding them as a protection or remedy in great emergencies or on supreme occasions, when nothing else will serve, as extraordinary and solemn acts of her religious sovereignty.[12] And our Lord, seeing what would be brought about by human means, even had He not willed it, and recognizing, from the laws which He Himself had imposed upon human society, that no large community could be strong which had no head, spoke the word in the beginning, as He did to Judah, "Thou art he whom thy brethren shall praise,"[13] and then left it to the course of events to fulfil it.

2. Mr. Gladstone ought to have chosen another issue for attack upon us, than the Pope's special power.[14] His real difficulty lies deeper; as little permission as he allows to the Pope, would he allow to any ecclesiastic who would wield the weapons of St. Ambrose and St. Augustine. That concentration of the Church's powers which history brings before us ought not to be the simple object of his indignation. It is not the existence of a Pope, but of a Church; which is his [210] aversion. It is the powers themselves, and not their distribution and allocation in the ecclesiastical body which he writes against. A triangle[15] is the same in its substance and nature, whichever side is made its base. "The Pontiffs," says

---

[12] Newman sees from history the special circumstances which call for the exercise of supreme papal authority.

[13] Gen 49: 8.

[14] 1875 ed.: "…the Pope's power"

[15] 1874 ed.: "A triangle or parallelogram …"

Mr. Bowden,[16] who writes as an Anglican, "exalted to the kingly throne of St. Peter, did not so much claim new privileges for themselves, as deprive their episcopal brethren of privileges originally common to the hierarchy. Even the titles by which those autocratical prelates, in the plenitude of their power, delighted to style themselves, 'Summus Sacerdos,' 'Pontifex Maximus,' 'Vicarius Christi,'[17] 'Papa' itself, had, nearer to the primitive times, been the honourable appellations of every bishop; as 'Sedes Apostolica'[18] had been the description of every Bishop's throne. The ascription of these titles, therefore, to the Pope only gave to the terms new force, because that ascription became exclusive; because, that is, the bishops in general were stripped of honours, to which their claims were as well founded as those of their Roman brother, who became, by the change, not so strictly universal as sole Bishop." (*Greg. VII*. vol. i. p. 64.)[19]

Say that the Christian polity now remained, as history represents it to us in the fourth century, or that it was, if that was possible, now to revert to such a state, would politicians have less trouble with 1800 centres of power than they have with one? Instead of one, with traditionary rules, the trammels of treaties and engagements, public opinion to consult and manage, the responsibility of great interests, and the guarantee for his behaviour in his temporal possessions, there would be a legion of ecclesiastics, each bishop with his following, each independent of the others, each with his own views, each with extraordinary powers, each with the risk of misusing them, all over Christendom. It would be the Anglican theory, made real. It would be an ecclesiastical

[211]

---

[16] John William Bowden (1798-1844) studied with Newman at Trinity College and became a lifelong friend; he was the author of *The Life and Pontificate of Gregory the Seventh*, London 1840.

[17] 'High Priest', 'Great High Priest', 'Vicar of Christ'.

[18] 'Apostolic See'.

[19] Gregory issued his *Dictatus Papae* (Papal Pronouncements) which contained twenty-seven propositions about the powers of the Pope in 1075. See supra p.[200] and infra p.[215].

communism; and, if it did not benefit religion, at least it would not benefit the civil power. Take a small illustration:— what interruption at this time to Parliamentary proceedings, does a small zealous party occasion, which its enemies call a mere "handful of clergy;"[20] and why? Because its members are responsible for what they do to God alone and to their conscience as His voice. Even suppose it was only here or there that episcopal autonomy was vigorous; yet consider what zeal is kindled by local interests and national spirit. One John of Tuam,[21] with a Pope's full apostolic powers, would be a greater trial to successive ministries than an Ecumenical Bishop at Rome. Parliament understands this well, for it exclaims against the Sacerdotal principle. Here, for a second reason, if our Divine Master has given those great powers to the Church, which ancient Christianity testifies, we see why His Providence has also brought it about that the exercise of them should be concentrated in one see.

But, anyhow, the progress of concentration was not the work of the Pope; it was brought about by the changes of times and the vicissitudes of nations. It was not his fault that the Vandals swept away the African sees,[22] and the Saracens those of Syria and Asia Minor,[23] or that Constantinople and its dependencies became the creatures of Imperialism,[24] or that France, England, and Germany would obey none but the [212]

---

[20] In the General Election of 1874, fifty-nine members of the (Irish) Home Rule League were elected to Parliament. The League was supported, and at local level even led by, Irish Catholic clergy.

[21] John MacHale (1791-1881) became Archbishop of Tuam in 1834. He was an Irish nationalist who opposed Archbishop Cullen over the Catholic University in Dublin and the appointment of Newman because he was an Englishman, although he personally had a high opinion of him. He was known as 'The Lion of the West.' At the Vatican Council he took an opposing stance to Archbishop Cullen.

[22] The Vandals were originally Teutonic tribes who migrated to Africa and besieged Hippo in 430, as Augustine lay dying.

[23] Name given by Greek authors to members of 1st century nomadic tribes on the eastern borders of the Roman empire.

[24] i.e. under the Byzantine emperors.

author of their own Christianity,[25] or that clergy and people at
a distance were obstinate in sheltering themselves under the
majesty of Rome against their own fierce kings and nobles or
imperious bishops, even to the imposing forgeries on the
world and on the Pope in justification of their proceedings.[26]
All this will be fact, whether the Popes were ambitious or not;
and still it will be fact that the issue of that great change was
a great benefit to the whole of Europe. No one but a Master,
who was a thousand bishops in himself at once, could have
tamed and controlled, as the Pope did, the great and little
tyrants of the middle age.

3. This is generally confessed now, even by Protestant
historians, viz., that the concentration of ecclesiastical power
in those centuries was simply necessary for the civilization
of Europe. Of course it does not follow that the benefits
rendered then to the European commonwealth by the political
supremacy of the Pope, would, if he was still supreme, be
rendered in time to come. I have no wish to make
assumptions; yet conclusions short of this will be
unfavourable to Mr. Gladstone's denunciation of him. We
reap the fruit at this day of his services in the past. With the
purpose of showing this I make a rather long extract from
Dean Milman's[27] "Latin Christianity;" he is speaking of the
era of Gregory I.,[28] and he says, the Papacy "was the only
power which lay not entirely and absolutely prostrate before
the disasters of the times—a power which had an inherent
strength, and might resume its majesty. It was this power

---

[25] i.e. the popes, such as St. Gregory the Great, who had sent missionaries to these countries.

[26] False Decretals, attributed to St Isidore of Seville but compiled in France in the ninth century, comprised letters of ante-Nicene Popes defending the rights of diocesan bishops and claiming authority for papal supremacy.

[27] Henry Hart Milman (1791-1868) was Rector of St. Margaret's Westminster in 1838 and Dean of St. Paul's in 1849. His *History of Latin Christianity* was published in 1855 and his *History of Christianity to the Abolition of Paganism in the Roman Empire* in 1840.

[28] Gregory I, Pope (590-604).

which was most imperatively required to preserve all which [213]
was to survive out of the crumbling wreck of Roman
civilization. To Western Christianity was absolutely
necessary a centre, standing alone, strong in traditionary
reverence, and in acknowledged claims to supremacy. Even
the perfect organization of the Christian hierarchy might in
all human probability have fallen to pieces in perpetual
conflict: it might have degenerated into a half-secular feudal
caste, with hereditary benefices more and more entirely
subservient to the civil authority, a priesthood of each nation
or each tribe, gradually sinking to the intellectual or religious
level of the nation or tribe. On the rise of a power both
controlling and conservative hung, humanly speaking, the
life and death of Christianity—of Christianity as a
permanent, aggressive, expansive, and, to a certain extent,
uniform system. There must be a counter-balance to barbaric
force, to the unavoidable anarchy of Teutonism, with its
tribal, or at the utmost national independence, forming a host
of small, conflicting, antagonistic kingdoms. All Europe
would have been what England was under the Octarchy,[29]
what Germany was when her emperors were weak; and even
her emperors she owed to Rome, to the Church, to
Christianity. Providence might have otherwise ordained; but
it is impossible for man to imagine by what other organizing
or consolidating force the commonwealth of the Western
nations could have grown up to a discordant, indeed, and
conflicting league, but still a league, with that unity and
conformity of manners, usages, laws, religion, which have
made their rivalries, oppugnancies',[30] and even their long
ceaseless wars, on the whole to issue in the noblest, highest, [214]
most intellectual form of civilization known to man ... It is
impossible to conceive what had been the confusion, the

---

[29] England was under eight different rulers before the Kings of Wessex united most
of the country in the ninth century.
[30] antagonisms

lawlessness, the chaotic state of the middle ages, without the medieval Papacy; and of the medieval Papacy the real father is Gregory the Great. In all his predecessors there was much of the uncertainty and indefiniteness of a new dominion ... Gregory is the Roman altogether merged in the Christian Bishop.[31] It is a Christian dominion of which he lays the foundations in the Eternal City, not the old Rome, associating Christian influence to her ancient title of sovereignty." (Vol. i. p. 401, 402.)

4. From Gregory I. to Innocent III.[32] is six hundred years; a very fair portion of the world's history, to have passed in doing good of primary importance to a whole continent, and that the continent of Europe; good, by which all nations and their governors, all statesmen and legislatures, are the gainers. And, again, should it not occur to Mr. Gladstone that these services were rendered to mankind by means of those very instruments of power on which he thinks it proper to pour contempt as "rusty tools"?[33] The right to warn and punish powerful men, to excommunicate kings, to preach aloud truth and justice to the inhabitants of the earth, to denounce immoral doctrines, to strike at rebellion in the garb of heresy, were the very weapons by which Europe was brought into a civilized condition; yet he calls them "rusty tools" which need "refurbishing." Does he wish then that such high expressions of ecclesiastical displeasure, such sharp penalties, should be of daily use? If they are rusty, because they have been long without using, then have they ever been rusty. Is a Council a rusty tool, because none had been held, till 1870, since the sixteenth century? or because

[215]

---

[31] Gregory I was the son of a senator who became prefect of the city in 573 and then entered the monastery in c. 574. See supra.

[32] Pope Innocent III (1198-1216) established his authority first in Italy and then more widely and was the first to call himself 'Vicar of Christ'. He declared, "No king can reign rightly unless he serves devoutly Christ's Vicar".

[33] In his article 'Ritual and Ritualism' in the *Contemporary Review* (October 1874 p. 674) Gladstone had written of Rome having "paraded anew every rusty tool she was fondly thought to have disused."

there have been but nineteen in 1900 years? How many times is it in the history of Christianity that the Pope has solemnly drawn and exercised his sword upon a king or an emperor? If an extraordinary weapon must be a rusty tool, I suppose Gregory VII.'s[34] sword was not keen enough for the German Henry; and the seventh Pius too used a rusty tool in his excommunication of Napoleon.[35] How could Mr. Gladstone ever "fondly think that Rome had disused" her weapons, and that they had hung up as antiquities and curiosities in her celestial armoury,—or, in his own words, as "hideous mummies," p. 46,—when the passage of arms between the great Conqueror and the aged Pope was so close upon his memory! Would he like to see a mummy come to life again? That unexpected miracle actually took place in the first years of this century. Gregory was considered to have done an astounding deed in the middle ages, when he brought Henry, the German Emperor, to do penance and shiver in the snow at Canossa; but Napoleon had his snow-penance too, and that with an actual interposition of Providence in the infliction of it. I describe it in the words of Alison:—

"'What does the Pope mean,' said Napoleon to Eugene,[36] in July, 1807, 'by the threat of excommunicating me? does he think the world has gone back a thousand years? does he suppose the arms will fall from the hands of my soldiers?' Within two years after these remarkable words were written, [216] the Pope did excommunicate him, in return for the confiscation of his whole dominions, and in less than four years more, the arms did fall from the hands of his soldiers; and the hosts, apparently invincible, which he had collected

---

[34] St. Gregory VII/Hildebrand (c.1021-85) insisted on the Church's independence of secular power. Henry IV of Germany was forced to submit to him at Canossa in 1077.

[35] Pius VII (1740-1823) excommunicated Napoleon in 1809. He was deported to Grenoble and then to Savona. He returned to Rome in 1814.

[36] Eugène de Bauharnais (1791-1824), Duke of Leuchtenberg, Napoleon's stepson who became his aide-de-camp and was made Arch-Chancellor of State in 1805.

were dispersed and ruined by the blasts of winter. 'The weapons of the soldiers,' says Segur,[37] in describing the Russian retreat, 'appeared of an insupportable weight to their stiffened arms. During their frequent falls they fell from their hands, and destitute of the power of raising them from the ground, they were left in the snow. They did not throw them away: famine and cold tore them from their grasp.' 'The soldiers could no longer hold their weapons,' says Salgues,[38] 'they fell from the hands even of the bravest and most robust. The muskets dropped from the frozen arms of those who bore them.'" (*Hist*. ch. lx. 9th ed.)

Alison adds: "There is something in these marvellous coincidences beyond the operations of chance, and which even a Protestant historian feels himself bound to mark for the observation of future ages. The world had not gone back a thousand years,[39] but that Being existed with whom a thousand years are as one day, and one day as a thousand years." As He was with Gregory in 1077, so He was with Pius in 1812, and He will be with some future Pope again, when the necessity shall come.

5. In saying this, I am far from saying that Popes are never in the wrong, and are never to be resisted; or that their excommunications always avail. I am not bound to defend the policy or the acts of particular Popes,[40] whether before or after the great revolt from their authority in the 16th century. There is no reason that I should contend, and I do not contend, for instance, that they at all times have understood our own people, our natural character and resources, and our position in Europe; or that they have never suffered from bad

[217]

---

[37] Louis Philippe, Comte de Ségur (1753-1830), diplomat and historian.

[38] Louis-Marie de Salgues (1766-1793), Marquis de Lescure, cavalry commander under General Westermann, known by reputation as 'Le saint de Poitou.'

[39] See 2 Pet 3:8.

[40] "A private Catholic is not answerable for the Pope's political errors, any more than the shareholder in a railway in 1875 is answerable for the railway's accidents in 1860." Newman to J. R. Mozley 4 April 1875 *LD* 27 p. 265.

counsellors or misinformation. I say this the more freely, because Urban VIII.,[41] about the year 1641 or 1642, seems to have blamed the policy of some Popes of the preceding century in their dealings with our country.* But, whatever we are bound to allow to Mr. Gladstone on this head, that does not warrant the passionate invective against the Holy See and us individually, which he has carried on through sixty-four pages. What we have a manifest right to expect from him is lawyer-like exactness and logical consecutiveness in his impeachment of us. The heavier that is, the less does it need the exaggerations of a great orator. If the Pope's conduct towards us three centuries ago has righteously wiped out the memory of his earlier benefits, yet he should have a fair trial. The more intoxicating was his solitary greatness, when it was in the zenith, the greater consideration should be shown [218] towards him in his present temporal humiliation, when concentration of ecclesiastical functions in one man, does but make him, in the presence of the haters of Catholicism, what a Roman Emperor contemplated, when he wished all his subjects had but one neck that he might destroy them by one blow.[42] Surely, in the trial of so august a criminal,[43] one might have hoped, at least, to have found gravity and measure in

* "When he was urged to excommunicate the Kings of France and Sweden, he made answer, 'We may declare them excommunicate, as Pius V. declared Queen Elizabeth of England, and before him Clement VII. the King of England, Henry VIII. ... but with what success? The whole world can tell. We yet bewail it with tears of blood. Wisdom does not teach us to imitate Pius V. or Clement VII., but Paul V. who, in the beginning, being many times urged by the Spaniards to excommunicate James, King of England, never would consent to it.'" (State Paper Office, *Italy*, 1641-1662.) *Vide* Mr. Simpson's very able and careful life of Campion, 1867, p. 371. [44]

---

[41] Urban VIII (1568-1644), Maffeo Barberini, became Pope in 1623.

[42] Caligula (37-41).

[43] i.e. Pius IX.

[44] Richard Simpson, *Edmund Campion, A Definitive Biography*,1867.

language, and calmness in tone—not a pamphlet written as if on impulse, in defence of an incidental parenthesis in a previous publication, and then, after being multiplied in 22,000 copies,[45] appealing to the lower classes in the shape of a sixpenny tract, the lowness of the price indicating the width of the circulation. Surely Nana Sahib[46] will have more justice done to him by the English people, than has been shown to the Father of European civilization.

6. I have been referring to the desolate state in which the Holy See has been cast during the last years, such that the Pope, humanly speaking, is at the mercy of his enemies, and morally a prisoner in his palace. That state of secular feebleness cannot last for ever; sooner or later there will be, in the divine mercy, a change for the better, and the Vicar of Christ will no longer be a mark for insult and indignity. But one thing, except by an almost miraculous interposition, cannot be; and that is, a return to the universal religious sentiment, the public opinion, of the medieval time. The Pope himself calls those centuries "the ages of faith." Such endemic faith may certainly be decreed for some future time; but, as far as we have the means of judging at present, [219] centuries must run out first. Even in the fourth century the ecclesiastical privileges, claimed on the one hand, granted on the other, came into effect more or less under two conditions, that they were recognized by public law, and that they had the consent of the Christian populations. Is there any chance whatever, except by miracles which were not granted then, that the public law and the inhabitants of Europe will allow the Pope that exercise of his rights, which they allowed him as a matter of course in the 11th and 12th centuries?[47] If the whole world will at once answer No, it is surely inopportune

---

[45] The second printing of 22,500 copies in November 1874.
[46] The last Mahratta Peshwa, Baji Rao II (1775-1851) who was deposed by the British in 1818 and given a pension.
[47] For instance under Gregory VII.

to taunt us this day with the acts of medieval Popes towards certain princes and nobles, when the sentiment of Europe was radically Papal. How does the past bear upon the present in this matter? Yet Mr. Gladstone is in earnest alarm, earnest with the earnestness which distinguishes him as a statesman, at the harm which society may receive from the Pope, at a time when the Pope can do nothing. He grants (p. 46) that "the fears are visionary ... that either foreign foe or domestic treason can, at the bidding of the Court of Rome, disturb these peaceful shores;" he allows that "in the middle ages the Popes contended, not by direct action of fleets and armies," but mainly "by interdicts," p. 35. Yet, because men then believed in interdicts, though now they don't, therefore the civil Power is to be roused against the Pope. But his *animus* is bad; his *animus*! what can *animus* do without matter to work upon? Mere *animus*, like big words, breaks no bones.

As if to answer Mr. Gladstone by anticipation, and to allay [220] his fears, the Pope made a declaration three years ago on the subject, which, strange to say, Mr. Gladstone quotes without perceiving that it tells against the very argument which he brings it to corroborate;—that is except as the Pope's *animus* goes. Doubtless he would wish to have the place in the political world which his predecessors had, because it was given to him by Providence, and is conducive to the highest interests of mankind, but he distinctly tells us in the declaration in question that he has not got it, and cannot have it, till the time comes, which we can speculate about as well as he, and which we say cannot come at least for centuries. He speaks of what is his highest political power, that of interposing in the quarrel between a prince and his subjects, and of declaring upon appeal made to him from them, that the Prince had or had not forfeited their allegiance. This power, most rarely exercised, and on very extraordinary occasions, it is not necessary for any Catholic to acknowledge; and I suppose, comparatively speaking, few

Catholics do acknowledge it; to be honest, I may say, I do; that is, under the conditions which the Pope himself lays down in the declaration to which I have referred, his answer to the address of the Academia.[48] He speaks of his right "to depose sovereigns, and release the people from the obligation of loyalty, a right which had undoubtedly sometimes been exercised in crucial circumstances," and he says, "This right (*diritto*) in those ages of faith,—(which discerned in the Pope, what he is, that is to say, the Supreme Judge of Christianity, and recognized the advantages of his tribunal in the great contests of peoples and sovereigns)—was freely extended,—(aided indeed as a matter of duty by the public law (*diritto*) and by the common consent of peoples)—to the most important (*i piu gravi*) interest of states and their rulers." (*Guardian*, Nov. 11, 1874.)

[221]

Now let us observe how the Pope restrains the exercise of this right. He calls it his right—that is in the sense in which right in one party is correlative with duty in the other, so that, when the duty is not observed, the right cannot be brought into exercise; and this is precisely what he goes on to intimate; for he lays down the conditions of that exercise. First it can only be exercised in rare and critical circumstances (*supreme circonstanze, i più gravi interessi*).[49] Next he refers to his being the supreme judge of Christendom and to his decision as coming from a tribunal; his prerogative then is not a mere arbitrary power, but must be exercised by a process of law and a formal examination of the case, and in the presence and the hearing of the two parties interested in it. Also in this limitation is implied that the Pope's definite sentence involves an appeal to the supreme standard of right

---

[48] "There are many errors regarding the Infallibility; but the most malicious of all is that which included, in the dogma the *right* of deposing sovereigns, and declaring the people no longer bound by the obligation of fidelity. This *right* has now and again, in critical circumstances, been exercised by the Pontiffs." His address to the Accademia Pontificia was on 21 July 1871.

[49] 'extreme circumstances and in the gravest interests'

and wrong, the moral law, as its basis and rule, and must contain the definite reasons on which it decides in favour of the one party or the other. Thirdly, the exercise of this right is limited to the ages of faith; ages which, on the one hand, inscribed it among the provisions of the *jus publicum*,[50] and on the other so fully recognized the benefits it conferred, as to be able to enforce it by the common consent of the peoples. These last words should be dwelt on: it is no consent which is merely local, as of one country, of Ireland or of Belgium, if that were probable; but a united consent of various nations of Europe, for instance, as a commonwealth, of which the Pope was the head. Thirty years ago we heard much of the Pope being made the head of an Italian confederation:[51] no word came from England against such an arrangement. It was possible, because the members of it were all of one religion; and in like manner a European commonwealth would be reasonable, if Europe were of one religion. Lastly, the Pope declares with indignation that a Pope is not infallible in the exercise of this right; such a notion is an invention of the enemy; he calls it "malicious."

[222]

What is there in all this to arouse the patriotic anxieties of Mr. Gladstone?[52]

---

[50] a country's public law

[51] Vincenzo Gioberti (b. 1801), Premier of Piedmont (1848-9), recommended in his *On the Moral and Civil Primacy of the Italian Race* (1843) an Italian federation with the Pope as head.

[52] This paragraph is not in the 1875 edition.

§ 4. *Divided Allegiance.*

BUT one attribute the Church has, and the Pope as head of the Church, whether he be in high estate, as this world goes, or not, whether he has temporal possessions or not, whether he is in honour or dishonour, whether he is at home or driven about, whether those special claims of which I have spoken are allowed or not,—and that is Sovereignty. As God has sovereignty, though He may be disobeyed or disowned, so has His Vicar upon earth; and farther than this, since Catholic populations are found everywhere, he ever will be in fact lord of a vast empire; as large in numbers, as far spreading as the British; and all his acts are sure to be such as are in keeping with the position of one who is thus supremely exalted.

I beg not to be interrupted here, as many a reader will interrupt me in his thoughts, for I am using these words, not at random, but as the commencement of a long explanation, and, in a certain sense, limitation, of what I have hitherto been saying concerning the Church's and the Pope's power. To this task the remaining pages, which I have to address to your Grace, will be directed; and I trust that it will turn out, when I come to the end of them, that, by first stating fully what the Pope's claims are, I shall be able most clearly to show what he does not claim.

Now the main point of Mr. Gladstone's Pamphlet is this:—that, since the Pope claims infallibility in faith and morals, and since there are no "departments and functions of human life which do not and cannot fall within the domain of morals," p. 36, and since he claims also "the domain of all that concerns the government and discipline of the Church," and moreover, "claims the power of determining the limits of those domains," and "does not sever them, by any acknowledged or intelligible line from the domains of civil duty and allegiance," p. 45, therefore Catholics are moral and mental slaves, and "every convert and member of the Pope's Church places his loyalty and civil duty at the mercy of another," p. 45.

I admit Mr. Gladstone's premises, but I reject his conclusion; and now I am going to show why I reject it.

In doing this, I shall, with him, put aside for the present and at first the Pope's prerogative of infallibility in general enunciations, whether of faith or morals, and confine myself to the consideration of his authority (in respect to which he is not infallible) in matters of conduct, and of our duty of obedience to him. "There is something wider still," he says, (than the claim of infallibility,) "and that is the claim to an Absolute and entire Obedience," p. 37. "Little does it matter to me, whether my Superior claims infallibility, so long as he is entitled to demand and exact conformity," p. 39. He speaks of a third province being opened, "not indeed to the abstract assertion of Infallibility, but to the far more practical and [225] decisive demand of Absolute Obedience," p. 41, "the Absolute Obedience, at the peril of salvation, of every member of his communion," p. 42.

Now, I proceed to examine this large, direct, religious, sovereignty of the Pope, both in its relation to his subjects, and to the Civil Power; but first, I beg to be allowed to say just one word on the principle of obedience itself, that is, by way of inquiring whether it is or is not now a religious duty.

Is there then such a duty at all as obedience to ecclesiastical authority now? or is it one of those obsolete ideas, which are swept away, as unsightly cobwebs, by the New Civilization? Scripture says, "Remember them which have the *rule* over you, who have spoken unto you the word of God, whose faith follow." And, "*Obey* them that have the *rule* over you, and *submit yourselves*; for they watch *for your souls*, as they that must give account, that they may do it with joy and not with grief; for that is unprofitable for you."[1] The margin in the Protestant Version reads, "those who are your *guides*;"[2] and the word may also be translated "leaders." Well, as rulers, or guides and leaders, whichever word be right, they are to be *obeyed*. Now Mr. Gladstone dislikes our way of fulfilling this precept, whether as regards our choice of ruler and leader, or our "Absolute Obedience" to him; but he does not give us his own. Is there any liberalistic reading of the Scripture passage? Or are the words only for the benefit of the poor and ignorant, not for the *Schola* (as it may be called) of political and periodical writers, not for individual members of Parliament, not for statesmen and Cabinet ministers, and people of Progress? Which party then is the more "Scriptural," those who recognize and carry out in their conduct texts like these, or those who don't? May not we Catholics claim some mercy from Mr. Gladstone, though we be faulty in the object and the manner of our obedience, since in a lawless day an object and a manner of obedience we have? Can we be blamed, if, arguing from those texts which say that ecclesiastical authority comes from above, we obey it in that one form in which alone we find it on earth, in that one person who, of all the notabilities of this nineteenth century into which we have been born, alone claims it of us? The Pope has no rival in his claim upon us; nor is it our doing that his claim has been made and allowed for centuries upon centuries, and that it was he who made the Vatican decrees, and not they him. If we give him up, to whom shall we go?[3] Can we dress up any civil functionary in the vestments of

[226]

---

[1] Heb 13:7, 17.
[2] Douai has 'prelates'. RSV has 'leaders'. Knox has 'those who have charge over you.'
[3] See John 6:68

divine authority? Can I, for instance, follow the faith, can I put my soul into the hands, of our gracious Sovereign? or of the Archbishop of Canterbury? or of the Bishop of Lincoln,[4] albeit he is not broad and low, but high? Catholics have "done what they could,"—all that any one could: and it should be Mr. Gladstone's business, before telling us that we are slaves, because we obey the Pope, first of all to tear away those texts from the Bible.

With this preliminary remark, I proceed to consider whether the Pope's authority is either a slavery to his subjects, or a menace to the Civil Power; and first, as to his power over his flock.

1. Mr. Gladstone says that "the Pontiff declares to belong [227] to him the *supreme direction* of Catholics in respect to all duty," p. 37. Supreme direction; true, but "supreme" is not "minute," nor does "direction" mean "supervision" or "management." Take the parallel of human law; the Law is *supreme*, and the Law *directs* our conduct under the manifold circumstances in which we have to act, and may and must be absolutely obeyed; but who therefore says that the Law has the "supreme direction" of us? The State, as well as the Church, has the power at its will of imposing laws upon us, laws bearing on our moral duties, our daily conduct, affecting our actions in various ways, and circumscribing our liberties; yet no one would say that the Law, after all, with all its power in the abstract and its executive vigour in fact, interferes either with our comfort or our conscience. There are numberless laws about property, landed and personal, titles, tenures, trusts, wills, covenants, contracts, partnerships, money transactions, life-insurances, taxes, trade, navigation, education, sanitary measures, trespasses, nuisances, all in addition to the criminal law. Law, to apply Mr. Gladstone's

---

[4] Edward King (1829-1910) was bishop of Lincoln. A Tractarian and friend of Pusey.

words, "is the shadow that cleaves to us, go where we will."[5] Moreover, it varies year after year, and refuses to give any pledge of fixedness or finality. Nor can any one tell what restraint is to come next, perhaps painful personally to himself. Nor are its enactments easy of interpretation; for actual cases, with the opinions and speeches of counsel, and the decisions of judges, must prepare the raw material, as it proceeds from the Legislature, before it can be rightly [228] understood; so that "the glorious uncertainty of the Law"[6] has become a proverb. And, after all, no one is sure of escaping its penalties without the assistance of lawyers, and that in such private and personal matters that the lawyers are, as by an imperative duty, bound to a secrecy which even courts of justice respect. And then, besides the Statute Law, there is the common and traditional; and, below this, usage. Is not all this enough to try the temper of a free-born Englishman, and to make him cry out with Mr. Gladstone, "Three-fourths of my life are handed over to the Law; I care not to ask if there be dregs or tatters of human life, such as can escape from the description and boundary of Parliamentary tyranny?" Yet, though we may dislike it, though we may at times suffer from it ever so much, who does not see that the thraldom and irksomeness is nothing compared with the great blessings which the Constitution and Legislature secure to us?

Such is the jurisdiction which the Law exercises over us. What rule does the Pope claim which can be compared to its strong and its long arm? What interference with our liberty of judging and acting in our daily work, in our course of life, comes to us from him? Really, at first sight, I have not known where to look for instances of his actual interposition in our private affairs, for it is our routine of personal duties about

---

[5] Gladstone in his *Expostulation* talked of *duty* as "the shadow which cleaves to us, go where we will and which only leaves us when we leave the light of life." p.37.
[6] The toast to "the glorious uncertainty of the Law" was given by Mr. Wilbraham at a dinner in Sergeant's hall in 1756 with reference to Lord Mansfield's judgements.

which I am now speaking. Let us see how we stand in this matter.

We are guided in our ordinary duties by the books of moral theology, which are drawn up by theologians of authority and experience, as an instruction for our Confessors. These books are based on the three Christian [229] foundations of Faith, Hope, and Charity, on the Ten Commandments, and on the six Precepts of the Church, which relate to the observance of Sunday, of fast days, of confession and communion, and, in one shape or other, to paying tithes.[7] A great number of possible cases are noted under these heads, and in difficult questions a variety of opinions are given, with plain directions, when it is that private Catholics are at liberty to choose for themselves whatever answer they like best, and when they are bound to follow some one of them in particular. Reducible as these directions in detail are to the few and simple heads which I have mentioned, they are little more than reflexions and memoranda of our moral sense, unlike the positive enactments of the Legislature; and, on the whole, present to us no difficulty—though now and then some critical question may arise, and some answer may be given (just as by the private conscience itself) which it is difficult to us or painful to accept. And again, cases may occur now and then, when our private judgment differs from what is set down in theological works, but even then it does not follow at once that our private judgment must give way, for those books are no utterance of Papal authority.

And this is the point to which I am coming. So little does the Pope come into this whole system of moral theology by which (as by our conscience) our lives are regulated, that the

---

[7] The Precepts of the Church are to keep Sundays and holidays of obligation holy by hearing Mass and resting from servile works, to receive the Sacrament of Penance once a year and Holy Communion during the Easter season, to observe the marriage laws of the Church, to contribute to the support of the clergy (tithes) and abstain from meat and fast on the appropriate days. (*Catechism of Christian Doctrine* n.229)

[230]

weight of his hand upon us, as private men, is absolutely unappreciable. I have had a difficulty where to find a measure or gauge of his interposition. At length I have looked through Busenbaum's "Medulla,"[8] to ascertain what light such a book would throw upon the question. It is a book of casuistry for the use of Confessors, running to 700 pages, and is a large repository of answers made by various theologians on points of conscience, and generally of duty. It was first published in 1645—my own edition is of 1844—and in this latter are marked those propositions, bearing on subjects treated in it, which have been condemned by Popes in the intermediate 200 years. On turning over the pages I find they are in all between fifty and sixty. This list includes matters sacramental, ritual, ecclesiastical, monastic, and disciplinarian, as well as moral, relating to the duties of ecclesiastics and regulars, of parish priests, and of professional men, as well as of private Catholics. And these condemnations relate for the most part to mere occasional details of duty, and are in reprobation of the lax or wild notions of speculative casuists, so that they are rather restraints upon theologians than upon laymen. For instance, the following are some of the propositions condemned:— "The ecclesiastic, who on a certain day is hindered from saying Matins and Lauds,[9] is not bound to say, if he can, the remaining hours;" "Where there is good cause, it is lawful to swear without the purpose of swearing, whether the matter is of light or grave moment;" "Domestics may steal from their masters, in compensation for their service, which they think greater than their wages;" "It is lawful for a public man to kill an opponent, who tries to fasten a calumny upon him, if he cannot otherwise escape the ignominy." I have taken these

---

[8] Hermann Busenbaum (1600-68), Jesuit theologian. His *Medulla Theologiae Moralis* was widely used as a textbook for practical moral theology for 200 years.

[9] The first prayers of the day in the Liturgy of the Hours (since 1971, Office of Readings and Morning Prayer).

instances at random. It must be granted, I think, that in the
long course of 200 years the amount of the Pope's [231]
authoritative enunciations has not been such as to press
heavily on the back of the private Catholic. He leaves us
surely far more than that "one fourth of the department of
conduct," which Mr. Gladstone allows us. Indeed, if my
account and specimens of his sway over us in morals be
correct, I do not see what he takes away at all from our private
consciences.

But here Mr. Gladstone will object, that the Pope does
really exercise a claim over the whole domain of conduct,
inasmuch as he refuses to draw any line across it in limitation
of his interference, and *therefore* it is that we are his slaves—
let us see if another illustration or parallel will not show this
to be a *non-sequitur*. Suppose a man, who is in the midst of
various and important lines of business, has a medical
adviser, in whom he has full confidence, as knowing well his
constitution. This adviser keeps a careful and anxious eye
upon him; and, as an honest man, says to him, "You must not
go off on a journey today," or "You must take some days'
rest," or "You must attend to your diet." Now, this is not a
fair parallel to the Pope's hold upon us; for the Pope does not
speak to us personally, but to all, and, in speaking definitively
on ethical subjects, what he propounds must relate to things
good and bad in themselves, not to things accidental,
changeable, and of mere expedience; so that the argument
which I am drawing from the case of a medical adviser is *à
fortiori*[10] in its character. However, I say that though a
medical man exercises a "supreme direction" over those who
put themselves under him, yet we do not therefore say, even [232]
of him, that he interferes with our daily conduct, and that we
are his slaves. He certainly does thwart many of our wishes
and purposes; and in a true sense we are at his mercy: he may
interfere any day, suddenly; he will not, he cannot, draw any

---

[10] all the more

intelligible line between the acts which he has a right to forbid us, and the acts which he has not. The same journey, the same press of business, the same indulgence at table, which he passes over one year, he sternly forbids the next. Therefore if Mr. Gladstone's argument is good, he has a finger in all the commercial transactions of the great trader or financier who has chosen him. But surely there is a simple fallacy here. Mr. Gladstone asks us whether our political and civil life is not at the Pope's mercy; every act, he says, of at least three-quarters of the day, is under his control. No, not *every*, but *any*, and this is all the difference—that is, we have no guarantee given us that there will never be a case, when the Pope's general utterances may come to have a bearing upon some personal act of ours. In the same way we are all of us in this age under the control of public opinion and the public prints;[11]; nay, much more intimately so. Journalism can be and is very personal; and, when it is in the right, more powerful just now than any Pope; yet we do not go into fits, as if we were slaves, because we are under a *surveillance* much more like tyranny than any sway, so indirect, so practically limited, so gentle, as his is.

[233] But it seems the cardinal point of our slavery lies, not simply in the domain of morals, but in the Pope's general authority over us in all things whatsoever. This count in his indictment Mr. Gladstone founds on a passage in the third chapter of the *Pastor æternus*,[12] in which the Pope, speaking of the Pontifical jurisdiction, says,—"Towards it (erga quam) pastors and people of whatsoever rite or dignity, each and all, are bound by the duty of hierarchical subordination and true obedience, not only in matters which pertain to faith and morals, but also in those which pertain to the *discipline* and the *regimen* of the Church spread throughout the world; so that, unity with the Roman Pontiff (both of communion and

---

[11] newspapers and periodicals
[12] First Dogmatic Constitution on the Church of Christ, 1 July 18th 1870.

of profession of the same faith) being preserved, the Church of Christ may be one flock under one supreme Shepherd. This is the doctrine of Catholic truth, from which no one can deviate without loss of faith and salvation."[13]

On Mr. Gladstone's use of this passage I observe first, that he leaves out a portion of it which has much to do with the due understanding of it (ita ut custoditâ, &c.)[14] Next, he speaks of "*absolute* obedience" so often, that any reader, who had not the passage before him, would think that the word "absolute" was the Pope's word, not his. Thirdly, three times (at pp. 38, 41, and 42) does he make the Pope say that no one can *disobey* him without risking his salvation, whereas what the Pope does say is, that no one can *disbelieve* the *duty* of obedience and unity without such risk. And fourthly, in order to carry out this false sense, or rather to hinder its being evidently impossible, he mistranslates, p. 38, "doctrina" (Hæc est doctrina[15]) by the word "rule."

But his chief attack is directed to the words "disciplina" and "regimen." "Thus," he says, "are swept into the Papal net [234] whole multitudes of facts, whole systems of government, prevailing, though in different degrees, in every country of the world," p. 41. That is, *disciplina* and *regimen* are words of such lax, vague, indeterminate meaning, that under them any matters can be slipped in, which may be required for the Pope's purpose in this or that country, such as, to take Mr. Gladstone's instances, blasphemy, poor-relief, incorporation, and mortmain;[16] as if no definitions were contained in our theological and ecclesiastical works of words in such common use, and as if in consequence the Pope was at liberty to give them any sense of his own. As to discipline, Fr. Perrone says, "Discipline comprises the exterior worship of

---

[13] Chapter 3 'The Power and Nature of the Primacy of the Roman Pontiff' *DS* 3060.
[14] "In this way the Church is protected, by unity with the Roman Pontiff in communion and in profession of the same faith…"
[15] 'This is doctrine'
[16] Lands held inalienably by a Church or corporation (from Latin: dead hand).

God, the liturgy, sacred rites, psalmody, the administration of the sacraments, the canonical form of sacred elections and the institution of ministers, vows, feast-days, and the like;" all of them (observe) matters internal to the Church, and without any relation to the Civil Power and civil affairs. Perrone adds, "Ecclesiastical discipline is a practical and external rule, prescribed by the Church, in order to retain the faithful in their *faith*, and the more easily lead them on to *eternal happiness*," *Præl. Theol.*,[17] t. 2, p. 381, 2nd ed., 1841. Thus discipline is in no sense a political instrument, except as the profession of our faith may accidentally become political. In the same sense Zallinger:[18] "The Roman Pontiff has by divine right the power of passing universal laws pertaining to the *discipline* of the Church; for instance, to divine worship, sacred rites, the ordination and manner of life of the clergy, the order of the ecclesiastical regimen, and the right administration of the temporal possessions of the church."—*Jur. Eccles.*, lib. i. t. 2, § 121.

[235]

So too the word "regimen" has a definite meaning, relating to a matter strictly internal to the Church: it means government, or the mode or form of government, or the course of government; and, as, in the intercourse of nation with nation, the nature of a nation's government, whether monarchical or republican, does not come into question, so the constitution of the Church simply belongs to its nature, not to its external action. Certainly there are aspects of the Church which involve relations toward secular powers and to nations, as, for instance, its missionary office; but regimen has relation to one of its internal characteristics, viz., its form of government, whether we call it a pure monarchy or with

---

[17] Giovanni Perrone S.J. See supra p. [234n]. *Praelectiones Theologicae* 9 vols 1835-42.

[18] Jakob Anton von Zallinger (1735-1813), Jesuit philosopher and canonist; author of *Iuri Publici Ecclesiastici Compendium* (1784).

others a monarchy tempered by aristocracy. Thus Tournely[19] says, "Three kinds of regimen or government are set down by philosophers, monarchy, aristocracy, and democracy."— *Theol.*, t. 2, p. 100. Bellarmine[20] says the same, *Rom. Pont.*, i. 2; and Perrone takes it for granted, *ibid.* pp. 70, 71.

Now, why does the Pope speak at this time of regimen and discipline? He tells us in that portion of the sentence, which, thinking it of no account, Mr. Gladstone has omitted. The Pope tells us that all Catholics should recollect their duty of obedience to him, not only in faith and morals, but in such matters of regimen and discipline as belong to the universal Church, "so that unity with the Roman Pontiff, both of communion and of profession of the same faith being preserved, the Church of Christ may be one flock under one [236] supreme Shepherd."[21] I consider this passage to be especially aimed at Nationalism: "Recollect," the Pope seems to say, "the Church is one, and that, not only in faith and morals, for schismatics may profess as much as this, but one, wherever it is, all over the world; and not only one, but one and the same, bound together by its one regimen and discipline and by the same regimen and discipline,—the same rites, the same sacraments, the same usages, and the same one Pastor; and in these bad times it is necessary for all Catholics to recollect, that this doctrine of the Church's individuality and, as it were, personality, is not a mere received opinion or understanding, which may be entertained or not, as we please, but is a fundamental, necessary truth." This being, speaking under correction, the drift of the passage, I observe that the words "spread throughout the world" or "universal"

---

[19] Honoré Tournély (1658-1729), Professor of Theology at the Sorbonne 1692-1716; author of *Praelectiones Theologicae* 16 vols. 1725-30.
[20] St. Robert Bellarmine (1542-1621), Professor of Controversial Theology at the Roman College and Cardinal Archbishop of Capua. *De Romano Pontifice* was published in his *Disputationes de Controversiis Christianae Fidei*. (3 vols. 1586-93).
[21] Ibid *DS* 3060.

are so far from turning "discipline and regimen" into what Mr. Gladstone calls a "net," that they contract the range of both of them, not including, as he would have it, "marriage," here, "blasphemy" there, and "poor-relief" in a third country, but noting and specifying that one and the same structure of laws, rites, rules of government, independency, everywhere, of which the Pope himself is the centre and life. And surely this is what every one of us will say as well as the Pope, who is not an Erastian,[22] and who believes that the Gospel is no mere philosophy thrown upon the world at large, no mere quality of mind and thought, no mere beautiful and deep sentiment or subjective opinion, but a substantive message from above, guarded and preserved in a visible polity.

[237]   2. And now I am naturally led on to speak of the Pope's supreme authority, such as I have described it, in its bearing towards the Civil Power all over the world,—a power which as truly comes from God, as his own does, though diverse, as the Church is invariable.[23]

That collisions can take place between the Holy See and national governments, the history of fifteen hundred years sufficiently teaches us; also, that on both sides there may occur grievous mistakes. But my question all along lies, not with "quicquid delirant reges,"[24] but with what, under the circumstance of such a collision, is the duty of those who are both children of the Pope and subjects of the Civil Power. As to the duty of the Civil Power, I have already intimated in my first section, that it should treat the Holy See as an independent sovereign,[25] and if this rule had been observed, the difficulty to Catholics in a country not Catholic, would be

---

[22] Erastianism is the belief, ascribed to the 16th-century Zwinglian theologian, Thomas Erastus, that the Church should be wholly subservient to the state. It is disputed whether he in fact taught this.

[23] 1875 ed.: "...all over the world – various, as the Church is invariable, - a power which as truly comes from God, as his own does."

[24] "Whatever monarchs err, the records are blamed." Horace *Letters* 1.2.14.

[25] Full diplomatic relations were only established in 1982 with the appointment of Sir Mark Heath; previously there had been a permanent mission. See supra p.[192].

most materially lightened. Great Britain recognizes and is recognized by the United States; the two powers have ministers at each other's court; here is one standing prevention of serious quarrels. Misunderstandings between the two coordinate powers may arise; but there follow explanations, removals of the causes of offence, acts of restitution. In actual collisions, there are conferences, compromises, arbitrations. Now the point to observe here is, that in such cases neither party gives up its abstract rights, but neither party practically insists on them. And each party thinks itself in the right in the particular case, protests against any other view, but still concedes. Neither party says, "I will not make it up with you, till you draw an intelligible line between your domain and mine." I suppose in the Geneva arbitration,[26] though we gave way, we still thought that, in our conduct in the American civil war,[27] we had acted within our rights. I say all this in answer to Mr. Gladstone's challenge to us to draw the line between the Pope's domain and the State's domain in civil or political questions. Many a private American, I suppose, lived in London and Liverpool, all through the correspondence between our Foreign Office and the government of the United States, and Mr. Gladstone never addressed any expostulation to them, or told them they had lost their moral freedom because they took part with their own government. The French, when their late war began, did sweep their German sojourners out of France, (the number, as I recollect, was very great,) but they were not considered to have done themselves much credit by such an act.[28] When

[238]

---

[26] The Geneva Convention or Treaty was adopted at a conference in 1864.

[27] The US government made claims against England concerning the MS Alabama, which was built in Britain for the Confederacy; also disputes with Canada were arbitrated in Geneva in 1872. The arbitration commission ordered Britain to pay $15.5 million in compensation over the sinking of the Alabama.

[28] As a result of a series of military defeats, French opinion turned against German nationals. Workmen were ostracised, and some families in Paris were ordered to leave because of the state of siege. There was no general order of expulsion, although many newspapers (including the *Liverpool Daily Post* on 23 September

we went to war with Russia,[29] the English in St. Petersburg made an address, I think to the Emperor, asking for his protection, and he gave it;—I don't suppose they pledged themselves to the Russian view of the war, nor would he have called them slaves instead of patriots, if they had refused to do so. Suppose England were to send her ironclads[30] to support Italy against the Pope and his allies, English Catholics would be very indignant, they would take part with the Pope before the war began, they would use all constitutional means to hinder it; but who believes that, when they were once in the war, their action would be anything else than prayers and exertions for a termination of it? What reason is there for saying that they would commit themselves to any step of a treasonable nature, any more than loyal [239] Germans, had they been allowed to remain in France? Yet, because those Germans would not relinquish their allegiance to their country, Mr. Gladstone, were he consistent, would at once send them adrift.

Of course it will be said that in these cases, there is no double allegiance, and again that the German government did not call upon Germans in France, as the Pope might call upon English Catholics, nay command them, to take a side; but my argument at least shows this, that till there comes to us a special, direct command from the Pope to oppose our country, we need not be said to have "placed our loyalty and civil duty at the mercy of another," p. 45. It is strange that a great statesman, versed in the new and true philosophy of compromise, instead of taking a practical view of the actual situation, should proceed against us, like a Professor in the

---

1870) would relate that 80,000 German nationals had been given three days' notice to leave by the government and were said to be petitioning the Emperor in Berlin for redress as "they were treated as criminals." See Emma Haddad *The Refugee in International Society.* Cambridge 2008 p.56.

[29] The Crimean War 1853-6.

[30] A large wooden warship with a keel armoured with iron plating.

schools, with the "parade" of his "relentless" (and may I add "rusty"?) "logic," p. 23.

I say, *till* the Pope told us to exert ourselves for his cause in a quarrel with this country, as in the time of the Armada, we need not attend to an abstract and hypothetical difficulty:—then and not till then. I add, as before, that, if the Holy See were frankly recognized by England, as other Sovereignties are, direct quarrels between the two powers would in this age of the world be rare indeed; and still rarer, their becoming so energetic and urgent as to descend into the hearts of the community, and to disturb the consciences and the family unity of private Catholics.

But now, lastly, let us suppose one of these extraordinary cases of direct and open hostility between the two powers [240] actually to occur;—here first, we must bring before us the state of the case. Of course we must recollect, on the one hand, that Catholics are not only bound by allegiance to the British Crown, but have special privileges as citizens, can meet together, speak and pass resolutions, can vote for members of Parliament, and sit in Parliament, and can hold office, all which are denied to foreigners sojourning among us; while on the other hand there is the authority of the Pope, which, though not "absolute" even in religious matters, as Mr. Gladstone would have it to be, has a call, a supreme call on our obedience. Certainly in the event of such a collision of jurisdictions, there are cases in which we should obey the Pope and disobey the State. Suppose, for instance, an Act was passed in Parliament, bidding Catholics to attend Protestant service every week, and the Pope distinctly told us not to do so, for it was to violate our duty to our faith:—I should obey the Pope and not the Law. It will be said by Mr. Gladstone, that such a case is impossible. I know it is; but why ask me for what I should do in extreme and utterly improbable cases such as this, if my answer cannot help bearing the character of an axiom? It is not my fault that I must deal in truisms.

The circumferences of State jurisdiction and of Papal are for the most part quite apart from each other; there are just some few degrees out of the 360 in which they intersect, and Mr. Gladstone, instead of letting these cases of intersection alone, till they occur actually, asks me what I should do, if I found myself placed in the space intersected. If I must answer then, [241] I should say distinctly that did the State tell me in a question of worship to do what the Pope told me not to do, I should obey the Pope, and should think it no sin, if I used all the power and the influence I possessed as a citizen to prevent such a Bill passing the Legislature, and to effect its repeal if it did.

But now, on the other hand, could the case ever occur, in which I should act with the Civil Power, and not with the Pope? Now, here again, when I begin to imagine instances, Catholics will cry out (as Mr. Gladstone, in the case I supposed, cried out in the interest of the other side), that instances never can occur. I know they cannot; I know the Pope never can do what I am going to suppose; but then, since it cannot possibly happen in fact, there is no harm in just saying what I should (hypothetically) do, if it did happen. I say then in certain (impossible) cases I should side, not with the Pope, but with the Civil Power. For instance, let us suppose members of Parliament, or of the Privy Council, took an oath[31] that they would not acknowledge the right of succession of a Prince of Wales, if he became a Catholic: in that case I should not consider the Pope could release me from that oath, had I bound myself by it.[32] Of course, I might exert myself to the utmost to get the act repealed which bound

---

[31] Gladstone pointed out to Newman that "there is no oath, it is simply a matter of Statute Law." 15 January 1875 *LD* 27 pp. 192-3. Affirming as an alternative to swearing was introduced by the Parliamentary Oaths Act of 1866. The original oath was changed in 1829 to include the words, "I solemnly abjure any intention to subvert the present Church establishment," which was acceptable to Roman Catholics.

[32] Newman raised this point with Lord Emly 9 October 1874 *LD* 27 p.133.

me; again, if I could not, I might retire from parliament or office, and so rid myself of the engagement I had made; but I should be clear that, though the Pope bade all Catholics to stand firm in one phalanx for the Catholic Succession, still, while I remained in office, or in my place in Parliament, I could not do as he bade me.

Again, were I actually a soldier or sailor in her Majesty's [242] service,[33] and sent to take part in a war which I could not in my conscience see to be unjust, and should the Pope suddenly bid all Catholic soldiers and sailors to retire from the service, here again, taking the advice of others, as best I could, I should not obey him.[34]

What is the use of forming impossible cases? One can find plenty of them in books of casuistry, with the answers attached in respect to them. In an actual case, a Catholic would, of course, not act simply on his own judgment; at the same time, there are supposable cases in which he would be obliged to go by it solely—viz., when his conscience could not be reconciled to any of the courses of action proposed to him by others.

In support of what I have been saying, I refer to one or two weighty authorities:—

Cardinal Turrecremata[35] says, "Although it clearly follows from the circumstance that the Pope can err at times, and command things which must not be done, that we are not to be simply obedient to him in all things, that does not show that he must not be obeyed by all when his commands are good. To know in what cases he is to be obeyed and in what not ... it is said in the Acts of the Apostles, 'One ought to obey God rather than man:' therefore, were the Pope to command anything against Holy Scripture, or the articles of faith, or the truth of the Sacraments, or the commands of the

---

[33] See Postscript pp.[357-8].

[34] See Postscript pp.[241-5].

[35] See p.[242] and reference in *Editor's Introduction*.

natural or divine law, *he ought not to be obeyed,* but in such commands is to be passed over (despiciendus)."—*Summ. de Eccl.*, pp. 47, 48.

[243]   Bellarmine, speaking of resisting the Pope, says, "In order to resist and defend oneself no authority is required ... Therefore, as it is lawful to resist the Pope, if he assaulted a man's person, so it is lawful to resist him, if he assaulted souls, or *troubled the state* (turbanti rempublicam), and much more if he strove to destroy the Church. It is lawful, I say, to resist him, by not doing what he commands, and hindering the execution of his will."—*De Rom. Pont.*, ii. 29.

Archbishop Kenrick[36] says, "His power was given for edification, not for destruction. If he uses it from the love of domination (quod absit[37]) *scarcely will he meet with obedient populations.*"—*Theolog. Moral.*, t. i. p. 158.

When, then, Mr. Gladstone asks Catholics how they can obey the Queen and yet obey the Pope, since it may happen that the commands of the two authorities may clash, I answer, that it is my *rule*, both to obey the one and to obey the other, but that there is no rule in this world without exceptions, and if either the Pope or the Queen demanded of me an "Absolute Obedience," he or she would be transgressing the laws of human society. I give an absolute obedience to neither. Further, if ever this double allegiance pulled me in contrary ways, which in this age of the world I think it never will, then I should decide according to the particular case, which is beyond all rule, and must be decided on its own merits. I should look to see what theologians could do for me, what the Bishops and clergy around me, what my confessor; what friends whom I revered: and if, after all, I could not take their

[244]   view of the matter, then I must rule myself by my own

---

[36] Francis Patrick Kenrick (1796-1863), Bishop of Philadelphia 1830-1851 and author of *Theologia Moralis* 3 vols. 1860.
[37] 'which [God] forbid'

judgment and my own conscience. But all this is hypothetical and unreal.

Here, of course, it will be objected to me, that I am, after all, having recourse to the Protestant doctrine of Private Judgment; not so; it is the Protestant doctrine that Private Judgment is our *ordinary* guide in religious matters, but I use it, in the case in question, in very extraordinary and rare, nay, impossible emergencies. Do not the highest Tories thus defend the substitution of William for James II.?[38] It is a great mistake to suppose our state in the Catholic Church is so entirely subjected to rule and system, that we are never thrown upon what is called by divines "the Providence of God."[39] The teaching and assistance of the Church does not supply all conceivable needs, but those which are ordinary; thus, for instance, the sacraments are necessary for dying in the grace of God and hope of heaven, yet, when they cannot be got, acts of faith, hope, and contrition, with the desire for those aids which the dying man has not, will convey in substance what those aids ordinarily convey. And so a Catechumen, not yet baptized, may be saved by his purpose and preparation to receive the rite. And so, again, though "Out of the Church there is no salvation,"[40] this does not hold in the case of good men who are in invincible ignorance. And so it is also in the case of our ordinations; Chillingworth[41] and Macaulay[42] say that it is morally impossible that we should

---

[38] By the Declaration of Right in 1689.

[39] God's plan which is all sustaining: "By his providence God watches over and governs all things that he made." Vatican I Chapter I *De Deo rerum omnium creatore*, *DS* 3003.

[40] Chapter 7 first draft of the Dogmatic Constitution on the Church of Christ.

[41] Chillingworth William Chillingworth (1602-1644), Anglican divine who wrote *Religion of Protestants a Safe Way to Salvation* in 1638. He was captured by Parliamentary forces and died in captivity.

[42] Macaulay (see p.[186]). In 'Catholicity of the Anglican Church' Newman mentions Macaulay's remarks on Apostolic Succession' in one of his reviews and says, "I cannot deny, certainly that Catholics, as well as the high Anglican school, do believe in the Apostolic Succession of ministry, continued through eighteen hundred years." *Ess* 2 p. 86.

have kept up for 1800 years an Apostolical succession of ministers without some breaks in the chain; and we in answer [245] say that, however true this may be humanly speaking, there has been a special Providence over the Church to secure it. Once more, how else could private Catholics save their souls when there was a Pope and Anti-popes, each severally claiming their allegiance?

§ 5. *Conscience.*

IT seems, then, that there are extreme cases in which Conscience may come into collision with the word of a Pope, and is to be followed in spite of that word. Now I wish to place this proposition on a broader basis, acknowledged by all Catholics, and, in order to do this satisfactorily, as I began with the prophecies of Scripture and the primitive Church, when I spoke of the Pope's prerogatives, so now I must begin with the Creator and His creature, when I would draw out the prerogatives and the supreme authority of Conscience.

I say, then, that the Supreme Being is of a certain character, which, expressed in human language, we call ethical. He has the attributes of justice, truth, wisdom, sanctity, benevolence and mercy, as eternal characteristics in His nature, the very Law of His being, identical with Himself; and next, when He became Creator, He implanted this Law, which is Himself, in the intelligence of all His rational creatures. The Divine Law, then, is the rule of ethical truth, the standard of right and wrong, a sovereign, irreversible, absolute authority in the presence of men and Angels. "The eternal law," says St. Augustine, "is the Divine Reason or Will of God, commanding the observance, forbidding the [247] disturbance, of the natural order of things."[1] "The natural law," says St. Thomas, "is an impression of the Divine Light in us, a participation of the eternal law in the rational creature."[2] (Gousset,[3] *Theol. Moral.*, t. i. pp. 24, &c.) This

---

[1] *Contra Faustum* I, 22 c.27 *ML* 42.418.

[2] *S. Th.* I-2 q.93 a.1c.

[3] Thomas-Marie-Joseph Gousset (1792-1866), Cardinal Archbishop of Rheims. *Théologie morale à l'usage des curés et des confesseurs* 2 vols 1848.

law, as apprehended in the minds of individual men, is called "conscience;" and though it may suffer refraction in passing into the intellectual medium of each, it is not therefore so affected as to lose its character of being the Divine Law, but still has, as such, the prerogative of commanding obedience. "The Divine Law," says Cardinal Gousset, "is the supreme rule of actions; our thoughts, desires, words, acts, all that man is, is subject to the domain of the law of God; and this law is the rule of our conduct by means of our conscience. Hence it is never lawful to go against our conscience; as the fourth Lateran Council says, 'Quidquid fit contra conscientiam, ædificat ad gehennam.'"[4]

This view of conscience, I know, is very different from that ordinarily taken of it, both by the science and literature, and by the public opinion, of this day. It is founded on the doctrine that conscience is the voice of God,[5] whereas it is fashionable on all hands now to consider it in one way or another a creation of man. Of course, there are great and broad exceptions to this statement. It is not true of many or most religious bodies of men; especially not of their teachers and ministers. When Anglicans, Wesleyans, the various Presbyterian sects in Scotland, and other denominations among us, speak of conscience, they mean what we mean, the

---

[4] The complete quotation is, "Quoniam omne, quod non est ex fide, peccatum est, et quidquid fit contra conscientiam, aedificat ad gehennam." "For everything which does not come from faith is sinful, and whatever goes against conscience builds the foundation for hell." In a case involving a woman ordered to resume marital relations which the wife considered incestuous, Innocent III in a letter of 1201, (not Lateran IV in 1212) quoting the adage, said "She should rather humbly accept the excommunication of the ecclesiastical court rather than disobey her conscience." Newman adds, "It may be objected indeed, that conscience is not infallible; it is true, but still it is ever to be obeyed." *Dev* p. 86.

[5] Joseph Butler (1692-1752) in his *Fifteen Sermons on Human Nature* (1715) says, "Conscience is the voice of God assigned to us by the Author of our nature." Also Newman: "In the main conscience is the voice of God speaking within you." *MS Sermon* 213 p.3 (25 October 1829).

voice of God[6] in the nature and heart of man, as distinct from the voice of Revelation. They speak of a principle planted [248] within us, before we have had any training, although training and experience are necessary for its strength, growth, and due formation. They consider it a constituent element of the mind, as our perception of other ideas may be, as our powers of reasoning, as our sense of order and the beautiful, and our other intellectual endowments. They consider it, as Catholics consider it, to be the internal witness of both the existence and the law of God. They think it holds of God, and not of man, as an Angel walking on the earth would be no citizen or dependent of the Civil Power. They would not allow, any more than we do, that it could be resolved into any combination of principles in our nature, more elementary than itself; nay, though it may be called, and is, a law of the mind, they would not grant that it was nothing more; I mean, that it was not a dictate, nor conveyed the notion of responsibility, of duty, of a threat and a promise, with a vividness which discriminated it from all other constituents of our nature.

This, at least, is how I read the doctrine of Protestants as well as of Catholics. The rule and measure of duty is not utility, nor expedience, nor the happiness of the greatest number,[7] nor State convenience, nor fitness, order, and the *pulchrum*.[8] Conscience is not a long-sighted selfishness, nor a desire to be consistent with oneself;[9] but it is a messenger

---

[6] "We obey God primarily because we actually feel his presence in our conscience bidding us to obey him." *PPS* I p.200. Callista, in Newman's novel says, "It is the echo of a person speaking to me." *Call* p.314

[7] "The greatest happiness of the greatest number is the foundation of morals and legislation." Jeremy Bentham (1748-1832), *Principles of Morals and Legislation* (1780) ch.13 § 2.

[8] The truly beautiful, as a combination of unity, truth and goodness. See Augustine *Confessions* 10.27.

[9] A reference to the message of self-reliance in Samuel Smiles' *Self-Help* (1859).

from Him,[10] who, both in nature and in grace, speaks to us behind a veil, and teaches and rules us by His representatives. Conscience is the aboriginal Vicar of Christ,[11] a prophet in its informations, a monarch in its peremptoriness, a priest in its blessings and anathemas, and, even though the eternal priesthood throughout the Church could cease to be, in it the sacerdotal principle would remain and would have a sway.

[249]

Words such as these are idle empty verbiage to the great world of philosophy now. All through my day there has been a resolute warfare, I had almost said conspiracy against the rights of conscience, as I have described it. Literature and science have been embodied in great institutions in order to put it down. Noble buildings have been reared as fortresses against that spiritual, invisible influence which is too subtle for science and too profound for literature. Chairs in Universities have been made the seats of an antagonist tradition. Public writers, day after day, have indoctrinated the minds of innumerable readers with theories subversive of its claims. As in Roman times, and in the middle age, its supremacy was assailed by the arm of physical force, so now the intellect is put in operation to sap the foundations of a power which the sword could not destroy. We are told that conscience is but a twist in primitive and untutored man; that its dictate is an imagination; that the very notion of guiltiness, which that dictate enforces, is simply irrational, for how can there possibly be freedom of will, how can there be consequent responsibility, in that infinite eternal network of cause and effect, in which we helplessly lie? and what

---

[10] "Conscience is a universal capacity inbuilt in mankind by divine creation." *New Dictionary of Theology* Sinclair Ferguson and David F. Wright eds. Leicester 1988. p.161.
[11] This much quoted phrase underlines the fundamental role that it plays in life. We are all its subjects, even the Vicar of Christ. Newman will contrast its power with the authority of the Pope himself, p.[261] and will refer to its 'divine authority' p.[252].

retribution have we to fear, when we have had no real choice to do good or evil?

So much for philosophers; now let us see what is the notion of conscience in this day in the popular mind. There, [250] no more than in the intellectual world, does "conscience" retain the old, true, Catholic meaning of the word. There too the idea, the presence of a Moral Governor is far away from the use of it, frequent and emphatic as that use of it is. When men advocate the rights of conscience, they in no sense mean the rights of the Creator, nor the duty to Him, in thought and deed, of the creature; but the right of thinking, speaking, writing, and acting, according to their judgment or their humour, without any thought of God at all.[12] They do not even pretend to go by any moral rule, but they demand, what they think is an Englishman's prerogative, for each to be his own master in all things, and to profess what he pleases, asking no one's leave, and accounting priest or preacher, speaker or writer, unutterably impertinent, who dares to say a word against his going to perdition, if he like it, in his own way. Conscience has rights because it has duties; but in this age, with a large portion of the public, it is the very right and freedom of conscience to dispense with conscience, to ignore a Lawgiver and Judge, to be independent of unseen obligations. It becomes a licence to take up any or no religion, to take up this or that and let it go again, to go to church, to go to chapel, to boast of being above all religions and to be an impartial critic of each of them. Conscience is a stern monitor, but in this century it has been superseded by a counterfeit, which the eighteen centuries prior to it never heard of, and could not have mistaken for it, if they had. It is the right of self-will.

---

[12] "It is because conscience to them is not the word of a lawgiver, as it ought to be, but the dictate of their own minds and nothing more... Their conscience has become a mere self respect." *Idea* p.192.

251

[251]   And now I shall turn aside for a moment to show how it is that the Popes of our century have been misunderstood by the English people, as if they really were speaking against conscience in the true sense of the word, when in fact they were speaking against it in the various false senses, philosophical or popular, which in this day are put upon the word. The present Pope, in his Encyclical of 1864, *Quantâ curâ*, speaks (as will come before us in the next section) against "liberty of conscience," and he refers to his predecessor, Gregory XVI., who, in his *Mirari vos*, calls it a "deliramentum."[13] It is a rule in formal ecclesiastical proceedings, as I shall have occasion to notice lower down, when books or authors are condemned, to use the very words of the book or author, and to condemn the words in that particular sense which they have in their context and their drift, not in the literal, not in the religious sense, such as the Pope might recognize, were they in another book or author. To take a familiar parallel, among many which occur daily. Protestants speak of the "Blessed Reformation;" Catholics too talk of "the Reformation," though they do not call it blessed. Yet every "reformation" ought, from the very meaning of the word, to be good, not bad; so that Catholics seem to be implying a eulogy on an event which, at the same time, they consider a surpassing evil. Here then they are taking the word and using it in the popular sense of it, not in the Catholic. They would say, if they expressed their full meaning, "the *so-called* reformation." In like manner, if the Pope condemned "the Reformation," it would be utterly sophistical to say in consequence that he had declared [252]   himself against all reforms; yet this is how Mr. Gladstone

---

[13] *Mirari vos* (1832). See also Encyclical *Quanta cura* (1864): "From this foulest source of indifferentism there flows the absurd and erroneous view, or rather insanity, according to which freedom of conscience must be asserted and vindicated for everybody." *DS* 2730. Leo XIII would later say, "Nothing more foolish can be uttered or conceived than the notion that because man is free by nature, he is therefore exempt from law." Encyclical *Libertas Praestantissimum* (1888).

treats him, when he speaks of (so-called) liberty of conscience. To make this distinction clear, viz., between the Catholic sense of the word "conscience," and that sense in which the Pope condemns it, we find in the *Recueil des Allocutions*, &c., the words accompanied with quotation-marks,[14] both in Pope Gregory's and Pope Pius's Encyclicals, thus:—Gregory's, "Ex hoc putidissimo 'indifferentismi' fonte,"[15] (mind, "indifferentismi" is under quotation-marks, because the Pope will not make himself answerable for so unclassical a word) "absurda illa fluit ac erronea sententia, seu potius deliramentum, asserendam esse ac vindicandam cuilibet 'libertatem conscientiæ.'"[16] And that of Pius, "Haud timent erroneam illam fovere opinionem a Gregorio XVI. deliramentum appellatam, nimirum 'libertatem conscientiæ' esse proprium cujuscunque hominis jus."[17] Both Popes certainly scoff at the so-called "liberty of conscience," but there is no scoffing of any Pope, in formal documents addressed to the faithful at large, at that most serious doctrine, the right and the duty of following that Divine Authority, the voice of conscience, on which in truth the Church herself is built.

So indeed it is; did the Pope speak against Conscience in the true sense of the word, he would commit a suicidal act. He would be cutting the ground from under his feet. His very mission is to proclaim the moral law, and to protect and strengthen that "Light which enlighteneth every man that cometh into the world."[18] On the law of conscience and its sacredness are founded both his authority in theory and his

---

[14] Newman consulted the original texts The quotation marks do not occur in most versions, including *Denzinger*. *Receuil des Allocutions* was a published collection of papal Allocutions.

[15] "From this putrid source of 'indifferentism"

[16] "That absurd and erroneous opinion, or rather it should be called a madness, claiming a sort of freedom of conscience"

[17] "We should not be afraid of that opinion of Gregory XVI calling 'freedom of conscience' a madness as being for each man his own law."

[18] John 1:9

power in fact. Whether this or that particular Pope in this bad world always kept this great truth in view in all he did, it is for history to tell. I am considering here the Papacy in its office and its duties, and in reference to those who acknowledge its claims. They are not bound by the Pope's personal character or private acts, but by his formal teaching. Thus viewing his position, we shall find that it is by the universal sense of right and wrong, the consciousness of transgression, the pangs of guilt, and the dread of retribution, as first principles deeply lodged in the hearts of men,[19] it is thus and only thus, that he has gained his footing in the world and achieved his success. It is his claim to come from the Divine Lawgiver, in order to elicit, protect, and enforce those truths which the Lawgiver has sown in our very nature, it is this and this only that is the explanation of his length of life more than antediluvian. The championship of the Moral Law and of conscience is his *raison d'être*. The fact of his mission is the answer to the complaints of those who feel the insufficiency of the natural light; and the insufficiency of that light is the justification of his mission.

All sciences, except the science of Religion, have their certainty in themselves; as far as they are sciences, they consist of necessary conclusions from undeniable premises, or of phenomena manipulated into general truths by an irresistible induction. But the sense of right and wrong, which is the first element in religion, is so delicate, so fitful, so easily puzzled, obscured, perverted, so subtle in its argumentative methods, so impressible by education, so biassed by pride and passion, so unsteady in its course, that, in the struggle for existence amid the various exercises and triumphs of the human intellect, this sense is at once the highest of all teachers, yet the least luminous; and the

---

[19] "This instinct of the mind recognizing an external Master in the dictate of conscience and imaging the thought of Him in the definite impressions which conscience creates, is parallel to that other law of, not only human but of brute nature." *GA* p.110.

Church, the Pope, the Hierarchy are, in the Divine purpose, the supply of an urgent demand. Natural Religion, certain as are its grounds and its doctrines as addressed to thoughtful, serious minds, needs, in order that it may speak to mankind with effect and subdue the world, to be sustained and completed by Revelation.

In saying all this, of course I must not be supposed to be limiting the Revelation of which the Church is the keeper to a mere republication of the Natural Law;[20] but still it is true, that, though Revelation is so distinct from the teaching of nature and beyond it, yet it is not independent of it, nor without relations towards it, but is its complement, reassertion, issue, embodiment, and interpretation. The Pope, who comes of Revelation, has no jurisdiction over Nature.[21] If, under the plea of his revealed prerogatives, he neglected his mission of preaching truth, justice, mercy, and peace, much more if he trampled on the consciences of his subjects,—if he had done so all along, as Protestants say, then he could not have lasted all these many centuries till now, so as to supply a mark for their reprobation. Dean Milman[22] has told us above, how faithful he was to his duty in the medieval time, and how successful. Afterwards, for a while the Papal chair was filled by men who gave themselves up to luxury, security, and a Pagan kind of Christianity;[23] and we all know what a moral earthquake was the consequence, and how the Church lost, thereby, and has lost to this day, one-half of Europe. The Popes could not have recovered from so terrible a catastrophe, as they have done, had they not returned to [255]

---

[20] "Christianity is a republication of natural religion. It instructs mankind in the moral system of the world... Revelation is further an authoritative publication of natural religion and so affords the evidence of testimony for the truth of it." Joseph Butler, *The Analogy of Religion Natural and Revealed to the Constitution and the Course of Nature* (1736) Part II ch. 1. "Natural Law is written and engraved in the mind of every man." Leo XIII Encyclical *Libertas Praestantissimum* (1888).

[21] See Postscript p.[358-9].

[22] See supra p.[212].

[23] Alexander VI (1492-1503) and Julius II (1503-13).

their first and better ways, and the grave lesson of the past is in itself the guarantee of the future.

Such is the relation of the ecclesiastical power to the human conscience:—however, a contrary view may be taken of it. It may be said that no one doubts that the Pope's power rests on those weaknesses of human nature, that religious sense, which in ancient days Lucretius[24] noted as the cause of the worst ills of our race; that he uses it dexterously, forming under shelter of it a false code of morals for his own aggrandisement and tyranny; and that thus conscience becomes his creature and his slave, doing, as if on a divine sanction, his will; so that in the abstract indeed and in idea it is free, but never free in fact, never able to take a flight of its own, independent of him, any more than birds whose wings are clipped;—moreover, that, if it were able to exert a will of its own, then there would ensue a collision more unmanageable than that between the Church and the State, as being in one and the same subject-matter—viz., religion; for what would become of the Pope's "absolute authority," as Mr. Gladstone calls it, if the private conscience had an absolute authority also?

I wish to answer this important objection distinctly.

1. First, I am using the word "conscience" in the high sense in which I have already explained it,—not as a fancy or an opinion, but as a dutiful obedience to what claims to be a divine voice, speaking within us; and that this is the view properly to be taken of it, I shall not attempt to prove here, but shall assume it as a first principle.

[256]

2. Secondly, I observe that conscience is not a judgment upon any speculative truth, any abstract doctrine, but bears immediately on conduct, on something to be done or not

---

[24] Lucretius Caius Titus (c.99-55 BC), Roman poet, author of *De Rerum Natura* in which he argued that the gods had no influence on mortal lives. Newman commented that he had "great poetical genius; but his work evinces that his miserable philosophy was rather the result of a bewildered judgment than a corrupt heart." *Ess* 1 p.23.

done. "Conscience," says St. Thomas, "is the practical judgment or dictate of reason, by which we judge what *hic et nunc*[25] is to be done as being good, or to be avoided as evil."[26] Hence conscience cannot come into direct collision with the Church's or the Pope's infallibility; which is engaged in general propositions, and in the condemnation of particular and given errors.[27]

3. Next, I observe that, conscience being a practical dictate, a collision is possible between it and the Pope's authority only when the Pope legislates, or gives particular orders, and the like. But a Pope is not infallible in his laws, nor in his commands, nor in his acts of state, nor in his administration, nor in his public policy. Let it be observed that the Vatican Council has left him just as it found him here. Mr. Gladstone's language on this point is to me quite unintelligible. Why, instead of using vague terms, does he not point out precisely the very words by which the Council has made the Pope in his acts infallible? Instead of so doing, he assumes a conclusion which is altogether false. He says, p. 34, "First comes the Pope's infallibility:" then in the next page he insinuates that, under his infallibility, come acts of excommunication, as if the Pope could not make mistakes in this field of action. He says, p. 35, "It may be sought to plead that the Pope does not propose to invade the country, to seize Woolwich,[28] or burn Portsmouth.[29] He will only, at the worst, excommunicate opponents ... Is this a good answer? After all, [257] even in the Middle Ages, it was not by the direct action of fleets and armies of their own that the Popes contended with kings who were refractory; it was mainly by interdicts,"[30] &c.

---

[25] 'in this particular situation', lit. 'here and now'.

[26] Although this does represent St. Thomas Aquinas' thoughts, Newman is quoting St. Alphonsus Liguori in his *Theologia Moralis* (1753) vol. 1 ch. 1 para 2.

[27] 1874 ed.: "On the condemnation of propositions simply particular."

[28] Home of the Royal Arsenal and Royal Dockyard.

[29] Premier naval port and dockyard.

[30] A personal censure with the same restrictions as excommunication. See *CIC* 3131.3132.

What have excommunication and interdict to do with Infallibility? Was St. Peter infallible on that occasion at Antioch when St. Paul withstood him?[31] was St. Victor infallible when he separated from his communion the Asiatic Churches?[32] or Liberius when in like manner he excommunicated Athanasius?[33] And, to come to later times, was Gregory XIII., when he had a medal struck in honour of the Bartholomew massacre?[34] or Paul IV. in his conduct towards Elizabeth?[35] or Sextus V. when he blessed the Armada[36] or Urban VIII. when he persecuted Galileo?[37] No Catholic ever pretends that these Popes were infallible in these acts. Since then infallibility alone could block the exercise of conscience, and the Pope is not infallible in that subject-matter in which conscience is of supreme authority, no deadlock, such as is implied in the objection which I am answering, can take place between conscience and the Pope.

4. But, of course, I have to say again, lest I should be misunderstood, that when I speak of Conscience, I mean conscience truly so called. When it has the right of opposing the supreme, though not infallible Authority of the Pope, it must be something more than that miserable counterfeit which, as I have said above, now goes by the name. If in a particular case it is to be taken as a sacred and sovereign monitor, its dictate, in order to prevail against the voice of the

---

[31] Gal 2:11.

[32] Victor I (189-98) excommunicated the Churches of Asia Minor for not accepting his ruling on the date of Easter.

[33] Liberius (352-66) under pressure from Constantius II accepted the condemnation of Athanasius. See *Ari* pp.322-3.

[34] Gregory XIII (1572-85) celebrated the massacre of 1572 with a *Te Deum* and a commemorative medal.

[35] Paul IV (1555-9) demanded in 1558 that Elizabeth should restore all Church properties and submit her claim to the throne for his approval.

[36] Sextus/Sixtus V (1585-90) supported the Armada of Philip II by a secret convention of 29 July 1597 which promised one million crowns, conditional on its success, and to be paid in instalments.

[37] Urban VIII (1623-44) condemned Galileo, although a personal friend, and forced him to renounce his astronomical views under threat of torture in 1633. Newman raised this point in a letter to Lord Emly 9 October 1874 *LD* 27 p.133.

Pope, must follow upon serious thought, prayer, and all [258] available means of arriving at a right judgment on the matter in question. And further, obedience to the Pope is what is called "in possession;" that is, the *onus probandi*[38] of establishing a case against him lies, as in all cases of exception, on the side of conscience. Unless a man is able to say to himself, as in the Presence of God, that he must not, and dare not, act upon the Papal injunction, he is bound to obey it, and would commit a great sin in disobeying it. *Primâ facie* it is his bounden duty, even from a sentiment of loyalty, to believe the Pope right and to act accordingly. He must vanquish that mean, ungenerous, selfish, vulgar spirit of his nature, which, at the very first rumour of a command, places itself in opposition to the Superior who gives it, asks itself whether he is not exceeding his right, and rejoices, in a moral and practical matter to commence with scepticism. He must have no wilful determination to exercise a right of thinking, saying, doing just what he pleases, the question of truth and falsehood, right and wrong, the duty if possible of obedience, the love of speaking as his Head speaks, and of standing in all cases on his Head's side, being simply discarded. If this necessary rule were observed, collisions between the Pope's authority and the authority of conscience would be very rare. On the other hand, in the fact that, after all, in extraordinary cases, the conscience of each individual is free, we have a safeguard and security, were security necessary (which is a most gratuitous supposition), that no Pope ever will be able, as the objection supposes, to create a false conscience for his own ends.

Now, I shall end this part of the subject, for I have not [259] done with it altogether, by appealing to various of our theologians in evidence that, in what I have been saying, I have not misrepresented Catholic doctrine on these important points.

---

[38] The burden of proof.

That is, on the duty of obeying our conscience at all hazards.

I have already quoted the words which Cardinal Gousset has adduced from the Fourth Lateran;[39] that "He who acts against his conscience loses his soul." This *dictum* is brought out with singular fulness and force in the moral treatises of theologians. The celebrated school, known as the Salmanticenses, or Carmelites of Salamanca,[40] lays down the broad proposition, that conscience is ever to be obeyed whether it tells truly or erroneously, and that, whether the error is the fault of the person thus erring or not.* They say that this opinion is certain, and refer, as agreeing with them, to St. Thomas, St. Bonaventura,[41] Caietan,[42] Vasquez[43] Durandus,[44] Navarrus,[45] Corduba,[46] Layman,[47] Escobar,[48] and

---

*"Aliqui opinantur quod conscientia erronea non obligat; Secondi sententiam, et certam, asserentem esse peccatum discordare à conscientiâ erroneâ, invincibili aut vincibili, tenet D. Thomas; quem sequuntur omnes Scholastici."—*Theol. Moral.*, t. v. p. 12, ed. 1728.[49]

---

[39] Fourth Lateran 1215. There is no direct reference in the Constitutions of the Council.
[40] The teachers of a school of theology of the Discalced Carmelites, based on St. Thomas Aquinas, at Salamanca between 1600 and 1725.
[41] St Bonaventure (c.1217-74), Franciscan Minister General and Cardinal.
[42] St Cajetan (1469-1534), author of *Commentary on St. Thomas' Summa Theologica* (1507-22).
[43] Gabriel Vasquez (1549-1604), Jesuit theologian who also wrote a commentary on the *Summa* (1598-1615).
[44] Durandus of Saint-Pourcain (c. 1275-1334), a Dominican who opposed Thomism and was censured, but the censure was later lifted. He was bishop of Meaux in 1326.
[45] Martin de Azpilcueta Navarrus/Dr. Navarrus (1493-1586), canonist and moral theologian.
[46] Antonio de Córdoba (1485-1578), Franciscan, author of a guide for confessors, *Tratado de Casos de Conciencia* (1562).
[47] James Laynez Layman (1512-65), Professor at the Sapienza in Rome, second General of the Jesuits and theologian at the Council of Trent.
[48] Antonio y Mendoza Escobar (1589-1669), Spanish Jesuit who supported the theory of Probabilism.
[49] "Some consider that an erroneous conscience does not bind; a second thesis claiming to be held certainly by St. Thomas (and all followers of Scholasticism)

fourteen others. Two of them even say this opinion is *de fide*.[50] Of course, if a man is culpable in being in error, which he might have escaped, had he been more in earnest, for that error he is answerable to God, but still he must act according to that error, while he is in it, because he in full sincerity thinks the error to be truth.[51]

Thus, if the Pope told the English Bishops to order their [260] priests to stir themselves energetically in favour of teetotalism, and a particular priest was fully persuaded that abstinence from wine, &c., was practically a Gnostic error, and therefore felt he could not so exert himself without sin; or suppose there was a Papal order to hold lotteries in each mission for some religious object, and a priest could say in God's sight that he believed lotteries to be morally wrong, that priest in either of these cases would commit a sin *hic et nunc* if he obeyed the Pope, whether he was right or wrong in his opinion, and, if wrong, although he had not taken proper pains to get at the truth of the matter.

Busenbaum, of the Society of Jesus, whose work I have already had occasion to notice,[52] writes thus:—"A heretic, as long as he judges his sect to be more or equally deserving of belief, has no obligation to believe [in the Church]." And he continues, "When men who have been brought up in heresy, are persuaded from boyhood that we impugn and attack the word of God, that we are idolators, pestilent deceivers, and therefore are to be shunned as pests, they cannot, while this persuasion lasts, with a safe conscience, hear us."—t. l, p. 54.

---

maintains that it is a sin to reject a conscience whether vincibly or invincibly erroneous."

[50] A proposition which is infallibly certain as pertaining to Catholic faith.

[51] Vatican II made it clear that "Those who, through no fault of their own, do not know the Gospel of Christ or his Church, but who nevertheless seek God or his Church with a sincere heart, and, moved by grace, try in their action to do his will as they know it though the dictates of their conscience – those too may achieve eternal salvation." *Lumen Gentium* n. 21.

[52] See p.[229].

Antonio Corduba,[53] a Spanish Franciscan, states the doctrine with still more point, because he makes mention of Superiors. "In no manner is it lawful to act against conscience, even though a Law, or a Superior commands it."—*De Conscient.*, p. 138.

And the French Dominican, Natalis Alexander:[54]—"If, in the judgment of conscience, through a mistaken conscience, a man is persuaded that what his Superior commands is displeasing to God, he is bound not to obey."—*Theol.* t. 2, p. 32.

[261]

The word "Superior" certainly includes the Pope; Cardinal Jacobatius[55] brings out this point clearly in his authoritative work on Councils, which is contained in Labbe's[56] Collection, introducing the Pope by name:—"If it were doubtful," he says, "whether a precept [of the Pope] be a sin or not, we must determine thus:—that, if he to whom the precept is addressed has a conscientious sense that it is a sin and injustice, first it is duty to put off that sense; but, if he cannot, nor conform himself to the judgment of the Pope, in that case it is his duty to follow his own private conscience, and patiently to bear it, if the Pope punishes him."—lib. iv. p. 241.

Would it not be well for Mr. Gladstone to bring passages from our recognized authors as confirmatory of his view of our teaching, as those which I have quoted are destructive of it? and they must be passages declaring, not only that the Pope is ever to be obeyed, but that there are no exceptions to the rule, for exceptions there must be in all concrete matters.[57]

---

[53] See supra p.[259].

[54] Alexander Natalis (1639-1724), Dominican Church historian.

[55] Domenico Giacobazzi Jacobatius (1444-1529), Cardinal in 1517 and Dean of the Roman Rota.

[56] Philippe Labbe (1607-67), Jesuit Church historian, author of *Sacrosancta Concilia ad Regiam Editionem Exacta* which later became part of J. D. Mansi's Conciliar collection.

[57] See Postscript pp.[359-362].

I add one remark. Certainly, if I am obliged to bring religion into after-dinner toasts, (which indeed does not seem quite the thing) I shall drink—to the Pope, if you please,—still, to Conscience first,[58] and to the Pope afterwards.

---

[58] Conscience: the sustaining principle for all religious authority.

§ 6. *The Encyclical of 1864.*[1]

THE subject of Conscience leads us to the Encyclical, which is one of the special objects of Mr. Gladstone's attack; and to do justice to it, I must, as in other sections, begin from an earlier date than 1864.

Modern Rome then is not the only place where the traditions of the old Empire, its principles, provisions, and practices, have been held in honour; they have been retained, they have been maintained in substance, as the basis of European civilization down to this day, and notably among ourselves. In the Anglican establishment the king took the place of the Pope, but the Pope's principles kept possession. When the Pope was ignored, the relations between Pope and king were ignored too, and therefore we had nothing to do any more with the old Imperial laws which shaped those relations; but the old idea of a Christian Polity was still in force. It was a first principle with England that there was one true religion, that it was inherited from an earlier time, that it came of direct Revelation, that it was to be supported to the disadvantage, to say the least, of other religions, of private judgment, of personal conscience. The Puritans held these principles as firmly as the school of Laud.[2] As to the Scotch [263] Presbyterians, we read enough about them in the pages of Mr. Buckle.[3] The Stuarts went, but still their principles suffered

---

[1] See supra p.[251].

[2] William Laud (1573-1645), Archbishop of Canterbury in 1633, held that the Roman and Anglican Churches were both part of the universal Church and strove to introduce some elements of pre-reformation liturgical practice.

[3] Henry Thomas Buckle (1821-62) published his *History of Civilisation in England* in 1857, with a second volume in 1861. Newman wrote to Pusey on 3 February 1865

no dethronement: their action was restrained, but they were still in force, when this century opened.

It is curious to see how strikingly in this matter the proverb has been fulfilled, "Out of sight, out of mind." Men of the present generation, born in the new civilization, are shocked to witness in the abiding Papal system the words, ways, and works of their grandfathers. In my own lifetime has that old world been alive, and has gone its way. Who will say that the plea of conscience was as effectual, sixty years ago, as it is now in England, for the toleration of every sort of fancy religion? Had the Press always that wonderful elbow-room which it has now? Might public gatherings be held, and speeches made, and republicanism avowed in the time of the Regency,[4] as is now possible?[5] Were the thoroughfares open to monster processions at that date, and the squares and parks at the mercy of Sunday manifestations? Could *savants* in that day insinuate in scientific assemblies what their hearers mistook for atheism, and artisans practise it in the centres of political action?[6] Could public prints day after day, or week after week, carry on a war against religion, natural and revealed, as now is the case? No; law or public opinion would not suffer it; we may be wiser or better now, but we were then in the wake of the Holy Roman Church, and had been so from the time of the Reformation. We were faithful to the tradition of fifteen hundred years. All this was called Toryism, and men gloried in the name; now it is called Popery and reviled.

When I was young the State had a conscience, and the Chief Justice of the day pronounced, not as a point of [264]

---

of Buckle's theory "that all things go on by fixed laws which cannot be broken [was] thus introducing a practical atheism." *LD* 21 p.401.

[4] The Regency 1811-20 under the Prince of Wales, the future George IV.

[5] The Riot Act of 1714 referred to gatherings of twelve people.

[6] "Great sceptics and their lesser followers were ill spoken of in society, while the batteries opened upon them by orthodox writers were overwhelming." G. M. Trevelyan *English Social History* 1944 p.359.

obsolete law, but as an energetic, living truth, that Christianity was the law of the land. And by Christianity was meant pretty much what Bentham[7] calls Church-of-Englandism, its cry being the dinner toast, "Church and king." Blackstone,[8] though he wrote a hundred years ago, was held, I believe, as an authority on the state of the law in this matter, up to the beginning of this century. On the supremacy of Religion he writes as follows, that is, as I have abridged him for my purpose.

"The belief of a future state of rewards and punishments, &c., &c., ... these are the grand foundation of all judicial oaths. All moral evidence, all confidence in human veracity, must be weakened by irreligion, and overthrown by infidelity. Wherefore all affronts to Christianity, or endeavours to depreciate its efficacy, are highly deserving of human punishment. It was enacted by the statute of William III.[9] that if any person *educated in*, and *having made profession of*, the Christian religion, shall by writing, printing, teaching, or advised speaking, deny the Christian religion to be true, or the Holy Scriptures to be of divine authority," or again in like manner, "if any person *educated* in the Christian religion shall by writing, &c., deny any one of the Persons of the Holy Trinity to be God, or maintain that there are more gods than one, he shall on the first offence be rendered incapable to hold any office or place of trust; and for the second, be rendered incapable of bringing any action, being guardian, executor, legatee, or purchaser of lands, and [265] shall suffer three years' imprisonment without bail. To give room, however, for repentance, if, within four months after the first conviction, the delinquent will in open court publicly

---

[7] Jeremy Bentham, the prophet of utilitarianism and promoter of social reform. His works fill eleven volumes. See supra p.[249n].

[8] Sir William Blackstone (1723-80). His *Commentaries on the Laws of England* (1765) remain a fundamental source for lawyers.

[9] William III reigned with Mary (1689-1702).

renounce his error, he is discharged for that once from all disabilities."[10]

Again: "those who absent themselves from the divine worship in the established Church, through total irreligion, and attend the service of no other persuasion, forfeit one shilling to the poor every Lord's day they so absent themselves, and £20 to the king, if they continue such a default for a month together. And if they keep any inmate, thus irreligiously disposed, in their houses, they forfeit £10 per month."[11]

Further, he lays down that "reviling the ordinances of the Church is a crime of a much grosser nature than the other of non-conformity; since it carries with it the utmost indecency, arrogance, and ingratitude;—indecency, by setting up private judgment in opposition to public; arrogance, by treating with contempt and rudeness what has at least a better chance to be right than the singular notions of any particular man; and ingratitude, by denying that indulgence and liberty of conscience to the members of the national Church, which the retainers to every petty conventicle enjoy."

Once more: "In order to secure the established Church against perils from non-conformists of all denominations, infidels, Turks, Jews, heretics, papists, and sectaries, there are two bulwarks erected, called the Corporation and Test Acts;[12] by the former, no person can be legally elected to any office relating to the Government of any city or corporation, unless, within a twelvemonth before, he has received the [266] sacrament of the Lord's Supper according to the rites of the Church of England; ... the other, called the Test Act, directs

---

[10] Statutes 9 and 10 William 3 ch. 32.
[11] See *Prepos* pp.367-8 for Penal Laws against Catholics; also John Wolffe *The Protestant Crusade in Great Britain* Oxford 1991 pp 145ff.
[12] The Corporation Act of 1661 obliged members of corporations to affirm that that had received communion in the Church of England during that year. The Test Act of 1673 required all who held office under the crown to swear the oath of Supremacy and to receive the Eucharist in the Church of England.

all officers, civil and military, to make the declaration against transubstantiation within six months after their admission, and also within the same time to receive the sacrament according to the usage of the Church of England." The same test being undergone by all persons who desired to be naturalized, the Jews also were excluded from the privileges of Protestant churchmen.

Laws, such as these, of course gave a tone to society, to all classes, high and low, and to the publications, periodical or other, which represented public opinion. Dr. Watson,[13] who was the liberal prelate of his day, in his answer to Paine,[14] calls him (unless my memory betrays me) "a child of the devil and an enemy of all righteousness." Cumberland,[15] a man of the world, (here again I must trust to the memory of many past years) reproaches a Jewish writer with ingratitude for assailing, as he seems to have done, a tolerant religious establishment; and Gibbon,[16] an unbeliever, feels himself at liberty, in his posthumous Autobiography, to look down on Priestly,[17] whose "Socinian shield,"[18] he says, "has been repeatedly pierced by the mighty spear of Horsley,[19] and

---

[13] Richard Watson (1737-1816), Bishop of Llandaff in 1782, proposed radical church reform and was elected a professor of chemistry. He wrote *An Apology for the Bible,* written against Thomas Paine, in 1796.

[14] Thomas Paine (1737-1809), political and religious radical, author of *Rights of Man* (1791-2).

[15] Richard Cumberland (1632-1718), Bishop of Peterborough, was a firm exponent of utilitarianism and author of *De legibus naturae disquisitio philosophica* (1672).

[16] Edward Gibbon (1737-94), historian, author of *The Decline and Fall of the Roman Empire* (1776 ff), called by Newman "an anti-Christ" (*US* p. 126), although frequently quoted. His memoirs were published in 1789.

[17] Joseph Priestley (1733-1804), Presbyterian minister, was the author of *History of Early Opinions concerning Jesus Christ* (1786). He became one of the founders of the Unitarian Society.

[18] From Faustus Sozzini (d. 1604) and Laelius Sozzini (d. 1662) who rejected the Trinity, the Divinity of Christ and Original Sin. Their teachings coincided with the Unitarians, of which Fausto became a leader in 1579. Joseph Blanco White (1775-1841), Newman's colleague at Oriel, became a Unitarian.

[19] Samuel Horslely (1733-1806), Bishop of St Asaph, pursued a long argument with Priestley over the divinity of Christ.

whose trumpet of sedition may at length awake the magistrates of a free country."

Such was the position of free opinion and dissenting worship in England till quite a recent date, when one after another the various disabilities which I have been recounting, and many others besides, melted away, like snow at spring-tide; and we all wonder how they could ever have been in force. The cause of this great revolution is obvious, and its effect inevitable. Though I profess to be an admirer of the principles now superseded in themselves, mixed up as they were with the imperfections and evils incident to everything human, nevertheless I say frankly I do not see how they could possibly be maintained in the ascendant. When the intellect is cultivated, it is as certain that it will develope[20] into a thousand various shapes, as that infinite hues and tints and shades of colour will be reflected from the earth's surface, when the sunlight touches it; and in matters of religion the more, by reason of the extreme subtlety and abstruseness of the mental action by which they are determined. During the last seventy years, first one class of the community, then another, has awakened up to thought and opinion. Their multiform views on sacred subjects necessarily affected and found expression in the governing order. The State in past time had a conscience; George the Third had a conscience;[21] but there were other men at the head of affairs besides him with consciences, and they spoke for others besides themselves, and what was to be done, if he could not work without them, and they could not work with him, as far as religious questions came up at the Council-board? This brought on a dead-lock in the time of his successor.[22] The

[267]

---

[20] Alternative nineteenth century spelling.

[21] George III (reigned 1760-1820) believed that his Coronation oath to uphold the Protestant religion meant that he could not in conscience support Catholic emancipation.

[22] Roman Catholic emancipation in England and Ireland was fiercely resisted by George IV (reigned 1820-1830). Robert Peel (1788-1850), formerly Chief Secretary

ministry of the day could not agree together in the policy or justice of keeping up the state of things which Blackstone describes. The State ought to have a conscience; but what if it happened to have half-a-dozen, or a score, or a hundred, in religious matters, each different from each? I think Mr. Gladstone has brought out the difficulties of the situation himself in his Autobiography.[23] No government could be formed, if religious unanimity was a *sine qua non*. What then was to be done? As a necessary consequence, the whole theory of Toryism, hitherto acted on, came to pieces and went the way of all flesh.[24] This was in the nature of things. Not a hundred Popes could have hindered it, unless Providence interposed by an effusion of divine grace on the hearts of men, which would amount to a miracle, and perhaps would interfere with human responsibility. The Pope has denounced the sentiment that he ought to come to terms with "progress, liberalism, and the new civilization."[25] I have no thought at all of disputing his words. I leave the great problem to the future. God will guide other Popes to act when Pius goes, as He has guided him. No one can dislike the democratic principle more than I do. No one mourns, for instance, more than I, over the state of Oxford, given up, alas! to "liberalism and progress,"[26] to the forfeiture of her great medieval motto,

---

for Ireland, was also opposed to emancipation but later as Home Secretary under Wellington became convinced of its necessity for the peace of Ireland and supported him in secret negotiations with the King. Finally, with threats of resignation, the Catholic Relief Act was passed in January 1829. See Antonia Fraser *Perilous Question* London 2014 pp. 9-10 24, 81, 241.

[23] *A Chapter of Autobiography* London 1868.

[24] i.e. it died, as everyone does; a popular phrase perhaps based on a misquotation of I Kings 2:2; and Joshua 22:14 'to go the way of all the earth'.

[25] In *Quanta cura* Pius IX attacks "the enemies of the useful sciences, of progress, and of civilization." *Syllabus* n. 80 declares that "The Roman Pontiff can and must be reconciled with progress, liberalism and recent civilization." *DS* 2980.

[26] Newman spoke of "a fierce and lawless principle everywhere at work – a spirit of rebellion against God and man, which the powers of government in each country can barely keep under with their greatest efforts." *Tract 83* (1838) 'The Times of Antichrist' *DA* p.51.

"Dominus illuminatio mea,"[27] and with a consequent call on her to go to Parliament or the Heralds' College for a new one; but what can we do? All I know is, that Toryism, that is, loyalty to persons, "springs immortal in the human breast";[28] that religion is a spiritual loyalty; and that Catholicity is the only divine form of religion. And thus, in centuries to come, there may be found out some way of uniting what is free in the new structure of society with what is authoritative in the old, without any base compromise with "Progress" and "Liberalism."

But to return:—I have noticed the great revolution in the [269] state of the Law which has taken place since 1828[29] for this reason:—to suggest that Englishmen, who within fifty years kept up the Pope's system, are not exactly the parties to throw stones at the Pope for keeping it up still.

But I go further:—in fact the Pope has not said on this subject of conscience (for that is the main subject in question) what Mr. Gladstone makes him say. On this point I desiderate that fairness in his Pamphlet which we have a right to expect from him; and in truth his unfairness is wonderful. He says, pp. 15, 16, that the Holy See has "condemned" the maintainers of "the Liberty of the Press, of conscience, and of worship." Again, that the "Pontiff has condemned free speech, free writing, a free press, toleration of non-conformity, liberty of conscience," p. 42. Now, is not this accusation of a very wholesale character? Who would not understand it to mean that the Pope had pronounced a universal anathema against *all* these liberties *in toto*, and that English law, on the contrary, allowed those liberties *in toto*, which the Pope had condemned? But the Pope has done no such thing. The real question is, in what respect, in what

---

[27] 'The Lord is my light'. The motto of Oxford University.

[28] Alexander Pope has "Hope springs eternal in the human breast," *An Essay on Man*. l. 95.

[29] Since 1828: when Test and Corporation Acts were repealed. See supra.

measure, has he spoken against liberty: the grant of liberty admits of degrees. Blackstone is careful to show how much more liberty the law allowed to the subject in his day, how much less severe it was in its safeguards against abuse, than it had used to be; but he never pretends that it is conceivable that liberty should have no boundary at all. The very idea of [270] political society is based upon the principle that each member of it gives up a portion of his natural liberty for advantages which are greater than that liberty; and the question is, whether the Pope, in any act of his which touches us Catholics, in any ecclesiastical or theological statement of his, has propounded any principle, doctrine, or view, which is not carried out in fact at this time in British courts of law, and would not be conceded by Blackstone. I repeat, the very notion of human society is a relinquishment, to a certain point, of the liberty of its members individually, for the sake of a common security. Would it be fair on that account to say that the British Constitution condemns *all* liberty of conscience in word and in deed?

We Catholics, on our part, are denied liberty of our religion by English law in various ways, but we do not complain, because a limit must be put to even innocent liberties, and we acquiesce in it for the social compensations which we gain on the whole. Our school boys cannot play cricket on Sunday, not even in country places, for fear of being taken before a magistrate and fined.[30] In Scotland we cannot play music on Sundays.[31] Here we cannot sound a bell for church.[32] I have had before now a lawyer's authority for saying that a religious procession is illegal even within our

---

[30] The Lord's Day Observance Act (1781) was drawn up by the Bishop of London, Beilby Porteus who was against Sunday concerts and debating societies. Sunday trading has been allowed since 2004 except for Christmas Day and Easter.

[31] 1875 ed.: "In Scotland we cannot play the piano on Sundays, much less the fiddle, even in our own rooms." Newman was fond of his 'dear fiddle' and would play it in his rooms at Oriel.

[32] 1874 ed.: this sentence is omitted.

own premises. Till the last year or two we could not call our Bishops by the titles which our Religion gave them.[33] A mandate from the Home Secretary obliged us to put off our cassocks when we went out of doors.[34] We are forced to pay rates for the establishment of secular schools which we cannot use, and then we have to find means over again for building schools of our own. Why is not all this as much an outrage on our conscience as the prohibition upon Protestants at Rome, Naples, and Malaga, before the late political changes[35]—(*not*, to hold their services in a private house, or in the ambassador's, or outside the walls),—but to flaunt them in public and thereby to irritate the natives? Mr. Gladstone seems to think it is monstrous for the Holy See to sanction such a prohibition. If so, may we not call upon him to gain for us in Birmingham "the free exercise of our religion," in making a circuit of the streets in our vestments, and chanting the "Pange Lingua,"[36] and the protection of the police against the mob which would be sure to gather round us—particularly since we are English born, whereas the Protestants at Malaga or Naples were foreigners.* But we have the good sense neither to feel such disabilities a hardship, nor to protest against them as a grievance.

[271]

But now for the present state of English Law:—I say seriously Mr. Gladstone's accusation of us avails quite as

* "Hominibus illuc immigrantibus." These words Mr. Gladstone omits; also he translates "publicum" "free," pp. 17, 18, as if worship could not be free without being public.[37]

---

[33] The Ecclesiastical Titles Act of 1851 was partially repealed in 1871.

[34] Proclamation 15 June 1852 "warning Roman Catholic Ecclesiastics of the Unlawfulness of wearing Ecclesiastical Habilments saving in the usual place of worship or in private houses."

[35] Rome was inaugurated as capital of Italy in 1871 with Victor Emmanuel II as King.

[36] Corpus Christi hymn by St. Thomas Aquinas, sung in Eucharistic processions: "Sing, my tongue, the Saviour's glory, of his flesh the mystery sing."

[37] "That persons coming to reside therein." *Syllabus* n. 78. *DS* 2978.

much against Blackstone's four volumes, against laws in general, against the social contract,[38] as against the Pope. What the Pope has said, I will show presently: first let us see what the statute book has to tell us about the present state of English liberty of speech, of the press, and of worship.

First, as to public speaking and meetings:—do we allow of seditious language, or of insult to the sovereign, or his representatives? Blackstone says, that a misprision[39] is committed against him by speaking or writing against him, [272] cursing or wishing him ill, giving out scandalous stories concerning him, or doing anything that may tend to lessen him in the esteem of his subjects, may weaken his government, or may raise jealousies between him and his people. Also he says, that "threatening and reproachful words to any judge sitting in the Courts" involve "a high misprision, and have been punished with large fines, imprisonment, and corporal punishment." And we may recollect quite lately the judges of the Queen's Bench[40] prohibited public meetings and speeches which had for their object the issue of a case then proceeding in Court.

Then, again, as to the Press, there are two modes of bridling it, one before the printed matter is published, the other after. The former is the method of censorship, the latter that of the law of libel. Each is a restriction on the liberty of the Press. We prefer the latter. I never heard it said that the law of libel was of a mild character; and I never heard that the Pope, in any Brief or Rescript, had insisted on a censorship.

---

[38] The agreement between the just state and the people; based on the views expressed in Jean-Jacques Rousseau's *Du contrat social* (1762).

[39] Act of contempt.

[40] One of the three divisions at that time of the High Court of Justice, (the others being of Chancery and of Justice), dating from 1178, with certain criminal jurisdiction in Crown cases. It was headed by the Lord Chief Justice.

Lastly, liberty of worship: as to the English restriction of it, we have had a notable example of it in the last session of Parliament, and we shall have still more edifying illustrations of it in the next, though certainly not from Mr. Gladstone. The ritualistic party, in the free exercise of their rights, under the shelter of the Anglican rubrics, of certain of the Anglican offices, of the teaching of their great divines, and of their conscientious interpretation of the Thirty-nine Articles have, at their own expense, built churches for worship after their own way;[41] and, on the other hand, Parliament and the newspapers are attempting to put them down, not so much because they are acting against the tradition and the law of the Establishment, but because of the national dislike and dread of the principles and doctrines which their worship embodies.[42]

[273]

When Mr. Gladstone has a right to say broadly, by reason of these restrictions, that British law and the British people condemn the maintainers of liberty of conscience, of the press, and of worship, *in toto*,[43] then may he say so of the Encyclical, on account of those words which to him have so frightful a meaning.

But now let us see, on the other hand, what the proposition really is,[44] the condemnation of which leads him to say, that the Pope has unrestrictedly "condemned those who maintain *the* liberty of the Press, *the* liberty of conscience and of worship, and *the* liberty of speech," p. 16,—has "condemned free speech, free writing, and a free press," p.42. The condemned proposition speaks as follows:—

---

[41] The Ecclesiological Society (1846) encouraged traditional church architecture and worship. It was responsible for Margaret Street Church.

[42] "The Judicial Committee of the Privy Council hearing the case of Rev. John Purchas declared that Eucharistic vestments, the eastward position, the Mixed Chalice, and Wafer Bread were illegal." Horton Davies *Worship and Theology in England from Newman to Martineau* Oxford 1962 p.126.

[43] entirely, completely.

[44] See Postscript pp.[273-275].

"Liberty of conscience and worship, is the *inherent right* of all men. 2. It ought to be proclaimed in *every* rightly constituted society. 3. It is a right to *all sorts of liberty* (omnimodam libertatem) such, that it ought not to be restrained by any authority, ecclesiastical *or civil*, as far as public speaking, printing, or any other public manifestation of opinions is concerned."

[274] Now, is there any government on earth that could stand the strain of such a doctrine as this? It starts by taking for granted that there are certain Rights of man; Mr. Gladstone so considers, I believe; but other deep thinkers of the day are quite of another opinion; however, if the doctrine of the proposition is true, then the right of conscience, of which it speaks, being inherent in man, is of universal force—that is, all over the world—also, says the proposition, it is a right which must be recognised by all rightly constituted governments. Lastly, what is the right of conscience thus inherent in our nature, thus necessary for all states? The proposition tells us. It is the liberty of *every* one to give *public* utterance, in *every* possible shape, by *every* possible channel, without *any* let or hindrance from God or man, to *all* his notions *whatsoever*.*

Which of the two in this matter is peremptory and sweeping in his utterance, the author of this thesis himself, or the Pope who has condemned what the other has uttered?[45] Which of the two is it who would force upon the world a universal? All that the Pope has done is to deny a universal,

---

* "Jus civibus *inesse* ad *omnimodam* libertatem, *nullâ* vel ecclesiasticâ vel civili auctoritate coarctandam, quo suos conceptus *quoscunque* sive voce, sive typis, sive aliâ ratione, *palam publiceque* manifestare ac declarare valeant."[46]

---

[45] See Postscript pp.[362-364].

[46] "The law gives citizens all manner of freedoms, and no authority, civil or ecclesiastical can interfere. This is manifestly the case whatever other reason is given whether spoken or written."

and what a universal! a universal liberty to all men to say out whatever doctrines they may hold by preaching, or by the press, uncurbed by church or civil power. Does not this bear out what I said in the foregoing section of the sense in which Pope Gregory denied a "liberty of conscience"? It is a liberty of self-will. What if a man's conscience embraces the duty of regicide? or infanticide? or free love? You may say that in England the good sense of the nation would stifle and extinguish such atrocities. True, but the proposition says that it is the very right of every one, by nature, in *every* well constituted society. If so, why have we gagged the Press in Ireland on the ground of its being seditious?[47] Why is not India brought within the British constitution?[48] It seems a light epithet for the Pope to use, when he calls such a doctrine of conscience *deliramentum*: of all conceivable absurdities it is the wildest and most stupid. Has Mr. Gladstone really no better complaint to make against the Pope's condemnations than this?

[275]

Perhaps he will say, Why should the Pope take the trouble to condemn what is so wild?* But he does: and to say that he condemns something which he does not condemn, and then to inveigh against him on the ground of that something else, is neither just nor logical.

* This question is directly answered, in the Postscript on this Section, infra pp. 362-364.[49]

---

[47] It was proposed in 1875 that the Peace Preservation Act of 1870 which authorized summary seizure of publication containing treasonable or seditious matter be continued.

[48] As a result of the Indian Mutiny of 1857 the position of the East India Company came to an end, to be replaced by direct rule from Britain in 1858. In 1877 Queen Victoria was proclaimed Empress of India.

[49] This footnote is not in 1875 edition.

§ 7. *The Syllabus.*[1]

NOW I come to the Syllabus of "Errors," the publication of which has been exclaimed against in England as such a singular enormity, and especially by Mr. Gladstone. The condemnation of theological statements which militate against the Catholic Faith is of long usage in the Church. Such was the condemnation of the heresies of Wickliffe in the Council of Constance,[2] such those of Huss,[3] of Luther,[4] of Baius,[5] of Jansenius;[6] such the condemnations which were published by Sextus IV., Innocent XI., Clement XI., Benedict XIV.,[7] and other Popes. Such condemnations are no invention of Pius IX.[8] The Syllabus is a collection of such erroneous propositions as he has noted during his Pontificate; there are eighty of them.

What does the word "Syllabus" mean? A collection; the French translation calls it a "*Resumé*;"—a Collection of what? I have already said, of propositions,—propositions which the Pope in his various Allocutions, Encyclicals, and like documents, since he has been Pope, has pronounced to be Errors. Who gathered the propositions out of these Papal documents, and put them together in one? We do not know; all we know is that, by the Pope's command, this Collection

---

[1] 'Syllabus of the principal errors of our time' issued on 8th December 1864 accompanying the encyclical *Quanta cura*.
[2] Council of Constance Session VIII, 4 May 1415 *DS* 1151-1195.
[3] Session XV 15 June 1425 *DS* 1201-1230.
[4] Bull *Exurge Domine* of Leo X, 15 June 1520 *DS* 1451-1492.
[5] Bull *Ex omnibus afflictionibus* of St Pius V 7 January 1567 *DS* 1901-1980
[6] Constitution *Cum occasione* of Innocent X 31 May 1653 *DS* 2001-2007
[7] *DS* 1411-1419; 2101-2167; 2400-2502; 2515-2520.
[8] In the 1875 edition there is a misprint: 'Pius XI.'

of Errors was sent by his Foreign Minister to the Bishops. He, Cardinal Antonelli,[9] sent to them at the same time the [277] Encyclical of December, 1864, which is a document of dogmatic authority. The Cardinal says, in his circular to them, that the Pope ordered him to do so. The Pope thought, he says, that perhaps the Bishops had not seen some of his Allocutions, and other authoritative letters and speeches of past years; in consequence the Pope had had the Errors which, at one time or other he had therein noted, brought together into one, and that for the use of the Bishops.

Such is the Syllabus and its object. There is not a word in it of the Pope's own writing; there is nothing in it at all but the Erroneous Propositions themselves—that is, except the heading "A Syllabus, containing the principal Errors of our times, which are noted in the Consistorial Allocutions, in the Encyclicals, and in other Apostolical Letters of our most Holy Lord, Pope Pius IX." There is one other addition—viz., after each Error a reference is given to the Allocution, Encyclical, or other document in which it is proscribed.[10]

The Syllabus, then, is to be received with profound submission, as having been sent by the Pope's authority to the Bishops of the world.[11] It certainly comes to them with his indirect extrinsic sanction;[12] but intrinsically, and viewed in itself, it is nothing more than a digest of certain Errors made by an anonymous writer. There would be nothing on the face of it, to show that the Pope had ever seen it, page by

---

[9] Giacomo Antonelli (1806-76) was created Cardinal by Pius IX while still a deacon and was appointed Secretary of State in Gaeta (where Pius had fled) in 1848.

[10] 1875 ed.: "… in which it is condemned"

[11] See Postscript pp.[364ff].

[12] "[Historians] see that it was not a papal bull, but an appendix; that it was afterwards interpreted variously, and that even the Pope himself approved in conversation a lax or minimizing interpretation." Owen Chadwick, *The Secularisation of the European Mind in the Nineteenth Century*, Cambridge University Press 1985 p.111.

page, unless the "Imprimatur"[13] implied in the Cardinal's letter had been an evidence of this. It has no mark or seal put [278] upon it which gives it a direct relation to the Pope. Who is its author? Some select theologian or high official doubtless; can it be Cardinal Antonelli himself? No surely: anyhow it is not the Pope, and I do not see my way to accept it for what it is not. I do not speak as if I had any difficulty in recognizing and condemning the Errors which it catalogues, did the Pope himself bid me; but he has not as yet done so, and he cannot delegate his *Magisterium*[14] to another. I wish with St. Jerome to "speak with the Successor of the Fisherman and the Disciple of the Cross."[15] I assent to that which the Pope propounds in faith and morals, but it must be he speaking officially, personally, and immediately, and not any one else, who has a hold over me. The Syllabus is not an official act, because it is not signed, for instance, with "Datum Romæ, Pius P.P. IX.," or "sub annulo Piscatoris,"[16] or in some other way; it is not a personal, for he does not address his "Venerabiles Fratres,"[17] or "Dilecto Filio,"[18] or speak as "Pius Episcopus;"[19] it is not an immediate, for it comes to the Bishops only through the Cardinal Minister of State.

If, indeed, the Pope should ever make that anonymous compilation directly his own, then of course I should bow to it and accept it as strictly his. He might have done so; he might do so still; again, he might issue a fresh list of Propositions in addition, and pronounce them to be Errors, and I should take that condemnation to be of dogmatic authority, because I believe him appointed by his Divine Master to determine in the detail of faith and morals what is

---

[13] Episcopal sanction 'Let it be printed' added to Catholic publications as testament to their orthodoxy.
[14] The Church's teaching authority.
[15] St Jerome in his letter 15 to Pope Damasus (376 or 377) *ML* 22.355.
[16] "under the ring of the fisherman"
[17] "Venerable Brothers"
[18] "Beloved Son"
[19] "Bishop Pius"

true and what is false. But such an act of his he would formally authenticate; he would speak in his own name, as Leo X.[20] or Innocent XI.[21] did, by Bull or Letter Apostolic. [279] Or, if he wished to speak less authoritatively, he would speak through a Sacred Congregation; but the Syllabus makes no claim to be acknowledged as the word of the Pope. Moreover, if the Pope drew up that catalogue, as it may be called, he would have pronounced in it some definite judgment on the propositions themselves. What gives cogency to this remark is, that a certain number of Bishops and theologians, when a Syllabus was in contemplation, did wish for such a formal act on the part of the Pope, and in consequence they drew up for his consideration the sort of document on which, if he so willed, he might suitably stamp his infallible sanction; but he did not accede to their prayer. This composition is contained in the "*Recueil des Allocutions,*" &c., and is far more than a mere "collection of errors." It is headed, "Theses ad Apostolicam Sedem delatæ *cum censuris,*"[22] &c., and each error from first to last has the ground of its condemnation marked upon it. There are sixty-one of them. The first is "impia, injuriosa religioni,"[23] &c.; the second is "complexivè sumpta, falsa,"[24] &c.; the third the same; the fourth, "hæretica,"[25] and so on, the epithets affixed having a distinct meaning, and denoting various degrees of error. Such a document, unlike the Syllabus, has a substantive character.

Here I am led to interpose a remark;—it is plain, then, that there are those near, or with access, to the Holy Father, who would, if they could, go much further in the way of assertion and command, than the divine *Assistentia,*[26] which

---

[20] Leo X, Giovanni de' Medici (reigned 1513-21).
[21] Innocent XI, Benedetto Odescalchi (reigned 1676-89)
[22] "Theses delated *with censures* to the Apostolic See" Rome 1875.
[23] "impious, injurious to religion"
[24] "taken comprensively, false"
[25] "heretical"
[26] The special help afforded by virtue of his office given by the Holy Spirit.

[280]   overshadows him, wills or permits; so that his acts and his
words on doctrinal subjects must be carefully scrutinized and
weighed, before we can be sure what really he has said.
Utterances which must be received as coming from an
Infallible Voice are not made every day, indeed they are very
rare; and those which are by some persons affirmed or
assumed to be such, do not always turn out what they are said
to be; nay, even such as are really dogmatic must be read by
definite rules and by traditional principles of interpretation,
which are as cogent and unchangeable as the Pope's own
decisions themselves. What I have to say presently will
illustrate this truth; meanwhile I use the circumstance which
has led to my mentioning it, for another purpose here. When
intelligence which we receive from Rome startles and pains
us from its seemingly harsh or extreme character, let us learn
to have some little faith and patience, and not take for granted
that all that is reported is the truth. There are those who wish
and try to carry measures and declare they have carried, when
they have not carried them. How many strong things, for
instance, have been reported with a sort of triumph on one
side and with irritation and despondency on the other, of what
the Vatican Council has done; whereas the very next year
after it, Bishop Fessler,[27] the Secretary General of the
Council, brings out his work on "True and False
Infallibility," reducing what was said to be so monstrous to
its true dimensions. When I see all this going on, those grand
lines in the Greek Tragedy always rise on my lips—

Οὔποτε τὰν Διὸς ἁρμονίαν
Θνατῶν παρεξίασι βουλαί,—[28]

---

[27] Josef Fessler (1813-72), Professor of Canon Law in the University of Vienna
1856-61, Bishop of Sankt Pölten 1864, Secretary to the Council 1869. He wrote *Die
wahre und de falshe unfehlbarkeit der Päpste*. 'The true and false infallibility of the
Pope' (Vienna 1871). It was translated by Ambrose St. John, London 1875.
[28] 'Never will the schemes of mortals transgress God's ordinances.' Aeschylus
Prometheus Unbound l. 551.

and still more the consolation given us by a Divine Speaker [281]
that, though the swelling sea is so threatening to look at, yet
there is One who rules it and says, "Hitherto shalt thou come
and no further, and here shall thy proud waves be stayed!"[29]

But to return:—the Syllabus then has no dogmatic force;[30]
it addresses us, not in its separate portions, but as a whole,
and is to be received from the Pope by an act of obedience,
not of faith, that obedience being shown by having recourse
to the original and authoritative documents, (Allocutions and
the like,) to which it pointedly refers. Moreover, when we
turn to those documents, which *are* authoritative, we find the
Syllabus cannot even be called an echo of the Apostolic
Voice; for, in matters in which wording is so important, it is
not an exact transcript of the words of the Pope, in its account
of the errors condemned,—just as is natural in what is
professedly an index for reference.

Mr. Gladstone indeed wishes to unite the Syllabus to that
Encyclical which so moved him in December, 1864, and says
that the Errors noted in the Syllabus are all brought under the
infallible judgment pronounced on certain errors specified in
the Encyclical. This is an untenable assertion. He says of the
Pope and of the Syllabus, p. 20: "These are not mere opinions
of the Pope himself, nor even are they opinions which he
might paternally recommend to the pious consideration of the
faithful. With the promulgation of his opinions is unhappily
combined, in the Encyclical Letter *which virtually, though
not expressly, includes the whole*, a *command* to all his
spiritual children (from which command we, the disobedient [282]
children, are in no way excluded) *to hold them*," and Mr.
Gladstone appeals in proof of this to the language of the
Encyclical; but let us see what that language is. The Pope
speaks thus, as Mr. Gladstone himself quotes him: "All and
each of the wrong opinions and doctrines, *mentioned one by*

---

[29] Job 38:11.
[30] See Postscript pp.[364-7].

one in this Encyclical (*hisce litteris*), by our Apostolical authority, we reprobate, &c."[31] He says then, as plainly as words can speak, that the wrong opinions which in this passage he condemns, are specified *in* the Encyclical, not outside of it; and, when we look into the earlier part of it, there they are, about ten of them; there is not a single word in the Encyclical to show that the Pope in it was alluding to the Syllabus. The Syllabus does not exist, as far as the language of the Encyclical is concerned. This gratuitous assumption seems to me marvellously unfair.

The only connexion between the Syllabus and the Encyclical is one external to them both, the connexion of time and organ; Cardinal Antonelli sending them both to the Bishops with the introduction of one and the same letter. In that letter he speaks to the Bishops thus, as I paraphrase his words:*—The Holy Father sends you by me a list, which he has caused to be drawn up and printed, of the errors which he has in various formal documents, in the course of the last eighteen years, noted. With that list of errors, he is also sending you a new Encyclical, which he has judged it

[283]

---

* His actual words (abridged) are these:—"Notre T.S.S. Pius IX., n'a jamais cessé de proscrire les principales erreurs de notre très-malheureuse époque, par ses Encycliques, et par ses Allocutions, &c. Mais comme il peut arriver que tous les actes pontificaux ne perviennent pas à chacun des Ordinaires, le même Souverain Pontife a voulu que l'on rédigeât un Syllabus de ces mêmes erreurs, destiné à être envoyé à tous les Evêques, &c. Il m'a ensuite ordonné de veiller à ce que ce Syllabus imprimé fût envoyé à V.E.R. dans ce temps où le même Souverain Pontife a jugé à propos d'écrire un autre Lettre Encyclique. Ainsi, je m'empresse d'envoyer à V.E. ce Syllabus avec ces Lettres."[32]

---

[31] 1875 ed.: "We, by our Apostolic Authority, reprobate, proscribe, and condemn, and it is our will and command that the same be in like manner held reprobated, proscribed, and condemned by all the children of the Holy Church. Ency Dec 8 1864."

[32] "Our Holy Father Pius IX has never ceased condemning the errors of our most unfortunate age by his Encyclicals and his Allocutions etc. But as it can happen that

apropos to write to the Catholic Bishops;—so I send you both at once."

The Syllabus, then, is a list, or rather an index, of the Pope's Encyclical or Allocutional "proscriptions," an index *raisonné*;[33]—(not alphabetical, as is found, for instance, in Bellarmine's[34] or Lambertini's[35] works,)—drawn up by the Pope's orders, out of his paternal care for the flock of Christ, and conveyed to the Bishops through his Minister of State. But we can no more accept it as *de fide*, as a dogmatic document, than any other index or table of contents. Take a parallel case, *mutatis mutandis*:[36] Counsel's opinion being asked on a point of law, he goes to his law books, writes down his answer, and, as authority, refers his client to 23 George III., c. 5, s. 11; 11 Victoria, c. 12, s. 19, and to Thomas *v.* Smith, Att. Gen. *v.* Roberts, and Jones *v.* Owen. Who would say that that sheet of foolscap has force of law, when it was nothing more than a list of references to the Statutes of the Realm, or Judges' decisions, in which the Law's voice really was found?

The value of the Syllabus, then, lies in its references; but of these Mr. Gladstone has certainly availed himself very little. Yet, in order to see the nature and extent of the blame cast on any proposition of the Syllabus, it is absolutely necessary to turn out the passage of the Allocution, Encyclical, or other document, in which the error is noted; [284] for the wording of the errors which the Syllabus contains is to be interpreted by its references. Instead of this Mr.

---

all these pontifical acts may not reach each one of the Ordinaries, the same Sovereign Pontiff has wished that a Syllabus of these same errors should be drawn up and sent to all the bishops etc. He has straightaway ordered that care should be taken to send to your excellencies this Syllabus once in print, when the same Sovereign Pontiff has thought suitable to write another Encyclical Letter. Hence I make haste to send you this Syllabus with these Letters." See infra p.[297].

[33] a systematic list

[34] See p.[235]

[35] Prospero Lorenzo Lambertini, Pope Benedict XIV (reigned 1740-58).

[36] things being changed that have to be changed.

Gladstone uses forms of speech about the Syllabus which only excite in me fresh wonder. Indeed, he speaks upon these ecclesiastical subjects generally in a style in which priests and parsons are accused by their enemies of speaking concerning geology. For instance, the Syllabus, as we have seen, is a list or index; but he calls it "extraordinary declarations," p. 21. How can a list of errors be a series of Pontifical "Declarations"?

However, perhaps he would say that, in speaking of "Declarations," he was referring to the authoritative allocutions, &c., which I have accused him of neglecting. With all my heart; but then let us see how the statements in these allocations fulfil the character he gives of them. He calls them "Extraordinary declarations on personal and private duty," p. 21, and "stringent condemnations," p. 19. Now, I certainly must grant that some are stringent, but only some. One of the most severe that I have found among them is that in the Apostolic Letter of June 10, 1851,[37] against some heretic priest out at Lima, whose elaborate work in six volumes against the Curia Romana, is pronounced to be in its various statements "scandalous, rash, false, schismatical, injurious to the Roman Pontiffs and Ecumenical Councils, impious and heretical." It well deserved to be called by these names, which are not terms of abuse, but each with its definite meaning; and, if Mr. Gladstone, in speaking of the condemnations, had confined his epithet "stringent" to it, no one would have complained of him. And another severe condemnation is that of the works of Professor Nuytz.[38] But

[285]

---

[37] A condemnatory letter (Damnatio) addressed to Francisco de Paula González Vigil, a clerical author and politician who wrote against the power of the Curia, *Defensa de la autoridad de los gobiernos contra las pretensiones de la Curia Romana* (A Defence of the Authority of Governments against the Claims of the Roman Curia) 1848-9. See also *Syllabus* nn. 23, 30, 54. The Papal Curia is the Papal Court which includes Congregations, Tribunals and other organisations and acts with delegated authority from the Pope.

[38] Nepomuk Nuytz, a Professor at Turin University, published *Juris Ecclesiastici Institutiones* on Church law in 1844 which was condemned 22 August 1851.

let us turn to some other of the so-called condemnations, in order to ascertain whether they answer to his general description of them.

1. For instance, take his own 16th (the 77th of the "erroneous Propositions"), that, "It is no longer expedient that the Catholic Religion should be established to the exclusion of all others." When we turn to the Allocution, which is the ground of its being put into the Syllabus, what do we find there? First, that the Pope was speaking, not of States universally, but of one particular State, Spain, definitely Spain;[39] secondly, that he was not noting the erroneous proposition directly, or categorically, but was protesting against the breach in many ways of the Concordat[40] on the part of the Spanish government; further, that he was not referring to any work containing the said proposition, nor contemplating any proposition at all; nor, on the other hand, using any word of condemnation whatever, nor using any harsher terms of the Government in question than an expression of "his wonder and distress."[41] And again, taking the Pope's remonstrance as it stands, is it any great cause of complaint to Englishmen, who so lately were severe in their legislation upon Unitarians, Catholics, unbelievers, and others,[42] that the Pope merely does not think it expedient for *every* state *from this time forth* to tolerate *every* sort of religion on its territory, and to disestablish the Church at once? for this is all that he denies. As in the instance in the foregoing section, he does but deny a universal, which the "erroneous proposition" asserts without any explanation.

---

[39] Allocution *Jamdudum cernimus* 18 March 1861.
[40] A treaty between the Holy See and a foreign government regarding the interests of religion in that country.
[41] 1875 ed.: "wonder and bitterness."
[42] The Trinity Act 1813 gave freedom of worship to Unitarians, and the Emancipation Act reduced penalties for Catholics in 1829. Non-Anglicans were not allowed to take up University teaching positions until 1871.

[286]   2. Another of Mr. Gladstone's "stringent Condemnations" (his 18th) is the Pope's denial of the proposition that "the Roman Pontiff can and ought to come to terms with Progress, Liberalism, and the New Civilization."[43] I turn to the Allocation of March 18, 1861, and find there no formal condemnation of this Proposition at all. The Allocution is a long *argument* to the effect that the moving parties in that Progress, Liberalism, and New Civilization, make use of it so seriously to the injury of the Faith and the Church, that it is both out of the power, and contrary to the duty, of the Pope to come to terms with them. Nor would those prime movers themselves differ from him here; certainly in this country it is the common cry that Liberalism is and will be the Pope's destruction, and they wish and mean it so to be.[44] This Allocution on the subject is at once beautiful, dignified, and touching: and I cannot conceive how Mr. Gladstone should make stringency his one characteristic of these condemnations, especially when after all there is here no condemnation at all.

     3. Take, again, Mr. Gladstone's 15th—"That the abolition of Temporal Power of the Popedom would be highly advantageous to the Church." Neither can I find in the Pope's Allocution any formal condemnation whatever of this proposition, much less a "stringent" one. Even the Syllabus does no more in the case of any one of the eighty, than to call it an "error;" and what the Pope himself says of this particular error is only this:—"We cannot but in particular *warn* and *reprove* (monere et redarguere) those who applaud the decree by which the Roman Pontiff has been despoiled of all the

[287]   honour and dignity of his civil rule, and assert that the said decree, more than anything else, conduces to the liberty and prosperity of the Church itself."—*Alloc.*, April 20, 1849.

---

[43] n. 89 *DS* 2980.
[44] See Newman's Biglietto Speech, *Campaign I* pp 513-6.

4. Take another of his instances, the 17th, the "error" that "in countries called Catholic the public exercise of other religions may laudably be allowed." I have had occasion to mention already his mode of handling the Latin text of this proposition—viz., that whereas the men who were forbidden the public exercise of their religion were foreigners, who had no right to be in a country not their own at all, and might fairly have conditions imposed upon them during their stay there, nevertheless Mr. Gladstone (apparently through haste) has left out the word "hominibus illuc immigrantibus,"[45] on which so much turns. Next, as I have observed above, it was only the sufferance of their *public* worship, and again of all worships whatsoever, however many and various, which the Pope blamed; and further, the Pope's words do not apply to all States, but specially, and, as far as the Allocution goes, definitely, to New Granada.[46]

However, the point I wish to insist upon here is, that there was in this case no condemned proposition at all, but it was merely, as in the case of Spain, an act of the Government which the Pope protested against. The Pope merely told that Government that that act, and other acts which they had committed, gave him very great pain; that he had expected better things of them; that the way they went on was all of a piece; and they had his best prayers. Somehow, it seems to me strange, for any one to call an expostulation like this one [288] of a set of "extraordinary declarations," "stringent condemnations."

I am convinced that the more the propositions and the references contained in the Syllabus are examined, the more signally will the charge break down, brought against the Pope on occasion of it: as to those Propositions which Mr.

---

[45] 'those who have come to the country as immigrants'
[46] The Spanish Viceroyalty established in 1717 included the modern countries of Colombia and Venezuela, Ecuador and parts of Peru and Brazil.

Gladstone specially selects, some of them I have already taken in hand, and but few of them present any difficulty.

5. As to those on Marriage, I cannot follow Mr. Gladstone's meaning here, which seems to me very confused, and it would be going out of the line of remark which I have traced out for myself, (and which already is more extended than I could wish), were I to treat of them.*

6. His fourth Error, (taken from the Encyclical) that "Papal judgments and decrees may, without sin, be disobeyed or differed from," is a denial of the principle of Hooker's celebrated work on Ecclesiastical Polity,[47] and would be condemned by him as well as by the Pope. And it is plain to common sense that no society can stand if its rules are disobeyed. What club or union would not expel members who refused so to be bound?

[289] 7. And the 5th,† 8th, and 9th propositions are necessarily errors, if the Sketch of Church Polity drawn out in my former Sections is true, and are necessarily considered to be such by those, as the Pope, who maintain that Polity.

8. The 10th Error, as others which I have noticed above, is a *universal* (that "in the conflict of laws, civil and ecclesiastical, the civil law should prevail"), and the Pope does but deny a universal.

9. Mr. Gladstone's 11th, which I do not quite understand in his wording of it, runs thus:—"Catholics can approve of that system of education for youth which is separated from

---

* I have observed on them in Postscript on § 7, infra pp. 368-370.
† Father Coleridge, in his Sermon on "The Abomination of Desolation," observes that, whereas Proposition 5th speaks of "jura," Mr. Gladstone translates "*civil* jura." Vid. also the *Month* for December, but above all Mgr. Dupanloup's works on the general subject.[48]

---

[47] Richard Hooker (c.1554-1600), Fellow of Corpus Christi, became Master of the Temple in 1585. He began to publish his *Laws of Ecclesiastical Policy* in 1594.
[48] Henry James Coleridge (1822-93), elected a fellow of Oriel in 1845, became a Jesuit and edited the *Month* 1865-81. Mgr. Dupanloup (1802-78) was Bishop of Orléans from 1849. He asked Newman to be his theological advisor at Vatican I.

the Catholic faith and the Church's power, and which regards the science only of physical things, and the outlines (fines) of earthly social life alone or at least primarily." How is this not an "Error"? Surely there are Englishmen enough who protest against the elimination of religion from our schools; is such a protest so dire an offence to Mr. Gladstone?

10. And the 12th Error is this:—That "the science of philosophy and of morals, also the laws of the State, can and should keep clear of divine and ecclesiastical authority." This too will not be anything short of an error in the judgment of great numbers of our own people.[49] Is Benthamism[50] so absolutely the Truth, that the Pope is to be denounced because he has not yet become a convert to it?

11. There are only two of the condemnations which really require a word of explanation; I have already referred to them. One is that of Mr. Gladstone's sixth Proposition, "Roman Pontiffs and Ecumenical Councils, have departed from the limits of their power, have usurped the rights of [290] Princes, and even in defining matters of faith and morals have erred." These words are taken from the Lima Priest's book. We have to see then what *he* means by "the Rights of Princes," for the proposition is condemned in *his* sense of the word. It is a rule of the Church in the condemnation of a book to state the proposition condemned in the words of the book itself, without the Church being answerable for those words as employed.* I have already referred to this rule in my 5th

---

* Propositiones, de quibus Ecclesia judicium suum pronunciat, duobus præsertim modis spectari possunt, vel absoluté ac in se ipsis, vel relativè ad sensum libri et auctoris. In censurâ propositionis alicujus auctoris vel libri, Ecclesia attendit ad sensum ab eo intentum, qui quidem ex verbis, ex totâ doctrinæ ipsius serie, libri textura et confirmatione, consilio, institutoque elicitur. Propositio libri vel auctoris *æquivoca* esse potest, duplicemque habere sensum, rectum unum et alterum malum. *Ubi*

---

[49] Newman had discussed this subject extensively in *The Idea of a University*.
[50] After Jeremy Bentham. See p.[249]

Section. Now this priest includes among the rights of Catholic princes that of deposing Bishops from their sacred Ministry, of determining the impediments to marriage, of forming Episcopal sees, and of being free from episcopal authority in spiritual matters. When, then, the Proposition is condemned "that Popes had usurped the rights of Princes;" what is meant is, "the so-called rights of Princes," which were really the rights of the Church, in assuming which there was no usurpation at all.

12. The other proposition, Mr. Gladstone's seventh, the condemnation of which requires a remark, is this: "The Church has not the power to employ force (vis inferendæ) nor any temporal power direct or indirect."

[291]   This is one of a series of Propositions found in the work of Professor Nuytz, entitled, "Juris Ecclesiastici Institutiones," all of which are condemned in the Pope's Apostolic Letter of August 22, 1851.[51] Now here "employing force" is not the Pope's phrase but Professor Nuytz's, and the condemnation is meant to run thus, "It is an error to say, with Professor Nuytz,[52] that what *he* calls 'employing force' is not allowable to the Church." That this is the right interpretation of the "error" depends of course on a knowledge of the Professor's work, which I have never had an opportunity of seeing; but here I will set down what the received doctrine of the Church is on ecclesiastical punishments, as stated in a work of the

contingit Ecclesiam propositiones hujusmodi æquivocas absque præviâdistinctione sensuum configere, censura unicè cadit in sensum libri vel auctoris.—Tournely, t. 2, p. 170, ed. 1752.[53]

---

[51] *Ad Apostolicae.*

[52] John Nepomucen Nuytz. See p.[285]

[53] "There are principally two ways in which it can be seen that the Church can pronounce judgement; either absolutely viewed in themselves or relatively from the sense of the written word or of the mind of the author. When censuring either propositions or the author the Church examines the sense which is intended from the words themselves and what can be drawn from the text, and how it impacts on

highest authority, since it comes to us with letters of approval from Gregory XVI. and Pius IX.

"The opinion," says Cardinal Soglia,[54] "that the coercive power divinely bestowed upon the Church consists in the infliction of spiritual punishments alone, and not in corporal or temporal, seems more in harmony with the gentleness of the Church. Accordingly I follow their judgment, who withdraw from the Church the corporal sword, by which the body is destroyed or blood is shed. Pope Nicholas thus writes: 'The Church has no sword but the spiritual. She does not kill, but gives life, hence that well-known saying, 'Ecclesia abhorret a sanguine.'[55] But the lighter punishments, though temporal and corporal, such as shutting up in a monastery, prison, flogging, and others of the same kind, short of effusion of blood, the Church *jure suo* can inflict."— (Institut. Jur., pp. 167-8, Paris.)[56]

And the Cardinal quotes the words of Fleury:[57] "The [292] Church has enjoined on penitent sinners almsgivings, fastings, and other corporal inflictions ... Augustine speaks of beating with sticks, as practised by the Bishops, after the manner of masters in the case of servants, parents in the case of children and school-masters in that of scholars. Abbots flogged monks in the way of paternal and domestic chastisement ... Imprisonment for a set time or for life is

---

doctrine. The theme of the book or its author could be *equivocal* having two meanings, a good and a bad one. When it comes to such equivocal meanings without beforehand determining the sense, the censure only falls on the wrong meaning of the book or its author." 1752." Honoré Tournely (1658-1729), French theologian and author of *Praelectiones theologicae* 16v 1725-1730. See supra p.[235].

[54] Cardinal Giovanni Soglia Ceroni (1779-1856), author of *Institutiones Iuris privati et ecclesiastici*, was briefly Secretary of State in 1848 from 4 June to 29 November. Newman writing to Thomas Arnold says Soglia maintained that the Church did not have the power to punish with temporal penalties. 15 November 1859 *LD* 32 p.209.

[55] "The Church abhors the shedding of blood."

[56] *Institutiones Juris Publici Ecclesiastici. 3v* (1840), 'Dispositions of the Public Law of the Church'.

[57] Claude Fleury (1640-1723), historian, known for his *Histoire ecclésiastique* in 20 vols (1691-1720).

mentioned among canonical penances; priests and other clerics, who had been deposed for their crimes, being committed to prison in order that they might pass the time to come in penance for their crime, which thereby was withdrawn from the memory of the public."

But now I have to answer one question. If what I have said is substantially the right explanation to give to the drift and contents of the Syllabus, have not I to account for its making so much noise, and giving such deep and wide offence on its appearance? It has already been reprobated by the voice of the world. Is there not, then, some reason at the bottom of the aversion felt by educated Europe towards it, which I have not mentioned? This is a very large question to entertain, too large for this place; but I will say one word upon it.

Doubtless one of the reasons of the excitement and displeasure which the Syllabus caused and causes so widely, is the number and variety of the propositions marked as errors, and the systematic arrangement to which they were subjected. So large and elaborate a work struck the public mind as a new law, moral, social, and ecclesiastical, which was to be the foundation of a European code, and the beginning of a new world, in opposition to the social principles of the 19th century; and there certainly were persons in high station who encouraged this idea. When this belief was once received, it became the interpretation of the whole Collection through the eighty Propositions, of which it recorded the erroneousness; as if it had for its object in all its portions one great scheme of aggression. Then, when the public mind was definitively directed to the examination of these erroneous *Theses*, they were sure to be misunderstood, from their being read apart from the context, occasion, and drift of each. They had been noted as errors[58] in the Pope's Encyclicals and Allocutions in the course of the preceding

[293]

---

[58] 1875 ed.: "The condemnations had been published in the Pope's Encyclicals…"

eighteen years,[59] and no one had taken any notice of them; but now, when they were brought all together, they made a great sensation. Why were they brought together, except for some purpose sinister and hostile to society? and if they themselves were hard to understand, still more so, and doubly so was their proscription.[60]

Another circumstance, which I am not theologian enough to account for, is this,—that the wording of many of the erroneous propositions, as they are drawn up in the Syllabus, gives an apparent breadth to the matter condemned which is not found in the Pope's own words in his Allocutions and Encyclicals. Not that really there is any difference between the Pope's words and Cardinal Antonelli's, for (as I have shown in various instances) what the former says in the concrete, the latter does but repeat in the abstract. Or, to speak logically, when the Pope enunciates as true the [294] particular affirmative, "Spain[61] ought to keep up the establishment of the Catholic Religion," then (since its contradictory is necessarily false) the Cardinal declares, "To say that no State should keep up the establishment of the Catholic Religion is an error." But there is a dignity and beauty in the Pope's own language which the Cardinal's abstract Syllabus cannot have, and this gave to opponents an opportunity to declaim against the Pope, which opportunity was in no sense afforded by what he said himself.

---

[59] 1875 ed.: "They were sure to be misunderstood; from the ignorance, in the case of all but ecclesiastics, of the nature and force of ecclesiastical language. The condemnations had been published in the Pope's Encyclicals and Allocutions in the course of the preceding eighteen years."

[60] 1875 ed.: "Now when they were brought all together they on that account made a great sensation. Next, that same fact seemed in itself a justification, with minds already prejudiced, for expecting in each of them something extraordinary as even hostile to society, and then again when they were examined one by one, certainly their real sense was often not obvious and could not be, to the intelligence of laymen, high and low, educated and simple."

[61] 1875 ed.: "New Granada"

Then, again, it must be recollected, in connexion with what I have said, that theology is a science, and a science of a special kind; its reasoning, its method, its modes of expression, and its language are all its own. Every science must be in the hands of a comparatively few persons—that is, of those who have made it a study. The courts of law have a great number of rules in good measure traditional; so has the House of Commons, and, judging by what one reads in the public prints, men must have a noviceship there before they can be at perfect ease in their position. In like manner young theologians, and still more those who are none, are sure to mistake in matters of detail; indeed a really first-rate theologian is rarely to be found. At Rome the rules of interpreting authoritative documents are known with a perfection which at this time is scarcely to be found elsewhere. Some of these rules, indeed, are known to all priests; but even this general knowledge is not possessed by laymen, much less by Protestants, however able and [295] experienced in their own several lines of study or profession. One of those rules I have had several times occasion to mention. In the censure of books, which offend against doctrine or discipline, it is a common rule to take sentences out of them in the author's own words, whether those are words in themselves good or bad, and to affix some note of condemnation to them in the sense in which they occur in the book in question. Thus it may happen that even what seems at first sight a true statement, is condemned for being made the shelter of an error; for instance: "Faith justifies when it works," or "There is no religion where there is no charity,"[62] may be taken in a good sense; but each proposition is condemned in Quesnell,[63] because it is false as he uses it.

---

[63] Pasquier Quesnel (1634-1719), Oratorian priest and theologian whose concept of grace, influenced by Jansenism, in his book *Moral Reflections on the New Testament* was condemned by Clement XI in a Brief of 1708 and then in the Constitution *Unigenitus* (1713). Eighty of its propositions include: "Faith justifies when it works

A further illustration of the necessity of a scientific education in order to understand the value of Propositions, is afforded by a controversy which has lately gone on among us as to the validity of Abyssinian Orders.[64] In reply to a document urged on one side of the question, it was allowed on the other, that, "if that document was to be read in the same way as we should read any ordinary judgment, the interpretation which had been given to it was the most obvious and natural." "But it was well known," it was said, "to those who are familiar with the practical working of such decisions, that they are only interpreted with safety in the light of certain rules, which arise out of what is called the *stylus curiæ*."[65] And then some of these rules were given; first, "that to understand the real meaning of a decision, no matter how clearly set forth, we should know the nature of the difficulty or *dubium*, as it was understood by the tribunal [296] that had to decide upon it. Next, nothing but the direct proposition, in its nudest and severest sense, as distinguished from indirect propositions, the grounds of the decision, or implied statements, is ruled by the judgment. Also, if there is anything in the wording of a decision which appears inconsistent with the teaching of an approved body of theologians, &c., the decision is to be interpreted so as to

---

but it does not work without charity." (51) "There is no God, no religion where there is no charity." (58) *DS* 2451, 2458. See also p.[295].

[64] Before 1703, a schismatical Orthodox Archbishop (or Abuna) ordained many hundred priests. Some of them who had later converted to Catholicism asked Rome to rule on whether their ordinations were valid. The decision was deferred at the time. In 1873 some Anglicans heard about the matter and gained the impression that the ordinations were valid and might lead to the acceptance of their own priesthood. Cardinal Manning in a letter of 24 August 1874 asked for a ruling. Johann Baptist Franzelin SJ (1816-86), Professor of Theology at the Roman College and later Cardinal, was asked to investigate and gave his verdict on 25 February 1875 that the formula used was not sufficient for validity.

[65] curial practice

leave such teaching intact;" and so on.* It is plain that the view thus opened upon us has further bearings than that for which I make use of it here.

These remarks on scientific theology apply also of course to its language. I have employed myself in illustration in framing a sentence, which would be plain enough to any priest, but I think would perplex any Protestant. I hope it is not of too light a character to introduce here. We will suppose then a theologian to write as follows:—"Holding, as we do, that there is only *material* sin in those who, being *invincibly* ignorant, reject the truth, therefore in charity we hope that they have the future portion of *formal* believers, as considering that by *virtue* of their good faith, though not of the *body* of the faithful, they *implicitly* and *interpretatively* believe what they seem to deny."[66] Now let us consider what sense would this statement convey to the mind of a member of some Reformation Society or Protestant League? He would read it as follows, and consider it all the more insidious and dangerous for its being so very unintelligible:—

[297] "Holding, as we do, that there is only a very considerable sin in those who reject the truth out of contumacious ignorance, therefore in charity we hope that they have the future portion of nominal Christians, as considering, that by the excellence of their living faith, though not in the number of believers, they believe without any hesitation, as interpreters [of Scripture?] what they seem to deny."

Now, considering that the Syllabus was intended for the Bishops, who would be the interpreters of it, as the need arose, to their people, and it got bodily into English newspapers even before it was received at many an episcopal

* *The Month*, Nov. and Dec., 1873.[67]

---

[66] See supra p.[259] on erroneous conscience.
[67] See Coleridge supra p.[288].

residence, we shall not be surprised at the commotion which accompanied its publication.

I have spoken of the causes intrinsic to the Syllabus, which have led to misunderstandings about it. As to external, I can be no judge myself as to what Catholics who have means of knowing are very decided in declaring, the tremendous power of the Secret Societies.[68] It is enough to have suggested here, how a wide-spread organization like theirs might malign and frustrate the most beneficial acts of the Pope. One matter I had information of myself from Rome at the time when the Syllabus had just been published, before there was yet time to ascertain how it would be taken by the world at large. Now, the Rock of St. Peter on its summit enjoys a pure and serene atmosphere, but there is a great deal of Roman *malaria*[69] at the foot of it. While the Holy Father was in great earnestness and charity addressing the Catholic world by his Cardinal Minister, there were circles of light-minded men in his city who were laying bets with each other   [298] whether the Syllabus would "make a row in Europe" or not. Of course it was the interest of those who betted on the affirmative side to represent the Pope's act to the greatest disadvantage; and it was very easy to kindle a flame in the mass of English and other visitors at Rome which with a very little nursing was soon strong enough to take care of itself.

---

[68] *Quanta cura* had reiterated the condemnation by the Papacy of secret societies and "branded with anathema their followers," even if tolerated by individual governments.

[69] The Pontine Marshes between Velletri and Terracina were sources of malaria until drained by the government under Mussolini. Cardinal Franchi in his letter to Bishop Ullathorne found this expression 'troppo irreverente'. *LD* 27 p, 409.

The Vatican Council.[1]

IN beginning to speak of the Vatican Council, I am obliged from circumstances to begin by speaking of myself. The most unfounded and erroneous assertions have publicly been made about my sentiments towards it, and as confidently as they are unfounded. Only a few weeks ago it was stated categorically by some anonymous correspondent of a Liverpool paper, with reference to the prospect of my undertaking the task on which I am now employed, that it was, "in fact understood that at one time Dr. Newman was on the point of uniting with Dr. Dollinger[2] and his party, and that it required the earnest persuasion of several members of the Roman Catholic Episcopate to prevent him from taking that step,"[3]—an unmitigated and most ridiculous untruth in every word of it, nor would it be worth while to notice it here, except for its connexion with the subject on which I am entering.[4]

But the explanation of such reports about me is easy. They arise from forgetfulness on the part of those who spread

---

[1] Vatican I, 8 December, 1869 - 20 October 1870. There were four sessions.

[2] Johann Joseph Ignaz Döllinger (1799-1890), Professor of Church history. Newman consulted him about his Rectorship of the Catholic University and hoped he would contribute lectures (*AW* pp. 281, 287; *Campaign II*, pp.10, 24, 25, 141, 147, 175, 391). Dollinger had attacked the temporal power of the Pope in 1861 and in his *Letters of Janus* criticized the Council and refused to submit to the doctrine of infallibility. He was excommunicated by the Bishop of Munich in 1871 and worked with the schismatic Old Catholic Church, becoming president of the Bavarian Royal Academy of Sciences.

[3] See also the rumours that Newman was about to return to the Church of England infra p.[349].

[4] See Newman's letter to the Editor of the *Liverpool Post* 19 November 1874 *LD* 27 pp.157-8.

them, that there are two sides of ecclesiastical acts, that right ends are often prosecuted by very unworthy means, and that in consequence those who, like myself, oppose a line of action, are not necessarily opposed to the issue for which it has been adopted. Jacob gained by wrong means his destined [300] blessing.[5] "All are not Israelites, who are of Israel,"[6] and there are partisans of Rome who have not the sanctity and wisdom of Rome herself.

I am not referring to anything which took place within the walls of the Council chambers; of that of course we know nothing;[7] but even though things occurred there which it is not pleasant to dwell upon, that would not at all affect, not by an hair's breadth, the validity of the resulting definition, as I shall presently show. What I felt deeply, and ever shall feel, while life lasts, is the violence and cruelty of journals and other publications, which, taking as they professed to do the Catholic side, employed themselves by their rash language (though, of course, they did not mean it so), in unsettling the weak in faith, throwing back inquirers, and shocking the Protestant mind. Nor do I speak of publications only; a feeling was too prevalent in many places that no one could be true to God and His Church, who had any pity on troubled souls, or any scruple of "scandalizing those little ones who believe in" Christ, and of "despising and destroying him for whom He died."

It was this most keen feeling, which made me say, as I did continually, "I will not believe that the Pope's Infallibility will be defined, till defined it is."

Moreover, a private letter of mine became public property.[8] That letter, to which Mr. Gladstone has referred with a compliment to me which I have not merited, was one of the most confidential I ever wrote in my life. I wrote it to

---

[5] Gen 27:18-30
[6] Rom 9:6
[7] There is an obligation of secrecy on the Council Fathers.
[8] To Bishop Ullathorne 28 January 1870 *LD* 25 pp.18-29.

[301] my own Bishop, under a deep sense of the responsibility I should incur, were I not to speak out to him my whole mind. I put the matter from me when I had said my say, and kept no proper copy of the letter. To my dismay I saw it in the public prints: to this day I do not know, nor suspect, how it got there;[9] certainly from no want of caution in the quarter to which it was addressed. I cannot withdraw it, for I never put it forward, so it will remain on the columns of newspapers whether I will or not; but I withdraw it as far as I can, by declaring that it was never meant for the public eye.

1. So much as to my posture of mind before the Definition: now I will set down how I felt after it. On July 24, 1870, I wrote as follows:[10]—

"I saw the new Definition yesterday, and am pleased at its moderation—that is, if the doctrine in question is to be defined at all. The terms are vague and comprehensive; and, personally, I have no difficulty in admitting it. The question is, does it come to me with the authority of an Ecumenical Council?

"Now the *primâ facie* argument is in favour of its having that authority. The Council was legitimately called; it was more largely attended than any Council before it; and innumerable prayers from the whole of Christendom, have preceded and attended it, and merited a happy issue of its proceedings.

"Were it not then for certain circumstances, under which the Council made the definition, I should receive that definition at once. Even as it is, if I were called upon to profess it, I should be unable, considering it came from the

[302] Holy Father and the competent local authorities, at once to refuse to do so. On the other hand, it cannot be denied that

---

[9] "There can be little doubt that Clifford [bishop of Clifton] was the culprit and he later admitted to Ullathorne that Errington [Archbishop of Trebizond] had taken a copy of his copy." Judith Champ *William Bernard Ullathorne* Gracewing 2006 p.373.

[10] To Ambrose Phillipps de Lisle 24 July 1870 *LD* 25 pp.164-6.

there are reasons for a Catholic, till better informed, to suspend his judgment on its validity.

"We all know that ever since the opening of the Council, there has been a strenuous opposition to the definition of the doctrine; and that, at the time when it was actually passed, more than eighty Fathers absented themselves from the Council, and would have nothing to do with its act. But, if the fact be so, that the Fathers were not unanimous, is the definition valid?[11] This depends on the question whether unanimity, at least moral, is or is not necessary for its validity? As at present advised I think it is; certainly Pius IV. lays great stress on the unanimity of the Fathers in the Council of Trent. 'Quibus rebus perfectis,' he says in his Bull of Promulgation, 'concilium tantâ *omnium qui illi interfuerent* concordiâ peractum fuit, ut consensum plane *a Domino* effectum esse constiterit; idque in nostris atque omnium oculis valdè mirabile fuerit."[12]

"Far different has been the case now,—though the Council is not yet finished. But, if I must now at once decide what to think of it, I should consider that all turned on what the dissentient Bishops now do.

"If they separate and go home without acting as a body, if they act only individually, or as individuals, and each in his own way, then I should not recognize in their opposition to the majority that force, firmness, and unity of view, which creates a real case of want of moral unanimity in the Council.

"Again, if the Council continues to sit, if the dissentient [303] Bishops more or less take part in it, and concur in its acts; if there is a new Pope, and he continues the policy of the present; and if the Council terminates without any reversal or modification of the definition, or any effective movement against it on the part of the dissentients, then again there will

---

[11] See Postscript pp.[370-2].
[12] "The Council took place in an atmosphere of total agreement among those who were present so that it could be plainly seen to be brought about by the Lord; in our eyes and those of all, it will be seen as truly wonderful."

be good reason for saying that the want of a moral unanimity has not been made out.

"And further, if the definition is consistently received by the whole body of the faithful, as valid, or as the expression of a truth, then too it will claim our assent by the force of the great dictum, 'Securus judicat orbis terrarum.'[13]

"This indeed is a broad principle by which all acts of the rulers of the Church are ratified.[14] But for it, we might reasonably question some of the past Councils or their acts."

Also I wrote as follows to a friend, who was troubled at the way in which the dogma was passed, in order to place before him in various points of view the duty of receiving it:—

July 27, 1870.[15]

"I have been thinking over the subject which just now gives you and me with thousands of others, who care for religion, so much concern.

"First, till better advised, nothing shall make me say that a mere majority in a Council, as opposed to a moral unanimity, in itself creates an obligation to receive its dogmatic decrees. This is a point of history and precedent, and of course on further examination I may find myself wrong in the view which I take of history and precedent; but I do not, cannot see, that a majority in the present Council can of itself *rule* its own sufficiency, without such external testimony.

[304]

"But there are other means by which I can be brought under the obligation of receiving a doctrine as a dogma. If I am clear that there is a primitive and uninterrupted tradition, as of the divinity of our Lord; or where a high probability drawn from Scripture or Tradition is partially or probably

---

[13] 'The judgement of the whole Church has no chance of being wrong'. Augustine, *Contra Epistolam Parmeniani* Book 3 ch. 3.

[14] Newman explains 'ratified' means 'brought home to us as authentic.' See Postscript infra p.[372].

[15] To Ambrose St John *LD* 25 pp. 167-8.

confirmed by the Church. Thus a particular Catholic might be so nearly sure that the promise to Peter in Scripture proves that the infallibility of Peter is a necessary dogma, as only to be kept from holding it as such by the absence of any judgment on the part of the Church, so that the present unanimity of the Pope and 500 Bishops, even though not sufficient to constitute a formal Synodal act, would at once put him in the position, and lay him under the obligation, of receiving the doctrine as a dogma, that is, to receive it with its anathema.[16]

"Or again, if nothing definitely sufficient from Scripture or Tradition can be brought to contradict a definition, the fact of a legitimate Superior having defined it, may be an obligation in conscience to receive it with an internal assent. For myself, ever since I was a Catholic, I have held the Pope's infallibility as a matter of theological opinion; at least, I see nothing in the Definition which necessarily contradicts Scripture, Tradition, or History; and the "Doctor Ecclesiæ" (as the Pope is styled by the Council of Florence) bids me accept it. In this case, I do not receive it on the word of the Council, but on the Pope's self-assertion.

"And I confess, the fact that all along for so many [305] centuries the Head of the Church and Teacher of the faithful and Vicar of Christ has been allowed by God to assert virtually his own infallibility, is a great argument in favour of the validity of his claim.

"Another ground for receiving the dogma, still not upon the direct authority of the Council, or with acceptance of the validity of its act *per se*, is the consideration that our Merciful Lord would not care so little for His elect people, the multitude of the faithful, as to allow their visible Head, and such a large number of Bishops to lead them into error, and an error so serious, if an error it be. This consideration leads me to accept the doctrine as a dogma, indirectly indeed from

---

[16] See infra n. 47.

the Council, but not so much from a Council, as from the Pope and a very large number of Bishops. The question is not whether they had a right to impose, or even were right in imposing dogma on the faithful; but whether, having done so, I have not an obligation to accept it, according to the maxim, 'Fieri non debuit, factum valet.'"[17]

This letter, written before the minority had melted away, insists on this principle, that a Council's definition would have a virtual claim on our reception, even though it were not passed *conciliariter*,[18] but in some indirect way; the great object of a Council being in some way[19] or other to declare the judgment of the Church. I think the Third Ecumenical[20] will furnish an instance of what I mean. There the question in dispute was settled and defined, even before certain constituent portions of the Episcopal body had made their appearance; and this, with a protest of sixty-eight of the Bishops then present against the opening of the Council. When the expected party[21] arrived, these did more than protest against the definition which had been carried;[22] they actually anathematized the Fathers who carried it, and in this state of disunion the Council ended. How then was its definition valid? In consequence of after events, which I suppose must be considered complements, and integral portions of the Council. The heads of the various parties entered into correspondence with each other, and at the end of two years their differences with each other were arranged.

[306]

---

[17] 'What ought not to be done becomes valid when it is done' (maxim of Roman civil law).

[18] decided by the Council in full session

[19] 1875 ed.: Newman adds "…but in some indirect way: as for instance, to use a Parliamentary expression, in general committee …."

[20] The Council of Ephesus, 431.

[21] 1875 ed.: "when the remaining 43 arrived."

[22] 1875 ed.: "… who carried it, whose number seems to have stood altogether at 124 against 111, and in this state…" In his Letter to Emily Bowles 5 April 1875 *LD* 27 p.267 Newman says, "I was rash in having given my own side of the numbers voting at Ephesus, and in the second Edition I cut them out". See Postscript pp.[372-5].

There are those who have no belief in the authority of Councils at all, and feel no call upon them to discriminate between one Council and another; but Anglicans, who are so fierce against the Vatican, and so respectful towards the Ephesine, should consider what good reason they have for swallowing the third Council, while they strain out the nineteenth.

The Council of Ephesus furnishes us with another remark, bearing upon the Vatican. It was natural for men who were in the minority at Ephesus to think that the faith of the Church had been brought into the utmost peril by the definition of the Council which they had unsuccessfully opposed. They had opposed it on the conviction that the definition gave great encouragement to religious errors in the opposite extreme to those which it condemned; and, in fact, I think that, humanly speaking, the peril was extreme. The event proved it to be so, when twenty years afterwards another Council was held under the successors of the majority at Ephesus[23] and carried triumphantly those very errors whose eventual success had been predicted by the minority. But Providence is never [307] wanting to His Church. St. Leo, the Pope of the day, interfered with this heretical Council, and the innovating party was stopped in its career. Its acts were cancelled at the great Council of Chalcedon, the Fourth Ecumenical,[24] which was held under the Pope's guidance, and which, without of course touching the definition of the Third, which had been settled once for all, trimmed the balance of doctrine by completing it, and excluded for ever from the Church those errors which seemed to have received some sanction at Ephesus. There is nothing of course that can be reversed in the definitions of the Vatican Council; but the series of its

---

[23] 'Robber Council' of Ephesus (Latrocinium), 449.
[24] Chalcedon, 451. Newman had given a dramatic account of these events in *Dev* pp.297-312.

acts was cut short by the great war,[25] and, should the need arise (which is not likely) to set right a false interpretation, another Leo will be given us for the occasion; "in monte Dominus videbit."[26]

In this remark, made for the benefit of those who need it, as I do not myself, I shelter myself under the following passage of Molina,[27] which a friend has pointed out to me:—"Though the Holy Ghost has always been present to the Church, to hinder error in her definitions, and in consequence they are all most true and consistent, yet it is not therefore to be denied, that God, when any matters have to be defined, requires of the Church a cooperation and investigation of those matters, and that, in proportion to the quality of the men who meet together in Councils, to the investigation and diligence which is applied, and the greater or less experience and knowledge which is possessed more at one time than at other times, definitions more or less perspicuous are drawn up and matters are defined more exactly and completely at [308] one time than at other times ... And, whereas by disputations, persevering reading, meditation, and investigation of matters, there is wont to be increased in course of time the knowledge and understanding of the same, and the Fathers of the later Councils are assisted by the investigation and definitions of the former, hence it arises that the definitions of later Councils are wont to be more luminous, fuller, more accurate and exact than those of the earlier. Moreover, it belongs to the later Councils to interpret and to define more exactly and fully what in earlier Councils have been defined less clearly, fully and exactly." (*De Concord. Lib. Arbit.*, &c., xiii. 15, p.

---

[25] The Franco-Prussian war caused the French troops guarding Rome to be withdrawn, allowing the forces of the Italian government to enter the city; the assembled bishops fled. The Council was initially prorogued and was only closed officially with the announcement of Vatican II.

[26] "On the mountain the Lord will see" Gen 22:14 in the Vulgate translation.

[27] Luis de Molina (1535-1600), Jesuit theologian who taught at Coimbra and published his *De concordia liberi arbitrii cum gratiae donis* ('Concerning the harmony of free will with the gifts of grace') in 1588.

59.) So much on the circumstances under which the Vatican Council passed its definition.

2. The other main objection made to the Council is founded upon its supposed neglect of history in the decision which its Definition embodies. This objection is touched upon by Mr. Gladstone in the beginning of his Pamphlet, where he speaks of its "repudiation of ancient history," and I have an opportunity given me of noticing it here.

He asserts that, during the last forty years, "more and more have the assertions of continuous uniformity of doctrine" in the Catholic Church "receded into scarcely penetrable shadow. More and more have another series of assertions, of a living authority, ever ready to open, adopt, and shape Christian doctrine according to the times, taken their place." Accordingly, he considers that a dangerous opening has been made in the authoritative teaching of the Church for the repudiation of ancient truth and the rejection of new. However, as I understand him, he withdraws this charge from the controversy he has initiated (though not from his Pamphlet) as far as it is aimed at the pure theology of the Church. So far it "belongs," he says, "to the theological domain," and "is a matter unfit for him to discuss, as it is a question of divinity." It has been, then, no duty of mine to consider it, except as it relates to matters ecclesiastical; but I am unwilling, when a charge has been made against our theology, unsupported indeed, yet unretracted, to leave it altogether without reply; and that the more, because, after renouncing "questions of divinity" at p. 14, nevertheless Mr. Gladstone brings them forward again at p. 15, speaking, as he does, of the "deadly blows of 1854 and 1870 at the old, historic, scientific, and moderate school" by the definitions of the Immaculate Conception and Papal Infallibility.

Mr. Gladstone then insists on the duty of "maintaining the truth and authority of history, and the inestimable value of the historic spirit;" and so far of course I have the pleasure of

[309]

heartily agreeing with him. As the Church is a sacred and divine creation, so in like manner her history, with its wonderful evolution of events, the throng of great actors who have a part in it, and its multiform literature, stained though its annals are with human sin and error, and recorded on no system, and by uninspired authors, still is a sacred work also; and those who make light of it, or distrust its lessons, incur a grave responsibility. But it is not every one that can read its pages rightly; and certainly I cannot follow Mr. Gladstone's [310] reading of it. He is too well informed indeed, too large in his knowledge, too acute and comprehensive in his views, not to have an acquaintance with history,[28] far beyond the run of even highly educated men; still when he accuses us of deficient attention to history, one cannot help asking, whether he does not, as a matter of course, take for granted as true the principles for using it familiar with Protestant divines, and denied by our own, and in consequence whether his impeachment of us does not resolve itself into the fact that he is Protestant and we are Catholics. Nay, has it occurred to him that perhaps it is the fact, that we have views on the relation of History to Dogma different from those which Protestants maintain? And is he so certain of the facts of History in detail, of their relevancy, and of their drift, as to have a right, I do not say to have an opinion of his own, but to publish to the world, on his own warrant, that we have "repudiated ancient history"? He publicly charges us, not merely with having "neglected" it, or "garbled" its evidence, or with having contradicted certain ancient usages or doctrines to which it bears witness, but he says "repudiated." He could not have used a stronger term, supposing the Vatican Council had, by a formal act, cut itself off from early times, instead of professing, as it does (hypocritically, if you will, but still professing) to speak, "supported by Holy

---

[28] Gladstone was the author of *Studies of Homer and the Homeric Age* (1858) and *Juventus Mundi: The Gods and Men of the Heroic Age* (1876).

Scripture and the decrees both of preceding Popes and General Councils," and "faithfully adhering to the aboriginal tradition of the Church." Ought any one but an *oculatus testis*,[29] a man whose profession was to acquaint himself with the details of history, to claim to himself the right of bringing, on his own authority, so extreme a charge against so august [311] a power, so inflexible and rooted in its traditions through the long past, as Mr. Gladstone would admit the Roman Church to be?

Of course I shall be reminded that, though Mr. Gladstone cannot be expected to speak on so large a department of knowledge with the confidence decorous in one who has made a personal study of it, there are others who have a right to do so; and that by those others he is corroborated and sanctioned. There are authors, it may be said, of so commanding an authority from their learning and their honesty, that, for the purposes of discussion or of controversy, what they say may be said by any one else without presumption or risk of confutation. I will never say a word of my own against those learned and distinguished men to whom I refer.[30] No: their present whereabout, wherever it is, is to me a thought full of melancholy. It is a tragical event, both for them and for us, that they have left us. It robs us of a great *prestige*; they have left none to take their place. I think them utterly wrong in what they have done and are doing; and, moreover, I agree as little in their view of history as in their acts. Extensive as may be their historical knowledge, I have no reason to think that they, more than Mr. Gladstone, would accept the position which History holds among the *Loci Theologici*[31] as Catholic theologians determine it; and I am denying not their report of facts, but their use of the facts

---

[29] eye witness

[30] A reference to Dr. Döllinger and those who rejected the dogma.

[31] The sources of theological knowledge: the Magisterium, Revelation in Scripture, Tradition, the Fathers of the Church, theologians, the liturgy and canon law. In Protestant theology this means the principal subdivisions of the faith.

they report, and that, because of that special stand-point from which they view the relations existing between the records of History and the enunciations of Popes and Councils. They [312] seem to me to expect from History more than History can furnish, and to have too little confidence in the Divine Promise and Providence as guiding and determining those enunciations.

Why should Ecclesiastical History, any more than the text of Scripture, contain in it "the whole counsel of God"?[32] Why should private judgment be unlawful in interpreting Scripture against the voice of authority, and yet be lawful in the interpretation of history?[33] There are those who make short work of questions such as these by denying authoritative interpretation altogether; that is their private concern, and no one has a right to inquire into their reason for so doing; but the case would be different were one of them to come forward publicly, and to arraign others, without first confuting their theological *præambula*,[34] for repudiating history, or for repudiating the Bible.

For myself, I would simply confess that no doctrine of the Church can be rigorously proved by historical evidence: but at the same time that no doctrine can be simply disproved by it. Historical evidence reaches a certain way, more or less, towards a proof of the Catholic doctrines; often nearly the whole way; sometimes it goes only as far as to point in their direction; sometimes there is only an absence of evidence for a conclusion contrary to them; nay, sometimes there is an apparent leaning of the evidence to a contrary conclusion, which has to be explained;—in all cases there is a margin left for the exercise of faith in the word of the Church. He who believes the dogmas of the Church only because he has reasoned them out of History, is scarcely a Catholic. It is the

---

[32] Acts 20:27

[33] Newman contrasts Dölllinger's position with his own.

[34] things which go before; in this context, pre-suppositions

Church's dogmatic use of History in which the Catholic believes; and she uses other informants also, Scripture, [313] tradition, the ecclesiastical sense or φρόνημα,[35] and a subtle ratiocinative[36] power, which in its origin is a divine gift. There is nothing of bondage or "renunciation of mental freedom" in this view, any more than in the converts of the Apostles believing what the Apostles might preach to them or teach them out of Scripture.

What has been said of History in relation to the formal Definitions of the Church, applies also to the exercise of Ratiocination. Our logical powers, too, being a gift from God, may claim to have their informations respected; and Protestants sometimes accuse our theologians, for instance, the medieval schoolmen, of having used them in divine matters a little too freely. Still it has ever been our teaching and our protest that, as there are doctrines which lie beyond the direct evidence of history, so there are doctrines which transcend the discoveries of reason; and, after all, whether they are more or less recommended to us by the one informant or the other, in all cases the immediate motive in the mind of a Catholic for his reception of them is, not that they are proved to him by Reason or by History, but because Revelation has declared them by means of that high ecclesiastical *Magisterium* which is their legitimate exponent.[37]

What has been said applies also to those other truths, with which Ratiocination has more to do than History, which are sometimes called developments of Christian doctrine, truths

---

[35] "A sort of instinct deep in the bosom of the mystical body of Christ", Newman 'On Consulting the Faithful in Matters of Doctrine' *The Rambler* July 1859, quoted by John Colson ed. London 1961 p.73.

[36] based on accurate, logical thinking

[37] Jan Walgrave says that Newman is arguing here that "The methods of theology by themselves are nearly always inadequate to demonstrate conclusively any single article of faith. The only decisive factor is the Church's dogmatic use of the results attained in theology. The word of the Church itself, uttered by the *magisterium*, gives each doctrine the weight that demands the belief of the faithful" op. cit. p.65.

which are not upon the surface of the Apostolic *depositum*[38]—that is, the legacy of Revelation,—but which from time to time are brought into form by theologians, and sometimes have been proposed to the faithful by the Church, as direct objects of faith. No Catholic would hold that they ought to be logically deduced in their fulness and exactness from the belief of the first centuries, but only this,—that, on the assumption of the Infallibility of the Church (which will overcome every objection except a contradiction in thought), there is nothing greatly to try the reason in such difficulties as occur in reconciling those evolved doctrines with the teaching of the ancient Fathers; such development being evidently the new form, explanation, transformation, or carrying out of what in substance was held from the first, what the Apostles said, but have not recorded in writing, or would necessarily have said under our circumstances, or if they had been asked, or in view of certain uprisings of error, and in that sense being really portions of the legacy of truth, of which the Church, in all her members, but especially in her hierarchy, is the divinely appointed trustee.

Such an evolution of doctrine has been, as I would maintain, a law of the Church's teaching from the earliest times, and in nothing is her title of "semper eadem"[39] more remarkably illustrated than in the correspondence of her ancient and modern exhibition of it. As to the ecclesiastical Acts of 1854 and 1870, I think with Mr. Gladstone that the principle of doctrinal development, and that of authority, have never in the proceedings of the Church been so freely and largely used as in the Definitions then promulgated to the faithful; but I deny that at either time the testimony of history was repudiated or perverted. The utmost that can be fairly said by an opponent against the theological decisions of those years is, that antecedently to the event, it might appear that

[314]

[315]

---

[38] the sum of revealed truths committed by Christ to his Church (see 1 Tim 6:20).
[39] See supra.

314

there were no sufficient historical grounds in behalf of either of them—I do not mean for a personal belief in either, but—for the purpose of converting a doctrine long existing in the Church into a dogma, and making it a portion of the Catholic Creed. This adverse anticipation was proved to be a mistake by the fact of the definition being made.

3. I will not pass from this question of History without a word[40] about Pope Honorius,[41] whose condemnation by anathema in the Sixth Ecumenical Council, is certainly a strong *primâ facie* argument against the Pope's doctrinal infallibility. His case is this:—Sergius, Patriarch of Constantinople, favoured, or rather did not condemn, a doctrine concerning our Lord's Person which afterwards the Sixth Council pronounced to be heresy.[42] He consulted Pope Honorius upon the subject, who in two formal letters declared his entire concurrence with Sergius's opinion. Honorius died in peace, but, more than forty years after him, the Sixth Ecumenical Council was held, which condemned him as a heretic on the score of those two letters. The simple question is, whether the heretical documents proceeded from him as an infallible authority or as a private Bishop.

Now I observe that, whereas the Vatican Council has determined that the Pope is infallible only when he speaks *ex cathedrâ*, and that, in order to speak *ex cathedrâ*, he must at least speak "as exercising the office of Pastor and Doctor of all Christians, defining, by virtue of his Apostolical authority, a doctrine whether of faith or of morals for the acceptance of

---

[40] 1875 ed.: "Here I will say just a few words on the case of Pope Honorius…"

[41] Honorius I (635-8)

[42] In a fragment of a letter to Sergius he accepted the formula of Chalcedon that in Christ there were two natures, one human and one divine but agreed with Sergius' belief in one energy (Monotheletism) while recommending silence as to one or two operations. It was felt that this would be acceptable to the Monophysites. Honorius was anathematized at the Third Council of Constantinople in 681 in its twelfth session. He had not however compromised the purity of Roman tradition because he had never claimed to represent it and did not intend his opinion to bind the whole Church. See John Chapman *The Condemnation of Honorius* London 1907.

[316]   the universal Church" (though Mr. Gladstone strangely says, p. 34, "There is *no* established or accepted definition of the phrase *ex cathedrâ*"), from this Pontifical and dogmatic explanation of the phrase it follows, that, whatever Honorius said in answer to Sergius, and whatever he held, his words were not *ex cathedrâ*, and therefore did not proceed from his infallibility.

   I say so first, because he could not fulfil the above conditions of an *ex cathedrâ* utterance, if he did not actually *mean* to fulfil them. The question is unlike the question about the Sacraments; external and positive acts, whether material actions or formal words, speak for themselves. Teaching on the other hand has no sacramental visible signs; it is an *opus operantis*,[43] and mainly a question of intention. Who would say that the architriclinus[44] at the wedding-feast who said, "Thou hast kept the good wine until now," was teaching the Christian world, though the words have a great ethical and evangelical sense? What is the worth of a signature, if a man does not consider he is signing? The Pope cannot address his people East and West, North and South, without meaning it, as if his very voice, the sounds from his lips, could literally be heard from pole to pole; nor can he exert his "Apostolical authority" without knowing he is doing so; nor can he draw up a form of words and use care and make an effort in doing so accurately, without intention to do so; and, therefore, no words of Honorius proceeded from his prerogative of infallible teaching, which were not accompanied with the intention of exercising that prerogative; and who will dream

[317]   of saying, be he Anglican, Protestant, unbeliever, or on the other hand Catholic, that Honorius on the occasion in question did actually intend to exert that infallible teaching

---

[43] lit. 'the work of the worker', i.e. depending on the disposition of the operator. In the 1875 edition in place of visible signs Newman said, "It is mainly a question of intention."

[44] The steward at the marriage feast of Cana. John 2:10.

voice which is heard so distinctly in the *Quantâ curâ* and the *Pastor Æternus*?[45]

What resemblance do these letters of his, written almost as private instructions, bear to the "Pius Episcopus, Servus Servorum Dei, Sacro approbante Concilio, ad *perpetuam rei memoriam*,"[46] or with the "Si quis huic nostræ definitioni contradicere (quod Deus avertat), præsumpserit, *anathema sit*"[47] of the *Pastor Æternus*? what to the "Venerabilibus fratribus, Patriarchis primatibus, Archiepiscopis, et Episcopis *universis*,[48] &c., with the "reprobamus, proscribimus, atque damnamus,"[49] and the date and signature, "Datum Romæ apud Sanctum Petrum, Die 8 Dec. anno 1864, &c., Pius P.P. IX." of the *Quantâ curâ*?

Secondly, it is no part of our doctrine, as I shall say in my next section, that the discussions previous to a Council's definition, or to an *ex cathedrâ* utterance of a Pope, are infallible, and these letters of Honorius on their very face are nothing more than portions of a discussion with a view to some final decision.

For these two reasons the condemnation of Honorius by the Council in no sense compromises the doctrine of Papal Infallibility. At the utmost it only decides that Honorius in his own person was a heretic, which is inconsistent with no Catholic doctrine; but we may rather hope and believe that the anathema fell, not upon him, but upon his letters in their objective sense, he not intending personally what his letters legitimately expressed.

4. And I have one remark to make upon the argumentative [318] method by which the Vatican Council was carried on to its

---

[45] In the 1875 edition: "…the infallible teaching voice which has been dogmatically recognized in the nineteenth?"

[46] "Pius, Bishop, Servant of the Servants of God, the Holy Council approving, for perpetual remembrance."

[47] "If any should presume to contradict this our definition (which God forbid) let him be anathema."

[48] "Venerable brothers, patriarchs, primates, and *all* bishops"

[49] "we reject, proscribe and condemn"

definition. The *Pastor Æternus* refers to various witnesses as contributing their evidence towards the determination of the contents of the *depositum*, such as Tradition, the Fathers and Councils, History, but especially Scripture. For instance, the Bull,[50] speaks of the Gospel ("juxta Evangelii testimonia,"[51] c. 1) and of Scripture ("manifesta S.S. Scripturarum doctrina,"[52] c. 1: "apertis S.S. Literarum testimoniis,"[53] c. 3. "S.S. Scripturis consentanea,"[54] c. 4.)[55] And it lays an especial stress on three passages of Scripture in particular—viz., "Thou art Peter," &c., Matthew xvi. 16-19; "I have prayed for thee," &c., Luke xxii. 32, and "Feed My sheep," &c., John xxi. 15-17. Now I wish all objectors to this method of ours, viz. of reasoning from Scripture, would view it in the light of the following passage in the great philosophical work of Butler,[56] Bishop of Durham.

He writes as follows:—"As it is owned the whole scheme of Scripture is not yet understood, so, if it ever comes to be understood, before the 'restitution of all things,' and without miraculous interpositions, it must be in the same way as natural knowledge is come at, by the continuance and progress of learning and of liberty, and by particular persons attending to, comparing, and pursuing intimations scattered up and down it, which are overlooked and disregarded by the generality of the world. For this is the way in which all improvements are made by thoughtful men tracing on obscure hints, as it were, dropped us by nature accidentally, or which seem to come into our minds by chance. Nor is it at all incredible that a book, which has been so long in the

[319]

---

[50] Pius IX issued a Bull in 1871 publishing the Constitution *Pastor Aeternus*. See p.[233].

[51] "according to the testimonies of the Gospel"

[52] "the clear teaching of the Most Holy Scriptures"

[53] "the open evidence of the Most Holy writings"

[54] "in harmony with the Most Holy Scriptures"

[55] *DS* 3059, 3054, 3053.

[56] *The Analogy of Religion Natural and Revealed to the Constitution and the Course of Nature* (1736).

possession of mankind, should contain many truths as yet undiscovered. For all the same phenomena, and the same faculties of investigation, from which such great discoveries in natural knowledge have been made in the present and last age, were equally in the possession of mankind several thousand years before. And possibly it might be intended that events, as they come to pass, should open and ascertain the meaning of several parts of Scripture," ii. 3, *vide* also ii. 4, fin.

What has the long history of the contest for and against the Pope's infallibility been, but a growing insight through centuries into the meaning of those three texts, to which I just now referred, ending at length by the Church's definitive recognition of the doctrine thus gradually manifested to her?

§ 9. *The Vatican Definition.*

NOW I am to speak of the Vatican definition, by which the doctrine of the Pope's infallibility has become *de fide*, that is, a truth necessary to be believed, as being included in the original divine revelation, for those terms, revelation, *depositum*, dogma, and *de fide*, are correlatives; and I begin with a remark which suggests the drift of all I have to say about it. It is this:—that so difficult a virtue is faith, even with the special grace of God, in proportion as the reason is exercised, so difficult is it to assent inwardly to propositions, verified to us neither by reason nor experience, but depending for their reception on the word of the Church as God's oracle, that she has ever shown the utmost care to contract, as far as possible, the range of truths and the sense of propositions, of which she demands this absolute reception. "The Church," says Pallavicini,[1] "as far as may be, has ever abstained from imposing upon the minds of men that commandment, the most arduous of the Christian Law—viz., to believe obscure matters without doubting."[*] To co-operate in this charitable duty has been one special work of her theologians, and rules are laid down by herself, by tradition, and by custom, to assist

[321]

[*] Quoted by Father Ryder (to whom I am indebted for other of my references), in his "Idealism in Theology," p. 25.[2]

---

[1] Francisco Maria Sforza Pallavicini (1607-69), Cardinal and author of *Assertiones theologicae* 1649.

[2] Henry Ignatius Dudley Ryder. See supra p.[17].

them in the task. She only speaks when it is necessary to speak; but hardly has she spoken out magisterially some great general principle, when she sets her theologians to work to explain her meaning in the concrete, by strict interpretation of its wording, by the illustration of its circumstances, and by the recognition of exceptions, in order to make it as tolerable as possible, and the least of a temptation, to self-willed, independent, or wrongly educated minds. A few years ago it was the fashion among us to call writers, who conformed to this rule of the Church, by the name of "Minimizers;" that day of tyrannous *ipse-dixits*,[3] I trust, is over: Bishop Fessler,[4] a man of high authority, for he was Secretary General of the Vatican Council, and of higher authority still in his work, for it has the approbation of the Sovereign Pontiff, clearly proves to us that a moderation of doctrine, dictated by charity, is not inconsistent with soundness in the faith. Such a sanction, I suppose, will be considered sufficient for the character of the remarks which I am about to make upon definitions in general, and upon the Vatican in particular.[5]

The Vatican definition, which comes to us in the shape of the Pope's Encyclical Bull called the *Pastor Æternus*, declares that "the Pope has that same infallibility which the Church has":[*] to determine therefore what is meant by the [322] infallibility of the Pope we must turn first to consider the

---

[*] Romanum Pontificem eâ infallibilitate pollere, quâ divinus Redemptor Ecclesiam suam in definiendâ doctrinâ de fide vel moribus instructam esse voluit.[6]

---

[3] lit. 'he himself said' - a dogmatic statement supported only by the speaker's authority, as quoted by Cicero in *De natura rerum* I v. 10.

[4] See supra p.[280].

[5] See Postscript pp.[375-6].

[6] "The Roman Pontiff enjoys that infallibility which the Divine Redeemer wished to be taught in his Church in matters of faith or morals." *DS* 3074.

infallibility of the Church. And again, to determine the character of the Church's infallibility, we must consider what is the characteristic of Christianity, considered as a revelation of God's will. Our Divine Master might have communicated to us heavenly truths without telling us that they came from Him, as it is commonly thought He has done in the case of heathen nations; but He willed the Gospel to be a revelation acknowledged and authenticated, to be public, fixed, and permanent; and accordingly, as Catholics hold, He framed a Society of men to be its home, its instrument, and its guarantee. The rulers of that Association are the legal trustees, so to say, of the sacred truths which He spoke to the Apostles by word of mouth. As He was leaving them, He gave them their great commission, and bade them "teach" their converts all over the earth, "to observe all things whatever He had commanded them;" and then He added, "Lo, I am with you always, even to the end of the world."[7]

Here, first, He told them to "teach" His revealed Truth; next, "to the consummation of all things;" thirdly, for their encouragement, He said that He would be with them "all days," all along, on every emergency or occasion, until that consummation. They had a duty put upon them of teaching their Master's words, a duty which they could not fulfil in the perfection which fidelity required, without His help; therefore came His promise to be with them in their performance of it. Nor did that promise of supernatural help end with the Apostles personally, for He adds, "to the consummation of the world," implying that the Apostles would have successors, and engaging that He would be with those successors as He had been with them.

[323]

---

[7] Matt 28:18-20

The same safeguard of the Revelation—viz. an authoritative, permanent tradition of teaching, is insisted on by an informant of equal authority with St. Matthew, but altogether independent of him, I mean St. Paul. He calls the Church "the pillar and ground of the Truth;"[8] and he bids his convert Timothy, when he had become a ruler in that Church, to "take heed unto his doctrine,"[9] to "keep the deposit"[10] of the faith, and to "commit" the things which he had heard from himself "to faithful men who should be fit to teach others."[11]

This is how Catholics understand the Scripture record, nor does it appear how it can otherwise be understood; but, when we have got as far as this, and look back, we find that we have by implication made profession of a further doctrine. For, if the Church, initiated in the Apostles and continued in their successors, has been set up for the direct object of protecting, preserving, and declaring the Revelation, and that, by means of the Guardianship and Providence of its Divine Author, we are led on to perceive that, in asserting this, we are in other words asserting, that, so far as the message entrusted to it is concerned, the Church is infallible; for what is meant by infallibility in teaching but that the teacher in his teaching is secured from error? and how can fallible man be thus secured except by a supernatural infallible guidance? And what can have been the object of the words, "I am with you all along to the end," but to give

---

[8] 1 Tim 3:15

[9] 1 Tim 4:16

[10] 1 Tim 6:20. Both the King James and the Douai bible translate 'deposit' as 'that which is committed to thy trust'. However, St. Paul uses a single word here, παραθήκην, meaning something which has been deposited, for example a sum of money. The Vulgate translated it as 'depositum'. Newman had made the same point quoting this verse in his 1871 revision of his 1836 essay on 'Apostolical Tradition'; see *Ess I* ed. Andrew Nash, Gracewing 2019, pp. xxiii, 130.

[11] 2 Tim 2:2.

thereby an answer by anticipation to the spontaneous, silent alarm of the feeble company of fishermen and labourers, to whom they were addressed, on their finding themselves laden with superhuman duties and responsibilities?

Such then being, in its simple outline, the infallibility of the Church, such too will be the Pope's infallibility, as the Vatican Fathers have defined it. And if we find that by means of this outline we are able to fill out in all important respects the idea of a Council's infallibility, we shall thereby be ascertaining in detail what has been defined in 1870 about the infallibility of the Pope. With an attempt to do this I shall conclude.

1. The Church has the office of teaching, and the matter of that teaching is the body of doctrine, which the Apostles left behind them as her perpetual possession. If a question arises as to what the Apostolic doctrine is on a particular point, she has infallibility promised to her to enable her to answer correctly. And, as by the teaching of the Church is understood, not the teaching of this or that Bishop, but their united voice, and a Council[12] is the form the Church must take, in order that all men may recognize that in fact she is teaching on any point in dispute, so in like manner the Pope must come before us in some special form or posture, if he is to be understood to be exercising his teaching office, and that form is called *ex cathedrâ*.[13] This term is most appropriate, as being on one occasion used by our Lord Himself. When the Jewish doctors taught, they placed themselves in Moses' seat, and spoke *ex cathedrâ*; and then, as He tells us, they were to be obeyed by their people, and that, whatever were their

---

[12] An Ecumenical Council (of which there have been twenty one, according to the Roman Catholic Church) are assemblies of all the bishops.
[13] 'from the throne'

324

private lives or characters. "The Scribes and Pharisees," He says, "are seated on the chair of Moses: all things therefore whatsoever they shall say to you, observe and do; but according to their works do you not, for they say and do not."[14]

2. The forms, by which a General Council is identified as representing the Church herself, are too clear to need drawing out; but what is to be that moral *cathedrâ*, or teaching chair, in which the Pope sits, when he is to be recognized as in the exercise of his infallible teaching? the new definition answers this question. He speaks *ex cathedrâ*, or infallibly, when he speaks, first, as the Universal Teacher; secondly, in the name and with the authority of the Apostles; thirdly, on a point of faith or morals; fourthly, with the purpose of binding every member of the Church to accept and believe his decision.

3. These conditions of course contract the range of his infallibility most materially. Hence Billuart[15] speaking of the Pope says, "Neither in conversation, nor in discussion, nor in interpreting Scripture or the Fathers, nor in consulting, nor in giving his reasons for the point which he has defined, nor in answering letters, nor in private deliberations, supposing he is setting forth his own opinion, is the Pope infallible," t. ii. p. 110.* And for this simple reason, because on these various occasions of speaking his mind, he is not in the chair of the universal doctor.

---

* Also the Swiss Bishops: "The Pope is not infallible as a man, or a theologian, or a priest, or a bishop, or a temporal prince, or a judge, or a legislator, or in his political views, or even in his government of the Church."—*Vid*. Fessler, French Transl., p. iv.

---

[14] Matt. 23:2-4.
[15] Charles René Billuart (1685-1757), Dominican theologian, author of *Summa S. Thomae hodiernis moribus accommodata* (1746-51).

[326]   4. Nor is this all; the greater part of Billuart's negatives refer to the Pope's utterances when he is out of the *Cathedra Petri*, but even, when he is in it, his words do not necessarily proceed from his infallibility.[16] He has no wider prerogative than a Council, and of a Council Perrone[17] says, "Councils are not infallible in the reasons by which they are led, or on which they rely, in making their definition, nor in matters which relate to persons, nor to physical matters which have no necessary connexion with dogma." *Præl. Theol.* t. 2, p. 492.[18] Thus, if a Council has condemned a work of Origen[19] or Theodoret,[20] it did not in so condemning go beyond the work itself; it did not touch the persons of either. Since this holds of a Council, it also holds in the case of the Pope; therefore, supposing a Pope has quoted the so called works of the Areopagite[21] as if really genuine, there is no call on us to believe him; nor again, if he condemned Galileo's Copernicanism,[22] unless the earth's immobility has a "necessary connexion with some dogmatic truth," which the present bearing of the Holy See towards that philosophy virtually denies.

     5. Nor is a Council infallible, even in the prefaces and introductions to its definitions. There are theologians of

---

[16] See Postscript pp.[376-7].

[17] Iam cit supra p.[234]n.

[18] *Praelectiones Theologicae* Rome 1838-43. See supra.

[19] Origen (c. 185-254), biblical exegete and head of the Catechetical School in Alexandria. His views on the fate of the soul after death were controversial: the Second Council of Constantinople in 553 condemned teaching said to have derived from him, Canon 11 *DS* 433.

[20] Theodoret (c 393-466), Bishop of Cyrrhus in 423. The Second Council of Constantinople in 553 also condemned the ideas expressed in opposition to Cyril of Alexandria. He was a friend of Nestorius. See Newman's 'Trials of Theodoret' in *HS* 2 pp.347-58.

[21] Areopagite. Dionysius (5th century) whose mystical writings divided the angels into various choirs and is named after the Dionysius in Acts 17:34.

[22] The earth moves round the sun, not vice versa.

name, as Tournely and Amort,* who contend that even those most instructive *capitula*[23] passed in the Tridentine Council, from which the Canons with anathemas are drawn up, are not portions of the Church's infallible teaching; and the parallel introductions prefixed to the Vatican anathemas have an authority not greater nor less than that of those capitula.

6. Such passages, however, as these are too closely [327] connected with the definitions themselves, not to be what is sometimes called, by a *catachresis*,[24] "proximum fidei;"[25] still, on the other hand, it is true also that, in those circumstances and surroundings of formal definitions, which I have been speaking of, whether on the part of a Council or a Pope, there may be not only no exercise of an infallible voice, but actual error. Thus, in the Third Council, a passage of an heretical author was quoted in defence of the doctrine defined, under the belief he was Pope Julius,[26] and narratives, not trustworthy, are introduced into the Seventh.

This remark and several before it will become intelligible if we consider that neither Pope nor Council are on a level with the Apostles. To the Apostles the whole revelation was given, by the Church it is transmitted; no simply new truth has been given to us since St. John's death; the one office of the Church is to guard "that noble deposit"[27] of truth, as St.

* * *

* *Vid.* Amort. Dem. Cr., pp. 205-6. This applies to the Unam Sanctam, *vid.* Fessler, Engl. Trans., p. 67.[28]

* * *

[23] sections or chapters.

[24] an incorrect use of words

[25] Lit. 'a neighbour of/close to the faith', i.e. connected with the faith, regarded as a truth of revelation but not finally defined as such.

[26] Julius I, Pope 337-51, summoned the Council of Sardica in 342 which rehabilitated Athanasius and confirmed Rome as a final court of appeal.

[27] 2 Tim 1:14: Greek text:'καλὴν παραθήκην'; Vulgate 'bonum depositum'.

[28] Eusebius Amort was a Bavarian theologian who published *Demonstratio critica religionis catholicae* in 1751. See Postscript pp.[376-7].

Paul speaks to Timothy, which the Apostles bequeathed to her, in its fulness and integrity. Hence the infallibility of the Apostles was of a far more positive and wide character than that needed by and granted to the Church. We call it, in the case of the Apostles, inspiration; in the case of the Church, *assistentia*.[29]

Of course there is a sense of the word "inspiration" in which it is common to all members of the Church, and therefore especially to its Bishops, and still more directly to those rulers, when solemnly called together in Council, after much prayer throughout Christendom, and in a frame of mind [328] especially serious and earnest by reason of the work they have in hand. The Paraclete certainly is ever with them, and more effectively in a Council, as being "in Spiritu Sancto congregata;"[30] but I speak of the special and promised aid necessary for their fidelity to Apostolic teaching; and, in order to secure this fidelity, no inward gift of infallibility is needed, such as the Apostles had, no direct suggestion of divine truth, but simply an external guardianship, keeping them off from error (as a man's good Angel, without at all enabling him to walk, might, on a night journey, keep him from pitfalls in his way), a guardianship, saving them, as far as their ultimate decisions are concerned, from the effects of their inherent infirmities, from any chance of extravagance, of confusion of thought, of collision with former decisions or with Scripture, which in seasons of excitement might reasonably be feared.

"Never," says Perrone, "have Catholics taught that the gift of infallibility is given by God to the Church after the manner of inspiration."—t. 2, p. 253. Again: "[Human] media of arriving at the truth are excluded neither by a Council's nor

---

[29] See supra and Postscript pp.[377-8].
[30] "gathered together in the Holy Spirit"

by a Pope's infallibility, for God has promised it, not by way of an infused" or habitual "gift, but by the way of *assistentia*."—*ibid* p. 541.

But since the process of defining truth is human, it is open to the chance of error; what Providence has guaranteed is only this, that there should be no error in the final step, in the resulting definition or dogma.

7. Accordingly, all that a Council, and all that the Pope, is infallible in, is the direct answer to the special question which he happens to be considering; his prerogative does not extend beyond a power, when in his *Cathedra*, of giving that very answer truly. "Nothing," says Perrone, "but the *objects* of dogmatic definitions of Councils are immutable, for in these are Councils infallible, not in their *reasons*," &c.—*ibid*. [329]

8. This rule is so strictly to be observed that, though dogmatic statements are found from time to time in a Pope's Apostolic Letters, &c., yet they are not accounted to be exercises of his infallibility if they are said only *obiter*—by the way, and without direct intention to define. A striking instance of this *sine qua non*[31] condition is afforded by Nicholas I.,[32] who, in a letter to the Bulgarians, spoke as if baptism were valid, when administered simply in our Lord's Name, without distinct mention of the Three Persons; but he is not teaching and speaking *ex cathedrâ*, because no question on this matter was in any sense the occasion of his writing. The question asked of him was concerning the *minister* of baptism—viz., whether a Jew or Pagan could validly baptize; in answering in the affirmative, he added *obiter*, as a private doctor, says Bellarmine,[33] "that the

---

[31] lit. 'without which not', i.e. indispensable
[32] St Nicholas I was Pope 858-67. He wrote his famous *Responsa Nicolai ad consulta Bulgarorum* in 866. *DS* 643, 646.
[33] See supra p.[235].

baptism was valid, whether administered in the name of the three Persons or in the name of Christ only." (*De Rom. Pont.*, iv. 12.)

9. Another limitation is given in Pope Pius's own conditions, set down in the *Pastor Æternus*, for the exercise of infallibility: viz., the proposition defined will be without any claim to be considered binding on the belief of Catholics, unless it is referable to the Apostolic *depositum*, through the channel either of Scripture or Tradition; and, though the Pope is the judge whether it is so referable or not, yet the necessity of his professing to abide by this reference is in itself a certain limitation of his dogmatic action. A Protestant will object indeed that, after his distinctly asserting that the Immaculate Conception and the Papal Infallibility are in Scripture and Tradition, this safeguard against erroneous definitions is not worth much, nor do I say that it is one of the most effective: but anyhow, in consequence of it, no Pope any more than a counsel,[34] could, for instance, introduce Ignatius's Epistles[35] into the Canon of Scripture;—and, as to his dogmatic condemnation of particular books, which, of course, are foreign to the *depositum*, I would say, that, as to their false doctrine there can be no difficulty in condemning that, by means of that Apostolic deposit; nor surely in his condemning the very wording, in which they convey it, when the subject is carefully considered. For the Pope's condemning the language, for instance, of Jansenius[36] is a

[330]

---

[34] presumably a slip for 'Council'

[35] St. Ignatius, Bishop of Antioch (c.35-107), wrote seven letters which are notable for their Catholic doctrine. For this reason some Protestants were unwilling to accept them as really by St. Ignatius. Newman discussed their teaching in *Ess I*, pp.223-64 and their genuineness in *TT* pp.93-136. Their authenticity was established definitively by Joseph Lightfoot in 1885.

[36] Cornelius Otto Jansen (1585-1638), Bishop of Ypres from 1635, was the author of *Augustinus*, published posthumously in 1640. It was condemned by Urban VIII

parallel act to the Church's sanctioning the word "Consubstantial,"[37] and if a Council and the Pope were not infallible so far in their judgment of language, neither Pope nor Council could draw up a dogmatic definition at all, for the right exercise of words is involved in the right exercise of thought.

10. And in like manner, as regards the precepts concerning moral duties, it is not in every such precept that the Pope is infallible.* As a definition of faith must be drawn [331] from the Apostolic *depositum* of doctrine, in order that it may be considered an exercise of infallibility, whether in the Pope or a Council, so too a precept of morals, if it is to be accepted as from an infallible voice, must be drawn from the Moral law, that primary revelation to us from God.

That is, in the first place, it must relate to things in themselves good or evil. If the Pope prescribed lying or revenge, his command would simply go for nothing, as if he had not issued it, because he has no power over the Moral Law. If he forbade his flock to eat any but vegetable food, or to dress in a particular fashion (questions of decency and modesty not coming into the question), he would also be going beyond the province of faith, because such a rule does not relate to a matter in itself good or bad. But if he gave a precept all over the world for the adoption of lotteries instead of tithes or offerings, certainly it would be very hard to prove that he was contradicting the Moral Law, or ruling a practice to be in

---

* It is observable that the *Pastor Æternus* does not speak of "præcepta" at all in its definition of the Pope's Infallibility, only of his "defining doctrine," and of his "definitions."

---

in 1642, but as his followers said he was misquoted, Clement XI condemned the Jansenist teaching as exhibited in the writings of Pasquier Quesnel in 1713. See p.[295n]

[37] By the Fathers at Nicæa in 325.

itself good which was in itself evil; and there are few persons but would allow that it is at least doubtful whether lotteries are abstractedly evil, and in a doubtful matter the Pope is to be believed and obeyed.

However, there are other conditions besides this, necessary for the exercise of Papal infallibility, in moral subjects:—for instance, his definition must relate to things necessary for salvation. No one would so speak of lotteries, nor of a particular dress, nor of a particular kind of food;— such precepts, then, did he make them, would be simply external to the range of his prerogative.

[332] And again, his infallibility in consequence is not called into exercise, unless he speaks to the whole world; for, if his precepts, in order to be dogmatic, must enjoin what is necessary to salvation, they must be necessary for all men. Accordingly orders which issue from him for the observance of particular countries, or political or religious classes, have no claim to be the utterances of his infallibility. If he enjoins upon the hierarchy of Ireland to withstand mixed education, this is no exercise of his infallibility.[38]

It may be added that the field of morals contains so little that is unknown and unexplored, in contrast with revelation and doctrinal fact, which form the domain of faith, that it is difficult to say what portions of moral teaching in the course of 1800 years actually have proceeded from the Pope, or from the Church, or where to look for such. Nearly all that either

---

[38] i. e. schools or colleges open indiscriminately to Catholics and non-Catholics, such as the non-denominational Queen's Colleges founded by the British government in Ireland in 1845. These were opposed by Pius IX who told the Irish bishops to found a Catholic University instead. Newman's experience as founding Rector of this caused him to modify his initial belief in the 'perpetual sagacity' of the papacy: 'I relied on the word of the Pope, but from the event I am led to think it not rash to say that I knew as much about Ireland as he did.' *AW* p.320, *My Campaign II*, p.92.

oracle has done in this respect, has been to condemn such propositions as in a moral point of view are false, or dangerous or rash; and these condemnations, besides being such as in fact will be found to command the assent of most men, as soon as heard, do not necessarily go so far as to present any positive statements for universal acceptance.

11. With the mention of condemned propositions I am brought to another and large consideration, which is one of the best illustrations that I can give of that principle of minimizing[39] so necessary, as I think, for a wise and cautious theology: at the same time I cannot insist upon it in the connexion into which I am going to introduce it, without submitting myself to the correction of divines more learned than I can pretend to be myself. [333]

The infallibility, whether of the Church or of the Pope, acts principally or solely in two channels, in direct statements of truth, and in the condemnation of error. The former takes the shape of doctrinal definitions, the latter stigmatizes propositions as heretical, next to heresy, erroneous, and the like. In each case the Church, as guided by her Divine Master, has made provision for weighing as lightly as possible on the faith and conscience of her children.

As to the condemnation of propositions all she tells us is, that the thesis condemned when taken as a whole, or, again, when viewed in its context, is heretical, or blasphemous, or impious, or whatever like epithet she affixes to it. We have only to trust her so far as to allow ourselves to be warned against the thesis, or the work containing it. Theologians employ themselves in determining what precisely it is that is condemned in that thesis or treatise; and doubtless in most cases they do so with success; but that determination is not

---

[39] not lessening the content but restricting its scope to what it actually determines or "determining what it is that its condemned in that thesis."

de fide; all that is of faith is that there is in that thesis itself, which is noted, heresy or error, or other like peccant matter, as the case may be, such, that the censure is a peremptory command to theologians, preachers, students, and all other whom it concerns, to keep clear of it. But so light is this obligation, that instances frequently occur, when it is successfully maintained by some new writer, that the Pope's act does not imply what it has seemed to imply, and questions which seemed to be closed, are after a course of years re-opened. In discussions such as these, there is a real exercise of private judgment and an allowable one; the act of faith, which cannot be superseded or trifled with, being, I repeat, the unreserved acceptance that the thesis in question is heretical, or the like, as the Pope or the Church has spoken of it.[*]

[334]

In these cases which in a true sense may be called the Pope's *negative* enunciations, the opportunity of a legitimate minimizing lies in the intensely concrete character of the matters condemned; in his affirmative enunciations a like opportunity is afforded by their being more or less abstract. Indeed, excepting such as relate to persons, that is, to the Trinity in Unity, the Blessed Virgin, the Saints, and the like, all the dogmas of Pope or of Council are but general, and so far, in consequence, admit of exceptions in their actual application,— these exceptions being determined either by other authoritative utterances, or by the scrutinizing vigilance, acuteness, and subtlety of the *Schola Theologorum*.

[*] Fessler seems to confine the exercise of infallibility to the *Note* "heretical," p. 11, Engl. Transl.[40]

---

[40] The translation was by Fr. Ambrose St. John.

One of the most remarkable instances of what I am insisting on is found in a dogma, which no Catholic can ever think of disputing, viz., that "Out of the Church, and out of the faith, is no salvation."[41] Not to go to Scripture, it is the doctrine of St. Ignatius, St. Irenæus, St. Cyprian[42] in the first three centuries, as of St. Augustine[43] and his contemporaries in the fourth and fifth. It can never be other than an elementary truth of Christianity; and the present Pope has proclaimed it[44] as all Popes, doctors, and bishops before him. But that truth has two aspects, according as the force of the negative falls upon the "Church" or upon the "salvation." The [335] main sense is, that there is no other communion or so called Church, but the Catholic, in which are stored the promises, the sacraments, and other means of salvation; the other and derived sense is, that no one can be saved who is not *in* that one and only Church. But it does not follow, because there is no Church but one, which has the Evangelical gifts and privileges to bestow, that therefore no one can be saved without the intervention of that one Church. Anglicans quite understand this distinction; for, on the one hand, their Article says, "They are to be had accursed (anathematizandi) that presume to say, that every man shall be saved[45] *by* (in) the law or sect which he professeth, so that he be diligent to frame his life according to that law and the light of nature;" while on the other hand they speak of and hold the doctrine

---

[41] "Extra Ecclesia nulla salus". See for example Origen *In Jesu Nave homiliae.*
[42] St. Ignatius *Ep. Ad Philadelphenses* 3,2 *PG* 5.700; St. Irenaeus *Adversus Haereses* 3.24.1 *PG* 7.966; St. Cyprian *Epist.* 73.21: "Salus extra ecclesia non est" *ML* 3.1169.
[43] Augustine *Sermo ad Caesariensis ecclesiae plebem* 6 *ML* 43. 695.
[44] Letter to the Bishops of Italy 10 August 1863 *DS* 2866.
[45] Article 18 *BCP.*

of the "uncovenanted mercies of God."[46] The latter doctrine in its Catholic form is the doctrine of invincible ignorance— or, that it is possible to belong to the soul of the Church without belonging to the body; and, at the end of 1800 years, it has been formally and authoritatively put forward by the present Pope (the first Pope, I suppose, who has done so), on the very same occasion on which he has repeated the fundamental principle of exclusive salvation itself. It is to the purpose here to quote his words; they occur in the course of his Encyclical, addressed to the Bishops of Italy, under date of August 10, 1863.[47]

[336]

"*We and you know*, that those who lie under invincible ignorance as regards our most Holy Religion, and who, diligently observing the natural law and its precepts, which are engraven by God on the hearts of all, and prepared to obey God, lead a good and upright life, are able, by the operation of the power of divine light and grace, to obtain eternal life."*

Who would at first sight gather from the wording of so forcible a universal, that an exception to its operation, such as this, so distinct, and, for what we know, so very wide, was

---

* The Pope speaks more forcibly still in an earlier Allocution. After mentioning invincible ignorance he adds:—"Quis tantum sibi arroget, ut hujusmodi ignorantiæ designare limites queat, juxta populorum, regionum, ingeniorum, aliarumque rerum tam multarum rationem et varietatem?"— Dec. 9, 1854.[48]

---

[46] "Let others be contented with the uncovenanted mercies of God". *Sovereign Grace* by Dwight Lyman Moody (1837-99), Congregationalist preacher and revivalist hymn writer.

[47] *Quanto conficiamur moerore*. The Pope says that invincible ignorance cannot be used as an excuse which those who support indifferentism argue. Compare teaching of Vatican II in 'Lumen Gentium' nn. 14, 16.

[48] "Who would claim to be able to describe the limits of this kind of ignorance, according to the nature and variety of people, regions, genius, and so many other things?"

consistent with holding it? Another instance of a similar kind is suggested by the general acceptance in the Latin Church, since the time of St. Augustine, of the doctrine of absolute predestination, as instanced in the teaching of other great saints besides him, such as St. Fulgentius,[49] St. Prosper, St. Gregory, St. Thomas, and St. Buonaventure. Yet in the last centuries a great explanation and modification of this doctrine has been effected by the efforts the Jesuit School,[50] which have issued in the reception of a distinction between predestination to grace and predestination to glory; and a consequent admission of the principle that, though our own works do not avail for bringing us under the action of grace here, that does not hinder their availing, when we are in a state of grace, for our attainment of eternal glory hereafter. Two saints of late centuries, St. Francis de Sales and St. Alfonso, seemed to have professed this less rigid opinion, which is now the more common doctrine of the day.

Another instance is supplied by the Papal decisions [337] concerning Usury. Pope Clement V., in the Council of Vienne,[51] declares, "If any one shall have fallen into the error of pertinaciously presuming to affirm that usury is no sin, we determine that he is to be punished as a heretic." However, in the year 1831 the Sacred *Pœnitentiaria* answered an inquiry on the subject, to the effect that the Holy See suspended its decision on the point, and that a confessor who allowed of

---

[49] St. Fulgentius of Ruspe (c. 390-463); St. Prosper of Aquitaine (c.390-463); St. Gregory (c. 540-64); St. Thomas (c. 1225-74); St. Bonaventure (c. 1217-74).
[50] The Congruists held an absolute predestination to glory irrespective of merits; but others (Suarez, Bellarmine) held that there is a predestination to grace, but final glory depends on our cooperation.
[51] Clement V Bertrand de Got (Pope 1305-14) in his *De usuris.* The fifteenth Ecumenical Council of Vienne took place 1311-12. *DS* 906.

usury was not to be disturbed, "non esse inquietandum."[52] Here again a double aspect seems to have been realized of the idea intended by the word *usury*.

To show how natural this process of partial and gradually developed teaching is, we may refer to the apparent contradiction of Bellarmine, who says "the Pope, whether he can err or not, is to be obeyed by all the faithful" (*Rom. Pont.* iv. 2), yet, as I have quoted him above, p. 52-53,[53] sets down (ii. 29) cases in which he is not to be obeyed. An illustration may be given in political history from the discussions which took place years ago as to the force of the Sovereign's Coronation Oath[54] to uphold the Established Church. The words were large and general, and seemed to preclude any act on his part to the prejudice of the distinction between the legislative and executive action of the Crown, which is now generally accepted.[55]

These instances out of many similar are sufficient to show what caution is to be observed, on the part of private and unauthorized persons, in imposing upon the consciences of others any interpretation of dogmatic enunciations which is beyond the legitimate sense of the words, inconsistent with the principle that all general rules have exceptions, and unrecognized by the Theological *Schola*.

12. From these various considerations it follows, that Papal and Synodal definitions, obligatory on our faith, are of rare occurrence; and this is confessed by all sober

[338]

---

[52] The Congregation of the Holy Office in 1830 with the approval of Pius VIII decided that those who regarded the fact that the law fixed a certain rate of interest as in itself a sufficient reason for taking it, were 'not to be disturbed'.

[53] See pp.[235, 242].

[54] The Coronation Oath Act of 1688 binds the sovereign to uphold the Church of England 'by Law established'.

[55] He taught that it in moral cases it was lawful to follow the milder of two equally probably opinions. Controversialists accused him unjustly of laxity.

theologians. Father O'Reilly,[56] for instance, of Dublin, one of the first theologians of the day, says:—

"The Papal Infallibility is comparatively seldom brought into action. I am very far from denying that the Vicar of Christ is largely assisted by God in the fulfilment of his sublime office, that he receives great light and strength to do well the great work entrusted to him and imposed on him, that he is continually guided from above in the government of the Catholic Church. But this is not the meaning of Infallibility ... What is the use of dragging in the Infallibility in connexion with Papal acts with which it has nothing to do,—papal acts, which are very good and very holy, and entitled to all respect and obedience, acts in which the Pontiff is commonly not mistaken, but in which he could be mistaken and still remain infallible in the only sense in which he has been declared to be so?" (The *Irish Monthly*, Vol. ii. No. 10, 1874.)[*]

This great authority goes on to disclaim any desire to minimize, but there is, I hope, no real difference between us here. He, I am sure, would sanction me in my repugnance to impose upon the faith of others more than what the Church distinctly claims of them: and I should follow him in thinking [339] it a more scriptural, Christian, dutiful, happy frame of mind, to be easy, than to be difficult, of belief. I have already spoken of that uncatholic spirit, which starts with a grudging faith in the word of the Church, and determines to hold nothing but what it is, as if by demonstration, compelled to

---

[*] *Vid.* Fessler also; and I believe Father Perrone says the same.

---

[56] Edmund Joseph O'Reilly D.D., S.J. (1811-78) resigned his Chair of Theology at Maynooth in 1851 to become a Jesuit. He taught theology at St. Beuno's in North Wales and was chosen by Newman as Professor of Dogmatic Theology at the Catholic University. See *Campaign I* p. 4. He was Jesuit provincial 1863-70.

believe. To be a true Catholic a man must have a generous loyalty towards ecclesiastical authority, and accept what is taught him with what is called the *pietas fidei*,[57] and only such a tone of mind has a claim, and it certainly has a claim, to be met and to be handled with a wise and gentle *minimism*.[58] Still the fact remains, that there has been of late years a fierce and intolerant temper abroad, which scorns and virtually tramples on the little ones of Christ.

———————————

I end with an extract from the Pastoral of the Swiss Bishops, a Pastoral which has received the Pope's approbation.

"It in no way depends upon the caprice of the Pope, or upon his good pleasure, to make such and such a doctrine, the object of a dogmatic definition. He is tied up and limited to the divine revelation, and to the truths which that revelation contains. He is tied up and limited by the Creeds, already in existence, and by the preceding definitions of the Church. He is tied up and limited by the divine law, and by the constitution of the Church. Lastly, he is tied up and limited by that doctrine, divinely revealed, which affirms that alongside religious society there is civil society, that [340] alongside the Ecclesiastical Hierarchy there is the power of temporal Magistrates, invested in their own domain with a full sovereignty, and to whom we owe in conscience obedience and respect in all things morally permitted, and belonging to the domain of civil society."

———————————

[57] respect for the body of Catholic teaching.
[58] W. G Ward said that the use of this term was a fundamental mistake, *The Dublin Review* July-October 1875 p.299.

§ 10. *Conclusion.*

I have now said all that I consider necessary in order to fulfil the task which I have undertaken, a task very painful to me and ungracious.[1] I account it a great misfortune, that my last words, as they are likely to be, should be devoted to a controversy with one whom I have always so much respected and admired.[2] But I should not have been satisfied with myself, if I had not responded to the call made upon me from such various quarters, to the opportunity at last given me of breaking a long silence on subjects deeply interesting to me, and to the demands of my own honour.

The main point of Mr. Gladstone's charge against us is that in 1870, after a series of preparatory acts, a great change and irreversible was effected in the political attitude of the Church by the third and fourth chapters of the Vatican *Pastor Æternus*, a change which no state or statesman can afford to pass over. Of this cardinal assertion I consider he has given no proof at all; and my object throughout the foregoing pages has been to make this clear. The Pope's infallibility indeed and his supreme authority have in the Vatican *capita* been declared matters of faith; but his prerogative of infallibility lies in matters speculative, and his prerogative of authority is no infallibility in laws, commands, or measures. His infallibility bears upon the domain of thought, not directly of action, and while it may fairly exercise the theologian, [342] philosopher, or man of science, it scarcely concerns the

---

[1] Gladstone used almost identical words in his Tract, "The task is not of a kind agreeable to me; but I proceed to perform it." p.5.

[2] Newman told Keble that he had "the greatest respect and liking for him (though I scarcely know him personally)." 4 August 1865 *LD* 22 p.24.

politician. Moreover, whether the recognition of his infallibility in doctrine will increase his actual power over the faith of Catholics, remains to be seen, and must be determined by the event; for there are gifts too large and too fearful to be handled freely. Mr. Gladstone seems to feel this, and therefore insists upon the increase made by the Vatican definition in the Pope's authority.[3] But there is no real increase; he has for centuries upon centuries had and used that authority, which the Definition now declares ever to have belonged to him.[4] Before the Council there was the rule of obedience and there were exceptions to the rule; and since the Council the rule remains, and with it the possibility of exceptions.

It may be objected that a representation such as this, is negatived by the universal sentiment, which testifies to the formidable effectiveness of the Vatican decrees, and to the Pope's intention that they should be effective; that it is the boast of some Catholics and the reproach levelled against us by all Protestants, that the Catholic Church has now become beyond mistake a despotic aggressive Papacy, in which freedom of thought and action is utterly extinguished. But I do not allow that this alleged unanimous testimony exists. Of course Prince Bismarck[*] and other statesmen such as Mr.

---

[*] Let me, from this accidental mention of Prince Bismarck, make for myself an opportunity, which my subject has not given me, of expressing my deep sympathy with the suffering Catholics of Germany. Who can doubt that, in their present resolute disobedience to that statesman's measures, they are only fulfilling their duty to God and His Church? Who can but pray that, were English Catholics in a similar trial, they might have grace to act as bravely in the cause of religion?[5]

---

[3] 1875 ed.: "...that authority which the Definition now declares ever to have belonged to him".

[4] "The perpetual practice of the Church confirms this." *DS* 3065.

[5] Prince Otto Eduard Leopold, Prince von Bismarck-Schönhausen (1815-98) became Chancellor of Prussia in 1871. His policy of *Kulturcampf* and the Falk Laws bringing education under the control of the State took place between 1871 and 1878.

Gladstone, rest their opposition to Pope Pius on the political [343] ground; but the Old-Catholic[6] movement is based, not upon politics, but upon theology, and Dr. Dollinger has more than once, I believe, declared his disapprobation of the Prussian acts against the Pope, while Father Hyacinth[7] has quarrelled with the anti-Catholic politics of Geneva. The French indeed have shown their sense of the political support which the Holy Father's name and influence would bring to their country; but does any one suppose that they expect to derive support definitely from the Vatican decrees, and not rather from the *prestige* of that venerable Authority, which those decrees have rather lowered than otherwise in the eyes of the world? So again the Legitimists[8] and Carlists[9] in France and Spain doubtless wish to associate themselves with Rome; but where and how have they signified that they can turn to profit the special dogma of the Pope's infallibility, and would not have been better pleased to be rid of the controversy which it has occasioned? In fact, instead of there being a universal impression that the proclamation of his infallibility and supreme authority has strengthened the Pope's secular position in Europe, there is room for suspecting that some of the politicians of the day, (I do not mean Mr. Gladstone) were not sorry that the Ultramontane party was successful at the Council in their prosecution of an object which those

The policy was condemned in the encyclical *Quod unquam* 1n 1875. See p.[343]. This footnote does not appear in the 1875 edition.

[6] The group of German, Austrian and Swiss Churches who refused to accept the doctrine of infallibility went in schism and termed themselves Old or Alt Catholic.; Ignaz von Döllinger presided over their Conferences at Bonn in 1874 and 1875. See p.[299].

[7] Charles Jean Marie Loyson a.k.a. Père Hyacinthe (1827-1912), Provincial of the Discalced Carmelites, left the Church after being excommunicated in 1869. He joined the Old Catholics, married and after lecturing in Geneva was elected to a parish under a new Swiss law in 1873.

[8] A party in France who after the revolution of 1830 upheld the claims of the Bourbon family.

[9] Followers of Don Carlos de Bourbon (1788-1855) and successive claimants to the Spanish throne. Don Carlos VII raised a Carlist war in 1872 but was driven out of the country in 1876.

politicians considered to be favourable to the interests of the Civil Power. There is certainly some plausibility in the view, that it is not the "Curia Romana," as Mr. Gladstone considers, or the "Jesuits," who are the "astute" party, but that rather they themselves have fallen into a trap, and are victims of the astuteness of secular statesmen.

[344]

The recognition, which I am here implying, of the existence of parties in the Church reminds me of what, while I have been writing these pages, I have all along felt would be at once the *primâ facie* and also the most telling criticism upon me. It will be said that there are very considerable differences in argument and opinion between me and others who have replied to Mr. Gladstone, and I shall be taunted with the evident breakdown, thereby made manifest, of that topic of glorification so commonly in the mouths of Catholics, that they are all of one way of thinking, while Protestant bodies are all at variance with each other, and by reason of that very variation of opinion can have no ground of certainty severally in their own.

This is a showy and serviceable retort in controversy; but it is nothing more. First, as regards the arguments which Catholics use, it has to be considered whether these are really incompatible with each other; if they are not, then surely it is generally granted by Protestants as well as Catholics, that two distinct arguments for the same conclusion, instead of invalidating that conclusion, actually strengthen it. And next, supposing the difference to be one of conclusions themselves, then it must be considered whether the difference relates to a matter of faith or to a matter of opinion. If a matter of faith is in question I grant there ought to be absolute agreement, or rather I maintain that there is; I mean to say that only one out of the statements put forth can be true, and that the other statements will be at once withdrawn by their authors, by virtue of their being Catholics, as soon as they learn on good authority that they are erroneous. But if the

[345]

differences which I have supposed are only in theological opinion, they do but show that after all private judgment is not so utterly unknown among Catholics and in Catholic Schools, as Protestants are desirous to establish.

I have written on this subject at some length in Lectures which I published many years ago, but, it would appear, with little practical effect upon those for whom they were intended. "Left to himself," I say, "each Catholic likes and would maintain his own opinion and his private judgment just as much as a Protestant; and he has it and he maintains it, just so far as the Church does not, by the authority of Revelation, supersede it. The very moment the Church ceases to speak, at the very point at which she, that is, God who speaks by her, circumscribes her range of teaching, then private judgment of necessity starts up; there is nothing to hinder it … A Catholic sacrifices his opinion to the Word of God, declared through His Church; but from the nature of the case, there is nothing to hinder him having his own opinion and expressing it, whenever, and so far as, the Church, the oracle of Revelation, does not speak."*

In saying this, it must not be supposed that I am denying what is called the *pietas fidei*,[10] that is, a sense of the great probability of the truth of enunciations made by the Church, which are not formally and actually to be considered as the "Word of God." Doubtless it is our duty to check many a [346] speculation, or at least many an utterance, even though we are not bound to condemn it as contrary to religious truth. But, after all, the field of religious thought which the duty of faith occupies, is small indeed compared with that which is open to our free, though of course to our reverent and conscientious, speculation.

* *Vide* 'Difficulties felt by Anglicans' Lecture X.[11]

---

[10] See supra p.[339].

[11] 'Differences among Catholics no prejudice to the unity of the Church' *Diff* I p.301.

Conclusion

I draw from these remarks two conclusions; first as regards Protestants,—Mr. Gladstone should not on the one hand declaim against us as having "no mental freedom," if the periodical press on the other hand is to mock us as admitting a liberty of private judgment, purely Protestant. We surely are not open to contradictory imputations. Every note of triumph over the differences which mark our answers to Mr. Gladstone is a distinct admission that we do not deserve his injurious reproach that we are captives and slaves of the Pope.

Secondly, for the benefit of some Catholics, I would observe that, while I acknowledge one Pope, *jure divino*,[12] I acknowledge no other, and that I think it a usurpation, too wicked to be comfortably dwelt upon, when individuals use their own private judgment, in the discussion of religious questions, not simply "abundare in suo sensu,"[13] but for the purpose of anathematizing the private judgment of others.

I say there is only one Oracle of God, the Holy Catholic Church and the Pope as her head. To her teaching I have ever desired all my thoughts, all my words to be conformed; to her judgment I submit what I have now written, what I have ever written, not only as regards its truth, but as to its prudence, its suitableness, and its expedience.[14] I think I have not pursued any end of my own in anything that I have published, but I know well, that, in matters not of faith, I may have spoken, when I ought to have been silent.

[347]

---

[12] 'by divine right'. See Vatican I ch. 4 *De Romani Pontificis infallibili magisterio* DS 3058.

[13] "to expand its meaning"

[14] "He now submits every part of the book to the judgement of the Church" *Dev* p.xi.

Conclusion

And now, my dear Duke, I release you from this long discussion, and, in concluding, beg you to accept the best Christmas wishes and prayers for your present and future from

Your affectionate Friend and Servant,

JOHN HENRY NEWMAN.

THE ORATORY,
Dec. 27, 1874.

POSTSCRIPT[1]

February 26, 1875. Mr. Gladstone's new Pamphlet, which has just appeared, is only partially directed against the foregoing Letter, and, when he remarks on what I have written, he does so with a gentleness which may be thought to be unfair to his argument. Moreover he commences with some pages about me personally of so special a character, that, did I dare dwell upon them in their direct import, they would of course gratify me exceedingly. But I cannot do so, because I believe that, with that seriousness which is characteristic of him, he has wished to say what he felt to be true, not what was complimentary; and because, looking on beyond his words to what they imply, I see in them, though he did not mean it so himself, a grave, or almost severe question addressed to me, which effectually keeps me from taking pleasure in them, however great is the honour they do me.

It is indeed a stern question which his words suggest, whether, now that I have come to the end of my days, I have used aright whatever talents God has given me, and as He would have had me use them, in building up religious truth, and not in pulling down, breaking up, and scattering abroad. All I can say in answer to it, is, that from the day I became a Catholic to this day, now close upon thirty years, I have never had a moment's misgiving that the communion of Rome is that Church which the Apostles set up at Pentecost, which

[349]

---

[1] Newman's thirty-one page pamphlet was published in March 1875 in response to Gladstone's *Vaticanism: An Answer to Replies and Reproofs.* He remarked to Malcolm Maccoll "I shall add a Postscript making two or three remarks on his 'Vaticanism' in defence of what I have said." 6 March 1875 *LD* 27 p.240.

alone has "the adoption of sons, and the glory, and the covenants, and the revealed law, and the service of God, and the promises",[2] and in which the Anglican communion, whatever its merits and demerits, whatever the great excellence of individuals in it, has, as such, no part. Nor have I ever, since 1845, for a moment hesitated in my conviction that it was my clear duty to join, as I did then join, that Catholic Church, which in my own conscience I felt to be divine.[3] Persons and places, incidents and circumstances of life, which belong to my first forty-four years, are deeply lodged in my memory and my affections; moreover, I have had more to try and afflict me in various ways as a Catholic than as an Anglican; but never for a moment have I wished myself back; never have I ceased to thank my Maker for His mercy in enabling me to make the great change, and never has He let me feel forsaken by Him, or in distress, or any kind of religious trouble. I do not know how to avoid thus meeting Mr. Gladstone's language about me: but I can say no more. The judgment must be left to a day to come.

In the remarks that follow I shall take the order of my Sections.

§ 1.

My first reason for writing in answer to Mr. Gladstone's Expostulation was his charge against us, "that Catholics, if they act consistently with their principles, cannot be loyal subjects," *supr.* p. 180. And he withdraws this in his new

---

[2] Rom. 9:4

[3] Newman once again returns to rumours that he was dissatisfied with Catholicism and was on the point of returning to the Church of England, being brutally frank when replying to his former Anglican friend, Henry Thomas Ellacombe, "I am as certain that the Church in communion with Rome is the successor and representative of the Primitive Church, as certain that the Anglican Church is *not.*" 22 August 1870 *LD* 25 p.194 n.1. A similar letter was sent as a reply to Mrs. Alice Smith on 3 November *LD* 25 p.225, which was later published in the *Tablet* and the *Guardian.* On 19 October 1874, The *Daily Telegraph* printed that Newman had applied to become a Jesuit and was refused admission, *LD* 27 p.143n; The *Liverpool Daily Post* stated that he was 'uniting with Dr. Döllinger' 19 January 1874 *LD* 27 p,157. He had to deny both stories.

[350]   Pamphlet (*Vaticanism*, p. 14), though not in very gracious language,[4] "The immediate purpose of my appeal," he says, "has been attained, in so far that the loyalty of our Roman Catholic fellow-subjects in the mass remains evidently untainted and secure."

My second reason was to protest against "his attack upon our moral uprightness," *supr. ibid.* Here again he seems to grant that, if what I say can be received as genuine Catholic teaching, I have succeeded in my purpose. He has a doubt, however, whether it does not "smack of Protestantism," *Vat.* p. 69. He does not give any distinct reason for this doubt; and, though I shall notice it in its place, *infr.* § 5, I think it but fair to maintain as a plain principle of controversy, that it is the accuser who has to prove his point, and that he must not content himself with professing that the accused parties have not succeeded to his satisfaction in disproving it.

Lastly, as springing out of these two charges and illustrating them, was his exaggerated notion of the force, drift, and range of the Vatican definition of the Pope's infallibility and supremacy. Here again I consider he leaves my interpretation of it without reply, though apparently it does not content him. Some of the objections to what I have said, which he throws out *obiter*,[5] as well as some made by others, shall now be noticed.

Supr. pp. 190, 191. I have said, apropos of the prospect of a definition of the Pope's Infallibility in the times of Pitt and Peel,[6] "If [the government] wanted to obtain some real information about the probabilities of the future, why did

---

[4] Gladstone said that these were "in the main remain evidently untainted and secure."
[5] by the way, incidentally
[6] William Pitt the Younger (1759-1806) resigned in 1801 because of royal opposition to a measure of Catholic emancipation. Sir Robert Peel (1788-1850) permitted Catholic-Irish endowments in 1844 but was defeated on an Irish Bill in 1846. Gladstone was made Postmaster General in Peel's second administration in 1843.

they not go to headquarters? why not go to Rome? ... It is impossible that they could have entered into normal [351] negotiations with the Pope, without its becoming perfectly clear that Rome could never be a party to such a pledge as England wanted, and that no pledge from Catholics was of value to which Rome was not a party." To my astonishment Mr. Gladstone seems to consider this a fatal admission. He cries out, "Statesmen of the future, recollect the words! ... The lesson received is this: although pledges were given, although their validity was formally and even passionately asserted, although the subject-matter was one of civil allegiance, 'no pledge from Catholics was of any value, to which Rome was not a party,'" p. 89.

I deny that the question of infallibility was one of civil allegiance, but let that pass; as to the main principle involved in what I have said, it certainly does perplex and confuse me that a statesman with Mr. Gladstone's experience should make light of credentials, and should not recognize the difference between party opinion and formal decisions and pledges. What is the use of accredited ministers and an official intercourse between foreign powers, if the acts of mere classes or interests will do instead of them? At a congress, I believe the first act of plenipotentiaries is to show to each other their credentials. What minister of foreign affairs would go to the Cesarowitch,[7] who happened to be staying among us, for an explanation of an expedition of Russia in upper Asia, instead of having recourse to the Russian ambassador?

The common saying, that "Whigs are Tories out of place"[8] illustrates again what is in itself so axiomatic. Successive ministries of opposite views show in history, for the most [352]

---

[7] Variant spelling of Tsarevitch, eldest son of the Tsar. There is a Flat handicap horse race run annually at Newmarket in October in honour of Tsarevitch Alexander, son of Nicholas I, who donated £300 to the Jockey Club in 1839; he had made a state visit to England in the previous year.

[8] John Wade. *A Political Dictionary or Pocket Companion*. London 1821.

part, as one consistent national government, and, when a foreign power mistakes the objections which public men in opposition make to the details, circumstances, or seasonableness of certain ministerial measures, for deliberate judgments in its favour, it is likely, as in the case of the great Napoleon, to incur eventually, when the opposition comes into office, great disappointment, and has no one to blame but itself. So again, the Czar Nicholas[9] seems to have mistaken the deputation of the peace party before the Crimean war for the voice of the English nation.[10] It is not a business-like way of acting to assume the assurances of partisans, however sincerely made, for conditions of a contract. There is nothing indeed to show that the Holy See in 1793 or 1829 had any notion that the infallibility of the Pope, even if ever made a dogma, would be so made within such limits of time as could affect the *bonâ fide* character of the prospects which English and Irish Catholics opened upon Mr. Pitt or Mr. Peel.[11] The events in Europe of the foregoing half century had given no encouragement to the Papal cause. Nor did Catholics alone avow anticipations which helped to encourage the latter statesman in the course, into which the political condition of Ireland, not any kindness to the Irish religion, primarily turned him. There were Anglican ecclesiastics, whom he deservedly trusted, who gave it to him as their settled opinion, as regards the Protestantism of England, that, if the emancipation of Catholics could but be passed in the night, there would be no excitement about it next morning. Did such an influential judgment, thus offered to Mr. Peel, involve a breach of a pledge, because it was not fulfilled?

---

[9] Czar Nicholas I (1796-1855) succeeded Alexander I in 1825.

[10] The deputation, including some from the Society of Friends, travelled to St. Petersburg in January 1853. The Crimean War began in October. See Letter to A. B. Hayward, the Secretary of the Peace Society who pointed out that it was not organized by his party. 8 April 1875 *LD* 27 p. 269.

[11] See supra p.[350].

Postscript

It was notorious all over the world that the North of [353] Catholic Christendom took a different view of Papal infallibility from the South. A long controversy had gone on; able writers were to be found on either side; each side was positive in the truth of its own cause; each hoped to prevail. The Gallican party, towards which England and Ireland inclined, thought the other simply extravagant; but with the Ultramontane stood Rome itself. Ministers do not commonly believe all the representations of deputations who come to them with the advocacy of particular measures, though those deputations may be perfectly sincere in what they aver. The Catholics of England and Ireland in 1826[12] were almost as one man in thinking lightly of the question, but even then there were those who spoke out in a different sense, and warned the government that there was a contrary opinion, and one strong both in its pretensions and its prospects. I am not bound to go into this subject at length, for I have allowed that the dominant feeling among our Catholics at that day was against the prudence or likelihood of a definition of Papal infallibility; but I will instance one or two writers of name who had spoken in a different sense.

I cannot find that Mr. Gladstone deals with my reference to Archbishop Troy,[13] whose pastoral bears the date (1793) of the very year in which as Mr. Gladstone tells us, *Vat.*, p. 48, a Relief Act was granted to Ireland. The Archbishop, as I have quoted him (*supr.*, p. 188), says, "*Many* Catholics contend that the Pope ... is infallible ... others deny this ... *Until* the Church shall *decide* ... either opinion may be adopted." This is a very significant, as well as an [354] authoritative passage.

Again: Father Mumford's *Catholic Scripturist*[14] is a popular Address to Protestants, in the vernacular, which has

---

[12] See p.[188n].

[13] See iam cit supra.

[14] James Mumford SJ (1606-66), a missioner in England, was imprisoned in Norwich in 1647. He wrote *The Catholick Scripturist, The Plea of the Roman*

gone through various editions in the 17th, 18th, and 19th centuries. The edition from which I quote is that of 1863. He says, p. 39, "Whether the definition of a council alone, defining without their chief pastor, or the definition of the chief pastor alone, defining without a council, be infallible or no, there be several opinions amongst us, in which we do and may vary without any prejudice to our faith, which is not built upon what is *yet* under opinion, but upon that which is delivered as infallible."

Again, Bishop Hay[15] is one of the most conspicuous Prelates and authoritative writers amongst us of the 18th century. In his "*Sincere Christian*," published between 1770 and 1780, he treats of the infallibility of the Pope at considerable length, and in its favour. He says, p. 188 (*ed.* 1871) that that doctrine "is not proposed to us as an article of divine faith, nor has the Church ever made any decision concerning it. Great numbers of the most learned divines are of opinion that, in such a case, the Head of the Church is infallible in what he teaches, but there are others who are of a contrary opinion." He proceeds, "On what grounds do those divines found their opinion, who believe that the Pope himself, when he speaks to the faithful as head of the Church, is infallible in what he teaches?" and he answers, "On very strong reasons both from Scripture, tradition, and reason." These he goes through *seriatim*;[16] then he adds, p. 194,[17] "What proof do the others bring for their opinion, that the Head of the Church is not infallible? They bring not a single text of Scripture, nor almost one argument from tradition to prove it."

[355]

Catholics shewing the Scriptures to hold the Roman faith in above 40 of the Chief Controversies now under debate. 2ⁿᵈ edition 1686, reprinted London 1863.

[15] George Hay (1729-1811) became Vicar Apostolic of the Lowland District of Scotland in 1769 and published a series of books on Catholic religious teaching.

[16] one after another, in an order.

[17] This and similar numbering refers to the American edition of 1875. See Printing History.

I might add that the chief instrument in rousing and rallying the Protestant sentiment against Catholic emancipation was from first to last the episcopate and clergy of the Church Established; now, if there was any body of men who were perfectly aware of the division of sentiment among Catholics as to the seat of infallibility, it was they. Their standard divines, writing in the vernacular, discharge it, as one of their most effective taunts, against their opponents, that, whilst the latter hold the doctrine of infallibility, they differ among themselves whether it is lodged in an Ecumenical Council or in the Roman See. It never can be said then that this opinion, which has now become a dogma, was not perfectly well known to be living and energetic in the Catholic communion, though it was not an article of faith, and was not spoken of as such by Catholics in this part of the world during the centuries of persecution.

Mr. Gladstone, as his mildest conclusion against us, is inclined to grant that it was not an act of duplicity in us, that in 1826 our Prelates spoke against the Pope's infallibility,[18] though in 1870 they took part in defining it; but then he maintains it to be at least a proof that the Church has changed its doctrine, and thereby forfeited its claim to be "semper eadem." But it is no change surely to decide between two prevalent opinions; however, if it is to be so regarded, then change has been the characteristic of the Church from the earliest times, as, for instance, in the third century, on the point of the validity of baptism by heretics.[19] And hence such change as has taken place (which I should prefer to call doctrinal development), is in itself a positive argument in favour of the Church's identity from first to last; for a growth in its creed is a law of its life. I have already insisted upon

[356]

---

[18] See supra p.[353].

[19] Pope St Stephen I (d. 257) maintained the validity of baptism by heretics, which was also St. Augustine's opinion, against the Donatists who insisted on a second baptism. St Cyprian of Carthage opposed Pope Stephen. See *DS* 1401.

this, *supra*, p. 314; also in former volumes, as in my *Apologia*[20] and *Difficulties of Anglicans*.[21]

§ 3.

Supr. p. 195. As Mr. Gladstone denied that the Papal prerogatives were consistent with ancient history, I said in answer that that history on the contrary was the clearest witness in their favour, as showing how the promises made to St. Peter were providentially fulfilled by political, &c., changes, external to the Pope, which worked for him. I did not mean to deny that those prerogatives were his from the beginning, but merely that they were gradually brought into full exercise by a course of events, which history records. Thus it was a mistake to say that Catholics could not appeal in favour of the Papal power to history. To make my meaning quite clear, as I hoped, I distinctly said I was not speaking theologically, but historically, nay, looking at the state of things with "non-Catholic eyes." However, as the following passage from the *Etudes Religieuses* shows, it seems that I have been misunderstood, though the writer himself, Père Ramière,[22] does me the justice and the favour to defend me, and I here adopt his words as my defence. He says,—"Pour [357] exprimer cette concentration providentielle, dans les mains du Pape, du pouvoir eccelesiastique partagé autrefois dans une plus large mesure par l'episcopat, le P. Newman se sert d'un terme légal qu'il ne faut pas prendre à la lettre. Il dit que le Pape est *héritier par défaut* de la hierarchie écuménique du iv⁽ᵉ⁾ siècle. Le savant directeur de la *Voce della Verità* blâme cette expression, qui impliquerait, selon lui, qui le Pape tient son pouvoir de la hierarchie: mais le P. Newman exclut cette interpretation, puis qu'il fait deriver le plenitude du pouvoir

---

[20] *Apo* pp.253-4.
[21] *Diff* I pp.217-8
[22] Henri Ramière (1821-84), French Jesuit priest, was theological advisor (peritus) to the Bishop Joseph Gignoux of Beauvais at the Vatican Council.

pontifical de la promesse faite par Jésus-Christ à Saint Pierre,"[23] p. 256, 7, note.

§ 4.

Supr., p. 242. I here say that "were I actually a soldier or sailor in her Majesty's service in a just war, and should the Pope suddenly bid all Catholic soldiers and sailors to retire from her service, taking the advice, &c., ... I should not obey him." Here I avail myself of a passage in Canon Neville's[24] recent pamphlet ("A few Comments, &c.," *Pickering*), in which he speaks with the authority belonging to a late theological Professor of Maynooth:[25]—

"In the impossible hypothesis of the Pope being engaged in a war with England, how would the allegiance of English Catholics be affected? ... how would it be, if they were soldiers or sailors? ... Some one will urge, the Pope may issue a mandate enforced by an annexed excommunication, forbidding all Catholics to engage in the war against him ... The supposed action of the Pope does not change the question materially ... The soldiers and sailors would not incur it, because '*grave fears*' excuse from censure [excommunication], censures being directed against the [358]

---

[23] "In order to explain this providential concentration in the hands of the Pope of Church authority formerly shared in a large part by the episcopate, Fr Newman uses a legal term which must not be taken literally. He says that the Pope *inherits by default* the ecumenical hierarchy of the fourth century. The learned director of *Voce della Verità* reproaches the use of this term which would imply according to him that the Pope holds power from the hierarchy: but Fr. Newman excludes this interpretation since the fulness of pontifical power must derive from the promise made by Jesus Christ to St Peter" [*Voce della Verità* was published by the Societá Primaria Romana, one of its editors being Carlo Curci, at that time a Jesuit.]

[24] Henry F Canon Neville (1822-89) was theologian to Bishop Moriarty at the Council and Vicar General of Cork. He was the author of *A Few Comments on Mr Gladstone's Expostulation* Pickering London 1875.

[25] "To quote a Maynooth Professor who could say the Pope need not be obeyed in the critical case of an English war against him, that his command was to be resisted on *any* motive, for *any* reason, that this was the *rule* in such a case, was to possess a great ally, who would block any attack, any annoyance, which my words might have caused." Newman to Lord Blatchford 11 April 1875 *LD* 27 p.274.

contumacious, not against those who act through fear or coercion ... It is a trite principle, that mere ecclesiastical laws do not bind, when there would be a very grave inconvenience in their observance; and it denies as a rule to any human legislator (*e.g.*, the Pope) the power of making laws or precepts, binding men to the performance of actions, which, from the danger and difficulty attendant on their fulfilment, are esteemed heroic," pp. 101, 2.

§ 5.

Supr., p. 254. I have said, "The Pope, who comes of Revelation, has no jurisdiction over Nature," i.e. the natural Law[26]. Mr. Gladstone on the other hand says, "Idle it is to tell us, finally, that the Pope is bound by the moral and divine law, by the commandments of God, by the rules of the Gospel: ... for of these, one and all, the Pope himself, by himself, is the judge without appeal," p. 102. That is, Mr. Gladstone thinks that the Pope may deny and anathematize the proposition, "There is one God:" and may proceed to circulate by Cardinal Antonelli a whole Syllabus of kindred "erroneous theses" for the instruction of the Bishops. Catholics think this impossible, as believing in a Divine Providence ever exercised over the Church. But let us grant, for argument-sake, that a Pope could commit so insane a violation of the Natural and the Revealed Law:—we know what would be the consequence to such a Pope. Cardinal Turrecremata[27] teaches, as I have quoted him, that "were the Pope to command anything against Holy Scripture, or the articles of faith, or the truth of the Sacraments, or the commands of the natural or divine law, he ought not to be obeyed, but in such commands to be ignored." *Supr.*, p. 242. Other, and they the highest Ultramontane theologians, hold that a Pope who teaches heresy *ipso facto* ceases to be Pope.

[359]

---

[26] See supra p.[254].
[27] See supra p.[242].

Supr., p. 261. Here, after stating that there are cases in which the Pope's commands are to be resisted by individual Catholics, I challenge Mr. Gladstone to bring passages from our authoritative writers to the contrary: and I add, "they must be passages declaring not only that the Pope is ever to be obeyed, but that there are no exceptions to this rule, for exceptions ever must be in all concrete matters." Instead of doing so, Mr. Gladstone contents himself with enunciating the contradictory to what I have said. "Dr. Newman says there are exceptions to this precept of obedience. But this is just what the Council has not said. The Church by the Council imposes Aye. The private conscience reserves to itself the title to say No. I must confess that in this apology there is to me a strong, undeniable smack of Protestantism," p. 69.

Mr. Gladstone says "there is to me;" yes, certainly to him and other Protestants, because they do not know our doctrine. I have given in my Pamphlet, three reasons in justification of what I said; first that exceptions *must* be from the nature of the case, "for in *all* concrete matters," not only in precepts of obedience, rules are but general, and exceptions must occur. Then, in a later page, p. 334, I give actual instances, which have occurred in the history of Catholic teaching, of [360] exceptions after large principles have been laid down. But my main reason lies in the absolute statements of theologians. I willingly endure to have about me a smack of Protestantism, which attaches to Cardinal Turrecremata in the 15th century, to Cardinals Jacobatius[28] and Bellarmine[29] in the 16th, to the Carmelites of Salamanca[30] in the 17th, and to all theologians prior to them; and also to the whole Schola after them, such

---

[28] See supra p.[260].
[29] See supra p.[235].
[30] See p.[259].

as to Fathers Corduba,[31] Natalis,[32] Alexander,[33] and Busenbaum,[34] and so down to St. Alfonso Liguori, the latest Doctor of the Church,[35] in the 18th, and to Cardinal Gousset[36] and Archbishop Kenrick[37] in the 19th.

On the subject of the supremacy of Conscience[38] a correspondent has done me the favour of referring me to a passage in the life of the well-known M. Emery[39] (Paris, 1862), Supérieur of St. Sulpice[40]. It runs as follows:—

"La célébration du mariage de Napoléon avec l'Archiduchesse d'Autriche[41] donna lieu à une autre difficulté sur la quelle M. Emery fut dans le cas de s'expliquer, non avec le gouvernement, mais avec quelques cardinaux qui désiraient connaître son sentiment. Il s'agissait de savoir si les cardinaux résident à Paris, au nombre de vingt-six, pouvaient en conscience assister à la cérémonie religieuse du mariage. Quelques jours avant cette cérémonie, M. Emery, consulté la-dessus par le cardinal della Somaglia,[42] qui paraissait regarder cette assistance comme illicite, lui répondit que, *s'il était effectivement dans cette persuasion, il ne pouvait en conscience assister à la cérémonie, parce qu'il n'est jamais permis d'agir contre sa conscience.* Mais il

[361]

---

[31] See pp.[259-60].

[32] Alexander Natalis: (1639-1724), Dominican Church historian and Gallican theologian.

[33] Not a separate person; Newman appears to have accidentally added the Christian name of Natalis.

[34] See p.[229]

[35] St. Alfonso (see supra) was made Doctor of the Church in 1871.

[36] Thomas Gousset (1792-1866), Archbishop of Rheims. See supra.p.[247].

[37] See p.[243]

[38] This section to § 6 did not appear in 1st. ed.

[39] Jacques André Emery (1732-1811), a Sulpician priest.

[40] A congregation of priests founded by J. J. Olier in 1642 in the parish of St. Sulpice in Paris mainly to prepare men for the priesthood.

[41] Marie Louise (1791-1847) married Napoleon in 1810 after his divorce and on his abdication in 1814 was appointed by the allies Duchess of Parma.

[42] Cardinal Giulio Maria della Somaglia (1744-1830), Dean of the College of Cardinals in 1820 and Secretary of State for Leo XII in 1830.

ajouta que cette assistance, au fond, ne lui paraissait pas illicite," &c.[43]

It got about in consequence that he had denied that any cardinal could with a safe conscience be present at the religious ceremony. This led Cardinal Fesch[44] to write him a letter asking for an explanation, inasmuch as a cardinal had distinctly stated "que M. Emery avait confirmé ce cardinal dans son opinion, qu'il ne pouvait pas, en conscience, assister au mariage de l'Empereur;" whereas, Cardinal Fesch proceeds, "hier même, à trois heures après midi, M. Emery, pour la seconde ou troisième fois, m'avait protesté qui'l était d'une opinion toute contraire, et qu'il pensait que les cardinaux pouvaient assister à la cérémonie."[45] In consequence he asked for "une réponse catégorique"[46] from M. Emery.

M. Emery in consequence wrote letters to both cardinals to show his consistency in the language he had used in conversation with each of them, insisting for that purpose on the distinction which has led to the introduction of his name and conduct into this place, viz., that every man must go by his own conscience, not by that of another. He says to Cardinal Somaglia, "Vous m'avez dit qu'après avoir fait les récherches les plus exactes, vous étiez convaincu que *vous ne*

---

[43] "The celebration of the marriage of Napoleon and the Archduchess of Austria gives rise to another difficulty which M. Emery was prepared to explain not to the government but to some Cardinals who wanted to know his mind on the matter. Twenty-six Cardinals resident in Paris wanted to know whether they could in conscience assist at the religious nuptials. A few days after the ceremony M. Emery, on being consulted by Cardinal della Somaglia, who appeared to regard such assistance as illicit, replied to him "*If he was of that opinion, he could not in conscience attend the ceremony, because it is never allowed to go against one's conscience.* But he added that such an assistance did not seem to him fundamentally illicit."

[44] Cardinal Joseph Fesch (1763-1839), uncle to Napoleon who created him Prince in 1807. He became Cardinal the same year. See supra p.[191n].

[45] "Yesterday at half past three, M. Emery for the second or third time has told me forthrightly that he had a contrary opinion and thought the Cardinals would attend the ceremony."

[46] "a categoric answer"

pouviez aller au mariage sans blesser votre conscience. J'ai dû vous dire, et je vous ai dit, que, *dans cette supposition*, vous ne deviez point y assister, parce que j'étais persuadé *comme vous*, qu'on ne pouvait, qu'on ne devait jamais, agir contre sa conscience, *même erronée.*"[47] He adds, "Non que les inconvénients soient une raison d'autoriser l'assistance [362] qui serait d'ailleurs illicite, mais ces inconvenients sont une raison très-forte d'examiner le plus attentivement qu'il est possible, si réellement l'assistance est illicite, et si la conscience qu'on s'est formée à cette sujet n'est point une conscience erronée."[48]—t. 2, pp. 249-254.

In the event Cardinal Somaglia[49] kept to his view, contrary to M. Emery, and did not attend the marriage ceremony.

§ 6.

Supr., pp. 274, 275. Speaking of the proposition condemned in the Encyclical of 1864, to the effect that it is the right of any one to have liberty to give public utterance, in every possible shape, by every possible channel, without any let or hindrance from God or man, to all his notions whatever, I have said that "it seems a light epithet for the Pope to use, when he called such a doctrine of conscience a *deliramentum.* Presently I add, "Perhaps Mr. Gladstone will say, Why should the Pope take the trouble to condemn what is so wild? but he does," &c.

On this Mr. Gladstone remarks, *Vat*, p. 21, 22, "It appears to me that this is, to use a mild phrase, merely trifling with

---

[47] "You have told me that having gone into the matter very carefully you have been convinced *that you could not go to the marriage without offending your conscience.* I had also to tell you, and I did tell you that *this being so* you must not in any way be present, because I was persuaded *like yourself,* that one might not and should not ever go against one's conscience, *even if it is erroneous.*"

[48] "It is not that these objections might offer a motive to allow of a presence which would be otherwise illicit, but they do offer a very strong motive to examine very carefully if one's presence is illicit and if a conscience formed on this mater is not an erroneous conscience at all."

[49] See supra p.[360].

the subject. We are asked to believe that what the Pope intended to condemn was a state of things which never has existed in any country in the world. Now he says he is condemning one of the commonly prevailing errors of the time, familiarly known to the Bishops whom he addresses. What bishop knows of a State which by law allows a perfectly free course to blasphemy, filthiness, and sedition?"

I do not find anything to show that the Pope is speaking of States, and not of writers; and, though I do not pretend to [363] know against what writers he is speaking, yet there are writers who do maintain doctrines which carried out consistently would reach that *deliramentum* which the Pope speaks of, if they have not rather already reached it. We are a sober people; but are not the doctrines of even so grave and patient a thinker as the late Mr. J. S. Mill very much in that direction? He says, "The appropriate region of human liberty comprises first the inward domain of consciousness; demanding liberty of conscience in the most comprehensive sense, liberty of thought and feeling, absolute freedom of opinion and sentiment on all subjects practical or speculative, scientific, moral, or theological. The liberty of *expressing* and *publishing* opinion may *seem* to fall under a different principle, since it belongs to that part of the conduct of an individual which concerns other people; but, being almost of as much importance as the liberty of thought itself, and resting in great part on the same reasons, *is practically inseparable from it*, &c. &c. ... No society in which these liberties are not on the whole respected, is free, whatever may be its form of government." (*On Liberty, Introd.*)[50] Of course he does not allow of a freedom to harm others, though we have to consider well what he means by harming: but his is a freedom which must meet with no "impediment from our fellow-creatures, so long as what we do does not harm them, even though they should think our conduct foolish, perverse,

---

[50] John Stuart Mill (1806-73) published *On Liberty* in 1859.

or wrong." "The only freedom," he continues, "which deserves the name is that of pursuing our own good in our own way, so long as we do not attempt to deprive others of theirs, or impede their efforts to obtain it. Each is the proper guardian of his own health, whether bodily, or mental and spiritual."

That is, no immoral doctrines, poems, novels, plays, conduct, acts, may be visited by the reprobation of public opinion; nothing must be put down, I do not say by the laws, but even by society, by the press, by religious influence, merely on the ground of shocking the sense of decency and the modesty of a Christian community. Nay, the police must not visit Holywell Street,[51] nor a licence be necessary for dancing-rooms: but the most revolting atrocities of heathen times and countries must for conscience-sake be allowed free exercise in our great cities. Averted looks indeed and silent disgust, or again rational expostulation, is admissible against them, but nothing of a more energetic character.

I do not impute this to Mr. Mill. He had too much English common sense to carry out his principles to these extreme but legitimate conclusions; he strove to find means of limiting them by the introduction of other and antagonist principles; but then that such a man held the theory of liberty which he has avowed, and that he has a great following, is a suggestion to us that the Holy See may have had abundant reason in the present state of the continent to anathematize a proposition, which to Mr. Gladstone seems so wild and unheard of.

§ 7.

Supr., pp. 277, 281. I have said that the Syllabus is to be received from the Pope with "profound submission." p. 277, and "by an act of obedience," p. 281; I add, "but not of faith," for it "has no dogmatic force." I maintain this still. I say, in

----

[51] Holywell Street (since demolished to make way for Aldwich) was the home of booksellers who sold pornography.

spite of Professor Schulte,[52] and the English Catholic writer to whom Mr. Gladstone refers, p. 32, I have as much right to maintain that the implicit condemnation with which it visits its eighty propositions is not *ex cathedra*, or an act of the Infallible Chair, as have those "gravest theologians," as Bishop Fessler speaks, who call its dogmatic force in question, *Fessler*, p. 91. I do not know what Fessler himself says of it more than that it is to be received with submission and obedience.[53] I do not deny another's right to consider it in his private conscience an act of infallibility, or to say, in Mr. Gladstone's words, p. 35, that "utterances *ex cathedra* are not the only form in which Infallibility can speak;" I only say that I have a right to think otherwise. And when the Pope by letters approves of one writer who writes one way, and of another who writes in another, he makes neither opinion dogmatic, but both allowable. Mr. Gladstone speaks as if what the Pope says to Fr. Schrader[54] undoes what he says to Bishop Fessler; why not say that his letter to Fessler neutralizes his letter to Schrader? I repeat, when I speak of minimizing, I am not turning the profession of it into a dogma; men, if they will, may maximize for me, provided they too keep from dogmatizing. This is my position all through these discussions, and must be kept in mind by any fair reasoner.

I grant the Pope has laid a great stress on the Syllabus; he is said in 1867 to have spoken of it as a "regula docendi;"[55] I

---

[52] Johann Friedrich Schulte (1827-94), Professor of History and Canon Law at Bonn, left the Church and became President of the Old Catholic Conference 1871-90.

[53] Joseph Fessler *The True and False Infallibility of the Pope* trans. Ambrose St. John 1875. See supra p.[280]

[54] Fr. Clement Schrader (1820-75), Jesuit theologian who collaborated with Pius IX, was rumoured to have provided a more positive version of the Syllabus. He also proposed a theory that it would be a mortal sin not to hold the Temporal Power necessary to the Papacy. See Wilfrid Ward *The Life of John Henry Cardinal Newman* vol 2 London 1921 pp.152, 239.

[55] "rule of teaching"

[366] cannot tell whether *vivâ voce*, or in writing;[56] any how this did not interfere with Fessler's "grave theologians" in 1871 considering the Pope was not in 1867 teaching dogmatically and infallibly. Moreover, how can a list of proscribed propositions be a "rule," except by turning to the Allocutions, &c., in which they are condemned? and in those Allocutions, when we turn to them, we find in what sense, and with what degree of force, severally. In itself the Syllabus can be no more than what the Pope calls it, a syllabus or collection of errors. Led by the references inserted in it to the Allocutions, &c., I have ventured to call it something more, viz., a list or index *raisonné*; an idea not attached to it by me first of all, for Père Daniel, in the October of that very year, 1867, tells us, in the *Etudes Religieuses*,[57] "Au Syllabus lui-même il ne faut pas demander que le degré de clarté qui convient à une bonne table des matières," p. 514.[58]

But, whether an index or not, and though it have a substantive character, it is at least clear that the only way in which it can be a "rule of teaching" is by its telling us what to avoid; and this consideration will explain what I mean by receiving it with "obedience," which to some persons is a difficult idea, when contrasted with accepting it with faith. I observe then that obedience is concerned with doing, but faith with affirming. Now, when we are told to avoid certain propositions, we are told primarily and directly not to do something; whereas, in order to affirm, we must have positive statements put before us. For instance, it is easy to understand, and in our teaching to avoid the proposition, "Wealth is the first of goods;"[59] but who shall attempt to

---

[56] It was in a speech made on the 21st anniversary of his accession in the Sistine Chapel on June 17 1867 where he said that "I lay it before you as a rule of your teaching".

[57] Père Daniel, with Ivan Gagarin, founded *Etudes de théologie, de philosophie et d'histoire* in 1857. It merged with *Etudes religieuses* in 1867.

[58] "As far as the Syllabus goes one should not demand the same degree of clarity which you expect of a contents list."

[59] Adam Smith *The Wealth of Nations* Book 4 ch. 1.

ascertain what the affirmative propositions are, one or more, [367] which are necessarily involved in the prohibition of such a proposition, and which must be clearly set down before we can make an act of faith in them?

However, Mr. Gladstone argues, that, since the Pope's condemnation of the propositions of the Syllabus has, as I have allowed, a claim on the obedience of Catholics, that very fact tells in favour of the propositions condemned by him; he thinks I have here made a fatal admission. It is *enough*, he says, that the Syllabus "unquestionably demands obedience;" that is, enough, whether the propositions condemned in it deserve condemnation or not. Here are his very words: "What is *conclusive* ... is this, that the obligation to *obey* it is asserted on all hands; ... it is *therefore* absolutely superfluous to follow Dr. Newman through his references to the Briefs and Allocutions marginally noted," in order to ascertain their meaning and drift ... "I *abide* by my account of the *contents* of the Syllabus," p. 86. That is, the propositions may be as false as heathenism, but they have this redeeming virtue, that the Pope denounces them. His judgment of them may be as true as Scripture, but it carries this unpardonable sin with it, that it is given with a purpose, and not as a mere literary flourish. Therefore I will not inquire into the propositions at all; but my original conclusion shall be dogmatic and irreformable. Sit pro ratione voluntas.[60]

Supra, p. 288. I have declined to discuss the difficulties which Mr. Gladstone raises upon our teaching respecting the [368] marriage contract (on which I still think him either obscure or incorrect), because they do not fall within the scope to which I professed to confine my remarks; however, his fresh statements, as they are found, *Vat.*, p. 28, lead me to say as follows:—

---

[60] "Let (good) will stand for reason." Juvenal *Satires* 6, l. 223

The non-Roman marriages in England, he says, "do not at present fall under the foul epithets of Rome. But why? not because we marry ... under the sanctions of religion, for our marriages are, in the eye of the Pope, purely civil marriages, but only for the technical ... reason that the disciplinary decrees of Trent are not canonically in force in this country," &c.[61]

Here Mr. Gladstone seems to consider that there are only two ways of marrying according to Catholic teaching; he omits a third, in which we consider the essence of the sacrament to lie. He speaks of civil marriage, and of marriage "under the sanctions of religion," by which phrase he seems to mean marriage with a rite and a minister. But it is also a *religious* marriage, if the parties, without a priest, by a mutual act of consent, as in the presence of God, marry themselves; and such a vow of each to other is, according to our theology, really the constituting act, the matter and form, the sacrament of marriage. That is, he omits the very contract which we specially call marriage. This being the case, it follows that every clause of the above passage is incorrect.

1. Mr. Gladstone says, that English non-Roman marriages are held valid at Rome, *not* because they are contracted "under the sanctions of religion." On the contrary, this is the very reason why they are held valid there; viz., only because parties who have already received the Christian rite of baptism, proceed to give themselves to each other in the sight of God sacramentally, though they may not call it a sacrament.

[369]

---

[61] The *Tametsi* decree (Session 24, 1563) on clandestine marriages stated that a marriage between baptized persons whether Catholic or not was valid only in the presence of the parish priest or local Ordinary and two witnesses. It was not published in Protestant countries (including the USA) as it had to be formally announced in each parish. The *Ne Temere* decree of 1907, DS 3468-3474 extended the obligation to the whole Latin Church and this is the current legal position. *CIC* 1108.

2. Mr. Gladstone says, "our marriages are in the eye of the Pope *purely civil* marriages. Just the reverse, speaking, as he is, of Church of England marriages. They are considered, in the case of baptized persons, sacramental marriages.

3. Mr. Gladstone says, that they are received at Rome as valid, "*only for the technical*, &c., reason that the disciplinary decrees of Trent are not canonically in force in this country. There is nothing, unless it be motives of mere policy, to prevent the Pope from giving them [those decrees] force here, when he pleases. If, and when that is done, *every marriage thereafter concluded in the English* Church, will, according to his own words, be '*a filthy concubinage.*'" This is not so; I quote to the point two sufficient authorities, St. Alfonso, Liguori and Archbishop Kenrick.[62]

Speaking of the clandestinity of marriage (that is, when it is contracted without parish priest and witnesses,) as an impediment to its validity, St. Alfonso says, "As regards non-Catholics (infideles), or Catholics who live in non-Catholic districts, or where the Council of Trent has not been received ... *such a marriage is valid.*"—tom. viii., p. 67, ed. 1845. Even then though the discipline of Trent *was* received in England, still it would not cease to be a Protestant country, and therefore marriages in Protestant churches would be valid.

Archbishop Kenrick is still more explicit. He says, [370] "Constat Patres Tridentinos legem ita tulisse, ut hæreticorum cœtus jam ab Ecclesia divulsos non respiceret ... Hoc igitur clandestinitatis impedimentum ad hæreticos seorsim

---

[62] Newman commented in a letter to Mrs.William Froude, "The only thing that Gladstone says new is about the marriage question – that I shall take up as far as I know anything about it. I am sorry to say there is some very unpleasant case at Rome to which G. refers. Some one (I believe) of the Aberdeen family is the principal in it, which has shocked numbers, including I hear, the Archbishop and our Bishop. It will be sure to come out, and will be a scandal, if it be what I am told it is." 9 March 1875 *LD* 27 p.245.

convenientes in locis ubi grassantur hæreses, non est extendendum."[63]—*Theol. Mor.*, t. 3, p. 351.

Such being the Catholic rule as to recognition of Protestant marriages, the Pope could not, as Mr. Gladstone thinks, any day invalidate English Protestant marriages by introducing into England the discipline of Trent. The only case, in which, consistently with the Council, any opportunity might occur to the Pope, according to his accusation, of playing fast and loose, is when there was a doubt whether the number of Protestants in a Catholic country was large enough to give them a clear footing there, or when the Government refused to recognize them. Whether such an opportunity has practically occurred and has ever been acted on, I have not the knowledge either to affirm or deny.

§ 8.

Supr., p. 302. "But if the fact be so that the Fathers were not unanimous, is the definition valid? This depends on the question whether unanimity, at least moral, is or is not necessary for its validity." Vid. also p. 303.

It should be borne in mind that these letters of mine were not intended for publication, and are introduced into my text as documents of 1870, with a view of refuting the false reports of my bearing at that time towards the Vatican Council and Definition. To alter their wording would have been to destroy their argumentative value. I said nothing to imply that on reflection I agreed to every proposition which I set down on my *primâ facie* view of the matter.

[371]

One passage of it, perhaps from my own fault, Mr. Gladstone has misunderstood. He quotes me, *Vat.*, p. 13, as holding that "a definition which the Pope approves, is not absolutely binding thereby, but requires a moral unanimity,

---

[63] "The Tridentine Fathers so legislated that already dissolved marriages of heretics should not be looked into …Therefore the impediment of clandestinity concerning heretics living in places where heresies are prevalent should not be extended."

and a subsequent reception by the Church." Nay, I considered that the Pope could define without either majority or minority; but that, if he chose to go by the method of a Council, in that case a moral unanimity was required of its Fathers. I say a few lines lower down, waiving the difficulty altogether, "Our merciful Lord would not care so little for His people ... as to allow their visible head and such a large number of Bishops to lead them into error." Père Ramière, in his very kind review of me in the *Études Religieuses* for February,[64] speaks of the notion of a moral unanimity as a piece of Gallicanism; but anyhow it has vanished altogether from theology now, since the Pope, if the Bishops in the Council, few or many, held back, might define a doctrine without them. A council of Bishops of the world around him, is only one of the various modes in which he exercises his infallibility. The seat of infallibility is in him, and they are adjuncts. The *Pastor Æternus* says, "Romani Pontifices, prout temporum et rerum conditio suadebat, *nunc* convocatis œcumenicis conciliis, *aut* rogatâ Ecclesiæ per orbem dispersæ sententiâ, *nunc* per synodos particulares, *nunc* aliis, quæ Divina suppeditabat Providentia, adhibitis auxiliis, ea [372] tenenda definiverunt, quæ sacris Scripturis et Apostolicis Traditionibus consentanea, Deo adjutore, cognoverant."[65]

Nor have I spoken of a subsequent reception by the Church as entering into the necessary conditions of a *de fide* decision. I said that by the "Securus judicat orbis terrarum"[66] "all acts of the rulers of the Church are ratified," p. 303. In this passage of my private letter I meant by "ratified" brought home to us as authentic. At this very moment it is certainly

---

[64] Père Henri Ramière SJ (1821-84) was Editor of the review. See supra p.[356].
[65] "The Roman Pontiffs in so far as times and seasons support, knew *either* ecumenical councils having been summoned or the judgement asked of the whole Church, *now* by particular synods *then* by other means, supported by divine providence or with the consent of the Sacred Scriptures and Apostolic Tradition with the help of God." *DS* 3069
[66] See supra.

the handy, obvious, and serviceable argument for our accepting the Vatican definition of the Pope's Infallibility.

Supr., p. 306. I said in my first edition, at this page, that the definition at Ephesus seemed to be carried by 124 votes against 111; as this was professedly only an inference of my own, I have withdrawn it. Confining myself to the facts of the history, which are perplexed, I observe:—The Council was opened by St. Cyril[67] on June 22 of the current year, without waiting for the Bishops representing the great Syrian patriarchate, who were a few days' journey from Ephesus, in spite of the protest on that account of sixty-eight of the Bishops already there. The numbers present at the opening are given in the Acts as about 150. The first Session in which Nestorius was condemned and a definition or exposition of faith made, was concluded before night. That exposition, as far as the Acts record, was contained in one of the letters of St. Cyril to Nestorius, which the Bishops in the Council one by one accepted as conformable to Apostolic teaching. Whether a further letter of St. Cyril's with his twelve anathematisms,[68] which was also received by the Bishops, was actually accepted by them as their dogmatic utterance, is uncertain; though the Bishops distinctly tell the Pope and the Emperor that they have accepted it as well as the others, as being in accordance with the Catholic Creed. At the end of the acts of the first Session the signatures of about 200 Bishops are found, and writers of the day confirm this number, though there is nothing to show that the additional forty or fifty were added on the day on which the definition was passed, June 22, and it is more probable that they were

[373]

---

[67] St Cyril of Alexandria (d. 444) became Patriarch in 412 He issued anathemas against Nestorius a month before the Council opened.
[68] *DS* 252-263.

added afterwards; *vid.* Tillemont,[69] *Cyril*, note 34, and Fleury,[70] *Hist.*, xxv. 42. And thus Tillemont, *ibid.*, thinks that the signatures in favour of Cyril altogether amounted to 220. The Legates of the Pope were not present; but they had arrived by July 10. The Syrian Bishops arrived on June 26th or 27th. As to Africa, then overrun by the Vandals,[71] it was represented only by the deacon of the Bishop of Carthage, who sent him to make his apologies for Africa, to warn the Council against the Pelagians,[72] and to testify the adherence of the African Churches to Apostolic doctrine. The countries which were represented at the Council, and took part in the definition were Egypt, Asia Minor, and Thrace, Greece, &c. The whole number of Bishops in Christendom at the time was about 1800; not 6000, as St. Dalmatius[73] says at random. Gibbon says, "The Catholic Church was administered by the spiritual and legal jurisdiction of 1800 bishops, of whom 1000 were seated in the Greek, and 800 in the Latin provinces of the empire." He adds, "The numbers are not ascertained by any ancient writer or original catalogue; for the partial lists of the eastern churches are comparatively modern. The patient diligence of Charles à S. Paolo,[74] of Luke Holstein,[75] [374]

---

[69] Louis Sébastien Le Nain de Tillemont (1637-98), French historian who published his *Mémoires pour server â l'histoire ecclésiastique des six premiers siècles* (16 vols 1693-1712).

[70] See supra p.[292].

[71] Originally a 3rd century East Germanic people who invaded Africa in 429 led by King Genseric and captured Hippo in 431.

[72] Followers of Pelagius who denied Original Sin and held that we are able to avoid sin and reach heaven by our natural ability.

[73] St. Dalmatius of Constantinople (d. 440).

[74] Charles Vialart de Saint-Paul (1592-1644), Bishop of Avranches and ecclesiastical historian.

[75] Lucas Hulsteinus (1596-1661) was born in Hamburg but converted to Catholicism in Paris and specialized in the study of Church manuscripts. He became librarian to the Pope and author of *On the Nicene Council.* He is referred to in Gibbon's *Decline and Fall* vol 4. Ch. 20.

and of Bingham,[76] has laboriously investigated all the episcopal sees of the Catholic Church."[77]

To the same purport[78] Fr. Ryder of this Oratory wrote, after my first edition, in answer to Fr. Botalla, S.J.[79], as follows:—

"As regards the Council of Ephesus, there are few points on which learned men are less agreed than its precise numbers.[80] The names given at the opening of the first Session (June 22, 431) in which Nestorius was condemned and St. Cyril approved, amounted to 159; standing aloof from those and protesting against this precipitation in not waiting for the Antiochenes, were sixty-eight ... Five days afterwards the Antiochenes with the Patriarch John at their head, about twenty-seven in number, arrived, and then and there anathematized St. Cyril and all his adherents, declaring null and void all they had done. This condemnation is signed by forty-three. The forty-three consists, besides the Antiochenes, of some who had signed the deposition of Nestorius and some of the sixty-eight protesters. The larger part of the sixty-eight, we may presume, went to swell St. Cyril's party, for we find 198 signatures to the deposition of Nestorius. Subsequently to this, in various official documents the majority refers to itself as 'about 200,' 'over 200'; but we have no signatures beyond the 198. On the other hand, we possess a document of the minority of July 17, containing

---

[76] Joseph Bingham (1668-1723), author of *The Antiquities of the Christian Church (Origines Ecclesiasticae)*10 vols 1708-22.

[77] *Decline and Fall* Book 2 ch. 20. He adds a footnote which ends, "which was almost commensurate with the Roman Empire."

[78] This section to §9 did not appear in the 1st ed.

[79] Fr. Paul Botalla SJ (1823-96), a Sicilian, was Professor of Theology at St. Beuno's College, North Wales, and the controversialist author of *Honorius Reconsidered with Reference to Recent Apologies* London 1869, which was an answer to Le Page Renouf's *Condemnation of Pope Honorius* London 1867 and *The Pope and the Church considered in their Mutual Relations with reference to the Errors of the High Church Party in England*. 1868 and 1870 (2 vols).

[80] See Newman's letter to Emily Bowles 5 April 1875 in which he has corrected the numbers he used in his first edition. *LD* 27 p.267.

fifty-three signatures. Afterwards the proportions of the [375] schism were still more serious ... John of Antioch's[81] twenty-seven were delegates and representatives of the whole Antiochene Patriarchate, except Cyprus. Thus, on leaving Ephesus, John was able to hold a Council at Antioch, and condemn Cyril with far larger numbers than before ... They cannot be well set at less than 100 ... [And elsewhere,] large portions of the Episcopate had no knowledge, or an utterly confused one, of what had been going on at Ephesus. St. Isidore, one of Cyril's own clergy, expostulates with him for his tyranny; and the works of Facundus[82] and Liberatus[83] show how deeply seated was the opposition of the African Church to the doctrine of Cyril."

§ 9.

Supra, pp. 320, &c. It has been objected to the explanation I have given from Fessler and others of the nature and range of the Pope's infallibility as now a dogma of the Church, that it was a lame and impotent conclusion of the Council, if so much effort was employed, as is involved in the convocation and sitting of an Ecumenical Council, in order to do so little. True, if it were called to do what it did and no more; but that such was its aim is a mere assumption. In the first place it can hardly be doubted that there were those in the Council who were desirous of a stronger definition; and the definition actually made, as being moderate, is so far the victory of those many bishops who considered any definition on the subject inopportune. And it was no slight fruit of their proceedings in the Council, if a definition was to be, to have [376] effected a moderate definition. But the true answer to the objection is that which is given by Bishop Ullathorne. The

---

[81] A friend of Nestorius, he arrived late at the Council. He held a counter-council which condemned Cyril but was later reconciled.

[82] 6th century Bishop of Hermiane who was sympathetic to Nestorian views.

[83] 6th century archdeacon from Carthage who wrote a history of the Nestorian and Monophysite controversies between the 6th and 8th centuries.

question of the Pope's infallibility was not one of the objects professed in convening the Council; and the Council is not yet ended.

He says in his "Expostulation Unravelled,"[84] "The Expostulation goes on to suggest that the Council was convened mainly with a view of defining the infallibility, and that the definition itself was brought about, chiefly for political objects, through the action of the Pontiff and a dominant party. A falser notion could not be entertained. I have the official catalogue before me of the *Schemata* prepared by the theologians for discussion in the Council. In them the infallibility is not even mentioned; for the greater part of them regard ecclesiastical discipline." P. 48, he adds, "Calamitous events suspended the Council."[85]

Supr., p. 326, note. I have referred to Bishop Fessler's statement that only the last sentences of Boniface's *Unam Sanctam*[86] are infallible. To this Mr. Gladstone replies, p. 45, that the word "Porro," introducing the final words to which the anathema is affixed, extends that anathema to the body of the Bull, which precedes the "Porro."[87] But he does not seem to have observed that there are two distinct heresies condemned in the Bull, and that the "Porro" is the connecting link between these two condemnations, that is, between the

---

[84] *Mr Gladstone's Expostulation Unravelled* London 1875.

[85] The definition was approved on July 18. France declared war on Prussia on 19 July. The Bishops were told to reassemble on 11 November but the Papal States fell to Victor Emmanuel's forces on 20 September, and Rome was declared the capital of the kingdom of Italy on 2 October. The Council was prorogued indefinitely.

[86] Bull of Boniface VIII in 1302 which declared that there was One Holy Catholic Church outside which there was no salvation and that the Pope had a temporal and spiritual sword: a universal power over all sovereigns and a spiritual preeminence over States. Bishop Fessler maintained that the definition at the end of *Unam Sanctam* only asserts the Catholic doctrine of the spiritual primacy of the Pope. *The True and False Infallibility of the Popes* (See supra p. [365], pp. 64-69. *LD* 27 p. 173n.

[87] "*Furthermore* we declare that this subjection to the Roman Pontiff as hereinbefore described is to be held as necessary for salvation. It is not the substance; but an addition to the substance." *Vaticanism* p.45.

penultima and final sentences. The Pope first says, "Nisi duo, sicut Manichæus, fingat esse principia, *quod falsum et hæreticum judicamus* ... porro, subesse Romano Pontifici, omni humanæ creaturæ declaramus, definimus, et pronunciamus omnino esse de necessitate salutis."[88] That the Latin is deficient in classical terseness and perspicuity we may freely grant. [377]

Supra, p. 327, I say, "We call 'infallibility' in the case of the Apostles, inspiration; in the case of the church, *assistentia*."

On this Mr. Gladstone says, "On such a statement I have two remarks to make; first, we have this assurance on the strength only of *his own private judgment*, p. 102." How can he say so when, p. 328, I quote Father Perrone, saying, "*Never have Catholics* taught that the gift of infallibility is given by God to the Church after the manner of inspiration!"

Mr. Gladstone proceeds, "Secondly, that, if bidden by the self-assertion of the Pope, he will be required by his principles to retract it, and to assert, if occasion should arise, the contrary." I can only say to so hypothetical an argument what is laid down by Fessler and the Swiss bishops, that the Pope cannot, by virtue of his infallibility, reverse what has always been held; and that the "inspiration" of the church, in the sense in which the Apostles were inspired, is contrary to our received teaching. If Protestants are to speculate about our future, they should be impartial enough to recollect, that if, on the one hand, we believe that a Pope can add to our articles of faith, so, on the other, we hold also that a heretical Pope, *ipso facto*, ceases to be Pope by reason of his heresy,[89] as I have said (*supr.*, p. 359).[90]

---

[88] "A Manichee imagines only two principles. *We judge them false and heretical* ... Further we declare, define and pronounce every human creature to be subject to the Roman Pontiff and this is altogether necessary for salvation."

[89] "as I have said (supr, p.359)." omitted in 1st ed.

[90] This numbering refers to the 1876 edition.

[378]   Mr. Gladstone thus ends: "Thirdly, that he lives under a system of development, through which somebody's private opinion of today may become matter of faith for all the tomorrows of the future." I think he should give some proof of this; let us have one instance in which "somebody's private opinion" has become *de fide*. Instead of this, he goes on to assert (interrogatively) that Popes, *e.g.* Clement XI. and Gregory II.,[91] and the present Pope, have claimed the inspiration of the Apostles, and that Germans, Italians, French, have ascribed such a gift to him;—of course he means theologians, not mere courtiers, or sycophants, for the Pope cannot help having such, till human nature is changed. If Mr. Gladstone is merely haranguing as an Orator, I do not for an instant quarrel with him or attempt to encounter him; but if he is a controversialist, we have a right to look for arguments, not mere assertions.

THE END.

---

[91] Clement XI (1649-1721), Pope from 1700; Gregory II (669-731), Pope from 715.

PRINTING HISTORY

A Letter to the Rev. E. B. Pusey DD, on his recent Eirenicon

1st edition: London, Longmans Green, Reader and Dyer, 1866, 159 pp.
American edition: New York, Lawrence Kehoe, 1866, 86 pp.

2nd edition: London, Longmans Green, Reader and Dyer, 1866 159 pp.

3rd edition: London, Longmans, Green, Reader and Dyer, 1866 160 pp. French and German translations 1866.[1]

4th edition: *Difficulties felt by Anglicans in Catholic teaching considered* I. In twelve lectures addressed to the party of the religious movement of 1833. II. In a letter addressed to the Rev. E. B. Pusey DD., on the occasion of his Eirenicon of 1864, London, Burns Oates & Co 1872 xvi, 496. pp.

5th edition: *Certain Difficulties felt by Anglicans in Catholic teaching considered; in a letter to the Rev. E. B. Pusey, DD., on occasion of his Eirenicon of 1864; and in a lecture to the Duke of Norfolk, on occasion of Mr. Gladstone's Expostulation of 1874,* London, Basil Montagu Pickering 1876, 378pp. Volume II:[2] London, Basil Montagu Pickering [1883 or 1884]

---

[1] Cf. Philip Boyce *Mary The Virgin Mary in the Life and Writing of John Henry Newman* London 2001 p.45.

[2] Newman wrote to B. M. Pickering on 12 June 1876 "I want to know whether you would advise just now, (what I mean to do ultimately) the publishing in one volume my two Letters to Dr Pusey and Mr. Gladstone. This would involve the anomaly (for

378pp.[3] London, Longmans, Green & Co 1885, 378pp. London & New York, Longmans, Green & Co 1888, 378pp

A Letter to His Grace the Duke of Norfolk

1st edition: London, B. M. Pickering,, 1875 131pp. New York, Catholic Publication Society, 1875, 171pp.

Postscript to a Letter: B. M. Pickering, 1875, 133-156pp.

Postscript to a Letter: The Catholic Publication Society. New York, 1875, 173-200pp.

2nd edition with *Postscript*: B. M. Pickering, 1875, 156pp. New York, The Catholic Publication Society, 1875, 200pp.

3rd edition: London, B. M. Pickering, 1875, 171 pp.

Postscript to a Letter...together with the decrees and canons of the Vatican Council: The Catholic Publication Society 1875 173-200 pp.

4th edition: London, B. M. Pickering, 1875, 172pp. Published in *Certain difficulties felt by Anglicans...* ** Vol II. (new and corrected edition with postscript) B. M. Pickering, 1876, 378pp.

---

the present) of one edition of a volume made up of 'Difficulties of Anglicans' – and Letter to Dr Pusey, (bound in red and sold by Burns and Oates) and another of a volume containing *only* 'Difficulties of Anglicans' – also by Burns and Oates, and bound in purple; and thirdly a volume, sold by you, made up of two Letters, and bound in purple." *LD* 28 p.76. Newman would later say "The only three controversial works I have written as a Catholic on the question of Rome and England – and should go together [=*Diff* 1 & 2], as Historical Sketches go together." To B. M Pickering 6 September 1876 *LD* 28 p.108. Two asterisks appeared on the volume.
[3] Referred to in correspondence but no copy found.

5th edition: London, B. M. Pickering in *Certain difficulties felt by Anglicans*...Vol II, 1883 or 1884.[4]

Vol II in *Certain difficulties felt by Anglicans*... London, Longmans, Green, and Co., 1885, 378pp.

Vol II in *Certain difficulties felt by Anglicans*... London and New York, Longmans, Green, and Co., 1888, 378pp.

---

[4] Referred to in correspondence but no copy found.

INDEX

Page numbers refer to this Gracewing edition.

383

Index

Index

Index

Index

Index

Index

Index

Index

THE MILLENNIUM EDITION OF THE WORKS OF ST. JOHN HENRY NEWMAN

Edited by scholars, these works by Newman have never previously been published in critical editions.
Order direct from www.gracewing.co.uk

Series Editor: James Tolhurst DD
Associate Editor: Andrew Nash PhD

Vol. I: **Lectures on the Present Position of Catholics in England**
Introduction, notes and textual appendix by Andrew Nash
978 085244 443 6   £25 hardback

Vol. II: **Sermon Notes 1849-1878**
Introduction and notes by James Tolhurst
978 085244 444 3   £25 hardback

Vol. III: **Rise and Progress of the Universities and Benedictine Essays**
Introduction and notes by Katherine Tillman
978 085244 449 8   £25 hardback

Vol. IV: **Arians of the Fourth Century**
Introduction and notes by Archbishop Rowan Williams
978 085244 448 1   £25 hardback

Vol. V: **Church of the Fathers**
Introduction and notes by Frank McGrath
978 085244 447 4   £25 hardback

Vol. VI: **Discourses Addressed to Mixed Congregations**
Introduction and notes by James Tolhurst
978 085244 455 9   £25 hardback

Vol. VII: **Discussions and Arguments**
Introduction and notes by Gerard Tracey
978 085244 453 5   £25 hardback

Vol. VIII: **Two Essays on Biblical and on Ecclesiastical Miracles**
Introduction by Bishop Geoffrey Rowell and notes by
James Tolhurst
978 085244 456 6   £25 hardback

Vol. IX: **Sermons Preached on Various Occasions**
Introduction and notes by James Tolhurst
978 085244 408 5   £25 hardback

Vol. X: **Tracts for the Times**
Introduction and notes by James Tolhurst
978 085244 749 9   £25 hardback

Vol. XI: **Loss and Gain**
Introduction and notes by Sheridan Gilley
978 085244 410 8   £25 hardback

Vol. XII: **An Essay on the Development of Christian Doctrine**
Introduction, notes and textual appendix by James Tolhurst
978 178182 012 4   £35 hardback

Vol. XIII: **Essays Critical and Historical Vol. I**
Introduction, notes and textual appendix by Andrew Nash
978 085244 457 3   £35 hardback

Vol. XIV: **Essays Critical and Historical Vol. II**
Introduction, notes and textual appendix by Nicholas
Schofield
978 085244 411 5   £35 hardback

Vol. XV: **Difficulties of Anglicans Vol. I**
Introduction and notes by Edward Short and textual
appendix by Andrew Nash
978 085244 412 2   £35 hardback

Vol. XVI: **My Campaign in Ireland Part I**
Introduction and notes by Paul Shrimpton
978 085244 409 2   £35 hardback

Vol. XVII: **My Campaign in Ireland Part II**
Introduction and notes by Paul Shrimpton
978 085244 966 0   £35 hardback

Vol. XVIII: **Difficulties of Anglicans Vol. II**
Introduction and notes by James Tolhurst
978 0 85244 413 9   £35 hardback

Forthcoming:

Vol. XIX: **Lectures on the Doctrine of Justification**
Introduction, notes and textual appendix by James Pereiro
978 0 85244 414 6   £35.00

Vol. XX **The Via Media Vol. I**
Introduction and notes by James Tolhurst
978 085244 787 1   £35.00 hardback

In preparation:

Vol. XXI **Callista**
Introduction, notes and textual appendix by Kathleen Dietz
FSO

Vol. XXII **The Via Media Vol. II**
Introduction and notes and textual appendix by Andrew Starkie

Vol. XXIII **Sermons Bearing on Subjects of the Day**
Introduction and notes by James Tolhurst